D1477087

54 : 530.145

30/-

QUANTUM

CHEMISTRY

BY

HENRY EYRING

DEAN OF GRADUATE SCHOOL
University of Utah

◈

THE LATE JOHN WALTER

PALMER PHYSICAL LABORATORY
Princeton University

◈

GEORGE E. KIMBALL

DEPARTMENT OF CHEMISTRY
Columbia University

◈

New York
JOHN WILEY & SONS, INC.
CHAPMAN & HALL, LTD.
London

FOURTH PRINTING, JUNE, 1948

PRINTED IN THE UNITED STATES OF AMERICA

PREFACE

In so far as quantum mechanics is correct, chemical questions are problems in applied mathematics. In spite of this, chemistry, because of its complexity, will not cease to be in large measure an experimental science, even as for the last three hundred years the laws governing the motions of celestial bodies have been understood without eliminating the need for direct observation. No chemist, however, can afford to be uninformed of a theory which systematizes all of chemistry even though mathematical complexity often puts exact numerical results beyond his immediate reach. In this book we have attempted to put into a systematic, condensed form the tools which have been found useful in efforts to understand and develop the concepts of chemistry and physics.

We have included a wider range of subject matter than is to be found in other introductory textbooks in quantum mechanics and have indicated this in the title. The effort has been to build a reasonably complete and unified logical system on which the serious student can continue building. This has necessitated a somewhat formal mathematical style. Much interesting illustrative material might have been added. Including it would have lengthened a book already long enough. Instead we have tried to present group theory, statistical mechanics, and rate theory in a usable, if condensed, form.

The book has been written at the level of the graduate student in chemistry. It contains somewhat more material than has been presented in the year course given at Princeton since 1931. The good student who has mastered calculus will be able to follow the arguments. The way will be made easier by whatever he has learned of differential equations, vector analysis, group theory, and physical optics. Often unfamiliarity is mistaken for inherent difficulty. The unavoidable formality of quantum mechanics looks much worse on first reading than it is. The important fact emerges from the experience of the last twenty years that mastery of the subject is worth what it costs in effort.

Our general indebtedness to others is great and is acknowledged in part throughout the text and in Appendix IX. We want, in addition, to thank Dr. Hugh Hulburt for much help in the writing of the chapter on rate processes.   We also thank our many friends who, over a period of years, have decreased the number of errors and obscurities in the material finally assembled here and hope that they and others will feel the unfinished task to be worth continuing.

HENRY EYRING
JOHN WALTER
GEORGE E. KIMBALL

CONTENTS

CHAPTER I

INTRODUCTION: THE OLD QUANTUM THEORY

1a. The Composition of Matter. It is now well established that all matter is composed of a small number of kinds of particles. We cannot discuss here the long chain of experimental evidence on which our belief in the existence of these particles is based, but at present the following types are known:

Electrons, with a mass of 9.107×10^{-28} gram and a negative charge of 4.8025×10^{-10} electrostatic unit.

Protons, with a mass of 1.6725×10^{-24} gram and a positive charge equal numerically to that of the electron.

Neutrons, with a mass very nearly equal to that of the proton but carrying no electric charge.

In addition, the following particles have been observed in nuclear phenomena but are not of chemical importance:

Positrons, with the mass of the electron and the charge of the proton.

Mesotrons or *mesons*, with the charge of the electron but with a mass intermediate between that of the electron and that of the proton.

Neutrinos, with a mass of the same order of magnitude as that of the electron but without electric charge.

The evidence for the last two particles is less conclusive than that for the first four.

From the viewpoint of the chemist, matter may be regarded as being composed of atomic nuclei, of charge $+Ze$ and mass M, where Z is the atomic number and e the magnitude of the electronic charge, and electrons of charge $-e$ and mass m. If matter is composed only of these particles, then it must follow that all the properties of matter are properties of assemblies of these particles. A knowledge of the forces between these particles and their laws of motion is at least in principle sufficient to determine the behavior of all matter under any conditions.

It was only natural that the first attempts in this direction should have been made with the laws of classical mechanics as laid down by Newton. It was soon found, however, that these laws were inadequate to cope with problems of atomic mechanics.

1b. Black-Body Radiation. The failure of classical mechanics in this realm was first recognized clearly by Planck[1] in 1901. By applying

---

[1] Planck, *Ann. Physik*, **4**, 553 (1901).

1

classical mechanics to the problem of the equilibrium between a perfect absorber and emitter of radiation, a so-called black body, and its radiation field, Rayleigh and Jeans had found that the amount of energy per unit volume, $E_\nu\, d\nu$, in the frequency range between ν and $\nu + d\nu$, in equilibrium with a black body at the absolute temperature T should be

$$E_\nu\, d\nu = \frac{8\pi\nu^2 kT}{c^3}\, d\nu \qquad\qquad 1\cdot1$$

where k is the Boltzmann constant and c is the velocity of light. This law is in hopeless disagreement with the experimental facts, since it states that E_ν becomes infinite as ν approaches infinity, whereas experimentally E_ν approaches zero for large values of ν.

Planck overcame this difficulty only by making a violent departure from the concepts of classical mechanics. In order to simplify the problem he assumed that the black body was composed of harmonic oscillators, that is, of small charged particles bound by Hooke's law forces to their equilibrium positions. According to classical theory such oscillators will absorb or emit radiation of their natural frequency, the absorption or emission taking place continuously. According to Planck's "quantum theory," however, this absorption or emission is not continuous. Instead, the energy of each oscillator must always be an integral multiple of a certain " quantum " of energy, the size of the quantum depending on the natural frequency ν_0 of the oscillator according to the law

$$\epsilon = h\nu_0 \qquad\qquad 1\cdot2$$

where ϵ is the quantum of energy and h is a factor of proportionality, the now famous Planck's constant, the value of which is 6.6242×10^{-27} erg $\cdot$ seconds. Application of the same statistical methods as those used by Rayleigh and Jeans now led Planck to the black-body radiation formula

$$E_\nu\, d\nu = \frac{8\pi h\nu^3}{c^3}\, \frac{1}{e^{\frac{h\nu}{kT}} - 1}\, d\nu \qquad\qquad 1\cdot3$$

which is in agreement with experiment. It will be noted that, when the condition $h\nu \ll kT$ is satisfied, the two expressions for the radiation density are identical.

1c. The Photoelectric Effect. The next successful application of Planck's quantum hypothesis was made by Einstein.[2] It was known that, when light falls on a clean metal surface, electrons are emitted.

---

[2] A. Einstein, *Ann. Physik*, **17**, 132 (1905).

If the kinetic energy of the electrons is plotted against the frequency of the incident light, we obtain a graph of the type shown in Figure 1·1. Varying the intensity of the incident light at constant frequency does not affect the kinetic energy of the emitted electrons but merely changes the number which are emitted in unit time. The equation of the curve in Figure 1·1 is

$$\text{Kinetic energy} = h(\nu - \nu_0) \qquad 1\cdot4$$

where ν_0 is a minimum frequency below which no electrons are emitted and h is numerically identical with the value required by Planck to make equation 1·3 reproduce the experimental data on the density of radiation in equilibrium with a black body. This photoelectric effect was completely explained by Einstein by the hypothesis that the energy

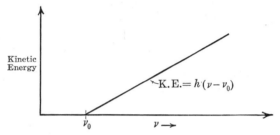

Fig. 1·1. Energy of photoelectric electrons.

of light is not spread out through the wave, as classical electrodynamics would have it, but is concentrated into corpuscles, or photons, of energy $h\nu$. It is further assumed that the emission of an electron from the surface takes place only when the electron is struck by and receives all the energy of the photon. The kinetic energy with which the electron is emitted will be less than $h\nu$ by an amount $h\nu_0$, the energy with which the electron is bound to the surface. The intensity of the light therefore determines only the number of electrons emitted; the frequency of the light determines their energies.

1d. Bohr's Theory of the Hydrogen Spectrum. Perhaps the greatest of these early successes of the quantum theory was the theory of the hydrogen spectrum as developed by Bohr.[3] Empirically, it has been found that all the lines in the hydrogen spectrum could be represented by the formula

$$\bar{\nu} = R_\text{H}\left(\frac{1}{n^2} - \frac{1}{m^2}\right) \qquad 1\cdot5$$

where n and m are integers with $n < m$, and where n has the values 1,

[3] N. Bohr, *Phil. Mag.*, **26**, 1 (1913).

2, 3, 4, 5 for the Lyman, Balmer, Paschen, Brackett, and Pfund series of lines, respectively. The Rydberg constant for hydrogen, R_H, has the value 109,677.581 if the frequencies are measured in wavenumbers $\bar{\nu}$. ($\bar{\nu}$ is the reciprocal of the wavelength in centimeters.) Bohr postulated, following Rutherford, that a hydrogen atom was composed of a positive nucleus around which moved one electron. Classically, it can be shown that an electron of mass m moving about a proton of mass M is equivalent to a particle of mass $\mu = \dfrac{mM}{m+M}$ moving about a fixed center. Considering only the case in which the particle moves in a circular orbit of radius r under the influence of the coulomb forces between the two charges, we have, since the centrifugal and attractive forces must balance,

$$\mu r \left(\frac{d\varphi}{dt}\right)^2 = \frac{e^2}{r^2} \qquad\qquad 1\cdot6$$

where φ is the azimuthal angle. The kinetic energy T, the potential energy V, and the total energy $E = T + V$ are

$$T = \tfrac{1}{2}\mu v^2 = \tfrac{1}{2}\mu r^2\left(\frac{d\varphi}{dt}\right)^2 = \frac{1}{2}\frac{e^2}{r}$$

$$V = -\frac{e^2}{r} \qquad\qquad 1\cdot7$$

$$E = T + V = -\frac{1}{2}\frac{e^2}{r} = -T$$

Bohr now made the assumption that only those orbits are allowed for which the angular momentum is an integral multiple of $\dfrac{h}{2\pi}$; that is, only those values of r are allowed for which

$$\mu r^2 \frac{d\varphi}{dt} = \frac{nh}{2\pi} \qquad (n \text{ an integer}) \qquad\qquad 1\cdot8$$

Using this relation, the allowed values for the energy are

$$E = -T = -\frac{1}{2}\frac{1}{\mu r^2}\frac{n^2 h^2}{4\pi^2} = -\frac{1}{2}\frac{e^2}{r} \qquad\qquad 1\cdot9$$

or, eliminating r from these equations,

$$E_n = -\frac{2\pi^2 \mu e^4}{n^2 h^2} \qquad\qquad 1\cdot10$$

Classically, such a system would radiate light of a frequency equal to the frequency of revolution of the electron about the nucleus. Bohr therefore made the additional assumption that the atom could exist in the states characterized by the above energy values without radiating energy, and that a transition from the state with the " quantum number " m to that with the quantum number n could take place with emission of light of frequency

$$\bar{\nu} = \frac{\nu}{c} = \frac{E_m - E_n}{ch} \qquad\qquad 1\cdot11$$

Substituting the values for the allowed energy levels into this expression gives the allowed frequencies

$$\bar{\nu} = R_{\mathrm{H}}\left(\frac{1}{n^2} - \frac{1}{m^2}\right) \qquad\qquad 1\cdot12$$

with $R_{\mathrm{H}} = \dfrac{2\pi^2\mu e^4}{ch^3}$. We see that (1·12) is identical in form with (1·5). The calculated value of R_{H} agrees with the experimental value within the limits of error involved in the determination of the values of the fundamental constants e, h, and m.

1e. The Old Quantum Theory. The work of Planck, Einstein, and Bohr formed the basis of what is now known as the old quantum theory. This method of attacking atomic problems consisted of two definite parts: first, the problem was solved by the methods of classical mechanics; and then, from all the possible motions of the system, only those which fulfilled certain " quantum conditions " were kept. These quantum conditions, for a system of f degrees of freedom, were of the form

$$\oint p_i \, dq_i = nh \qquad (i = 1, 2 \cdots f) \qquad\qquad 1\cdot13$$

where q_i is any of the coordinates representing a degree of freedom of the system and p_i is the corresponding momentum. The symbol $\oint$ means that the integral was taken over a complete cycle if the motion was periodic; non-periodic motions were not quantized. The analogous quantum condition in the above treatment of the hydrogen atom is given by equation 1·8. The number n on the right side of equation 1·13 was called the quantum number corresponding to that particular degree of freedom. In most cases n was taken to be an integer, but in some problems it proved better to use half quantum numbers, that is, to give n a value from the series $1/2, 3/2, 5/2 \cdots$. In this way a number (generally an infinite number) of quantized motions of the system were found. The energies of these motions were called the energy levels of the system. These energies substituted in equation 1·11 determined the spectrum of the system. By the absorption of light of the proper frequency the system could be raised from a low energy level to a higher one, and by the emission of light the system could pass from a high energy level, or excited state, to a lower one. Although it did not prove possible to calculate the actual energy levels of any atom except hydrogen (and other one-electron atoms such as He^+ and Li^{++}), the scheme of energies could be found from the spectrum, and in this way a large amount of knowledge concerning atomic structure was gained.

In spite of the success of the old quantum theory in simple problems, it finally became evident that it could not produce correct quantitative results in the more complicated ones. For this reason the old quantum theory was finally abandoned in favor of what is known as quantum mechanics.

1f. The Dual Nature of Light. The essential feature of quantum mechanics is the dualism of all the fundamental particles. At times these particles behave like forms of wave motion; at other times they exhibit the ordinary properties of particles. Consider, for example, the photon. Although Einstein was forced to assume that the energy of a light wave was concentrated into corpuscles, his success in explaining the photoelectric effect in no way invalidated the old well-tested evidence that light is a form of wave motion. It is just as inconceivable that a stream of particles should show the phenomena of diffraction as that a wave should suddenly concentrate its energy at one point to knock an electron out of a surface.

Let us examine the conditions under which light behaves as a wave. In a typical diffraction experiment, light from a point or line source passes through a slit system and the diffraction pattern is recorded on a photographic plate. Now it has been found experimentally that the sensitization of a photographic plate is a quantum process as much as is the photoelectric effect. Regarded from the photon theory, therefore, the experiment may be considered as the passage of a stream of photons from the source to the plate. If it were possible to perform the experiment with a single photon we could not possibly obtain the complete diffraction pattern; at most one grain of the emulsion on the plate would be sensitized. The experiment with a large number of photons can be regarded as the experiment with a single photon repeated a large number of times. The diffraction pattern is then an expression of the probability that a photon emitted from the source will strike a given part of the plate. The waves themselves are not observed in this or any other optical experiment: the actual observations of the light are always quantized, whether we detect the light with a photographic plate, a photoelectric cell, or the human eye.

Since we always observe photons, and not light waves, we must logically conclude that light is " really " a stream of photons. The waves are the mathematical expressions of the way in which the photons move. The photons of a beam of light do not obey Newton's laws of motion but the laws of wave motion.

1g. The Dual Nature of Electrons. It is now known, as a result of the experiments of Davisson and Germer[4] and of G. P. Thomson,[5] that diffraction experiments very similar to those on light may be performed with a beam of electrons. These experiments form a brilliant confirmation of the hypothesis, first advanced by de Broglie,[6] and put into mathematical expression by Schrödinger,[7] that electrons, instead of having laws of motion similar to the classical laws, actually obeyed the laws of wave motion in the same way that photons do.

Instead of starting with the classical motion and applying quantum conditions to it, as in the old quantum theory, the new quantum mechanics abandons classical concepts almost entirely. In the new quantum mechanics all our information concerning an electron is contained in the mathematical expression of a function Ψ. The square of the absolute value of this function expresses the probability of finding the electron at a given point. The law according to which Ψ changes with time is known, so that a statistical knowledge, but nothing more, can be obtained of the position of the electron at any future time.

In the chapters to come we shall see how this new mechanics gives all the results of the old quantum theory and goes on to solve problems in which the old theory failed. Before starting a discussion of the principles of quantum mechanics and its application to problems of chemical interest, it will be of value to review, in the next chapter, the principles of classical mechanics, since the new mechanics is expressed largely in the terminology of the old.

[4] C. Davisson and L. Germer, *Phys. Rev.*, **30**, 705 (1927).

[5] G. P. Thomson, *Proc. Roy. Soc. London*, **117**, 600 (1928).

[6] L. de Broglie, *Ann. phys.*, **3**, 22 (1925).

[7] E. Schrödinger, *Ann. physik*, **79**, 361, 478; **80**, 437; **81**, 109 (1926).

CHAPTER II

THE PRINCIPLES OF CLASSICAL MECHANICS

2a. Generalized Coordinates. In classical mechanics, the motion of a particle is determined by Newton's law of motion, which may be written in the form

$$m\frac{d^2x}{dt^2} = f_x \qquad m\frac{d^2y}{dt^2} = f_y \qquad m\frac{d^2z}{dt^2} = f_z \qquad 2\cdot1$$

where x, y, and z are the Cartesian coordinates of the particle, m is its mass, and f_x, f_y, and f_z are the three components of the total force acting on the particle.

In many problems it is not convenient to use rectangular coordinates. In the problem of planetary motion, for example, the forces are simple expressions in polar coordinates but are quite complicated in rectangular coordinates. Again, if the motion is not free but is subjected to constraints, such as the requirement that the particle move on a given surface, it is usually preferable to use a coordinate system such that the condition of constraint takes the form of a requirement that one or more of the coordinates remains constant.

The most frequently met example of a motion subject to constraints is the motion of a rigid body. We may regard a rigid body as a system of particles moving in such a way that the distance between any two of them remains constant. If there are N particles, their positions are specified by $3N$ rectangular coordinates x_1, y_1, $z_1 \cdots x_N$, y_N, z_N. These variables are not all independent, since we must allow them to vary only in such ways that the distances between particles remain constant. If we fix the coordinates of three particles which do not lie in a straight line, the coordinates of all the other particles are then determined. Between the nine coordinates of the three chosen particles there are three relations corresponding to the three distances between the particles, so that the positions of the three particles, and hence of the whole body, are fixed by only six variables. The only exception to this rule occurs when all the particles lie on a straight line; then the position of the whole system is seen to be determined by five variables. The number of variables necessary to specify the

8

position of a system is known as the number of degrees of freedom of the system; thus, a rigid body has six degrees of freedom.

In general the position of a system of N particles with F degrees of freedom is determined by F coordinates, which we shall denote by $q_1, \cdots q_F$. The conditions of constraint may then be expressed by the constancy of $3N - F$ other variables $q_{F+1} \cdots q_{3N}$. In terms of the q's the rectangular coordinates of the particles are given by the $3N$ functions

$$x_1 = \varphi_1(q_1 \cdots q_{3N}) \qquad y_1 = \varphi_2(q_1 \cdots q_{3N}) \qquad z_1 = \varphi_3(q_1 \cdots q_{3N})$$

$$\cdot \qquad \qquad \cdot$$
$$\cdot \qquad \qquad \cdot \qquad \qquad 2 \cdot 2$$
$$\cdot \qquad \qquad \cdot$$

$$x_N = \varphi_{3N-2}(q_1 \cdots q_{3N}) \quad y_N = \varphi_{3N-1}(q_1 \cdots q_{3N}) \quad z_N = \varphi_{3N}(q_1 \cdots q_{3N})$$

2b. Lagrange's Equations. We shall now find the equations of motion in terms of the generalized coordinates q_i. In the derivations which follow, it is convenient to make a slight change of notation. Instead of representing the Cartesian coordinates of the first particle by x_1, y_1, z_1, we shall use x_1, x_2, x_3. For the second particle we use x_4, x_5, x_6, and so on. We number the forces and masses in the same way. Newton's laws may then be expressed by the single equation

$$m_i \frac{d^2 x_i}{dt^2} = f_i \qquad 2 \cdot 3$$

Likewise, equations 2·2 become

$$x_i = \varphi_i(q_1 \cdots q_{3N}) \qquad 2 \cdot 4$$

and a variation in the x's may be expressed in terms of a variation in the q's by the relation

$$dx_i = \sum_j \frac{\partial x_i}{\partial q_j} dq_j \qquad 2 \cdot 5$$

Suppose that the system is subjected to an infinitesimal displacement of the coordinates. In this displacement, the forces do an amount of work

$$dW = \sum_i f_i \, dx_i = \sum_i \sum_j f_i \frac{\partial x_i}{\partial q_j} dq_j = \sum_j Q_j \, dq_j \qquad 2 \cdot 6$$

where

$$Q_j = \sum_i f_i \frac{\partial x_i}{\partial q_j} \qquad 2 \cdot 7$$

is the generalized force associated with the generalized coordinate q_j. Using equation 2·3, the work done may also be written as

$$dW = \sum_i m_i \frac{d^2 x_i}{dt^2} dx_i = \sum_i \sum_j m_i \frac{d^2 x_i}{dt^2} \frac{\partial x_i}{\partial q_j} dq_j \qquad 2\cdot 8$$

so that we have the relation

$$\sum_i \sum_j m_i \frac{d^2 x_i}{dt^2} \frac{\partial x_i}{\partial q_j} dq_j = \sum_j Q_j dq_j \qquad 2\cdot 9$$

Since the q's are independent variables there is no relation between the dq's; equation 2·9 will therefore be true only if the coefficients of each dq_j on both sides of the equation are equal. This condition gives us the set of j equations:

$$\sum_i m_i \frac{d^2 x_i}{dt^2} \frac{\partial x_i}{\partial q_j} = Q_j \qquad 2\cdot 10$$

The left side of this equation can be simplified. By the ordinary rule for the differentiation of an implicit function, we have

$$\frac{dx_i}{dt} = \sum_j \frac{\partial x_i}{\partial q_j} \frac{dq_j}{dt} \qquad 2\cdot 11$$

so that, upon differentiating with respect to $\dfrac{dq_k}{dt} = \dot{q}_k$, we obtain

$$\frac{\partial \dot{x}_i}{\partial \dot{q}_k} = \frac{\partial x_i}{\partial q_k} \qquad 2\cdot 12$$

We can obtain the additional relation

$$\frac{d}{dt} \frac{\partial x_i}{\partial q_k} = \frac{\partial \dot{x}_i}{\partial q_k} \qquad 2\cdot 13$$

by noting that

$$\frac{\partial \dot{x}_i}{\partial q_k} = \sum_j \frac{\partial}{\partial q_k} \frac{\partial x_i}{\partial q_j} \frac{dq_j}{dt} \qquad 2\cdot 14$$

and

$$\frac{d}{dt} \frac{\partial x_i}{\partial q_k} = \sum_j \frac{\partial}{\partial q_j} \frac{\partial x_i}{\partial q_k} \frac{dq_j}{dt} \qquad 2\cdot 15$$

We now write the left side of equation 2·10 as

$$\sum_i m_i \frac{d^2 x_i}{dt^2} \frac{\partial x_i}{\partial q_j} = \sum_i m_i \frac{d}{dt} \left(\frac{dx_i}{dt} \frac{\partial x_i}{\partial q_j} \right) - \sum_i m_i \frac{dx_i}{dt} \frac{d}{dt} \frac{\partial x_i}{\partial q_j} \qquad 2\cdot 16$$

which becomes, after using the relations expressed by equations 2·12 and 2·13,

$$\sum_i m_i \frac{d^2 x_i}{dt^2}\frac{\partial x_i}{\partial q_j} = \sum_i m_i \frac{d}{dt}\left(\frac{dx_i}{dt}\frac{\partial \dot{x}_i}{\partial \dot{q}_j}\right) - \sum_i m_i \frac{dx_i}{dt}\frac{\partial \dot{x}_i}{\partial q_j}$$

$$= \frac{d}{dt}\left(\frac{\partial}{\partial \dot{q}_j}\left[\sum_i \tfrac{1}{2}m_i\left(\frac{dx_i}{dt}\right)^2\right]\right) - \frac{\partial}{\partial q_j}\left[\sum_i \tfrac{1}{2}m_i\left(\frac{dx_i}{dt}\right)^2\right] \qquad 2\cdot17$$

The kinetic energy of the system is $T = \sum_i \tfrac{1}{2}m_i\left(\dfrac{dx_i}{dt}\right)^2$; the set of equations 2·10 may therefore finally be written

$$\frac{d}{dt}\frac{\partial T}{\partial \dot{q}_j} - \frac{\partial T}{\partial q_j} = Q_j \qquad\qquad 2\text{-}18$$

If the f_i's are derivable from a potential, that is, if there exists a function $V(x_1 \cdots x_{3N})$ such that

$$f_i = -\frac{\partial V}{\partial x_i} \qquad\qquad 2\text{-}19$$

then

$$Q_j = -\sum_i \frac{\partial V}{\partial x_i}\frac{\partial x_i}{\partial q_j} = -\frac{\partial V}{\partial q_j} \qquad\qquad 2\text{-}20$$

In this particular case, which is the most important one, equation 2·18 reduces to

$$\frac{d}{dt}\frac{\partial T}{\partial \dot{q}_j} - \frac{\partial}{\partial q_j}(T - V) = 0 \qquad\qquad 2\text{-}21$$

Since V is a function of the coordinates only, this equation can be written more simply in terms of the function $L = T - V$; it then becomes

$$\frac{d}{dt}\frac{\partial L}{\partial \dot{q}_j} - \frac{\partial L}{\partial q_j} = 0 \qquad\qquad 2\text{-}22$$

The function L is known as the Lagrangian function for the system, and the set of equations represented by 2·22 as the Lagrangian equations of motion.

Example 1. Two particles of masses m_1 and m_2 are connected by a massless rod of length R. The system moves in a vertical plane under the influence of gravity. Discuss the motion.

Let the coordinates of the center of gravity of the system be x and y, the y axis being vertical, and let the angle made by the line from the center of gravity to the first particle with the vertical be φ. In terms of these coordinates, the rectangular coordinates of the two particles are

$$x_1 = x + \frac{m_2}{m_1 + m_2} R \sin \varphi \qquad y_1 = y + \frac{m_2}{m_1 + m_2} R \cos \varphi$$

$$2\cdot 23$$

$$x_2 = x - \frac{m_1}{m_1 + m_2} R \sin \varphi \qquad y_2 = y - \frac{m_1}{m_1 + m_2} R \cos \varphi$$

The kinetic energy

$$T = \frac{m_1}{2}\left[\left(\frac{dx_1}{dt}\right)^2 + \left(\frac{dy_i}{dt}\right)^2\right] + \frac{m_2}{2}\left[\left(\frac{dx_2}{dt}\right)^2 + \left(\frac{dy_2}{dt}\right)^2\right]$$

is easily found to be, in the new coordinate system,

$$T = \frac{M}{2}\left[\left(\frac{dx}{dt}\right)^2 + \left(\frac{dy}{dt}\right)^2\right] + \frac{I}{2}\left(\frac{d\varphi}{dt}\right)^2$$

$$2\cdot 24$$

where $M = m_1 + m_2$ and $I = \dfrac{m_1 m_2}{m_1 + m_2} R^2$. The forces acting on the particles are, first, the forces due to gravity, which may be derived from the potential $V = Mgy$, where g is the gravitational constant; and the forces exerted by the connecting rod. Suppose that the x component of this force on the first particle is F. In order that the force may be directed along the rod, the y component must be $F \cot \varphi$. The law of action and reaction then requires that the components of the force on the second particle be $-F$ and $-F \cot \varphi$. It is easily verified that the generalized forces due to the connecting rod vanish. This result is perfectly general: the generalized forces due to the con- straints of any system always vanish and hence never need be con- sidered. The Lagrangian function for the system is therefore

$$L = T - V = \frac{M}{2}\left[\left(\frac{dx}{dt}\right)^2 + \left(\frac{dy}{dt}\right)^2\right] + \frac{I}{2}\left(\frac{d\varphi}{dt}\right)^2 - Mgy \qquad 2\cdot 25$$

and Lagrange's equations of motion become

$$M \frac{d^2 x}{dt^2} = 0$$

$$M \frac{d^2 y}{dt^2} + Mg = 0 \qquad\qquad 2\cdot 26$$

$$I \frac{d^2 \varphi}{dt^2} = 0$$

The first two of these equations show that the center of gravity of the system moves as a particle of mass M under the influence of the gravitational field. The last equation shows that the angular velocity of the system is constant.

Example 2. A particle of mass m moves in a plane under the influence of a potential which is a function only of the distance of the particle from a fixed point in the plane. Discuss the motion.

Let the origin of coordinates be at the fixed point; let r be the distance of the particle from the fixed point, and let φ be the angle between the x axis and the line from the fixed point to the particle. The relation between the two coordinate systems is therefore

$$x = r \cos \varphi \qquad y = r \sin \varphi \qquad\qquad 2\cdot27$$

so that the kinetic energy is

$$T = \frac{m}{2}\left[\left(\frac{dx}{dt}\right)^2 + \left(\frac{dy}{dt}\right)^2\right] = \frac{m}{2}\left[\left(\frac{dr}{dt}\right)^2 + r^2\left(\frac{d\varphi}{dt}\right)^2\right] \qquad 2\cdot28$$

If we represent the potential energy by $V(r)$, the Lagrangian function is

$$L = \frac{m}{2}\left[\left(\frac{dr}{dt}\right)^2 + r^2\left(\frac{d\varphi}{dt}\right)^2\right] - V(r) \qquad\qquad 2\cdot29$$

and the Lagrangian equations of motion are

$$\frac{d}{dt}\left(mr^2\frac{d\varphi}{dt}\right) = 0$$

$$m\frac{d^2r}{dt^2} - mr\left(\frac{d\varphi}{dt}\right)^2 + \frac{\partial}{\partial r}V(r) = 0 \qquad\qquad 2\cdot30$$

The first of these may be integrated to give the result

$$mr^2\frac{d\varphi}{dt} = c = p_\varphi \qquad\qquad 2\cdot31$$

that is, the angular momentum of the particle about the fixed point is a constant. By use of this result $\frac{d\varphi}{dt}$ may be eliminated from the second equation, giving

$$m\frac{d^2r}{dt^2} - \frac{p_\varphi^2}{mr^3} + \frac{\partial}{\partial r}V(r) = 0 \qquad\qquad 2\cdot32$$

which may be solved when an explicit form is taken for $V(r)$. The second term in this equation represents the centrifugal force.

2c. Generalized Momenta and Hamilton's Equations. In many problems it is convenient to express the kinetic energy in terms of momenta instead of velocities. For generalized coordinates we define the momentum p_i associated with the coordinate q_i as

$$p_i = \frac{\partial L}{\partial \dot{q}_i} \qquad 2 \cdot 33$$

In order to find the laws of motion in terms of the p_i's and q_i's instead of the q_i's and $\dot{q}_i$'s, consider the differential

$$dL = \sum_i \left(\frac{\partial L}{\partial \dot{q}_i} d\dot{q}_i + \frac{\partial L}{\partial q_i} dq_i \right) \qquad 2 \cdot 34$$

The coefficient of $d\dot{q}_i$ is by definition p_i, while from Lagrange's equations

$$\frac{\partial L}{\partial q_i} = \frac{d}{dt} \frac{\partial L}{\partial \dot{q}_i} = \dot{p}_i \qquad 2 \cdot 35$$

Hence

$$dL = \sum_i (p_i d\dot{q}_i + \dot{p}_i dq_i) \qquad 2 \cdot 36$$

If we subtract equation 2·36 from the identity

$$d(\sum_i p_i \dot{q}_i) = \sum_i (p_i d\dot{q}_i + \dot{q}_i dp_i) \qquad 2 \cdot 37$$

we obtain

$$d(\sum_i p_i \dot{q}_i - L) = \sum_i (\dot{q}_i dp_i - \dot{p}_i dq_i) \qquad 2 \cdot 38$$

The quantity $(\sum_i p_i \dot{q}_i - L)$ is known as the Hamiltonian of the system and is represented by the symbol H. If H is regarded as a function of the p's and q's, then, from 2·38,

$$dH = \sum_i (\dot{q}_i dp_i - \dot{p}_i dq_i) \qquad 2 \cdot 39$$

and by the definition of a partial derivative

$$\frac{\partial H}{\partial p_i} = \dot{q}_i \qquad \frac{\partial H}{\partial q_i} = -\dot{p}_i \qquad 2 \cdot 40$$

This set of equations is known as Hamilton's equations of motion.

Since the kinetic energy T is a homogeneous quadratic function of the $\dot{x}$'s, and the $\dot{x}$'s are homogeneous linear functions of the $\dot{q}$'s, it follows that T is a homogeneous quadratic function of the $\dot{q}$'s; that is, $T = \sum_i \sum_j a_{ij} \dot{q}_i \dot{q}_j$, where a_{ij} may be a function of the q's but not of the

$\dot{q}$'s. If the forces are derivable from a potential, then

$$p_k = \frac{\partial L}{\partial \dot{q}_k} = \frac{\partial T}{\partial \dot{q}_k} = \sum_j a_{kj}\dot{q}_j + \sum_i a_{ik}\dot{q}_i$$

$$\sum_k p_k \dot{q}_k = \sum_k \sum_j a_{kj}\dot{q}_k\dot{q}_j + \sum_i \sum_k a_{ik}\dot{q}_i\dot{q}_k = 2T \qquad 2\cdot41$$

$$H = \sum_k p_k \dot{q}_k - L = 2T - L = 2T - (T - V) = T + V$$

that is, the Hamiltonian function H is equal to the total energy of the system.

Example 3. Solve example 1 by the use of Hamilton's equations. The generalized momenta are:

$$p_x = \frac{\partial L}{\partial \dot{x}} = M\frac{dx}{dt}$$

$$p_y = \frac{\partial L}{\partial \dot{y}} = M\frac{dy}{dt} \qquad 2\cdot42$$

$$p_\varphi = \frac{\partial L}{\partial \dot{\varphi}} = I\frac{d\varphi}{dt}$$

so that

$$H = \frac{1}{2M}(p_x^2 + p_y^2) + \frac{1}{2I}p_\varphi^2 + Mgy \qquad 2\cdot43$$

and Hamilton's equations of motion become

$$\frac{dx}{dt} = \frac{p_x}{M} \qquad \frac{dp_x}{dt} = 0$$

$$\frac{dy}{dt} = \frac{p_y}{M} \qquad \frac{dp_y}{dt} = -Mg \qquad 2\cdot44$$

$$\frac{d\varphi}{dt} = \frac{p_\varphi}{I} \qquad \frac{dp_\varphi}{dt} = 0$$

The equations are readily seen to be equivalent to those obtained from Lagrange's equation.

Any p_i and the corresponding q_i are said to be conjugate variables. By extending this definition to include any pair of variables which satisfy equations of the form 2·39 the concept becomes more general. For example, if a system of F degrees of freedom is described by the coordinates $q_1 \cdots q_F$ and the time t, with t being formally treated on the same basis as the q's, the analysis shows that for systems in which the total energy is constant the variable conjugate to t is the negative of the Hamiltonian function.

2d. Vibration Theory and Normal Coordinates. Many problems of mechanics are concerned with the vibrations of a system of particles. By a vibration we mean the oscillations of a system when it is slightly disturbed from a position of stable equilibrium. In such a motion no coordinate ever departs by a large amount from the value it would have if the system were in the equilibrium position. It is convenient in these problems to choose a system of coordinates such that all the q_i's vanish at the point of equilibrium; then all the q_i's will remain small throughout the motion.

If we were to express the coordinates of each particle by a set of rectangular coordinates with the origin at the equilibrium position of the particle, the kinetic energy of the system would be

$$T = \tfrac{1}{2}\sum_i m_i \left(\frac{dx_i}{dt}\right)^2 \qquad\qquad 2\cdot45$$

Usually a more general coordinate system would be used; the kinetic energy of the system in generalized coordinates is of the form

$$T = \tfrac{1}{2}\sum_i\sum_j a_{ij} \frac{dq_i}{dt}\frac{dq_j}{dt} \qquad\qquad 2\cdot46$$

where the a_{ij}'s are functions of the q_i's, but for small vibrations it will be a sufficiently good approximation to regard the a_{ij}'s as constants, with the value they have at the equilibrium position.

The potential energy may be expanded in a Taylor's series in the q's about the point of equilibrium:

$$V = V_0 + \sum_i \left(\frac{\partial V}{\partial q_i}\right)_0 q_i + \sum_i\sum_j \frac{1}{2}\left(\frac{\partial^2 V}{\partial q_i\,\partial q_j}\right)_0 q_i q_j + \cdots \qquad 2\cdot47$$

where the derivatives are evaluated at $q_i = 0$, the position of equilibrium. The constant term V_0 is arbitrary, and so for the sake of simplicity we take it to be zero. Since $q_i = 0$ is a point of equilibrium, V must be a minimum at this point, so that $\left(\dfrac{\partial V}{\partial q_i}\right)_0 = 0$. If we denote the constant $\left(\dfrac{\partial^2 V}{\partial q_i\,\partial q_j}\right)_0$ by b_{ij}, we may therefore represent V approximately by

$$V = \tfrac{1}{2}\sum_i\sum_j b_{ij} q_i q_j \qquad\qquad 2\cdot48$$

Lagrange's equations for the system are then

$$\sum_j a_{ij} \frac{d^2 q_j}{dt^2} + \sum_j b_{ij} q_j = 0 \qquad 2 \cdot 49$$

If the system has F degrees of freedom, there are F of these differential equations corresponding to $i = 1, 2, \cdots F$. In order to solve these equations let us try to find a set of constants c_i such that, if each equation of the set is multiplied by c_i and the results added together, the new equations will be of the form

$$\frac{d^2 Q}{dt^2} + \lambda Q = 0 \qquad 2 \cdot 50$$

where Q is an expression of the form

$$Q = \sum_j h_j q_j \qquad 2 \cdot 51$$

The equations which must be satisfied in order to obtain this result are

$$\sum_i c_i a_{ij} = \frac{1}{\lambda} \sum_i c_i b_{ij} = h_j \qquad 2 \cdot 52$$

The equations given by the equality sign on the left are just sufficient to determine the c_i's; the remaining equations will then give the h_j's. If we write the left-hand equation in the form

$$\sum_i (\lambda a_{ij} - b_{ij}) c_i = 0 \qquad 2 \cdot 53$$

it is seen that one solution is $c_i = 0$. Now by an algebraic theorem (Appendix IV) this is the only solution unless the determinant of the coefficients vanishes, that is, unless

$$|\lambda a_{ij} - b_{ij}| = 0 \qquad 2 \cdot 54$$

This equation may be satisfied if we choose λ properly. Let λ_1 be one of the F roots of this equation. Then the equations

$$\sum_i (\lambda_1 a_{ij} - b_{ij}) c_i = 0 \qquad 2 \cdot 55$$

have a set of non-vanishing solutions for the c_i's, which are unique except for one arbitrary constant factor.

When this set of c_i's has been determined, the h_i's are fixed by equation $2 \cdot 52$. Let these be denoted by $h_i^{(1)}$ and the corresponding Q by Q_1. In the same way each of the other roots of $2 \cdot 54$ gives a set of h_i's which in turn determines a possible Q, so that we arrive at a set of F Q's, each of which satisfies the equation

$$\frac{d^2 Q_i}{dt^2} + \lambda_i Q_i = 0 \qquad (i = 1, 2, \cdots F) \qquad \text{2·56}$$

If we regard the Q's as a new set of coordinates, these equations are just Lagrange's equations in the new coordinates. Because of the simple form of these equations the Q's are known as the normal coordinates of the system. In terms of the normal coordinates, the kinetic and potential energies have the simple form:

$$T = \tfrac{1}{2}\sum_i \left(\frac{dQ_i}{dt}\right)^2 \qquad V = \tfrac{1}{2}\sum_i \lambda_i Q_i^2 \qquad \text{2·57}$$

If the equilibrium is stable, then all the λ_i's $\left(\lambda_i = \dfrac{\partial^2 V}{\partial Q_i^2}\right)$ are real and positive. But for positive λ's it is easily seen that the solution of equation 2·56 is

$$Q_i = A_i \cos\left(\sqrt{\lambda_i}\,t + \epsilon_i\right) \qquad \text{2·58}$$

where A_i and ϵ_i are arbitrary constants.

If the solution is desired in terms of the original coordinates, the q_i's must be expressed in terms of the Q_i's by solving simultaneously the equations defining the Q_i's. Suppose that the result is

$$q_i = \sum_j g_{ij} Q_j \qquad \text{2·59}$$

Then the equations of motion are

$$q_i = \sum_j g_{ij} A_j \cos\left(\sqrt{\lambda_j}\,t + \epsilon_j\right) \qquad \text{2·60}$$

If all the A_j's are zero except one, then each q_i varies sinusoidally with time, each with the same phase. Such a motion is called a normal mode of vibration of the system. Corresponding to such a mode of vibration there is a definite frequency given by $\nu_j = \dfrac{\sqrt{\lambda_j}}{2\pi}$. The most general vibration of the system can be regarded as a superposition of the various normal modes, with arbitrary amplitudes and phases.

If the equilibrium is unstable, the above formal treatment can still be carried out. In this case, however, at least one of the λ's is real and negative, so that the corresponding frequency is imaginary. The motion then is not sinusoidal, since the Q corresponding to the negative λ will be an exponentially increasing function of the time.

Example 4. Three springs, whose force constants are k, $2k$, and k, are joined in a straight line, and the ends of the system are fixed.

The joints between the springs are balls of mass m (Figure 2·1).   Determine the motion if the balls are set vibrating in the line of the springs.

FIG. 2·1.

Let the displacement of the first ball from its equilibrium position be x_1 and that of the second ball x_2.   The changes in length of the three springs are then x_1, $x_2 - x_1$, and $-x_2$, so that the potential energy of the system is

$$V = \tfrac{1}{2}kx_1^2 + \tfrac{1}{2}(2k)(x_2 - x_1)^2 + \tfrac{1}{2}k(-x_2)^2$$
$$= \tfrac{3}{2}kx_1^2 - 2kx_1x_2 + \tfrac{3}{2}kx_2^2 \qquad\qquad 2\text{·}61$$

If we consider the springs to have zero mass, the kinetic energy is

$$T = \frac{m}{2}\left[\left(\frac{dx_1}{dt}\right)^2 + \left(\frac{dx_2}{dt}\right)^2\right] \qquad\qquad 2\text{·}62$$

Lagrange's equations of motion are therefore

$$m\frac{d^2x_1}{dt^2} + 3kx_1 - 2kx_2 = 0$$

$$\qquad\qquad 2\text{·}63$$

$$m\frac{d^2x_2}{dt^2} - 2kx_1 + 3kx_2 = 0$$

If we multiply the first of these equations by c_1 and the second by c_2 and add, we obtain

$$mc_1\frac{d^2x_1}{dt^2} + mc_2\frac{d^2x_2}{dt^2} + (3kc_1 - 2kc_2)x_1 + (-2kc_1 + 3kc_2)x_2 = 0 \quad 2\text{·}64$$

In order that this be of the form 2·50 we must have

$$mc_1 = \frac{1}{\lambda}(3kc_1 - 2kc_2) = h_1$$

$$\qquad\qquad 2\text{·}65$$

$$mc_2 = \frac{1}{\lambda}(-2kc_1 + 3kc_2) = h_2$$

There will be a non-trivial solution for c_1 and c_2 only if

$$\begin{vmatrix} \lambda m - 3k & 2k \\ 2k & \lambda m - 3k \end{vmatrix} = 0 \qquad\qquad 2\text{·}66$$

The roots of this determinant are $\lambda_1 = \dfrac{5k}{m}$; $\lambda_2 = \dfrac{k}{m}$. Substituting λ_1 in equation 2·65 gives $c_1 = -c_2$. Hence if we take c_1, which is arbitrary, to be 1, c_2 must be -1, and

$$Q_1 = h_1^{(1)}x_1 + h_2^{(1)}x_2 = mx_1 - mx_2 \qquad\qquad 2\cdot67$$

In the same way we find for Q_2 the value

$$Q_2 = mx_1 + mx_2 \qquad\qquad 2\cdot68$$

The equations of motion in the new coordinates are

$$\frac{d^2Q_1}{dt^2} + \frac{5k}{m}Q_1 = 0$$

$$\qquad\qquad\qquad\qquad\qquad\qquad 2\cdot69$$

$$\frac{d^2Q_2}{dt^2} + \frac{k}{m}Q_2 = 0$$

The first normal mode is that in which $Q_2 = 0$, that is, $x_1 + x_2 = 0$. In this normal mode the balls move in opposite directions with a frequency $\dfrac{1}{2\pi}\sqrt{\dfrac{5k}{m}}$. In the second normal mode $x_1 = x_2$; the balls move in the same direction with a frequency $\dfrac{1}{2\pi}\sqrt{\dfrac{k}{m}}$.

CHAPTER III

THE PRINCIPLES OF QUANTUM MECHANICS

3a. The Uncertainty Principle. A typical problem in classical mechanics involves the finding of the values of the various dynamical variables of a system, given the values of the p's and q's at one instant. In general the motion of a system of f degrees of freedom requires the knowledge of $2f$ variables at some time in order to be completely specified. It is assumed in classical mechanics that it is possible to determine these $2f$ variables to any desired degree of accuracy. Within the last two decades it has been found that this specification cannot be carried out beyond a certain limit.

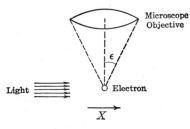

Fig. 3·1.

Suppose that we set out to measure the position and momentum of an electron in order to determine its motion. The natural instrument to use in the determination of its position is a microscope, illustrated diagrammatically in Figure 3·1. The accuracy with which a microscope can measure distance along the x direction is limited by the wavelength of the light used, this limit being $\dfrac{\lambda}{2 \sin \epsilon}$. At first it might seem that this difficulty could be overcome by using light of a very short wavelength. However, a new difficulty then arises: the Compton effect. If a photon of energy $h\nu$ and momentum $\dfrac{h\nu}{c}$ strikes an electron at rest, the photon after the collision will have an energy $h\nu'$ and momentum $\dfrac{h\nu'}{c}$, while the electron will have a kinetic energy $\frac{1}{2}mv^2$ and momentum mv, where m is the relativistic mass of the electron and v is its velocity.

The motions of the photon and electron are illustrated in Figure 3·2. The law of conservation of energy gives the relation

$$h\nu = h\nu' + \tfrac{1}{2}mv^2 \qquad\qquad 3\cdot1$$

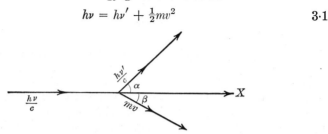

Fig. 3·2. The Compton effect.

while the law of conservation of momentum gives the relations

$$\frac{h\nu}{c} = \frac{h\nu'}{c}\cos\alpha + mv\cos\beta \qquad\qquad 3\cdot2$$

$$0 = \frac{h\nu'}{c}\sin\alpha - mv\sin\beta \qquad\qquad 3\cdot3$$

The x component of the momentum of the electron is therefore

$$p_x = \frac{h}{c}(\nu - \nu'\cos\alpha) \qquad\qquad 3\cdot4$$

As may be seen from equation 3·1, ν' is less than ν; that is, the scattered light is of longer wavelength than the incident light. For our purposes, however, we will obtain a sufficiently accurate value for the momentum of the electron if we put $\nu' = \nu$ in equation 3·4, giving

$$p_x = \frac{h}{\lambda}(1 - \cos\alpha) \qquad\qquad 3\cdot5$$

If we are to see the light in the microscope it must be scattered by the electron into the objective, so that α must lie between the limits $90° - \epsilon$ and $90° + \epsilon$. Since there is no way of telling through which part of the objective the light from the electron has passed, we know only that the x component of the momentum of the electron lies between the limits

$$\frac{h}{\lambda}(1 - \sin\epsilon) \le p_x \le \frac{h}{\lambda}(1 + \sin\epsilon) \qquad\qquad 3\cdot5$$

so that there is an uncertainty in the momentum of the electron of an amount

$$\Delta p_x \sim \frac{h}{\lambda}\sin\epsilon \qquad\qquad 3\cdot7$$

Owing to the finite resolving power of the microscope, there will be an uncertainty in the position of the electron, as mentioned above, of an amount

$$\Delta x \sim \frac{\lambda}{\sin \epsilon} \qquad 3\cdot8$$

The product of these uncertainties is

$$\Delta p_x \, \Delta x \sim h \qquad 3\cdot9$$

which is independent of the wavelength of the light used. The attempt to gain accuracy in position by using light of short wavelength is therefore defeated by the loss of accuracy in the measurement of momentum.

This difficulty is quite general. Whatever experiments are devised to measure at the same time two conjugate variables, the limit of accuracy always appears to be given by a relation similar to 3·9. This result has been assumed by Heisenberg[1] to be a fundamental law of nature, and is generally known as the uncertainty principle.

3b. Wave Mechanics. In order to explain this principle a new mechanics is necessary. This mechanics must not, like the old mechanics, assign a definite position and momentum to each particle, but must allow an uncertainty in these variables. This is accomplished by introducing functions which express, not the fact that a particle is at a given point, but the probability that the particle is at that point. Such functions are used in the theory of electromagnetic waves. As stated in Chapter I, light is corpuscular in nature, at least when it interacts with matter. The motion of these light corpuscles, or photons, is governed by the electromagnetic field, which according to Maxwell's equations moves in the form of waves which obey the usual equation of wave motion

$$\frac{\partial^2 W}{\partial x^2} + \frac{\partial^2 W}{\partial y^2} + \frac{\partial^2 W}{\partial z^2} = \frac{1}{c^2} \frac{\partial^2 W}{\partial t^2} \qquad 3\cdot10$$

where c is the velocity of light and W is the amplitude of the wave. The photon is not definitely located in any part of the wave, but the probability of finding a photon at any point is given by the square of the amplitude at that point. The energy E of the photon is connected with the frequency ν of the wave motion by the Einstein relation

$$E = h\nu \qquad 3\cdot11$$

and the momentum of the photon is

$$p = \frac{h}{\lambda} \qquad 3\cdot12$$

[1] W. Heisenberg, Z. *Physik*, **43**, 172 (1927).

As stated in Chapter I, the de Broglie assumption that electrons were accompanied by waves controlling their motions in the same manner that photons are controlled by electromagnetic waves has been verified by the electron diffraction experiments of Davisson and Germer, G. P. Thomson, and others. By using crystal lattices as gratings and comparing the wavelength of the electrons as calculated from the diffraction pattern with that calculated from the momentum of the electron, the validity of equation 3·12 for electron waves has been verified.

If we assume that the Einstein relation (3·11) is valid for electron waves, the velocity of the waves is given by

$$v = \lambda\nu = \frac{E}{p} \qquad\qquad 3\cdot13$$

The differential equation of the wave motion is then

$$\frac{\partial^2\Psi}{\partial x^2} + \frac{\partial^2\Psi}{\partial y^2} + \frac{\partial^2\Psi}{\partial z^2} = \frac{1}{v^2}\frac{\partial^2\Psi}{\partial t^2} = \frac{p^2}{E^2}\frac{\partial^2\Psi}{\partial t^2} \qquad 3\cdot14$$

where Ψ is the amplitude of the wave; the square of this amplitude gives the probability of finding the electron at a given point. If we wish a solution that will represent standing waves (such as those on a string fastened at both ends), we may write Ψ in the form

$$\Psi = \psi e^{-2\pi i\nu t} \qquad\qquad 3\cdot15$$

where ψ is a function of x, y, and z, but not of the time t. For the probability of finding the electron at a point we must take the square of the absolute value of Ψ in order that the probability be real and positive. Substituting 3·15 into 3·14 gives

$$\frac{\partial^2\psi}{\partial x^2} + \frac{\partial^2\psi}{\partial y^2} + \frac{\partial^2\psi}{\partial z^2} = -\frac{4\pi^2 p^2}{h^2}\psi \qquad 3\cdot16$$

as the differential equation for ψ. The kinetic energy of the electron is $T = E - V$, where V is the potential energy and is connected with the momentum by the relation $T = \dfrac{p^2}{2m}$. We may therefore write equation 3·16 in the form

$$\frac{\partial^2\psi}{\partial x^2} + \frac{\partial^2\psi}{\partial y^2} + \frac{\partial^2\psi}{\partial z^2} + \frac{8\pi^2 m}{h^2}(E - V)\psi = 0 \qquad 3\cdot17$$

This is the first of Schrödinger's equations,[2] by means of which most of the applications of quantum mechanics are made. From the form of

[2] See Chapter I, reference 7.

equation 3·15, it may be noted that this equation may also be written as

$$\frac{\partial^2 \Psi}{\partial x^2} + \frac{\partial^2 \Psi}{\partial y^2} + \frac{\partial^2 \Psi}{\partial z^2} + \frac{8\pi^2 m}{h^2}\left(\frac{h}{2\pi i}\frac{\partial}{\partial t} - V\right)\Psi = 0 \qquad 3·18$$

which is the second of Schrödinger's equations. Although the greater part of this text will be devoted to the solution of equations 3·17 and 3·18 for particular systems, the above " derivation " of these equations does not furnish a very satisfactory foundation for an exposition of quantum mechanics. We shall therefore proceed to formulate the principles of quantum mechanics in more general terms.

3c. Functions and Operators. Because the mathematics used in the general formulation of quantum mechanics is rather unusual, we shall first develop the elements of the theory of operators. A function is nothing but a rule by which, given any number, we can find another number. Thus the function x^2 is merely the rule: take the number x and multiply it by itself. Similarly, we define an operator as a rule by which, given any function, we can find another function. Thus we may define an operator ξ as follows: multiply the function by the independent variable. This rule is written symbolically

$$\xi f(x) = x f(x) \qquad 3·19$$

Another operator, δ, is differentiation with respect to the independent variable:

$$\delta f(x) = f'(x) \qquad 3·20$$

We may develop an algebra of operators, just as we can develop an algebra of numbers. The sum of two operators α and β is defined by the equation

$$(\alpha + \beta)f(x) = \alpha f(x) + \beta f(x) \qquad 3·21$$

The product of two operators is defined by the equation

$$\alpha\beta f(x) = \alpha[\beta f(x)] \qquad 3·22$$

The resemblance of operator algebra to ordinary algebra is only superficial. Although the operator $\alpha + \beta$ is the same as the operator $\beta + \alpha$ by definition, the operators $\alpha\beta$ and $\beta\alpha$ may be quite different. If $\alpha\beta$ and $\beta\alpha$ are the same, α and β are said to commute. An example of two operators which do not commute is given by the operators ξ and δ defined above, since

$$\xi\delta f(x) = \xi[\delta f(x)] = \xi f'(x) = x f'(x) \qquad 3·23$$

$$\delta\xi f(x) = \delta[\xi f(x)] = \delta[x f(x)] = x f'(x) + f(x) \qquad 3·24$$

Operators are not limited to functions of one variable. We may have such operators as δ_x, defined by the equation

$$\delta_x f(x, y) = \frac{\partial}{\partial x} f(x, y) \qquad 3\cdot25$$

An important group of operators are the vector operators (Appendix II), of which the one most frequently used in quantum mechanics is the Laplacian operator, defined by the equation

$$\nabla^2 f(x, y, z) = \frac{\partial^2 f}{\partial x^2} + \frac{\partial^2 f}{\partial y^2} + \frac{\partial^2 f}{\partial z^2} \qquad 3\cdot26$$

We define a class of functions as all those functions which obey certain specified conditions. Thus there is the class of continuous, single-valued functions of one variable x which vanish at $x = 1$ and $x = -1$. It may happen that in a given class there are functions which, when operated on by an operator α, are merely multiplied by some constant a, or in symbols

$$\alpha f(x) = a f(x) \qquad 3\cdot27$$

Those members of the class which obey such a relation are known as the characteristic functions or eigenfunctions of the operator α. The various possible values of a are called the characteristic values or eigenvalues of the operator. For example, if our class is the class of functions of x which are finite, continuous, and single-valued in the range $-\pi \leq x \leq \pi$, and if our operator is $\delta = \dfrac{d}{dx}$, the eigenfunctions are of the form e^{kx}, where k may be real or complex, since

$$\frac{d}{dx} e^{kx} = k e^{kx} \qquad 3\cdot28$$

and every number is an eigenvalue. The class of the functions is very important, for, if in this example we had restricted our class by adding the condition that the value of the function must be the same at $x = \pi$ and $x = -\pi$, the eigenfunctions would have been only those functions of the form e^{imx}, where m is an integer, and the eigenvalues would have been the imaginary integers im.

In quantum mechanics the eigenfunctions which are allowed are always chosen from the class of functions which are single-valued and continuous (except at a finite number of points where the function may become infinite) in the complete range of the variables, and which give a finite result when the squares of their absolute values are integrated over the complete range of the variables. If ψ is such a function and ψ^* its complex conjugate, the last condition requires that $\int \psi\psi^* \, d\tau$ be finite, where the element of volume $d\tau = dx_1 \, dx_2 \cdots dx_n$, the x's being the cartesian coordinates of the particles. By appropriate transformations $d\tau$ is expressible in other coordinate systems. We shall refer to this class of functions as the class Q.

If ψ and φ are any two functions belonging to the class Q, and $\mathbf{a}$ is an operator operating on ψ and φ, the operator $\mathbf{a}$ is said to be Hermitian if

$$\int \varphi^*(\mathbf{a}\psi) \, d\tau = \int \psi(\mathbf{a}^*\varphi^*) \, d\tau \qquad 3\cdot 29$$

Hermitian operators have the property that their eigenvalues for functions in class Q are always real, for, if $\mathbf{a}$ is an Hermitian operator and ψ is an eigenfunction of $\mathbf{a}$ from class Q with the eigenvalue a, then

$$\mathbf{a}\psi = a\psi \qquad 3\cdot 30$$

Taking the complex conjugate of every quantity in this equation,

$$\mathbf{a}^*\psi^* = a^*\psi^* \qquad 3\cdot 31$$

Then

$$\int \psi^*(\mathbf{a}\psi) \, d\tau = a \int \psi^*\psi \, d\tau \qquad 3\cdot 32$$

and

$$\int \psi(\mathbf{a}^*\psi^*) \, d\tau = a^* \int \psi\psi^* \, d\tau \qquad 3\cdot 33$$

But if $\mathbf{a}$ is Hermitian these quantities must be equal, so that $a = a^*$, which is true only if a is real.

Operators do not generally have the property expressed by the equation

$$\mathbf{a}[c_1 f_1(x) + c_2 f_2(x)] = c_1 \mathbf{a} f_1(x) + c_2 \mathbf{a} f_2(x) \qquad 3\cdot 34$$

For example, if $\mathbf{a}$ is the operator which squares the function, that is, if

$$\mathbf{a} f(x) = [f(x)]^2$$

then

$$\mathbf{a}[f_1(x) + f_2(x)] = [f_1(x)]^2 + 2f_1(x)f_2(x) + [f_2(x)]^2 \qquad 3\cdot 35$$

and

$$\mathbf{a} f_1(x) + \mathbf{a} f_2(x) = [f_1(x)]^2 + [f_2(x)]^2 \neq \mathbf{a}[f_1(x) + f_2(x)] \qquad 3\cdot 36$$

If equation 3·34 holds for a given operator, the operator is said to be linear.

3d. The General Formulation of Quantum Mechanics. We are now ready to put forward the general principles of quantum mechanics.

We shall do this by making certain postulates, which, like the axioms of geometry, are not proved. From these postulates the whole theory will follow, and finally we shall be led to conclusions which can be checked experimentally. The theory will stand or fall on the strength of these experimental checks. There is no unique set of postulates in quantum mechanics, but the following formulation seems most convenient for our purposes.

Let us consider a system of particles of f degrees of freedom which could be described classically by the values at a given time t of the f coordinates $q_1 \cdots q_f$ and the f conjugate momenta $p_1 \cdots p_f$. We then state

POSTULATE I. Any state of the system is described as fully as possible by a function $\Psi(q_1 \cdots q_f, t)$ of the class Q. This function $\Psi(q_1 \cdots q_f, t)$ is called the state function of the system, and has the property that $\Psi^*\Psi \, d\tau$ is the probability that the variables lie in the volume element $d\tau$ at time t; that is, q_1 has a value between q_1 and $q_1 + dq_1$, etc. Since each variable must have some value, the total probability must be unity, so that

$$\int \Psi^*(q_1 \cdots q_f, t)\Psi(q_1 \cdots q_f, t) \, d\tau = 1 \qquad 3\cdot37$$

where the integral is taken over all possible values of the q's.

POSTULATE II. To every dynamical variable M there can be assigned a linear operator μ. Since we are interested only in observable quantities, which are real, we may restrict ourselves to the case where these linear operators are also Hermitian. The rules for finding these operators are the following:

(a) If M is one of the q's or t, the operator is multiplication by the variable itself.

(b) If M is one of the p's, the operator is $\dfrac{h}{2\pi i}\dfrac{\partial}{\partial q_i}$, where q_i is conjugate to p_i.

(c) If M is any dynamical variable expressible in terms of the q's, the p's, and t, the operator is found by substituting the operators for the q's, the p's, and t as defined above in the algebraic expression for M, and replacing the processes of ordinary algebra by those of operator algebra. If there is any ambiguity in the order of the factors, they must be arranged so that the resulting operator is Hermitian.

POSTULATE III. The state functions $\Psi(q, t)$ satisfy the equation

$$\mathrm{H}\left(q, \frac{h}{2\pi i}\frac{\partial}{\partial q}, t\right)\Psi(q, t) = -\frac{h}{2\pi i}\frac{\partial}{\partial t}\Psi(q, t) \qquad 3\cdot38$$

where $\mathbf{H}\left(q, \dfrac{h}{2\pi i}\dfrac{\partial}{\partial q}, t\right)$ is the Hamiltonian operator for the system

This is Schrödinger's equation including the time.

POSTULATE IV. If the state function $\Psi(q, t)$ is an eigenfunction of the operator $\boldsymbol{\mu}$ corresponding to a dynamical variable M, that is, if

$$\boldsymbol{\mu}\Psi(q, t) = m\Psi(q, t) \qquad 3\cdot39$$

then in this state the variable M has the constant value m precisely; and conversely. Such a state is known as an eigenstate of M.

COROLLARY I. If the state function is an eigenfunction of the energy operator, the Hamiltonian operator $\mathbf{H}$, with the eigenvalue E, then $\Psi(q, t)$ satisfies the equation

$$\mathbf{H}\left(q, \frac{h}{2\pi i}\frac{\partial}{\partial q}, t\right)\Psi(q, t) = E\Psi(q, t) \qquad 3\cdot40$$

If equations 3·40 and 3·38 are to be consistent, $\Psi(q, t)$ must be of the form

$$\Psi(q, t) = \psi(q)e^{-\frac{2\pi i}{h}Et} \qquad 3\cdot41$$

where $\psi(q)$ is a solution of the equation

$$\mathbf{H}\left(q, \frac{h}{2\pi i}\frac{\partial}{\partial q}, t\right)\psi(q) = E\psi(q) \qquad 3\cdot42$$

Equation 3·42 is Schrödinger's equation for a stationary state, that is, for a state which is an eigenstate of the energy operator.

As an example of the manner in which these postulates work let us consider the system consisting of a particle of mass m moving in a potential field $V(x, y, z)$. The kinetic energy of the particle is

$$T = \frac{1}{2m}(p_x^2 + p_y^2 + p_z^2) \qquad 3\cdot43$$

and the classical Hamiltonian function is

$$H = \frac{1}{2m}(p_x^2 + p_y^2 + p_z^2) + V(x, y, z) \qquad 3\cdot44$$

According to the above postulates, the Hamiltonian operator is

$$\mathbf{H}\left(q, \frac{h}{2\pi i}\frac{\partial}{\partial q}, t\right) = \frac{1}{2m}\left[\left(\frac{h}{2\pi i}\frac{\partial}{\partial x}\right)^2 + \left(\frac{h}{2\pi i}\frac{\partial}{\partial y}\right)^2 + \left(\frac{h}{2\pi i}\frac{\partial}{\partial z}\right)^2\right]$$

$$+ V(x, y, z) \qquad 3\cdot45$$

$$= \frac{-h^2}{8\pi^2 m}\left(\frac{\partial^2}{\partial x^2} + \frac{\partial^2}{\partial y^2} + \frac{\partial^2}{\partial z^2}\right) + V(x, y, z)$$

The Schrödinger equation including the time is therefore

$$\frac{-h^2}{8\pi^2 m}\left(\frac{\partial^2}{\partial x^2} + \frac{\partial^2}{\partial y^2} + \frac{\partial^2}{\partial z^2}\right)\Psi(x, y, z, t) + V(x, y, z)\Psi(x, y, z, t)$$

$$= \frac{-h}{2\pi i}\frac{\partial}{\partial t}\Psi(x, y, z, t) \qquad 3\cdot 46$$

If we look for a solution of this equation in the form

$$\Psi(x, y, z, t) = \psi(x, y, z)e^{\frac{-2\pi i}{h}Et} \qquad 3\cdot 47$$

we obtain the equation

$$\left[\frac{-h^2}{8\pi^2 m}\left(\frac{\partial^2}{\partial x^2} + \frac{\partial^2}{\partial y^2} + \frac{\partial^2}{\partial z^2}\right) + V(x, y, z)\right]\psi(x, y, z) = E\psi(x, y, z) \qquad 3\cdot 48$$

This is identical with equation 3·42, so that, if $\psi(x, y, z)$ is a solution of equation 3·48 and is a function of class Q, it is an eigenfunction of the energy operator and describes a state with the precise value E for the energy. Equation 3·48 may also be written as

$$\frac{\partial^2\psi}{\partial x^2} + \frac{\partial^2\psi}{\partial y^2} + \frac{\partial^2\psi}{\partial z^2} + \frac{8\pi^2 m}{h^2}(E - V)\psi = 0 \qquad 3\cdot 49$$

so that in this special case the general theory gives the same result as the theory of section 3b.

In most of our discussions we shall be dealing with state functions which are eigenfunctions of the energy operator for a given system. For such state functions equations 3·37 and 3·39 are equally valid if $\Psi(q, t)$ is replaced by $\psi(q)$, as may be seen from the relation 3·41 between these functions.

From the postulated form of the operators for position and momentum we can obtain an important rule for their product. Since

$$\mathbf{pq}\psi = \frac{h}{2\pi i}\frac{\partial}{\partial q}(q\psi) = \frac{h}{2\pi i}\psi + \frac{h}{2\pi i}q\frac{\partial\psi}{\partial q} \qquad 3\cdot 50$$

and

$$\mathbf{qp}\psi = q\left(\frac{h}{2\pi i}\frac{\partial}{\partial q}\psi\right) = \frac{h}{2\pi i}q\frac{\partial\psi}{\partial q} \qquad 3\cdot 51$$

we have the result that

$$(\mathbf{pq} - \mathbf{qp})\psi = \frac{h}{2\pi i}\psi \qquad 3\cdot 52$$

a rule first discovered by Heisenberg.[1]

3e. Expansion Theorems. If two functions $\varphi_1(x)$ and $\varphi_2(x)$ have the property that

$$\int_a^b \varphi_2^*(x)\varphi_1(x)\, dx = 0 \qquad\qquad 3\cdot53$$

for a certain interval (a, b), the functions are said to be orthogonal in this interval. A set of functions

$$\varphi_1(x), \varphi_2(x), \cdots \varphi_i(x) \cdots$$

such that any two functions in the set are orthogonal in the interval (a, b) is called an orthogonal set for the interval (a, b). If in addition

$$\int_a^b \varphi_i^*(x)\varphi_i(x)\, dx = 1 \qquad\qquad 3\cdot54$$

for all values of i, the set is said to be normalized.

The great importance of orthogonal functions lies in the possibility of expanding arbitrary functions in a series of these orthogonal functions. Suppose that $f(x)$ is any function and that it is possible to expand $f(x)$ in the interval (a, b) in a series

$$f(x) = c_1\varphi_1(x) + c_2\varphi_2(x) + \cdots + c_i\varphi_i(x) + \cdots \qquad 3\cdot55$$

where the c's are constants. If we now multiply both sides of equation 3·55 by $\varphi_n^*(x)$, where $\varphi_n(x)$ is a member of the set of normalized and orthogonal functions given above, we have

$$\int_a^b \varphi_n^*(x)f(x)\, dx =$$

$$c_1 \int_a^b \varphi_n^*(x)\varphi_1(x)\, dx + \cdots + c_n \int_a^b \varphi_n^*(x)\varphi_n(x)\, dx + \cdots \qquad 3\cdot56$$

All the integrals on the right side of 3·56 vanish because of the orthogonality of the functions except

$$\int_a^b \varphi_n^*(x)\varphi_n(x)\, dx = 1$$

hence

$$c_n = \int_a^b \varphi_n^*(x)f(x)\, dx \qquad\qquad 3\cdot57$$

so that the coefficients are easily found if the expansion is valid. The question as to when such an expansion is possible is beyond the scope of this text, but it is possible for all functions of the class Q.

We shall now show that the eigenfunctions of any Hermitian operator are orthogonal functions in the interval corresponding to the complete range of the variables. Let the operator be $\mathbf{a}$, the eigenfunctions ψ_1 and ψ_2, with the eigenvalues a_1 and a_2, that is

$$\mathbf{a}\psi_1 = a_1\psi_1 \qquad \mathbf{a}\psi_2 = a_2\psi_2 \qquad\qquad 3\cdot58$$

Now consider the integral

$$\int \psi_2^* \mathbf{a}\psi_1 \, d\tau = a_1 \int \psi_2^*\psi_1 \, d\tau \qquad\qquad 3\cdot59$$

Since $\mathbf{a}$ is Hermitian, we have

$$\int \psi_2^* \mathbf{a}\psi_1 \, d\tau = \int \psi_1 \mathbf{a}^*\psi_2^* \, d\tau = a_2^* \int \psi_1\psi_2^* \, d\tau = a_2 \int \psi_1\psi_2^* \, d\tau \quad 3\cdot60$$

the last equality arising from the fact that a_2, being an eigenvalue of an Hermitian operator, is real.   Hence

$$a_1 \int \psi_2^*\psi_1 \, d\tau = a_2 \int \psi_1\psi_2^* \, d\tau$$

$$3\cdot61$$

$$(a_1 - a_2) \int \psi_2^*\psi_1 \, d\tau = 0$$

If $a_1 \neq a_2$, this requires that

$$\int \psi_2^*\psi_1 \, d\tau = 0 \qquad\qquad 3\cdot62$$

so that eigenfunctions corresponding to different eigenvalues are orthogonal.   When two or more eigenfunctions have the same eigenvalues this argument breaks down.   In this case, however, a set of orthogonal eigenfunctions can always be found.   Suppose that

$$\mathbf{a}\psi_1 = a\psi_1; \quad \mathbf{a}\psi_2 = a\psi_2; \quad \int \psi^*\psi_1 \, d\tau = b \qquad 3\cdot63$$

If we replace ψ_2 by $\psi_2' = \psi_2 - b\psi_1$, then

$$\int \psi_2'^*\psi_1 \, d\tau = \int \psi_2^*\psi_1 \, d\tau - b \int \psi_1^*\psi_1 \, d\tau = b - b = 0 \qquad 3\cdot64$$

and

$$\mathbf{a}\psi_2' = \mathbf{a}(\psi_2 - b\psi_1) = \mathbf{a}\psi_2 - b\mathbf{a}\psi_1$$

$$= a(\psi_2 - b\psi_1) = a\psi_2' \qquad\qquad 3\cdot65$$

so that ψ_2' is also an eigenfunction of α and is orthogonal to ψ_1, and if we use ψ_2' instead of ψ_2 our eigenfunctions are all orthogonal.   The process by which ψ_2' was found is known as orthogonalization.

If ψ_1 and ψ_2 are two eigenfunctions of the operator μ corresponding to the dynamical variable M, with eigenvalues m_1 and m_2 ($m_1 \neq m_2$), the state represented by $\psi = c_1\psi_1 + c_2\psi_2$ is not an eigenstate of μ, since

$$\mu\psi = \mu(c_1\psi_1 + c_2\psi_2) = c_1 m_1 \psi_1 + c_2 m_2 \psi_2 \neq m(c_1\psi_1 + c_2\psi_2) \quad 3\cdot66$$

In order that $\int \psi^*\psi \, d\tau = 1$ we must have the relation

$$\int (c_1^*\psi_1^* + c_2^*\psi_2^*)(c_1\psi_1 + c_2\psi_2) \, d\tau = c_1^*c_1 + c_2^*c_2 = 1 \qquad 3\cdot67$$

between the coefficients. We may give the following interpretation to the state ψ by a postulate, known as the principle of superposition.

POSTULATE V. If ψ_1 and ψ_2 are eigenfunctions of the operator μ corresponding to the variable M with the eigenvalues m_1 and m_2, then the state represented by $\psi = c_1\psi_1 + c_2\psi_2$ is that state in which the probability of observing the value of M to be m_1 is $c_1^*c_1$ and the probability of observing the value m_2 is $c_2^*c_2$. Since the set of eigenfunctions $\psi_1, \psi_2, \cdots \psi_i, \cdots$ of an operator μ is a normalized, orthogonal set, we may expand any state function φ in terms of these ψ_i's:

$$\varphi = \sum_i c_i\psi_i$$

where

$$c_i = \int \psi_i^*\varphi \, d\tau$$

Consider now the integral $\int \varphi^*\mu\varphi \, d\tau$. Expanding φ in terms of the eigenfunctions of μ we have

$$\int \varphi^*\mu\varphi \, d\tau = \int (\sum_i c_i^*\psi_i^*)\mu(\sum_i c_i\psi_i) \, d\tau$$

$$= \int (\sum_i c_i^*\psi_i^*)(\sum_i c_i m_i \psi_i) \, d\tau = \sum_i m_i c_i^* c_i \qquad 3\cdot68$$

But $\sum_i m_i c_i^* c_i$ is merely the average value of M in the state φ, so that we have the important theorem:

THEOREM I. The average value of any dynamical variable M in any state φ is given by $\int \varphi^*\mu\varphi \, d\tau$, where μ is the operator corresponding to M.

An important example of an expansion of this type occurs when φ is formed by operating on one of the eigenfunctions ψ_j of an operator μ

by the operator $\boldsymbol{\alpha}$ of some other variable, so that $\varphi_j = \boldsymbol{\alpha}\psi_j$. In this special case we have

$$\varphi_j = \boldsymbol{\alpha}\psi_j = \sum_i a_{ij}\psi_i \qquad 3\cdot 69$$

where

$$a_{ij} = \int \psi_i^* \boldsymbol{\alpha}\psi_j \, d\tau \qquad 3\cdot 70$$

The set of quantities a_{ij} found by expanding all the functions $\boldsymbol{\alpha}\psi_j$ is called the matrix of $\boldsymbol{\alpha}$. The quantities a_{ij} are usually written in the form of a table:

$$\begin{pmatrix} a_{11} & a_{12} & a_{13} \cdots \\ a_{21} & a_{22} & a_{23} \cdots \\ a_{31} & a_{32} & a_{33} \cdots \\ \cdot & \cdot & \cdot & \cdots \\ \cdot & \cdot & \cdot & \cdots \\ \cdot & \cdot & \cdot & \cdots \end{pmatrix} \qquad 3\cdot 71$$

If $\boldsymbol{\alpha}$ is Hermitian

$$a_{ij} = \int \psi_i^* \alpha \psi_j \, d\tau = \int \psi_j \alpha^* \psi_i^* \, d\tau = a_{ji}^* \qquad 3\cdot 72$$

Suppose that we also have an operator $\boldsymbol{\beta}$ such that

$$\boldsymbol{\beta}\psi_j = \sum_i b_{ij}\psi_i; \quad b_{ij} = \int \psi_i^* \boldsymbol{\beta}\psi_j \, d\tau \qquad 3\cdot 73$$

and we wish to find the matrix c_{ij} of the operator $\boldsymbol{\gamma} = \boldsymbol{\alpha}\boldsymbol{\beta}$. We have

$$\boldsymbol{\alpha}\boldsymbol{\beta}\psi_j = \boldsymbol{\alpha}\sum_k b_{kj}\psi_k = \sum_k b_{kj}\boldsymbol{\alpha}\psi_k$$

$$= \sum_k \sum_i b_{kj} a_{ik}\psi_i = \sum_i (\sum_k a_{ik}b_{kj})\psi_i = \sum_i c_{ij}\psi_i \qquad 3\cdot 74$$

so that

$$c_{ij} = \sum_k a_{ik}b_{kj} \qquad 3\cdot 75$$

3f. Eigenfunctions of Commuting Operators. In most of the problems in atomic and molecular structure with which we shall be concerned we will be interested in several operators at the same time. The eigenfunctions of one operator are usually different from those of another operator, but there is a very important exception in which one set of functions is a set of eigenfunctions of two operators at the same time, namely, when the operators commute. In this case we have the theorem:

THEOREM II.   If two operators α and β commute, there exists a set of functions which are simultaneously eigenfunctions of both operators.

Let α and β be two commuting operators and let ψ_i^a and ψ_i^b be the eigenfunctions of these operators, so that

$$\alpha\psi_i^a = a_i\psi_i^a; \quad \beta\psi_i^b = b_i\psi_i^b \qquad 3\cdot76$$

If we expand ψ_i^a in terms of the ψ_j^b's, $\psi_i^a = \sum_j c_{ji}\psi_j^b$ we have

$$\alpha\psi_i^a = \alpha\sum_j c_{ji}\psi_j^b = a_i\sum_j c_{ji}\psi_j^b$$

or

$$\sum_j c_{ji}(\alpha - a_i)\psi_j^b = 0 \qquad 3\cdot77$$

The function $(\alpha - a_i)\psi_j^b$ is an eigenfunction of β, or is identically zero, for, since α and β commute

$$\beta\{(\alpha - a_i)\psi_j^b\} = (\alpha - a_i)\beta\psi_j^b$$
$$= (\alpha - a_i)b_j\psi_j^b = b_j\{(\alpha - a_i)\psi_j^b\} \qquad 3\cdot78$$

and the eigenvalue of this function is the same as that of ψ_j^b itself.   Let us suppose that there are no two of the b_j's which are equal, that is, the ψ_j^b's form a set of non-degenerate eigenfunctions.   Then it follows that ψ_j^b and its multiples are the only functions which satisfy the equation

$$\beta\psi = b_j\psi \qquad 3\cdot79$$

The function $(\alpha - a_i)\psi_j^b$ must therefore be some multiple of ψ_j^b; that is

$$(\alpha - a_i)\psi_j^b = g_{ij}\psi_j^b \qquad 3\cdot80$$

where g_{ij} is some numerical constant.   Substituting this relation in $3\cdot77$, we have $\sum_j c_{ji}g_{ij}\psi_j^b = 0$.   If we now multiply by ψ_k^{b*} and integrate over the variables we have

$$\sum_j c_{ji}g_{ij}\int \psi_k^{b*}\psi_j^b \, d\tau = c_{ki}g_{ik} = 0 \qquad 3\cdot81$$

so that either c_{ki} or g_{ik} is zero.   If g_{ik} is zero, then

$$(\alpha - a_i)\psi_j^b = 0; \quad \alpha\psi_j^b = a_i\psi_j^b \qquad 3\cdot82$$

and ψ_j^b is an eigenfunction of α with the eigenvalue a_i, as well as an eigenfunction of β.   If $c_{ki} = 0$, then

$$\int \psi_k^{b*}\psi_i^a \, d\tau = \sum_j c_{ji}\int \psi_k^{b*}\psi_j^b \, d\tau = c_{ki} = 0 \qquad 3\cdot83$$

and we see that ψ_i^a is orthogonal to ψ_k^b.   Since the set of functions ψ_i^a form a complete set, no function can be orthogonal to all of them;

there must be at least one value of k for which $g_{ki} = 0$. We thus see that when there is non-degeneracy every eigenfunction of $\boldsymbol{\beta}$ is also an eigenfunction of $\boldsymbol{\alpha}$.

If, as usually happens, there are several ψ_j's with the same eigenvalue, the above argument does not hold. Suppose, for example, that ψ_1^b and ψ_2^b have the same eigenvalue. Let us then make the following change in the ψ_j^b's. We write

$$\psi_1^{b'} = c_1\psi_1^b + c_2\psi_2^b$$

and construct another function

$$\psi_2^{b'} = d_1\psi_1^b + d_2\psi_2^b$$

with the constants d_1 and d_2 chosen so that $\psi_1^{b'}$ is orthogonal to $\psi_2^{b'}$. If there are other degeneracies we adopt an analogous scheme. We now carry out the analysis using the $\psi_1^{b'}$'s. Owing to the degeneracy of $\psi_1^{b'}$ and $\psi_2^{b'}$, we have in place of 3·80 the two equations

$$(\boldsymbol{\alpha} - a_i)\psi_1^{b'} = g_{i1}\psi_1^{b'} + g_{i2}\psi_2^{b'}$$
$$(\boldsymbol{\alpha} - a_i)\psi_2^{b'} = h_{i1}\psi_1^{b'} + h_{i2}\psi_2^b$$

3·80a

where $g_{i1} = \int \psi_1^{b'*}(\boldsymbol{\alpha} - a_i)\psi_1^{b'}\, d\tau$, etc. It is now possible to form linear combinations of $\psi_1^{b'}$ and ψ_2^b which are eigenfunctions of $\boldsymbol{\alpha}$, that is, we can find constants k_{i1} and k_{i2} such that

$$(\boldsymbol{\alpha} - a_i)\{k_{i1}\psi_1^{b'} + k_{i2}\psi_2^{b'}\} = A_i\{k_{i1}\psi_1^{b'} + k_{i2}\psi_2^{b'}\}\qquad 3·84$$

By multiplying the first of equations 3·80a by k_{i1} and the second by k_{i2} and adding, we find that k_{i1} and k_{i2} must satisfy the relations

$$A_ik_{i1} = k_{i1}g_{i1} + k_{i2}h_{i1}$$
$$A_ik_{i2} = k_{i1}g_{i2} + k_{i2}h_{i2}$$

3·85

When these relations are satisfied, the functions $(k_{i1}\psi_1^{b'} + k_{i2}\psi_2^{b'})$ are eigenfunctions of $\boldsymbol{\alpha}$ with the eigenvalues $A_i + a_i$. They are of course eigenfunctions of $\boldsymbol{\beta}$ with the eigenvalue b_1.

Theorem II has thus been proved. The analogous theorem holds for the case of more than two operators; we shall use this theorem without proof.

We may also prove the converse of this theorem:

THEOREM III. If there exists a complete set of orthogonal functions ψ_i which are eigenfunctions of two operators $\boldsymbol{\alpha}$ and $\boldsymbol{\beta}$, then $\boldsymbol{\alpha}$ and $\boldsymbol{\beta}$ commute.

Let us expand any function φ in terms of the ψ_i's, and then operate on φ with $(\alpha\beta - \beta\alpha)$. We have

$$(\alpha\beta - \beta\alpha)\varphi = (\alpha\beta - \beta\alpha)\sum_i c_i\psi_i = \sum_i c_i(a_ib_i - b_ia_i)\psi_i = 0 \qquad 3\cdot86$$

Since φ is an arbitrary function we see that α and β commute.

The physical interpretation of these theorems is that, if two physical quantities have operators which commute (as do the operators for the energy and the total angular momentum of a system), then it is possible to have states of the system in which both variables have definite values. Conversely, if it is possible for two variables (physical quantities) to have definite values for a complete set of states at the same time, then the corresponding operators commute.

Another theorem which we shall find useful is:

THEOREM IV. If β is an operator which commutes with an operator α (where both are Hermitian), and ψ_1 and ψ_2 are eigenfunctions of α, then the matrix element $\int \psi_1^*\beta\psi_2 \, d\tau$ vanishes unless $a_1 = a_2$, where a_1 and a_2 are the eigenvalues of ψ_1 and ψ_2.

To prove this theorem consider the integral

$$\int \psi_1^*\beta\alpha\psi_2 \, d\tau = a_2 \int \psi_1^*\beta\psi_2 \, d\tau \qquad 3\cdot87$$

Using the fact that α is Hermitian,

$$\int \psi_1^*\beta\alpha\psi_2 \, d\tau = \int \psi_1^*\alpha(\beta\psi_2) \, d\tau = \int (\beta\psi_2)(\alpha^*\psi_1^*) \, d\tau$$

$$= a_1 \int \psi_1^*\beta\psi_2 \, d\tau \qquad 3\cdot88$$

Therefore $\qquad\qquad (a_1 - a_2) \int \psi_1^*\beta\psi_2 \, d\tau = 0 \qquad\qquad 3\cdot89$

so that $\int \psi_1^*\beta\psi_2 \, d\tau = 0$ if $a_1 \neq a_2$.

3g. The Hamiltonian Operator. We have seen that the Hamiltonian operator for a single particle is, in rectangular coordinates,

$$\mathbf{H} = \frac{-h^2}{8\pi^2 m}\left(\frac{\partial^2}{\partial x^2} + \frac{\partial^2}{\partial y^2} + \frac{\partial^2}{\partial z^2}\right) + V(x, y, z) \qquad 3\cdot90$$

but we have not as yet proved that this operator is actually Hermitian. Such a proof is necessary, for if we had written the classical Hamiltonian in the form

$$H = \frac{1}{2m}\left(\frac{1}{x} p_x^2 x + \frac{1}{y} p_y^2 y + \frac{1}{z} p_z^2 z\right) + V(x, y, z) \qquad 3\cdot91$$

which is algebraically equivalent to equation 3·44, and then substituted the operators for the p's, we would have the quite different result

$$\mathbf{H} = \frac{-h^2}{8\pi^2 m}\left(\frac{\partial^2}{\partial x^2} + \frac{1}{x}\frac{\partial}{\partial x} + \frac{\partial^2}{\partial y^2} + \frac{1}{y}\frac{\partial}{\partial y} + \frac{\partial^2}{\partial z^2} + \frac{1}{z}\frac{\partial}{\partial z}\right) + V(x, y, z) \quad 3·92$$

Since $\mathbf{H} = \mathbf{H}^*$, the condition that $\mathbf{H}$ be Hermitian is

$$\iiint_{-\infty}^{\infty} \varphi^* H\psi \, dx \, dy \, dz = \iiint_{-\infty}^{\infty} \psi H\varphi^* \, dx \, dy \, dz$$

provided that φ and ψ belong to class Q. This condition requires that φ and ψ vanish at infinity. Consider the operator $\dfrac{\partial^2}{\partial x_2}$. We have

$$\iiint_{-\infty}^{\infty} \varphi^* \frac{\partial^2 \psi}{\partial x^2} \, dx \, dy \, dz = \iint_{-\infty}^{\infty} \varphi^* \frac{\partial \psi}{\partial x} \, dy \, dz \Big]_{x=-\infty}^{x=+\infty}$$
$$- \iiint_{-\infty}^{\infty} \frac{\partial \varphi^*}{\partial x}\frac{\partial \psi}{\partial x} \, dx \, dy \, dz$$

Since φ^* vanishes at infinity, and $\dfrac{\partial \psi}{\partial x}$ is finite or zero, the first integral on the right is zero, hence

$$\iiint_{-\infty}^{\infty} \varphi^* \frac{\partial^2 \psi}{\partial x^2} \, dx \, dy \, dz = - \iiint_{-\infty}^{\infty} \frac{\partial \varphi^*}{\partial x}\frac{\partial \psi}{\partial x} \, dx \, dy \, dz$$

In the same way, we find

$$\iiint_{-\infty}^{\infty} \psi \frac{\partial^2 \varphi^*}{\partial x^2} \, dx \, dy \, dz = - \iiint_{-\infty}^{\infty} \frac{\partial \varphi^*}{\partial x}\frac{\partial \psi}{\partial x} \, dx \, dy \, dz$$

so that the operator $\dfrac{\partial^2}{\partial x^2}$, and analogously the operators $\dfrac{\partial^2}{\partial y^2}$ and $\dfrac{\partial^2}{\partial z^2}$, are Hermitian. The Hamiltonian operator 3·90, being the sum of Hermitian operators multiplied by real constants, is therefore Hermitian.

For the operator $\dfrac{\partial}{\partial x}$, we find

$$\iiint_{-\infty}^{\infty} \varphi^* \frac{\partial \psi}{dx} \, dx \, dy \, dz = \iint_{-\infty}^{\infty} \varphi^* \psi \, dy \, dz \Big]_{x=-\infty}^{x=+\infty}$$
$$- \iiint_{-\infty}^{\infty} \psi \frac{\partial \varphi^*}{\partial x} \, dx \, dy \, dz$$
$$= - \iiint_{-\infty}^{\infty} \psi \frac{\partial \varphi^*}{\partial x} \, dx \, dy \, dz \neq \iiint_{-\infty}^{\infty} \psi \frac{\partial \varphi^*}{\partial x} \, dx \, dy \, dz \quad 3·93$$

so that the operator $\dfrac{\partial}{\partial x}$ is not Hermitian.   (From the above equations,

however, it is apparent that the operator $i\dfrac{\partial}{\partial x}$ is Hermitian.)   The

operator $\dfrac{1}{x}\dfrac{\partial}{\partial x}$ will likewise be non-Hermitian, so that the Hamiltonian
written as 3·92 is not valid from the quantum-mechanical viewpoint.

Written in vector notation, the Hamiltonian operator 3·90 is

$$\mathbf{H} = \frac{-h^2}{8\pi^2 m}\, \nabla^2(x,\, y,\, z) + V(x,\, y,\, z) \qquad\qquad 3\text{·}94$$

Rectangular coordinates are not always the most convenient coordinates to use.   Since the Laplacian operator is invariant under a transformation of coordinates (Appendix III), the Hamiltonian operator
in an arbitrary coordinate system will be

$$\mathbf{H} = \frac{-h^2}{8\pi^2 m}\, \nabla^2(\xi,\, \eta,\, \zeta) + V(\xi,\, \eta,\, \zeta) \qquad\qquad 3\text{·}95$$

where ξ, η, ζ are the new coordinates.   The transformations from rectangular to various other important coordinate systems are given in
Appendix III, as are the expressions for the Laplacian operator ∇^2 and
the volume element $d\tau$ in these coordinate systems.

3h. Angular Momenta. Of almost as great importance as the
Hamiltonian operator are the operators connected with angular momenta.
For a single particle, the angular momentum about the origin is
$\mathbf{M} = \mathbf{r} \times \mathbf{p}$, where $\mathbf{r}$ is the distance from the origin and $\mathbf{p}$ is the linear
momentum, or, in terms of its components M_x, M_y, and M_z in rectan-
gular coordinates,

$$
\begin{aligned}
M_x &= yp_z - zp_y \\
M_y &= zp_x - xp_z \qquad\qquad 3\text{·}96 \\
M_z &= xp_y - yp_x
\end{aligned}
$$

Replacing the p's by the corresponding quantum-mechanical operators,
we obtain the operators for the components of angular momenta:

$$
\begin{aligned}
\mathbf{M}_x &= \frac{h}{2\pi i}\left(y\frac{\partial}{\partial z} - z\frac{\partial}{\partial y} \right) \\[6pt]
\mathbf{M}_y &= \frac{h}{2\pi i}\left(z\frac{\partial}{\partial x} - x\frac{\partial}{\partial z} \right) \qquad\qquad 3\text{·}97 \\[6pt]
\mathbf{M}_z &= \frac{h}{2\pi i}\left(x\frac{\partial}{\partial y} - y\frac{\partial}{\partial x} \right)
\end{aligned}
$$

The total angular momentum is, of course,

$$\mathbf{M} = \mathbf{i}M_x + \mathbf{j}M_y + \mathbf{k}M_z$$

We shall never have occasion to use $\mathbf{M}$ itself, but only its scalar product with some other vector, or its square:

$$\mathbf{M}^2 = \mathbf{M}_x^2 + \mathbf{M}_y^2 + \mathbf{M}_z^2 \qquad\qquad 3\cdot98$$

The angular momentum operators are usually expressed in spherical coordinates. By means of the transformations given in Appendix III the operators in spherical coordinates are readily found to be:[3]

[3] We may illustrate this calculation for M_x. From the transformations

$$x = r \sin\theta \cos\varphi$$
$$y = r \sin\theta \sin\varphi$$
$$z = r \cos\theta$$

we obtain the reverse transformations

$$r^2 = x^2 + y^2 + z^2$$

$$\cos\theta = \frac{z}{\sqrt{x^2 + y^2 + z^2}}$$

$$\tan\varphi = \frac{y}{x}$$

from which we calculate the partial derivatives:

$$\frac{\partial r}{\partial z} = \cos\theta \qquad\qquad \frac{\partial r}{\partial y} = \sin\theta \sin\varphi$$

$$\frac{\partial\theta}{\partial z} = -\frac{\sin\theta}{r} \qquad\qquad \frac{\partial\theta}{\partial y} = \frac{\cos\theta \sin\varphi}{r}$$

$$\frac{\partial\varphi}{\partial z} = 0 \qquad\qquad \frac{\partial\varphi}{\partial y} = \frac{\cos\varphi}{r\sin\theta}$$

Therefore

$$\mathbf{M}_x = \frac{h}{2\pi i}\left[y\frac{\partial}{\partial z} - z\frac{\partial}{\partial y} \right]$$

$$= \frac{h}{2\pi i}\left[r\sin\theta\sin\varphi\left(\frac{\partial r}{\partial z}\frac{\partial}{\partial r} + \frac{\partial\theta}{\partial z}\frac{\partial}{\partial\theta} + \frac{\partial\varphi}{\partial z}\frac{\partial}{\partial\varphi} \right) \right.$$

$$\left. - r\cos\theta\left(\frac{\partial r}{\partial y}\frac{\partial}{\partial r} + \frac{\partial\theta}{\partial y}\frac{\partial}{\partial\theta} + \frac{\partial\varphi}{\partial y}\frac{\partial}{\partial\varphi} \right) \right]$$

$$= \frac{h}{2\pi i}\left[(r\sin\theta\sin\varphi\cos\theta - r\cos\theta\sin\theta\sin\varphi)\frac{\partial}{\partial r} \right.$$

$$\left. + (-\sin^2\theta\sin\varphi - \cos^2\theta\sin\varphi)\frac{\partial}{\partial\theta} + (-\cot\theta\cos\varphi)\frac{\partial}{\partial\varphi} \right]$$

$$= \frac{h}{2\pi i}\left[-\sin\varphi\frac{\partial}{\partial\theta} - \cot\theta\cos\varphi\frac{\partial}{\partial\varphi} \right]$$

$$\mathbf{M}_x = \frac{h}{2\pi i}\left(-\sin\varphi\,\frac{\partial}{\partial\theta} - \cot\theta\cos\varphi\,\frac{\partial}{\partial\varphi}\right)$$

$$\mathbf{M}_y = \frac{h}{2\pi i}\left(\cos\varphi\,\frac{\partial}{\partial\theta} - \cot\theta\sin\varphi\,\frac{\partial}{\partial\varphi}\right)$$

$$\mathbf{M}_z = \frac{h}{2\pi i}\frac{\partial}{\partial\varphi}$$

$$\mathbf{M}^2 = \frac{-h^2}{4\pi^2}\left[\frac{1}{\sin\theta}\frac{\partial}{\partial\theta}\left(\sin\theta\,\frac{\partial}{\partial\theta}\right) + \frac{1}{\sin^2\theta}\frac{\partial^2}{\partial\varphi^2}\right]$$

3·99

The commutation rules for $\mathbf{M}_x$, $\mathbf{M}_y$, and $\mathbf{M}_z$ are most readily found from the expressions in rectangular coordinates

$$\mathbf{M}_x\mathbf{M}_y = \frac{-h^2}{4\pi^2}\left(y\,\frac{\partial}{\partial x} + yz\,\frac{\partial^2}{\partial x\,\partial z} - xy\,\frac{\partial^2}{\partial z^2} - z^2\,\frac{\partial^2}{\partial x\,\partial y} + xz\,\frac{\partial^2}{\partial y\,\partial z}\right) \quad 3\cdot100$$

$$\mathbf{M}_y\mathbf{M}_x = \frac{-h^2}{4\pi^2}\left(yz\,\frac{\partial^2}{\partial x\,\partial z} - z^2\,\frac{\partial^2}{\partial x\,\partial y} - xy\,\frac{\partial^2}{\partial z^2} + x\,\frac{\partial}{\partial y} + xz\,\frac{\partial^2}{\partial y\,\partial z}\right) \quad 3\cdot101$$

so that

$$\mathbf{M}_x\mathbf{M}_y - \mathbf{M}_y\mathbf{M}_x = \frac{-h^2}{4\pi^2}\left(y\,\frac{\partial}{\partial x} - x\,\frac{\partial}{\partial y}\right)$$

$$= \frac{ih}{2\pi}\cdot\frac{h}{2\pi i}\left(x\,\frac{\partial}{\partial y} - y\,\frac{\partial}{\partial x}\right) = \frac{ih}{2\pi}\mathbf{M}_z \quad\quad 3\cdot102$$

Similarly, we find

$$\mathbf{M}_y\mathbf{M}_z - \mathbf{M}_z\mathbf{M}_y = \frac{ih}{2\pi}\mathbf{M}_x$$

$$\mathbf{M}_z\mathbf{M}_x - \mathbf{M}_x\mathbf{M}_z = \frac{ih}{2\pi}\mathbf{M}_y$$

3·103

If we now consider the commutation of $\mathbf{M}^2$ and $\mathbf{M}_z$, we see immediately from the expressions for the operators in spherical coordinates that

$$\mathbf{M}^2\mathbf{M}_z - \mathbf{M}_z\mathbf{M}^2 = 0 \quad\quad 3\cdot104$$

so that $\mathbf{M}^2$ commutes with $\mathbf{M}_z$. Because of the equivalence of $\mathbf{M}_x$, $\mathbf{M}_y$, and $\mathbf{M}_z$, $\mathbf{M}^2$ will also commute with $\mathbf{M}_x$ and $\mathbf{M}_y$, as may be proved explicitly from the expressions for the operators. These commutation rules will be shown later to hold for systems of particles as well as for a single particle.

From the commutation rules derived above, it is possible to deduce the most important properties of angular momenta. Since $\mathbf{M}^2$ and

$\mathbf{M}_z$ commute, it is possible to find a set of functions which are eigen-functions of both operators simultaneously. We shall denote these eigenfunctions by $Y_{l,\,m}$, where $Y_{l,\,m}$ satisfies the equations

$$\mathbf{M}^2 Y_{l,\,m} = k_l Y_{l,\,m} \qquad\qquad 3\cdot105$$

$$\mathbf{M}_z Y_{l,\,m} = k_m Y_{l,\,m} \qquad\qquad 3\cdot106$$

where the subscripts l and m identify the eigenvalues k_l and k_m asso-ciated with $Y_{l,\,m}$. Writing $\mathbf{M}^2$ in terms of its components, 3·105 be-comes

$$(\mathbf{M}_x^2 + \mathbf{M}_y^2 + \mathbf{M}_z^2) Y_{l,\,m} = k_l Y_{l,\,m} \qquad\qquad 3\cdot107$$

and applying $\mathbf{M}_z$ to equation 3·106 yields

$$\mathbf{M}_z^2 Y_{l,\,m} = k_m^2 Y_{l,\,m} \qquad\qquad 3\cdot108$$

Subtracting 3·108 from 3·107 gives the result

$$(\mathbf{M}_x^2 + \mathbf{M}_y^2) Y_{l,\,m} = (k_l - k_m^2) Y_{l,\,m} \qquad\qquad 3\cdot109$$

so that $Y_{l,\,m}$ is an eigenfunction of $(\mathbf{M}_x^2 + \mathbf{M}_y^2)$ as well as of $\mathbf{M}^2$ and $\mathbf{M}_z$. Let us now write $Y_{l,\,m} = \sum_i c_i \psi_i$, where the ψ_i's are eigenfunctions of $\mathbf{M}_x$ with eigenvalues m_{xi}. Then

$$\mathbf{M}_x^2 Y_{l,\,m} = \sum_i c_i m_{xi}^2 \psi_i = \sum_n \sum_p a_{n,p} Y_{n,p} \qquad\qquad 3\cdot110$$

where

$$a_{l,\,m} = \int Y_{l,m}^* \mathbf{M}_x^2 Y_{l,\,m}\, d\tau = \int \Big(\sum_i c_i^* \psi_i^*\Big)\Big(\sum_i c_i m_{xi}^2 \psi_i\Big)\, d\tau = \sum_i |c_i|^2 m_{xi}^2 \quad 3\cdot111$$

Similarly, we can find for $\mathbf{M}_y^2 Y_{l,\,m}$ the expression

$$\mathbf{M}_y^2 Y_{l,\,m} = \sum_n \sum_p b_{n,\,p} Y_{n,\,p}; \quad \text{where} \quad b_{n,\,p} = \sum_i |d_i|^2 m_{yi}^2 \quad 3\cdot112$$

Comparing 3·109 with the sum of 3·110 and 3·112, we see that

$$k_l - k_m^2 = \sum_i (|c_i|^2 m_{xi}^2 + |d_i|^2 m_{yi}^2) \qquad\qquad 3\cdot113$$

Since $\mathbf{M}_x$ and $\mathbf{M}_y$ are Hermitian, m_{xi}^2 and m_{yi}^2 are positive; the right side of 3·113 is therefore positive, so that

$$k_l \geq k_m^2 \qquad\qquad 3\cdot114$$

We now make use of the commutation rules for $\mathbf{M}_x$, $\mathbf{M}_y$, and $\mathbf{M}_z$. It is easily verified that

$$\mathbf{M}_z(\mathbf{M}_x + i\mathbf{M}_y) = (\mathbf{M}_x + i\mathbf{M}_y)\Big(\mathbf{M}_z + \frac{h}{2\pi}\Big) \qquad\qquad 3\cdot115$$

$$\mathbf{M}_z(\mathbf{M}_x - i\mathbf{M}_y) = (\mathbf{M}_x - i\mathbf{M}_y)\Big(\mathbf{M}_z - \frac{h}{2\pi}\Big) \qquad\qquad 3\cdot116$$

Operating on $Y_{l,\,m}$ with both sides of 3·115 gives

$$\mathbf{M}_z\big\{(\mathbf{M}_x + i\mathbf{M}_y)Y_{l,\,m}\big\} = (\mathbf{M}_x + i\mathbf{M}_y)\Big(\mathbf{M}_z + \frac{h}{2\pi}\Big)Y_{l,\,m}$$

$$= \Big(k_m + \frac{h}{2\pi}\Big)\big\{(\mathbf{M}_x + i\mathbf{M}_y)Y_{l,\,m}\big\} \qquad 3\cdot117$$

so that $(\mathbf{M}_x + i\mathbf{M}_y)Y_{l,\,m}$ is seen to be an eigenfunction of $\mathbf{M}_z$ with the eigenvalue $k_m + \dfrac{h}{2\pi}$ or zero. Since $\mathbf{M}^2$ commutes with all the operators in 3·115, $(\mathbf{M}_x + i\mathbf{M}_y)Y_{l,\,m}$ is still an eigenfunction of $\mathbf{M}^2$ with the eigenvalue k_l. In an analogous manner we see that $(\mathbf{M}_x - i\mathbf{M}_y)Y_{l,\,m}$ is an eigenfunction of $\mathbf{M}_z$ with the eigenvalue $k_m - \dfrac{h}{2\pi}$ or zero, and of $\mathbf{M}^2$ with the eigenvalue k_l. We may therefore obtain a whole series of eigenfunctions of $\mathbf{M}^2$ and $\mathbf{M}_z$, all having the eigenvalue k_l for $\mathbf{M}^2$ but having the eigenvalues

$$\cdots,\; k_m - \frac{2h}{2\pi},\quad k_m - \frac{h}{2\pi},\quad k_m,\quad k_m + \frac{h}{2\pi},\quad k_m + \frac{2h}{2\pi},\cdots \qquad 3\cdot118$$

for $\mathbf{M}_z$. This series must terminate in both directions, since 3·114 states that the square of the eigenvalue for $\mathbf{M}_z$ must be less than k_l. Let us denote by $k_{m'}$ the lowest and by $k_{m''}$ the highest allowed eigenvalue of $\mathbf{M}_z$, and the corresponding eigenfunctions by $Y_{l,\,m'}$ and $Y_{l,\,m''}$. $(\mathbf{M}_x + i\mathbf{M}_y)Y_{l,\,m''}$ should be an eigenfunction of $\mathbf{M}_z$ with the eigenvalue $k_{m''} + \dfrac{h}{2\pi}$ or zero, and since by hypothesis $k_{m''}$ is the highest eigenvalue we must conclude that

$$(\mathbf{M}_x + i\mathbf{M}_y)Y_{l,\,m''} = 0 \qquad 3\cdot119$$

For similar reasons, we must have

$$(\mathbf{M}_x - i\mathbf{M}_y)Y_{l,\,m'} = 0 \qquad 3\cdot120$$

Operating on 3·119 with the operator $(\mathbf{M}_x - i\mathbf{M}_y)$ gives

$$(\mathbf{M}_x - i\mathbf{M}_y)(\mathbf{M}_x + i\mathbf{M}_y)Y_{l,\,m''}$$

$$= \big\{\mathbf{M}_x^2 + \mathbf{M}_y^2 + i(\mathbf{M}_x\mathbf{M}_y - \mathbf{M}_y\mathbf{M}_x)\big\}Y_{l,\,m''}$$

$$= \Big(\mathbf{M}_x^2 + \mathbf{M}_y^2 - \frac{h}{2\pi}\mathbf{M}_z\Big)Y_{l,\,m''} = \Big(\mathbf{M}^2 - \mathbf{M}_z^2 - \frac{h}{2\pi}\mathbf{M}_z\Big)Y_{l,\,m''}$$

$$= \Big(k_l - k_{m''}^2 - \frac{h}{2\pi}k_{m''}\Big)Y_{l,\,m''} = 0 \qquad 3\cdot121$$

so that

$$k_l = k_{m''}^2 + \frac{h}{2\pi} k_{m''} \qquad 3\cdot122$$

By operating on 3·120 with $(\mathbf{M}_x + i\mathbf{M}_y)$, we find

$$k_l = k_{m'}^2 - \frac{h}{2\pi} k_{m'} \qquad 3\cdot123$$

In order that equations 3·122 and 3·123 will be consistent, with $k_{m''} > k_{m'}$, we must have $k_{m''} = -k_{m'}$. According to 3·118, $k_{m''}$ must be greater than $k_{m'}$ by an integral multiple of $\frac{h}{2\pi}$ so that $k_{m''}$ must be of the form $\frac{nh}{2\pi}$, where n is a number in one of the series 0, 1, 2, 3, or $\frac{1}{2}$ $\frac{3}{2}$, $\frac{5}{2}$, $\cdots$. Since we have so far put no particular significance on l, and since $k_{m''}$ depends on l only, we may put $l = n$, so that $k_{m''} = \frac{lh}{2\pi}$. Then

$$k_l = \left(\frac{lh}{2\pi}\right)^2 + \frac{h}{2\pi}\left(\frac{lh}{2\pi}\right)$$

by 3·122, or

$$k_l = l(l+1)\frac{h^2}{4\pi^2} \qquad 3\cdot124$$

The possible values of k_m are then

$$\frac{lh}{2\pi}, \quad (l-1)\frac{h}{2\pi}, \quad \cdots -\frac{lh}{2\pi} \qquad 3\cdot125$$

and we may specify m by

$$k_m = \frac{mh}{2\pi}, \quad l \geq m \geq -l \qquad 3\cdot126$$

If l is an integer, m is also an integer; if l has half-integral values, m likewise has half-integral values.

We may now write equations 3·105 and 3·106 as

$$\mathbf{M}^2 Y_{l,\,m} = l(l+1)\frac{h^2}{4\pi^2} Y_{l,\,m}$$

$$\mathbf{M}_z Y_{l,\,m} = m\frac{h}{2\pi} Y_{l,\,m} \qquad 3\cdot127$$

As these results were derived entirely from the commutation rules, they will be valid for any operators whose commutation rules are similar to those for angular momentum.

With the aid of the operators $(\mathbf{M}_x \pm i\mathbf{M}_y)$ we may obtain the form of $Y_{l,\,m}$ for the case of a single particle where the explicit form of the operators is known. We have seen that $(\mathbf{M}_x - i\mathbf{M}_y)Y_{l,\,m}$ is an eigenfunction of $\mathbf{M}^2$ with the eigenvalue $l(l+1)\dfrac{h^2}{4\pi^2}$ and of $\mathbf{M}_z$ with the eigenvalue $\dfrac{mh}{2\pi} - \dfrac{h}{2\pi} = (m-1)\dfrac{h}{2\pi}$. The eigenfunction $(\mathbf{M}_x - i\mathbf{M}_y)Y_{l,\,m}$ is therefore related to the eigenfunction $Y_{l,\,m-1}$ by the relation

$$(\mathbf{M}_x - i\mathbf{M}_y)Y_{l,\,m} = NY_{l,\,m-1} \qquad 3\cdot128$$

where N is a constant numerical factor. In order to determine N we use the requirement that $Y_{l,\,m}$ be normalized. We therefore multiply 3·128 by its conjugate and integrate over the coordinates. This gives

$$\int \big\{ (\mathbf{M}_x - i\mathbf{M}_y)Y_{l,\,m} \big\}^* (\mathbf{M}_x - i\mathbf{M}_y)Y_{l,\,m}\,d\tau$$

$$= NN^* \int Y_{l,\,m-1}^* Y_{l,\,m-1}\,d\tau = N^2 \qquad 3\cdot129$$

since we may choose our normalizing factor to be real. $\mathbf{M}_x$ and $\mathbf{M}_y$ are Hermitian, so that the first integral may be written as

$$N^2 = \int \big\{ (\mathbf{M}_x - i\mathbf{M}_y)Y_{l,\,m} \big\}^* \mathbf{M}_x Y_{l,\,m}\,d\tau$$

$$- i \int \big\{ (\mathbf{M}_x - i\mathbf{M}_y)Y_{l,\,m} \big\}^* \mathbf{M}_y Y_{l,\,m}\,d\tau$$

$$= \int Y_{l,\,m} \mathbf{M}_x^* \big\{ (\mathbf{M}_x - i\mathbf{M}_y)Y_{l,\,m} \big\}^*\,d\tau$$

$$- i \int Y_{l,\,m} \mathbf{M}_y^* \big\{ (\mathbf{M}_x - i\mathbf{M}_y)Y_{l,\,m} \big\}^*\,d\tau$$

$$= \int Y_{l,\,m} \big\{ \mathbf{M}_x^{*2} + \mathbf{M}_y^{*2} + i(\mathbf{M}_x^*\mathbf{M}_y^* - \mathbf{M}_y^*\mathbf{M}_x^*) \big\} Y_{l,\,m}^*\,d\tau \qquad 3\cdot130$$

Taking the complex conjugate of this equation, and making the obvious substitutions, we have

$$N^2 = \int Y_{l,\,m}^* \left(\mathbf{M}^2 - \mathbf{M}_z^2 + \frac{h}{2\pi}\mathbf{M}_z \right) Y_{l,\,m}\,d\tau$$

$$= \frac{h^2}{4\pi^2}\{ l(l+1) - m(m-1) \} \qquad 3\cdot131$$

so that

$$(\mathbf{M}_x - i\mathbf{M}_y)Y_{l,\,m} = \frac{h}{2\pi}\sqrt{l(l+1) - m(m-1)}\;Y_{l,\,m-1}$$

$$= \frac{h}{2\pi}\sqrt{(l+m)(l-m+1)}\;Y_{l,\,m-1} \qquad 3\cdot132$$

In a similar way, we find

$$(\mathbf{M}_x + i\mathbf{M}_y)Y_{l,\,m} = \frac{h}{2\pi}\sqrt{l(l+1) - m(m+1)}\;Y_{l,\,m+1}$$

$$= \frac{h}{2\pi}\sqrt{(l+m+1)(l-m)}\;Y_{l,\,m+1} \qquad 3\cdot133$$

Let us now assume that $Y_{l,\,m}(\theta,\varphi)$ may be written as the product $\Theta_{l,\,m}(\theta)\,\Phi_m(\varphi)$. Using the operator for $\mathbf{M}_z$ in spherical coordinates, we then have

$$\frac{h}{2\pi i}\frac{\partial}{\partial\varphi}\left\{\Theta_{l,\,m}(\theta)\Phi_m(\varphi)\right\} = \frac{mh}{2\pi}\left\{\Theta_{l,\,m}(\theta)\Phi_m(\varphi)\right\} \qquad 3\cdot134$$

or

$$\frac{\partial}{\partial\varphi}\Phi_m(\varphi) = im\Phi_m(\varphi) \qquad 3\cdot135$$

The solution of this equation is

$$\Phi_m(\varphi) = Ne^{im\varphi} \qquad 3\cdot136$$

In order that $\Phi_m(\varphi)$ be a single-valued function of position, we must have

$$\Phi_m(\varphi) = \Phi_m(\varphi + 2\pi) \qquad \text{or} \qquad e^{im\varphi} = e^{im(\varphi+2\pi)} \qquad 3\cdot137$$

This requires $e^{2\pi mi}$ to be unity, which is true only if m is an integer. The normalization condition

$$\int_0^{2\pi}\Phi_m^*(\varphi)\Phi_m(\varphi)\,d\varphi = N^2\int_0^{2\pi}d\varphi = 1 \qquad 3\cdot138$$

gives the value $\dfrac{1}{\sqrt{2\pi}}$ for N.

In order to calculate $\Theta_{l,\,m}(\theta)$ we apply 3·119 in the form

$$(\mathbf{M}_x + i\mathbf{M}_y)Y_{l,\,l} = 0 \qquad 3\cdot139$$

In spherical coordinates the operator $(\mathbf{M}_x + i\mathbf{M}_y)$ is

$$(\mathbf{M}_x + i\mathbf{M}_y) = \frac{h}{2\pi}\left(e^{i\varphi}\frac{\partial}{\partial\theta} + ie^{i\varphi}\cot\theta\frac{\partial}{\partial\varphi}\right) \qquad 3\cdot140$$

Equation 3·139 is therefore

$$\frac{h}{2\pi}\frac{1}{\sqrt{2\pi}}\,e^{i\varphi}\left\{\left(\frac{\partial}{\partial\theta}+i\cot\theta\,\frac{\partial}{\partial\varphi}\right)\Theta_{l,\,l}(\theta)e^{il\varphi}\right\}=0 \qquad 3\cdot141$$

which reduces to

$$\frac{d}{d\theta}\,\Theta_{l,\,l}(\theta)-l\cot\theta\,\Theta_{l,\,l}(\theta)=0 \qquad 3\cdot142$$

or

$$\frac{d\,\Theta_{l,\,l}(\theta)}{\Theta_{l,\,l}(\theta)}=l\,\frac{\cos\theta}{\sin\theta}\,d\theta \qquad 3\cdot143$$

Integrating both sides of this equation with respect to θ, we readily find the solution

$$\Theta_{l,\,l}(\theta)=N_{ll}\sin^l\theta \qquad 3\cdot144$$

The normalization factor N_{ll} is given by

$$\frac{1}{N_{ll}^2}=\int_0^\pi\sin^{2l}\theta\,\sin\theta\,d\theta=-\sin^{2l}\theta\cos\theta]_0^\pi+2l\int_0^\pi\cos^2\theta\,\sin^{2l-1}\theta\,d\theta$$

$$=\frac{2l}{2l+1}\int_0^\pi\sin^{2l-1}\theta\,d\theta \qquad 3\cdot145$$

If the integration is repeated l times, we obtain

$$\frac{1}{N_{ll}^2}=\frac{2l(2l-2)\cdots2}{(2l+1)(2l-1)\cdots3}\int_0^\pi\sin\theta\,d\theta$$

$$=\frac{2(2^ll!)^2}{(2l+1)!} \qquad 3\cdot146$$

The normalized solution of 3·142 is therefore

$$\Theta_{l,\,l}(\theta)=(-1)^l\sqrt{\frac{(2l+1)!}{2}}\,\frac{1}{2^ll!}\sin^l\theta \qquad 3\cdot147$$

where the factor $(-1)^l$ has been introduced for our convenience later. From the expression thus obtained for $Y_{l,\,l}$, $Y_{l,\,m}$ may be found by repeated application of 3·132. The result obtained in this way is equivalent to the following compact expression, as will appear in the next chapter (section 4e).

$$Y_{l,\,m}(\theta,\varphi)=$$
$$\frac{(-1)^l}{2^ll!}\sqrt{\frac{(2l+1)}{4\pi}\frac{(l-|m|)!}{(l+|m|)!}}\sin^{|m|}\theta\,\frac{d^{l+|m|}\sin^{2l}\theta}{(d\cos\theta)^{l+|m|}}\,e^{im\varphi} \qquad 3\cdot148$$

where $|m|$ is the absolute value of m.

CHAPTER IV

THE DIFFERENTIAL EQUATIONS OF QUANTUM MECHANICS[1]

4a. The Linear Differential Equation of the Second Order. We have seen that the Hamiltonian operator is a second-order differential operator, so that the equation $\mathbf{H}\psi = E\psi$ is a second-order differential equation. In order to find the eigenfunctions of $\mathbf{H}$ we must therefore develop the technique of solving differential equations of this type. For the present we shall confine ourselves to the case of one independent variable. The general equation to be solved is then of the form

$$\frac{d^2y}{dx^2} + p(x)\frac{dy}{dx} + q(x)y = 0 \qquad 4\cdot1$$

where $p(x)$ and $q(x)$ are given functions of x.

Suppose that, in the neighborhood of the point $x = x_0$, y can be expanded in the form of a power series

$$y = a_0 + a_1(x - x_0) + a_2(x - x_0)^2 + \cdots \qquad 4\cdot2$$

Taylor's theorem then states that

$$a_0 = y_{(x=x_0)}; \quad a_1 = \left(\frac{dy}{dx}\right)_{x=x_0}; \quad a_2 = \frac{1}{2!}\left(\frac{d^2y}{dx^2}\right)_{x=x_0}; \quad \cdots \qquad 4\cdot3$$

If we solve 4·1 for $\dfrac{d^2y}{dx^2}$, we find an expression for $\dfrac{d^2y}{dx^2}$ in terms of $\dfrac{dy}{dx}$ and y. If we differentiate 4·1, we then find an expression for $\dfrac{d^3y}{dx^3}$ in terms of $\dfrac{d^2y}{dx^2}$, $\dfrac{dy}{dx}$, and y. By repeated differentiations we may therefore find any derivative of y in terms of the lower derivatives. Now suppose that at the point $x = x_0$ we are given the values of y and $\dfrac{dy}{dx}$. The differential equation then gives all the higher derivatives, and from these the constants $a_0, a_1, a_2 \cdots$ in the series 4·2 are determined by 4·3. Thus from the values of y and $\dfrac{dy}{dx}$ at one point we may determine

---

[1] Some readers may prefer to delay the study of this chapter until they require the specific results for the solution of the equations in later chapters of the text.

the whole function throughout the interval in which the series converges.

In practice this method usually turns out to be rather clumsy. If, however, the differential equation can be put in the form

$$P(x) \frac{d^2y}{dx^2} + Q(x) \frac{dy}{dx} + R(x)y = 0 \qquad 4\cdot4$$

where $P(x)$, $Q(x)$, and $R(x)$ are polynomials in x, the solution is much simpler. We expand y as a power series in x

$$y = a_0 + a_1 x + \cdots + a_\nu x^\nu + \cdots \qquad 4\cdot5$$

and differentiate the series term by term, obtaining

$$\frac{dy}{dx} = a_1 + 2a_2 x + \cdots + (\nu + 1)a_{\nu+1} x^\nu + \cdots \qquad 4\cdot6$$

$$\frac{d^2y}{dx^2} = 2a_2 + 3\cdot2a_3 x + \cdots + (\nu + 2)(\nu + 1)a_{\nu+2} x^\nu + \cdots \qquad 4\cdot7$$

If we substitute these series in the differential equation, the coefficient of every power of x must vanish. Putting the coefficient of x^ν equal to zero then gives a relation of the form

$$a_\nu = c_1 a_{\nu-1} + c_2 a_{\nu-2} + \cdots + c_k a_{\nu-k} \qquad 4\cdot8$$

where the c's are constants. The number of c's occurring in this expression will depend on the form of the differential equation. Such a relation is known as a recursion formula; by means of it the whole series can be found when the first few terms are known.

As a simple example of this process consider the equation

$$\frac{d^2y}{dx^2} - y = 0 \qquad 4\cdot9$$

where $P(x) = 1$, $Q(x) = 0$, $R(x) = -1$. If we put

$$y = a_0 + a_1 x + a_2 x^2 + \cdots \qquad 4\cdot10$$

and substitute in the equation, we find

$$0 = (2a_2 - a_0) + (3\cdot2a_3 - a_1)x + \cdots$$
$$+ [(\nu + 2)(\nu + 1)a_{\nu+2} - a_\nu]x^\nu + \cdots \qquad 4\cdot11$$

Equating the coefficient of x^ν to zero gives

$$a_{\nu+2} = \frac{a_\nu}{(\nu + 2)(\nu + 1)} ; \quad \text{or} \quad a_\nu = \frac{a_{\nu-2}}{\nu(\nu - 1)} \qquad 4\cdot12$$

If we take $a_0 = a_1 = 1$, we obtain the particular solution

$$y = 1 + x + \frac{x^2}{2} + \frac{x^3}{3 \cdot 2} + \cdots + \frac{x^\nu}{\nu!} + \cdots = e^x \qquad 4 \cdot 13$$

which is seen to satisfy the differential equation 4·9.

If we attempt to use this method on the equation

$$x^2 \frac{d^2y}{dx^2} + x \frac{dy}{dx} + (x^2 - \tfrac{1}{4})y = 0 \qquad 4 \cdot 14$$

we find

$$0 = -\tfrac{1}{4}a_0 + \tfrac{3}{4}a_1 x + (\tfrac{15}{4}a_2 + a_0)x^2 + \cdots$$
$$+ [(\nu^2 - \tfrac{1}{4})a_\nu + a_{\nu-2}]x^\nu + \cdots \qquad 4 \cdot 15$$

so that the recursion formula is

$$a_\nu = -\frac{a_{\nu-2}}{\nu^2 - \tfrac{1}{4}} \qquad 4 \cdot 16$$

In order that the constant term and the coefficient of x vanish, we must have $a_0 = a_1 = 0$. The recursion formula then requires that all the remaining a's vanish, so that we get no solution at all. A little consideration shows why this has happened. If we write equation 4·14 in the form of 4·1, we have

$$\frac{d^2y}{dx^2} + \frac{1}{x}\frac{dy}{dx} + \left(1 - \frac{1}{4x^2}\right)y = 0 \qquad 4 \cdot 17$$

When $x = 0$, $p(x)$ and $q(x)$ become infinite, so that $\dfrac{d^2y}{dx^2}$ cannot be found from this equation. The point $x = 0$ is called a singular point of the equation. If it is possible to write a differential equation in the form

$$x^2 \frac{d^2y}{dx^2} + xp'(x)\frac{dy}{dx} + q'(x)y = 0 \qquad 4 \cdot 18$$

where $p'(x)$ and $q'(x)$ are finite at $x = 0$, the point $x = 0$ is called a regular point of the equation. A singular point which is not regular is called an essential singularity.

In the neighborhood of a regular point a differential equation can usually be solved by the following method. Instead of starting the power series with a constant term, we use a series of the form

$$y = a_0 x^L + a_1 x^{L+1} + a_2 x^{L+2} + \cdots \qquad 4 \cdot 19$$

where $a_0 \neq 0$ and L may have any value. Then

$$\frac{dy}{dx} = La_0 x^{L-1} + (L + 1)a_1 x^L + \cdots \qquad 4\cdot20$$

$$\frac{d^2y}{dx^2} = L(L - 1)a_0 x^{L-2} + (L + 1)La_1 x^{L-1} + \cdots \qquad 4\cdot21$$

If we substitute these series in equation 4·14, we find

$$0 = (L^2 - \tfrac{1}{4})a_0 x^L + \{(L + 1)^2 - \tfrac{1}{4}\}a_1 x^{L+1}$$
$$+\{[(L + 2)^2 - \tfrac{1}{4}]a_2 + a_0\}x^{L+2} + \cdots$$
$$+ \{[(L + \nu)^2 - \tfrac{1}{4}]a_\nu + a_{\nu-2}\}x^{L+\nu} + \cdots \qquad 4\cdot22$$

which leads to the series of equations

$$(L^2 - \tfrac{1}{4})a_0 = 0$$
$$[(L + 1)^2 - \tfrac{1}{4}]a_1 = 0$$
$$\cdots\cdots\cdots\cdots\cdots\cdots$$
$$\{[(L + \nu)^2 - \tfrac{1}{4}]a_\nu + a_{\nu-2}\} = 0 \qquad 4\cdot23$$

The first of these is called the indicial equation. Since $a_0 \neq 0$ we must have $L^2 = \tfrac{1}{4}$, or $L = \pm\tfrac{1}{2}$. The other equations then determine the other a's in terms of a_0. There are thus two solutions:

$$y = a_0 x^{1/2}\left\{1 - \frac{x^2}{6} + \frac{x^4}{120} + \cdots\right\} \qquad 4\cdot24$$

$$y = a_0 x^{-1/2}\left\{1 - \frac{x^2}{2} + \frac{x^4}{24} + \cdots\right\} \qquad 4\cdot25$$

If we are interested only in the solutions of a differential equation which belong to the class Q, it is essential to investigate the behavior of the solutions at all the singular points of the equation, for if the exponent L is negative or fractional the function y is either infinite or multiple-valued and therefore cannot be of class Q.

Infinite series are at best awkward things with which to work. For example, it is very difficult to derive the properties of the function sin x from the series

$$\sin x = x - \frac{x^3}{3!} + \frac{x^5}{5!} - \frac{x^7}{7!} + \cdots \qquad 4\cdot26$$

whereas the properties are easily derived from the ordinary trigonometric definition. For this reason the various functions which are met in quantum mechanics are defined by some other definition than the power series derived from the differential equation, and are then identified with this series.

4b.   The Legendre Polynomials.   Consider the equation

$$(1 - x^2) \frac{dy}{dx} + 2nxy = 0 \qquad 4\cdot27$$

If we write this in the form

$$\frac{dy}{y} = - \frac{2nx\,dx}{(1 - x^2)} \qquad 4\cdot28$$

it may immediately be integrated to give

$$y = c(1 - x^2)^n \qquad 4\cdot29$$

where c is any constant.   If we differentiate equation $4\cdot27$ $(n + 1)$ times, the result is

$$(1 - x^2) \frac{d^{n+2}y}{dx^{n+2}} - 2x \frac{d^{n+1}y}{dx^{n+1}} + n(n + 1)\frac{d^n y}{dx^n} = 0 \qquad 4\cdot30$$

which may be written as

$$(1 - x^2) \frac{d^2 z}{dx^2} - 2x \frac{dz}{dx} + n(n + 1)z = 0 \qquad 4\cdot31$$

where

$$z = \frac{d^n y}{dx^n} = c \frac{d^n}{dx^n} (1 - x^2)^n \qquad 4\cdot32$$

Equation $4\cdot31$ is known as Legendre's equation.   The particular solution

$$z = P_n(x) = \frac{1}{2^n n!} \frac{d^n}{dx^n} (x^2 - 1)^n \qquad 4\cdot33$$

is called the Legendre polynomial of degree n.   [$P_0(x)$ is defined to be unity.]   It is possible to show that these functions form a system of orthogonal functions in the interval $-1 \le x \le 1$, and also that these polynomials are the only functions of class Q which satisfy equation $4\cdot31$ in this interval.   As these functions are special cases of a more general set of functions which we shall now discuss, we shall prove these statements only for the general case.

4c.   The Associated Legendre Polynomials.   If equation $4\cdot27$ is differentiated $(m + n + 1)$ times, we obtain the equation

$$(1 - x^2) \frac{d^{m+n+2}y}{dx^{m+n+2}} - 2(m + 1)x \frac{d^{m+n+1}y}{dx^{m+n+1}} +$$

$$(m + n + 1)(n - m) \frac{d^{m+n}y}{dx^{m+n}} = 0 \qquad 4\cdot34$$

which may also be written as

$$(1 - x^2)\frac{d^2z}{dx^2} - 2(m + 1)x\frac{dz}{dx} + (m + n + 1)(n - m)z = 0 \qquad 4\cdot35$$

where

$$z = \frac{d^{m+n}y}{dx^{m+n}} = \frac{d^m}{dx^m}P_n(x) = c\frac{d^{m+n}}{dx^{m+n}}(1 - x^2)^n \qquad 4\cdot36$$

Let us now put

$$z = u(1 - x^2)^{-\frac{m}{2}} \qquad 4\cdot37$$

Then

$$\frac{dz}{dx} = \left\{\frac{du}{dx} + \frac{mxu}{1 - x^2}\right\}(1 - x^2)^{-\frac{m}{2}}$$

$$\frac{d^2z}{dx^2} = \left\{\frac{d^2u}{dx^2} + \frac{2mx}{1 - x^2}\frac{du}{dx} + \left(\frac{m}{1 - x^2} + \frac{m(m + 2)x^2}{(1 - x^2)^2}\right)u\right\}(1 - x^2)^{-\frac{m}{2}}$$

so that the differential equation for u is

$$(1 - x^2)\frac{d^2u}{dx^2} - 2x\frac{du}{dx} + \left(n(n + 1) - \frac{m^2}{1 - x^2}\right)u = 0 \qquad 4\cdot38$$

This equation is known as the associated Legendre equation, and the function u, denoted by $u = P_n^m(x)$, is called the associated Legendre polynomial of degree n and order m. From equations 4·36 and 4·37, we see that

$$P_n^m(x) = (1 - x^2)^{\frac{m}{2}}z = (1 - x^2)^{\frac{m}{2}}\frac{d^m}{dx^m}P_n(x) \qquad 4.39$$

or, using 4·33,

$$P_n^m(x) = \frac{(1 - x^2)^{\frac{m}{2}}}{2^n n!}\frac{d^{n+m}}{dx^{n+m}}(x^2 - 1)^n \qquad 4\cdot40$$

It is apparent that $P_n^0(x) = P_n(x)$. Also, since $P_n(x)$ is a polynomial of degree n, $P_n^m(x)$ is zero if $m > n$.

We shall now show that the functions $P_n^m(x)$ and $P_l^m(x)$ are orthogonal in the interval $-1 \leq x \leq 1$ if $l \neq n$. The equations arising from 4·38 satisfied by these functions may be put in the form

$$\frac{d}{dx}\left\{(1 - x^2)\frac{dP_n^m}{dx}\right\} + \left\{n(n + 1) - \frac{m^2}{1 - x^2}\right\}P_n^m = 0 \qquad 4\cdot41$$

$$\frac{d}{dx}\left\{(1 - x^2)\frac{dP_l^m}{dx}\right\} + \left\{l(l + 1) - \frac{m^2}{1 - x^2}\right\}P_l^m = 0 \qquad 4\cdot42$$

If we multiply 4·41 by P_l^m and 4·42 by P_n^m and subtract, we obtain

$$\frac{d}{dx}\left\{(1-x^2)\left(P_l^m\frac{dP_n^m}{dx}-P_n^m\frac{dP_l^m}{dx}\right)\right\}$$
$$+\{n(n+1)-l(l+1)\}P_n^mP_l^m = 0 \qquad 4\cdot43$$

Upon integrating between -1 and $+1$, the first term vanishes because of the factor $(1-x^2)$, so that, if $n \neq l$, we have

$$\int_{-1}^{+1} P_n^m(x)P_l^m(x)\,dx = 0 \qquad 4\cdot44$$

In order to normalize these functions, let us now consider the integral

$$\int_{-1}^{+1}[P_n^m(x)]^2\,dx = \int_{-1}^{+1}(1-x^2)^m\frac{d^mP_n}{dx^m}\frac{d^mP_n}{dx^m}\,dx$$
$$= \left[(1-x^2)^m\frac{d^mP_n}{dx^m}\frac{d^{m-1}P_n}{dx^{m-1}}\right]_{x=-1}^{x=+1}$$
$$- \int_{-1}^{+1}\frac{d^{m-1}P_n}{dx^{m-1}}\frac{a}{dx}\left\{(1-x^2)^m\frac{d^mP_n}{dx^m}\right\}dx \qquad 4\cdot45$$

If 4·27 is differentiated $m+n$ times, and the result multiplied by $(1-x^2)^{m-1}$, we obtain

$$(1-x^2)^m\frac{d^{m+1}P_n}{dx^{m+1}} - 2mx(1-x^2)^{m-1}\frac{d^mP_n}{dx^m}$$
$$+ (n+m)(n-m+1)(1-x^2)^{m-1}\frac{d^{m-1}P_n}{dx^{m-1}} = 0 \quad 4\cdot46$$

which is equivalent to

$$\frac{d}{dx}\left\{(1-x^2)^m\frac{d^mP_n}{dx^m}\right\}$$
$$= -(n+m)(n-m+1)(1-x^2)^{m-1}\frac{d^{m-1}P_n}{dx^{m-1}} \quad 4\cdot47$$

Substituting this result in 4·45, we find

$$\int_{-1}^{+1}[P_n^m(x)]^2\,dx$$
$$= (n+m)(n-m+1)\int_{-1}^{+1}(1-x^2)^{m-1}\left[\frac{d^{m-1}P_n}{dx^{m-1}}\right]^2\,dx$$
$$= (n+m)(n-m+1)\int_{-1}^{+1}[P_n^{m-1}(x)]^2\,dx \qquad 4\cdot48$$

If this process is continued, we finally arrive at the result

$$\int_{-1}^{+1} [P_n^m(x)]^2 \, dx = \frac{(n+m)!}{(n-m)!} \int_{-1}^{+1} [P_n(x)]^2 \, dx \qquad 4\text{·}49$$

This last integral can be evaluated by means of the explicit expression 4·33 for $P_n(x)$. We have

$$\int_{-1}^{+1} [P_n(x)]^2 \, dx = \frac{1}{[2^n n!]^2} \int_{-1}^{+1} \frac{d^n}{dx^n}(x^2-1)^n \frac{d^n}{dx^n}(x^2-1)^n \, dx \quad 4\text{·}50$$

Integrating by parts n times, this reduces to

$$\int_{-1}^{+1} [P_n(x)]^2 = \frac{(-1)^n}{[2^n n!]^2} \int_{-1}^{+1} (x^2-1)^n \frac{d^{2n}}{dx^{2n}}(x^2-1)^n \, dx$$

$$= \frac{(-1)^n}{[2^n n!]^2} \int_{-1}^{+1} (x^2-1)^n (2n)! \, dx$$

$$= \frac{(2n)!}{[2^n n!]^2} \int_{-1}^{+1} (1-x)^n (1+x)^n \, dx \qquad 4\text{·}51$$

Since

$$\int_{-1}^{+1} (1-x)^n (1+x)^n \, dx = \frac{n}{n+1} \int_{-1}^{+1} (1-x)^{n-1}(1+x)^{n+1}$$

$$= \frac{n(n-1)\cdots 1}{(n+1)(n+2)\cdots 2n} \int_{-1}^{+1}(1+x)^{2n} = \frac{(n!)^2}{(2n)!} \frac{2^{2n+1}}{(2n+1)} \qquad 4\text{·}52$$

equation 4·49 may finally be written as

$$\int_{-1}^{+1} [P_n^m(x)]^2 \, dx = \frac{(n+m)!}{(n-m)!} \frac{2}{2n+1} \qquad 4\text{·}53$$

so that the normalized functions are $\sqrt{\dfrac{2n+1}{2} \dfrac{(n-m)!}{(n+m)!}}\, P_n^m(x)$.

4d. The General Solution of the Associated Legendre Equation. Up to this point we have been concerned with particular solutions of Legendre's equations 4·31 and 4·38. We shall now show that these are the only solutions for the interval $-1 \le x \le 1$ which belong to class Q. Since 4·31 is a special case of 4·38, we shall discuss 4·38 for the sake of generality; the results, of course, will hold for 4·31 as well.

Equation 4·38 has two singular points, $x = 1$ and $x = -1$. If we make the transformation $x = \xi + 1$, the resulting equation is

$$\xi^2 \frac{d^2 u}{d\xi^2} + 2\frac{\xi(\xi+1)}{\xi+2}\frac{du}{d\xi} + \left(-n(n+1)\frac{\xi}{\xi+2} - \frac{m^2}{(\xi+2)^2}\right) u = 0 \quad 4\text{·}54$$

which is of the form 4·18, with

$$p'(\xi) = \frac{2(\xi + 1)}{\xi + 2} \qquad q'(\xi) = -n(n + 1)\frac{\xi}{\xi + 2} - \frac{m^2}{(\xi + 2)^2} \qquad 4\cdot55$$

Since these functions are finite for $\xi = 0$, the point $\xi = 0$ $(x = 1)$ is a regular point. If we now clear of fractions we obtain our equation in the form of 4·4

$$(\xi^4 + 4\xi^3 + 4\xi^2)\frac{d^2u}{d\xi^2} + (2\xi^3 + 6\xi^2 + 4\xi)\frac{du}{d\xi}$$
$$+ [-n(n + 1)\xi^2 - 2n(n + 1)\xi - m^2]u = 0 \qquad 4\cdot56$$

Substituting for u the power series

$$u = a_0\xi^L + a_1\xi^{L+1} + \cdots \qquad 4\cdot57$$

we obtain the indicial equation

$$4L(L - 1) + 4L - m^2 = 0; \quad L = \pm\frac{m}{2} \qquad 4\cdot58$$

If we take m real and positive the series beginning with $\xi^{-\frac{m}{2}}$ becomes infinite at $\xi = 0$ in such a way that the square of the function is not integrable, and so the resulting function is not of class Q in a range including the point $\xi = 0$ $(x = 1)$. The solution which remains is, returning to x as the independent variable,

$$u = (x - 1)^{\frac{m}{2}}(a_0' + a_1'x + \cdots) \qquad 4\cdot59$$

A similar analysis of the other singular point shows that u must also be of the form

$$u = (x + 1)^{\frac{m}{2}}(a_0'' + a_1''x + \cdots) \qquad 4\cdot60$$

Now the function

$$u = (1 - x^2)^{\frac{m}{2}}(b_0 + b_1x + \cdots) \qquad 4\cdot61$$

is of the form 4·59 if we expand the factor $(1 + x)^{\frac{m}{2}}$ and also of the form 4·60 if we expand the factor $(1 - x)^{\frac{m}{2}}$, so that the requirements at both singular points are satisfied if we put

$$u = (1 - x^2)^{\frac{m}{2}}z; \quad z = b_0 + b_1x + \cdots \qquad 4\cdot62$$

The differential equation satisfied by z is

$$(1 - x^2)\frac{d^2z}{dx^2} - 2(m + 1)x\frac{dz}{dx} + [n(n + 1) - m(m + 1)]z = 0 \qquad 4\cdot63$$

giving the recursion formula for the coefficients in 4·62

$$(\nu + 1)(\nu + 2)b_{\nu+2} = [\nu(\nu - 1) + 2(m + 1)\nu$$
$$- n(n + 1) + m(m + 1)]b_{\nu}, \qquad 4·64$$

If $n - m$ is an integer, we find that, for the particular case in which $\nu = n - m$, b_{n-m+2} is zero, and thus the alternate coefficients b_{n-m+4}, $b_{n-m+6}, \cdots$ are also zero. Therefore if the solution is written in the form

$$z = b_0 \left(1 + \frac{m(m + 1) - n(n + 1)}{2} x^2 + \cdots \right)$$
$$+ b_1 \left(x + \frac{(m + 1)(m + 2) - n(n + 1)}{3·2} x^3 + \cdots \right) \qquad 4·65$$

either the even series or the odd series degenerates to a polynomial of degree $n - m$. The complete solution of 4·38 is therefore

$$u = (1 - x^2)^{\frac{m}{2}} z = A P_n^m(x) + B Q_n^m(x) \qquad 4·66$$

where $Q_n^m(x)$ represents the series which does not terminate. The terminating series must, of course, be the polynomial $P_n^m(x)$ which we have already studied. Since

$$\frac{b_{\nu+2}}{b_{\nu}} = \frac{\nu(\nu - 1) + 2(m + 1)\nu - n(n + 1) + m(m + 1)}{(\nu + 1)(\nu + 2)};$$

$$\lim_{\nu \to \infty} \frac{b_{\nu+2}}{b_{\nu}} = 1 \qquad 4·67$$

the series for Q_n^m converges for $-1 < x < 1$, but at the points $x = \pm 1$ the series becomes divergent. The function $[Q_n^m(x)]^2$ is therefore not integrable over the range $-1 \leq x \leq 1$ and hence is not of class Q in this range. We therefore see that, aside from a numerical factor, $P_n^m(x)$ is the only function of class Q which satisfies equation 4·38 in the range $(-1, 1)$. If $n - m$ is not an integer neither series terminates. The same considerations which were applied to the function Q_n^m apply here to both series, so that there is no solution of 4·38 which belongs to the class Q.

4e. The Functions $\Theta_{l,m}(\theta)$ and $Y_{l,m}(\theta, \varphi)$. We will now establish the connection between the functions $\Theta_{l,m}(\theta)$ introduced in the previous chapter and the functions $P_n^m(x)$ discussed above. We there derived the results:

$$\mathbf{M}^2 Y_{l,m} = l(l + 1) \frac{h^2}{4\pi^2} Y_{l,m} \qquad 4·68$$

$$\mathbf{M}_z Y_{l,m} = m \frac{h}{2\pi} Y_{l,m} \qquad 4·69$$

$Y_{l, m}$ was found to be equal to $\dfrac{1}{\sqrt{2\pi}}\Theta_{l, m}(\theta)e^{im\varphi}$, where m is an integer.

Using for $\mathbf{M}^2$ the expression in spherical coordinates (3·99), we obtain as the differential equation for $\Theta_{l, m}(\theta)$

$$\frac{1}{\sin\theta}\frac{d}{d\theta}\left(\sin\theta\frac{d\Theta_{l, m}}{d\theta}\right) - \frac{m^2}{\sin^2\theta}\Theta_{l, m} + l(l+1)\Theta_{l, m} = 0 \quad 4\cdot70$$

or

$$\frac{d^2\Theta_{l, m}}{d\theta^2} + \frac{\cos\theta}{\sin\theta}\frac{d\Theta_{l, m}}{d\theta} + \left\{l(l+1) - \frac{m^2}{\sin^2\theta}\right\}\Theta_{l, m} = 0 \quad 4\cdot71$$

In order to be an acceptable solution, $\Theta_{l, m}(\theta)$ must be of the class Q over the range $0 \leq \theta \leq \pi$. Let us now make the change of variable $x = \cos\theta$. Then

$$\frac{d}{d\theta} = -\sin\theta\frac{d}{dx} \qquad \frac{d^2}{d\theta^2} = \sin^2\theta\frac{d^2}{dx^2} - \cos\theta\frac{d}{dx} \qquad 4\cdot72$$

and equation 4·71 becomes

$$(1-x^2)\frac{d^2\Theta_{l, m}}{dx^2} - 2x\frac{d\Theta_{l, m}}{dx} + \left\{l(l+1) - \frac{m^2}{1-x^2}\right\}\Theta_{l, m} = 0 \quad 4\cdot73$$

Expressed as a function of x, $\Theta_{l, m}$ must be of the class Q over the range $-1 \leq x \leq 1$. Comparing 4·73 and 4·38 we see that $\Theta_{l, m}$ must be identified with $u = P_n^m$. Since m enters equation 4·73 only as m^2, we must have $\Theta_{l, m} = \Theta_{l, -m}$. The exact identification is, therefore, for the normalized functions:

$$\Theta_{l, m}(\theta) = \sqrt{\frac{2l+1}{2}\frac{(l-|m|)!}{(l+|m|)!}}\,P_l^{|m|}(\cos\theta) \qquad 4\cdot74$$

where $|m|$ indicates the absolute value of m. Further, since m is an integer, and since equation 4·38 or 4·73 has an acceptable solution only if $l - m$ is an integer, l must be integral valued. From 4·40, we see that the explicit expression for $\Theta_{l, m}(\theta)$ is

$$\Theta_{l, m}(\theta) = \frac{(-1)^l}{2^l l!}\sqrt{\frac{2l+1}{2}\frac{(l-|m|)!}{(l+|m|)!}}\,\sin^{|m|}\theta\,\frac{d^{l+|m|}(\sin^{2l}\theta)}{(d\cos\theta)^{l+|m|}} \qquad 4\cdot75$$

The explicit expressions for the normalized associated Legendre polynomials are given in Table 4·1 for $l = 0, 1, 2, 3$. The normalized spherical harmonics $Y_{l, m}(\theta, \varphi)$ are obtained by multiplying $\Theta_{l, m}(\theta)$ by $\Phi_m(\varphi) = \dfrac{1}{\sqrt{2\pi}}e^{im\varphi}$.

TABLE 4·1

THE NORMALIZED ASSOCIATED LEGENDRE POLYNOMIALS $\Theta_{l,\,m}(\theta)$

$l = 0, \quad m = 0 \qquad \Theta_{0,\,0} = \dfrac{1}{\sqrt{2}}$

$l = 1, \quad m = 0 \qquad \Theta_{1,\,0} = \sqrt{\tfrac{3}{2}} \cos\theta$

$l = 1, \quad m = \pm 1 \qquad \Theta_{1,\,\pm 1} = \sqrt{\tfrac{3}{4}} \sin\theta$

$l = 2, \quad m = 0 \qquad \Theta_{2,\,0} = \sqrt{\tfrac{5}{8}} \,(3\cos^2\theta - 1)$

$l = 2, \quad m = \pm 1 \qquad \Theta_{2,\,\pm 1} = \sqrt{\tfrac{15}{4}} \sin\theta \cos\theta$

$l = 2, \quad m = \pm 2 \qquad \Theta_{2,\,\pm 2} = \sqrt{\tfrac{15}{16}} \sin^2\theta$

$l = 3, \quad m = 0 \qquad \Theta_{3,\,0} = \sqrt{\tfrac{63}{8}} \,(\tfrac{5}{3}\cos^3\theta - \cos\theta)$

$l = 3, \quad m = \pm 1 \qquad \Theta_{3,\,\pm 1} = \sqrt{\tfrac{21}{32}} \,(5\cos^2\theta - 1)\sin\theta$

$l = 3, \quad m = \pm 2 \qquad \Theta_{3,\,\pm 2} = \sqrt{\tfrac{105}{16}} \sin^2\theta \cos\theta$

$l = 3, \quad m = \pm 3 \qquad \Theta_{3,\,\pm 3} = \sqrt{\tfrac{35}{32}} \sin^3\theta$

4f. Recursion Formulas for the Legendre Polynomials. In our later work, we shall have occasion to evaluate integrals of the form

$$\int \Theta_{l,\,m} \cos\theta \, \Theta_{l',\,m'} \, d\tau \quad \text{and} \quad \int \Theta_{l,\,m} \sin\theta \, \Theta_{l',\,m'} \, d\tau$$

The evaluation will be greatly simplified if we have available explicit expressions for the quantities $\cos\theta \, P_l^{|m|}(\cos\theta)$ and $\sin\theta \, P_l^{|m|}(\cos\theta)$ in terms of a series of Legendre polynomials. From the formula

$$P_l(x) = \frac{1}{2^l l!} \frac{d^l}{dx^l} (x^2 - 1)^l \qquad 4\cdot76$$

it can readily be shown that the equations

$$(2l + 1)P_l = \frac{d}{dx}(P_{l+1} - P_{l-1}) \qquad 4\cdot77$$

and

$$(l + 1)P_l = \frac{d}{dx}P_{l+1} - x\frac{d}{dx}P_l \qquad 4\cdot78$$

are valid. If 4·77 is differentiated m times and the resulting equation multiplied by $(1 - x^2)^{\frac{m+1}{2}}$ we immediately have, using the definition 4·39 for the associated Legendre polynomials,

$$(2l + 1)(1 - x^2)^{\frac12} P_l^m = P_{l+1}^{m+1} - P_{l-1}^{m+1} \qquad 4\cdot79$$

Differentiating 4·78 $(m - 1)$ times, we have

$$(l + 1)\frac{d^{m-1}P_l}{dx^{m-1}} = \frac{d^m P_{l+1}}{dx^m} - x\frac{d^m P_l}{dx^m} - (m - 1)\frac{d^{m-1}P_l}{dx^{m-1}} \qquad 4\cdot80$$

Multiplying this expression by $(2l + 1)(1 - x^2)^{\frac{m}{2}}$ and rearranging gives

$$
\begin{aligned}
(2l + 1)xP_l^m &= (2l + 1)P_{l+1}^m - (l + m)\{(2l + 1)(1 - x^2)^{\frac{1}{2}}P_l^{m-1}\} \\
&= (2l + 1)P_{l+1}^m - (l + m)\{P_{l+1}^m - P_{l-1}^m\} \\
&= (l - m + 1)P_{l+1}^m + (l + m)P_{l-1}^m
\end{aligned}
$$
4·81

If equation 4·27 is differentiated $(m + l)$ times, the resulting equation for P_l is

$$
(1 - x^2)\frac{d^{m+1}P_l}{dx^{m+1}} - 2mx\frac{d^mP_l}{dx^m} + (l + m)(l - m + 1)\frac{d^{m-1}P_l}{dx^{m-1}} = 0 \quad 4\cdot82
$$

We now multiply by $(2l + 1)(1 - x^2)^{\frac{m}{2}}$ and rearrange, obtaining

$$
(2l + 1)(1 - x^2)^{\frac{1}{2}}P_l^{m+1}
$$
$$
= 2m\,(2l + 1)xP_l^m - (l + m)(l - m + 1)(2l + 1)(1 - x^2)^{\frac{1}{2}}P_l^{m-1} \quad 4\cdot83
$$

Substituting for the terms on the right their values as given by 4·79 and 4·81, we obtain

$$
\begin{aligned}
(2l + 1)(1 - x^2)^{\frac{1}{2}}P_l^{m+1} &= P_{l+1}^m\{(m - l)(l - m + 1)\} \\
&\quad + P_{l-1}^m\{(l + m)(l + m + 1)\}
\end{aligned}
$$

or, replacing m by $(m - 1)$,

$$
\begin{aligned}
(2l + 1)(1 - x^2)^{\frac{1}{2}}P_l^m &= -(l - m + 1)(l - m + 2)P_{l+1}^{m-1} \\
&\quad + (l + m)(l + m - 1)P_{l-1}^{m-1} \quad 4\cdot84
\end{aligned}
$$

Expressing equations 4·79, 4·81, and 4·84 in terms of $\cos\theta = x$ gives us the desired relations

$$
\begin{aligned}
\cos\theta P_l^{|m|}(\cos\theta) = \frac{1}{2l + 1} &\{(l - |m| + 1)P_{l+1}^{|m|}(\cos\theta) \\
&+ (l + |m|)P_{l-1}^{|m|}(\cos\theta)\} \quad 4\cdot85
\end{aligned}
$$

$$
\sin\theta\, P_l^{|m|}(\cos\theta) = \frac{1}{2l + 1}\{P_{l+1}^{|m|+1}(\cos\theta) - P_{l-1}^{|m|+1}(\cos\theta) \quad 4\cdot86
$$

$$
\begin{aligned}
= \frac{1}{2l + 1}&\{(l + |m|)(l + |m| - 1)P_{l-1}^{|m|-1}(\cos\theta) \\
&- (l - |m| + 1)(l - |m| + 2)P_{l+1}^{|m|-1}(\cos\theta)\} \quad 4\cdot87
\end{aligned}
$$

4g. The Hermite Polynomials. Consider the equation

$$
\frac{dy}{dx} + 2xy = 0 \quad\quad 4\cdot88
$$

The solution of this equation is readily seen to be

$$y = ce^{-x^2} \qquad 4\cdot89$$

If we differentiate equation 4·88 $(n+1)$ times, we get

$$\frac{d^2z}{dx^2} + 2x\frac{dz}{dx} + 2(n+1)z = 0 \qquad 4\cdot90$$

where

$$z = \frac{d^ny}{dx^n} = c\frac{d^n}{dx^n}(e^{-x^2}) \qquad 4\cdot91$$

z is a function of the form $u(x)e^{-x^2}$, where $u(x)$ is a polynomial of degree n. Substituting this expression for z in equation 4·90 we find that $u(x)$ satisfies the equation

$$\frac{d^2u}{dx^2} - 2x\frac{du}{dx} + 2nu = 0 \qquad 4\cdot92$$

Equation 4·92 is known as Hermite's equation, and the particular solution obtained by putting $c = (-1)^n$ is known as the Hermite polynomial of degree n. The usual symbol for these polynomials is $H_n(x)$; explicitly

$$H_n(x) = (-1)^n e^{x^2}\frac{d^n}{dx^n}(e^{-x^2}) \qquad 4\cdot93$$

The first five Hermite polynomials are:

$$H_0(x) = 1 \qquad\qquad H_1(x) = 2x$$
$$H_2(x) = 4x^2 - 2 \qquad\qquad H_3(x) = 8x^3 - 12x$$
$$H_4(x) = 16x^4 - 48x^2 + 12 \qquad 4\cdot94$$

In general

$$H_n(x) = (2x)^n - \frac{n(n-1)(2x)^{n-2}}{1!}$$
$$+ \frac{n(n-1)(n-2)(n-3)(2x)^{n-4}}{2!} + \cdots \qquad 4\cdot95$$

Differentiating this series term by term, we find

$$\frac{dH_n(x)}{dx} = 2n\left\{(2x)^{n-1} - \frac{(n-1)(n-2)}{1!}(2x)^{n-3} + \cdots\right.$$
$$= 2nH_{n-1}(x) \qquad 4\cdot96$$

Differentiating once again, we find

$$\frac{d^2H_n(x)}{dx^2} = 2n\frac{dH_{n-1}(x)}{dx} = 4n(n-1)H_{n-2} \qquad 4{\cdot}97$$

If we now substitute 4·96 and 4·97 in the differential equation 4·92, we obtain the useful recursion formulas

$$4n(n-1)H_{n-2} - 4nxH_{n-1} + 2nH_n = 0$$
$$xH_{n-1} = (n-1)H_{n-2} + \tfrac{1}{2}H_n \qquad 4{\cdot}98$$

or, upon replacing n by $n+1$, we obtain the relation analogous to equation 4·85

$$xH_n = nH_{n-1} + \tfrac{1}{2}H_{n+1} \qquad 4{\cdot}99$$

We shall now show that the functions $H_n(x)e^{-\frac{x^2}{2}}$ form an orthogonal set in the interval $(-\infty, \infty)$. Let m be less than n; then

$$(-1)^n \int_{-\infty}^{\infty} H_m(x)H_n(x)e^{-x^2}\,dx = \int_{-\infty}^{\infty} H_m(x)\frac{d^n(e^{-x^2})}{dx^n}\,dx \qquad 4{\cdot}100$$

Integrating by parts, we have

$$(-1)^n \int_{-\infty}^{\infty} H_m(x)H_n(x)e^{-x^2}\,dx = \frac{H_m(x)d^{n-1}(e^{-x^2})}{dx^{n-1}}\Bigg]_{-\infty}^{\infty}$$
$$- \int_{-\infty}^{\infty} \frac{dH_m}{dx}\frac{d^{n-1}(e^{-x^2})}{dx^{n-1}}\,dx \qquad 4{\cdot}101$$

The first term on the right is zero, since e^{-x^2} and all its derivatives vanish at $x = \pm\infty$. Replacing $\frac{dH_m}{dx}$ by $2mH_{m-1}$, we have

$$\int_{-\infty}^{\infty} H_m(x)H_n(x)e^{-x^2}\,dx = (-1)^{n+1}2m \int_{-\infty}^{\infty} H_{m-1}\frac{d^{n-1}}{dx^{n-1}}(e^{-x^2})\,dx \qquad 4{\cdot}102$$

Repeating this process, we finally obtain

$$\int_{-\infty}^{\infty} H_m(x)H_n(x)e^{-x^2}\,dx = (-1)^{n+m}2^m m! \int_{-\infty}^{\infty} H_0(x)\frac{d^{n-m}}{dx^{n-m}}(e^{-x^2})\,dx$$
$$= (-1)^{n+m}2^m m!\left[\frac{d^{n-m-1}}{dx^{n-m-1}}(e^{-x^2})\right]_{-\infty}^{\infty} = 0 \qquad 4{\cdot}103$$

If $m = n$, the same process leads to

$$\int_{-\infty}^{\infty} [H_n(x)]^2\,dx = (-1)^{2n}2^n n! \int_{-\infty}^{\infty} e^{-x^2}\,dx = 2^n n!\sqrt{\pi} \qquad 4{\cdot}104$$

We have thus proved that the functions $\dfrac{1}{(2^n n!\sqrt{\pi})^{\frac{1}{2}}} H_n(x)e^{-\frac{x^2}{2}}$ form a normalized, orthogonal set.

We must now show that these polynomials are the only solutions of equation 4·92 belonging to the class Q for the range $(-\infty, \infty)$. As there are no singular points in this equation (except $x = \pm\infty$), we may expand our solution about any point. Expanding about the origin, we find the recursion formula for the coefficients in the series

$$u = a_0 + a_1 x + a_2 x^2 + \cdots \qquad 4\cdot105$$

to be
$$(\nu + 2)(\nu + 1)a_{\nu+2} + (2n - 2\nu)a_\nu = 0 \qquad 4\cdot106$$

so that the solution is

$$u = a_0\left(1 - nx^2 + \frac{n^2 - 2n}{6} x^4 + \cdots\right) + a_1\left(x - \frac{(n-1)}{3} x^3 + \cdots\right) \quad 4\cdot107$$

Since $\lim\limits_{\nu \to \infty} \dfrac{a_{\nu+2}}{a_\nu} = \dfrac{2}{\nu}$, the series always converges. In the series

$$e^{x^2} = 1 + x^2 + \frac{x^4}{2!} + \cdots + \frac{x^{2\nu}}{\nu!} \qquad 4\cdot108$$

$a_\nu = \dfrac{1}{(\nu/2)!}$ for ν even; $a_\nu = 0$ for ν odd, so that $\lim\limits_{\nu \to \infty} \dfrac{a_{\nu+2}}{a_\nu} = \dfrac{2}{\nu}$ We therefore see that the series 4·107 behaves like e^{x^2} near $x = \pm\infty$. But neither e^{2x^2} nor e^{x^2} is integrable from $-\infty$ to ∞, so that neither u nor $ue^{-\frac{x^2}{2}}$ is a function of class Q. If n is a positive integer, one of the two series in 4·107 reduces to a polynomial, which will be a constant times the particular solution $H_n(x)$. Then, as we have seen, $H_n(x)e^{-\frac{x^2}{2}}$ is quadratically integrable and hence is a function of class Q.

4h. The Laguerre Polynomials. The polynomials $L_\alpha(x)$, of the αth degree in x, are defined by the equation

$$L_\alpha(x) = e^x \frac{d^\alpha}{dx^\alpha} (x^\alpha e^{-x}) \qquad 4\cdot109$$

and are known as the Laguerre polynomials. The βth derivative of $L_\alpha(x)$, called an associated Laguerre polynomial, is denoted by $L_\alpha^\beta(x)$. The general formula for the associated Laguerre polynomials is

$$L_\alpha^\beta(x) = (-1)^\alpha \frac{\alpha!}{(\alpha - \beta)!}\left\{x^{\alpha-\beta} - \frac{\alpha(\alpha - \beta)}{1!} x^{\alpha-\beta-1}\right.$$
$$\left. + \frac{\alpha(\alpha - 1)(\alpha - \beta)(\alpha - \beta - 1)}{2!} x^{\alpha-\beta-2} + \cdots\right\} \quad 4\cdot110$$

The Laguerre polynomials are not orthogonal functions, but the functions $e^{-\frac{x}{2}}L_\alpha(x)$ form an orthogonal set for the interval $(0, \infty)$. In order to prove this, consider the integral

$$\int_0^\infty e^{-x}x^\gamma L_\alpha(x)\, dx = \int_0^\infty x^\gamma \frac{d^\alpha}{dx^\alpha}(x^\alpha e^{-x})\, dx \qquad 4\cdot111$$

If we integrate by parts γ times, we find

$$\int_0^\infty e^{-x}x^\gamma L_\alpha(x)\, dx = (-1)^\gamma \gamma! \int_0^\infty \frac{d^{\alpha-\gamma}}{dx^{\alpha-\gamma}}(x^\alpha e^{-x})\, dx$$

For $\gamma < \alpha$, this gives

$$\int_0^\infty e^{-x}x^\gamma L_\alpha(x)\, dx = (-1)^\gamma \gamma! \left[\frac{d^{\alpha-\gamma-1}}{dx^{\alpha-\gamma-1}}(x^\alpha e^{-x})\right]_0^\infty = 0 \qquad 4\cdot112$$

while for $\gamma = \alpha$ we have

$$\int_0^\infty e^{-x}x^\gamma L_\alpha(x)\, dx = (-1)^\alpha \alpha! \int_0^\infty x^\alpha e^{-x}\, dx = (-1)^\alpha(\alpha!)^2 \qquad 4\cdot113$$

Since L_γ is a polynomial of the γth degree, $4\cdot112$ gives

$$\int_0^\infty e^{-x}L_\gamma(x)L_\alpha(x)\, dx = 0 \qquad \gamma < \alpha \qquad 4\cdot114$$

or, exchanging the roles of α and γ,

$$\int_0^\infty e^{-x}L_\gamma(x)L_\alpha(x)\, dx = 0 \qquad \gamma \neq \alpha \qquad 4\cdot115$$

The highest power of x in $L_\alpha(x)$ is $(-1)^\alpha x^\alpha$, so that

$$\int_0^\infty e^{-x}[L_\alpha(x)]^2\, dx = (-1)^\alpha \int_0^\infty e^{-x}x^\alpha L_\alpha(x)\, dx = [\alpha!]^2 \qquad 4\cdot116$$

The functions $\dfrac{1}{\alpha!}e^{-\frac{x}{2}}L_\alpha(x)$ therefore form a normalized, orthogonal set.

To show the orthogonality properties of the associated Laguerre polynomials, we consider the integral

$$\int_0^\infty e^{-x}x^\gamma L_\alpha^\beta\, dx = \int_0^\infty e^{-x}x^\gamma \frac{d^\beta}{dx^\beta}L_\alpha\, dx \qquad 4\cdot117$$

Integrating this by parts β times gives

$$\int_0^\infty e^{-x}x^\gamma L_\alpha^\beta\, dx = (-1)^\beta \int_0^\infty L_\alpha \frac{d^\beta}{dx^\beta}(e^{-x}x^\gamma)\, dx \qquad 4\cdot118$$

as the integrated part always vanishes. The first term in $\dfrac{d^\beta}{dx^\beta}(e^{-x}x^\gamma)$

is $(-1)^\beta e^{-x} x^\gamma$. For $\gamma < \alpha$, we therefore see from 4·112 that

$$\int_0^\infty e^{-x} x^\gamma L_\alpha^\beta \, dx = 0$$

Now the function $x^\beta L_\gamma^\beta$ is a polynomial of degree γ, so that we have the result

$$\int_0^\infty e^{-x} x^\beta L_\gamma^\beta L_\alpha^\beta \, dx = 0 \qquad \gamma < \alpha \qquad\qquad 4·119$$

or, since α and γ may be exchanged

$$\int_0^\infty e^{-x} x^\beta L_\gamma^\beta L_\alpha^\beta \, dx = 0 \qquad \gamma \neq \alpha \qquad\qquad 4·120$$

For $\gamma = \alpha$, the first term in $x^\beta L_\alpha^\beta$ is $\dfrac{(-1)^\alpha \alpha!}{(\alpha - \beta)!} x^\alpha$. We therefore have, by 4·118 and 4·113,

$$\int_0^\infty e^{-x} x^\beta L_\alpha^\beta L_\alpha^\beta \, dx = \frac{(-1)^\alpha \alpha!}{(\alpha - \beta)!} \int_0^\infty e^{-x} x^\alpha L_\alpha^\beta \, dx$$

$$= \frac{(-1)^\alpha \alpha!}{(\alpha - \beta)!} \int_0^\infty e^{-x} x^\alpha L_\alpha \, dx = \frac{(\alpha!)^3}{(\alpha - \beta)!} \qquad 4·121$$

The functions $\sqrt{\dfrac{(\alpha - \beta)!}{(\alpha!)^3}} \, e^{-\frac{x}{2}} x^{\frac{\beta}{2}} \, L_\alpha^\beta$ therefore form a normalized orthogonal set in the interval $(0, \infty)$.

In the theory of the hydrogen atom we will need the value of the integral $\int_0^\infty e^{-x} x^{\beta+1} L_\alpha^\beta L_\alpha^\beta \, dx$. By expanding $x^{\beta+1} L_\alpha^\beta$ by means of 4·110, and retaining only the terms in $x^{\alpha+1}$ and x^α, since lower powers of x will integrate to zero, we have

$$\int_0^\infty e^{-x} x^{\beta+1} L_\alpha^\beta L_\alpha^\beta \, dx = \frac{(-1)^\alpha \alpha!}{(\alpha - \beta)!} \left\{ \int_0^\infty e^{-x} x^{\alpha+1} L_\alpha^\beta \, dx \right.$$

$$\left. - \alpha(\alpha - \beta) \int_0^\infty e^{-x} x^\alpha L_\alpha^\beta \, dx \right\} \qquad 4·122$$

Using 4·118, and retaining the first two terms in the expansion of $\dfrac{d^\beta}{dx^\beta} (e^{-x} x^{\alpha+1})$, this reduces to

$$\int_0^\infty e^{-x} x^{\beta+1} L_\alpha^\beta L_\alpha^\beta \, dx = \frac{(-1)^\alpha \alpha!}{(\alpha - \beta)!} \left\{ \int_0^\infty e^{-x} x^{\alpha+1} L_\alpha \, dx \right.$$

$$\left. - [\beta(\alpha + 1) + \alpha(\alpha - \beta)] \int_0^\infty e^{-x} x^\alpha L_\alpha \, dx \right\} \qquad 4·123$$

The last integral has the value $(-1)^{\alpha}[\alpha!]^2$, according to 4·113. For the first integral, we have

$$\int_0^\infty e^{-x} x^{\alpha+1} L_\alpha \, dx = \int_0^\infty x^{\alpha+1} \frac{d^\alpha}{dx^\alpha} (x^\alpha e^{-x}) \, dx$$

or, after integrating by parts α times,

$$\int_0^\infty e^{-x} x^{\alpha+1} L_\alpha \, dx = (-1)^\alpha (\alpha+1)! \int_0^\infty x^{\alpha+1} e^{-x} \, dx$$

$$= (-1)^\alpha [(\alpha+1)!]^2 \quad \text{4·124}$$

Substituting these values in 4·123 gives us the final result

$$\int_0^\infty e^{-x} x^{\beta+1} L_\alpha^\beta L_\alpha^\beta \, dx = \frac{(\alpha!)^3}{(\alpha-\beta)!} \left\{ (\alpha+1)^2 - [\beta(\alpha+1) + \alpha(\alpha-\beta)] \right\}$$

$$= \frac{(2\alpha - \beta + 1)(\alpha!)^3}{(\alpha-\beta)!} \quad \text{4·125}$$

In order to find the differential equations satisfied by the Laguerre polynomials and their derivatives, consider the equation

$$x \frac{dy}{dx} + (x - \alpha)y = 0 \quad \text{4·126}$$

which is satisfied by $y = x^\alpha e^{-x}$. If we differentiate this equation $(\alpha + 1)$ times, we find

$$x \frac{d^2 z}{dx^2} + (x+1) \frac{dz}{dx} + (\alpha+1)z = 0 \quad \text{4·127}$$

where

$$z = \frac{d^\alpha y}{dx^\alpha} = \frac{d^\alpha}{dx^\alpha} (x^\alpha e^{-x}) = e^{-x} L_\alpha(x)$$

Substituting this value of z in equation 4·127 gives us the differential equation for the Laguerre polynomials

$$x \frac{d^2 L_\alpha}{dx^2} + (1 - x) \frac{dL_\alpha}{dx} + \alpha L_\alpha = 0 \quad \text{4·128}$$

and differentiating this equation β times gives

$$x \frac{d^2 u}{dx^2} + (\beta + 1 - x) \frac{du}{dx} + (\alpha - \beta)u = 0 \quad \text{4·129}$$

where $u = \dfrac{d^\beta L_\alpha}{dx^\beta} = L_\alpha^\beta$ as the differential equation for the associated Laguerre polynomials.

We shall now consider the general solution of this equation. The point $x = 0$ is a singular point, but it is regular, so that we take as our solution the series

$$u = a_0 x^L + a_1 x^{L+1} + \cdots \qquad 4 \cdot 130$$

Substituting this series in 4·129 gives the indicial equation

$$L(L + \beta) = 0 \qquad L = 0, \quad L = -\beta$$

The series beginning with $x^{-\beta}$ cannot be of class Q in any region including the point $x = 0$; therefore there remains only the series

$$u = a_0 + a_1 x + a_2 x^2 + \cdots \qquad 4 \cdot 131$$

The recursion formula for the coefficients is readily found to be

$$(\nu + \beta + 1)(\nu + 1)a_{\nu+1} = (\nu + \beta - \alpha)a_\nu; \qquad 4 \cdot 132$$

so that

$$\lim_{\nu \to \infty} \frac{a_{\nu+1}}{a_\nu} = \frac{1}{\nu}$$

The series always converges, but, as $\nu \to \infty$, the limiting ratio of the coefficients is the same as that in the series expansion of e^x. Hence the function u is not of class Q, nor is $e^{-\frac{x}{2}} x^{\frac{\beta}{2}} u$ unless the series terminates. This is possible only if $\alpha - \beta$ is an integer greater than zero, in which event we have a constant multiple of L_α^β. Where we shall use this function, β will be a positive integer, so that α must be an integer greater than β if there is to be a solution of class Q.

CHAPTER V

THE QUANTUM MECHANICS OF SOME SIMPLE SYSTEMS

In this chapter we propose to treat by the methods of quantum mechanics certain of the simple systems for which the Schrödinger equation can be solved exactly. These systems are an idealization of naturally occurring systems, but the consideration of them is not without value, as they furnish an insight into the methods of quantum mechanics and give results which are useful in the discussion of many problems of physical and chemical interest.

5a. The Free Particle. The simplest imaginable system would be a particle of mass m moving in the x direction under the influence of no forces. The classical Hamiltonian function for this system is

$$H = \frac{1}{2m}\, p_x^2 \qquad\qquad 5\cdot1$$

where the value zero has been chosen for the constant potential V. The eigenvalues E_x for the energy are given by the solution of the equation

$$-\frac{h^2}{8\pi^2 m}\frac{d^2\psi}{dx^2} = E_x\psi \qquad\qquad 5\cdot2$$

A possible solution of this equation is

$$\psi = N(E_x)e^{\frac{2\pi i}{h}\sqrt{2mE_x}\,x} \qquad\qquad 5\cdot3$$

In order that the wave function remain finite at $x = \pm\infty$, the quantity $\sqrt{2mE_x}$ must be real, and so E_x must be positive. As this is the only restriction on E_x, we conclude that all possible values of E_x from 0 to $+\infty$ are permissible; that is, we have a continuous spectrum of energy values. Classically, the energy is related to the momentum by the relation $E_x = \frac{1}{2m}\, p_x^2$, so that in terms of the momentum we may write

$$\psi = N(p_x)e^{\frac{2\pi i}{h}\sqrt{p_x^2}\,x} \qquad\qquad 5\cdot4$$

Let us now calculate the average value of the momentum associated

68

with the wave function 5·3. According to equation 3·68, this is

$$\bar{p}_x = \frac{\int \psi^* \left(\frac{h}{2\pi i}\frac{\partial}{\partial x}\right)\psi\,dx}{\int \psi^*\psi\,dx} = \sqrt{2mE_x} = \sqrt{p_x^2} \qquad 5\cdot5$$

An equally valid solution of equation 5·2 is

$$\psi = N(E_x)e^{-\frac{2\pi i}{h}\sqrt{2mE_x}x} = N(p_x)e^{-\frac{2\pi i}{h}\sqrt{p_x^2}x} \qquad 5\cdot6$$

The average value of the momentum associated with this wave function is $-\sqrt{p_x^2}$. The wave function 5·4 therefore represents a state in which the particle is moving in the $+x$ direction with the definite momentum $\sqrt{p_x^2}$; the wave function 5·6 represents a state in which the particle is moving in the $-x$ direction with the same absolute value of the momentum. Let us now consider the probability that the particle, in the state represented by 5·3, will be in the region between x and $x + dx$. According to Postulate I, this is $\psi^*\psi\,dx = N^*N\,dx$. We thus see that all regions of space are equally probable, so that the uncertainty in the position of the particle is infinite. This is, of course, required by the uncertainty principle, for, if Δp_x is zero, as we have found it to be, Δx will be infinite in order that the relation $\Delta p_x\,\Delta x \sim h$ will be true. Any linear combination of the solutions in 5·3 and 5·6 involving the time

$$\psi = N(E_x)e^{\frac{2\pi i}{h}\sqrt{2mE_x}x}\,e^{-\frac{2\pi iE_x}{h}t} \qquad 5\cdot3a$$

$$\psi = N(E_x)e^{-\frac{2\pi i}{h}\sqrt{2mE_x}x}\,e^{-\frac{2\pi iE_x}{h}t} \qquad 5\cdot6a$$

is also a solution of the wave equation

$$-\frac{h^2}{8\pi^2 m}\frac{\partial^2\psi}{\partial x^2} = \frac{h}{2\pi i}\frac{\partial}{\partial t}\psi$$

If we take the combination representing the sum of all possible wave functions 5·3a and 5·6a, the waves will reinforce one another at some particular point $x = x_0$ and will interfere everywhere else, so that in this event the particle can be located exactly. However, the uncertainty in the momentum is infinite. A more complete analysis[1] shows that the smallest possible simultaneous uncertainties in position and momentum are governed by the relation $\Delta p_x\,\Delta x \sim h$; in this way the uncertainty principle is derivable from our fundamental postulates.

[1] R. C. Tolman, *Principles of Statistical Mechanics.* Oxford, 1938. p. 231.

5b.   The Particle in a Box.   We now consider a particle of mass m constrained to move in a fixed region of space, which for simplicity we take to be a rectangular box with edges of length a, b, and c and volume $v = abc$.   The potential V may be put equal to zero within the box; at the boundaries of the box and in the remainder of space we put $V = \infty$.   We take our coordinate system to be the cartesian coordinate system with the origin at one corner of the box and the x, y, and z axes along the edges of length a, b, and c, respectively.   The potential energy is then

$$V_x = 0, \quad 0 < x < a; \quad V_x = \infty \quad \text{otherwise}$$

$$V_y = 0, \quad 0 < y < b; \quad V_y = \infty \quad \text{otherwise}$$

$$V_z = 0, \quad 0 < z < c; \quad V_z = \infty \quad \text{otherwise}$$

Schrödinger's equation for the system is

$$\frac{\partial^2 \psi}{\partial x^2} + \frac{\partial^2 \psi}{\partial y^2} + \frac{\partial^2 \psi}{\partial z^2} + \frac{8\pi^2 m}{h^2}(E - V)\psi = 0 \qquad 5{\cdot}7$$

We have a differential equation in three variables.   In order to solve this equation we seek a solution of the form

$$\psi = X(x)Y(y)Z(z) \qquad 5{\cdot}8$$

where $X(x)$ is a function of x alone, etc.   If we now put $V = V_x + V_y + V_z$, and substitute 5·8 in 5·7, we obtain

$$\frac{1}{X(x)}\frac{\partial^2 X(x)}{\partial x^2} + \frac{1}{Y(y)}\frac{\partial^2 Y(y)}{\partial y^2} + \frac{8\pi^2 m}{h^2}(E - V_x - V_y)$$

$$= -\frac{1}{Z(z)}\frac{\partial^2 Z(z)}{\partial z^2} + \frac{8\pi^2 m}{h^2}V_z \qquad 5{\cdot}9$$

On the left we have a function of x and y only; on the right, a function of z only.   If we vary x and y, keeping z constant, the right side remains constant; therefore the left side must be a constant.   Let us call this constant $\dfrac{8\pi^2 m}{h^2}E_z$.   We then have the equations

$$\frac{d^2 Z(z)}{dz^2} + \frac{8\pi^2 m}{h^2}(E_z - V_z)Z(z) = 0 \qquad 5{\cdot}10$$

$$\frac{1}{X(x)}\frac{\partial^2 X(x)}{\partial x^2} + \frac{8\pi^2 m}{h^2}(E - E_z - V_x)$$

$$= -\frac{1}{Y(y)}\frac{\partial^2 Y(y)}{\partial y^2} + \frac{8\pi^2 m}{h^2}V_y \qquad 5{\cdot}11$$

By the same reasoning followed above, both sides of this last equation must be equal to a constant, which we call $\dfrac{8\pi^2 m}{h^2}E_y$. This gives us the additional equations

$$\frac{d^2 Y(y)}{dy^2} + \frac{8\pi^2 m}{h^2}(E_y - V_y)Y(y) = 0 \qquad 5\cdot12$$

$$\frac{d^2 X(x)}{dx^2} + \frac{8\pi^2 m}{h^2}(E_x - V_x)X(x) = 0 \qquad 5\cdot13$$

where, in 5·13, we have put $E = E_x + E_y + E_z$. We thus have three differential equations, each involving one variable only, and which are thus readily solvable. Let us consider first the equation in x. Since $V_x = \infty$ for $x \geq a$, $x \leq 0$, 5·13 will hold in this region only if we put $X(x) = 0$, $\dfrac{d^2 X(x)}{dx^2} = 0$. For the region inside the box the equation is

$$\frac{d^2 X(x)}{dx^2} = -\frac{8\pi^2 m}{h^2}E_x X(x) \qquad 5\cdot14$$

for which the general solution is

$$X(x) = A e^{\frac{2\pi i}{h}\sqrt{2mE_x}x} + B e^{-\frac{2\pi i}{h}\sqrt{2mE_x}x} \qquad 5\cdot15$$

or

$$X(x) = A' \cos\frac{2\pi}{h}\sqrt{2mE_x}\,x + B' \sin\frac{2\pi}{h}\sqrt{2mE_x}\,x \qquad 5\cdot16$$

In order that the solution for the region inside the box join smoothly with the solution for the region outside the box, we must have $X(x) = 0$ at $x = 0$, $x = a$. The first of these considerations requires that $A' = 0$; the second requires that $\dfrac{2\pi}{h}\sqrt{2mE_x}\,a = n_x\pi$, where n_x is an integer (not including zero, as this value of n_x would make $X(x)$ equal to zero everywhere). This limitation on the nature of the wave function at the edge of the box requires that the energy be quantized that is, only those values of the energy given by

$$E_x = \frac{n_x^2 h^2}{8ma^2} \qquad n_x = 1, 2, 3, \cdots \qquad 5\cdot17$$

will give an acceptable wave function. This wave function may now be written as

$$X(x) = B' \sin\frac{n_x\pi}{a}x \qquad 5\cdot18$$

The normalization factor is given by the integral

$$\int_0^a [X(x)]^2 \, dx = B'^2 \int_0^a \sin^2 \left(\frac{n_x \pi}{a} x \right) dx = 1 \qquad 5\cdot19$$

which gives $B' = \sqrt{\dfrac{2}{a}}$. The equations in y and z are solved in the same manner. The final results are therefore

$$\psi(x, y, z) = X(x)Y(y)Z(z) = \sqrt{\frac{8}{abc}} \sin \frac{n_x \pi}{a} x \sin \frac{n_y \pi}{b} y \sin \frac{n_z \pi}{c} z$$

$$= \sqrt{\frac{8}{v}} \sin \frac{n_x \pi}{a} x \sin \frac{n_y \pi}{b} y \sin \frac{n_z \pi}{c} z \qquad 5\cdot20$$

$$E = E_x + E_y + E_z = \frac{h^2}{8m} \left(\frac{n_x^2}{a^2} + \frac{n_y^2}{b^2} + \frac{n_z^2}{c^2} \right) \qquad 5\cdot21$$

where $n_x, n_y, n_z = 1, 2, 3, 4, \cdots$. These results will be of importance in connection with the theory of a perfect gas, and also in the theory of absolute reaction rates.

5c. The Rigid Rotator. The theory of the rigid rotator in space will be of value in the discussion of the spectra of diatomic molecules. As an idealization of a diatomic molecule, we consider that the molecule consists of two atoms rigidly connected so that the distance between them is a constant, R. As we are not interested here in the translational motion of the molecule in space, we may regard the center of gravity as fixed at the origin of our coordinate system. Suppose that the polar coordinates of one atom are a, θ, φ, where $a = \dfrac{m_2}{m_1 + m_2} R$, and m_1 and m_2 are the masses of the two atoms. The polar coordinates of the other atom are then b, θ, φ, where $b = -\dfrac{m_1}{m_1 + m_2} R$. The kinetic energy of the first particle is

$$\frac{m_1}{2} \left[\left(\frac{dx_1}{dt} \right)^2 + \left(\frac{dy_1}{dt} \right)^2 + \left(\frac{dz_1}{dt} \right)^2 \right] = \frac{m_1 a^2}{2} \left[\left(\frac{d\theta}{dt} \right)^2 + \sin^2 \theta \left(\frac{d\varphi}{dt} \right)^2 \right] \qquad 5\cdot22$$

Similarly, the kinetic energy of the second particle is

$$\frac{m_2 b^2}{2} \left[\left(\frac{d\theta}{dt} \right)^2 + \sin^2 \theta \left(\frac{d\varphi}{dt} \right)^2 \right]$$

so that the total kinetic energy is

$$T = \frac{m_1 a^2 + m_2 b^2}{2} \left[\left(\frac{d\theta}{dt} \right)^2 + \sin^2 \theta \left(\frac{d\varphi}{dt} \right)^2 \right] \qquad 5\cdot23$$

If we put $m_1 a^2 + m_2 b^2 = I$ (the moment of inertia), then the kinetic energy may be written as

$$T = \frac{I}{2}\left[\left(\frac{d\theta}{dt}\right)^2 + \sin^2\theta\left(\frac{d\varphi}{dt}\right)^2\right] \qquad 5\cdot24$$

which is the same as that of a single particle of mass I confined to the surface of a sphere of unit radius. From the expression for the Laplacian operator in spherical coordinates (Appendix III) we see that the Hamiltonian operator is

$$\mathbf{H} = \frac{-h^2}{8\pi^2 m}\left[\frac{1}{r^2}\frac{\partial}{\partial r}\left(r^2\frac{\partial}{\partial r}\right) + \frac{1}{r^2\sin\theta}\frac{\partial}{\partial\theta}\left(\sin\theta\frac{\partial}{\partial\theta}\right)\right.$$
$$\left. + \frac{1}{r^2\sin^2\theta}\frac{\partial^2}{\partial\varphi^2}\right] + V \qquad 5\cdot25$$

If no forces are acting on the rotator we may put $V = 0$, and, putting $r = 1$, $mr^2 = m = I$, we find that Schrödinger's equation is

$$\frac{1}{\sin\theta}\frac{\partial}{\partial\theta}\left(\sin\theta\frac{\partial\psi}{\partial\theta}\right) + \frac{1}{\sin^2\theta}\frac{\partial^2\psi}{\partial\varphi^2} + \frac{8\pi^2 IE}{h^2}\psi = 0 \qquad 5\cdot26$$

We have once again a differential equation with more than one independent variable, so that we look for a solution of the form

$$\psi = \Theta(\theta)\Phi(\varphi) \qquad 5\cdot27$$

After making this substitution we may write equation 5·26 as

$$\frac{\sin\theta}{\Theta}\frac{\partial}{\partial\theta}\left(\sin\theta\frac{\partial\Theta}{\partial\theta}\right) + \frac{8\pi^2 IE}{h^2}\sin^2\theta = -\frac{1}{\Phi}\frac{\partial^2\Phi}{\partial\varphi^2} \qquad 5\cdot28$$

By the same line of reasoning as was employed in the previous section both sides of this equation must be equal to a constant, which we take equal to m^2. We thus obtain two differential equations

$$\frac{d^2\Phi}{d\varphi^2} = -m^2\Phi \qquad 5\cdot29$$

$$\frac{1}{\sin\theta}\frac{\partial\Theta}{\partial\theta}\left(\sin\theta\frac{\partial\Theta}{\partial\theta}\right) - \frac{m^2}{\sin^2\theta}\Theta + \frac{8\pi^2 IE}{h^2}\Theta = 0 \qquad 5\cdot30$$

Equation 5·29 is seen to have the solution

$$\Phi(\varphi) = ce^{\pm im\varphi} \qquad 5\cdot31$$

We have previously shown (section 3h) that this is an acceptable wave function if m is an integer; the normalized solution of 5·29 is therefore

$$\Phi(\varphi) \equiv \Phi_{\pm m}(\varphi) = \frac{1}{\sqrt{2\pi}}e^{\pm im\varphi} \qquad m = 0, 1, 2, 3\cdots \qquad 5\cdot32$$

In equation 5·30, let us replace $\dfrac{8\pi^2 I E}{h^2}$ by $l(l+1)$. This equation then becomes

$$\frac{1}{\sin\theta}\frac{\partial}{\partial\theta}\left(\sin\theta\frac{\partial\Theta}{\partial\theta}\right) - \frac{m^2}{\sin^2\theta}\Theta + l(l+1)\,\Theta = 0 \qquad 5\cdot33$$

which is identical with equation 4·70, and therefore has acceptable solutions only for integral values of l; $l \geq |m|$. The normalized solutions of 5·33 are therefore

$$\Theta(\theta) \equiv \Theta_{l,\,\pm m}(\theta) = \sqrt{\frac{2l+1}{2}\frac{(l-|m|)!}{(l+|m|)!}}\,P_l^{|m|}(\cos\theta) \qquad 5\cdot34$$

The restriction on l requires that only those values of the energy given by the relation

$$E = \frac{h^2}{8\pi^2 I}l(l+1) \qquad l = 0,\,1,\,2,\,3\cdots \qquad 5\cdot35$$

are allowed. The total wave function is, of course,

$$\psi = \Theta_{l,\,\pm m}(\theta)\Phi_{\pm m}(\varphi) \equiv Y_{l,\,\pm m}(\theta,\,\varphi)$$

As we have seen in sections 3h and 4e, these wave functions satisfy simultaneously the equations

$$\mathbf{M}^2 Y_{l,\,\pm m} = l(l+1)\frac{h^2}{4\pi^2}\,Y_{l,\,\pm m}$$

$$\mathbf{M}_z Y_{l,\,\pm m} = \pm m\,\frac{h}{2\pi}\,Y_{l,\,\pm m}$$

$$5\cdot36$$

In addition to being eigenfunctions of the Hamiltonian, with the eigenvalues for the energy $E = \dfrac{h^2}{8\pi^2 I}l(l+1)$, these functions are also eigenfunctions of the total angular momentum, with the eigenvalues $M^2 = l(l+1)\dfrac{h^2}{4\pi^2}$, and of the z component of the angular momentum, with the eigenvalues $M_z = \pm m\dfrac{h}{2\pi}$. All these variables thus have a constant value simultaneously. In general, when only two coordinates are needed to describe a system, we would expect only two dynamical variables to be simultaneous eigenvalues. The reason that we have three here is that classically there is a relation between the energy and the square of the total angular momentum, this relation being $E = \dfrac{M^2}{2I}$, which is also true for the eigenvalues given above.

5d. The Rigid Rotator in a Plane. As a special case of the above problem, let us restrict the motion to rotation in a given plane, which we may without loss of generality take to be the xy plane. In this event, θ has the constant value of $90°$, so that equation 5·26 becomes

$$\frac{d^2\psi}{d\varphi^2} = -\frac{8\pi^2 I E}{h^2}\,\psi \qquad 5·37$$

Comparing this with 5·29 we see that the eigenfunctions are $\psi = \Phi_{\pm m}(\varphi)$ with the energy eigenvalues $E = \dfrac{h^2}{8\pi^2 I}\,m^2$. These eigenfunctions for the energy are also eigenfunctions for M_z, with the eigenvalues $\pm m\,\dfrac{h}{2\pi}$.

5e. The Harmonic Oscillator. Many systems of interest can be approximated by harmonic oscillators; for example, the vibrations of a diatomic molecule and the motions of atoms in a crystal lattice can be treated to a first approximation as motions of a particle in a harmonic field. A harmonic oscillator is a particle of mass m moving in a straight line (along, say, the x axis) subject to a potential $V = \frac{1}{2}kx^2$, so that the force on the particle is $-kx$. Classically, the equation of motion is

$$m\frac{d^2x}{dt^2} = -kx \qquad 5·38$$

with the general solution

$$x = a\cos 2\pi\nu(t - t_0) \qquad 5·39$$

where a and t_0 are constants and $\nu = \dfrac{1}{2\pi}\sqrt{\dfrac{k}{m}}$. The kinetic energy is $\frac{1}{2}m\left(\dfrac{dx}{dt}\right)^2 = 2m\pi^2\nu^2 a^2 \sin^2 2\pi\nu(t - t_0)$; the potential energy is $\frac{1}{2}kx^2 = 2m\pi^2\nu^2 a^2 \cos^2 2\pi\nu(t - t_0)$, so that the total energy is $E = 2m\pi^2\nu^2 a^2 = \dfrac{k}{2}a^2$; all positive values of E are allowed.

The classical Hamiltonian for the system is

$$H = \frac{1}{2m}\,p^2 + \frac{k}{2}\,x^2 \qquad 5·40$$

so that the Hamiltonian operator is

$$\mathbf{H} = -\frac{h^2}{8\pi^2 m}\frac{d^2}{dx^2} + \frac{k}{2}\,x^2 \qquad 5·41$$

The wave equation for the system is therefore

$$\frac{d^2\psi}{dx^2} + \frac{8\pi^2 m}{h^2}\left(E - \frac{k}{2}x^2\right)\psi = 0 \qquad 5\cdot42$$

and our problem is to find those functions of class Q which satisfy this equation. This equation may be rewritten as

$$\frac{d^2\psi}{dx^2} + (\alpha - \beta^2 x^2)\psi = 0 \qquad 5\cdot43$$

where $\alpha = \dfrac{8\pi^2 m}{h^2}E$, $\beta = \dfrac{2\pi\sqrt{mk}}{h}$. We can further simplify this equation by making the change of variable $\xi = \sqrt{\beta}\,x$. Then $\dfrac{d^2}{dx^2} = \beta\dfrac{d^2}{d\xi^2}$, and the equation in ξ becomes

$$\frac{d^2\psi}{d\xi^2} + \left(\frac{\alpha}{\beta} - \xi^2\right)\psi = 0 \qquad 5\cdot44$$

Let us first see what form we must take for $\psi(\xi)$ for very large values of ξ in order that we may have an acceptable wave function. For sufficiently large values of ξ, $\dfrac{\alpha}{\beta}$ may be neglected in comparison with ξ^2, so that in this region $\psi(\xi)$ must approximately satisfy the equation

$$\frac{d^2\psi}{d\xi^2} = \xi^2\psi \qquad 5\cdot45$$

The solutions of this equation are approximately $\psi = ce^{\pm\frac{\xi^2}{2}}$, since $\dfrac{d^2}{d\xi^2}\left(e^{\pm\frac{\xi^2}{2}}\right) = e^{\pm\frac{\xi^2}{2}}(\xi^2 \pm 1)$, and the factor ± 1 may be neglected in comparison to ξ^2 in the region of large ξ. We cannot use the solution $e^{+\frac{\xi^2}{2}}$, as this is certainly not of class Q; the solution $e^{-\frac{\xi^2}{2}}$ will, however, behave satisfactorily at large values of ξ. These considerations suggest that a solution of 5·44 of the form $\psi(\xi) = u(\xi)e^{-\frac{\xi^2}{2}}$ might be found. Making this substitution, we find that $u(\xi)$ must satisfy the differential equation

$$\frac{d^2 u}{d\xi^2} - 2\xi\frac{du}{d\xi} + \left(\frac{\alpha}{\beta} - 1\right)u = 0 \qquad 5\cdot46$$

Comparing this with equation 4·92, we see that the two equations are identical if we replace $\left(\dfrac{\alpha}{\beta} - 1\right)$ by $2n$. $u(\xi)$ is therefore $H_n(\xi)$, and

the wave function $\psi(\xi)$ is $cH_n(\xi)e^{-\frac{\xi^2}{2}}$, which, as we have seen, is a

function of class Q for all positive integral values of n, including zero. This restriction on n gives us a corresponding restriction on E. We have

$$\frac{\alpha}{\beta} = 2n + 1 \qquad\qquad 5\cdot47$$

or, substituting the full expressions for α and β and simplifying

$$E = \frac{h}{2\pi}\sqrt{\frac{k}{m}}\,(n + \tfrac{1}{2}) = (n + \tfrac{1}{2})h\nu \qquad\qquad 5\cdot48$$

The allowed energy values are thus $\frac{1}{2}$, $\frac{3}{2}$, $\frac{5}{2}$, $\cdots$ times the energy $h\nu$ associated with the classical frequency of oscillation.

We now need to find the constant c such that

$$\int_{-\infty}^{\infty} \psi_n^* \psi_n \, dx = \frac{c^2}{\sqrt{\beta}} \int_{-\infty}^{\infty} [H_n(\xi)]^2 e^{-\xi^2} d\xi = 1 \qquad\qquad 5\cdot49$$

From equation 4·104, we see that we must take $c = \dfrac{\sqrt[4]{\beta}}{\sqrt{2^n n!\sqrt{\pi}}}$. The

normalized wave functions for the harmonic oscillator are therefore

$$\psi_n(\xi) = \left(\frac{\sqrt{\beta/\pi}}{2^n n!}\right)^{\frac{1}{2}} H_n(\xi)e^{-\frac{\xi^2}{2}} \qquad \xi = \sqrt{\beta}\,x \qquad\qquad 5\cdot50$$

The first few energy levels and the corresponding wave functions are shown graphically in Figure 5·1. We note that the wave functions are alternately symmetrical and antisymmetrical about the origin. Of particular interest is the fact that, on the basis of quantum mechanics, the harmonic oscillator is not allowed to have zero energy, the smallest allowed energy value being the " zero-point " energy $\frac{1}{2}h\nu$. This is in accord with the uncertainty principle; if the oscillator had zero energy it would have zero momentum and would also be located exactly at the position of minimum potential energy. The necessary uncertainties in position and momentum give rise to the zero-point energy. A similar situation exists for the particle in a box, which also has a zero-point energy. In the rotator, the lowest state corresponds to the situation in which all orientations in space are equally probable; the uncertainty in position is therefore infinite, hence the momentum, and therefore the energy, may have the precise value zero.

Let us now calculate the average value of the displacement of the particle from its equilibrium position.   We have

$$\bar{x} = \frac{1}{\sqrt{\beta}}\,\bar{\xi} = \frac{1}{\beta}\,\frac{\sqrt{\beta/\pi}}{2^n n!} \int_{-\infty}^{\infty} H_n(\xi)\xi H_n(\xi)e^{-\xi^2}\,d\xi \qquad 5{\cdot}51$$

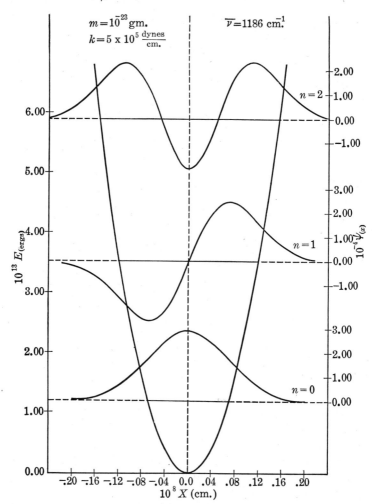

FIG. 5·1.   Energy levels and eigenfunctions for the harmonic oscillator.

The recursion formula 4·99 for the Hermite polynomials states that

$$\xi H_n(\xi) = n H_{n-1}(\xi) + \tfrac{1}{2}H_{n+1}(\xi)$$

The integral therefore vanishes because of the orthogonality of the wave functions, so that $\bar{x} = 0$. This was, of course, to be expected, since the squares of the functions are symmetrical about the origin. For the average value of x^2, we have

$$\overline{x^2} = \frac{1}{\beta^{3/2}} \frac{\sqrt{\beta/\pi}}{2^n n!} \int_{-\infty}^{\infty} H_n(\xi)\xi^2 H_n(\xi)e^{-\xi^2}\, d\xi \qquad 5\cdot52$$

From the recursion formula, we have

$$\xi^2 H_n = n\xi H_{n-1} + \tfrac{1}{2}\xi H_{n+1}$$
$$= n[(n-1)H_{n-2} + \tfrac{1}{2}H_n] + \tfrac{1}{2}[(n+1)H_n + \tfrac{1}{2}H_{n+2}] \qquad 5\cdot53$$

Since only the terms in H_n contribute, the integral 5·52 becomes

$$\overline{x^2} = \frac{1}{\beta^{3/2}} \frac{\sqrt{\beta/\pi}}{2^n n!} (n + \tfrac{1}{2}) \int_{-\infty}^{\infty} [H_n(\xi)]^2 e^{-\xi^2}\, d\xi = \frac{n + \tfrac{1}{2}}{\beta} \qquad 5\cdot54$$

Using the relations derived above, this may be written as $\overline{x^2} = \dfrac{E}{k}$ or

$E = k\overline{x^2}$. Now, classically, $\overline{x^2} = \dfrac{a^2}{2}$, so that in terms of the mean square displacement from the equilibrium position we see that the energy is given by the same relation in both cases.

CHAPTER VI

THE HYDROGEN ATOM

6a. The Hydrogen Atom. In this chapter we will treat by the methods of quantum mechanics the simplest atomic system, the hydrogen atom. The hydrogen atom consists of a proton, of charge $+e$ and mass M, and an electron, of charge $-e$ and mass m. These two particles attract each other according to the Coulomb law of electrostatic interaction. If we denote the coordinates of the proton by x_1, y_1, and z_1, and the coordinates of the electron by x_2, y_2, and z_2, the potential energy is

$$V = \frac{-e^2}{\sqrt{(x_1 - x_2)^2 + (y_1 - y_2)^2 + (z_1 - z_2)^2}}$$

The classical Hamiltonian function, in this coordinate system, will then be

$$H = \frac{M}{2}\left[\left(\frac{dx_1}{dt}\right)^2 + \left(\frac{dy_1}{dt}\right)^2 + \left(\frac{dz_1}{dt}\right)^2\right]$$
$$+ \frac{m}{2}\left[\left(\frac{dx_2}{dt}\right)^2 + \left(\frac{dy_2}{dt}\right)^2 + \left(\frac{dz_2}{dt}\right)^2\right] + V \quad 6\cdot 1$$

Because of the form of the potential energy, the Hamiltonian function is not at all simple in this coordinate system. We therefore introduce the following change of variables. Let x, y, and z be the coordinates of the center of gravity. Referred to the center of gravity of the system as origin of a spherical coordinate system, let the spherical coordinates of the electron be a, θ, φ and those of the proton b, θ, φ, where $a = \dfrac{M}{M + m}r$, $b = -\dfrac{m}{M + m}r$ and where r is the distance between the proton and the electron. In this coordinate system, the potential energy now has the simple form $V = -\dfrac{e^2}{r}$. In terms of the new coordinates, the rectangular coordinates of the proton and electron are

$$x_1 = x - \frac{\mu}{M} r \sin\theta \cos\varphi \qquad x_2 = x + \frac{\mu}{m} r \sin\theta \cos\varphi$$

$$y_1 = y - \frac{\mu}{M} r \sin\theta \sin\varphi \qquad y_2 = y + \frac{\mu}{m} r \sin\theta \sin\varphi \qquad 6\cdot 2$$

$$z_1 = z - \frac{\mu}{M} r \cos\theta \qquad z_2 = z + \frac{\mu}{m} \cos\theta$$

where $\mu = \dfrac{mM}{M + m}$ is the " reduced mass " of the system. With the introduction of this change of variables, the classical Hamiltonian function becomes

$$H = \frac{M + m}{2}\left[\left(\frac{dx}{dt}\right)^2 + \left(\frac{dy}{dt}\right)^2 + \left(\frac{dz}{dt}\right)^2\right]$$
$$+ \frac{\mu}{2}\left[\left(\frac{dr}{dt}\right)^2 + r^2\left(\frac{d\theta}{dt}\right)^2 + r^2\sin^2\theta\left(\frac{d\varphi}{dt}\right)^2\right] - \frac{e^2}{r} \quad 6\cdot3$$

The first term is the kinetic energy, in rectangular coordinates, of a particle of mass $M + m$; the second term is the kinetic energy, in spherical coordinates, of a particle of mass μ. The Hamiltonian operator for the system is therefore

$$\mathbf{H} = \frac{-h^2}{8\pi^2(M + m)}\left\{\frac{\partial^2}{\partial x^2} + \frac{\partial^2}{\partial y^2} + \frac{\partial^2}{\partial z^2}\right\}$$
$$- \frac{h^2}{8\pi^2\mu}\left\{\frac{1}{r^2}\frac{\partial}{\partial r}\left(r^2\frac{\partial}{\partial r}\right) + \frac{1}{r^2\sin\theta}\frac{\partial}{\partial\theta}\left(\sin\theta\frac{\partial}{\partial\theta}\right)\right.$$
$$\left. + \frac{1}{r^2\sin^2\theta}\frac{\partial^2}{\partial\varphi^2}\right\} - \frac{e^2}{r} \quad 6\cdot4$$

so that Schrödinger's equation for the hydrogen atom is

$$\frac{h^2}{8\pi^2(M + m)}\left\{\frac{\partial^2}{\partial x^2} + \frac{\partial^2}{\partial y^2} + \frac{\partial^2}{\partial z^2}\right\}\psi'$$
$$+ \frac{h^2}{8\pi^2\mu}\left\{\frac{1}{r^2}\frac{\partial}{\partial r}\left(r^2\frac{\partial}{\partial r}\right) + \frac{1}{r^2\sin\theta}\frac{\partial}{\partial\theta}\left(\sin\theta\frac{\partial}{\partial\theta}\right)\right.$$
$$\left. + \frac{1}{r^2\sin^2\theta}\frac{\partial^2}{\partial\varphi^2}\right\}\psi' + \left(E' + \frac{e^2}{r}\right)\psi' = 0 \quad 6\cdot5$$

It is apparent that we can separate this wave equation into two equations, one containing x, y, and z only, the other containing r, θ, φ only. Carrying out this separation in the manner employed in the previous chapter, we set $\psi' = \chi(x, y, z)\psi(r, \theta, \varphi)$ and obtain the two equations

$$\frac{\partial^2\chi}{\partial x^2} + \frac{\partial^2\chi}{\partial y^2} + \frac{\partial^2\chi}{\partial z^2} + \frac{8\pi^2(M + m)}{h^2}(E' - E)\chi = 0 \quad 6\cdot6$$

$$\frac{1}{r^2}\frac{\partial}{\partial r}\left(r^2\frac{\partial\psi}{\partial r}\right) + \frac{1}{r^2\sin\theta}\frac{\partial}{\partial\theta}\left(\sin\theta\frac{\partial\psi}{\partial\theta}\right)$$
$$+ \frac{1}{r^2\sin\theta}\frac{\partial^2\psi}{\partial\varphi^2} + \frac{8\pi^2\mu}{h^2}\left(E + \frac{e^2}{r}\right)\psi = 0 \quad 6\cdot7$$

Equation 6·7 contains only the relative coordinates of the two particles, so that E is the internal energy of the hydrogen atom. Equation 6·6 is just the wave equation for a free particle of mass $M + m$, with translational energy $E' - E$. This equation has already been discussed, and we will not consider it further in this chapter. It is apparent that in the treatment of any atomic or molecular problem the translational degrees of freedom of the system may be separated from the internal degrees of freedom in the same manner and thus need not be considered in general.

To separate the variables in 6·7, we make the substitution

$$\psi(r, \theta, \varphi) = R(r) Y(\theta, \varphi)$$

obtaining

$$\frac{1}{R} \frac{\partial}{\partial r}\left(r^2 \frac{\partial R}{\partial r}\right) + \frac{8\pi^2 \mu}{h^2}\left(E + \frac{e^2}{r}\right) r^2$$
$$= -\frac{1}{Y \sin \theta} \frac{\partial}{\partial \theta}\left(\sin \theta \frac{\partial Y}{\partial \theta}\right) - \frac{1}{Y \sin^2 \theta} \frac{\partial^2 Y}{\partial \varphi^2} \qquad 6·8$$

By our usual argument, both sides of this equation must be equal to a constant, which we call λ. We then have the two equations

$$\frac{1}{\sin \theta} \frac{\partial}{\partial \theta}\left(\sin \theta \frac{\partial Y}{\partial \theta}\right) + \frac{1}{\sin^2 \theta} \frac{\partial^2 Y}{\partial \varphi^2} + \lambda Y = 0 \qquad 6·9$$

$$\frac{1}{r^2} \frac{d}{dr}\left(r^2 \frac{dR}{dr}\right) + \left\{\frac{8\pi^2 \mu}{h^2}\left(E + \frac{e^2}{r}\right) - \frac{\lambda}{r^2}\right\} R = 0 \qquad 6·10$$

Equation 6·9 is by now quite familiar. The allowed solutions are $Y = Y_{l, \pm m}(\theta, \varphi)$, where $\lambda = l(l + 1)$, with l and m integers, and $l \geq |m|$. It should be mentioned at this point that, in all problems in which, in spherical coordinates, the potential energy can be written as a function of r only, the separation of the wave equation will proceed in the same manner as above, giving $Y_{l, \pm m}$ as the angular part of the wave function. Introducing the required value $\lambda = l(l + 1)$ into 6·10, and expanding the first term, we have

$$\frac{d^2 R}{dr^2} + \frac{2}{r} \frac{dR}{dr} + \left[\frac{8\pi^2 \mu}{h^2}\left(E + \frac{e^2}{r}\right) - \frac{l(l + 1)}{r^2}\right] R = 0 \qquad 6·11$$

We must now consider separately the two cases where E is positive and where E is negative. With negative E, equation 6·11 may be simplified by the introduction of a new parameter n, defined by the relation

$$E = -\frac{2\pi^2 \mu e^4}{n^2 h^2} \qquad 6·12$$

and a new variable x defined by

$$r = \frac{nh^2}{8\pi^2 \mu e^2} x \qquad 6\cdot 13$$

Equation 6·11 is reduced by these substitutions to

$$\frac{d^2R}{dx^2} + \frac{2}{x}\frac{dR}{dx} + \left(-\frac{1}{4} + \frac{n}{x} - \frac{l(l+1)}{x^2}\right)R = 0 \qquad 6\cdot 14$$

If we look for a solution of the form

$$R = u(x)x^l e^{-\frac{x}{2}} \qquad 6\cdot 15$$

we find that $u(x)$ must satisfy the differential equation

$$x\frac{d^2u}{dx^2} + (2l + 2 - x)\frac{du}{dx} + (n - l - 1)u = 0 \qquad 6\cdot 16$$

This is the same as equation 4·129 if we put $\beta = 2l + 1$ and $\alpha = n + l$. We have seen that equation 4·129 possesses satisfactory solutions only if $\alpha - \beta$ is a positive integer. Now $\alpha - \beta$ is equal to $n - l - 1$, and, since l may have the values 0, 1, 2, 3, $\cdots$, n may have the values 1, 2, 3, $\cdots$, with the restriction that $n \geq l + 1$. This gives the allowed negative values of the energy

$$E = -\frac{2\pi^2 \mu e^4}{n^2 h^2} \qquad n = 1, 2, 3, \cdots \qquad 6\cdot 17$$

which are identical with the values obtained in Chapter I by means of the Bohr theory.

The radial wave functions for the hydrogen atom are therefore

$$R(r) = cx^l e^{-\frac{x}{2}} L_{n+l}^{2l+1}(x); \quad x = \frac{8\pi^2 \mu e^2}{nh^2} r \qquad 6\cdot 18$$

To determine c, we take

$$\int_0^\infty [R(r)]^2 r^2 \, dr = 1 \qquad 6\cdot 19$$

But

$$\int_0^\infty [R(r)]^2 r^2 \, dr = c^2 \int_0^\infty x^{2l} e^{-x} [L_{n+l}^{2l+1}(x)]^2 r^2 \, dr \qquad 6\cdot 20$$

We may write $r = \frac{na_0}{2} x$, where $a_0 = \frac{h^2}{4\pi^2 \mu e^2}$ is the radius of the first Bohr orbit, as is easily verified from the equations in Chapter I. Then, by means of equation 4·125,

$$\int_0^\infty [R(r)]^2 r^2 \, dr = c^2 \left(\frac{na_0}{2}\right)^3 \int_0^\infty x^{2l+2} e^{-x} [L_{n+l}^{2l+1}(x)]^2 \, dx$$

$$= c^2 \left(\frac{na_0}{2}\right)^3 \frac{2n[(n+l)!]^3}{(n-l-1)!} \qquad 6\cdot21$$

so that

$$R(r) = -\sqrt{\left(\frac{2}{na_0}\right)^3 \frac{(n-l-1)!}{2n[(n+l)!]^3}} \left(\frac{2r}{na_0}\right)^l e^{-\frac{r}{na_0}} L_{n+l}^{2l+1}\left(\frac{2r}{na_0}\right) \qquad 6\cdot22$$

where the minus sign has been introduced to make the functions positive.

6b. Hydrogenlike Atoms. The problem of the ionized atoms He^+, Li^{++}, etc., is identical in principle with that of the hydrogen atom, the only distinction being a slight difference in the reduced mass μ, and a numerical factor Ze^2 in place of e^2 in the potential energy. We can therefore write down immediately the solution for the general hydrogen-like atom of nuclear charge Z and nuclear mass M_Z. The solutions are

$$\psi = R_{n,\,l}(r) Y_{l,\,\pm m}(\theta, \varphi) \qquad 6\cdot23$$

$$Y_{l,\,\pm m}(\theta, \varphi) = \sqrt{\frac{2l+1}{4\pi} \frac{(l-|m|)!}{(l+|m|)!}} \, P^{|m|}(\cos\theta) e^{\pm im\varphi} \qquad 6\cdot24$$

$$R_{n,\,l}(r) = -\sqrt{\frac{(n-l-1)!}{2n[(n+l)!]^3}} \left(\frac{2Z}{na_0}\right)^3 \left(\frac{2Zr}{na_0}\right)^l e^{-\frac{Zr}{na_0}} L_{n+l}^{2l+1}\left(\frac{2Zr}{na_0}\right)$$

$$= -\sqrt{\frac{4(n-l-1)!}{n^4[(n+l)!]^3}} \left(\frac{Z}{a_0}\right)^{3/2} \left(\frac{2\rho}{n}\right)^l e^{-\frac{\rho}{n}} L_{n+l}^{2l+1}\left(\frac{2\rho}{n}\right) \qquad 6\cdot25$$

where $\rho = \dfrac{Z}{a_0} r$. Certain of the normalized radial wave functions for hydrogenlike atoms are given in Table 6·1. The energy levels for these atoms are

$$E_Z = \frac{-2\pi^2 \mu_Z Z^2 e^4}{n^2 h^2} = Z^2 \frac{\mu_Z}{\mu_H} E_H; \quad \mu_Z = \frac{M_Z m}{M_Z + m} \qquad 6\cdot26$$

Since $\dfrac{\mu_Z}{\mu_H}$ is very close to unity, the energy levels of hydrogenlike atoms are given to an excellent approximation by the relation $E_Z = Z^2 E_H$, where E_H represents the energy levels of hydrogen.

The energy levels as given by 6·26 are in essentially perfect agreement with the experimental results. The above treatment of the hydrogen atom neglects certain small energy terms, the first being that due to " electron spin," which, although very small for hydrogen, is important in the general theory of atomic structure and will be considered in a later chapter, the second being a small relativity correction which we shall entirely disregard, as these relativistic effects are negligible for small energies and hence can be ignored in problems of chemical interest.

6c. Some Properties of the Wave Functions of Hydrogen. From the form of the wave functions, we see that they satisfy simultaneously the equations

$$\mathbf{H}\,\psi_{n,\,l,\,\pm m} = E_n\,\psi_{n,\,l,\,\pm m}$$

$$\mathbf{M}^2\,\psi_{n,\,l,\,\pm m} = l(l+1)\,\frac{h^2}{4\pi^2}\,\psi_{n,\,l,\,\pm m} \qquad \text{6·27}$$

$$\mathbf{M}_z\,\psi_{n,\,l,\,\pm m} = \pm m\,\frac{h}{2\pi}\,\psi_{n,\,l,\,\pm m}$$

so that the energy, square of the total angular momentum, and z component of the total angular momentum are simultaneous eigenvalues. Each wave function of hydrogen is specified by the three quantum

TABLE 6·1

NORMALIZED RADIAL WAVE FUNCTIONS $R(r)$ FOR HYDROGENLIKE ATOMS

$$\rho = \frac{Z}{a_0}\,r; \quad n \geq l + 1$$

$n = 1, \quad l = 0 \qquad R_{1,\,0} = 2\left(\frac{Z}{a_0}\right)^{3/2} e^{-\rho}$

$n = 2, \quad l = 0 \qquad R_{2,\,0} = \dfrac{1}{2\sqrt{2}}\left(\dfrac{Z}{a_0}\right)^{3/2}(2 - \rho)e^{-\frac{\rho}{2}}$

$n = 2, \quad l = 1 \qquad R_{2,\,1} = \dfrac{1}{2\sqrt{6}}\left(\dfrac{Z}{a_0}\right)^{3/2}\rho\,e^{-\frac{\rho}{2}}$

$n = 3, \quad l = 0 \qquad R_{3,\,0} = \dfrac{2}{81\sqrt{3}}\left(\dfrac{Z}{a_0}\right)^{3/2}(27 - 18\rho + 2\rho^2)e^{-\frac{\rho}{3}}$

$n = 3, \quad l = 1 \qquad R_{3,\,1} = \dfrac{4}{81\sqrt{6}}\left(\dfrac{Z}{a_0}\right)^{3/2}(6\rho - \rho^2)e^{-\frac{\rho}{3}}$

$n = 3, \quad l = 2 \qquad R_{3,\,2} = \dfrac{4}{81\sqrt{30}}\left(\dfrac{Z}{a_0}\right)^{3/2}\rho^2\,e^{-\frac{\rho}{3}}$

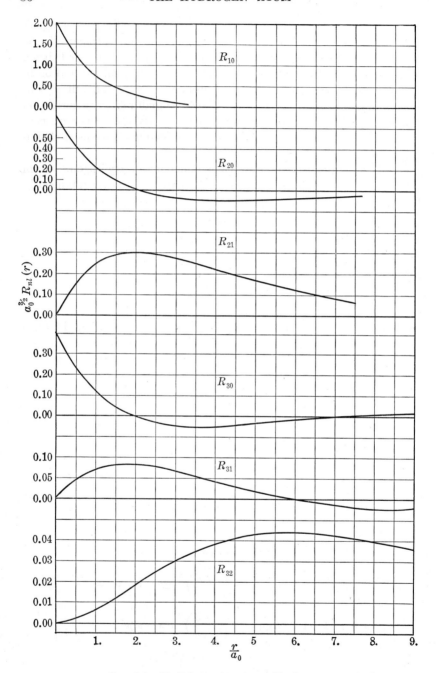

FIG. 6·1.   Radial eigenfunctions of hydrogen.

numbers n, l, and m. The quantum number n determines the energy of the atom; the quantum number l determines the total angular momentum; and the quantum number m determines the z component of the angular momentum. In Figure 6·1 we have plotted the radial wave function $R(r)$ for several of the lowest energy levels of hydrogen. It is noted that the radial wave function has a non-zero value at $r = 0$ only for those states for which $l = 0$, that is, only for those states which have no angular momentum. The radial wave functions become zero $n - l - 1$ times between $r = 0$ and $r = \infty$.

According to Postulate I, the probability of finding the electron at a distance between r and $r + dr$ from the nucleus, with its angular coordinates having values between θ and $\theta + d\theta$, φ and $\varphi + d\varphi$, is

$$\psi^*\psi \, d\tau = [R_{n,\,l}(r)]^2[Y_{l,\,\pm m}(\theta, \varphi)]^2 r^2 \sin \theta \, dr \, d\theta \, d\varphi \qquad 6\cdot 28$$

An alternative way of viewing this situation is to consider the electron as having a spatial distribution, the density of the "electron cloud" at any point in space being given by the square of the wave function at that point. The angular distribution of the electron density is given by the square of the spherical harmonics $Y_{l,\,\pm m}(\theta, \varphi)$. Referring to Table 4·1, we see that the state with $l = 0$, $m = 0$, is spherically symmetrical about the origin. The state with $l = 1$, $m = 0$, has the maximum value for the electron density along the z axis; the states with $l = 1$, $m = 1$, have the maximum value for the electron density in the xy plane.

To determine the probability that the electron be between the distances r and $r + dr$, regardless of angle, we must integrate over θ and φ. Since the spherical harmonics are normalized to unity, this integration gives us simply

$$P(r) \, dr = [R_{n,\,l}(r)]^2 r^2 \, dr \qquad 6\cdot 29$$

In Figure 6·2 we have plotted this probability distribution for several of the lower states of the hydrogen atom. The average distance of the electron from the nucleus is given by the integral

$$\bar{r} = \int \psi^* r \psi \, d\tau = \int_0^\infty [R_{n,\,l}(r)]^2 r^3 \, dr \qquad 6\cdot 30$$

For the hydrogen atom in the lowest state ($n = 1, l = 0$), the average value of r is

$$\bar{r} = \frac{4}{a_0^3} \int_0^\infty e^{-\frac{2r}{a_0}} r^3 \, dr = \frac{4}{a_0^3} \left\{ 3! \left(\frac{a_0}{2}\right)^4 \right\} = \tfrac{3}{2} a_0 \qquad 6\cdot 31$$

that is, the average distance of the electron from the nucleus is three-halves the radius of the first Bohr orbit. The *most probable* value of r is found from the equation

$$\frac{dP(r)}{dr} = -\frac{2}{a_0} e^{-\frac{2r}{a_0}} r^2 + 2re^{-\frac{2r}{a_0}} = 0 \qquad 6.32$$

so that the most probable distance of the electron from the nucleus is exactly a_0. The average value of r^2 is

$$\overline{r^2} = \frac{4}{a_0^3} \int_0^\infty e^{-\frac{2r}{a_0}} r^4 \, dr = \frac{4}{a_0^3} 4! \left(\frac{a_0}{2}\right)^5 = 3a_0^2 \qquad 6.33$$

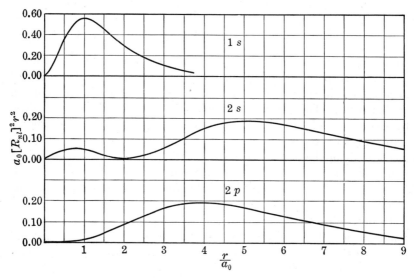

FIG. 6·2. Probability distribution in hydrogen.

States of the hydrogen atom with $l = 0, 1, 2, 3, 4, 5, \cdots$ are known as $s, p, d, f, g, h, \cdots$ states, respectively. A state with $n = 3, l = 1$, is called a $3p$ state; a state with $n = 1, l = 0$, is called a $1s$ state; etc. It will be noted that there are three p states, with $m = 1, 0, -1$. These may be designated as p_{+1}, p_0, and p_{-1} states, respectively. The angular factors associated with these states are, aside from a numerical factor,

$$p_{+1} \sim \sin \theta e^{i\varphi}$$

$$p_0 \sim \cos \theta \qquad 6.34$$

$$p_{-1} \sim \sin \theta e^{-i\varphi}$$

For many purposes it is more convenient to replace these functions by the following linear combinations:

$$p_x = \frac{p_{+1} + p_{-1}}{\sqrt{2}} \sim \sin \theta \cos \varphi \sim x$$

$$p_z = p_0 \sim \cos \theta \sim z \qquad\qquad \text{6·35}$$

$$p_y = -i \frac{p_{+1} - p_{-1}}{\sqrt{2}} \sim \sin \theta \sin \varphi \sim y$$

the designations p_x, p_y, and p_z indicating that the angular part of these wave functions have their maximum values in the x, y, and z directions respectively. Similarly, for the d functions, we take the linear combinations

$$d_{z^2} = d_0 \sim (3 \cos^2 \theta - 1) \sim 3z^2 - 1$$

$$d_{xz} = \frac{d_{+1} + d_{-1}}{\sqrt{2}} \sim \sin \theta \cos \theta \cos \varphi \sim xz$$

$$d_{yz} = -i \frac{d_{+1} - d_{-1}}{\sqrt{2}} \sim \sin \theta \cos \theta \sin \varphi \sim yz \qquad\qquad \text{6·36} \cdot$$

$$d_{x^2-y^2} = \frac{d_{+2} + d_{-2}}{\sqrt{2}} \sim \sin^2 \theta \cos 2\varphi \sim \sin^2 \theta(\cos^2 \varphi - \sin^2 \varphi) \sim x^2 - y^2$$

$$d_{xy} = -i \frac{d_{+2} - d_{-2}}{\sqrt{2}} \sim \sin^2 \theta \sin 2\varphi \sim \sin^2 \theta \cos \varphi \sin \varphi \sim xy$$

In Table 6·2 we give the complete normalized hydrogenlike wave functions for $n = 1, 2, 3$, using the above form for the angular part of the wave functions.

TABLE 6·2

NORMALIZED HYDROGENLIKE WAVE FUNCTIONS

$$\rho = \frac{Z}{a_0} r$$

$n = 1,$	$l = 0,$	$m = 0$	$\psi_{1s} = \dfrac{1}{\sqrt{\pi}} \left(\dfrac{Z}{a_0}\right)^{3/2} e^{-\rho}$
$n = 2,$	$l = 0,$	$m = 0$	$\psi_{2s} = \dfrac{1}{4\sqrt{2\pi}} \left(\dfrac{Z}{a_0}\right)^{3/2} (2 - \rho)e^{-\frac{\rho}{2}}$
$n = 2,$	$l = 1,$	$m = 0$	$\psi_{2p_z} = \dfrac{1}{4\sqrt{2\pi}} \left(\dfrac{Z}{a_0}\right)^{3/2} \rho e^{-\frac{\rho}{2}} \cos \theta$

TABLE 6·2 (Continued)

$n = 2, \quad l = 1, \quad m = \pm 1 \quad \psi_{2p_x} = \dfrac{1}{4\sqrt{2\pi}} \left(\dfrac{Z}{a_0}\right)^{3/2} \rho e^{-\frac{\rho}{2}} \sin\theta \cos\varphi$

$\psi_{2p_y} = \dfrac{1}{4\sqrt{2\pi}} \left(\dfrac{Z}{a_0}\right)^{3/2} \rho e^{-\frac{\rho}{2}} \sin\theta \sin\varphi$

$n = 3, \quad l = 0, \quad m = 0 \quad \psi_{3s} = \dfrac{2}{81\sqrt{3\pi}} \left(\dfrac{Z}{a_0}\right)^{3/2} (27 - 18\rho + 2\rho^2) e^{-\frac{\rho}{3}}$

$n = 3, \quad l = 1, \quad m = 0 \quad \psi_{3p_z} = \dfrac{2}{81\sqrt{\pi}} \left(\dfrac{Z}{a_0}\right)^{3/2} (6\rho - \rho^2) e^{-\frac{\rho}{3}} \cos\theta$

$n = 3, \quad l = 1, \quad m = \pm 1 \quad \psi_{3p_x} = \dfrac{2}{81\sqrt{\pi}} \left(\dfrac{Z}{a_0}\right)^{3/2} (6\rho - \rho^2) e^{-\frac{\rho}{3}} \sin\theta \cos\varphi$

$\psi_{3p_y} = \dfrac{2}{81\sqrt{\pi}} \left(\dfrac{Z}{a_0}\right)^{3/2} (6\rho - \rho^2) e^{-\frac{\rho}{3}} \sin\theta \sin\varphi$

$n = 3, \quad l = 2, \quad m = 0 \quad \psi_{3d_{z^2}} = \dfrac{1}{81\sqrt{6\pi}} \left(\dfrac{Z}{a_0}\right)^{3/2} \rho^2 e^{-\frac{\rho}{3}} (3\cos^2\theta - 1)$

$n = 3, \quad l = 2, \quad m = \pm 1 \quad \psi_{3d_{xz}} = \dfrac{\sqrt{2}}{81\sqrt{\pi}} \left(\dfrac{Z}{a_0}\right)^{3/2} \rho^2 e^{-\frac{\rho}{3}} \sin\theta \cos\theta \cos\varphi$

$\psi_{3d_{yz}} = \dfrac{\sqrt{2}}{81\sqrt{\pi}} \left(\dfrac{Z}{a_0}\right)^{3/2} \rho^2 e^{-\frac{\rho}{3}} \sin\theta \cos\theta \sin\varphi$

$n = 3, \quad l = 2, \quad m = \pm 2 \quad \psi_{3d_{x^2-y^2}} = \dfrac{1}{81\sqrt{2\pi}} \left(\dfrac{Z}{a_0}\right)^{3/2} \rho^2 e^{-\frac{\rho}{3}} \sin^2\theta \cos 2\varphi$

$\psi_{3d_{xy}} = \dfrac{1}{81\sqrt{2\pi}} \left(\dfrac{Z}{a_0}\right)^{3/2} \rho^2 e^{-\frac{\rho}{3}} \sin^2\theta \sin 2\varphi$

6d. The Continuous Spectrum of Hydrogen. We must now consider those states of the hydrogen atoms for which E is positive. In this case we make the substitutions

$$E = \frac{2\pi^2 \mu e^4}{k^2 h^2} \qquad\qquad 6\cdot37$$

$$r = \frac{k h^2}{8\pi^2 \mu e^2} x \qquad\qquad 6\cdot38$$

Equation 6·11 then becomes

$$\frac{d^2 R}{dx^2} + \frac{2}{x}\frac{dR}{dx} + \left[\frac{1}{4} + \frac{k}{x} - \frac{l(l+1)}{x^2}\right] R = 0 \qquad\qquad 6\cdot39$$

For very large values of x this is approximately

$$\frac{d^2 R}{dx^2} + \tfrac{1}{4} R = 0 \qquad\qquad 6\cdot40$$

for which the solutions are $R = ce^{\pm i\frac{x}{2}}$. The solutions of 6·39 are therefore finite at infinity. The only possible difficulty is at the origin, where there is a singular point. If we let

$$R = a_0 x^L + a_1 x^{L+1} + a_2 x^{L+2} + \cdots \qquad 6·41$$

the indicial equation is found to be

$$L(L - 1) + 2L - l(l + 1) = 0 \qquad 6·42$$

so that $L = l$ or $L = -(l + 1)$. The solution beginning with $L = l$ is finite at the origin and at infinity. There is therefore a solution of Schrödinger's equation of class Q for all positive values of E. We thus have a continuous range of positive eigenvalues, corresponding to ionization of the hydrogen atom, as well as the discrete set of negative eigenvalues for the un-ionized atom.

CHAPTER VII

APPROXIMATE METHODS

7a. Perturbation Theory. The number of problems which can be solved exactly by the methods of quantum mechanics is not very large. This is not surprising if we recall that even in classical mechanics such problems as the three-body problem have resisted solution in a closed form. The great majority of the problems of quantum mechanics, including the problem of the structure of all atomic systems more complicated than the hydrogen atom, must therefore be treated by approximate methods. The most important of these approximate methods, at least for our purposes, is the quantum-mechanical perturbation theory.

Suppose that we wish to solve the problem of the motion of a system whose Hamiltonian operator $\mathbf{H}$ is only slightly different from the Hamiltonian operator $\mathbf{H}_0$ of some problem which has already been solved. Associated with $\mathbf{H}_0$ we have a set of eigenvalues E_1^0, $E_2^0 \cdots E_n^0 \cdots$, and the corresponding eigenfunctions ψ_1^0, $\psi_2^0 \cdots \psi_n^0 \cdots$ satisfying the equation

$$\mathbf{H}_0 \psi_n^0 = E_n^0 \psi_n^0 \qquad 7 \cdot 1$$

Since by assumption $\mathbf{H}$ is only slightly different from $\mathbf{H}_0$, we write

$$\mathbf{H} = \mathbf{H}_0 + \lambda \mathbf{H}^{(1)} \qquad 7 \cdot 2$$

where λ is some parameter, and the term $\lambda \mathbf{H}^{(1)}$, which is called a "perturbation," is small in comparison to $\mathbf{H}_0$. The equation which we wish to solve is therefore

$$(\mathbf{H}_0 + \lambda \mathbf{H}^{(1)}) \psi_n = E_n \psi_n \qquad 7 \cdot 3$$

If λ is placed equal to zero, equation 7·3 reduces to 7·1, so that it is natural to assume that for small values of λ the solutions of 7·3 will lie close to those of 7·1; that is, the effect of the perturbation $\lambda \mathbf{H}^{(1)}$ will be to change slightly the "unperturbed" eigenvalues E_n^0 and eigenfunctions ψ_n^0. Now suppose that ψ_n and E_n are the eigenfunction and eigenvalue which approach ψ_n^0 and E_n^0 as $\lambda \to 0$; and for the present we shall assume that no two of the E_n^0's are equal. Since ψ_n and E_n will be functions of λ, we may expand them in the form of a power series as

$$\psi_n = \psi_n^0 + \lambda\psi_n^{(1)} + \lambda^2\psi_n^{(2)} + \cdots \qquad 7\cdot4$$

$$E_n = E_n^0 + \lambda E_n^{(1)} + \lambda^2 E_n^{(2)} + \cdots \qquad 7\cdot5$$

where $\psi_n^{(1)}, \psi_n^{(2)}, \cdots; E_n^{(1)}, E_n^{(2)}, \cdots$ are independent of λ. If we substitute these series in 7·3 we find

$$\mathbf{H}_0\psi_n^0 + \lambda(\mathbf{H}^{(1)}\psi_n^0 + \mathbf{H}_0\psi_n^{(1)}) + \lambda^2(\mathbf{H}^{(1)}\psi_n^{(1)} + \mathbf{H}_0\psi_n^{(2)}) + \cdots$$
$$= E_n^0\psi_n^0 + \lambda(E_n^{(1)}\psi_n^0 + E_n^0\psi_n^{(1)})$$
$$+ \lambda^2(E_n^{(2)}\psi_n^0 + E_n^{(1)}\psi_n^{(1)} + E_n^0\psi_n^{(2)}) + \cdots \quad 7\cdot6$$

In order that this equation may be satisfied for all values of λ the coefficients of the various powers of λ on the two sides of the equation must be equal. Equating the coefficients of the various powers of λ gives the series of equations

$$\mathbf{H}_0\psi_n^0 = E_n^0\psi_n^0 \qquad 7\cdot7$$

$$(\mathbf{H}_0 - E_n^0)\psi_n^{(1)} = E_n^{(1)}\psi_n^0 - \mathbf{H}^{(1)}\psi_n^0 \qquad 7\cdot8$$

$$(\mathbf{H}_0 - E_n^0)\psi_n^{(2)} = E_n^{(2)}\psi_n^0 + E_n^{(1)}\psi_n^{(1)} - \mathbf{H}^{(1)}\psi_n^{(1)} \qquad 7\cdot9$$

The first of these, by assumption, is already solved. If the second can be solved, we can find $\psi_n^{(1)}$ and $E_n^{(1)}$. The solution of the third equation then gives $\psi_n^{(2)}$ and $E_n^{(2)}$, and so on.

In order to solve equation 7·8, let us assume that the expansion of the function $\psi_n^{(1)}$ in terms of the normalized and orthogonal set of functions $\psi_1^0, \psi_2^0, \cdots \psi_n^0, \cdots$ is

$$\psi_n^{(1)} = A_1\psi_1^0 + A_2\psi_2^0 + \cdots + A_m\psi_m^0 + \cdots \qquad 7\cdot10$$

where the A_m's are to be determined. The function $\mathbf{H}^{(1)}\psi_n^0$ can also be expanded into the series

$$\mathbf{H}^{(1)}\psi_n^0 = H_{1n}^{(1)}\psi_1^0 + H_{2n}^{(1)}\psi_2^0 + \cdots + H_{mn}^{(1)}\psi_m^0 + \cdots \qquad 7\cdot11$$

where

$$H_{mn}^{(1)} = \int \psi_m^{0*}\mathbf{H}^{(1)}\psi_n^0 \, d\tau$$

Substituting these series into 7·8 gives

$$(\mathbf{H}_0 - E_n^0)(A_1\psi_1^0 + A_2\psi_2^0 + \cdots) = E_n^{(1)}\psi_n^0 - H_{1n}^{(1)}\psi_1^0 - H_{2n}^{(1)}\psi_2^0 \cdots \quad 7\cdot12$$

which can be reduced by means of equation 7·7 to

$$(E_1^0 - E_n^0)A_1\psi_1^0 + (E_2^0 - E_n^0)A_2\psi_2^0 + \cdots$$
$$= E_n^{(1)}\psi_n^0 - H_{1n}^{(1)}\psi_1^0 - H_{2n}^{(1)}\psi_2^0 \cdots \quad 7\cdot13$$

The coefficient of each ψ_n^0 must be equal on both sides of the equation. On the left the coefficient of ψ_n^0 is zero; on the right it is $(E_n^{(1)} - H_{nn}^{(1)})$; so that

$$E_n^{(1)} - H_{nn}^{(1)} = 0 \qquad 7\cdot14$$

The first-order perturbation energy has thus been determined to be

$$E_n^{(1)} = H_{nn}^{(1)} = \int \psi_n^{0*} \mathbf{H}^{(1)} \psi_n^0 \, d\tau \qquad 7\cdot15$$

By equating the coefficients of ψ_m^0 $(m \neq n)$, we obtain

$$(E_m^0 - E_n^0) A_m = -H_{mn}^{(1)}; \quad A_m = \frac{H_{mn}^{(1)}}{E_n^0 - E_m^0} \qquad 7\cdot16$$

This relation gives us the values of all the A's except A_n. The coefficient A_n may be determined by the requirement that ψ_n be normalized. We may express ψ_n as

$$\psi_n = \psi_n^0 + \lambda \sum_m{}' A_m \psi_m^0 + \lambda A_n \psi_n^0 + \lambda^2(\cdots)$$

where $\sum_m{}'$ means that we are to sum over all values of m except n. Then

$$\int \psi_n^* \psi_n \, d\tau = \int \psi_n^{0*} \psi_n^0 \, d\tau + \lambda \sum_m{}' A_m \int \psi_m^{0*} \psi_n^0 \, d\tau$$

$$+ \lambda \sum_m{}' A_m \int \psi_n^{0*} \psi_m^0 \, d\tau + 2\lambda A_n \int \psi_n^{0*} \psi_n^0 \, d\tau + \lambda^2(\cdots) \quad 7\cdot17$$

Since the functions ψ_m^0 are normalized and orthogonal, equation 7·17 reduces to

$$\int \psi^* \psi_n \, d\tau = 1 + 2\lambda A_n + \lambda^2(\cdots) \qquad 7\cdot18$$

If the functions ψ_n are to be normalized, the right side of this equation must be equal to unity for all values of λ, so that we must put A_n equal to zero. The results to the first order in λ are therefore

$$E_n = E_n^0 + \lambda H_{nn}^{(1)} + \lambda^2(\cdots) \qquad 7\cdot19$$

$$\psi_n = \psi_n^0 + \lambda \sum_m{}' \frac{H_{mn}^{(1)}}{E_n^0 - E_m^0} \psi_m^0 + \lambda^2(\cdots) \qquad 7\cdot20$$

We obtain $\psi_n^{(2)}$ and $E_n^{(2)}$ by a similar process. If we assume that

$$\psi_n^{(2)} = B_1 \psi_1^0 + B_2 \psi_2^0 + \cdots + B_m \psi_m^0 + \cdots \qquad 7\cdot21$$

where the B's are to be determined, then

$$(\mathbf{H}_0 - E_n^0)\psi_n^{(2)} = (E_1^0 - E_n^0)B_1\psi_1^0 + (E_2 - E_n^0)B_2\psi_2^0 + \cdots \quad 7\cdot 22$$

From equations 7·10, 7·11, 7·15, and 7·16, we have

$$E_n^{(1)}\psi_n^{(1)} = \sum_m{}' \frac{H_{nn}^{(1)}H_{mn}^{(1)}}{E_n^0 - E_m^0}\psi_m^0 \quad 7\cdot 23$$

$$\mathbf{H}^{(1)}\psi_n^{(1)} = \sum_m{}' \frac{H_{mn}^{(1)}}{E_n^0 - E_m^0}\mathbf{H}^{(1)}\psi_m^0$$

$$= \sum_m{}' \frac{H_{mn}^{(1)}}{E_n^0 - E_m^0}\sum_k H_{km}^{(1)}\psi_k^0$$

$$= \sum_k\sum_m{}' \frac{H_{km}^{(1)}H_{mn}^{(1)}}{E_n^0 - E_m^0}\psi_k^0 \quad 7\cdot 24$$

so that, with the use of these results, equation 7·9 becomes

$$\sum_k (E_k^0 - E_n^0)B_k\psi_k^0 = E_n^{(2)}\psi_n^0 + \sum_m{}' \frac{H_{nn}^{(1)}H_{mn}^{(1)}}{E_n^0 - E_m^0}\psi_m^0$$

$$- \sum_k\sum_m{}' \frac{H_{km}^{(1)}H_{mn}^{(1)}}{E_n^0 - E_m^0}\psi_k^0 \quad 7\cdot 25$$

If we now equate the coefficients of ψ_n^0 on either side of the equation, we find

$$0 = E_n^{(2)} - \sum_m{}' \frac{H_{nm}^{(1)}H_{mn}^{(1)}}{E_n^0 - E_m^0} \quad 7\cdot 26$$

or

$$E_n^{(2)} = \sum_m{}' \frac{H_{nm}^{(1)}H_{mn}^{(1)}}{E_n^0 - E_m^0} \quad 7\cdot 27$$

Equating coefficients of ψ_k^0 $(k \neq n)$ gives

$$(E_k^0 - E_n^0)B_k = \frac{H_{nn}^{(1)}H_{kn}^{(1)}}{E_n^0 - E_k^0} - \sum_m{}' \frac{H_{km}^{(1)}H_{mn}^{(1)}}{E_n^0 - E_m^0} \quad 7\cdot 28$$

so that

$$B_k = \sum_m{}' \frac{H_{km}^{(1)}H_{mn}^{(1)}}{(E_n^0 - E_m^0)(E_n^0 - E_k^0)} - \frac{H_{nn}^{(1)}H_{kn}^{(1)}}{(E_n^0 - E_k^0)^2} \quad 7\cdot 29$$

The normalization of ψ_n requires that B_n vanish. The results, correct to the second order in λ, for the energy levels and wave functions are therefore

$$E_n = E_n^0 + \lambda H_{nn}^{(1)} + \lambda^2 \sum_m{}' \frac{H_{nm}^{(1)}H_{mn}^{(1)}}{E_n^0 - E_m^0} + \lambda^3(\cdots) + \cdots \quad 7\cdot 30$$

$$\psi_n = \psi_n^0 + \lambda \sum_m{}' \frac{H_{mn}^{(1)}}{E_n^0 - E_m^0} \psi_m^0$$

$$+ \lambda^2 \sum_k{}' \left[\sum_m{}' \frac{H_{km}^{(1)}H_{mn}^{(1)}}{(E_n^0 - E_k^0)(E_n^0 - E_m^0)} - \frac{H_{nn}^{(1)}H_{kn}^{(1)}}{(E_n^0 - E_k^0)^2} \right] \psi_k^0 + \lambda^3(\cdots) + \cdots$$

$$7 \cdot 31$$

In most applications it proves convenient to absorb the parameter λ into the function $\mathbf{H}^{(1)}$, in other words, to place λ equal to unity in the above equations.

7b. Perturbation Theory for Degenerate Systems. In the last section we made the assumption that the unperturbed energy levels E_n^0 were all different. Problems frequently arise in which two or more orthogonal eigenfunctions have the same eigenvalue. Such eigenvalues are called degenerate. Suppose, for example, that

$$\mathbf{H}\psi_1 = E\psi_1 \qquad\qquad 7 \cdot 32$$

and

$$\mathbf{H}\psi_2 = E\psi_2 \qquad\qquad 7 \cdot 33$$

Then, if c_1 and c_2 are any constants such that $c_1^* c_1 + c_2^* c_2 = 1$,

$$\mathbf{H}(c_1\psi_1 + c_2\psi_2) = E(c_1\psi_1 + c_2\psi_2) \qquad\qquad 7 \cdot 34$$

so that $c_1\psi_1 + c_2\psi_2$ is also an eigenfunction. Hence, if there are two eigenfunctions having the same eigenvalue, there are an infinite number of eigenfunctions having that eigenvalue.

A set of n eigenfunctions is said to be linearly independent if there is no relation of the type

$$c_1\psi_1 + c_2\psi_2 + \cdots + c_n\psi_n = 0 \qquad\qquad 7 \cdot 35$$

connecting them. In the above example there are no three eigenfunctions which are linearly independent since all the eigenfunctions are expressible in the form $c_1\psi_1 + c_2\psi_2$. If the number of linearly independent eigenfunctions corresponding to a given eigenvalue is n, the eigenvalue is said to be n-fold degenerate. Once a set of n linearly independent eigenfunctions has been chosen, any other eigenfunction with the given eigenvalue can be expressed in the form

$$c_1\psi_1 + c_2\psi_2 + \cdots + c_n\psi_n \qquad\qquad 7 \cdot 36$$

where the c's are constants.

Now suppose that we wish to find the solution of

$$(\mathbf{H}_0 + \lambda\mathbf{H}^{(1)})\psi = E\psi \qquad\qquad 7 \cdot 37$$

where the eigenvalue approaches an m-fold degenerate eigenvalue of

$$\mathbf{H}_0 \psi^0 = E^0 \psi^0 \qquad 7\cdot38$$

as λ approaches zero. With no loss of generality we may assume that the m linearly independent eigenfunctions corresponding to this eigenvalue are $\psi_1^0, \psi_2^0 \cdots \psi_m^0$, so that $E_1^0 = E_2^0 = \cdots = E_m^0$. We may also assume that $\psi_1^0, \psi_2^0 \cdots \psi_m^0$ have been made orthogonal. As λ approaches zero, ψ must approach some solution of 7·38 whose eigenvalue equals E_1^0, that is, some linear combination

$$\varphi = c_1 \psi_1^0 + c_2 \psi_2^0 + \cdots + c_m \psi_m^0 \qquad 7\cdot39$$

where the c's are constants. This linear combination may be spoken of as the "zeroth-order" approximation to ψ. The expansion of E and ψ in powers of λ must therefore be of the form

$$E = E_1^0 + \lambda E^{(1)} + \lambda^2 E^{(2)} \qquad 7\cdot40$$

$$\psi = \sum_{j=1}^{m} c_j \psi_j^0 + \lambda \psi^{(1)} + \lambda^2 \psi^{(2)} + \cdots \qquad 7\cdot41$$

Substituting these expansions in 7·37 and equating coefficients of like powers of λ gives

$$\mathbf{H}_0 \sum_{j=1}^{m} c_j \psi_j^0 = E_1^0 \sum_{j=1}^{m} c_j \psi_j^0 \qquad 7\cdot42$$

$$(\mathbf{H}_0 - E_1^0) \psi^{(1)} = \sum_{j=1}^{m} c_j (E^{(1)} - \mathbf{H}^{(1)}) \psi_j^0 \qquad 7\cdot43$$

Since $E_1^0 = E_2^0 = \cdots = E_m^0$, equation 7·42 is already satisfied. As before, let us put

$$\psi^{(1)} = \sum_j A_j \psi_j^0; \quad \mathbf{H}^{(1)} \psi_j^0 = \sum_k H_{kj}^{(1)} \psi_k^0 \qquad 7\cdot44$$

where $H_{kj}^{(1)} = \int \psi_k^{0*} \mathbf{H}^{(1)} \psi_j^0 \, d\tau$, and the A's are constants to be determined. Then

$$\sum_{j=1}^{m} c_j \mathbf{H}^{(1)} \psi_j^0 = \sum_{j=1}^{m} \sum_k c_j H_{kj}^{(1)} \psi_k^0$$

$$= \sum_{k=1}^{m} \sum_j c_k H_{jk}^{(1)} \psi_j^0 \qquad 7\cdot45$$

Substituting these expressions in 7·43 gives

$$\sum (E_j^0 - E_1^0) A_j \psi_j^0 = \sum_{j=1}^{m} E^{(1)} c_j \psi^0 - \sum_j \left(\sum_{k=1}^{m} c_k H_{jk}^{(1)} \right) \psi_j^0 \qquad 7\cdot46$$

If $j \geq m$, equating the coefficients of ψ_j^0 on both sides gives

$$(E_j^0 - E_1^0)A_j = E^{(1)}c_j - \sum_{k=1}^{m} H_{jk}^{(1)}c_k \qquad 7\cdot47$$

But, for $j \leq m$, $E_j^0 = E_1^0$, so that

$$\sum_{k=1}^{m} H_{jk}^{(1)}c_k - E^{(1)}c_j = 0 \qquad 7\cdot48$$

We thus have the system of m simultaneous equations for the c_j's

$$(H_{11}^{(1)} - E^{(1)})c_1 + H_{12}^{(1)}c_2 + \cdots + H_{1m}^{(1)}c_m = 0$$
$$H_{21}^{(1)}c_1 + (H_{22}^{(1)} - E^{(1)})c_2 + \cdots + H_{2m}^{(1)}c_m = 0$$

$$\vdots$$

$$H_{m1}^{(1)}c_1 + H_{m2}^{(1)}c_2 + \cdots + (H_{mm}^{(1)} - E^{(1)})c_m = 0 \qquad 7\cdot49$$

A possible solution of this set of equations is $c_1 = c_2 = \cdots = c_m = 0$. According to a theorem of algebra (Appendix IV) this is the only solution unless the determinant of the coefficients of the c's vanishes, that is, unless

$$\begin{vmatrix} (H_{11}^{(1)} - E^{(1)}) & H_{12}^{(1)} & \cdots & H_{1m}^{(1)} \\ H_{21}^{(1)} & (H_{22}^{(1)} - E^{(1)}) & \cdots & H_{2m}^{(1)} \\ \vdots & & & \\ H_{m1}^{(1)} & H_{m2}^{(1)} & \cdots & (H_{mm}^{(1)} - E^{(1)}) \end{vmatrix} = 0 \qquad 7\cdot50$$

This is known as the secular equation. Since the $H_{jk}^{(1)}$'s are known constants, it is an equation of the mth degree in $E^{(1)}$, and therefore has m roots. Let these roots be $E_1^{(1)}$, $E_2^{(1)}$, $\cdots E_m^{(1)}$. Unless some of these roots happen to be equal, there are therefore m different perturbed states whose energies approach E_1^0 as λ approaches zero.

In order to find the eigenfunction corresponding to the root $E_l^{(1)}$, we substitute this value for $E^{(1)}$ in the set of equations 7·49 and solve for the ratios $\dfrac{c_2}{c_1}, \dfrac{c_3}{c_1}, \cdots$. A knowledge of these ratios, plus the normalizing condition

$$c_1^* c_1 + c_2^* c_2 + \cdots + c_m^* c_m = 1 \qquad 7\cdot51$$

is sufficient to determine completely the c's and hence the zeroth-order eigenfunctions φ_l, the subscript indicating the root of 7·50 to which the eigenfunction corresponds.

The first-order eigenfunction may now be found by equating the coefficients of the remaining ψ_j^0 $(j > m)$ in equation 7·46. The result is

$$(E^0 - E_1^0)A_j = -\sum_{k=1}^{m} c_k H_{jk}^{(1)}; \quad A_j = \frac{\sum_{k=1}^{m} c_k H_{jk}^{(1)}}{(E_1^0 - E_j^0)} \qquad 7\cdot52$$

In order that ψ be normalized we must put $A_j = 0$ $(j \le m)$. Hence, if ψ_l is the eigenfunction whose zeroth-order approximation is φ_l, the first-order perturbation theory gives

$$\psi_l = \varphi_l + \lambda \sum_{j>m} \frac{\sum_{k=1}^{m} c_k H_{jk}^{(1)}}{(E_1^0 - E_j^0)} \psi_j^0 + \lambda^2(\cdots) \qquad 7\cdot53$$

$$E_l = E_1^0 + \lambda E_l^{(1)} + \lambda^2(\cdots) \qquad 7\cdot54$$

for the perturbed eigenfunctions and eigenvalues.

7c. The Variation Method. Another, completely different, method of finding approximate solutions of the wave equation is based upon the following theorem: If φ is any function of class Q such that $\int \varphi^* \varphi \, d\tau = 1$, and if the lowest eigenvalue of the operator $\mathbf{H}$ is E_0, then

$$\int \varphi^* \mathbf{H} \varphi \, d\tau \ge E_0 \qquad 7\cdot55$$

The proof of this theorem is very simple. Consider the integral

$$\int \varphi^*(\mathbf{H} - E_0)\varphi \, d\tau = \int \varphi^* \mathbf{H} \varphi \, d\tau - E_0 \int \varphi^* \varphi \, d\tau$$

$$= \int \varphi^* \mathbf{H} \varphi \, d\tau - E_0 \qquad 7\cdot56$$

If we expand the function φ in a series of the eigenfunctions $\psi_1, \psi_2, \cdots$ $\psi_i \cdots$ of $\mathbf{H}$, we will have

$$\int \varphi^*(\mathbf{H} - E_0)\varphi \, d\tau = \int \left(\sum_i c_i^* \psi_i^*\right)(\mathbf{H} - E_0)\left(\sum_i c_i \psi_i\right) d\tau \qquad 7\cdot57$$

Since the ψ_i's are eigenfunctions of $\mathbf{H}$, $\mathbf{H}\psi_i = E_i \psi_i$, and so equation 7·57 becomes

$$\int \varphi^*(\mathbf{H} - E_0)\varphi \, d\tau = \int \left(\sum_i c_i^* \psi_i^*\right)\left(\sum_i (E_i - E_0)c_i \psi_i\right) d\tau$$

$$= \sum_i c_i^* c_i (E_i - E_0) \qquad 7\cdot58$$

Now $c_i^* c_i$ is a positive number, and by definition $E_i \geq E_0$, hence

$$\int \varphi^*(\mathbf{H} - E_0)\varphi \, d\tau \geq 0 \qquad 7\cdot59$$

and

$$\int \varphi^*\mathbf{H}\varphi \, d\tau \geq E_0 \qquad 7\cdot60$$

The equality sign can hold only when $\varphi = \psi_0$, where ψ_0 is the eigenfunction with the eigenvalue E_0.

The method of applying this theorem is equally simple in principle. A trial eigenfunction $\varphi(\lambda_1, \lambda_2, \cdots)$, normalized to unity, is chosen, this trial eigenfunction being a function of a number of parameters λ_1, $\lambda_2, \cdots$. The integral $J = \int \varphi^*\mathbf{H}\varphi \, d\tau$ is then found. The result will, of course, be a function of the parameters $\lambda_1, \lambda_2, \cdots$. The integral J is then minimized with respect to the parameters. The result is an approximation to the lowest eigenvalue, and the corresponding φ is an approximation to the corresponding eigenfunction. By taking a sufficiently large number of parameters in a function of a well-chosen form, a very close approximation to the correct eigenvalue and eigenfunction can be found.

In simple cases, and with a judiciously chosen trial eigenfunction, the results of the variation method are identical with the results obtained by the solution of the Schrödinger equation. As an example, let us consider the harmonic oscillator, for which the Hamiltonian operator is

$$\mathbf{H} = -\frac{h^2}{8\pi^2 m}\frac{d^2}{dx^2} + \frac{k}{2}x^2 \qquad 7\cdot61$$

If we try $\varphi = ce^{-\lambda x^2}$, the condition that φ be normalized is fulfilled if we put $c = \sqrt[4]{\dfrac{2\lambda}{\pi}}$. Then

$$\mathbf{H}\varphi = -\frac{ch^2}{8\pi^2 m}(4\lambda^2 x^2 - 2\lambda)e^{-\lambda x^2} + \frac{ck}{2}x^2 e^{-\lambda x^2}$$

and

$$J = \int_{-\infty}^{+\infty}\left[-\frac{c^2 h^2}{8\pi^2 m}(4\lambda^2 x^2 - 2\lambda)e^{-2\lambda x^2} + \frac{c^2 k}{2}x^2 e^{-2\lambda x^2}\right]dx \qquad 7\cdot62$$

Upon evaluating these integrals (Appendix VIII), we obtain

$$J = \frac{h^2\lambda}{8\pi^2 m} + \frac{k}{8\lambda} \qquad 7\cdot63$$

The condition that J be a minimum is

$$\frac{dJ}{d\lambda} = \frac{h^2}{8\pi^2 m} - \frac{k}{8\lambda^2} = 0 \quad \text{or} \quad \lambda = \frac{\pi}{h}\sqrt{mk} \qquad 7\cdot 64$$

so that the lowest eigenvalue is

$$E_0 \leq \frac{h}{4\pi}\sqrt{\frac{k}{m}} = \tfrac{1}{2}h\nu \qquad 7\cdot 65$$

and the corresponding eigenfunction is

$$\varphi = \sqrt[4]{\frac{2}{h}\sqrt{mk}}\, e^{-\frac{\pi}{h}\sqrt{mk}x^2} \qquad 7\cdot 66$$

The fact that these results are identical with those of section 5e is, of course, due to the "well-chosen" form which we took for our trial eigenfunction.

It is also possible to use the variation method for the calculation of energy levels and eigenfunctions for excited states. After we have obtained an approximation to the ground state by the above method, we choose a second trial eigenfunction which is orthogonal to the one that we obtained for the ground state. A repetition of the above procedure will then give us an approximation to the first excited state. This process may be continued indefinitely, although the errors involved will be cumulative.

7d. The Ground State of the Helium Atom. As a further example of the use of these approximate methods we shall calculate the energy of the ground state of the helium atom both by the application of the first-order perturbation theory and by the variation method. The Hamiltonian operator for the helium atom (or for other two-electron atoms such as Li^+, etc.), is, if we neglect the terms arising from the motion of the nucleus,

$$\mathbf{H} = -\frac{h^2}{8\pi^2 m}(\nabla_1^2 + \nabla_2^2) - \frac{Ze^2}{r_1} - \frac{Ze^2}{r_2} + \frac{e^2}{r_{12}} \qquad 7\cdot 67$$

where ∇_1 and ∇_2 are the Laplacian operators for electrons 1 and 2; r_1 and r_2 are the distances of these electrons from the nucleus; r_{12} is the distance between the two electrons; and Z is the nuclear charge. For the purpose of simplifying the calculation of the integrals involved in problems of this type it is usually more convenient to use atomic units. The transformation to atomic units is obtained by expressing distances in terms of the Bohr radius $a_0 = \dfrac{h^2}{4\pi^2 me^2}$. We therefore write $r_1 = a_0R_1$, $r_2 = a_0R_2$, $r_{12} = a_0R_{12}$, $\dfrac{\partial^2}{\partial x_1^2} = \dfrac{1}{a_0^2}\dfrac{\partial^2}{\partial X_1^2}$, etc. With this transformation, the Hamiltonian operator becomes

$$\mathbf{H} = -\frac{h^2}{8\pi^2 m}\frac{1}{a_0^2}(\nabla_1^2 + \nabla_2^2) - \frac{Ze^2}{a_0R_1} - \frac{Ze^2}{a_0R_2} + \frac{e^2}{a_0R_{12}} \qquad 7 \cdot 68$$

or, in units of $\dfrac{e^2}{a_0}$,

$$\mathbf{H} = -\tfrac{1}{2}(\nabla_1^2 + \nabla_2^2) - \frac{Z}{R_1} - \frac{Z}{R_2} + \frac{1}{R_{12}} \qquad 7 \cdot 69$$

In applying the methods of the perturbation theory to this problem we set $\mathbf{H} = \mathbf{H}_0 + \mathbf{H}^{(1)}$, where

$$\mathbf{H}_0 = -\tfrac{1}{2}(\nabla_1^2 + \nabla_2^2) - \frac{Z}{R_1} - \frac{Z}{R_2} \qquad 7 \cdot 70$$

$$\mathbf{H}^{(1)} = \frac{1}{R_{12}} \qquad 7 \cdot 71$$

The zeroth-order eigenfunctions are the solutions of the equation

$$H_0\psi^0 = E^0\psi^0 \qquad 7 \cdot 72$$

If we now set $\psi^0 = \psi^0(1)\psi^0(2)$, $E^0 = E^0(1) + E^0(2)$, equation 7·72 is immediately separable into the two equations

$$\tfrac{1}{2}\nabla_1^2\psi^0(1) + \left(E^0(1) + \frac{Z}{R_1}\right)\psi^0(1) = 0$$

$$\tfrac{1}{2}\nabla_2^2\psi^0(2) + \left(E^0(2) + \frac{Z}{R_2}\right)\psi^0(2) = 0 \qquad 7 \cdot 73$$

These equations are just those for a hydrogenlike atom with nuclear charge Z. For the ground state of the helium atom, we therefore have

$$\psi^0(1) = \frac{1}{\sqrt{\pi}}Z^{3/2}e^{-ZR_1} \qquad \psi^0(2) = \frac{1}{\sqrt{\pi}}Z^{3/2}e^{-ZR_2}$$

$$\psi^0 = \psi^0(1)\psi^0(2) = \frac{Z^3}{\pi}e^{-Z(R_1+R_2)} \qquad 7 \cdot 74$$

$$E^0 = E^0(1) + E^0(2) = 2Z^2E_{1s}(\mathrm{H})$$

where $E_{1s}(\mathrm{H})$ is the energy of the ground state of hydrogen, and, in ordinary units, is $-\tfrac{1}{2}\dfrac{e^2}{a_0}$. The first-order correction to the energy is, according to equation 7·15

$$E^{(1)} = \int\int \psi^{0*} H^{(1)} \psi^0 \, d\tau_1 \, d\tau_2$$

$$= \frac{e^2}{a_0} \frac{Z^6}{\pi^2} \int\int \frac{e^{-2ZR_1}e^{-2ZR_2}}{R_{12}} \, d\tau_1 \, d\tau_2 \qquad 7\cdot 75$$

where

$$d\tau_1 = R_1^2 \sin \Theta_1 \, dR_1 \, d\Theta_1 \, d\Phi_1$$

$$d\tau_2 = R_2^2 \sin \Theta_2 \, dR_2 \, d\Theta_2 \, d\Phi_2$$

Written in the above form, the integral cannot be evaluated because of the presence of the term $\dfrac{1}{R_{12}}$. According to the theorem proved in Appendix V, this quantity can be expanded in terms of the associated Legendre polynomials as

$$\frac{1}{R_{12}} = \sum_l \sum_m \frac{(l-|m|)!}{(l+|m|)!} \frac{R_<^l}{R_>^{l+1}} P_l^{|m|}(\cos \Theta_1) \, P_l^{|m|}(\cos \Theta_2) \, e^{im(\Phi_1 - \Phi_2)} \qquad 7\cdot 76$$

where $R_<$ is the smaller and $R_>$ is the larger of the quantities R_1 and R_2. The wave functions themselves do not involve the angles explicitly; in other words, only the constant functions $P_0^0(\cos \Theta_1)$ and $P_0^0(\cos \Theta_2)$ are involved in the wave functions. Since the associated Legendre polynomials are orthogonal, all the terms in the summation will vanish except those for $l = 0$, $m = 0$. For these terms $P_0(\cos \theta) = 1$, so that equation 7·75 reduces to

$$E^{(1)} = \frac{e^2}{a_0} \frac{Z^6}{\pi^2} \int\int \frac{e^{-2ZR_1}e^{-2ZR_2}}{R_>} \, d\tau_1 \, d\tau_2 \qquad 7\cdot 77$$

The integration over the angles gives a factor $(4\pi)^2$, so that we have only the integral over R_1 and R_2, which may be written as

$$E^{(1)} = 16Z^6 \frac{e^2}{a_0} \int_0^\infty e^{-2ZR_1} \left[\frac{1}{R_1} \int_0^{R_1} e^{-2ZR_2} R_2^2 \, dR_2 \right. $$
$$\left. + \int_{R_1}^\infty e^{-2ZR_2} R_2 \, dR_2 \right] R_1^2 \, dR_1 \qquad 7\cdot 78$$

which may be evaluated in a straightforward manner to give

$$E^{(1)} = \tfrac{5}{8}Z \frac{e^2}{a_0} \qquad 7\cdot 79$$

To the first order, the energy of the lowest state of helium (or helium-like atoms) is therefore

$$E = E^0 + E^{(1)} = (2Z^2 - \tfrac{5}{4}Z)\left(-\frac{1}{2}\frac{e^2}{a_0}\right)$$

$$= (2Z^2 - \tfrac{5}{4}Z)E_{1s}(\mathrm{H}) \qquad\qquad 7\cdot80$$

The energy of the ground state of He^+ is $Z^2 E_{1s}(\mathrm{H})$. The first ionization potential of helium, that is, the energy necessary to remove one electron from the atom, is thus calculated to be

$$(Z^2 - \tfrac{5}{4}Z)E_{1s}(\mathrm{H}) = \tfrac{3}{2}E_{1s}(\mathrm{H}) = \tfrac{3}{2}(13.60) = 20.40 \text{ electron volts}$$

The observed value is 24.58 e.v., so that our calculated value is in error by 4.18 e.v. or about 16 per cent. Our results will look better if we compare the calculated and observed total binding energy. These values are: calculated $\tfrac{11}{2}(13.60) = 74.80$ e.v., observed 78.98 e.v. — an error of 4.18 e.v. or about 5 per cent. The actual error is the same in both cases; the percentage error is, of course, decreased in the latter case.

For the two-electron atoms Li^+, etc., the percentage error is considerably less than for helium, since the interactions between the electrons and the nucleus become relatively more important than the interaction between the electrons. In 7·80 we see that for helium the perturbation energy is $\tfrac{5}{16}$ of the zeroth-order energy. As this is certainly not a " small " perturbation, we should not be greatly disappointed at the failure of the first-order perturbation theory to give more accurate results. We shall now show how the binding energy of the helium atom can be calculated to any desired degree of accuracy by means of the variation method.

In order that we may choose a reasonable trial eigenfunction for use in the variation method, let us consider that one of the electrons of the helium atom is in an excited state and the other in the ground state. The electron in the ground state is subjected to the full attractive force of the nucleus, so that $\psi^0(1)$ should be essentially the same as in 7·74. The electron in the excited state, however, moves essentially in the field of a nucleus of charge e, as the $(1s)$ electron screens the nucleus more or less completely, and so $\psi^0(2)$ for an excited state should approximate more closely a hydrogen wave function with $Z = 1$. These considerations suggest that a good trial eigenfunction would be

$$\varphi = \frac{Z'^3}{\pi} e^{-Z'(R_1+R_2)} \qquad\qquad 7\cdot81$$

where Z' is between 1 and 2, the best value being determined by minimizing the energy with respect to Z'. The functions written above are the solutions of the equation

$$\mathbf{H}_0'\varphi = E_0'\varphi \qquad 7 \cdot 82$$

where, in units of $\dfrac{e^2}{a_0}$,

$$H_0' = -\tfrac{1}{2}(\nabla_1^2 + \nabla_2^2) - \frac{Z'}{R_1} - \frac{Z'}{R_2}$$

$$E_0' = 2Z'^2 E_{1s}(\mathrm{H})$$

We must evaluate the integral

$$E = \int\int \varphi^* \mathbf{H}\varphi \, d\tau_1 \, d\tau_2 \qquad 7 \cdot 83$$

where $\mathbf{H}$ is given by 7·69. We can write $\mathbf{H}\varphi$ as

$$\mathbf{H}\varphi = \left[-\tfrac{1}{2}\,(\nabla_1^2 + \nabla_2^2) - \frac{Z'}{R_1} - \frac{Z'}{R_2} \right]\varphi - (Z - Z')\left(\frac{1}{R_1} + \frac{1}{R_2} \right)\varphi + \frac{1}{R_{12}}\varphi$$

$$= E_0'\varphi - (Z - Z')\left(\frac{1}{R_1} + \frac{1}{R_2} \right)\varphi + \frac{1}{R_{12}}\varphi \qquad 7 \cdot 84$$

so that the integral 7·83 is reduced to

$$E = E_0' - (Z - Z')\left[\int\int \frac{\varphi^2}{R_1}\, d\tau_1 \, d\tau_2 + \int\int \frac{\varphi^2}{R_2} d\tau_1 \, d\tau_2 \right]$$

$$+ \int\int \frac{\varphi^2}{R_{12}}\, d\tau_1 \, d\tau_2 \quad 7 \cdot 85$$

The two integrals in the brackets are equal, as they differ only in the interchange of the subscripts. The first of these is

$$16\pi^2 \frac{Z'^6}{\pi^2} \int_0^\infty e^{-2Z'R_1}R_1 \, dR_1 \int_0^\infty e^{-2Z'R_2}R_2^2 \, dR_2 = Z' \qquad 7 \cdot 86$$

The last integral is identical with 7·75 if Z is replaced by Z'. The result for the energy is thus

$$E = E_0' - 2Z'(Z - Z')\frac{e^2}{a_0} + \tfrac{5}{8}Z'\frac{e^2}{a_0}$$

$$= [2Z'^2 + 4Z'(Z - Z') - \tfrac{5}{4}Z']E_{1s}(\mathrm{H})$$

$$= [-2Z'^2 + 4ZZ' - \tfrac{5}{4}Z']E_{1s}(\mathrm{H}) \qquad 7 \cdot 87$$

According to the theorem of the variation method, we obtain the best approximation to the true energy by giving Z' the value which will make the energy a minimum.   This condition requires that

$$\frac{\partial E}{\partial Z'} = (-4Z' + 4Z - \tfrac{5}{4})E_{1s}(\text{H}) = 0$$

or

$$Z' = Z - \tfrac{5}{16} \qquad\qquad 7 \cdot 88$$

Substituting this result in 7·87, we obtain for the energy the value

$$E = 2Z'^2 E_{1s}(\text{H}) = 2(Z - \tfrac{5}{16})^2 E_{1s}(\text{H}) \qquad 7 \cdot 89$$

For the first ionization potential of helium we therefore obtain

$$[2(\tfrac{27}{16})^2 - 4]E_{1s}(\text{H}) = 1.695(13.60) = 23.05 \text{ e.v.}$$

The discrepancy between calculated and observed values is thus reduced to 1.53 e.v., or about 6 per cent.   The total binding energy is calculated to be 77.45 e.v. as compared to the experimental value 78.98 e.v., or an error of about 2 per cent.

By introducing more parameters into the trial eigenfunction φ, we can approach more and more closely to the experimental result.   Particularly good results are obtained, even with quite simple trial eigenfunctions, if the variable R_{12} is explicitly introduced into the trial eigenfunction.   For example, Hylleras,[1] using the trial eigenfunction

$$\varphi = A\{e^{-Z'(R_1 + R_2)}(1 + cR_{12})\} \qquad 7 \cdot 90$$

where A is the normalization factor and Z' and c are adjustable constants, obtained a value for the ionization potential which was in error by only 0.34 e.v.   By using the more general function

$$\varphi = A\{e^{-Z'(R_1 + R_2)}(\text{polynomial in } R_1, R_2, R_{12})\} \qquad 7 \cdot 91$$

he was able to reduce the error still further.   The function involving a polynomial of fourteen terms gave a value for the energy which agreed with the experimental value within 0.002 e.v.   It is thus apparent that the accuracy of the results obtainable by the variation method are limited only by the patience of the calculator, a very important limitation, however.   In our later work, we shall therefore be satisfied with a smaller degree of accuracy in most of our numerical calculations.

[1] E. Hylleras, Z. *Physik*, **65**, 209 (1930).

CHAPTER VIII

TIME–DEPENDENT PERTURBATIONS: RADIATION THEORY

8a. Time-Dependent Perturbations. In the previous chapter we discussed the problem of determining the new energy levels and wave functions for a system subjected to a perturbation which depended only on the space coordinates of the system. For certain problems, particularly those dealing with the emission and absorption of radiation, we need to calculate the effects produced by a perturbation which is a function of the time; therefore, we shall now develop the time-dependent perturbation theory.

The wave equation, in the form which expresses the manner in which the complete wave function Ψ changes with time, is

$$\mathbf{H}\Psi = -\frac{h}{2\pi i}\frac{\partial \Psi}{\partial t} = i\hbar\frac{\partial \Psi}{\partial t} \qquad 8 \cdot 1$$

where $\hbar = \dfrac{h}{2\pi}$. Let us now write the Hamiltonian operator as $\mathbf{H} = \mathbf{H}_0 + \mathbf{H}'$, where $\mathbf{H}_0$ is independent of time and $\mathbf{H}'$ is a time-dependent perturbation. The unperturbed eigenfunctions Ψ^0 satisfy the equation

$$\mathbf{H}_0\Psi^0 = i\hbar\frac{\partial \Psi^0}{\partial t} \qquad 8 \cdot 2$$

and are of the form $\Psi_n^0(q, t) = \Psi_n^0(q)e^{-i\frac{E_n}{\hbar}t}$. In order to obtain a solution of 8·1 we expand the function Ψ in terms of the unperturbed eigenfunctions Ψ_n^0, with coefficients which are functions of the time; that is, we write

$$\Psi(q, t) = \sum_n c_n(t)\Psi_n^0(q, t) \qquad 8 \cdot 3$$

Substituting this expression for Ψ in equation 8·1 gives

$$\sum_n c_n\mathbf{H}_0\Psi_n^0 + \sum_n c_n\mathbf{H}'\Psi_n^0 = i\hbar\sum_n \frac{dc_n}{dt}\Psi_n^0 + i\hbar\sum_n c_n\frac{\partial \Psi_n^0}{\partial t} \qquad 8 \cdot 4$$

Since the unperturbed eigenfunctions Ψ_n^0 satisfy equation 8·2, the above

107

equation immediately reduces to

$$\sum_n c_n \mathbf{H}' \Psi_n^0 = i\hbar \sum_n \frac{dc_n}{dt} \Psi_n^0 \qquad 8\cdot5$$

Let us now multiply both sides of this equation by Ψ_m^{0*} and integrate over coordinate space.   Then

$$\sum_n c_n \int \Psi_m^{0*} \mathbf{H}' \Psi_n^0 \, d\tau = i\hbar \sum_n \frac{dc_n}{dt} \int \Psi_m^{0*} \Psi_n^0 \, d\tau = i\hbar \frac{dc_m}{dt} \qquad 8\cdot6$$

or

$$\frac{dc_m}{dt} = -\frac{i}{\hbar} \sum_n c_n \int \Psi_m^{0*} \mathbf{H}' \Psi_n^0 \, d\tau \qquad 8\cdot7$$

In any particular problem we will thus have a set of simultaneous differential equations which can be solved to give explicit expressions for the c_n's.

8b.   The Wave Equation for a System of Charged Particles under the Influence of an External Electric or Magnetic Field.   The most important problem to which the time-dependent perturbation theory will be applied is that of radiation.   In order to discuss radiation theory we need the Hamiltonian operator for a charged particle in an electromagnetic field.   In deriving the classical Hamiltonian function it is more convenient to use the vector potential $\mathbf{A}$ and the scalar potential φ rather than the electric and magnetic field strengths $\mathbf{E}$ and $\mathbf{H}$.   The relations between these quantities are given by the equations

$$\mathbf{H} = \nabla \times \mathbf{A}; \quad \mathbf{E} = -\frac{1}{c}\frac{\partial}{\partial t}\mathbf{A} - \nabla\varphi \qquad 8\cdot8$$

where c is the velocity of light.

A particle of mass m and charge e moving with a velocity $\mathbf{v}$ in an electromagnetic field is subjected to a force

$$\mathbf{F} = e\left(\mathbf{E} + \frac{1}{c}[\mathbf{v} \times \mathbf{H}]\right)$$

The equations of motion are therefore

$$m\frac{d^2x}{dt^2} = -e\frac{\partial\varphi}{\partial x} - \frac{e}{c}\frac{\partial A_x}{\partial t} + \frac{e}{c}\left(\frac{dy}{dt}H_z - \frac{dz}{dt}H_y\right) \qquad 8\cdot9$$

with similar expressions for $\dfrac{d^2y}{dt^2}$ and $\dfrac{d^2z}{dt^2}$.   Using the relation $\mathbf{H} = \nabla \times \mathbf{A}$, these equations become

$$m\frac{d^2x}{dt^2} = -e\frac{\partial\varphi}{\partial x} - \frac{e}{c}\frac{\partial A_x}{\partial t} + \frac{e}{c}\left[\frac{dy}{dt}\left(\frac{\partial A_y}{\partial x} - \frac{\partial A_x}{\partial y}\right)\right.$$
$$\left. + \frac{dz}{dt}\left(\frac{\partial A_z}{\partial x} - \frac{\partial A_x}{\partial z}\right)\right] \qquad 8\cdot10$$

etc. It is not difficult to demonstrate that these equations of motion are derivable from the Lagrangian function

$$L = \frac{m}{2}\left[\left(\frac{dx}{dt}\right)^2 + \left(\frac{dy}{dt}\right)^2 + \left(\frac{dz}{dt}\right)^2\right]$$
$$+ \frac{e}{c}\left(\frac{dx}{dt}A_x + \frac{dy}{dt}A_y + \frac{dz}{dt}A_z\right) - e\varphi \quad 8\cdot11$$

From the definition of generalized momentum, $p_i = \dfrac{\partial L}{\partial \dot{q}_i}$, we see that $p_x = m\dfrac{dx}{dt} + \dfrac{e}{c}A_x$, with analogous values for p_y and p_z. The Hamiltonian function is therefore

$$H = p_x\frac{dx}{dt} + p_y\frac{dy}{dt} + p_z\frac{dz}{dt} - L$$
$$= \frac{m}{2}\left[\left(\frac{dx}{dt}\right)^2 + \left(\frac{dy}{dt}\right)^2 + \left(\frac{dz}{dt}\right)^2\right] + e\varphi \quad 8\cdot12$$

or, in terms of coordinates and momenta,

$$H = \frac{1}{2m}\left[\left(p_x - \frac{e}{c}A_x\right)^2 + \left(p_y - \frac{e}{c}A_y\right)^2 + \left(p_z - \frac{e}{c}A_z\right)^2\right] + e\varphi \quad 8\cdot13$$

The procedure for constructing the Hamiltonian operator is identical with that followed before; in the classical Hamiltonian function the momentum p_x is replaced by $\dfrac{h}{2\pi i}\dfrac{\partial}{\partial x} = -i\hbar\dfrac{\partial}{\partial x}$, etc Operating on a wave function Ψ, the first term in the Hamiltonian gives

$$\frac{1}{2m}\left(-i\hbar\frac{\partial}{\partial x} - \frac{e}{c}A_x\right)^2\Psi$$
$$= \frac{1}{2m}\left(-\hbar^2\frac{\partial^2}{\partial x^2} + i\hbar\frac{e}{c}\frac{\partial}{\partial x}A_x + i\hbar\frac{e}{c}A_x\frac{\partial}{\partial x} + \frac{e^2}{c^2}|A_x|^2\right)\Psi$$
$$= \frac{1}{2m}\left(-\hbar^2\frac{\partial^2\Psi}{\partial x^2} + i\hbar\frac{e}{c}\frac{\partial A_x}{\partial x}\Psi\right.$$
$$\left. + i\hbar\frac{e}{c}A_x\frac{\partial\Psi}{\partial x} + i\hbar\frac{e}{c}A_x\frac{\partial\Psi}{\partial x} + \frac{e^2}{c^2}|A_x|^2\Psi\right) \quad 8\cdot14$$

After collecting terms, and expressing our results in vector notation, we see that the Hamiltonian operator is

$$\mathbf{H} = \frac{1}{2m}\left(-\hbar^2\nabla^2 + i\hbar\frac{e}{c}\nabla\cdot\mathbf{A} + 2i\hbar\frac{e}{c}\mathbf{A}\cdot\nabla + \frac{e^2}{c^2}|\mathbf{A}|^2\right) + e\varphi \quad 8\cdot15$$

For an electromagnetic field such as that associated with a light wave, $\nabla \cdot \mathbf{A} = 0$ and $\varphi = 0$. Since the perturbation of a system by a light wave will be a small perturbation, the term $\dfrac{e^2}{c^2} |\mathbf{A}|^2$ may be neglected in discussing radiation, although it must be retained when discussing perturbations due to strong magnetic fields. For a system of charged particles, with an internal potential energy V, we will therefore have the Hamiltonian operator $\mathbf{H} = \mathbf{H}_0 + \mathbf{H}'$, where

$$\mathbf{H}_0 = -\sum_j \frac{\hbar^2}{2m_j} \nabla_j^2 + V; \quad \mathbf{H}' = \sum_j \frac{e}{m_j c} i\hbar \mathbf{A}_j \cdot \nabla_j \qquad 8\cdot16$$

The operator $\mathbf{H}^0$ is just the operator for the system in the absence of an electromagnetic field; the perturbation $\mathbf{H}'$ may equally well be written as $\mathbf{H}' = -\sum_j \dfrac{e}{m_j c} \mathbf{A}_j \cdot \mathbf{p}_j$.

8c. Induced Emission and Absorption of Radiation. Let us consider an atomic or molecular system subjected to the perturbation $\mathbf{H}'$ of an electromagnetic field. For simplicity, we first will assume that the field is that of a plane-polarized light wave with A_y and A_z equal to zero.* We shall need to calculate the values of such matrix elements as

$$\int \Psi_m^{0*} \mathbf{H}' \Psi_n^0 \, d\tau = (\Psi_m^{0*}|\mathbf{H}'|\Psi_n^0) = \left(\Psi_m^{0*} \left| -\sum_j \frac{e}{m_j c} A_{xj} p_{xj} \right| \Psi_n^0 \right) \qquad 8\cdot17$$

Since molecular dimensions are of the order of 1/1000 the wavelengths of visible light, a sufficiently good approximation for our present purposes will be to take $\mathbf{A}$ as constant over the molecule. The matrix elements

---

* That this situation represents a plane-polarized wave may be seen as follows: We take $\mathbf{A} = \mathbf{i} A_x$ with

$$A_x = A_x^0 \cos 2\pi\nu \left(t - \frac{z}{c} \right)$$

This represents a wave moving in the z direction with a velocity equal to c. The associated electric and magnetic fields are then

$$\mathbf{E} = -\frac{1}{c} \frac{\partial}{\partial t} \mathbf{A} = \mathbf{i} \frac{2\pi\nu}{c} A_x^0 \sin 2\pi\nu \left(t - \frac{z}{c} \right)$$

$$\mathbf{H} = \nabla \times \mathbf{A} = \mathbf{j} \frac{2\pi\nu}{c} A_x^0 \sin 2\pi\nu \left(t - \frac{z}{c} \right)$$

The electric and magnetic fields therefore have equal amplitudes and are at right angles to each other as well as to the direction of propagation, and hence represent a plane-polarized light wave moving along the z axis with a velocity c.

can then be written as

$$-\frac{e}{c}A_x \sum_j \frac{1}{m_j}(\Psi_m^{0*}|p_{xj}|\Psi_n^0) \equiv -\frac{e}{c}\frac{\hbar}{i}A_x \sum_j \frac{1}{m_j}\left(\Psi_m^{0*}\left|\frac{\partial}{\partial x_j}\right|\Psi_n^0\right)$$

$$= -\frac{e}{c}\frac{\hbar}{i}A_x e^{i\frac{E_m-E_n}{\hbar}t}\sum_j \frac{1}{m_j}\left(\psi_m^{0*}\left|\frac{\partial}{\partial x_j}\right|\psi_n^0\right) \quad 8\cdot18$$

In order to obtain usable results, we wish to express the matrix elements of $\frac{\partial}{\partial x_j}$ in terms of those of x_j. Let us for the moment consider that the ψ's are functions only of one coordinate x. Then ψ_m^{*0} and ψ_n^0 satisfy the equations

$$\frac{d^2\psi_m^{0*}}{dx^2} + \frac{2m}{\hbar^2}[E_m - V(x)]\psi_m^{0*} = 0 \quad 8\cdot18a$$

$$\frac{d^2\psi_n^0}{dx^2} + \frac{2m}{\hbar^2}[E_n - V(x)]\psi_n^0 = 0 \quad 8\cdot18b$$

If we multiply the first of these equations by $x\psi_n^0$ and the second by $x\psi_m^{0*}$ and subtract, we obtain, upon integrating the resulting equation,

$$\int_{-\infty}^{\infty}\left(x\psi_n^0\frac{d^2\psi_m^{0*}}{dx^2} - x\psi_m^{0*}\frac{d^2\psi_n^0}{dx^2}\right)dx = \frac{2m}{\hbar^2}(E_n - E_m)\int_{-\infty}^{\infty}\psi_m^{0*}x\psi_n^0\,dx \quad 8\cdot18c$$

The first two terms may now be integrated by parts; since the wave functions vanish at infinity, we have

$$\int_{-\infty}^{\infty}\left[\frac{d}{dx}(x\psi_n^0)\frac{d\psi_m^{0*}}{dx} - \frac{d}{dx}(x\psi_m^{0*})\frac{d\psi_n^0}{dx}\right]dx$$

$$= \frac{2m}{\hbar^2}(E_m - E_n)\int_{-\infty}^{\infty}\psi_m^{0*}x\psi_n^0\,d\tau \quad 8\cdot18d$$

or

$$\int_{-\infty}^{\infty}\left(\psi_n^0\frac{d\psi_m^{0*}}{dx} - \psi_m^{0*}\frac{d\psi_n^0}{dx}\right)dx = \frac{2m}{\hbar^2}(E_m - E_n)\int_{-\infty}^{\infty}\psi_m^{0*}x\psi_n^0\,dx \quad 8\cdot18e$$

of we integrate the first term by parts, we see that it is equal to the second. For this one-dimensional example, we have thus obtained the result

$$\left(\psi_m^{0*}\left|\frac{\partial}{\partial x}\right|\psi_n^0\right) = -\frac{m}{\hbar^2}(E_m - E_n)(\psi_m^{0*}|x|\psi_n^0) \quad 8\cdot18f$$

This result can be generalized. The matrix element $(\Psi_m^{0*}|\mathbf{H}'|\Psi_n^0)$ may therefore be written as

$$(\Psi_m^{0*}|\mathbf{H}'|\Psi_n^0) = -\frac{1}{c}A_x\frac{i}{\hbar}(E_m - E_n)X_{mn}e^{i\frac{E_m-E_n}{\hbar}t} \quad 8\cdot18g$$

where $X_{mn} = (\psi_m^{0*}|e\sum_j x_j|\psi_n^0)$ is the matrix element for the x component of the dipole moment.

If we now assume that the system was originally in the state n, so that $c_n = 1$ and all the other c's are zero at the time $t = 0$, we have, for times sufficiently small so that all the c's are negligible except c_n:

$$\frac{dc_m}{dt} = -\frac{1}{c\hbar^2} A_x X_{mn}(E_m - E_n)e^{i\frac{E_m - E_n}{\hbar}t} \qquad 8\cdot19$$

If the light has the frequency ν, the time dependence of A_x may be expressed as

$$A_x = A_x^0 \cos 2\pi\nu t = \tfrac{1}{2}A_x^0(e^{2\pi i\nu t} + e^{-2\pi i\nu t})$$

Then

$$\frac{dc_m}{dt} = -\frac{1}{2c\hbar^2} A_x^0 X_{mn}(E_m - E_n)\left\{e^{i\frac{E_m - E_n + h\nu}{\hbar}t} + e^{i\frac{E_m - E_n - h\nu}{\hbar}t}\right\} \qquad 8\cdot20$$

Integrating, and choosing the constant of integration so that c_m equal zero when $t = 0$, we have

$$c_m = \frac{i}{2c\hbar} A_x^0 X_{mn}(E_m - E_n)\left\{\frac{e^{i\frac{E_m - E_n + h\nu}{\hbar}t} - 1}{(E_m - E_n + h\nu)} + \frac{e^{i\frac{E_m - E_n - h\nu}{\hbar}t} - 1}{(E_m - E_n - h\nu)}\right\} \qquad 8\cdot21$$

Let us consider that $E_m > E_n$, so that the transition corresponds to absorption. c_m will be large only when the denominator of the second term in brackets is nearly zero, that is, when $E_m - E_n \simeq h\nu$. The probability that the system will be in the state m at time t will be the value of the product $c_m^* c_m$. The first term in brackets being neglected, this product is

$$c_m^* c_m = \frac{t^2}{4c^2\hbar^4} |A_x^0|^2 |X_{mn}|^2 (E_m - E_n)^2 \frac{\sin^2\left\{\dfrac{E_m - E_n - h\nu}{2\hbar}t\right\}}{\left\{\dfrac{E_m - E_n - h\nu}{2\hbar}t\right\}^2} \qquad 8\cdot22$$

So far we have considered only a single frequency ν. To obtain the correct value of $c_m^* c_m$ we will have to integrate over a range of frequencies. Since $c_m^* c_m$ is very small except for frequencies such that $E_m - E_n \simeq h\nu$, it will be satisfactory to integrate from $-\infty$ to $+\infty$ and regard A_x^0 as constant and equal to $A_x^0(\nu_{mn})$. This integration gives

$$c_m^* c_m = \frac{\pi^2 \nu_{mn}^2}{c^2\hbar^2} |A_x^0(\nu_{mn})|^2 |X_{mn}|^2 t \qquad 8\cdot23$$

where $E_m - E_n$ has been replaced by $h\nu_{mn}$.

Equation 8·23 has been derived upon the assumption that the light was plane polarized. In the general case in which A_y and A_z are not zero, equation 8·23 will, of course, contain additional terms in A_y and A_z. In calculating $c_m^* c_m$ the cross terms will vanish because of the randomness of the phase differences between the various components of **A**; the final expression for $c_m^* c_m$ will therefore be

$$c_m^* c_m = \frac{\pi^2 \nu_{mn}^2}{c^2 \hbar^2} \left\{ |A_x^0(\nu_{mn})|^2 |X_{mn}|^2 + |A_y^0(\nu_{mn})|^2 |Y_{mn}|^2 \right.$$
$$\left. + |A_z^0(\nu_{mn})|^2 |Z_{mn}|^2 \right\} t \qquad 8\cdot24$$

If the radiation is isotropic, then

$$|A_x^0(\nu_{mn})|^2 = |A_y^0(\nu_{mn})|^2 = |A_z^0(\nu_{mn})|^2 = \tfrac{1}{3} |A^0(\nu_{mn})|^2 \qquad 8\cdot25$$

We may express $|A^0(\nu_{mn})|^2$ in terms of the radiation density $\rho(\nu_{mn})$. From Equation 8·8,

$$\mathbf{E}(\nu_{mn}) = \frac{2\pi\nu_{mn}}{c} \mathbf{A}^0(\nu_{mn}) \sin 2\pi\nu t$$

Then

$$\overline{E^2(\nu_{mn})} = \frac{2\pi^2 \nu_{mn}^2}{c^2} |A^0(\nu_{mn})|^2$$

since the average value of $\sin^2 2\pi\nu t$ is $\tfrac{1}{2}$. In electromagnetic theory, it is shown that $\rho(\nu_{mn}) = \frac{1}{4\pi} \overline{E^2(\nu_{mn})}$, so that $|A_x^0(\nu_{mn})|^2 = \frac{2}{3} \frac{c^2}{\pi \nu_{mn}^2} \rho(\nu_{mn})$. The product $c_m^* c_m$ may now be written in terms of the radiation density as

$$c_m^* c_m = \frac{2\pi}{3\hbar^2} \left\{ |X_{mn}|^2 + |Y_{mn}|^2 + |Z_{mn}|^2 \right\} \rho(\nu_{mn}) t \qquad 8\cdot26$$

Since the probability that the system will be in the state m is zero at time $t = 0$, and is the value given by 8·26 at time t, the probability that a transition from the state n to the state m will take place in unit time, resulting in absorption of energy from the electromagnetic field, is

$$B_{n\to m}\rho(\nu_{mn}) = \frac{2\pi}{3\hbar^2} |R_{mn}|^2 \rho(\nu_{mn}) \qquad 8\cdot27$$

where

$$|R_{mn}|^2 = |X_{mn}|^2 + |Y_{mn}|^2 + |Z_{mn}|^2 \qquad 8\cdot28$$

If the system is originally in the state m, then the same treatment shows that the probability of transition to the state n, resulting in the emission of energy, due to the perturbing effect of the electromagnetic field, is

$$B_{m \to n} \rho(\nu_{mn}) = B_{n \to m} \rho(\nu_{mn}) \qquad 8 \cdot 29$$

8d. The Einstein Transition Probabilities. The coefficients $B_{m \to n}$ and $B_{n \to m}$ are known as the Einstein transition probability coefficients for induced emission and absorption, respectively. Since a system in an excited state can emit radiation even in the absence of an electromagnetic field, the completion of the theory of radiation requires the calculation of the transition probability coefficient $A_{m \to n}$ for spontaneous emission. The direct quantum-mechanical calculation of this quantity is a problem of great difficulty, but its value has been determined by Einstein[1] by a consideration of the equilibrium between two states of different energy. If the number of systems in the state with energy E_m is N_m, and the number in the state with energy E_n is N_n, then the Boltzmann distribution law states that at equilibrium

$$\frac{N_m}{N_n} = \frac{e^{-\frac{E_m}{kT}}}{e^{-\frac{E_n}{kT}}} = e^{-\frac{h\nu_{mn}}{kT}} \qquad 8 \cdot 30$$

where T is the absolute temperature and k is the Boltzmann constant. Expressed in terms of the transition probability coefficients discussed above, the number of systems making the transition from m to n in unit time is

$$N_m \{ A_{m \to n} + B_{m \to n} \rho(\nu_{mn}) \}$$

Similarly, the number of systems making the reverse transition is

$$N_n B_{n \to m} \rho(\nu_{mn})$$

Since at equilibrium these two numbers are equal, we have, after eliminating the ratio $\dfrac{N_m}{N_n}$ by means of equation 8·30,

$$e^{-\frac{h\nu_{mn}}{kT}} = \frac{B_{n \to m} \rho(\nu_{mn})}{A_{m \to n} + B_{m \to n} \rho(\nu_{mn})}$$

or
$$\rho(\nu_{mn}) = \frac{A_{m \to n} e^{-\frac{h\nu_{mn}}{kT}}}{-B_{m \to n} e^{-\frac{h\nu_{mn}}{kT}} + B_{n \to m}} \qquad 8 \cdot 31$$

Using relation 8·29, the energy density may therefore be written as

$$\rho(\nu_{mn}) = \frac{\dfrac{A_{m \to n}}{B_{m \to n}}}{e^{\frac{h\nu_{mn}}{kT}} - 1} \qquad 8 \cdot 32$$

[1] A. Einstein, *Physik. Z.*, **18**, 121 (1917).

The energy density in a radiation field in equilibrium with a black body at a temperature T may be calculated by the methods of quantum statistical mechanics (Chapter XV) and, as mentioned in Chapter I, is given by Planck's radiation distribution law as

$$\rho(\nu_{mn}) = \frac{8\pi h\nu_{mn}^3}{c^3} \frac{1}{e^{\frac{h\nu_{mn}}{kT}} - 1} \qquad 8\cdot33$$

Comparing 8·32 and 8·33, we see that

$$A_{m\to n} = \frac{8\pi h\nu_{mn}^3}{c^3} B_{m\to n}$$

or

$$A_{m\to n} = \frac{32\pi^3\nu_{mn}^3}{3c^3\hbar} |R_{mn}|^2 \qquad 8\cdot34$$

To the degree of approximation used above, the coefficient for spontaneous emission depends only on the matrix element for the electric dipole moment between the two states. If the variation of the field over the molecule is not neglected, there will be additional terms in the expression for $A_{m\to n}$, the first two additional terms being those corresponding to magnetic dipole and electric quadripole radiation. Including these terms gives[2]

$$A_{m\to n} = \frac{32\pi^3\nu_{mn}^3}{3c^3\hbar} \left\{ |(m|e\mathbf{r}|n)|^2 + \left|\left(m\left|\frac{e}{2mc}\mathbf{r}\times\mathbf{p}\right|n\right)\right|^2 \right.$$
$$\left. + \tfrac{3}{10}\pi^3\frac{\nu_{mn}^2}{c^2}|(m|e\mathbf{rr}|n)|^2 \right\} \qquad 8\cdot35$$

We may estimate the relative orders of magnitude of these terms as follows. Disregarding the constant term, we have

$$|(m|e\mathbf{r}|n)|^2 \sim (ea_0)^2 \sim 6\cdot5 \times 10^{-36} \text{ c.g.s.}$$

$$\left|\left(m\left|\frac{e}{2mc}\mathbf{r}\times\mathbf{p}\right|n\right)\right|^2 \sim \left(\frac{e\hbar}{2mc}\right)^2 \sim 8\cdot7 \times 10^{-41} \text{ c.g.s.}$$

$$\tfrac{3}{10}\pi^3\frac{\nu_{mn}^2}{c^2}|(m|e\mathbf{rr}|n)|^2 \sim 6\cdot8 \times 10^{-43} \text{ c.g.s.} \quad (\lambda = 5000 \text{ Å})$$

We thus see that the probability of transition due to magnetic dipole or electric quadripole radiation will be negligible in comparison to the probability of transition due to electric dipole radiation. The higher terms in 8·35 will therefore be of importance only in those cases in which

[2] E. U. Condon and G. H. Shortley, *The Theory of Atomic Spectra*, p. 96, Cambridge University Press, 1935.

the electric dipole matrix element $(m|er|n)$ vanishes because of the symmetry properties of the states m and n.

The actual intensity of radiation of frequency ν_{mn} due to spontaneous emission will, of course, be

$$I(\nu_{mn}) = N_m(h\nu_{mn})A_{m \to n} \qquad 8\cdot36$$

8e. Selection Rules for the Hydrogen Atom. According to the results derived above, the only transitions of importance in the hydrogen atom will be between those states a and b for which

$$(a|er|b) = e\{i(a|x|b) + j(a|y|b) + k(a|z|b)\}$$

is different from zero. The eigenfunctions for the hydrogen atom may be written as

$$\psi_{n,l,m} = f(r)P_l^{|m|}(\cos\theta)\,e^{im\varphi}$$

so that we must investigate the values of such integrals as

$$\int \psi_{n,l,m} z\psi_{n',l,m'}^* \, d\tau = \int \psi_{n,l,m}(r\cos\theta)\psi_{n',l',m'}^* \, d\tau$$

This integral may be written as the product of integrals in r, θ, and φ. The integrals in r will be non-vanishing, so that we may concentrate our attention on the integrals over the angular coordinates. For the z component of the electric dipole moment we must therefore investigate the integral

$$\int P_l^{|m|}\cos\theta\, P_{l'}^{|m'|}\sin\theta\,d\theta \int e^{i(m-m')\varphi}\,d\varphi \qquad 8\cdot37$$

From the recursion formulas for the associated Legendre polynomials (equation 4·85), we have

$$\cos\theta P_{l'}^{|m'|} = \frac{l' - |m'| + 1}{2l' + 1}P_{l'+1}^{|m'|} + \frac{l' + |m'|}{2l' + 1}P_{l'-1}^{|m'|} \qquad 8\cdot38$$

The integral 8·37 is therefore non-vanishing only if

$$m = m'; \quad l = l' \pm 1 \qquad 8\cdot39$$

These relations are the selection rules for the emission of light polarized in the z direction. Rather than calculate the matrix components for x and y separately it is more convenient to calculate those for the combinations $(x + iy) = r\sin\theta\, e^{i\varphi}$ and $(x - iy) = r\sin\theta\, e^{-i\varphi}$. For the combination $(x - iy)$ we have the integrals

$$\int P_l^{|m|}\sin\theta\, P_{l'}^{|m'|}\sin\theta\,d\theta \int e^{i(m-m'-1)\varphi}\,d\varphi \qquad 8\cdot40$$

The integral over φ is non-vanishing only if $m = m' + 1$. From the recursion formula 4·86

$$\sin \theta \, P_{l'}^{|m'|} = \frac{1}{2l + 1} \{P_{l'+1}^{|m'|+1} - P_{l'-1}^{|m'|+1}\} \qquad 8\text{·}41$$

we see that the integral over θ is non-vanishing only if $l = l' \pm 1$. Similarly for the combination $(x + iy)$ we have the selection rules $m = m' - 1$, $l = l' \pm 1$. The selection rules for the hydrogen atom may therefore be written as

$$\Delta l = \pm 1; \quad \Delta m = 0, \pm 1 \qquad 8\text{·}42$$

The selection rules for the different types of polarization are, of course, significant only when there is a unique z direction, due, for example, to the presence of a uniform magnetic field. This subject will be discussed more fully in the following chapter, where the Zeeman effect is considered. It is apparent from the derivation of the above selection rules that they are not limited to the hydrogen atom but are valid for any central field problem where the angular portion of the wave function is identical with that of the hydrogen atom.

8f. Selection Rules for the Harmonic Oscillator. Let us now consider the system consisting of a particle moving along the x axis with a harmonic motion. Let the charge on the particle be $+e$, and let the charge at the position of equilibrium be $-e$. The instantaneous value of the electric dipole moment will then be ex. The wave functions for the system will be the eigenfunctions of the harmonic oscillator (section 5e). A transition between the states n and m will be possible only if the integral

$$(n|ex|m) = e \int \psi_n x \psi_m \, dx \qquad 8\text{·}43$$

is different from zero. From the recursion formula (equation 4·99)

$$xH_m = mH_{m-1} + \tfrac{1}{2}H_{m+1} \qquad 8\text{·}44$$

we see immediately that the integral 8·43 will be zero unless $m = n \pm 1$. This is the selection rule for the harmonic oscillator; only the fundamental frequency ν can be emitted or absorbed by this system. We shall later require the exact values of the integrals in 8·43. The wave functions are

$$\psi_n(x) = N_n e^{-\frac{\xi^2}{2}} H_n(\xi) \qquad 8\text{·}45$$

where

$$\xi = \sqrt{\alpha}\, x \qquad N_n = \left(\frac{\alpha}{\pi}\right)^{\frac{1}{4}} \left(\frac{1}{2^n n!}\right)^{\frac{1}{2}}$$

so that

$$(n|ex|n + 1) = N_n N_{n+1} \frac{e}{\sqrt{\alpha}} \int e^{-\xi^2} H_n(\xi) \xi H_{n+1}(\xi) \, dx \qquad 8\cdot46$$

By the use of the recursion formula 8·44, this reduces to

$$(n|ex|n + 1) = N_n N_{n+1} \frac{e}{\sqrt{\alpha}} \int e^{-\xi^2} H_n(\xi)(n + 1) H_n(\xi) \, dx$$

$$= \frac{e}{\sqrt{\alpha}} (n + 1) \frac{N_{n+1}}{N_n} \int [\psi_n(x)]^2 \, dx = \frac{e}{\sqrt{\alpha}} (n + 1) \frac{N_{n+1}}{N_n} \qquad 8\cdot47$$

Introducing the explicit expressions for the normalizing factors, we obtain

$$(n|ex|n + 1) = e \sqrt{\frac{n + 1}{2\alpha}} \qquad 8\cdot48$$

Similarly,

$$(n|ex|n - 1) = N_n N_{n-1} \frac{e}{\sqrt{\alpha}} \int e^{-\xi^2} H_n(\xi) \xi H_{n-1}(\xi) \, dx$$

$$= \frac{e}{2\sqrt{\alpha}} \frac{N_{n-1}}{N_n} = e \sqrt{\frac{n}{2\alpha}} \qquad 8\cdot49$$

8g. Polarizability; Rayleigh and Raman Scattering. If α is the polarizability of an atomic system, then an electric field $\mathbf{E}$ induces a dipole moment $\mathbf{R} = \alpha\mathbf{E}$ in the system. Let us consider classically a system in which an electron of charge $-e$ is bound elastically to an equilibrium position at which there is a charge $+e$. If the system is subjected to an alternating electric field of strength $\mathbf{E} = \mathbf{E}_0 \cos \omega t$, the classical equation of motion is

$$m \frac{d^2\mathbf{r}}{dt^2} + k\mathbf{r} = -e\mathbf{E}_0 \cos \omega t \qquad 8\cdot50$$

where $\mathbf{r}$ is the displacement of the electron from the origin and k is the force constant of the forces binding the electron to the equilibrium position. The steady-state solution of this equation is

$$\mathbf{r} = \frac{-e\mathbf{E}_0 \cos \omega t}{k - m\omega^2} = \frac{-\dfrac{e}{m} \mathbf{E}_0 \cos \omega t}{\omega_0^2 - \omega^2} \qquad 8\cdot51$$

where $\omega_0 = \sqrt{\dfrac{k}{m}}$. The dipole moment of the system is $\mathbf{R} = -e\mathbf{r}$;

the classical polarizability of the system is therefore $\dfrac{e^2/m}{\omega_0^2 - \omega^2}$. If we now write $\mathbf{r} = \mathbf{A}\cos\omega t$, then the acceleration of the electron is $\dfrac{d^2\mathbf{r}}{dt^2} = -\mathbf{A}\omega^2\cos\omega t$. The time average of the square of the acceleration is

$$\overline{\left(\frac{d^2\mathbf{r}}{dt^2}\right)^2} = |A|^2\omega^4\,\overline{\cos^2\omega t} = \tfrac{1}{2}|A|^2\omega^4 \qquad 8{\cdot}52$$

According to classical electromagnetic theory, an electron moving with acceleration a radiates in one second the amount of energy $\dfrac{2e^2a^2}{3c^3}$. Classically, the system described above would therefore radiate light of frequency $\nu = \dfrac{\omega}{2\pi}$, the amount of energy radiated per second being $\dfrac{e^2|A|^2\omega^4}{3c^3}$.

According to quantum mechanics, if a system is in a state a, then the probability of a transition to a state b with the emission of light of frequency ν_{ab} is, as we have seen earlier in this chapter,

$$A_{a\rightarrow b} = \frac{32\pi^3\nu_{ab}^2}{3c^3\hbar}|R_{ab}|^2 \qquad 8{\cdot}53$$

The amount of energy radiated per second is

$$2\pi\hbar\nu_{ab}A_{a\rightarrow b} = \frac{64\pi^4\nu_{ab}^4}{3c^3}|R_{ab}|^2 \qquad 8{\cdot}54$$

Let us now calculate the dipole moment associated with the transition between the states a and b, which we define as

$$\mathbf{R}_{ab} = (\Psi_a^{0*}|er|\Psi_b^0) + (\Psi_b^{0*}|er|\Psi_a^0)$$

$$= (a|er|b)\left\{e^{i\frac{E_{ab}}{\hbar}t} + e^{-i\frac{E_{ab}}{\hbar}t}\right\}$$

$$= 2(a|er|b)\cos\frac{E_{ab}}{\hbar}t = 2(a|er|b)\cos\omega_{ab}t \qquad 8{\cdot}55$$

where $\omega_{ab} = \dfrac{E_{ab}}{\hbar} = \dfrac{E_a - E_b}{\hbar}$. By analogy with the classical argument, we therefore calculate the rate of emission of energy of frequency

ν_{ab} to be

$$\frac{2\left(\dfrac{d^2\mathbf{R}_{ab}}{dt^2}\right)^2}{3c^3} = \frac{4\omega_{ab}^4}{3c^3}\,|(a|er|b)|^2 = \frac{64\pi^4\nu_{ab}^4}{3c^3}\,|R_{ab}|^2 \qquad 8\cdot56$$

which is identical with the quantum-mechanical result in equation 8·54. This is a justification for the definition given in 8·55 for the dipole moment associated with the transition between two states a and b. $\mathbf{R}_{ab}$ may also be written as $\mathbf{R}_{ab} = 2Re\{(\Psi_a^{0*}|er|\Psi_b^0)\}$, where Re means that we are to take the real part of the quantity in brackets. For the dipole moment associated with a given state

$$\mathbf{R}_a = Re\{(\Psi_a^{0*}|er|\Psi_a^0)\}$$

A system which in the absence of an electromagnetic field is in the state represented by Ψ_a^0 has, in the presence of the field, the perturbed wave function

$$\Psi_a = \Psi_a^0 + \sum_b c_b \Psi_b^0 \qquad 8\cdot57$$

where c_b, according to equation 8·21, is given by the relation

$$c_b = \frac{iE_{ba}}{2c\hbar}\mathbf{A}_0^0 \cdot (b|er|a)\left\{\frac{e^{i\frac{E_{ba}+\epsilon}{\hbar}t}}{E_{ba}+\epsilon} + \frac{e^{i\frac{E_{ba}-\epsilon}{\hbar}t}}{E_{ba}-\epsilon}\right\} + \text{constant} \qquad 8\cdot58$$

where $E_{ba} = E_b - E_a$; $\epsilon = h\nu$. The dipole moment associated with the state Ψ_a is

$$\mathbf{R}_a = Re\{(\Psi_a^*|er|\Psi_a\} = (a|\mathbf{R}|a) + 2Re\left\{\sum_b c_b(a|\mathbf{R}|b)e^{i\frac{E_{ab}}{\hbar}t}\right\}$$

$$= (a|\mathbf{R}|a) + Re\left\{\sum_b \frac{iE_{ba}}{c\hbar}(a|\mathbf{R}|b)(b|\mathbf{R}|a)\cdot\mathbf{A}_0^0\left[\frac{e^{i\frac{\epsilon}{\hbar}t}}{E_{ba}+\epsilon} + \frac{e^{-i\frac{\epsilon}{\hbar}t}}{E_{ba}-\epsilon}\right]\right\} \qquad 8\cdot59$$

where $\mathbf{R} = er$. In writing this last expression the constant in equation 8·58 has been placed equal to zero. This can be done in this case without loss of generality, as the inclusion of this constant would give us no additional terms which would be functions of the perturbing fields. Equation 8·59 may be simplified to

$$\mathbf{R}_a = (a|\mathbf{R}|a) + \sum_b \frac{E_{ba}}{c\hbar}\left(\frac{1}{E_{ba}-\epsilon} - \frac{1}{E_{ba}+\epsilon}\right) \times$$

$$(a|\mathbf{R}|b)(b|\mathbf{R}|a)\cdot\mathbf{A}_0^0 \sin\frac{\epsilon}{\hbar}t \qquad 8\cdot60$$

Since $\mathbf{E}_0 = -\dfrac{1}{c}\dfrac{d\mathbf{A}_0}{dt} = \dfrac{\epsilon}{c\hbar}\mathbf{A}_0^0\sin\frac{\epsilon}{\hbar}t$, the dipole moment as a function of the electric field becomes

$$\mathbf{R}_a = (a|\mathbf{R}|a) + \sum_b \frac{E_{ba}}{\epsilon} \left(\frac{1}{E_{ba} - \epsilon} - \frac{1}{E_{ba} + \epsilon} \right) (a|\mathbf{R}|b)(b|\mathbf{R}|a) \cdot \mathbf{E}_0$$

$$= (a|\mathbf{R}|a) + \sum_b \frac{2E_{ba}}{E_{ba}^2 - \epsilon^2} (a|\mathbf{R}|b)(b|\mathbf{R}|a) \cdot \mathbf{E}_0$$

$$= (a|\mathbf{R}|a) + \frac{2}{h} \sum_b \frac{\nu_{ba}}{\nu_{ba}^2 - \nu^2} (a|\mathbf{R}|b)(b|\mathbf{R}|a) \cdot \mathbf{E}_0 \qquad 8\cdot61$$

The first term in this expression is the permanent dipole moment μ of the system. In order to determine the polarizability, we must write the remaining terms in the form $\alpha \mathbf{E}_0$, which can be done by averaging the vector quantities over all orientations of the system with respect to the field, assuming all orientations to be equally probable. The quantity which we must average is of the form $\mathbf{R}\mathbf{R} \cdot \mathbf{E}$. If θ is the angle between $\mathbf{R}$ and $\mathbf{E}$, this is equal to $\mathbf{R}|R| \, |E| \cos \theta$, which is a vector in the direction of $\mathbf{R}$. The component of this vector along $\mathbf{E}$ is $|R| \, |R| \, |E| \cos^2 \theta$. Averaging over all values of θ, we obtain for the magnitude of the vector along $\mathbf{E}$ the value $\frac{1}{3}|R| \, |R| \, |E|$, so that the average value of the vector quantity $\mathbf{R}\mathbf{R} \cdot \mathbf{E}$ is $\frac{1}{3}\mathbf{R} \cdot \mathbf{R}\mathbf{E}$. Making this transformation in 8·61, we obtain

$$\mathbf{R}_a = (a|\mathbf{R}|a) + \frac{2}{3h} \sum_b \frac{\nu_{ba}|(a|\mathbf{R}|b)|^2}{\nu_{ba}^2 - \nu^2} \mathbf{E}_0 \qquad 8\cdot62$$

The second term is now of the form $\alpha \mathbf{E}_0$, so that we have obtained the quantum-mechanical expression for the polarizability

$$\alpha = \frac{2}{3h} \sum_b \frac{\nu_{ba}|R_{ab}|^2}{\nu_{ba}^2 - \nu^2} \qquad 8\cdot63$$

The dipole moment $\mathbf{R}_a$ contains a term which varies with the frequency ν of the incident light. According to the above discussion, the system will therefore radiate light of frequency ν, which will be in phase with the incident light and which is therefore called coherent. This coherent scattering of light by an atomic system is known as Rayleigh scattering.

Of more importance for the elucidation of problems in molecular structure is the study of the phenomenon known as incoherent or Raman scattering. In order to understand the origin of this phenomenon, let us calculate the dipole moment for the transition $a \rightarrow b$ when the system is subjected to radiation of frequency ν. The wave functions are

$$\Psi_a = \Psi_a^0 + \sum_k c_k \Psi_k^0$$

$$\Psi_b = \Psi_b^0 + \sum_l c_l \Psi_l^0$$

8·64

The dipole moment for the transition is therefore

$$\mathbf{R}_{ab} = 2Re\{(\Psi_a^* | \mathbf{R} | \Psi_b)\}$$

$$= 2Re\{(a|\mathbf{R}|b)e^{i\frac{E_{ab}}{\hbar}t} + \sum_k c_k^*(k|\mathbf{R}|b)e^{i\frac{E_{kb}}{\hbar}t} + \sum_l c_l(a|\mathbf{R}|l)e^{i\frac{E_{al}}{\hbar}t}\}$$ 8·65

where the coefficients c_k^* and c_l are

$$c_k^* = \frac{-iE_{ka}}{2c\hbar}(k|\mathbf{R}|a) \cdot \mathbf{A}_0^0 \left\{ \frac{e^{-i\frac{E_{ka}+\epsilon}{\hbar}t}}{E_{ka}+\epsilon} + \frac{e^{-i\frac{E_{ka}-\epsilon}{\hbar}t}}{E_{ka}-\epsilon} \right\}$$ 8·66

$$c_l = \frac{iE_{lb}}{2c\hbar}(l|\mathbf{R}|b) \cdot \mathbf{A}_0^0 \left\{ \frac{e^{i\frac{E_{lb}+\epsilon}{\hbar}t}}{E_{lb}+\epsilon} + \frac{e^{i\frac{E_{lb}-\epsilon}{\hbar}t}}{E_{lb}-\epsilon} \right\}$$ 8·67

Substituting these expressions for the coefficients in equation 8·65, we obtain for the dipole moment of the transition between the two states a and b the result

$$\mathbf{R}_{ab} = 2Re\left\{ (a|\mathbf{R}|b)e^{i\frac{E_{ab}}{\hbar}t} - \sum_k \frac{iE_{ka}}{2c\hbar}(k|\mathbf{R}|b)(k|\mathbf{R}|a) \cdot \mathbf{A}_0^0 \times \right.$$

$$\left[\frac{e^{i\frac{E_{ab}-\epsilon}{\hbar}t}}{E_{ka}+\epsilon} + \frac{e^{i\frac{E_{ab}+\epsilon}{\hbar}t}}{E_{ka}-\epsilon} \right] + \sum_l \frac{iE_{lb}}{2c\hbar}(a|\mathbf{R}|l)(l|\mathbf{R}|b) \cdot \mathbf{A}_0^0 \times$$

$$\left. \left[\frac{e^{i\frac{E_{ab}+\epsilon}{\hbar}t}}{E_{lb}+\epsilon} + \frac{e^{i\frac{E_{ab}-\epsilon}{\hbar}t}}{E_{lb}-\epsilon} \right] \right\}$$ 8·68

Since

$$Re\left\{ ie^{i\frac{E_{ab}-\epsilon}{\hbar}t} \right\} = -\sin\left(\frac{E_{ab}-\epsilon}{\hbar}\right)t$$

$$= \sin\left(\frac{\epsilon - E_{ab}}{\hbar}\right)t = \sin 2\pi (\nu - \nu_{ab})t; \quad \text{etc.}$$ 8·69

the expression for the dipole moment $\mathbf{R}_{ab}$ may be simplified to

$$\mathbf{R}_{ab} = 2(a|\mathbf{R}|b)\cos 2\pi\nu_{ab}t - \sum_k \frac{E_{ka}}{c\hbar}(k|\mathbf{R}|b)(k|\mathbf{R}|a) \cdot \mathbf{A}_0^0 \times$$

$$\left\{ \frac{\sin 2\pi(\nu - \nu_{ab})t}{E_{ka}+\epsilon} - \frac{\sin 2\pi(\nu + \nu_{ab})t}{E_{ka}-\epsilon} \right\} - \sum_l \frac{E_{lb}}{c\hbar}(a|\mathbf{R}|l)(l|\mathbf{R}|b) \cdot \mathbf{A}_0^0 \times$$

$$\left\{ \frac{\sin 2\pi(\nu + \nu_{ab})t}{E_{lb}+\epsilon} - \frac{\sin 2\pi(\nu - \nu_{ab})t}{E_{lb}-\epsilon} \right\}$$ 8·70

Since the summations over k and l are entirely equivalent we may replace both of them by a summation over j and write 8·70 as

$$\mathbf{R}_{ab} = 2(a|\mathbf{R}|b) \cos 2\pi\nu_{ab}t + \sum_j \left(\frac{\nu_{aj}}{\nu_{aj} + \nu} - \frac{\nu_{jb}}{\nu_{jb} + \nu} \right) \times$$

$$(a|\mathbf{R}|j)(j|\mathbf{R}|b) \cdot \frac{A_0^0}{c\hbar} \sin 2\pi(\nu + \nu_{ab})t + \sum_j \left(\frac{\nu_{bj}}{\nu_{bj} + \nu} - \frac{\nu_{ja}}{\nu_{ja} + \nu} \right) \times$$

$$(a|\mathbf{R}|j)(j|\mathbf{R}|b) \cdot \frac{A_0^0}{c\hbar} \sin 2\pi(\nu - \nu_{ab})t \quad 8\cdot71$$

where $\nu_{aj} = \dfrac{E_{aj}}{h}$, etc. The dipole moment for the transition thus contains three terms varying with the time. If the matrix element $(a|\mathbf{R}|b)$ is not zero, light of frequency ν_{ab} will be emitted. This, of course, is just the term corresponding to ordinary emission, as stated earlier in this chapter. We see, however, that if there exists some state j for which $(a|\mathbf{R}|j)$ and $(j|\mathbf{R}|b)$ are simultaneously different from zero, then light of frequency $\nu + \nu_{ab}$ and $\nu - \nu_{ab}$ are also emitted by the system. The first frequency arises when the system goes from an excited state to a lower state, thus adding energy to the field; the second arises when a system absorbs energy from the field.

For a harmonic oscillator, the selection rule for the Raman effect is the following. Let us assume that the harmonic oscillator is originally in the state a with quantum number n. Then the matrix element $(a|\mathbf{R}|j)$ will be different from zero only if the state j has the quantum number $n \pm 1$. Similarly, if state b has the quantum number m, $(j|\mathbf{R}|b)$ will be different from zero only if state j has the quantum number $m \pm 1$. Both matrix elements will be simultaneously different from zero only if $m = n$ or $m = n \pm 2$, so that we may conclude that the selection rule for Raman scattering by a harmonic oscillator is $\Delta n = 0, \pm 2$. The first possibility corresponds to scattering of light of the incident frequency ν; the second corresponds to scattering of light of frequency $\nu \pm 2\nu_e$, where ν_e is the fundamental frequency of the harmonic oscillator.

If we assume that $\nu \gg \nu_{aj}$ we may write

$$\sum \frac{\nu_{aj} - \nu_{jb}}{\nu} (a|\mathbf{R}|j)(j|\mathbf{R}|b) = \frac{\nu_{ab}}{\nu} \sum_j (a|\mathbf{R}|j)(j|\mathbf{R}|b)$$

$$= \frac{\nu_{ab}}{\nu} (a|\mathbf{R}\mathbf{R}|b) \quad 8\cdot72$$

According to 8·72, the frequency $\nu + \nu_{ab}$ will appear in the Raman effect if any matrix element of the type $(a|x_1x_2|b)$, where x_1, x_2 equal x, y, or z, is different from zero. We shall use this formulation of the selection rules for Raman scattering.

CHAPTER IX

ATOMIC STRUCTURE

The spectrum of a many-electron atom will in general consist of hundreds of lines with little apparent regularity. Before the development of the quantum theory it was found empirically that when the observed wavelengths were expressed as frequencies, a set of numbers could be assigned to a given atom such that all observed frequencies would be given by the difference of two numbers in this set, although not all differences would appear in the observed spectrum. In modern terms these experimental facts are expressed as follows. For a given atomic system, there exists a set of discrete energy levels, or "stationary states," of energy $E_1, E_2 \cdots E_n, \cdots$. Transitions between certain of these states are allowed, these transitions resulting in the emission of radiation of frequency $\nu = \dfrac{E_m - E_n}{h}$ if the transition is from the state designated by the letter m to that designated by the letter n. In this chapter we shall determine the number and characteristics of the states present in a given atom, derive the selection rules regulating the transitions between these states, and calculate theoretically, so far as these calculations are feasible, the eigenvalues and eigenfunctions of these states. This program will necessitate the inclusion of several additional features in our general theory, the first of these being the hypothesis of "electron spin."

9a. The Hypothesis of Electron Spin. If the energy level diagram of an alkali metal, which has one valence electron, is drawn from the spectroscopic data, it is found that most of the levels appear in closely spaced groups of two. In the alkali-earth metals, with two valence electrons, the levels may be divided into two series; in one series the levels appear separately, in the other in groups of three. This multiplicity of levels does not appear if the electron is assumed to have no properties other than mass and charge, as was done in our previous treatment of the hydrogen and helium atoms. This difficulty was resolved by Goudsmit and Uhlenbeck,[1] who introduced into the old quantum theory the hypothesis that the electron possesses an intrinsic

---

[1] G. Goudsmit and S. Uhlenbeck, *Naturwissenschaften*, **13**, 953 (1925).

angular momentum $\dfrac{h}{4\pi}$, with which there is associated a magnetic

moment of magnitude $\dfrac{eh}{4\pi mc}$. The interaction of the magnetic moment
of the electron with the magnetic fields produced by the motion of the
electrons in their orbits was then found to give rise to the splitting of the
energy levels into the observed multiplets.

The spin of the electron was measured experimentally by Stern and
Gerlach.[2] A beam of silver atoms was passed through a strong inho-
mogeneous magnetic field. It was found that the beam divided sharply
into two beams. One beam was deflected as though each atom were a

magnetic dipole of magnitude $\dfrac{eh}{4\pi mc}$ oriented along the field direction;

the other was deflected like a magnetic dipole of the same strength
but oriented in the opposite direction. There are good grounds for
believing that the total angular momentum due to the electrons moving in their orbits vanishes for the normal silver atom, and that the
observed magnetic moment is due solely to the single valence electron.
The Stern-Gerlach experiment is therefore a direct measurement of the
electron's intrinsic magnetic moment.

It is impossible to explain by classical mechanics why the beam of
silver atoms is split into two distinct beams; classical mechanics would
predict only a broadening of the beam. If, however, we assume that
the spin angular momentum obeys the quantum-mechanical laws of
angular momentum, and assume that $l = \frac{1}{2}$, then we would expect that
the beam would be split into two beams corresponding to the states with
$m = +\frac{1}{2}$ and $m = -\frac{1}{2}$.

In view of this fact we make the assumption that the electron has spin
angular momentum, represented by a set of operators $\mathbf{S}_x$, $\mathbf{S}_y$, $\mathbf{S}_z$, and $\mathbf{S}^2$
which are analogous to the operators $\mathbf{M}_x$, $\mathbf{M}_y$, $\mathbf{M}_z$, and $\mathbf{M}^2$ for orbital
angular momentum and obey the same commutation rules. According
to the discussion in the previous paragraph, we assume that there is

only one eigenvalue $\frac{1}{2}(1 + \frac{1}{2})\dfrac{h^2}{4\pi^2}$ for $\mathbf{S}^2$, so that there are only two

eigenvalues of $\mathbf{S}_z$, namely, $\frac{1}{2}\dfrac{h}{2\pi}$ and $-\frac{1}{2}\dfrac{h}{2\pi}$. In referring to a general

spin eigenfunction we shall use the quantum number s, writing $s\dfrac{h}{2\pi}$ for

the eigenvalues of $\mathbf{S}_z$. s may therefore have the values $\pm\frac{1}{2}$.

Let us denote by α the spin eigenfunction corresponding to $s = +\frac{1}{2}$,

[2] O. Stern and W. Gerlach, Z. *Physik*, **8**, 110; **9**, 349 (1922).

and by β the spin eigenfunction corresponding to $s = -\frac{1}{2}$. These eigenfunctions then satisfy the equations

$$\mathbf{S}^2\alpha = \frac{3}{4}\frac{h^2}{4\pi^2}\alpha \qquad \mathbf{S}^2\beta = \frac{3}{4}\frac{h^2}{4\pi^2}\beta \qquad 9\text{·}1$$

$$\mathbf{S}_z\alpha = \frac{1}{2}\frac{h}{2\pi}\alpha \qquad \mathbf{S}_z\beta = -\frac{1}{2}\frac{h}{2\pi}\beta \qquad 9\text{·}2$$

In order to find the effect of $\mathbf{S}_x$ and $\mathbf{S}_y$ on these eigenfunctions we use the equations analogous to 3·132 and 3·133. These are, making the proper substitutions,

$$(\mathbf{S}_x - i\mathbf{S}_y)\alpha = \frac{h}{2\pi}\beta$$
$$(\mathbf{S}_x - i\mathbf{S}_y)\beta = 0$$
$$(\mathbf{S}_x + i\mathbf{S}_y)\alpha = 0 \qquad 9\text{·}3$$
$$(\mathbf{S}_x + i\mathbf{S}_y)\beta = \frac{h}{2\pi}\alpha$$

From these equations we find by addition and subtraction that

$$\mathbf{S}_x\alpha = \frac{h}{4\pi}\beta \qquad \mathbf{S}_x\beta = \frac{h}{4\pi}\alpha \qquad 9\text{·}4$$

$$\mathbf{S}_y\alpha = \frac{ih}{4\pi}\beta \qquad \mathbf{S}_y\beta = -\frac{ih}{4\pi}\alpha \qquad 9\text{·}5$$

The effect of such operators as $\mathbf{S}_x\mathbf{S}_y$, etc., can be easily found by the successive application of the above rules. For example,

$$\mathbf{S}_x\mathbf{S}_y\alpha = \frac{ih^2}{16\pi^2}\alpha; \quad \mathbf{S}_y\mathbf{S}_x\alpha = -\frac{ih^2}{16\pi^2}\alpha \qquad 9\text{·}6$$

so that

$$(\mathbf{S}_x\mathbf{S}_y - \mathbf{S}_y\mathbf{S}_x)\alpha = \frac{ih}{2\pi}\frac{h}{4\pi}\alpha = \frac{ih}{2\pi}\mathbf{S}_z\alpha \qquad 9\text{·}7$$

as, of course, it must be if the commutation rules are to be satisfied. This formal method of treating electron spin was developed by Pauli.[3]

In order to fix in our minds more clearly the relation between angular momentum and magnetic moment, let us consider a particle of mass m and algebraic charge e moving in a circular orbit of radius a with a velocity v. The motion of the charged particle is equivalent to a current flowing along the orbit, the magnitude of the current being equal to the

---

[3] W. Pauli, *Z. Physik*, **43**, 601 (1925).

charge divided by the time required for a complete cycle, **or**

$$I = \frac{e}{2\pi a/v} = \frac{ev}{2\pi a}$$

According to electromagnetic theory, a current I moving about a loop of area A is equivalent to a magnetic moment $\dfrac{IA}{c}$. The magnetic moment associated with the motion of the charged particle is therefore

$$\mu = \frac{ev}{2\pi a}\frac{\pi a^2}{c} = \frac{e}{2c}av = \frac{e}{2mc}p \qquad 9\cdot8$$

where p is the angular momentum of the particle. The ratio of magnetic moment to angular momentum, $\dfrac{e}{2mc}$, is called the gyromagnetic ratio. The classical result above gives the correct relation between orbital angular momentum and associated magnetic moment in quantum mechanics as well. For spin angular momentum, however, we obtain correct results only if we take the gyromagnetic ratio to be twice as large. The magnetic moment of the spinning electron is therefore represented by the operators

$$\mu_x = \frac{e}{mc}\,\mathbf{S}_x$$

$$\mu_y = \frac{e}{mc}\,\mathbf{S}_y \qquad 9\cdot9$$

$$\mu_z = \frac{e}{mc}\,\mathbf{S}_z$$

where e and m are the charge and mass of the electron. In a magnetic field with the components H_x, H_y, and H_z, the classical energy of a magnetic dipole is

$$-(H_x\mu_x + H_y\mu_y + H_z\mu_z)$$

The corresponding operator is obtained by replacing the μ's by the operators in 9·9, so that in a magnetic field the Hamiltonian operator contains the operator

$$-\frac{e}{mc}\,(H_x\mathbf{S}_x + H_y\mathbf{S}_y + H_z\mathbf{S}_z) \qquad 9\cdot10$$

If the z axis is taken to be the field direction, so that H_x and H_y vanish, this reduces to

$$-\frac{e}{mc}H\mathbf{S}_z \qquad 9\cdot11$$

The spin eigenfunctions α and β are therefore the correct eigenfunctions of the Hamiltonian operator as well as of the operators $\mathbf{S}_z$ and $\mathbf{S}^2$. If the field strength is allowed to become zero this argument still holds, so that even if there is no magnetic field we still use α and β as our spin eigenfunctions of the Hamiltonian operator.

9b. The Electronic States of Complex Atoms. For an atom of atomic number Z, the approximate Hamiltonian is

$$\mathbf{H} = -\frac{h^2}{8\pi^2 m}\sum_i \nabla_i^2 - \sum_i \frac{Ze^2}{r_i} + \sum_{i>j} \frac{e^2}{r_{ij}} \qquad 9\cdot12$$

where ∇_i^2 is the Laplacian operator for the ith electron, r_i is the distance of the ith electron from the nucleus (motion of the nucleus can be neglected in heavy atoms), and r_{ij} is the distance between the ith and jth electrons. The exact Hamiltonian contains additional terms representing the magnetic interactions of the electronic orbits and spins, which we will disregard for the present.

Because of the presence of the terms $\dfrac{e^2}{r_{ij}}$ in the Hamiltonian operator it is not possible to separate the variables in the wave equation. The problem must therefore be treated by approximate methods, but it is gratifying to find that all the qualitative features of atomic structure can be obtained with little actual computation. As the starting point of the perturbation theory we use the set of one-electron eigenfunctions which are the solutions of the wave equation with the Hamiltonian

$$\mathbf{H}_0 = -\frac{h^2}{8\pi^2 m}\sum_i \nabla_i^2 + \sum_i V(r_i) \qquad 9\cdot13$$

where $V(r_i)$ is an effective potential for the ith electron. The difference between 9·12 and 9·13 is treated as the perturbation

$$\mathbf{H}' = -\sum_i \frac{Ze^2}{r_i} + \sum_{i>j} \frac{e^2}{r_{ij}} - \sum_i V(r_i) \qquad 9\cdot14$$

In order to obtain a good set of zero-order functions, $V(r_i)$ should be taken to be such a function of r_i that H' is as small as possible. If r_i is much greater than any of the other r_j's, the field due to the remaining electrons will approximate that of a charge $-(Z-1)e$ at the origin, so that $V(r_i) = -\dfrac{e^2}{r_i}$, in which case we say that the nucleus has been screened by the other electrons. If r_i is much smaller than any of the other r_j's, the field due to the other electrons is approximately the field inside of a spherical shell of charge, which is a constant, so that

$$V(r_i) = -\frac{Ze^2}{r_i} + \text{constant.}$$ As the general features of the electronic states are not dependent upon the explicit form chosen for $V(r)$, a further discussion of the radial part of the wave equation will be reserved for later sections of this chapter.

The eigenfunctions of the approximate Hamiltonian 9·13 are known as atomic orbitals. Since we have chosen a potential function which is a function of r only, they will be similar in many ways to the hydrogen eigenfunctions. The factors of the orbital depending on θ and φ are of the form $P_l^{|m|} (\cos \theta)e^{im\varphi}$, and the radial factor is similar to the radial function of hydrogen. Each orbital may therefore be labeled by quantum numbers n, l, m, analogous to those in hydrogen, and we may speak of $2s$ orbitals, $3p$ orbitals, etc. One important difference between these atomic orbitals and the hydrogen eigenfunctions is that the energy of a hydrogen eigenfunction is a function of n only, whereas the energy of an atomic orbital depends on l as well, so that, for example, a $2s$ and $2p$ orbital have different energies. Since the energy of an atomic orbital is not a function of m, the value of this quantum number is not specified when we describe an orbital.

9c. The Pauli Exclusion Principle. Having once chosen an appropriate set of atomic orbitals we must combine these orbitals into approximate eigenfunctions for the entire atom. This can, of course, be done in a variety of ways, depending on the choice of orbitals from the chosen set. Let us suppose, however, that we have decided to construct an eigenfunction corresponding to a state in which the numbers of $1s$, $2s$, $2p$, etc., electrons are all fixed. To be concrete, suppose that the state is one with two $1s$ electrons and one $2p$ electron. Let us denote our orbital by $\varphi(n, l, m|i)$, giving the first part of the parentheses the three quantum numbers, and in the other part the number of the electron occupying the orbital. Then we might take the product

$$\varphi(100|1)\varphi(100|2)\varphi(211|3) \qquad 9\cdot15$$

as an approximation to the eigenfunction for the desired state. We might equally well have chosen

$$\varphi(100|3)\varphi(100|2)\varphi(21\bar{1}|1) \qquad 9\cdot16$$

$\{\varphi(21\bar{1}|1) \equiv \varphi(2, 1, -1|1)\}$ or any similar product. Up to the present we have not considered the spin of the electrons. Since the Hamiltonian 9·12 does not involve the spin in any way as yet, we may take the functions α and β of section $9a$ as representing the two possible spin states of each electron. If we insert the s value after the three quantum numbers n, l, m in our symbols for the orbitals the eigenfunctions for our chosen state might take on the appearance

$$\varphi(100\tfrac{1}{2}|1)\varphi(100\overline{\tfrac{1}{2}}|2)\varphi(100\overline{\tfrac{1}{2}}|3) \qquad 9{\cdot}17$$

In this way we can write an eigenfunction, in fact a number of eigen-functions, for any state. But we could by this procedure write eigen-functions corresponding to states which are never observed. For example

$$\varphi(100\tfrac{1}{2}|1)\varphi(100\tfrac{1}{2}|2)\varphi(100\tfrac{1}{2}|3) \qquad 9{\cdot}18$$

would represent a state in which the atom had three $1s$ electrons, all with positive spin. If we were to calculate the energy of this state in lithium by the variation method we would find a lower energy than that of any known level, and yet the theory of the variation method tells us that our calculated energy must be too high.

The way out of this difficulty was discovered by Pauli.[4] Before quantum mechanics took on its present form Pauli put forth the follow-ing exclusion principle: no two electrons can have all their quantum numbers, including spin quantum number, the same. With the new quantum mechanics this has been changed to the following statement, from which the previous one may be derived: every eigenfunction must be antisymmetrical in every pair of electrons (or more generally in every pair of identical elementary particles); that is, if any two electrons are interchanged, the eigenfunction must remain unchanged except for the factor -1. The electron density distribution for a given state is given by the square of the corresponding eigenfunction. If two electrons are interchanged, the electron density distribution must, of course, remain unchanged. This means that the eigenfunction must either be unaf-fected by this interchange of electrons or must change only in sign. It is found empirically that we obtain a correct description of nature only if we always adopt the second alternative.

It is not immediately apparent that the new form of the exclusion principle includes the old. Let us, however, consider the determinant

$$D = \frac{1}{\sqrt{3!}} \begin{vmatrix} \varphi(100\tfrac{1}{2}|1) & \varphi(100\tfrac{1}{2}|2) & \varphi(100\tfrac{1}{2}|3) \\ \varphi(100\overline{\tfrac{1}{2}}|1) & \varphi(100\overline{\tfrac{1}{2}}|2) & \varphi(100\overline{\tfrac{1}{2}}|3) \\ \varphi(211\tfrac{1}{2}|1) & \varphi(211\tfrac{1}{2}|2) & \varphi(211\tfrac{1}{2}|3) \end{vmatrix} \qquad 9{\cdot}19$$

If we interchange any two electrons in this eigenfunction, say electrons 1 and 2, then two columns of the determinant are interchanged. This causes a change of sign of the determinant, so that this eigenfunction satisfies the exclusion principle in the new form. Any antisymmetric eigenfunction can be written as such a determinant or as a linear combi-

[4] W. Pauli, *Z. Physik*, **31**, 765 (1925).

nation of such determinants. Now if we attempt to set up an eigenfunction in which two electrons have the same set of quantum numbers, and write the eigenfunction in its determinantal form, it is seen that two rows of the determinant are identical. But such a determinant, one with two identical rows, vanishes, and the eigenfunction vanishes. Therefore the old form of the exclusion principle is included in the new.

Accepting the exclusion principle in its new form as a new postulate to our theory, we are no longer permitted to use the simple products such as 9·15 in our future discussion, but only linear combinations of determinants such as 9·19. In other words, though we can construct eigenfunctions corresponding to states in which a definite set of orbitals is occupied, we cannot specify which electron occupies a particular orbital.

In most atoms the energies of the various orbitals lie in the order $1s, 2s, 2p, 3s, 3p, 4s, 3d, 4p, 5s, 4d, 5p, 6s, 4f, 5d, 6p, 7s, 6d$, the $1s$ orbitals having the lowest energy. When the atom is in its normal state, its Z electrons occupy the lowest orbitals possible without violating the exclusion principle. Thus hydrogen, with one electron, normally has this electron in the $1s$ orbital, but in lithium one electron must go into the $2s$ orbital, since there is no way in which three electrons can occupy the $1s$ orbital without violating the Pauli exclusion principle. The group of two $1s$ electrons is presen in all the elements of higher atomic number than 1. Such a complette group is known as a closed shell. With beryllium, the $2s$ shell is completed, and the fifth electron in boron must occupy a $2p$ orbital. Since there are three different $2p$ orbitals, corresponding to the values 1, 0, -1, for the quantum number m, and since each of these may have either of two values for the spin quantum number associated with it, the $2p$ shell can hold six electrons. In the elements from boron to neon the $2p$ orbitals are being filled. When we come to sodium, however, there is no more room for $2p$ electrons, and so the eleventh electron goes into a $3s$ orbital. Magnesium completes the $3s$ shell, and from aluminum to argon the $3p$ orbitals are filled. In this way we build up all the atoms in the periodic table. There are a few irregularities which will be discussed in section 9m, where we shall consider the properties of the atoms in the periodic table from the viewpoint of their electronic structure.

A state of an atom in which the number of electrons in each shell is specified is called a configuration. The usual notation for a configuration is the following. We write the designations $1s$, $2p$, etc., for the various shells, with exponents indicating the number of electrons in the shell. Thus the normal configuration of lithium is $(1s)^2(2s)$, and the normal configuration of phosphorus is $(1s)^2(2s)^2(2p)^6(3s)^2(3p)^3$.

9d. The Calculation of Energy Levels.[5] For a closed shell of electrons only one eigenfunction may be written. Thus for a shell of six $2p$ electrons we may write

$$\frac{1}{\sqrt{6!}} \begin{vmatrix} \varphi(211\tfrac{1}{2}|1) & \cdots\cdots & \varphi(211\tfrac{1}{2}|6) \\ \varphi(211\overline{\tfrac{1}{2}}|1) & \cdots\cdots & \cdot \\ \varphi(210\tfrac{1}{2}|1) & \cdots\cdots & \cdot \\ \varphi(210\overline{\tfrac{1}{2}}|1) & \cdots\cdots & \cdot \\ \varphi(21\overline{1}\tfrac{1}{2}|1) & \cdots\cdots & \cdot \\ \varphi(21\overline{1}\,\overline{\tfrac{1}{2}}|1) & \cdots\cdots & \varphi(21\overline{1}\,\overline{\tfrac{1}{2}}|6) \end{vmatrix} \qquad 9\cdot20$$

No other determinant is possible. $\left(\text{The factor } \dfrac{1}{\sqrt{6!}} \text{ is a normalizing}\right.$ factor; the determinant as written will be normalized if the functions φ are normalized. For N electrons the factor is $\dfrac{1}{\sqrt{N!}}\cdot\Big)$ Hence for a closed shell the eigenfunction is completely determined by the configuration. For an incomplete shell, however, there are always a number of possible eigenfunctions. For example, the configuration $(1s)(2p)$ has twelve possibilities. Abbreviating the determinants by writing just the principal diagonal between bars, these are

$$D_1 = \frac{1}{\sqrt{2!}}\,\left|\varphi(100\tfrac{1}{2}|1)\varphi(211\tfrac{1}{2}|2)\right| \qquad D_7 = \frac{1}{\sqrt{2!}}\,\left|\varphi(100\overline{\tfrac{1}{2}}|1)\varphi(211\tfrac{1}{2}|2)\right|$$

$$D_2 = \frac{1}{\sqrt{2!}}\,\left|\varphi(100\tfrac{1}{2}|1)\varphi(211\overline{\tfrac{1}{2}}|2)\right| \qquad D_8 = \frac{1}{\sqrt{2!}}\,\left|\varphi(100\overline{\tfrac{1}{2}}|1)\varphi(211\overline{\tfrac{1}{2}}|2)\right|$$

$$D_3 = \frac{1}{\sqrt{2!}}\,\left|\varphi(100\tfrac{1}{2}|1)\varphi(210\tfrac{1}{2}|2)\right| \qquad D_9 = \frac{1}{\sqrt{2!}}\,\left|\varphi(100\overline{\tfrac{1}{2}}|1)\varphi(210\tfrac{1}{2}|2)\right|$$

$$D_4 = \frac{1}{\sqrt{2!}}\,\left|\varphi(100\tfrac{1}{2}|1)\varphi(210\overline{\tfrac{1}{2}}|2)\right| \qquad D_{10} = \frac{1}{\sqrt{2!}}\,\left|\varphi(100\overline{\tfrac{1}{2}}|1)\varphi(210\overline{\tfrac{1}{2}}|2)\right|$$

$$D_5 = \frac{1}{\sqrt{2}}\,\left|\varphi(100\tfrac{1}{2}|1)\varphi(21\overline{1}\tfrac{1}{2}|2)\right| \qquad D_{11} = \frac{1}{\sqrt{2!}}\,\left|\varphi(100\overline{\tfrac{1}{2}}|1)\varphi(21\overline{1}\tfrac{1}{2}|2)\right|$$

$$D_6 = \frac{1}{\sqrt{2}}\,\left|\varphi(100\tfrac{1}{2}|1)\varphi(21\overline{1}\,\overline{\tfrac{1}{2}}|2)\right| \qquad D_{12} = \frac{1}{\sqrt{2}}\,\left|\varphi(100\overline{\tfrac{1}{2}}|1)\varphi(21\overline{1}\,\overline{\tfrac{1}{2}}|2)\right|$$

[5] The methods used in this and several subsequent sections are essentially due to J. C. Slater, *Phys. Rev.*, **34**, 1293 (1929).

Let us suppose that in the general case there are n determinants $D_1, D_2, \cdots D_n$ corresponding to a given configuration. The first-order perturbation theory for degenerate systems then tells us that the energy levels will be given by the roots of the equation

$$
\begin{vmatrix}
H_{11} - S_{11}E & H_{12} - S_{12}E & \cdots\cdots & H_{1n} - S_{1n}E \\
H_{21} - S_{21}E & H_{22} - S_{22}E & \cdots\cdots & H_{2n} - S_{2n}E \\
\cdots\cdots\cdots\cdots\cdots\cdots\cdots\cdots\cdots\cdots\cdots\cdots \\
H_{n1} - S_{n1}E & H_{n2} - S_{n2}E & \cdots\cdots & H_{nn} - S_{nn}E
\end{vmatrix} = 0 \qquad 9\cdot21
$$

where $H_{ij} = \int D_i^* H D_j \, d\tau$; $S_{ij} = \int D_i^* D_j \, d\tau$. Equation 9·21 is analogous to 7·50, except that the D functions have not been assumed to be orthogonal.

9e. Angular Momenta. The large number of states arising from most configurations makes the direct solution of equation 9·21 a very difficult task. Equation 9·21 can be simplified by the use of the operators representing the various angular momenta of the atom. Representing the operators for the components of orbital angular momentum of the various electrons by $\mathbf{M}_{x1}, \mathbf{M}_{y1}, \mathbf{M}_{z1}$; $\mathbf{M}_{x2}, \mathbf{M}_{y2}, \mathbf{M}_{z2}$, etc., we define the operators for the components of the total angular momentum by

$$\mathbf{M}_x = \mathbf{M}_{x1} + \mathbf{M}_{x2} + \cdots$$

$$\mathbf{M}_y = \mathbf{M}_{y1} + \mathbf{M}_{y2} + \cdots \qquad 9\cdot22$$

$$\mathbf{M}_z = \mathbf{M}_{z1} + \mathbf{M}_{z2} + \cdots$$

The operator for the square of the orbital angular momentum of the atom is

$$\mathbf{M}^2 = \mathbf{M}_x^2 + \mathbf{M}_y^2 + \mathbf{M}_z^2 \qquad 9\cdot23$$

At the same time we define the components of the total spin angular momentum by

$$\mathbf{S}_x = \mathbf{S}_{x1} + \mathbf{S}_{x2} + \cdots$$

$$\mathbf{S}_y = \mathbf{S}_{y1} + \mathbf{S}_{y2} + \cdots \qquad 9\cdot24$$

$$\mathbf{S}_z = \mathbf{S}_{z1} + \mathbf{S}_{z2} + \cdots$$

For the square of the total spin angular momentum the operator is

$$\mathbf{S}^2 = \mathbf{S}_x^2 + \mathbf{S}_y^2 + \mathbf{S}_z^2 \qquad 9\cdot25$$

Finally there are the operators for the components of total angular momentum and its square

$$\mathbf{J}_x = \mathbf{M}_x + \mathbf{S}_x$$
$$\mathbf{J}_y = \mathbf{M}_y + \mathbf{S}_y$$
$$\mathbf{J}_z = \mathbf{M}_z + \mathbf{S}_z \qquad \qquad 9\cdot 26$$
$$\mathbf{J}^2 = \mathbf{J}_x^2 + \mathbf{J}_y^2 + \mathbf{J}_z^2$$

Classically all these angular momenta are constant. The quantum analogue of this is that all these operators commute with the Hamiltonian operator $\mathbf{H}$. That $\mathbf{S}_x$, $\mathbf{S}_y$, $\mathbf{S}_z$, and $\mathbf{S}^2$ commute with $\mathbf{H}$ is obvious, since $\mathbf{H}$ does not contain the spin coordinates. To show that the others commute with $\mathbf{H}$ we first consider $\mathbf{M}_z$. In polar coordinates this operator is

$$\mathbf{M}_z = \frac{h}{2\pi i}\left(\frac{\partial}{\partial \varphi_1} + \frac{\partial}{\partial \varphi_2} + \cdots\right)$$

The only terms in $\mathbf{H}$ which involve the φ's are the parts of the Laplacian containing $\dfrac{\partial^2}{\partial \varphi^2}$, which commutes with $\dfrac{\partial}{\partial \varphi}$, and the terms in $\dfrac{e^2}{r_{ij}}$. Now $\dfrac{1}{r_{12}}$ involves φ_1 and φ_2 only in the combination $(\varphi_1 - \varphi_2)$, so that

$$\left(\frac{\partial}{\partial \varphi_1} + \frac{\partial}{\partial \varphi_2} + \cdots\right)\frac{e^2}{r_{12}}$$
$$= \frac{\partial}{\partial(\varphi_1 - \varphi_2)}\left(\frac{e^2}{r_{12}}\right)\left\{\frac{\partial(\varphi_1 - \varphi_2)}{\partial \varphi_1} + \frac{\partial(\varphi_1 - \varphi_2)}{\partial \varphi_2}\right\} + \cdots$$
$$= 0$$

Hence $\mathbf{M}_z$ commutes with $\mathbf{H}$. Since $\mathbf{H}$ is spherically symmetrical, $\mathbf{M}_x$ and $\mathbf{M}_y$ must therefore also commute with $\mathbf{H}$, as must $\mathbf{M}^2$. The $\mathbf{J}$'s must likewise commute with $\mathbf{H}$, for they are combinations of operators all of which commute with $\mathbf{H}$.

These operators do not, however, commute among themselves. Making use of equations 3·103, and the fact that the various angular momenta of one electron commute with those of any other electron, we find that

$$\mathbf{M}_x\mathbf{M}_y - \mathbf{M}_y\mathbf{M}_x = \frac{ih}{2\pi}\mathbf{M}_z$$

$$\mathbf{M}_y\mathbf{M}_z - \mathbf{M}_z\mathbf{M}_y = \frac{ih}{2\pi}\mathbf{M}_x \qquad \qquad 9\cdot 27$$

$$\mathbf{M}_z\mathbf{M}_x - \mathbf{M}_x\mathbf{M}_z = \frac{ih}{2\pi}\mathbf{M}_y$$

Similar equations hold between S_x, S_y, and S_z, and between J_x, J_y, and J_z. Just as M^2 commutes with M_x, M_y, and M_z for one electron, M^2, S^2, and J^2 commute with their components. Of course M^2 and its components commute with S^2 and its components. M^2 and S^2 also commute with J^2 and its components, but the components of M^2 and S^2 do not commute with either J^2 or its components (except like components such as M_x, S_x, and J_x).

We can therefore select from among the angular momentum operators various sets which commute among themselves and also with H. Thus we might choose M^2, M_z, S^2, S_z, and J_z or M^2, S^2, J^2, and J_z. Now according to Theorem II of Chapter III, the eigenfunctions of H can be chosen so that they are simultaneously eigenfunctions of all the operators in any one of these sets. Moreover, if this is done the matrix components of H between eigenfunctions which have different eigenvalues for any one of these operators will vanish. Therefore, if we take a set of linear combinations of the D functions described above such that each combination is an eigenfunction of all the operators of a set of commuting angular momenta, then in equation 9·21 the H_{ij}'s and S_{ij}'s will vanish except between those combinations which have the same eigenvalues for all operators of the set. The appearance of 9·21 will then be

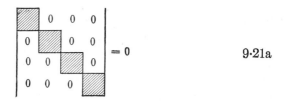

$$= 0 \qquad\qquad 9\cdot21a$$

if we arrange the combinations of D's in such a way that the combinations with the same eigenvalues for the angular momenta are together. The shaded portion of the diagram represents non-vanishing H's and S's; the remainder of the determinant is occupied by zeros. Now a determinant such as the one in 9·21a is equal to the product of the shaded determinants along the diagonal, so that the roots of 9·21a are just the roots obtained by putting each of the shaded determinants successively equal to zero. The solution of 9·21 is thus reduced to the solution of a number of equations similar in form but of smaller degree.

9f. Multiplet Structure. As long as we use the Hamiltonian 9·12, which does not contain the spin terms, it does not matter what set of angular momenta we use to reduce the secular equation 9·21 to the form 9·21a. If the complete Hamiltonian were used, the only angular momenta which would commute with it would be J^2 and its components.

Although the other angular momenta do not commute with the exact Hamiltonian, it is found that usually $\mathbf{M}^2$ and $\mathbf{S}^2$ "almost commute" with $\mathbf{H}$; that is, $\mathbf{HM}^2 - \mathbf{M}^2\mathbf{H}$ is small. On the other hand, $\mathbf{M}_z$, $\mathbf{S}_z$, etc., do not "almost commute" with the exact Hamiltonian. It would therefore seem logical to pick the set $\mathbf{M}^2$, $\mathbf{S}^2$, $\mathbf{J}^2$, and $\mathbf{J}_z$ as the set of angular momenta to be used to reduce the secular equation. We shall presently see, however, that the eigenfunctions of the type described above are already eigenfunctions of $\mathbf{M}_z$ and $\mathbf{S}_z$. For this reason it is more convenient to choose $\mathbf{M}^2$, $\mathbf{S}^2$, $\mathbf{M}_z$, and $\mathbf{S}_z$ as our set of angular momenta as long as we are using the approximate Hamiltonian 9·13. If it is desired to find the eigenfunctions of $\mathbf{J}^2$ and $\mathbf{J}_z$, these may be found later in terms of this set.

Our next problem is then to combine the determinantal eigenfunctions, the D functions, into new trial eigenfunctions which are eigenfunctions of $\mathbf{M}^2$, $\mathbf{S}^2$, $\mathbf{M}_z$, and $\mathbf{S}_z$. We shall first show that these trial eigenfunctions are already eigenfunctions of $\mathbf{M}_z$ and $\mathbf{S}_z$. Let us take a general determinantal eigenfunction

$$D = \frac{1}{\sqrt{N!}} \left| \varphi(n_1 l_1 m_1 s_1 | 1) \varphi(n_2 l_2 m_2 s_2 | 2) \cdots \right| \qquad 9\cdot 28$$

A typical term in the expansion of this determinant is

$$\varphi(n_1 l_1 m_1 s_1 | 1) \varphi(n_2 l_2 m_2 s_2 | 2) \cdots$$

Operating on this term with $\mathbf{M}_z$, we find that the term $\mathbf{M}_{z1}$ gives the same product multiplied by $m_1 \dfrac{h}{2\pi}$, the term $\mathbf{M}_{z2}$ the same product multiplied by $m_2 \dfrac{h}{2\pi}$, and so on. The total result of operating with $\mathbf{M}_z$ is the sum of these, or $(m_1 + m_2 + \cdots) \dfrac{h}{2\pi}$ times the original product. Since this holds for every term in the expansion of the determinant, it holds for the whole determinant, which is therefore an eigenfunction of $\mathbf{M}_z$ with the eigenvalue $M_L \dfrac{h}{2\pi}$, where $M_L = m_1 + m_2 + \cdots$. By an exactly similar argument the D functions are eigenfunctions of $\mathbf{S}_z$ with the eigenvalue $M_S \dfrac{h}{2\pi}$, where $M_S = s_1 + s_2 + \cdots$. For the list of possible D functions for the configuration $(1s)(2p)$ given above, we have, for example,

$$\mathbf{M}_z D_1 = \frac{h}{2\pi} D_1 \qquad \mathbf{M}_z D_6 = -\frac{h}{2\pi} D_6 \qquad 9\cdot29$$

$$\mathbf{S}_z D_1 = \frac{h}{2\pi} D_1 \qquad \mathbf{S}_z D_6 = 0 \qquad 9\cdot30$$

Let us now consider the effect of $\mathbf{M}^2$ on the D's. A typical term in the expansion of a D function is

$$\varphi(n_1 l_1 m_1 s_1 | 1)\varphi(n_2 l_2 m_2 s_2 | 2) \cdots \qquad 9\cdot31$$

Now

$$\mathbf{M}^2 = (\mathbf{M}_{x1} + \mathbf{M}_{x2} + \cdots)^2 + (\mathbf{M}_{y1} + \mathbf{M}_{y2} + \cdots)^2$$
$$+ (\mathbf{M}_{z1} + \mathbf{M}_{z2} + \cdots)^2$$
$$= \mathbf{M}_1^2 + \mathbf{M}_2^2 + \mathbf{M}_3^2 + \cdots$$
$$+ 2\mathbf{M}_{z1}\mathbf{M}_{z2} + 2\mathbf{M}_{z1}\mathbf{M}_{z3} + 2\mathbf{M}_{z2}\mathbf{M}_{z3} + \cdots$$
$$+ (\mathbf{M}_{x1} + i\mathbf{M}_{y1})(\mathbf{M}_{x2} - i\mathbf{M}_{y2})$$
$$+ (\mathbf{M}_{x1} - i\mathbf{M}_{y1})(\mathbf{M}_{x2} + i\mathbf{M}_{y2}) + \cdots$$

Using equations 3·127, 3·132, 3·133, we find

$$\mathbf{M}^2\{\varphi(n_1 l_1 m_1 s_1 | 1)\varphi(n_2 l_2 m_2 s_2 | 2) \cdots\}$$
$$= \frac{h^2}{4\pi^2}\{[l_1(l_1 + 1) + l_2(l_2 + 1) + \cdots + 2m_1 m_2 + 2m_1 m_3$$
$$+ 2m_2 m_3 + \cdots][\varphi(n_1 l_1 m_1 s_1 | 1)\varphi(n_2 l_2 m_2 s_2 | 2) \cdots]$$
$$+ [(l_1(l_1 + 1) - m_1(m_1 + 1))(l_2(l_2 + 1) - m_2(m_2 - 1))]^{\frac{1}{2}}$$
$$[\varphi(n_1 l_1, m_1 + 1, s_1 | 1)\varphi(n_2 l_2, m_2 - 1, s_2 | 2)\varphi(n_3 l_3 m_3 s_3 | 3) \cdots]$$
$$+ [(l_1(l_1 + 1) - m_1(m_1 - 1))(l_2(l_2 + 1) - m_2(m_2 + 1))]^{\frac{1}{2}}$$
$$[\varphi(n_1 l_1, m_1 - 1, s_1 | 1)\varphi(n_2 l_2, m_2 + 1, s_2 | 2)\varphi(n_3 l_3 m_3 s_3 | 3) \cdots]$$
$$+ \cdots\} \qquad 9\cdot32$$

If we represent by $D\{(n_1 l_1 m_1 s_1)(n_2 l_2 m_2 s_2) \cdots\}$ the D function whose principal diagonal is 9·31, we see that $\mathbf{M}^2$ affects each term in its expansion in the same way, and hence that

$$\mathbf{M}^2 D\{(n_1 l_1 m_1 s_1)(n_2 l_2 m_2 s_2) \cdots\}$$
$$= \frac{h^2}{4\pi^2}\{[\Sigma l_i(l_i + 1) + 2\sum_{i>j} m_i m_j]D\{(n_1 l_1 m_1 s_1)(n_2 l_2 m_2 s_2) \cdots\}$$
$$+ \sum_{i \neq j} [(l_i(l_i + 1) - m_i(m_i + 1))(l_j(l_j + 1) - m_j(m_j - 1))]^{\frac{1}{2}}$$
$$D\{(n_1 l_1 m_1 s_1) \cdots (n_i l_i, m_i + 1, s_i) \cdots (n_j l_j, m_j - 1, s_j) \cdots\}\} \qquad 9\cdot33$$

Analogously

$$\mathbf{S}^2D\{(n_1l_1m_1s_1)(n_2l_2m_2s_2)\cdots\}$$

$$= \frac{h^2}{4\pi^2}\{[\sum_i|s_i|(|s_i|+1) + 2\sum_{i>j}s_is_j]D\{(n_1l_1m_1s_1)(n_2l_2m_2s_2)\cdots\}$$

$$+ \sum_{i\neq j}[(\tfrac{3}{2}+s_i)(\tfrac{1}{2}-s_i)(\tfrac{3}{2}-s_j)(\tfrac{1}{2}+s_j)]^{\frac{1}{2}}D\{(n_1l_1m_1s_1)\cdots$$

$$(n_il_im_i, s_i+1)\cdots(n_jl_jm_j, s_j-1)\cdots\}\} \quad 9\cdot34$$

In the same way we find the effect of $(\mathbf{M}_x \pm i\mathbf{M}_y)$ and $(\mathbf{S}_x \pm i\mathbf{S}_y)$ on the D functions to be

$$(\mathbf{M}_x \pm i\mathbf{M}_y)D\{(n_1l_1m_1s_1)\cdots\} = \frac{h}{2\pi}\sum_i[l_i(l_i+1) - m_i(m_i\pm1)]^{\frac{1}{2}}$$

$$D\{(n_1l_1m_1s_1)\cdots(n_il_im_i\pm1, s_i)\cdots\} \quad 9\cdot35$$

$$(\mathbf{S}_x \pm i\mathbf{S}_y)D\{(n_1l_1m_1s_1)\cdots\} = \frac{h}{2\pi}\sum_i[(\tfrac{3}{2}\pm s_i)(\tfrac{1}{2}\mp s_i)]^{\frac{1}{2}}$$

$$D\{(n_1l_1m_1s_1)\cdots(n_il_im_i, s_i\pm1)\cdots\} \quad 9\cdot36$$

We thus see that the D's are not themselves eigenfunctions of $\mathbf{M}^2$ or $\mathbf{S}^2$. We can, however, form linear combinations of D's which are such eigenfunctions. First, it is obvious from 9·33 that $\mathbf{M}^2$ does not change the value of M_L or M_S. The combinations that we desire will therefore involve only D functions with the same M_L and M_S. We therefore put

$$A = \sum_i c_iD_i \quad 9\cdot37$$

where D_i is one of a set of D functions arising from a given configuration and having the same M_L and M_S. We wish A to satisfy

$$\mathbf{M}^2A = \lambda A \quad 9\cdot38$$

and we know in advance from 3·127 that λ is of the form $L(L+1)\dfrac{h^2}{4\pi^2}$. Since M_L has an integral value, L must also be integral. Substituting 9·37 into 9·38 gives

$$\mathbf{M}^2\sum_i c_iD_i = \lambda\sum_i c_iD_i$$

Multiplying through by each of the D_i^* in turn gives a set of equations analogous to 7·49

$$\sum_i(M_{ji}^2 - \lambda\delta_{ji})c_i = 0 \quad 9\cdot39$$

where $M_{ji}^2 = \displaystyle\int D_j^*\mathbf{M}^2D_i\,d\tau$. These equations are solved in the same way as 7·49.

Having found a set of A's which are eigenfunctions of $\mathbf{M}^2$, $\mathbf{M}_z$, and $\mathbf{S}_z$, we repeat this same process with $\mathbf{S}^2$ taking the place of $\mathbf{M}^2$. The resulting linear combinations of A's are then eigenfunctions of $\mathbf{M}^2$, $\mathbf{S}^2$, $\mathbf{M}_z$, and $\mathbf{S}_z$. We thus obtain a set of trial eigenfunctions B_i which satisfy the relations

$$\mathbf{M}^2 B_i = L_i(L_i + 1) \frac{h^2}{4\pi^2} B_i \qquad\qquad 9\cdot40$$

$$\mathbf{S}^2 B_i = S_i(S_i + 1) \frac{h^2}{4\pi^2} B_i \qquad\qquad 9\cdot41$$

$$\mathbf{M}_z B_i = M_{Li} \frac{h}{2\pi} B_i \qquad\qquad 9\cdot42$$

$$\mathbf{S}_z B_i = M_{S_i} \frac{h}{2\pi} B_i \qquad\qquad 9\cdot43$$

The final step is to use the B's (taking only a set with the same L, S, M_L, and M_S) in equation 9·21 to determine the approximate energy levels and eigenfunctions of $\mathbf{H}$. Before going into this last step in detail, we shall note some of the properties of the B functions.

The L and S values of a B function (or an energy level whose eigenfunction of $\mathbf{H}$ is a combination of B functions) is denoted by a capital letter showing the L value, the letter being chosen from the same code which is used in denoting the l value of an atomic orbital. The value of $2S + 1$, the multiplicity of the term or group of levels with the same L value, is placed as a left-hand superscript. Thus a B function with $L = 1$, $S = \frac{3}{2}$ is denoted by ^4P (quartet P); a B function with $L = 0$, $S = 0$ is denoted by ^1S (singlet S).

If any one of the B's is picked out, a set of associated B's can be found by applying the operators $(\mathbf{M}_x \pm i\mathbf{M}_y)$ and $(\mathbf{S}_x \pm i\mathbf{S}_y)$ to the original B function until no new functions arise. All the members of such a set will have the same L and S values but will have all the possible M_L and M_S values consistent with the L and S values. Such a set is known as a " term." If there is more than one term of a given L and S value arising from a given configuration, the B's arising from one of the B functions with a given M_L and M_S upon multiplication by $(\mathbf{M}_x \pm i\mathbf{M}_y)$ and $(\mathbf{S}_x \pm i\mathbf{S}_y)$ may not be the same as those found directly from perturbation theory. These may, however, always be combined in such a way that the terms do not get mixed. In future work we shall assume that this has been done.

Now let us consider a matrix component of H between any two B functions, $\int B_1^* \mathbf{H} B_2 \, d\tau$, where B_1 and B_2 have the same value of L, S,

M_L, and M_S. Let B_1' be the member of the term of B_1 derived from B_1 by the application of the operator $(\mathbf{M}_x + i\mathbf{M}_y)$, thus having an M_L value greater by 1 than B_1 has. Let B_2' be the corresponding function derived from B_2. Then from equations 3·133

$$B_1' = \frac{2\pi}{h} [L(L+1) - M_L(M_L+1)]^{-\frac{1}{2}} (\mathbf{M}_x + i\mathbf{M}_y)B_1$$

$$B_2' = \frac{2\pi}{h} [L(L+1) - M_L(M_L+1)]^{-\frac{1}{2}} (\mathbf{M}_x + i\mathbf{M}_y)B_2$$

The matrix element of $\mathbf{H}$ between B_1' and B_2' is

$$\int B_1'^* \mathbf{H} B_2' \, d\tau = \frac{4\pi^2}{h^2} [L(L+1) - M_L(M_L+1)]^{-1}$$

$$\int [(\mathbf{M}_x + i\mathbf{M}_y)B_1]^* \mathbf{H} (\mathbf{M}_x + i\mathbf{M}_y)B_2 \, d\tau$$

$$= \frac{4\pi^2}{h^2} [\cdots]^{-1} \int B_1^* \mathbf{H} (\mathbf{M}_x - i\mathbf{M}_y)(\mathbf{M}_x + i\mathbf{M}_y)B_2 \, d\tau$$

$$= \frac{4\pi^2}{h^2} [\cdots]^{-1} \int B_1^* \mathbf{H} (\mathbf{M}^2 - \mathbf{M}_z^2 - \frac{h}{2\pi} \mathbf{M}_z)B_2 \, d\tau$$

$$= \frac{4\pi^2}{h^2} [L(L+1) - M_L(M_L+1)]^{-1}[L(L+1) - M_L^2 - M_L]$$

$$\frac{h^2}{4\pi^2} \int B_1^* \mathbf{H} B_2 \, d\tau$$

$$= \int B_1^* \mathbf{H} B_2 \, d\tau$$

This same relation holds for all the members of the term. Hence if we use any set of B's belonging to a term, regardless of the M_L and M_S values, the matrix of $\mathbf{H}$ is the same, and therefore the approximate energy levels are the same. This is the reason that the M_L and M_S values of a B function are not specified.

As an illustration of the construction of B functions let us consider the configuration $(2p)^2$. The possible D functions are:

		M_L	M_S
D_1	$= D\{(211\frac{1}{2})(211\overline{\frac{1}{2}})\}$	2	0
D_2	$= D\{(211\frac{1}{2})(210\frac{1}{2})\}$	1	1
D_3	$= D\{(211\frac{1}{2})(210\overline{\frac{1}{2}})\}$	1	0
D_4	$= D\{(211\overline{\frac{1}{2}})(210\frac{1}{2})\}$	1	0
D_5	$= D\{(211\overline{\frac{1}{2}})(210\overline{\frac{1}{2}})\}$	1	-1

$$
\begin{array}{lcc}
 & M_L & M_S \\
D_6 = D\{(211\tfrac{1}{2})(21\bar{1}\tfrac{1}{2})\} & 0 & 1 \\
D_7 = D\{(211\tfrac{1}{2})(21\bar{1}\tfrac{\bar{1}}{2})\} & 0 & 0 \\
D_8 = D\{(211\tfrac{\bar{1}}{2})(21\bar{1}\tfrac{1}{2})\} & 0 & 0 \\
D_9 = D\{(210\tfrac{1}{2})(210\tfrac{\bar{1}}{2})\} & 0 & 0 \\
D_{10} = D\{(211\tfrac{\bar{1}}{2})(21\bar{1}\tfrac{\bar{1}}{2})\} & 0 & -1 \\
D_{11} = D\{(210\tfrac{1}{2})(21\bar{1}\tfrac{1}{2})\} & -1 & 1 \\
D_{12} = D\{(210\tfrac{1}{2})(21\bar{1}\tfrac{\bar{1}}{2})\} & -1 & 0 \\
D_{13} = D\{(210\tfrac{\bar{1}}{2})(21\bar{1}\tfrac{1}{2})\} & -1 & 0 \\
D_{14} = D\{(210\tfrac{\bar{1}}{2})(21\bar{1}\tfrac{\bar{1}}{2})\} & -1 & -1 \\
D_{15} = D\{(21\bar{1}\tfrac{1}{2})(21\bar{1}\tfrac{\bar{1}}{2})\} & -2 & 0 \\
\end{array}
$$

Since D_1 is the only D function with $M_L = 2$, $M_S = 0$, it must be a B function. Applying $\mathbf{M}^2$ and $\mathbf{S}^2$ to it, and using 9·33 and 9·34, we find

$$
\mathbf{M}^2 D_1 = \frac{h^2}{4\pi^2}(2 + 2 + 2)D_1 = 2(2 + 1)\frac{h^2}{4\pi^2}D_1
$$

$$
\mathbf{S}^2 D_1 = \frac{h^2}{4\pi^2}[\tfrac{3}{4}2 - \tfrac{1}{4}2]D\{(211\tfrac{1}{2})(211\tfrac{\bar{1}}{2})\}
$$

$$
+ (1)(1)(1)(1)D\{(211\tfrac{\bar{1}}{2})(211\tfrac{1}{2})\}
$$

and since $D\{(211\tfrac{\bar{1}}{2})(211\tfrac{1}{2})\} = -D_1$

$$
\mathbf{S}^2 D_1 = \frac{h^2}{4\pi^2}(D_1 - D_1) = 0(0 + 1)D_1
$$

we conclude, therefore, that, having $L = 2$, $S = 0$, D_1 is a B function belonging to a ^1D term.

As an example of the procedure when there is more than one D function with given M_L and M_S values, consider D_7, D_8, and D_9. Equation 9·33 gives

$$
\mathbf{M}^2 D_7 = 2\frac{h^2}{4\pi^2}D_7 + 2\frac{h^2}{4\pi^2}D_9
$$

$$
\mathbf{M}^2 D_8 = 2\frac{h^2}{4\pi^2}D_8 - 2\frac{h^2}{4\pi^2}D_9
$$

$$
\mathbf{M}^2 D_9 = 2\frac{h^2}{4\pi^2}D_7 - 2\frac{h^2}{4\pi^2}D_8 + 4\frac{h^2}{4\pi^2}D_9
$$

The secular equation for the eigenvalues is therefore

$$
\begin{vmatrix}
2 - L(L+1) & 0 & 2 \\
0 & 2 - L(L+1) & -2 \\
2 & -2 & 4 - L(L+1)
\end{vmatrix} = 0
$$

which is satisfied by $L = 0, 1,$ and 2.　For $L = 0$, equations 9·39 become

$$2c_1 + 2c_3 = 0$$

$$2c_2 - 2c_3 = 0$$

$$2c_1 - 2c_2 + 4c_3 = 0$$

which gives $c_1 : c_2 : c_3 = -1 : 1 : 1$.　Hence we put

$$A_7 = \frac{1}{\sqrt{3}} (-D_7 + D_8 + D_9)$$

choosing the magnitudes of the c's so that A_7 is normalized.　It is easily verified that A_7 is an eigenfunction of $\mathbf{M}^2$ with the eigenvalue zero.　In a similar way we find for $L = 1$

$$A_8 = \frac{1}{\sqrt{2}} (D_7 + D_8)$$

and for $L = 2$

$$A_9 = \frac{1}{\sqrt{6}} (D_7 - D_8 + 2D_9)$$

We now calculate $\mathbf{S}^2 D_7$, $\mathbf{S}^2 D_8$, and $\mathbf{S}^2 D_9$ by the use of equation 9·34.

$$\mathbf{S}^2 D_7 = \frac{h^2}{4\pi^2} D_7 + \frac{h^2}{4\pi^2} D_8$$

$$\mathbf{S}^2 D_8 = \frac{h^2}{4\pi^2} D_7 + \frac{h^2}{4\pi^2} D_8$$

$$\mathbf{S}^2 D_9 = 0$$

Hence

$$\mathbf{S}^2 A_7 = 0; \quad \mathbf{S}^2 A_8 = 1(1 + 1) \frac{h^2}{4\pi^2} A_8; \quad \mathbf{S}^2 A_9 = 0$$

It follows that A_7, A_8, and A_9 are eigenfunctions of $\mathbf{S}^2$ and may be used immediately as B functions.　$B_7 = A_7$ belongs to a ^1S term; $B_8 = A_8$ belongs to a ^3P term; and $B_9 = A_9$ belongs to a ^1D term.　The complete list of B functions is found to be

(^1D)　$B_1 = D_1$　　　　　　　　　　(^1D)　$B_9 = \frac{1}{\sqrt{6}} (D_7 - D_8 + 2D_9)$

(^3P)　$B_2 = D_2$　　　　　　　　　　(^3P)　$B_{10} = D_{10}$

(^3P)　$B_3 = \frac{1}{\sqrt{2}} (D_3 + D_4)$　　　　(^3P)　$B_{11} = D_{11}$

$$(^1D) \quad B_4 = \frac{1}{\sqrt{2}} (D_3 - D_4) \qquad\qquad (^3P) \quad B_{12} = \frac{1}{\sqrt{2}} (D_{12} + D_{13})$$

$$(^3P) \quad B_5 = D_5 \qquad\qquad\qquad\quad (^1D) \quad B_{13} = \frac{1}{\sqrt{2}} (D_{12} - D_{13})$$

$$(^3P) \quad B_6 = D_6 \qquad\qquad\qquad\quad (^3P) \quad B_{14} = D_{14}$$

$$(^1S) \quad B_7 = \frac{1}{\sqrt{3}} (-D_7 + D_8 + D_9) \quad (^1D) \quad B_{15} = D_{15}$$

$$(^3P) \quad B_8 = \frac{1}{\sqrt{2}} (D_7 + D_8)$$

By operating with $(\mathbf{M}_x \pm i\mathbf{M}_y)$ and $(\mathbf{S}_x \pm i\mathbf{S}_y)$ on these functions we find that all the ^1D B functions belonging to a single term. In the same way the ^3P B functions form a term, and the single ^1S B function represents a complete term.

A configuration representing a closed shell has been seen to have only a single D function. This D function is always a B function of the type ^1S, having $L = 0$ and $S = 0$. If we compare the D functions arising from a configuration which includes one or more closed shells with the D functions arising from the configuration obtained by omitting the closed shells, we find that their properties are the same for operations with the operators $\mathbf{M}^2$, $\mathbf{S}^2$, $\mathbf{M}_z$, etc. The terms arising from these configurations are therefore the same. Hence, in the treatment of any atom, the closed shells may be omitted during the processes described in this section. Thus our example of the configuration $(2p)^2$ serves as well for the configuration $(1s)^2(2s)^2(2p)^2$ of the carbon atom.

9g. Calculation of the Energy Matrix. The matrix H_{ij} of equations 9·21 is formed from integrals of the type

$$H_{ij} = \int B_i^* \mathbf{H} B_j \, d\tau$$

Since the B's are linear combinations of the D functions, these integrals may be expressed in terms of the integrals

$$H_{ij}' = \int D_i^* \mathbf{H} D_j \, d\tau$$

Let us therefore consider this integral, taking as D_i

$$D_i = \frac{1}{\sqrt{N!}} \left| \varphi(a_1'|1)\varphi(a_2'|2) \cdots \right| \qquad\qquad 9\cdot44$$

and as D_j

$$D_j = \frac{1}{\sqrt{N!}} \left| \varphi(a_1''|1)\varphi(a_2''|2) \cdots \right| \qquad 9\text{·}45$$

where we have abbreviated the sets of quantum numbers n, l, m, s to the single symbol a, and N is the number of electrons in the configuration. If the determinants are expanded, 9·44 and 9·45 become

$$D_i = \frac{1}{\sqrt{N!}} \sum_{\nu=1}^{n} (-1)^\nu P_\nu \{\varphi(a_1'|1)\varphi(a_2'|2) \cdots\} \qquad 9\text{·}46$$

$$D_j = \frac{1}{\sqrt{N!}} \sum_{\nu=1}^{n} (-1)^\nu P_\nu \{\varphi(a_1''|1)\varphi(a_2''|2) \cdots\} \qquad 9\text{·}47$$

where P_ν is an operator which permutes the variables $1, 2, 3, \cdots$ among themselves, and ν is the ordinal number of the permutations. H_{ij}' may then be written

$$H_{ij}' = \left[\frac{1}{N!} \int \sum_\mu \sum_\nu (-1)^\mu P_\mu \{\varphi(a_1'|1)\varphi(a_2'|2) \cdots\} \right]^*$$
$$H[(-1)^\nu P_\nu \{\varphi(a_1''|1)\varphi(a_2''|2) \cdots\}] \, d\tau \qquad 9\text{·}48$$

Since all the variables are integrated out in each of the terms in this expression, we may interchange them in any way that we wish without changing the values of the integrals, provided that all the functions in any one integral have their variables changed in the same way. Suppose, therefore, that in each of the terms in 9·48 we change the variables by the permutation P_μ^{-1} which restores the order of the variables in the first product to the normal order. Then

$$H_{ij}' = \frac{1}{N!} \sum_\mu \sum_\nu \int [\{\varphi(a_1'|1)\varphi(a_2'|2) \cdots \}]^*$$
$$H[(-1)^\nu P_\mu^{-1} P_\nu \{\varphi(a_1''|1)\varphi(a_2''|2) \cdots \}] \, d\tau \qquad 9\text{·}49$$

since H is not changed by permuting the variables. If we now sum over μ we find that all the terms in the sum are equal, for the application of P_μ^{-1} to the whole set of permutations P_ν gives the same set in a different order. Since there are $N!$ permutations P_μ^{-1}, we find

$$H_{ij}' = \sum_\nu \int \{\varphi(a_1'|1)\varphi(a_2'|2) \cdots \}^*$$
$$H(-1)^\nu P_\nu \{\varphi(a_1''|1)\varphi(a_2''|2) \cdots \} \, d\tau \qquad 9\text{·}50$$

The last product in this expression is of the form

$$(-1)^\nu \varphi(a_1^\nu|1)\varphi(a_2^\nu|2) \cdots$$

where the a_i^ν are the same as the a_i'', or at most in some new order.

If we put

$$-\frac{h^2}{8\pi^2 m}\nabla_i^2 - \frac{Ze^2}{r_i} = \mathbf{U}_i \qquad \frac{e^2}{r_{ij}} = \mathbf{V}_{ij}$$

equation 9·50 becomes

$$H'_{ij} = \sum_k \sum_\nu (-1)^\nu \int \{\varphi^*(a'_1|1)\varphi^*(a'_2|2) \cdots \}\mathbf{U}_k\{\varphi(a_1^\nu|1)\varphi(a_2^\nu|2) \cdots \} \, d\tau$$

$$+ \sum_{l<k} \sum_\nu (-1)^\nu \int \{\varphi^*(a'_1|1)\varphi^*(a'_2|2) \cdots \}$$
$$\mathbf{V}_{kl}\{\varphi(a_1^\nu|1)\varphi(a_2^\nu|2) \cdots \} \, d\tau \quad 9\cdot51$$

Since $\mathbf{U}_k$ is a function only of the coordinates of the kth electron, we may now integrate over all the variables in the first of these integrals except those of the kth electron. The result is

$$(-1)^\nu U(a'_k, a_k^\nu) = (-1)^\nu \int \varphi^*(a'_k|k)\mathbf{U}_k\varphi(a_k^\nu|k) \, d\tau \qquad 9\cdot52$$

if $a_i^\nu = a'_i$ for all i except $i = k$. Otherwise the integral will vanish because of the orthogonality of the orbitals. But if one of the $\mathbf{P}_\mu$ makes all the a_i^ν except one equal to the corresponding a'_i, then any other permutation $\mathbf{P}_\mu$ will destroy this equality, since no two a_i^ν are equal. Hence only one term in the summation over ν will remain. If we now sum over k, we find the total contribution of $\mathbf{U}_k$ to H'_{ij}. This contribution is

(a) $\sum_k U(a'_k, a'_k)$ if $D_i = D_j$.

(b) $U(a'_i, a''_i)$ if D_j differs from D_i only in that $a'_i \neq a''_i$.

(c) If, by permuting the order of the orbitals in D_j by a permutation $\mathbf{P}$, D_j may be made to satisfy the conditions of (a) or of (b), then the contribution is that of (a) or (b) times $+1$ if the permutation is even, or times -1 if the permutation is odd.

(d) If two or more orbitals of D_j are different from those of D_i, there is no contribution.

Rule (a) is a consequence of the orthogonality of the orbitals and the fact that no term in H involves the coordinates of more than two electrons. In the second integral of 9·51, we integrate first over all the coordinates except those of the kth and lth electrons. This integration gives zero unless every $a'_i = a_i^\nu$ except for $i = k$ and $i = l$, when it becomes

$$(-1)^\nu V(a'_k, a'_l; a_k^\nu, a_l^\nu)$$
$$= (-1)^\nu \int \varphi^*(a'_k|k)\varphi^*(a'_l|l)\mathbf{V}_{kl}\varphi(a_k^\nu|k)\varphi(a_l^\nu|l) \, d\tau \qquad 9\cdot53$$

In considering the various permutations $\mathbf{P}_\nu$, we see that, if any $\mathbf{P}_\nu$ gives a set of a_i^ν such that $a_i^\nu = a_i'$ except for $i = k, l$, then any other permutation will destroy this property except the permutation which differs from this $\mathbf{P}_\nu$ only in the interchange of l and k. The sum over ν therefore gives only two terms. Summation over k and l now leads to the following rules for determining the contribution of $\mathbf{V}_{kl}$ to H_{ij}'. This contribution is

(a) $\sum\limits_{l<k} \{V(a_k', a_l'; a_k', a_l') - V(a_k', a_l'; a_l', a_k')\}$ if $D_j = D_i$.

(b) $\sum\limits_{k \neq m} \{V(a_k', a_m'; a_k', a_m'') - V(a_k', a_m'; a_m'', a_k')\}$ if D_j differs from D_i only in that $a_m' \neq a_m''$.

(c) $V(a_m', a_n'; a_m'', a_n'') - V(a_m', a_n'; a_n'', a_m'')$ if D_j differs from D_i in that $a_m' \neq a_m''$ and $a_n' \neq a_n''$ but is otherwise the same.

(d) That of (a), (b), or (c), if, by permuting the a_i'', D_j can be made to obey the conditions of (a), (b), or (c), times $+1$ if the permutation is even, or times -1 if the permutation is odd.

(e) Zero if D_j contains three φ's different from those of D_i.

Since neither $\mathbf{U}_k$ nor $\mathbf{V}_{kl}$ depends on the spin coordinates of the orbitals, these coordinates may be integrated out of the expressions for $\mathbf{U}_k$ and $\mathbf{V}_{kl}$. Using the orthogonality properties of α and β we see at once that $U(a_1, a_2) = 0$ if $s_1 \neq s_2$ and that $V(a_1, a_2; a_3, a_4) = 0$ unless $s_1 = s_3$ and $s_2 = s_4$.

As the operators $\mathbf{U}_k$ do not depend on the θ or φ coordinates of the electrons, these may also be integrated out of 9·52. If we put

$$\varphi(nlms|i) = R(nl|i)Y(lm|i)\begin{Bmatrix}(\alpha)\\(\beta)\end{Bmatrix} \qquad 9\cdot54$$

then

$$U(n_1 l_1 m_1 s_1; n_2 l_2 m_2 s_2)$$

$$= \int R^*(n_1 l_1|1)\mathbf{U}_1 R(n_2 l_2|1)Y^*(l_1 m_1|1)Y(l_2 m_2|1)\begin{Bmatrix}\alpha_1^*\\\beta_1^*\end{Bmatrix}\begin{Bmatrix}\alpha_2\\\beta_2\end{Bmatrix} d\tau$$

$$= I(n_1 l_1; n_2 l_2)\int Y^*(l_1 m_1|1)Y(l_2 m_2|1)\sin\theta\, d\theta\, d\varphi\, \delta(s_1, s_2) \qquad 9\cdot55$$

where

$$I(n_1 l_1; n_2 l_2) = \int R^*(n_1 l_1|1)\mathbf{U}_1 R(n_2 l_2|1)r^2\, dr \qquad 9\cdot56$$

and where $\delta(s_1, s_2) = 1$ if $s_1 = s_2$; $= 0$ otherwise. Because of the orthogonality of the Y's, the integral

$$\int Y^*(l_1 m_1|1)Y(l_2 m_2|1)\sin\theta\, d\theta\, d\varphi$$

vanishes unless $l_1 = l_2$ and $m_1 = m_2$, in which case it is unity. Hence
$$U(n_1 l_1 m_1 s_1;\ n_2 l_2 m_2 s_2)$$
$$= I(n_1 l_1;\ n_2 l_2)\ \delta(l_1, l_2)\ \delta(m_1, m_2)\ \delta(s_1, s_2) \qquad 9\cdot 57$$

Since $\mathbf{V}_{kl}$ involves $\dfrac{1}{r_{kl}}$, which depends on the variables θ and φ, we cannot integrate out these variables in $V(a_1 a_2,\ a_3 a_4)$ directly. If, however, we use the expansion of $\dfrac{1}{r_{kl}}$ as given in Appendix V, we find, after integrating out the spins,

$$V(n_1 l_1 m_1 s_1;\ n_2 l_2 m_2 s_2;\ n_3 l_3 m_3 s_3;\ n_4 l_4 m_4 s_4)$$

$$= \sum_{l,m} \frac{4\pi}{2l+1} \left\{ \int\!\!\int R^*(n_1 l_1 | 1) R^*(n_2 l_2 | 2) \frac{r_<^l}{r_>^{l+1}} R(n_3 l_3 | 1) \right.$$
$$R(n_4 l_4 | 1) r_1^2 r_2^2\, dr_1\, dr_2 \times$$

$$\int\!\!\int Y^*(l_1 m_1 | \theta_1 \varphi_1) Y(l_3 m_3 | \theta_1 \varphi_1) Y^*(lm | \theta_1 \varphi_1) \sin\theta_1\, d\theta_1\, d\varphi_1 \times$$

$$\left. \int\!\!\int Y^*(l_2 m_2 | \theta_2 \varphi_2) Y(l_4 m_4 | \theta_2 \varphi_2) Y(lm | \theta_2 \varphi_2) \sin\theta_2\, d\theta_2\, d\varphi_2 \right\} \times$$
$$\delta(s_1 s_3)\ \delta(s_2 s_4) \qquad 9\cdot 58$$

The integrals vanish unless $m = m_3 - m_1 = m_2 - m_4$, so that the summation over m is reduced to a single term. The remaining integral over the angles is of the form of a product of two integrals which we denote by

$$c_k(l_1 m_1;\ l_2 m_2)$$
$$= \left\{ \frac{4\pi}{2k+1} \right\}^{\frac{1}{2}} \int Y^*(l_1 m_1 | \theta\varphi) Y(lm | \theta\varphi) Y(l_2 m_2 | \theta\varphi) \sin\theta\, d\theta\, d\varphi$$

where $m = m_1 - m_2$. Now unless $m_1 + m_2 = m_3 + m_4$ in equation 9·58 it is impossible to find an m such that $m = m_3 - m_1 = m_2 - m_4$. Hence $V(n_1 \cdots) = 0$ unless $m_1 + m_2 = m_3 + m_4$, and of course $s_1 = s_3;\ s_2 = s_4$. When these conditions are fulfilled

$$V(n_1 l_1 m_1 s_1;\ n_2 l_2 m_2 s_2;\ n_3 l_3 m_3 s_3;\ n_4 l_4 m_4 s_4)$$
$$= \sum c_l^*(l_3 m_3;\ l_1 m_1) c_l(l_2 m_2;\ l_4 m_4) R_l(n_1 l_1,\ n_2 l_2;\ n_3 l_3,\ n_4 l_4) \qquad 9\cdot 59$$

where

$$R_l(n_1 l_1,\ \cdots n_4 l_4) = \int\!\!\int R^*(n_1 l_1 | 1) R^*(n_2 l_2 | 2) \frac{r_<^l}{r_>^{l+1}}$$
$$R(n_3 l_3 | 1) R(n_4 l_4 | 2) r_1^2 r_2^2\, dr_1\, dr_2 \qquad 9\cdot 60$$

The integrals $I(n_1l_1; n_2l_2)$ and $R_l(n_1l_1, n_2l_2; n_3l_3, n_4l_4)$ cannot be evaluated unless the forms of the φ's are known, so that we have reduced the calculation of H'_{ij} to its simplest form.

To summarize the procedure for calculating H'_{ij}, there are four steps:

1. We are given two D functions, $D(a'_1, a'_2, a'_3, \cdots)$ and $D(a''_1, a''_2, a''_3 \cdots)$. We first permute the sets of quantum numbers a''_1, a''_2, $\cdots$ until as many sets a''_i as possible are identical with the corresponding sets a'_i. If the permutation which effects this arrangement is an odd permutation, we multiply the result by -1.

2. We now express H'_{ij} in terms of the $U(a_i, a_j)$ and $V(a_i, a_j; a_k, a_l)$. There are four cases:

(a) After the permutation, the two D functions are identical. Then

$$H'_{ij} = \sum_k U(a_k, a_k) + \sum_{k<l}\{V(a_k, a_l; a_k, a_l) - V(a_k, a_l; a_l, a_k)\} \quad 9\cdot 61$$

(b) After the permutation the two D functions are identical except for one set of quantum numbers, say the kth, so that $a'_k \neq a''_k$. Then

$$H'_{ij} = U(a'_k, a''_k) + \sum_{l\neq k}\{V(a'_k, a_l; a''_k, a_l) - V(a'_k, a_l; a_l, a''_k)\} \quad 9\cdot 62$$

(c) After the permutation the two D functions differ in two sets of quantum numbers, say $a'_k = a''_k$ and $a'_l \neq a''_l$. Then

$$H'_{ij} = V(a'_k, a'_l; a''_k, a''_l) - V(a'_k, a'_l; a''_l, a''_k) \quad 9\cdot 63$$

(d) After the permutation, the two D functions differ in more than two sets of quantum numbers. The contribution to H'_{ij} is then zero.

3. The $U(a_i, a_j)$ and $V(a_ia_j; a_ka_l)$ are expressed in terms of the integrals $I(n_il_i, n_jl_j)$ and $R_l(n_il_i, n_jl_j; n_kl_k, n_ll_l)$. We have

$$U(a_ia_j) = I(n_il_i; n_jl_j)\,\delta(l_i, l_j)\,\delta(m_i, m_j)\,\delta(s_i, s_j)$$

$$V(a_1a_2; a_3a_4) = \sum_l c_l^*(l_3m_3, l_1m_1)c_l(l_2m_2, l_4m_4)$$
$$R_l(n_1l_1, n_2l_2; n_3l_3; n_4l_4)\,\delta(s_1, s_3)\,\delta(s_2, s_4)$$
$$\delta(m_1 + m_2, m_3 + m_4) \quad 9\cdot 64$$

4. The integrals $I(n_il_i; n_jl_j)$ and $R(n_il_i \cdots)$ are evaluated and the results for H_{ij} are substituted in 9·21. The integrals S_{ij} are equal to δ_{ij}, since the D's and B's are orthogonal.

In most of the calculations of this type it will be necessary to calculate only diagonal elements for the energy matrix. This will be the matrix element between one D function and itself, so that we have case 2a.

The energy matrix in this case may be written quite simply as

$$H_{ii} = \sum_k I(a_k, a_k) + \sum_{k<l} J(k, l) - \sum_{k<l} K(k, l) \qquad 9\text{·}65$$

where the " coulombic " integral $J(k, l)$ is defined as

$$J(k, l) = V(a_k a_l;\ a_k a_l) = \sum_l a^l(a_k, a_l) F^l(a_k, a_l) \qquad 9\text{·}66$$

and the " exchange " integral $K(k, l)$ is defined as

$$K(k, l) = V(a_k, a_l;\ a_l, a_k) = \delta(s_k, s_l) \sum_l b^l(a_k, a_l) G^l(a_k, a_l) \qquad 9\text{·}67$$

where

$$a^l(a_k, a_l) = c_l^*(a_k, a_k) c_l(a_l, a_l)$$
$$b^l(a_k, a_l) = c_l^*(a_l, a_k) c_l(a_l, a_k)$$
$$F^l(a_k, a_l) = R_l(a_k a_l;\ a_k a_l)$$
$$G^l(a_k, a_l) = R_l(a_k a_l;\ a_l a_k)$$

In Tables 9·1 and 9·2 are listed the values of the a's and b's for states involving s and p electrons. Values of the c's, as well as more complete tables for the a's and b's, may be found in Condon and Shortley.[6]

As an example of these rules, let us calculate the energies of the terms arising from the configuration $(2p)^2$. Referring to the list of B functions for this configuration, we see that the secular equation has the form

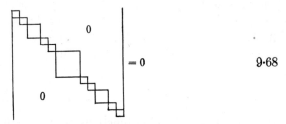

$$= 0 \qquad 9\text{·}68$$

including eight determinants of the first order, two of the second, and one of the third. Now D_1 is a B function corresponding to the ^1D term, so that the energy of this term is immediately given by the root of the determinant in the upper left-hand corner as

$$E(^1D) = H_{11}' \qquad 9\text{·}69$$

Similarly, the energy of the ^3P term is immediately given as

$$E(^3P) = H_{22}' \qquad 9\text{·}70$$

[6] E. U. Condon and G. H. Shortley, *Theory of Atomic Spectra*, Cambridge University Press, p. 178, 1935.

TABLE 9·1

$$a^l(l, m; l', m')$$

ELECTRON CONFIGURATION	l	m	l'	m'	a^0	a^2
ss	0	0	0	0	1	0
sp	0	0	1	±1	1	0
	0	0	1	0	1	0
pp	1	±1	1	±1	1	$\frac{1}{25}$
	1	±1	1	0	1	$-\frac{2}{25}$
	1	0	1	0	1	$\frac{4}{25}$

The remaining a's are zero for s and p electrons.

TABLE 9·2

$$b^l(l, m; l', m')$$

ELECTRON CONFIGURATION	l	m	l'	m'	b^0	b^1	b^2
ss	0	0	0	0	1	0	0
sp	0	0	1	±1	0	$\frac{1}{3}$	0
	0	0	1	0	0	$\frac{1}{3}$	0
pp	1	$+1$	1	$+1$	1	0	$\frac{1}{25}$
	1	-1	1	-1	1	0	$\frac{1}{25}$
	1	±1	1	0	0	0	$\frac{3}{25}$
	1	$+1$	1	-1	0	0	$\frac{6}{25}$
	1	0	1	0	1	0	$\frac{4}{25}$

The energy of the ^1S term will be given by one of the roots of the third-order determinant. The other two roots of this determinant correspond to the ^1D and ^3P terms. Now the sum of the roots of a determinant is equal to the sum of the terms on the principal diagonal, so that the energy of the ^1S term is given as

$$E(^1S) = H'_{77} + H'_{88} + H'_{99} - H'_{11} - H'_{22} \qquad 9·71$$

Referring to the list of D functions, we readily find, by means of equations 9·65–9·67 and Tables 9·1 and 9·2 that the pertinent matrix components of H are

$$H'_{11} = 2I(2, 1; 2, 1) + F^0(2, 1; 2, 1) + \tfrac{1}{25}F^2(2, 1; 2, 1)$$

$$H'_{22} = 2I(2, 1; 2, 1) + F^0(2, 1; 2, 1) - \tfrac{2}{25}F^2(2, 1; 2, 1) \\ - \tfrac{3}{25}G^2(2, 1; 2, 1)$$

$$H'_{77} = 2I(2, 1; 2, 1) + F^0(2, 1; 2, 1) + \tfrac{1}{25}F^2(2, 1; 2, 1)$$

$$H'_{88} = 2I(2, 1; 2, 1) + F^0(2, 1; 2, 1) + \tfrac{1}{25}F^2(2, 1; 2, 1)$$

$$H'_{99} = 2I(2, 1; 2, 1) + F^0(2, 1; 2, 1) + \tfrac{4}{25}F^2(2, 1; 2, 1)$$

from which we calculate the energies for the various terms to be

$$E(^1D) = 2I(2, 1;\ 2, 1) + F^0(2, 1;\ 2, 1) + \tfrac{1}{25}F^2(2, 1;\ 2, 1) \qquad 9\cdot72$$

$$E(^3P) = 2I(2, 1;\ 2, 1) + F^0(2, 1;\ 2, 1) - \tfrac{2}{25}F^2(2, 1;\ 2, 1)$$
$$- \tfrac{3}{25}G^2(2, 1;\ 2, 1) \qquad 9\cdot73$$

$$E(^1S) = 2I(2, 1;\ 2, 1) + F^0(2, 1;\ 2, 1) + \tfrac{7}{25}F^2(2, 1;\ 2, 1)$$
$$+ \tfrac{3}{25}G^2(2, 1;\ 2, 1) \qquad 9\cdot74$$

It is, of course, impossible to make an exact comparison of theory with experiment without evaluating the integrals for a particular choice of trial eigenfunctions. It is, however, possible to make some qualitative calculations. As the integrals F and G are positive quantities, we see that the orders of the levels will be ^3P, ^1D, ^1S, with the ^3P the lowest. This is in accord with Hund's rule in atomic spectroscopy: Of the terms arising from a given electron configuration the term with the highest multiplicity will lie lowest; of terms with the same multiplicity, the one with the highest L value will lie lowest. For equivalent electrons, $F^l(n1,\ n1) = G^l(n1,\ n1)$. For the electron configuration $(np)^2$, our results state that

$$\frac{E(^1S) - E(^1D)}{E(^1D) - E(^3P)} = \frac{\tfrac{6}{25}F^2 + \tfrac{3}{25}G^2}{\tfrac{3}{25}F^2 + \tfrac{3}{25}G^2} = \frac{3}{2} \qquad 9\cdot75$$

For the atoms C, Si, Ge, Sn, all having this electron configuration, Condon and Shortley give the values for this ratio as 1.13, 1.48, 1.50, 1.39, respectively, although for certain other atoms having this same configuration the agreement is less satisfactory. Although this method of approach by no means gives exact quantitative results, it does give the number and type of terms correctly, and usually the relative positions of these terms are qualitatively correct.

9h. Fine Structure. To the approximation we have been considering, we have seen that the various B functions of a term all have the same energy. If, however, we add to our Hamiltonian operator the terms representing the interaction between the magnetic dipoles associated with the motions of the electrons in their orbits and the magnetic dipoles associated with the spin of the electron, this is no longer true.

We can determine the general form of this " spin-orbit " interaction by the following argument. Consider an electron moving about a nucleus of charge $Z|e|$ at a distance r. The electric field at the electron will be $\mathbf{E} = \dfrac{Z|e|}{r^3}\mathbf{r}$. If the electron is moving with a velocity $\mathbf{v}$, it will be subjected to the action of a magnetic field of strength

$$\mathbf{H} = \frac{\mathbf{E} \times \mathbf{v}}{c} = \frac{Z|e|}{cr^3} \mathbf{r} \times \mathbf{v} = \frac{Z|e|}{mcr^3} \mathbf{M} \qquad 9 \cdot 76$$

where $\mathbf{M}$ is the angular momentum of the electron. The classical energy of a dipole in a magnetic field is $-\boldsymbol{\mu} \cdot \mathbf{H}$, so that the energy correction should be

$$H' = - \frac{Z|e|}{mcr^3} \mathbf{M} \cdot \boldsymbol{\mu}$$

A more careful analysis,[7] including a relativity correction, shows that this expression should be reduced by a factor $\frac{1}{2}$. Since $\mu_x = - \frac{|e|}{mc} S_x$, etc., the spin-orbit interaction thus contributes a term to the Hamiltonian ·

$$\mathbf{H}' = \sum_i \frac{1}{2m^2c^2} \frac{Ze^2}{r_i^3} (\mathbf{M}_{xi}\mathbf{S}_{xi} + \mathbf{M}_{yi}\mathbf{S}_{yi} + \mathbf{M}_{zi}\mathbf{S}_{zi}) \qquad 9 \cdot 77$$

For the more general case of a non-coulomb field, the term $\frac{Ze^2}{r_i^3}$ will be replaced by $\frac{1}{r_i} \frac{\partial V(r_i)}{\partial r_i}$, so that we obtain for the spin-orbit interaction operator the result

$$\mathbf{H}' = \sum_i \frac{1}{2m^2c^2} \left\{ \frac{1}{r_i} \frac{\partial V(r_i)}{\partial r_i} \right\} (\mathbf{M}_{xi}\mathbf{S}_{xi} + \mathbf{M}_{yi}\mathbf{S}_{yi} + \mathbf{M}_{zi}\mathbf{S}_{zi}) \qquad 9 \cdot 78$$

This operator commutes with $\mathbf{J}^2$ and $\mathbf{J}_z$, but not with $\mathbf{M}^2$, $\mathbf{S}^2$ or their components. The eigenfunctions of the complete Hamiltonian will not therefore be eigenfunctions of $\mathbf{M}^2$, $\mathbf{S}^2$, $\mathbf{M}_z$, or $\mathbf{S}_z$. If, however, the term $\mathbf{H}'$ is small compared to the other terms in the Hamiltonian, the energy levels of the complete Hamiltonian will approximate those of the approximate Hamiltonian which we have previously considered. Therefore each term will break up into a number of energy levels whose energies will be close to that of the unperturbed term. The eigenfunctions corresponding to these energy levels will be approximately represented by linear combinations of the B functions corresponding to the unperturbed terms.

Since $\mathbf{J}^2$ and $\mathbf{J}_z$ commute with the complete Hamiltonian, the final eigenfunctions of $\mathbf{H}$ must also be eigenfunctions of those operators with eigenvalues of the form $J(J+1) \frac{h^2}{4\pi^2}$ for $\mathbf{J}^2$ and $M \frac{h}{2\pi}$ for $\mathbf{J}_z$. If we

[7] E. Kemble, *Fundamental Principles of Quantum Mechanics*, p. 502, McGraw-Hill Book Company, 1937.

represent the final eigenfunctions of **H** by $C(J, M)$, we must therefore have

$$\mathbf{J}^2 C(J, M) = J(J + 1) \frac{h^2}{4\pi^2} C(J, M) \qquad 9\cdot79$$

$$\mathbf{J}_z C(J, M) = M \frac{h}{2\pi} C(J, M) \qquad 9\cdot80$$

Since $\mathbf{J}_z = \mathbf{M}_z + \mathbf{S}_z$, the B functions involved in $C(J, M)$ must have $M_L + M_S = M$, since there is but one B function with a given M_L and M_S value. We may label the B functions by their M_L and M_S value as $B(M_L, M_S)$, so that the C's must have the form

$$C(J, M) = \sum k(M_L, M_S) B(M_L, M_S) \qquad 9\cdot81$$

where $k(M_L, M_S)$ is a constant.

The values of the constants k are most easily found by means of the operators

$$\mathbf{J}_x \pm i\mathbf{J}_y = \mathbf{M}_x \pm i\mathbf{M}_y + \mathbf{S}_x \pm i\mathbf{S}_y$$

We have

$$(\mathbf{J}_x \pm i\mathbf{J}_y) C(J, M) = \sum k(M_L, M_S)(\mathbf{M}_x \pm i\mathbf{M}_y) B(M_L, M_S)$$
$$+ \sum k(M_L, M_S)(\mathbf{S}_x \pm i\mathbf{S}_y) B(M_L, M_S)$$

from which

$$[J(J + 1) - M(M \pm 1)]^{\frac{1}{2}} C(J, M \pm 1)$$
$$= \sum k(M_L, M_S)[L(L + 1) - M_L(M_L \pm 1)]^{\frac{1}{2}} B(M_L \pm 1, M_S)$$
$$+ \sum k(M_L, M_S)[S(S + 1) - M_S(M_S \pm 1)]^{\frac{1}{2}} B(M_L, M_S \pm 1) \quad 9\cdot82$$

and therefore, from a knowledge of $C(J, M)$, equation 9·82 gives $C(J, M \pm 1)$ and hence all C's with the same J value.

The highest value of M is $M = L + S$, and there is only one B function with this value of $M_L + M_S$. Moreover, there is no B function with a greater value of M. Hence if $J = L + S$

$$C(J, J) = B(L, S)$$

and by 9·82 all the $C(J, M)$ with $J = L + S$ can be found. In particular, $C(J, J - 1)$ is found as a linear combination of $B(L - 1, S)$ and $B(L, S - 1)$. Now $C(J', J')$, where $J' = L + S - 1$, must also be a linear combination of the same two B functions; in addition it must be orthogonal to $C(J, J - 1)$. We therefore put

$$C(J', J') = k_1' B(L - 1, S) + k_2' B(L, S - 1)$$

If

$$C(J, J - 1) = k_1 B(L - 1, S) + k_2 B(L, S - 1)$$

the orthogonality condition is, since the B's are normalized and orthogonal,

$$k_1 k_1' + k_2 k_2' = 0 \qquad 9\cdot83$$

which, with the condition $k_1'^2 + k_2'^2 = 1$, determines k_1' and k_2'. Having determined $C(J', J')$ we now determine all the $C(J', M)$ by 9·82. We may now determine $C(J'', J'')$, where $J'' = L + S - 2$, by finding that combination of $B(L - 2, S)$, $B(L - 1, S - 1)$, and $B(L, S - 2)$ which is orthogonal to $C(J, J - 2)$ and $C(J', J' - 1)$. This in turn gives all the $C(J'', M)$. This process is continued until $2S + 1$ or $2L + 1$, whichever is smaller, sets of functions have been found, with the J values $|L + S|$, $|L + S| - 1 \cdots |L - S|$. If we attempt to carry the process beyond this point, we find that the number of B functions corresponding to $M = J^{(n+1)}$ is only $2x + 1$, where x is the smaller of L and S, and we already have $(2x + 1)$ $C(J^{(n)}, M)$'s. It is therefore impossible to find a new linear combination of B's which is orthogonal to the linear combinations already found.

To illustrate this process, let us consider a ^2P term, so that $L = 1$, $S = \frac{1}{2}$. The B functions are $B(1, \frac{1}{2})$, $B(1, -\frac{1}{2})$, $B(0, \frac{1}{2})$, $B(0, -\frac{1}{2})$, $B(-1, \frac{1}{2})$, $B(-1, -\frac{1}{2})$. The process therefore starts with $C(\frac{3}{2}, \frac{3}{2}) = B(1, \frac{1}{2})$. Equation 9·82 (with the lower signs) then gives

$$C(\tfrac{3}{2}, \tfrac{3}{2}) = B(1, \tfrac{1}{2})$$
$$C(\tfrac{3}{2}, \tfrac{1}{2}) = \sqrt{\tfrac{2}{3}} B(0, \tfrac{1}{2}) + \sqrt{\tfrac{1}{3}} B(1, -\tfrac{1}{2})$$
$$C(\tfrac{3}{2}, -\tfrac{1}{2}) = \sqrt{\tfrac{1}{3}} B(-1, \tfrac{1}{2}) + \sqrt{\tfrac{2}{3}} B(0, -\tfrac{1}{2})$$
$$C(\tfrac{3}{2}, -\tfrac{3}{2}) = B(-1, -\tfrac{1}{2})$$

We now put

$$C(\tfrac{1}{2}, \tfrac{1}{2}) = k_1 B(0, \tfrac{1}{2}) + k_2 B(1, -\tfrac{1}{2})$$

and 9·83 gives for orthogonality to $C(\frac{3}{2}, \frac{1}{2})$

$$\sqrt{\tfrac{2}{3}} k_1 + \sqrt{\tfrac{1}{3}} k_2 = 0; \quad k_2 = -\sqrt{2} k_1$$

The values $k_1 = \sqrt{\frac{1}{3}}$ and $k_2 = -\sqrt{\frac{2}{3}}$ satisfy this as well as the relation $k_1^2 + k_2^2 = 1$. Hence

$$C(\tfrac{1}{2}, \tfrac{1}{2}) = \sqrt{\tfrac{1}{3}} B(0, \tfrac{1}{2}) - \sqrt{\tfrac{2}{3}} B(1, -\tfrac{1}{2})$$

If we apply 9·82 again, we obtain

$$C(\tfrac{1}{2}, -\tfrac{1}{2}) = \sqrt{\tfrac{2}{3}} B(-1, \tfrac{1}{2}) - \sqrt{\tfrac{1}{3}} B(0, -\tfrac{1}{2})$$

We have now formed six C functions out of the six B functions, and no more linear combinations can be made. The process is therefore complete.

The energy levels derived from the C functions are dependent only on J and are the same for C functions with the same J but different M. Thus the four C functions $C(\frac{3}{2}, \frac{3}{2})$, $C(\frac{3}{2}, \frac{1}{2})$, $C(\frac{3}{2}, -\frac{1}{2})$, $C(\frac{3}{2}, -\frac{3}{2})$ have one energy, and the two $C(\frac{1}{2}, \frac{1}{2})$ and $C(\frac{1}{2}, -\frac{1}{2})$ have a different energy. The energy levels are denoted by adding the value of J as a subscript to the term symbol. Thus the two energy levels arising from the ^2P term are denoted by $^2P_{3/2}$ and $^2P_{1/2}$.

In retrospect, the energy levels of an atom may be thought of as arising from the various electron configurations. If the interactions between the electrons were completely neglected, the various eigenfunctions arising from the configuration would have the same energy. The electrostatic interactions split the configurations into terms, denoted by their L and S values, with different energies. Finally, the spin-orbit interaction splits each term into $2L + 1$ or $2S + 1$ energy levels, distinguished by their J values, which run from $|L + S|$ to $|L - S|$. Each of these energy levels is still degenerate, having $2J + 1$ eigenfunctions corresponding to M values which run from J to $-J$. As we shall see in the next section, this degeneracy can be removed by the application of an external magnetic field.

In many atoms, particularly atoms of high atomic number and with almost complete shells, the spin-orbit interaction may become of more importance than the electrostatic interaction. In considering these atoms, it is a better approximation to neglect the electrostatic energy at first and consider the spin-orbit interaction alone for the first approximation. We shall not treat this case here. Atoms of this type are said to have j–j coupling, as contrasted with the type we have been considering, which are said to have L–S, or Russell-Saunders, coupling.

9i. The Vector Model of the Atom. The results obtained above form a basis for a discussion of the " vector model " of the atom. This model is of value in visualizing some of the energy relations involved, as well as in giving a simple method of calculating the terms arising from a given electron configuration. From the configuration $(np)^2$, we saw that one obtained the terms ^1D, ^3P, ^1S; that is, we had possible L values of 2, 1, and 0, and possible S values of 1 and 0. Since we had $l_1 = 1$, $l_2 = 1$, where l_1 and l_2 are the l values of the two electrons, we see that the above L values are obtained by adding l_1 and l_2 vectorially, if we require the resultant vectors to differ in length by steps of unity. In the same manner the above S values can be obtained by vector addition of $|s_1| = \frac{1}{2}$ and $|s_2| = \frac{1}{2}$. The resulting L and S values cannot be combined arbitrarily, since the exclusion principle must be taken into account. The possible terms can be determined by the following scheme.[8] We write as a table all the possible values of M_L which can be formed by combination of m_1 and m_2.

The table shows that the values of M_L are

$$\begin{array}{ccccc} 2 & 1 & 0 & -1 & -2 \\ & 1 & 0 & -1 & \\ & & 0 & & \end{array}$$

which are just the values required to form one D, one P, and one S term. The spins can be combined to form either $S = 0$ or $S = 1$. For $S = 1$, both electrons have the same spin quantum number, so that they must differ in their values of m. We cannot, therefore, combine any of the M_L values from the diagonal of the above table with $S = 1$. Also, we can use only the M_L values from one side of the diagonal, as those on the other side merely correspond to a different numbering of the electrons. When $S = 1$, we are thus limited to the M_L values 1, 0, -1, so that we have a ^3P term. When $S = 0$, the electrons differ in their spin quantum numbers and there is no restriction on the values of M_L which may be combined with this value of S. As the set of values 1, 0, -1 has already been used to form the ^3P term, we thus have the sets of M_L values 2, 1, 0, -1, -2, and 0 to combine with $S = 0$, giving ^1D and ^1S terms.

For the configuration $(ns)^2$, there is, of course, only the one term ^1S. For the configuration $(nd)^2$, our table for the M_L values is

For $S = 1$, we are again limited to the M_L values from one side of the diagonal, which are sufficient to give ^3F and ^3P terms. For $S = 0$, we have the remaining sets of M_L values, which are sufficient to give ^1G, ^1D, ^1S terms. This method can be extended to more than two equivalent electrons, although the calculations are slightly more complicated. The possible terms that can arise from combinations of equivalent s and p electrons are

$$
\begin{array}{llll}
(ns) & {}^2S & & \\
(ns)^2 & {}^1S & & \\
(np) & {}^2P & & \\
(np)^2 & {}^1S & {}^3P & {}^1D \\
(np)^3 & {}^4S & {}^2D & {}^2P \\
(np)^4 & {}^1S & {}^3P & {}^1D \\
(np)^5 & {}^2P & & \\
(np)^6 & {}^1S & &
\end{array}
$$

For such electron configurations as (np, mp), the exclusion principle is already satisfied by the differing values of the principal quantum number. There is thus no restriction on the combinations of M_L and S, so that this electron configuration gives the terms ^3D, ^3P, ^3S, ^1D, ^1P, ^1S. Similarly, for the combination (np, nd), the exclusion principle is satisfied by the differing l values. From this configuration we thus obtain the terms ^3F, ^3D, ^3P, ^3S, ^1F, ^1D, ^1P, ^1S.

For a given term we have an electronic angular momentum $\mathbf{L}^* \dfrac{h}{2\pi}$, where $|\mathbf{L}^*| = \sqrt{L(L + 1)}$; and a spin angular momentum $\mathbf{S}^* \dfrac{h}{2\pi}$, where $|\mathbf{S}^*| = \sqrt{S(S + 1)}$. As we have seen in the previous section, these angular momenta combine to give a total angular momentum $\mathbf{J}^* \dfrac{h}{2\pi}$, where $|\mathbf{J}^*| = \sqrt{J(J + 1)}$, and where J has the values from $|L + S|$ to $|L - S|$, the J values differing by unity. These are just the J values we would obtain if we imagined the orbital and spin angular momenta to combine vectorially to give the resultant angular momentum, the resultant values being limited by the quantum principle. As we have seen, a magnetic moment is associated with the orbital angular momentum as well as with the spin angular momentum. Also, the motion of the electrons in their orbits produces a magnetic field. According to equation 9·78, we see that the spin-orbit interaction will be of the form

$$\Delta E = A\mathbf{L}^* \cdot \mathbf{S}^* \qquad\qquad 9\cdot84$$

where A will be some function of L and S and the electronic state.   Since

$$\mathbf{L}^* \cdot \mathbf{S}^* = \frac{|\mathbf{J}^*|^2 - |\mathbf{L}^*|^2 - |\mathbf{S}^*|^2}{2}$$

this becomes

$$\Delta E = \frac{A}{2}\{J(J+1) - L(L+1) - S(S+1)\} \qquad 9 \cdot 85$$

The magnetic field produced by the orbital motion is in the same direction as the orbital angular momentum.   The state of lowest energy will be that in which the magnetic moment of the electron spin is parallel to the field.   Now the magnetic moments of both orbital and spin angular momenta are in the direction opposite to that of the associated angular momenta, owing to the negative charge of the electron.   The state of lowest energy will thus be that in which L and S are in opposite directions.   The lowest state is therefore that with the lowest value of J. [In the list of terms arising from configurations of equivalent electrons as given above, it will be noted that $(np)^5$ gives the same terms as (np); that is, a closed shell minus one electron gives terms similar to those from the same shell containing only one electron.   In terms arising from these " almost-closed shells " the order of the states is reversed, the lowest state being that with the highest J value.   For example, the halogens, with the $(np)^5$ configuration, have $^2P_{3/2}$ as the ground state.]

Since L and S are the same for all members of a multiplet, the separation between the state with quantum number J and that with $J + 1$ is

$$\frac{A}{2}\{(J+1)(J+2) - J(J+1)\} = A(J+1) \qquad 9 \cdot 86$$

that is, it is proportional to the larger J value.   For example, the states $^3P_0$, $^3P_1$, $^3P_2$ have relative separations $1 : 2$; the states $^4D_{1/2}$, $^4D_{3/2}$, $^4D_{5/2}$, $^4D_{7/2}$ have relative separations $3 : 5 : 7$.   This relation, the Lande interval rule, is closely obeyed in atoms with Russell-Saunders coupling.

As stated above, a state with angular momentum quantum number J is $(2J + 1)$-fold degenerate, there being this number of C functions with the same value of J.   Returning to our example of the terms arising from the electron configuration $(np)^2$, we have $^1S_0$, non-degenerate; $^1D_2$, $^3P_2$, five-fold degenerate; $^3P_1$, three-fold degenerate; $^3P_0$, non-degenerate.   This accounts for the fifteen states corresponding to the possible linear combinations of the fifteen D functions for this configuration.   If the atom is now placed in a magnetic field, the energy will depend on M as well as on J, and this degeneracy will be removed.   If μ_{J^*} is the magnetic moment associated with a state with quantum number J, the energy in a magnetic field will be

$$E(J, M) = E_0(J) - \mu_{J*} \cdot \mathbf{H} \qquad 9\text{·}87$$

where $E_0(J)$ is the energy in the absence of the field. As we have noted previously, the magnetic moment associated with the orbital motion is

$$\mu_{L*} = \mathbf{L}^* \frac{eh}{4\pi mc}$$

that associated with spin angular momentum is

$$\mu_{S*} = 2\mathbf{S}^* \frac{eh}{4\pi mc}$$

The magnetic moment associated with the total angular momentum is therefore

$$\mu_{J*} = \frac{\mathbf{J}^*}{|\mathbf{J}^*|} \left(|\mu_{L*}| \cos (\mathbf{L}^*, \mathbf{J}^*) + |\mu_{S*}| \cos (\mathbf{S}^*, \mathbf{J}^*) \right)$$

$$= g\mathbf{J}^* \frac{eh}{4\pi mc} \qquad 9\text{·}88$$

where

$$g = 1 + \frac{J(J+1) + S(S+1) - L(L+1)}{2J(J+1)}$$

is the " Landé g factor." The energy levels in the presence of a magnetic field are therefore

$$E(J, M) = E_0(J) - g \frac{eh}{4\pi mc} \mathbf{J}^* \cdot \mathbf{H}$$

$$= E_0(J) + g \frac{|e|h}{4\pi mc} HM, \quad M = J, J - 1 \cdots - J \qquad 9\text{·}89$$

Each level with quantum number J is thus split into $2J + 1$ equally spaced levels by the magnetic field, the lowest level being that with $M = -J$. In Figure 9·1 we have plotted the levels arising from the configuration $(np)^2$ for the various degrees of approximation. For each degree of approximation, the relative separations within a given multiplet are correct; the other separations are not to scale.

9j. Selection Rules for Complex Atoms. As the field of atomic spectroscopy lies to a certain extent outside the scope of this book, we shall not treat the selection rules for the allowed transitions in complex atoms in any detail but shall merely summarize some of the more important results. According to the general theory of Chapter VIII, a transition between two states a and b may take place with the emission or absorption of electric dipole radiation only if the integral $\int \psi_a^* \mathbf{r} \psi_b \, d\tau$ is different from zero. Now any atom has spherical symmetry; the Hamiltonian operator is unchanged if the position coordinates of every electron are subjected to an inversion through the origin of coordinates. Because of this spherical symmetry, the product $\psi_a^*\psi_a$ must be unchanged

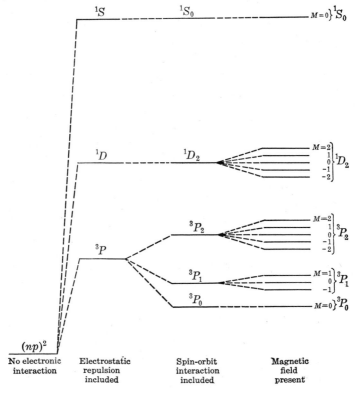

FIG. 9·1. Schematic energy levels from the electron configuration $(np)^2$.

if every coordinate is replaced by its inverse. Upon inversion, therefore, the function ψ_a must either remain unchanged or must change only in sign, so that the atomic wave functions can be classed as *even* or *odd* with respect to inversion. The vector **r** is, of course, an odd function with respect to this operation. Now, if ψ_a and ψ_b are both even functions or both odd functions, the product $\psi_a^* \mathbf{r} \psi_b$ will be an odd function. If we carry out an inversion, the integrand will change sign, its magnitude, however, remaining unchanged. Thus for every contribution to the integral from a particular volume element $d\tau_i$ there will be a contribution of equal magnitude but opposite sign from the inverse volume element; the integral will be *identically* zero. We have thus derived the selection rule for dipole radiation: only transitions between an *even* state and an *odd* state are allowed. This selection rule is perfectly general, depending as it does only on the symmetry properties of an atom and not on the particular set of wave functions which we use to give an approximate description of the electronic state of the atom. The following selection rules are less strict but hold approximately for many atoms.

If we consider that the states of the atom can be described by wave functions which are the proper linear combinations of products of one-electron orbitals which are solutions of a central field problem, we can make the following statements. Many transitions can be described by assuming that only one electron is involved. The angular portions of the orbitals are then identical with those of the hydrogen atom, the selection rule will therefore be the same, so for a one-electron transition, to this approximation, we have the rule $\Delta l = \pm 1$. For example, a transition of the type $(np)^2 \to (np, md)$ is allowed; transitions of the type $(np)^2 \to (np, mp)$ or $(np)^2 \to (np, mf)$ are forbidden. As may readily be seen, either from the expressions for the hydrogenlike wave functions or from the nature of the spherical harmonics, these functions are even for l even and odd for l odd. To the approximation we are here considering, an atomic wave function is therefore even or odd according as $\sum_i l_i$ is even or odd. If we have a transition involving two electrons simultaneously, then the general theorem that transitions are allowed only between even and odd states tells us that Δl must be even for one electron and odd for the other. Since we have $\Delta l = \pm 1$ for a one-electron transition, for a two-electron transition we would have $\Delta l_1 = \pm 1$; $\Delta l_2 = 0, \pm 2$.

Of more general interest are the selection rules for S, L, and J, as these quantum numbers describe an atomic state with greater accuracy. To the approximation that we neglect spin in the Hamiltonian operator, the spin wave functions are independent of the coordinate wave functions. The dipole moment integral will vanish because of the orthogonality of the spin functions unless the spin quantum numbers match in the initial and final states. To this approximation, we thus have the selection rule $\Delta S = 0$; that is, only transitions between terms of the same multiplicity are allowed. The selection rules for L and J cannot be derived so simply; the results are[9]

$$\Delta L = 0, \pm 1; \quad \Delta J = 0, \pm 1 \qquad 9 \cdot 90$$

[9] E. Kemble, *Fundamental Principles of Quantum Mechanics*, p. 543, McGraw-Hill Book Company, 1937.

In the presence of a magnetic field, the energy depends also on M. The observed phenomena in the Zeeman effect are explained by the selection rule for M

$$\Delta M = 0, \pm 1 \qquad\qquad 9\cdot 91$$

this selection rule being derivable in the same manner as the selection rule for m in the theory of the hydrogen atom. The selection rule $\Delta M = 0$ corresponds to the non-vanishing of the z component of the dipole moment integral; the light emitted during a transition for which $\Delta M = 0$ is polarized along the z axis (the direction of the magnetic field). Similarly, for transitions for which $\Delta M = \pm 1$, the emitted light is circularly polarized in the xy plane. In passing, we might mention that investigations of the Zeeman effect provide one of the most powerful tools for the determination of the characteristics of the states involved in atomic spectra.

9k. The Radial Portion of the Atomic Orbitals. Up to the present we have not specified the exact nature of our atomic orbitals, aside from the specification that the angular portion of the orbitals would be the ordinary spherical harmonics, since they were assumed to arise from the solution of a central field problem. For any quantitative calculation of energy levels some form must be chosen for the radial portion of the orbital. The best one-electron orbitals are found by the method of Hartree, which is discussed in the next section. In approximate work it is often desirable to use orbitals which, although less accurate than those obtained by Hartree's method, are simpler in form and hence easier to use. For example, Zener[10] and Slater[11] have used orbitals of the form

$$N r^{(n^*-1)} e^{-(Z-s)\frac{r}{n^* a_0}} Y(l, m | \theta, \varphi) \qquad\qquad 9\cdot 92$$

where n^* and s are adjustable constants and N is a normalizing factor. These eigenfunctions are solutions of the central field problem where $V(r)$ is given by the relation

$$V(r) = -\frac{(Z-s)e^2}{r} + \frac{n^*(n^*-1)h^2}{8\pi^2 m r^2} \qquad\qquad 9\cdot 93$$

For large values of r this approaches

$$V(r) \sim -\frac{(Z-s)e^2}{r} \qquad\qquad 9\cdot 94$$

corresponding to a screening of the nucleus equivalent to s atomic units;

---

[10] C. Zener, *Phys. Rev.*, **36**, 51 (1930).

[11] J. C. Slater, *Phys. Rev.*, **36**, 57 (1930).

in other words, the effective nuclear charge is equal to $Z - s$. From its resemblance to the quantum number n of the hydrogen atom, n^* is known as the " effective quantum number." Qualitatively, the eigenfunctions 9·92 differ from the hydrogen eigenfunctions in that there are no nodes in the radial portion, whereas the hydrogen eigenfunctions have $n - l - 1$ nodes.

By varying n^* and s so as to minimize the energy, Slater has been able to give the following rules for the determination of these constants:

1. n^* is assigned according to the following table, according to the value of the real quantum number n:

$$n = 1 \quad 2 \quad 3 \quad 4 \quad 5 \quad 6$$
$$n^* = 1 \quad 2 \quad 3 \quad 3.7 \quad 4.0 \quad 4.2$$

2. For determining s, the electrons are divided into the following groups: $1s$; $2s, 2p$; $3s, 3p$; $3d$; $4s, 4p$; $4d, 4f$; $\cdots$

3. The shielding constant s is formed, for any group of electrons, from the following contributions:

(a) Nothing from any shell outside the one considered.

(b) An amount 0.35 from each other electron in the group considered (except in the $1s$ group, where 0.30 is used).

(c) If the shell considered is an s or p shell, an amount 0.85 from each electron with principal quantum number less by 1, and an amount 1.00 from each electron still farther in; but if the shell is a d or f shell, an amount 1.00 from each electron inside it.

For example, carbon has two $1s$ electrons, two $2s$ electrons, and two $2p$ electrons. The approximate radial orbital (unnormalized) for a $1s$ electron is, according to the above rules:

$$\varphi(1s) \frown e^{-5.70\frac{r}{a_0}}$$

while for a $2s$ or $2p$ electron the radial function is

$$\varphi(2s) = \varphi(2p) \frown re^{-\frac{3.25\,r}{2\,a_0}}$$

Since the constants in these functions were determined by the use of experimental data, the functions will be satisfactory for rough quantitative calculations. Various other sets of screening constants have been proposed for use in wave functions of the above type, for example, those of Pauling and Sherman.[12]

91. The Hartree Method. According to our discussion of the helium atom in Chapter VII, the best wave functions for an atomic system

---

[12] L. Pauling and J. Sherman, *Z. Krist.*, **81**, 1 (1932).

should include the distance between the electrons r_{ij}, explicitly. Because of the complexity that would result from the use of such wave functions for many-electron atoms, we are limited in practice to the use of the one-electron wave functions of the type 9·19. The best possible wave functions of this type would be obtained by means of the variation method. In the earlier work of Hartree, the simpler product form of one-electron functions was used instead of the determinantal form. If we write the wave function for an n-electron atom as

$$\psi = \varphi_1(a_1|1)\varphi_2(a_2|2) \cdots \varphi_n(a_n|n) \qquad 9\text{·}95$$

then the best wave function of this type is that which makes the energy $E = \int \psi^* \mathbf{H}\psi \, d\tau$ a minimum, in other words, that which satisfies the equation

$$\delta E = \delta \int \psi^* \mathbf{H}\psi \, d\tau = 0 \qquad 9\text{·}96$$

The above method of expressing the energy is valid only if ψ is normalized. We can insure that this condition is fulfilled if we require that each φ be normalized, that is

$$\int \varphi_i^* \varphi_i \, d\tau = 1; \quad i = 1, 2, \cdots n \qquad 9\text{·}97$$

The Hamiltonian operator for the system of n electrons is

$$\mathbf{H} = \sum_{i=1}^{n} \left\{ \frac{h^2}{-8\pi^2 m} \nabla_i^2 - \frac{Ze^2}{r_i} \right\} + \tfrac{1}{2}\sum_i \sum_{j \neq i} \frac{e^2}{r_{ij}} \qquad 9\text{·}98$$
$$= \sum_{i=1}^{n} \mathbf{H}_i + \tfrac{1}{2}\sum_i \sum_{j \neq i} \frac{e^2}{r_{ij}}$$

The solution of equation 9·96, subject to the condition 9·97, shows that the best possible wave function of the type 9·95 is obtained by using the set of φ's which are the solutions of the n simultaneous equations

$$\mathbf{H}_i \varphi_i + \left\{ \sum_{j \neq i} e^2 \int \frac{|\varphi_j|^2}{r_{ij}} \, d\tau_j \right\} \varphi_i = \epsilon \varphi_i \qquad 9\text{·}99$$

Now $e^2|\varphi_j|^2$ is just the charge distribution of the jth electron, and $e^2\dfrac{|\varphi_j|^2}{r_{ij}}$ is the potential energy of the ith electron in the field of the jth electron. The term in brackets thus represents the potential energy of the ith electron in the field of all the remaining electrons. The method of solution of the set of simultaneous equations is the following. First an arbitrary set of φ_i's is chosen (the choice, of course, being guided by any previous knowledge of approximate wave functions for the atom). The field arising from all the electrons except the ith electron is calculated from this set of φ's, and φ_i is then calculated from equation 9·99. This procedure is carried out for each of the n electrons. The calculated set of φ's will not in general be identical with the original set; the calculations are repeated with a new set of φ's which have been altered in a manner suggested by the results of the first calculation. This process is continued until the assumed set of φ's and the calculated set are identical, at which point the solution of the set of simultaneous equations has been achieved. Since an assumed charge distribution gives a set of φ's which will reproduce this charge distribution, the above method is frequently called the " method of the self-consistent field."

The energy associated with the wave function 9·95 is

$$E = \int \psi^* \mathbf{H} \psi \, d\tau$$

$$= \sum_{i=1}^{n} \varphi_i^* \mathbf{H}_i \varphi_i \, d\tau_i + \tfrac{1}{2} \sum_i \sum_{j \neq i} e^2 \int \int \frac{|\varphi_i|^2 |\varphi_j|^2}{r_{ij}} \, d\tau_i \, d\tau_j \qquad 9·100$$

Comparing this equation with 9·65, we see that it contains terms representing the energy of the one-electron wave functions and terms representing the " coulombic " interaction of the electron cloud distributions, but that the term representing the " exchange " energy is missing. If the φ's are the solutions of equations 9·99 the energy will be given by

$$E = \sum_{i=1}^{n} \epsilon_i - \tfrac{1}{2} \sum_i \sum_{j \neq i} e^2 \int \int \frac{|\varphi_i|^2 |\varphi_j|^2}{r_{ij}} \, d\tau_i \, d\tau_j \qquad 9·101$$

The reason why there are no energy terms in 9·100 corresponding to the exchange energy is that the original wave function ψ was written as a simple product rather than as a determinant, as it should be if the exclusion principle is to be satisfied. By writing ψ as a determinant, and proceeding as above, with the additional requirement that the φ's be orthogonal, one is led to Fock's equations,[13] which are similar in form to the Hartree equation 9·99, but contain additional terms corresponding to the potential energies arising from the electron interchange. The results for the energy levels and wave functions do not differ appreciably from those obtained by the Hartree method. Since our main interest is in the problem of molecular structure rather than in that of atomic structure, we shall postpone a more thorough discussion of exchange energies to later chapters, where they will be of more significance.

[13] V. Fock, *Z. Physik*, **61**, 126 (1930).

It should be mentioned at this point that, although the above wave functions, particularly those obtained by the solution of Fock's equations, are the " best possible " one-electron wave functions, they give values for the energies of atoms which are incorrect by approximately 0.5 volt per electron. For this reason any results obtained from calculations based upon one-electron wave functions can be only quali-

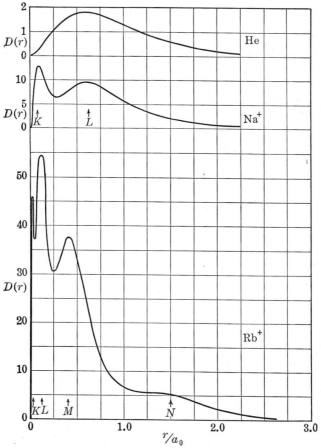

Fig. 9·2. Electron distribution in He, Na⁺, and Rb⁺ by the Hartree method.

tatively correct; it is somewhat unfortunate that these are the only wave functions which can be used in most problems concerning the energy levels of complex systems.

In Figure 9·2 we show the electron density distribution, as calculated by the Hartree method,[14] for He, Na⁺, and Rb⁺. It will be noted that

[14] D. R. Hartree, *Proc. Cambridge Phil. Soc.*, **24**, 89, 111 (1928).

the various shells of electrons can be clearly distinguished, and that the " radii " of these shells decrease as the nuclear charge Z increases. The diameter of the first shell, the K shell, is essentially $\dfrac{a_0}{Z}$, where a_0 is the radius of the first Bohr orbit. In Figure 9·2 the electron density $D(r)$ is normalized in such a way that the area under each curve is equal to the number of electrons in the atom.

9m. The Periodic System of the Elements. We will conclude this chapter on atomic structure with a brief discussion of the periodic system of the elements from the viewpoint of the electronic states of the various elements. In Figure 9·3 we have reproduced the periodic chart, the arrangement being essentially that suggested by White[15] on the basis of the spectroscopic characteristics of the various elements. In this table are included the electron configurations of the ground states of the elements, the designation of the lowest level, and the ionization potentials[16] both numerically and graphically. As a matter of convenience, the members of the rare-earth group between La and Lu have been omitted. In giving the electron configurations, only those electrons which have been added to the electrons of the preceding rare-gas configuration have been explicitly noted. For example, the electron configuration of Ne is $(1s)^2(2s)^2(2p)^6$; the designation $(3s)$ for the electron configuration of Na implies $(1s)^2(2s)^2(2p)^6(3s)$.

As mentioned in section 9c, the electron configuration of the ground state of any atom is obtained by adding the electrons one at a time to the lowest possible orbitals, taking account, however, of the exclusion principle. As previously mentioned, the orbitals lie approximately in the order $1s$, $2s$, $2p$, $3s$, $3p$, $4s$, $3d$, $4p$, $5s$, $4d$, $5p$, $6s$, $4f$, $5d$, $6p$, $7s$, $6d$. In the hydrogen atom the energy depends only on n, so that, for example, the $3s$, $3p$, and $3d$ orbitals all have the same energy. The new order of the orbitals in the heavier atoms may be qualitatively understood in the following way. The outer electrons move in an effective field which is the resultant of the nuclear field and the field of the inner electrons, or, as we have previously said, the inner electrons " screen " the outer electrons from the nucleus. The energy binding an outer electron to the atom will thus depend on how effectively this electron is screened from the nucleus; for example, if a $3d$ electron is more completely screened than a $3p$, and the $3p$ is more completely screened than a $3s$, then the order of the orbitals will be $3s$, $3p$, $3d$, with the $3s$ orbital the most stable. This is exactly the case in heavy atoms. If we look at the hydrogenlike

[15] H. E. White, *Introduction to Atomic Spectra*, p. 85, McGraw-Hill Book Company, 1934.

[16] G. Herzberg, *Atomic Spectra and Atomic Structure*, p. 287, Prentice-Hall, 1937.

Fig. 9·3.   The periodic system of the elements.

The periodic system of the elements (each cell lists: atomic number, symbol, term symbol, ionization potential, electron configuration):

Period	IA	IIA	IIIB	IVB	VB	VIB	VIIB	VIII	VIII	VIII	IB	IIB	IIIA	IVA	VA	VIA	VIIA	0
1	1. H $^2S_{1/2}$ 13.527 (1s)																	2. He $^1S_0$ 24.46 $(1s)^2$
2	3. Li $^2S_{1/2}$ 5.363 (2s)	4. Be $^1S_0$ 9.28 $(2s)^2$											5. B $^2P_{1/2}$ 8.257 $(2s)^2(2p)$	6. C $^3P_0$ 11.217 $(2s)^2(2p)^2$	7. N $^4S_{3/2}$ 14.48 $(2s)^2(2p)^3$	8. O $^3P_2$ 13.55 $(2s)^2(2p)^4$	9. F $^2P_{3/2}$ 17.34 $(2s)^2(2p)^5$	10. Ne $^1S_0$ 21.45 $(2s)^2(2p)^6$
3	11. Na $^2S_{1/2}$ 5.12 (3s)	12. Mg $^1S_0$ 7.61 $(3s)^2$											13. Al $^2P_{1/2}$ 5.96 $(3s)^2(3p)$	14. Si $^3P_0$ 8.12 $(3s)^2(3p)^2$	15. P $^4S_{3/2}$ 10.9 $(3s)^2(3p)^3$	16. S $^3P_2$ 10.30 $(3s)^2(3p)^4$	17. Cl $^2P_{3/2}$ 12.95 $(3s)^2(3p)^5$	18. A $^1S_0$ 15.68 $(3s)^2(3p)^6$
4	19. K $^2S_{1/2}$ 4.318 (4s)	20. Ca $^1S_0$ 6.09 $(4s)^2$	21. Sc $^2D_{3/2}$ (6.7) $(3d)(4s)^2$	22. Ti $^3F_2$ 6.81 $(3d)^2(4s)^2$	23. V $^4F_{3/2}$ 6.71 $(3d)^3(4s)^2$	24. Cr $^7S_3$ 6.74 $(3d)^5(4s)$	25. Mn $^6S_{5/2}$ 7.41 $(3d)^5(4s)^2$	26. Fe $^5D_4$ 7.83 $(3d)^6(4s)^2$	27. Co $^4F_{9/2}$ 7.81 $(3d)^7(4s)^2$	28. Ni $^3F_4$ 7.61 $(3d)^8(4s)^2$	29. Cu $^2S_{1/2}$ 7.68 $(3d)^{10}(4s)$	30. Zn $^1S_0$ 9.36 $(3d)^{10}(4s)^2$	31. Ga $^2P_{1/2}$ 5.97 $-(4p)$	32. Ge $^3P_0$ 8.09 $-(4p)^2$	33. As $^4S_{3/2}$ 10.5 $-(4p)^3$	34. Se $^3P_2$ 9.70 $-(4p)^4$	35. Br $^2P_{3/2}$ 11.80 $-(4p)^5$	36. Kr $^1S_0$ 13.93 $-(4p)^6$
5	37. Rb $^2S_{1/2}$ 4.159 (5s)	38. Sr $^1S_0$ 5.667 $(5s)^2$	39. Y $^2D_{3/2}$ (6.5) $(4d)(5s)^2$	40. Zr $^3F_2$ 6.92 $(4d)^2(5s)^2$	41. Cb $^6D_{1/2}$ $(4d)^4(5s)$	42. Mo $^7S_3$ 7.35 $(4d)^5(5s)$	43. Ma	44. Ru $^5F_5$ $(4d)^7(5s)$	45. Rh $^4F_{9/2}$ 7.7 $(4d)^8(5s)$	46. Pd $^1S_0$ 8.3 $(4d)^{10}$	47. Ag $^2S_{1/2}$ 7.54 $(4d)^{10}(5s)$	48. Cd $^1S_0$ 8.96 $(4d)^{10}(5s)^2$	49. In $^2P_{1/2}$ 5.76 $-(5p)$	50. Sn $^3P_0$ 7.30 $-(5p)^2$	51. Sb $^4S_{3/2}$ $-(5p)^3$	52. Te $^3P_2$ 8.96 $-(5p)^4$	53. I $^2P_{3/2}$ 10.6 $-(5p)^5$	54. Xe $^1S_0$ 12.08 $-(5p)^6$
6	55. Cs $^2S_{1/2}$ 3.87 (6s)	56. Ba $^1S_0$ 5.19 $(6s)^2$	57. La $^2D_{3/2}$ $(5d)(6s)^2$; 71. Lu $^2D_{3/2}$ $(4f)^{14}(5d)(6s)^2$	72. Hf $^3F_2$ $(4f)^{14}(5d)^2(6s)^2$	73. Ta $^4F_{3/2}$ $(5d)^3(6s)^2$	74. W $^5D_0$ $(5d)^4(6s)^2$	75. Re $^6S_{5/2}$ $(5d)^5(6s)^2$	76. Os $^5D_4$ (8.7) $(5d)^6(6s)^2$	77. Ir $^4F_{9/2}$ $(5d)^7(6s)^2$	78. Pt $^3D_3$ 8.88 $(5d)^9(6s)$	79. Au $^2S_{1/2}$ 9.18 $(5d)^{10}(6s)$	80. Hg $^1S_0$ 10.38 $(5d)^{10}(6s)^2$	81. Tl $^2P_{1/2}$ 6.07 $-(6p)$	82. Pb $^3P_0$ 7.38 $-(6p)^2$	83. Bi $^4S_{3/2}$ $-(6p)^3$	84. Po $^3P_2$ $-(6p)^4$	85.	86. Rn $^1S_0$ 10.69 $-(6p)^6$
7	57.	88. Ra $^1S_0$ 5.252 $(7s)^2$	89.	90. Th	91. Pa	92. U												

eigenfunctions in Table 6·1, we see that, disregarding the constant factor, the angular factor, and the common exponential factor, for small values of r the $3s$ eigenfunction is a constant, the $3p$ eigenfunction varies as r, and the $3d$ eigenfunction varies as r^2. This means that the probability of finding the electron in the immediate neighborhood of the nucleus is greatest for the $3s$ electron and least for the $3d$ electron, so that the $3s$ electron is screened least by the inner electrons and the $3d$ is screened most; the order of stability is thus $3s$, $3p$, $3d$. Because of this difference in energy between the $3p$ and $3d$, it is possible for the $4s$ orbital to be even more stable than the $3d$, and we observe that this is so. Similar arguments hold for the relative stability of f orbitals; it is observed that the $4f$ orbitals are so completely screened by the inner electrons that the $6s$ orbital is more stable.

By adding electrons into the various possible orbitals, taking proper account of the exclusion principle, we get the electron configurations as shown in Figure 9·3. The $1s$ shell is complete at He, the $2s$ shell at Be, and the $2p$ shell at Ne. From the viewpoint of electron configuration alone, He should properly be in the same column as Be; from the viewpoint of chemical properties, it belongs with Ne. This point will be discussed later. The $3s$ shell is completed at Mg, the $3p$ shell at A, and the $4s$ shell at Ca. At this point the $3d$ shell begins to fill up. Since the $4s$ and $3d$ orbitals are close together, it happens that the $3d$ shell does not fill up smoothly; there is a tendency for the $3d$ shell to fill up at the expense of the $4s$ shell. At Cu the $3d$ shell is complete, and there is one $4s$ electron present; at Zn both the $3d$ and the $4s$ shells are filled. The $4p$ electrons are now added, this shell being completed at Kr. The same procedure is repeated with the $5s$, $4d$, and $5p$ electrons. The $6s$ shell is completed at Ba, then one $5d$ electron is added, followed by the fourteen $4f$ electrons. The $4f$ shell is completed at Lu, which, as far as electrons outside closed shells are concerned, has the same configuration as La. The addition of the remaining $5d$ electrons and the addition of the $6p$ electrons brings us finally to Rn. Little is known about the remaining elements.

We now note that all the elements in a given column have the same ground state. For example, the elements H, Li, Na, K, Rb, and Cs have $^2S_{\frac{1}{2}}$ as the ground state; the elements Zn, Cd, and Hg have $^1S_0$ as the ground state; the elements C, Si, Ge, Sn, and Pb have $^3P_0$ as the ground state. Since the chemical properties of an element are determined by the electron configuration of the element, we see why the elements in any given column have similar chemical properties. The above statements are not strictly true for the elements in those portions of the table where the d shells are being filled. Owing to the competition between the d and s shells, certain irregularities arise; for example, while Ti, Zr, and Hf have the same electron configuration, that of Cb differs from that of V and Ta. In the first four and last eight columns the correspondence is exact; the intermediate columns show more or less variation.

We also note that the chemical characteristics of an element are not completely determined by the electron configuration of the ground state, since, for example, K and Cu both have $^2S_{\frac{1}{2}}$ as the lowest level, and Ca, Zn, and Kr all have $^1S_0$. In order to understand the differences between such elements several other factors must be considered. The differences between K and Cu are undoubtedly to be attributed to the fact that in Cu we have a $4s$ electron on top of the rather loosely held $3d$ shell, whereas in K we have a $4s$ electron on top of the tightly held A configuration. The result of this is that the $4s$ electron in Cu moves in a stronger effective field than the $4s$ electron of K, hence the ionization potential of Cu is considerably higher than that of K. The $4s$ electron in K is therefore more readily removed than that of Cu, so that, though there are many similarities between the two elements, K is the more reactive.

As will be seen in the following chapters, the normal covalence of an atom is equal to the number of unpaired electron spins in the atom. F, O, and N have multiplicities of 2, 3, 4, respectively, so that the spin quantum number S has the values $\frac{1}{2}$, 1, $\frac{3}{2}$, respectively, for these atoms. These values of S can arise from 1, 2, 3 unpaired spins, so that F, O, and N have normal covalences of 1, 2, and 3, respectively. Be, on the other hand, should have a normal covalence of zero. However, comparing the ionization potentials of Be and B, we see that the $2p$ orbital is only slightly less stable than the $2s$. One of the $2s$ electrons in Be can thus be rather readily moved up to the $2p$ level, giving two unpaired spins and hence a covalence of two. Similarly, by moving one electron from the $2s$ to the $2p$ level in B and C, we obtain the normal covalences of 3 and 4 for these elements. The behavior of Zn is analogous to that of Be. For the rare-gas elements, a quite different condition exists. For example, the ionization potential of Ne is 21.45 e.v., while that of Na is only 5.12 e.v. There is thus a great gap between the $2p$ and $3s$ levels. The promotion of a $2p$ electron in Ne to the $3s$ level, which would give Ne a covalence of 2, requires so much energy that this condition does not occur. Similarly, there is a large gap between the $1s$ and the $2s$ levels; for this reason He has the chemical properties of Ne rather than of Be.

As we fill in a given shell, say the $2p$ shell, the ionization potential increases with increasing atomic number; since the electrons in a given shell screen each other very little, the effective nuclear charge is increasing. An exception will be noted in the oxygen group; the ionization potential of O is less than that of N. As long as there are three or less electrons in a p shell they can all be in different ones of the three available p orbitals (p_x, p_y, p_z), so that the electrostatic repulsions are a minimum. The fourth p electron must go into an orbital which is already occupied by one electron; the increased electrostatic repulsion causes the electron to be bound less firmly than would be expected from considerations of effective nuclear charge alone.

CHAPTER X

GROUP THEORY

The Schrödinger equation can be solved exactly in only a very few simple cases; in general, we are limited to the approximate methods of solution discussed in Chapter VII. There exists, however, a large class of results which depend only on the symmetry properties of the system under consideration; these results can be obtained exactly by use of the branch of mathematics known as group theory. We present in this chapter an elementary treatment of group theory, although we make no claim to completeness. Several of the important theorems are presented without proof; the interested reader may refer to one of the complete expositions of the field (see General References). Group theory, in the form which will be of interest to us, makes considerable use of matrix notation, so that we shall first present the elements of matrix algebra, with particular reference to the matrices involved in linear transformations of coordinates.

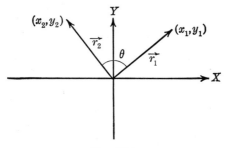

FIG. 10·1.

10a. Matrices. Let us consider a point in the xy plane, this point being specified by the coordinates (x_1, y_1) (Figure 10·1). These two numbers may also be thought of as defining the vector $\mathbf{r}_1$. A rotation of this vector through an angle θ will transform it into the new vector $\mathbf{r}_2$, defined by the numbers x_2 and y_2. The relation between (x_2, y_2) and (x_1, y_1) and the angle of rotation θ is given by the set of linear equations

$$x_2 = x_1 \cos \theta - y_1 \sin \theta$$

$$y_2 = x_1 \sin \theta + y_1 \cos \theta$$

10·1

The reverse transformation is

$$x_1 = x_2 \frac{\cos \theta}{\Delta} + y_2 \frac{\sin \theta}{\Delta}$$

10·2

$$y_1 = -x_2 \frac{\sin \theta}{\Delta} + y_2 \frac{\cos \theta}{\Delta}$$

where Δ is the determinant of the coefficients in 10·1:

$$\Delta = \begin{vmatrix} \cos \theta & -\sin \theta \\ \sin \theta & \cos \theta \end{vmatrix} = \cos^2 \theta + \sin^2 \theta = 1$$

The set of equations 10·1 can be written as

$$\begin{pmatrix} x_2 \\ y_2 \end{pmatrix} = \begin{pmatrix} \cos \theta & -\sin \theta \\ \sin \theta & \cos \theta \end{pmatrix} \begin{pmatrix} x_1 \\ y_1 \end{pmatrix}$$

10.3

where

$$\begin{pmatrix} \cos \theta & -\sin \theta \\ \sin \theta & \cos \theta \end{pmatrix}$$

10·4

is the matrix of the transformation which takes r_1 into r_2. The corresponding matrix for the reverse transformation is

$$\begin{pmatrix} \cos \theta & \sin \theta \\ -\sin \theta & \cos \theta \end{pmatrix}$$

10·5

In the n-dimensional case, we have the corresponding set of equations

$$\begin{aligned} x_1' &= a_{11}x_1 + a_{12}x_2 + \cdots + a_{1n}x_n \\ x_2' &= a_{21}x_1 + a_{22}x_2 + \cdots + a_{2n}x_n \\ &\cdots\cdots\cdots\cdots\cdots\cdots\cdots\cdots\cdots \\ x_n' &= a_{n1}x_1 + a_{n2}x_2 + \cdots + a_{nn}x_n \end{aligned}$$

10·6

where the x_i''s are the new coordinates and where the a's satisfy the relations

$$\sum_{j=1}^{n} a_{jk}^2 = 1 \qquad\qquad k = 1, 2, \cdots n$$

$$\sum_{j=1}^{n} a_{kj}^2 = 1 \qquad\qquad k = 1, 2, \cdots n$$

10·7

$$\sum_{j=1}^{n} a_{jk}a_{jl} = 0 \qquad\qquad k, l = 1, 2, \cdots n; \ k \neq l$$

$$\sum_{i=1}^{n} a_{kj}a_{lj} = 0 \qquad\qquad k, l = 1, 2, \cdots n; \ k \neq$$

In addition, the determinant of the a's is unity. The matrix formed by a set of a's which satisfy the relations 10·7 is said to be a unitary matrix; the matrices representing rotations, reflections, and inversions are unitary. It will be noted that the matrices 10·3 and 10·4 satisfy the relations 10·7. The transformation which is the reverse of 10·6 is given by the set of equations

$$
\begin{aligned}
x_1 &= a_{11}x_1' + a_{21}x_2' + \cdots + a_{n1}x_n' \\
x_2 &= a_{12}x_1' + a_{22}x_2' + \cdots + a_{n2}x_n' \\
&\cdots\cdots\cdots\cdots\cdots\cdots\cdots\cdots\cdots\cdots \\
x_n &= a_{1n}x_1' + a_{2n}x_2' + \cdots + a_{nn}x_n'
\end{aligned}
\qquad 10\cdot 8
$$

The matrix of the reverse transformation is thus obtained from the matrix for the original transformation merely by changing columns into rows.

The set of equations in 10·6 can be written in the compact form

$$
x_j' = \sum_k a_{jk}x_k \qquad k, j = 1, 2, \cdots n \qquad 10\cdot 9
$$

An even simpler notation which expresses the same thing is obtained if we write

$$
x' = \mathbf{a}x \qquad\qquad 10\cdot 10
$$

where $\mathbf{a}$ is the matrix

$$
\mathbf{a} = \begin{pmatrix}
a_{11} & a_{12} & \cdots & a_{1n} \\
a_{21} & a_{22} & \cdots & a_{2n} \\
\cdots & \cdots & \cdots & \cdots \\
a_{n1} & a_{n2} & \cdots & a_{nn}
\end{pmatrix}
$$

of the transformation from the unprimed to the primed coordinates. A second transformation could be written as

$$
x'' = \mathbf{b}x'; \quad \text{or} \quad x_i'' = \sum_j b_{ij}x_j' \qquad 10\cdot 11
$$

These two successive transformations are equivalent to some one transformation

$$
x'' = \mathbf{c}x; \quad \text{or} \quad x_i'' = \sum_k c_{ik}x_k \qquad 10\cdot 12
$$

Combining the above equations, we have

$$
x_i'' = \sum_j b_{ij}x_j' = \sum_j\sum_k b_{ij}a_{jk}x_k = \sum_k c_{ik}x_k \qquad 10\cdot 13
$$

The components of the product matrix $\mathbf{c} = \mathbf{ba}$ are thus given by the relation

$$
c_{ik} = \sum b_{ij}a_{jk} \qquad\qquad 10\cdot 14
$$

which is the rule for matrix multiplication. The product of the matrices of the transformations 10·6 and 10·8 must be a matrix which represents no transformation of coordinates at all, that is

$$\begin{pmatrix} a_{11} & a_{12} & \cdots & a_{1n} \\ a_{21} & a_{22} & \cdots & a_{2n} \\ \cdots\cdots\cdots\cdots\cdots \\ a_{n1} & a_{n2} & \cdots & a_{nn} \end{pmatrix} \begin{pmatrix} a_{11} & a_{21} & \cdots & a_{n1} \\ a_{12} & a_{22} & \cdots & a_{n2} \\ \cdots\cdots\cdots\cdots\cdots \\ a_{1n} & a_{2n} & \cdots & a_{nn} \end{pmatrix} = \begin{pmatrix} 1 & 0 & \cdots & 0 \\ 0 & 1 & \cdots & 0 \\ \cdots\cdots\cdots\cdots \\ 0 & 0 & \cdots & 1 \end{pmatrix} \quad 10·15$$

From the rule for matrix multiplication, and the relations in 10·7, we see that the matrix equation 10·15 is indeed true.

Before proceeding with the formulation of group theory, we need certain general concepts concerning vectors. In three-dimensional space, any three numbers may be thought of as defining a vector, the vector from the origin of coordinates to the point specified by the three numbers. If we have the two vecors $\mathbf{A}$ and $\mathbf{B}$, defined by the numbers (A_1, A_2, A_3) and (B_1, B_2, B_3), the vectors are said to be orthogonal if

$$A_1B_1 + A_2B_2 + A_3B_3 = 0$$

In the three-dimensional case, this means that vectors are perpendicular, or, in the notation outlined in Appendix II, the scalar product $\mathbf{A} \cdot \mathbf{B}$ is zero. In more general terms, we may consider n numbers $(A_1, A_2 \cdots A_n)$ as defining a vector $\mathbf{A}_n$ in n-dimensional space. If $\mathbf{B}_n$ is another n-dimensional vector, the two vectors are said to be orthogonal if their scalar product

$$\mathbf{A}_n \cdot \mathbf{B}_n = A_1B_1 + A_2B_2 + \cdots + A_nB_n$$

is equal to zero. If the numbers which define the vectors are complex, the vectors are said to be orthogonal if the Hermitian scalar product

$$(\mathbf{A}_n \cdot \mathbf{B}_n) = A_1^*B_1 + A_2^*B_2 + \cdots + A_n^*B_n$$

is zero.

In three dimensions any arbitrary vector can be expressed in terms of a linear combination of three orthogonal vectors, for example, the three unit vectors along the coordinate axes. In other words, it is possible to construct only three independent orthogonal vectors in three-dimensional space. Analogously, in n-dimensional space, it is possible to construct only n independent vectors. This concept of a set of numbers defining a vector will prove useful later.

10b. The General Principles of Group Theory. The set of operations which send a symmetrical figure into itself are said to form a group. Let us consider the symmetrical figure formed by three points at the corners of an equilateral triangle, as in Figure 10·2. The operations which send this figure into itself are:

1. The identity operation E, which leaves each point unchanged.
2. Operation A, which is a reflection in the yz plane.
3. B — reflection in the plane passing through the point b and perpendicular to the line joining a and c.
4. C — reflection in the plane passing through c and perpendicular to the line joining a and b.
5. D — clockwise rotation through 120°.
6. F — counterclockwise rotation through 120°.

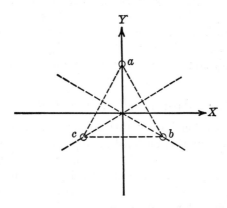

FIG. 10·2.

Other symmetry operations are possible, but they are all equivalent to one of the operations given above. For example, a clockwise rotation through 240° is a symmetry operation, but it is identical with operation F; a rotation through 180° about the y axis is identical with operation A.

The successive application of any two of the operations listed above will be equivalent to some single operation. Rotation in the clockwise direction through 240° is obtained by applying operation D twice; this is equivalent to the single operation F — we denote this fact by the equation $DD = F$. Operation A interchanges points b and c; if operation D is applied to the resulting figure, c is returned to its original position, b goes to the position originally occupied by a, and a goes to that originally occupied by b. Operation A followed by operation D is thus equivalent to operation C, or $DA = C$. If we work out all possible products of two operations, we obtain the following multi-

plication table, Table 10·1, where the operation which is to be applied
to the figure first is written across the top of the table. The set of
operations E, A, B, C, D, F forms a group, and Table 10·1 is known
as the multiplication table for this group. The number of operations
in the group is called the order h of the group; here the order of the
group is 6.

TABLE 10·1

	E	A	B	C	D	F
E	E	A	B	C	D	F
A	A	E	D	F	B	C
B	B	F	E	D	C	A
C	C	D	F	E	A	B
D	D	C	A	B	F	E
F	F	B	C	A	E	D

More generally, any set of elements P, Q, R, $S \cdots$ is said to form a
group if the following conditions are satisfied:

1. The product of any two elements in the set is another element in
the set.
2. The set must contain the identity operation E which satisfies the
relation $ER = RE = R$, where R is any element of the set.
3. The associative law of multiplication, $P(QR) = (PQ)R$, must
hold; that is, P times the product of Q and R must be equal to the
product of P and Q times R.
4. Every element must have a reciprocal such that, if R is the reciprocal of S, then $RS = SR = E$.

That all these conditions are satisfied by the group given above is
easily verified. The commutative law of multiplication does not necessarily hold. From Table 10·1 we see that $AB = D$; $BA = F$, so that
$AB \neq BA$. If $PQ = QP$ for all elements of the group, the group is
said to be Abelian.

In the group of symmetry operations on three points as given above,
we have three distinct types of operations: the identity operation E;
the reflections A, B, and C; and the rotations D and F. We say that
each of these sets of elements forms a class; that is, E forms a class by
itself, A, B, and C form a class, and D and F form a class. Usually
the geometric considerations will enable us to pick out the classes;
more precisely, two elements P and Q which satisfy the relation
$X^{-1}PX = P$ or Q, where X is any element of the group and X^{-1} is
its reciprocal, are said to belong to the same class. From the multi-

plication table, we have

$$EDE = D \qquad EFE = F$$
$$ADA = F \qquad AFA = D$$
$$BDB = F \qquad BFB = D$$
$$CDC = F \qquad CFC = D$$
$$FDD = D \qquad FFD = F$$
$$DDF = D \qquad DFF = F$$

The elements D and F therefore form a class; in the same way it is found that A, B, and C form a class, and that E forms a class. If the group is Abelian, then $X^{-1}PX = X^{-1}XP = P$ for all X's and P's. Each element of the group then forms a class by itself, and the number of classes is equal to the number of elements. The concept of a class of operations has the following geometric meaning. If two operations belong to the same class, it is possible to pick out a new coordinate system in which one operation is replaced by the other. For example, in the group given above, we could equally well have taken our y axis through the point b and perpendicular to the line joining a and c. The operation A in the new coordinate system is the same as the operation B in the old coordinate system, since A has been defined to be a reflection in the yz plane.

Any set of elements which multiply according to the group multiplication table is said to form a representation Γ of the group. For the group given above, we immediately see that the sets of numbers assigned to the various elements in the following way form representations of the group:

E	A	B	C	D	F
1	1	1	1	1	1
1	-1	-1	-1	1	1

The corresponding matrices will also form a representation of the group if we replace ordinary multiplication by matrix multiplication. If we denote by $\mathbf{e}$, $\mathbf{a}$, $\mathbf{b}$, $\mathbf{c}$, $\mathbf{d}$, $\mathbf{f}$ the matrices of the transformations of coordinates associated with the corresponding operations, we see that these matrices form a representation of the group. That is, the product of, say, A and B is $AB = D$; the product of the matrices $\mathbf{a}$ and $\mathbf{b}$ must therefore be $\mathbf{ab} = \mathbf{d}$, so that the matrices multiply according to the group multiplication table. We have therefore found three matrix representations:

$$
\begin{array}{ccccccc}
 & E & A & B & C & D & F \\
\Gamma_1 & (1) & (1) & (1) & (1) & (1) & (1) \\
\Gamma_2 & (1) & (-1) & (-1) & (-1) & (1) & (1)
\end{array}
$$

$$
\Gamma_3 \quad
\begin{pmatrix} 1 & 0 \\ 0 & 1 \end{pmatrix}
\begin{pmatrix} -1 & 0 \\ 0 & +1 \end{pmatrix}
\begin{pmatrix} \frac{1}{2} & -\frac{\sqrt{3}}{2} \\ -\frac{\sqrt{3}}{2} & -\frac{1}{2} \end{pmatrix}
\begin{pmatrix} \frac{1}{2} & \frac{\sqrt{3}}{2} \\ \frac{\sqrt{3}}{2} & -\frac{1}{2} \end{pmatrix}
\begin{pmatrix} -\frac{1}{2} & \frac{\sqrt{3}}{2} \\ -\frac{\sqrt{3}}{2} & -\frac{1}{2} \end{pmatrix}
\begin{pmatrix} -\frac{1}{2} & -\frac{\sqrt{3}}{2} \\ \frac{\sqrt{3}}{2} & -\frac{1}{2} \end{pmatrix}
$$

In Γ_3, the matrices $\mathbf{e}$ and $\mathbf{a}$ can be written down immediately. $\mathbf{d}$ and $\mathbf{f}$ are obtained from 10·4 by inserting the proper value of θ; $\mathbf{b}$ and $\mathbf{c}$ can then be found by means of the group multiplication table and the rule for matrix multiplication.

It is possible to find other representations of the group. For example, if we assign to the points a, b, and c the coordinates (x_a, y_a), etc., the matrices of the transformations would be of dimension 6 (six-row matrices) and would form a representation of the group. Let us suppose that we have found some such representation, and let us call the corresponding matrices $\mathbf{e}'$, $\mathbf{a}'$, $\mathbf{b}'$, $\mathbf{c}'$, $\mathbf{d}'$, $\mathbf{f}'$. The new set of matrices $\mathbf{e}'' = \boldsymbol{\beta}^{-1}\mathbf{e}'\boldsymbol{\beta}$; $\mathbf{a}'' = \boldsymbol{\beta}^{-1}\mathbf{a}'\boldsymbol{\beta}$; $\mathbf{b}'' = \boldsymbol{\beta}^{-1}\mathbf{b}'\boldsymbol{\beta}$, etc., also form a representation of the group, as may be seen as follows. Assume that

$$\mathbf{a}''\mathbf{b}'' = \mathbf{d}'' \qquad\qquad 10\cdot16$$

Then $\boldsymbol{\beta}^{-1}\mathbf{a}'\boldsymbol{\beta}\boldsymbol{\beta}^{-1}\mathbf{b}'\boldsymbol{\beta} = \boldsymbol{\beta}^{-1}\mathbf{d}'\boldsymbol{\beta}$. From the associative law of multiplication, we have

$$\boldsymbol{\beta}^{-1}\mathbf{a}'\mathbf{b}'\boldsymbol{\beta} = \boldsymbol{\beta}^{-1}\mathbf{d}'\boldsymbol{\beta}$$

If we now multiply from the left by $\boldsymbol{\beta}$ and from the right by $\boldsymbol{\beta}^{-1}$ we have

$$\mathbf{a}'\mathbf{b}' = \mathbf{d}' \qquad\qquad 10\cdot17$$

Since 10·17 is true, 10.16 must also be true; the transformed matrices $\mathbf{e}''$, etc., therefore also form a representation of the group. The transformations of the type $\mathbf{a}'' = \boldsymbol{\beta}^{-1}\mathbf{a}'\boldsymbol{\beta}$ are called similarity transformations. Let us now suppose that it is possible to find a similarity transformation which will transform all the matrices $\mathbf{e}'$, $\mathbf{a}' \cdots$ into the form

$$\mathbf{a}'' = \beta^{-1}\mathbf{a}'\beta = \begin{pmatrix} \mathbf{a}_1'' & 0 & 0 & \vdots \\ 0 & \mathbf{a}_2'' & 0 & \vdots \\ 0 & 0 & \mathbf{a}_3'' & \vdots \\ \cdots\cdots\cdots\cdots\cdots\cdots \end{pmatrix} \qquad 10\cdot 18$$

where $\mathbf{a}_1''$ is a square matrix which has the same dimension as $\mathbf{b}_1''$, $\mathbf{c}_1'' \cdots$, and where there are only zeros outside the squares. Since $\mathbf{a}''\mathbf{b}'' = \mathbf{d}'' \cdots$, we have from the law of matrix multiplication the relations

$$\mathbf{a}_1''\mathbf{b}_1'' = \mathbf{d}_1''$$
$$\mathbf{a}_2''\mathbf{b}_2'' = \mathbf{d}_2'' \qquad\qquad 10\cdot 19$$
$$\cdots\cdots\cdots\cdots$$

The sets of matrices $\mathbf{e}_1''$, $\mathbf{a}_1''$, $\mathbf{b}_1'' \cdots$; $\mathbf{e}_2''$, $\mathbf{a}_2''$, $\mathbf{b}_2'' \cdots$; etc., therefore form representations of the group. The matrix representation $\mathbf{e}'$, $\mathbf{a}'$, $\mathbf{b}' \cdots$ is said to be reducible and to have been reduced by the similarity transformation with the matrix β. If it is not possible to find a similarity transformation which will further reduce all the matrices of a given representation, the representation is said to be irreducible.

The representations Γ_1, Γ_2, Γ_3 given above are all irreducible. Since matrices representing transformations of interest to us are unitary, we may restrict ourselves to representations which involve only unitary matrices and to similarity transformations with unitary matrices. Two irreducible representations which differ only by a similarity transformation are said to be equivalent. We shall now show that the non-equivalent irreducible representations Γ_1, Γ_2, Γ_3 given above are the only non-equivalent irreducible representations of the corresponding group, and we shall then state, without proof, certain general theorems regarding irreducible representations.

We denote by $\Gamma_i(R)$ the matrix corresponding to the operation R of the ith irreducible representation, and by $\Gamma_i(R)_{mn}$ the mnth component of this matrix. For the above representations, we therefore have the relations:[1]

$$\sum_R \Gamma_1(R)_{11}\Gamma_1(R)_{11} = 6$$

$$\sum_R \Gamma_2(R)_{11}\Gamma_2(R)_{11} = 6$$

$$\sum_R \Gamma_3(R)_{11}\Gamma_3(R)_{11} = \sum_R \Gamma_3(R)_{12}\Gamma_3(R)_{12}$$

$$= \sum_R \Gamma_3(R)_{21}\Gamma_3(R)_{21} = \sum_R \Gamma_3(R)_{22}\Gamma_3(R)_{22} = 3$$

10·20

In addition, we note that

$$\sum_R \Gamma_1(R)_{11}\Gamma_2(R)_{11} = 0$$

$$\sum_R \Gamma_1(R)_{11}\Gamma_3(R)_{11} = 0$$

$$\sum_R \Gamma_1(R)_{11}\Gamma_3(R)_{12} = 0$$

$$\sum_R \Gamma_3(R)_{11}\Gamma_3(R)_{12} = 0, \text{ etc.}$$

10·21

All the relations of the type 10·21 can be expressed by the equations

$$\sum_R \Gamma_i(R)_{mn}\Gamma_j(R)_{m'n'} = 0; \quad i \neq j$$

$$\sum_R \Gamma_i(R)_{mn}\Gamma_i(R)_{m'n'} = 0; \quad m \neq m'; \quad n \neq n'$$

10·22

while the relations 10·20 can be written as

$$\sum_R \Gamma_i(R)_{mn}\Gamma_i(R)_{mn} = \frac{h}{l_i}$$

10·23

where h is the order of the group and l_i is the dimension of the ith representation. Equations 10·22 and 10·23 can be combined into the general relation (see Appendix VI)

$$\sum_R \Gamma_i(R)_{mn}\sqrt{\frac{l_i}{h}}\,\Gamma_j(R)_{m'n'}\sqrt{\frac{l_j}{h}} = \delta_{ij}\,\delta_{mm'}\,\delta_{nn'}$$

10·24

where $\delta_{ij} = 1$ if $i = j$; $\delta_{ij} = 0$ otherwise. *Equation 10·24 may be shown to be true for the non-equivalent irreducible representations of any group.*

From equation 10·22 we see that the matrix components $\Gamma_i(R_1)_{mn}$, $\Gamma_i(R_2)_{mn} \cdots \Gamma_i(R_h)_{mn}$ of the h elements of the group can be regarded as the components of an h-dimensional vector which is orthogonal to any one of the vectors obtained by a different choice of the subscripts

[1] To be more general, these expressions should be replaced by $\sum_R [\Gamma_1(R)]^*_{11}\Gamma_1(R)_{1,1}$ etc., but this form of the equations will be sufficiently general for our purposes.

m and n, as well as being orthogonal to any of the similar vectors obtained from a different irreducible representation. If there are c such irreducible representations, each of dimension l_i, there are $l_1^2 + l_2^2 + \cdots + l_c^2$ such orthogonal vectors. But it is possible to construct only h orthogonal h-dimensional vectors. Actually,

$$l_1^2 + l_2^2 + \cdots + l_c^2 = h \qquad 10\cdot25$$

This result is perfectly general and follows directly from 10·24. The representations Γ_1, Γ_2, and Γ_3 are therefore the only non-equivalent irreducible representations of the symmetric group of three points.

The sum of the diagonal elements of a matrix is known as the character of the matrix. We denote by $\chi_i(R)$ the character of the matrix of the operation R belonging to the ith irreducible representation of the group, that is

$$\chi_i(R) = \sum_m \Gamma_i(R)_{mm} \qquad 10\cdot26$$

The characters of the representations Γ_1, Γ_2, Γ_3 of the group which we have been discussing are

	E	A	B	C	D	F
χ_1	1	1	1	1	1	1
χ_2	1	-1	-1	-1	1	1
χ_3	2	0	0	0	-1	-1

The character of a matrix is unchanged by a similarity transformation. The character of a matrix P is $\chi_P = \sum P_{jj}$. The character of $Q = X^{-1}PX$ is

$$\chi_Q = \sum_i Q_{ii} = \sum_i \sum_j \sum_k X_{ij}^{-1} P_{jk} X_{ki} = \sum_j \sum_k \sum_i X_{ki} X_{ij}^{-1} P_{jk}$$
$$= \sum_j \sum_k \delta_{kj} P_{jk} = \sum_j P_{jj} = \chi_P$$

If two operations belong to the same class, the corresponding matrices for a given representation have the same character, as may also be verified from the character table above.

From 10·24, we have the result

$$\sum_R \Gamma_i(R)_{mm} \Gamma_j(R)_{m'm'} = \frac{h}{l_j} \delta_{ij} \delta_{mm'}$$

Summing over m from 1 to l_i and over m' from 1 to l_j gives

$$\sum_R \chi_i(R)\chi_j(R) = \frac{h}{l_j} \delta_{ij} \sum_{m=1}^{i} \sum_{m'=1}^{l_j} \delta_{mm'} = \frac{h}{l_j} \delta_{ij} \sum_{m'=1}^{i} 1 = h\,\delta_{ij} \qquad 10\cdot27$$

We see, therefore, that the characters of the matrices of the irreducible representations form sets of orthogonal vectors. Since the character is unchanged by a similarity transformation, we see that two non-equivalent representations have different character systems and that two irreducible representations with the same character system are equivalent.

Since the characters of all matrices of a given representation which correspond to operations in the same class are equal, 10·27 can be written as

$$\sum_{\rho=1}^{k} \chi_i(R_\rho)\chi_j(R_\rho)g_\rho = h\,\delta_{ij}$$

or

$$\sum_{\rho=1} \chi_i(R_\rho)\sqrt{\frac{g_\rho}{h}}\,\chi_j(R_\rho)\sqrt{\frac{g_\rho}{h}} = \delta_{ij} \qquad 10·28$$

where g_ρ is the number of elements in class ρ, R_ρ is any one of the operations in this class, $\chi(R_\rho)$ is the corresponding character, and k is the number of classes. The normalized characters $\chi_i(R_\rho)\sqrt{\dfrac{g_\rho}{h}}$ are therefore the components of a set of orthogonal vectors in k-dimensional space. Since there can be k such vectors, we see that the number of irreducible representations is equal to the number of classes.

From the relations already developed it is possible to obtain further interesting results. Any matrix representation of a group must be some one of the irreducible representations or some combination of them; otherwise it would be an additional irreducible representation, but the number of irreducible representations is limited to the number of classes. Any reducible representation can be reduced to its irreducible representations by a similarity transformation which leaves the character unchanged. Thus we can write for the character of a matrix R of the reducible representation the expression

$$\chi(R) = \sum_{=1}^{k} a_j\chi_j(R) \qquad 10·29$$

where a_j is the number of times the jth irreducible representation occurs in the reducible representation. From 10·27 we have

$$\sum_{R}\chi(R)\chi_i(R) = \sum_{R}\sum_{j}a_j\chi_j(R)\chi_i(R) = ha_i \qquad 10·30$$

so that the number of times the irreducible representation Γ_i occurs in the reducible representation is

$$a_i = \frac{1}{h}\sum_R \chi(R)\chi_i(R) \qquad 10\cdot31$$

Since there is a one-to-one correspondence between the character systems of a group and the irreducible representations of the group, we will usually find it sufficient to deal with the characters themselves rather than with the irreducible representations. For any group, the character table can be built up by means of the relations already derived. We here summarize these rules in a convenient form.

RULE 1. The number of irreducible representations is equal to the number of classes of the group.

RULE 2. The sum of the squares of the dimensions of the irreducible representations of a group is equal to the order of the group, that is,

$$l_1^2 + l_2^2 + \cdots + l_k^2 = h$$

Since $l_j = \chi_j(E)$, this is equivalent to the relation

$$\sum_j [\chi_j(E)]^2 = h \qquad 10\cdot32$$

RULE 3. The character systems of non-equivalent irreducible representations form orthogonal vectors; that is

$$\sum_R \chi_i(R)\chi_j(R) = 0; \quad i \neq j \qquad 10\cdot33$$

RULE 4. The sum of the squares of the characters of a given irreducible representation is equal to the order of the group; that is

$$\sum_R [\chi_i(R)]^2 = h \qquad 10\cdot34$$

10c. Group Theory and Quantum Mechanics. We consider now the Schrödinger equation

$$\mathbf{H}\psi_i = E_i\psi_i$$

for some atomic or molecular system. Suppose that R is some transformation of coordinates which has the effect of interchanging like particles in the system. For example, in helium, R could be the transformation which interchanges the two electrons; in H_2O, R could be the transformation which interchanges the hydrogen atoms. We subject both sides of the Schrödinger equation to the transformation R, obtaining $RH\psi_i = RE_i\psi_i$. Since R interchanges only like particles, it can have no effect on the Hamiltonian, so that $RH = HR$. R, of course, commutes with the constant E_i, so that we have

$$\mathbf{H}R\psi_i = E_iR\psi_i \qquad 10\cdot35$$

that is, the function $R\psi_i$ is a solution of the Schrödinger equation with the eigenvalue E_i. If E_i is a non-degenerate eigenvalue, then ψ_i or constant multiples of ψ_i are the only eigenfunctions satisfying 10·35, so that for this case we have $R\psi_i = c\psi_i$; in order that $R\psi_i$ be normalized, $c = \pm1$. If E_i is k-fold degenerate, then any linear combination of the functions $\psi_{i1}, \psi_{i2}, \cdots \psi_{ik}$ will be a solution of 10·35, so that in this case we have

$$R\psi_{il} = \sum_{j=1}^{k} a_{jl}\psi_{ij} \qquad 10\cdot36$$

where the a_{il}'s must satisfy the relation

$$\sum_{j=1}^{k} a_{jl}^2 = 1$$

If S is another operation which interchanges like particles, we also have

$$S\psi_{ij} = \sum_{m=1}^{k} b_{mj}\psi_{im} \qquad 10\cdot37$$

Applying operation S to 10·36 gives

$$SR\psi_{il} = \sum_{j=1}^{k} a_{jl}S\psi_{ij} = \sum_{j=1}^{k}\sum_{m=1}^{k} a_{jl}b_{mj}\psi_{im} \qquad 10\cdot38$$

Now the product of S and R, which we may denote by $SR = T$, is likewise an operation which interchanges like particles, so that

$$T\psi_{il} = \sum_{m=1}^{k} c_{ml}\psi_{im} \qquad 10\cdot39$$

Comparing 10·38 and 10·39, we see that

$$c_{ml} = \sum_{j=1}^{k} b_{mj}a_{jl} \qquad 10\cdot40$$

If we now form the matrix $\mathbf{a}$ from the coefficients a_{jl}, and the matrix $\mathbf{b}$ from the coefficients b_{mj}, we see that the product of these two matrices is equal to the matrix $\mathbf{c}$ formed from the coefficient c_{ml}; moreover, all the matrices are unitary. In other words, the matrices obtained from the coefficients in the expansion of $R\psi_{il}$, etc., form a representation of the group of operations which leave the Hamiltonian unchanged. The set of eigenfunctions $\psi_{i1}, \cdots \psi_{ik}$ is said to form a basis for a representation of the group, since the representation is generated by the application of operations R, S, etc. The dimension

of the representation is equal to the degeneracy of the corresponding
eigenvalue. The representations generated by the eigenfunctions
corresponding to a single eigenvalue are irreducible representations, as
otherwise it would be possible to form sets of linear combinations

$$\psi'_{i1}, \psi'_{i2} \cdots; \quad \psi'_{is}, \psi'_{i,\,s+1} \cdots; \quad \cdots; \quad \cdots \psi'_{ik}$$

of the original eigenfunctions such that operations of the group would
send one of the new eigenfunctions into a linear combination involving
only members of the same set. But, if this were possible, the eigenvalues corresponding to the new sets could be different, which would
contradict our original assumption, except for the extremely rare case
of " accidental degeneracy " (where two eigenvalues are the same
even though the corresponding eigenfunctions behave differently under
the operations of the group). We may therefore in general assume
that sets of eigenfunctions with the same eigenvalue form a basis for
an irreducible representation of the group of operations which leave
the Hamiltonian unchanged. Returning to our original notation, if
Γ_j is an irreducible representation of dimension k, and if $\psi^j_1, \psi^j_2 \cdots \psi^j_k$
is a set of degenerate eigenfunctions which form the basis for the jth
irreducible representation of the group of symmetry operations, these
eigenfunctions transform according to the relation

$$R\psi^j_i = \sum_{l=1}^{k} \Gamma_j(R)_{li} \psi^j_l \qquad\qquad 10\cdot 41$$

If we are dealing with a symmetrical atomic or molecular system, these
considerations place a severe restriction on the possible eigenfunctions
of the system. All possible eigenfunctions must form bases for some
irreducible representation of the group of symmetry operations. From
a knowledge of the irreducible representations of the group, we therefore know immediately what degrees of degeneracy are possible. The
form of the possible eigenfunctions is also determined to a large extent,
since they must transform in a quite definite way under the operations
of the group. For example, if our system had the symmetry of the
group of three points which we have discussed in detail in this chapter,
our eigenfunctions would be of the following types. There would be
a set of eigenfunctions which would form bases for the representation
Γ_1. These eigenfunctions would be non-degenerate and would remain
unchanged if subjected to any of the operations of the group.
There would be another set of non-degenerate eigenfunctions which
form bases for the representation Γ_2; these would remain unchanged
if subjected to operations E, D, and F, but would change sign if subjected to operations A, B, or C. Finally, there would be a set of doubly

degenerate eigenvalues; two eigenfunctions with the same eigenvalue would behave in the manner determined by the matrices for the irreducible representation Γ_3 and equation 10·41. No other types of eigenfunctions would be possible; for example, there would be no triply degenerate eigenvalues, nor would there be any non-degenerate eigenfunctions which changed sign when subjected to operations D or F.

10d. The Direct Product. Let us suppose that R is some operation of a group, and that $A_1, A_2 \cdots A_m$; $B_1, B_2 \cdots B_n$ are two sets of functions which form bases for representations of the group. Then

$$RA_i = \sum_{j=1}^{m} a_{ji}A_j$$

$$RB_k = \sum_{l=1}^{n} b_{lk}B_l$$

and

$$RA_iB_k = \sum_{j=1}^{m} \sum_{l=1}^{n} a_{ji}b_{lk}A_jB_l = \sum_j \sum_l c_{jl,\ ik}\, A_jB_l$$

The set of functions A_iB_k forms a basis for a representation of the group of dimension mn. The matrix $\mathbf{c}$ of this representation has the character

$$\chi(c) = \sum_j \sum_l c_{jl,\ jl} = \sum_{j=1}^{m} \sum_{l=1}^{n} a_{jj}b_{ll} = \chi(a)\chi(b) \qquad 10\cdot42$$

The set of functions A_iB_k is called the direct product of the sets of functions A_i and B_k. Equation 10·42 then tells us that the character of the representation of the direct product is equal to the product of the characters of the individual representations. The representation of the direct product of two irreducible representations will in general be a reducible representation but may be expressed in terms of the irreducible representations by means of equation 10·31. For example, for the direct products of the irreducible representations Γ_1, Γ_2, Γ_3 of the symmetric group of three points, we have

$$\Gamma_1\Gamma_1 = \Gamma_1 \qquad\qquad \Gamma_1\Gamma_2 = \Gamma_2$$
$$\Gamma_2\Gamma_2 = \Gamma_1 \qquad\qquad \Gamma_1\Gamma_3 = \Gamma_3$$
$$\Gamma_3\Gamma_3 = \Gamma_1 + \Gamma_2 + \Gamma_3 \qquad\qquad \Gamma_2\Gamma_3 = \Gamma_3$$

The importance of the direct product appears when we wish to evaluate integrals involving functions which are bases for representations of the group. If we have an integral $\int \varphi_A\varphi_B \, d\tau$, this integral will be different from zero only if the integrand is invariant under all the operations of the group or may be expressed as a sum of terms of which at least one is invariant. The integrand belongs to the representation $\Gamma_{\text{int}} = \Gamma_A \Gamma_B$ where $\Gamma_A \Gamma_B$ is the direct product of the representations of φ_A and φ_B. In general, $\Gamma_A \Gamma_B$ will be reducible, that is, will be expressible as

$$\Gamma_A \Gamma_B = \sum_i a_i \Gamma_i$$

where the Γ_i's are irreducible representations of the group. The integral will be different from zero only if $\Gamma_A \Gamma_B$ contains the totally symmetrical representation Γ_1. It may readily be verified from the tables in Appendix VII that, if the characters of the representation are real, as they will be in all cases of interest to us, then $\Gamma_A \Gamma_B$ contains Γ_1 only if $\Gamma_A = \Gamma_B$. For our purposes, therefore, we may state the following corollary to this theorem: The integral $\int \varphi_A f \varphi_B \, d\tau$ is different from zero only if $\Gamma_A \Gamma_B = \Gamma_f$. Moreover, since the Hamiltonian operator belongs to the totally symmetrical representation Γ_1, the integral $\int \varphi_A \mathbf{H} \varphi_B \, d\tau$ is different from zero only if $\Gamma_A = \Gamma_B$. In the secular determinant of the type

$$\begin{vmatrix} H_{11} - S_{11}E & H_{12} - S_{12}E & \cdots & H_{1n} - S_{1n}E \\ H_{21} - S_{21}E & H_{22} - S_{22}E & \cdots & H_{2n} - S_{2n}E \\ \cdot & & & \\ \cdot & & & \\ \cdot & & & \\ H_{n1} - S_{n1}E & H_{n2} - S_{n2}E & \cdots & H_{nn} - S_{nn}E \end{vmatrix} = 0$$

the terms H_{ij} and S_{ij} will be different from zero only if φ_i and φ_j belong to the same irreducible representation. By classifying the eigenfunctions φ according to the representation to which they belong, it is often possible to reduce the order of the secular equation.

It may happen that in certain problems we start a perturbation calculation with zero-order eigenfunctions which do not themselves form bases for irreducible representations of a group. If we take the proper linear combinations of these eigenfunctions so that the new eigenfunctions form bases for irreducible representations, the secular equation will be simplified. These linear combinations can be found by the following procedure. Denote the original eigenfunctions by φ' and the new by φ, where φ_{km}^i is the eigenfunction belonging to the ith irreducible representation of dimension l_i with the eigenvalue E_{ik}. Suppose further that there are s_i eigenvalues corresponding to the representation Γ_i; that is, the representation Γ_i occurs s_i times in the reducible representation to which the φ''s belong. Then any of the

φ'''s may be expressed in terms of the φ's by

$$\varphi' = \sum_i \sum_{k=1}^{s_i} \sum_{m=1}^{l_i} c_{ikm}\varphi_{km}^i \qquad 10\cdot43$$

If R is any operation of the group, then by $10\cdot41$

$$R\varphi' = \sum_i \sum_{k=1}^{s_i} \sum_{m=1}^{l_i} c_{ikm} \sum_{n=1}^{l_i} \Gamma_i(R)_{nm}\varphi_{kn}^i \qquad 10\cdot44$$

If we now multiply by $\chi_j(R) = \sum_{t=1}^{l_j} \Gamma_j(R)_{tt}$ and sum over all operations of the group, we have

$$\sum_R \chi_j(R)R\varphi' = \sum_i \sum_{k=1}^{s_i} \sum_{m=1}^{l_i} c_{ikm} \sum_{n=1}^{l_i} \sum_{t=1}^{l_j} \sum_R \Gamma_j(R)_{tt}\Gamma_i(R)_{nm}\varphi_{kn} \qquad 10\cdot45$$

From $10\cdot24$, we see that this expression reduces to

$$\sum_R \chi_j(R)R\varphi' = \sum_{k=1}^{s_j} \sum_{m=1}^{l_j} c_{jkm}\frac{h}{l_j} \sum_{n=1}^{i} \sum_{t=1}^{i} \delta_{tn}\delta_{tm}\,\varphi_{kn}^j \qquad 10\cdot46$$

$$= \sum_{k=1}^{s_j} \sum_{t=1}^{l_j} \frac{h}{l_j} c_{jkt}\,\varphi_{kt}^j \qquad 10\cdot47$$

Equation $10\cdot47$ has the following meaning. If both s_j and l_j are unity, then $\sum_R \chi_j(R)R\varphi'$ will give a constant times φ_{11}^j, regardless of which φ' we use. If l_j is unity, but s_j is, say, two, then $\sum_R \chi_j(R)R\varphi'$ will give expressions of the form $a\varphi_{11}^j + b\varphi_{21}^j$. There will be two linearly independent expressions of this form; the combinations of those which correspond to the two eigenvalues are determined in the usual way after the corresponding two-row determinant has been solved. For s_j equal to unity, l_j equal to 2, we obtain two independent linear combinations which have the same eigenvalue. For s_j and l_j equal to 2, we obtain four independent linear combinations, the solution of the corresponding secular determinant will then enable us to form two sets of two combinations each, one set for each of the two eigenvalues. The other cases are analogous.

A description of the various symmetry groups of interest in the theory of molecular structure has been included in Appendix VII. Appendix VII also contains the character tables for these groups, as well as the transformation properties of certain quantities which will be of interest in our later work. We shall make considerable use of group theory in later chapters; the actual applications are much easier to perform than might be expected from some of the rather complicated equations which appear above.

CHAPTER XI

ELECTRONIC STATES OF DIATOMIC MOLECULES

11a. Separation of Electronic and Nuclear Motions. A molecule is usually defined as a stable group of atoms held together by valence forces. We shall here, however, use the word molecule in a somewhat wider sense, to denote any system of atomic nuclei and electrons, whether stable or not. If we regard the problem of the motion of such a system from the classical viewpoint, we see that, because of the great masses of the nuclei as compared with the mass of the electron, the electrons will move with much greater velocities than the nuclei, so that, to a first approximation at least, the motion of the electrons is the same as it would be if the nuclei were held fixed in space.

This same approximation is stated quantum mechanically by the assumption that the eigenfunction ψ for the whole system may be expressed as the product of the two factors ψ_n and ψ_e, where ψ_n involves only the coordinates of the nuclei, while ψ_e is an eigenfunction of the electronic coordinates found by solving Schrödinger's equation with the assumption that the nuclei are held fixed in space. The coordinates of the nuclei would thus enter ψ_e only as parameters.

In order to test the validity of this assumption we need to see if such an eigenfunction can satisfy, to a good approximation, the wave equation for the whole system. The exact Hamiltonian operator may be written as

$$\mathbf{H} = -\sum_\alpha \frac{h^2}{8\pi^2 M_\alpha} \nabla_\alpha^2 - \sum_i \frac{h^2}{8\pi^2 m} \nabla_i^2 + V_{nn} + V_{ne} + V_{ee} \qquad 11\cdot1$$

where the first term represents the kinetic energy of the nuclei, the second represents the kinetic energy of the electrons, and V_{nn}, V_{ne}, and V_{ee} are the contributions to the potential energy arising from nuclear, nuclear-electronic, and electronic interactions, respectively. If the nuclei were assumed to be fixed in space, the Hamiltonian for the electrons would be

$$\mathbf{H}_e = -\sum_i \frac{h^2}{8\pi^2 m} \nabla_i^2 + V_{ne} + V_{ee} \qquad 11\cdot2$$

If we now represent the remaining terms in 11·1 by $\mathbf{H}_n$ we have

$$\mathbf{H}_n = -\sum_\alpha \frac{h^2}{8\pi^2 M_\alpha} \nabla_\alpha^2 + V_{nn} \qquad 11\cdot 3$$

and

$$\mathbf{H} = \mathbf{H}_n + \mathbf{H}_e \qquad 11\cdot 4$$

We define ψ_e as the function which satisfies the equation

$$\mathbf{H}_e\psi_e = E_e\psi_e \qquad 11\cdot 5$$

where E_e is the electronic energy. Now if we write the wave equation for the complete system, assuming ψ to be of the form $\psi_n\psi_e$, where ψ_n is a function of nuclear coordinates only, we have

$$\mathbf{H}\psi_e\psi_n = E\psi_e\psi_n \qquad 11\cdot 6$$

or

$$-\sum_\alpha \frac{h^2}{8\pi^2 M_\alpha} \nabla_\alpha^2\psi_e\psi_n - \sum_i \frac{h^2}{8\pi^2 m} \nabla_i^2\psi_e\psi_n$$
$$+ (V_{nn} + V_{ne} + V_{ee})\psi_e\psi_n = E\psi_e\psi_n \qquad 11\cdot 7$$

Now

$$\nabla_\alpha^2\psi_e\psi_n = \psi_e\nabla_\alpha^2\psi_n + 2\nabla_\alpha\psi_e \cdot \nabla_\alpha\psi_n + \psi_n\nabla_\alpha^2\psi_e$$
$$\nabla_i^2\psi_e\psi_n = \psi_n\nabla_i^2\psi_e$$

so that 11·7 becomes

$$\left\{-\sum_\alpha \frac{h^2}{4\pi^2 M_\alpha} \nabla_\alpha\psi_e \cdot \nabla_\alpha\psi_n - \sum_\alpha \frac{h^2}{8\pi^2 M_\alpha} \psi_n\nabla_\alpha^2\psi_e\right\} + \psi_e\sum_\alpha - \frac{h^2}{8\pi^2 M_\alpha} \nabla_\alpha^2\psi_n$$
$$+ \psi_n\sum_i - \frac{h^2}{8\pi^2 m} \nabla_i^2\psi_e + (V_{nn} + V_{ne} + V_{ee})\psi_e\psi_n = E\psi_e\psi_n \qquad 11\cdot 8$$

If we neglect the terms in braces, this reduces to

$$\frac{\psi_e}{\psi_n}\sum_\alpha - \frac{h^2}{8\pi^2 M_\alpha} \nabla_\alpha^2\psi_n + \left[\sum_i - \frac{h^2}{8\pi^2 m} \nabla_i^2\psi_e + (V_{ne} + V_{ee})\psi_e\right]$$
$$- E\psi_e + V_{nn}\psi_e = 0 \qquad 11\cdot 9$$

or, from 11·2 and 11·5,

$$\sum_\alpha - \frac{h^2}{8\pi^2 M_\alpha} \nabla_\alpha^2\psi_n + V_{nn}\psi_n + E_e\psi_n - E\psi_n = 0 \qquad 11\cdot 10$$

which, because of 11·3, is equivalent to

$$(\mathbf{H}_n + E_e)\psi_n = E\psi_n \qquad 11\cdot 11$$

We thus see that, if our approximation is valid, the effective Hamiltonian for nuclear motion is just that which would arise if we assumed

that the electronic energy E_e, which will be a function of the internuclear distances regarded as parameters, behaved as a part of the
potential energy of the nuclei. For equation 11·11 to be valid, the
terms in braces in 11·8 must be small in comparison to the term
$\psi_e \sum_\alpha - \dfrac{h^2}{8\pi^2 M_\alpha} \nabla_\alpha^2 \psi_n$, which represents the kinetic energy of the nuclei.
ψ_e is usually only a slowly varying function of the nuclear coordinates,
so that $\nabla_\alpha \psi_e$ is much smaller than $\nabla_\alpha \psi_n$; hence the approximation will
be valid. Otherwise the neglected terms may be treated as a perturba-
tion and will give rise to energy terms representing the interactions
of electronic and nuclear motions. We shall postpone further consideration of equation 11·11 to Chapter XIV, devoting the remainder
of this and the following two chapters to the solution of equation 11·5.

11b. Molecular Orbitals; The H_2^+ Ion. The problem of the
electronic structure of molecules bears many resemblances to the problem of atomic structure. Just as the eigenfunctions of atoms are
usually built up as linear combinations of atomic orbitals, so may the
eigenfunctions of molecules be approximated by a series of molecular
orbitals. No method for the construction of molecular orbitals, however, is comparable in accuracy to the Hartree method for atoms. It
is true that the principles of the Hartree method apply equally to atoms
and molecules, but the difficulties encountered in the numerical integrations needed to calculate the Hartree field of even the simplest
molecules have not yet been overcome.

The chief source of trouble in molecular problems is the absence of
the spherical symmetry of the isolated atom. The operators $\mathbf{M}^2$
and its components, which played such an important part in our treatment of atomic structure, no longer commute with the Hamiltonian,
and so they lose their usefulness. It is true that many molecules have
some elements of symmetry, when the problem can be simplified with
the aid of group theory, but these symmetry elements are properties
of individual molecules and cannot be used in the general theory of
molecular structure.

In order to set up a system of molecular orbitals we are almost
forced to use linear combinations of some set of functions in terms of
which an arbitrary function may be expressed. Such a set might be
the atomic orbitals of any one of the atoms composing the molecule.
This set, however, would converge very slowly if we tried to expand
in terms of it an orbital belonging to some other atom of the molecule.
If we use as our set the orbitals of all the atoms of the molecule we
should expect rather rapid convergence of our molecular orbitals. The
value of this method can be estimated only by actual trial.

Let us therefore suppose that we have set up an approximate potential field V for the molecule, in which an electron is to move. ' This field might, for example, be that obtained by the superposition of the Hartree fields of the component atoms. Let us also suppose that we are given a set of functions $\varphi_1, \varphi_2, \cdots \varphi_n$, which we shall think of as atomic orbitals of the various atoms of the molecule, although any set of independent functions could be used. The approximate orbitals can then be found by the method of trial eigenfunctions, using $\varphi_1, \cdots \varphi_n$ as the zero-order functions. The approximate energies of the molecular orbitals will therefore be the roots of the secular equation

$$
\begin{vmatrix}
H_{11} - S_{11}E & \cdots & H_{1n} - S_{1n}E \\
\cdot & & \\
\cdot & & \\
\cdot & & \\
H_{n1} - S_{n1}E & \cdots & H_{nn} - S_{nn}E
\end{vmatrix} = 0 \qquad 11\text{·}12
$$

where, if $\mathbf{H}$ is the one-electron Hamiltonian $\mathbf{H} = -\dfrac{h^2}{8\pi^2 m}\nabla^2 + V$,

$$
H_{ij} = \int \varphi_i^* \mathbf{H} \varphi_j \, d\tau \qquad 11\text{·}13
$$

$$
S_{ij} = \int \varphi_i^* \varphi_j \, d\tau \qquad 11\text{·}14
$$

Unless the atoms of the molecule are infinitely far apart, the integral S_{ij} will not in general vanish, since φ_i and φ_j are not necessarily eigenfunctions of the same Hamiltonian and are therefore not necessarily orthogonal.

If, however, the atoms are a large distance apart, all the off-diagonal terms of 11·12 will vanish; those between orbitals of different atoms because each orbital vanishes over the region where the other has a finite value, those on the same atom because then $\mathbf{H}$ is just the atomic Hamiltonian in the region where the orbitals do not vanish, and the orbitals are eigenfunctions of the atomic Hamiltonian. If the atomic orbitals are normalized, equation 11·12 is of the form

$$
\begin{vmatrix}
H_{11} - E & 0 & \cdots & 0 \\
0 & H_{22} - E & \cdots & 0 \\
\cdot & & & \\
\cdot & & & \\
\cdot & & & \\
0 & 0 & \cdots & H_{nn} - E
\end{vmatrix} = 0 \qquad 11\text{·}15
$$

and the roots are $E = H_{11}, H_{22}, \cdots H_{nn}$. In other words, the energies of the molecular orbitals are equal to the energies of the atomic orbitals if the atoms are far apart.

If we now bring the atoms together, the roots of equation 11·12 will change continuously. We may thus correlate each of the n roots of 11·12 for any configuration of the nuclei with one of the energies of one of the separated atoms. This does not, however, imply that each molecular orbital will become an atomic orbital on separation of the nuclei, for, if any two of the atomic orbitals have the same energy, the molecular orbitals whose energies approach this energy on separation will usually go over into some linear combination of these orbitals. To illustrate this effect let us consider two orbitals which have the same energy at infinite separation. When the separation is large, equation 11·12 has the form

$$\begin{vmatrix} E_1 - E & \epsilon \\ \epsilon & E_1 - E \end{vmatrix} = 0 \qquad\qquad 11\cdot16$$

where E_1 is the energy of each orbital and ϵ is the small value of H_{12}. The roots of this equation are $E = E_1 \pm \epsilon$. If we take $E = E_1 + \epsilon$, the linear combination of φ_1 and φ_2 given by equation 7·49 is $\dfrac{1}{\sqrt{2}}\,(\varphi_1 + \varphi_2)$; while if we take $E = E_1 - \epsilon$, the linear combination is $\dfrac{1}{\sqrt{2}}\,(\varphi_1 - \varphi_2)$. If we go to the other extreme and let the distances between the nuclei become zero, the Hamiltonian of the molecule reduces to that of an atom whose nuclear charge is the sum of the nuclear charges of the atoms composing the molecule. The proper orbitals are then just the atomic orbitals of this " united atom." Each molecular orbital may therefore be designated by the united atom orbital into which it degenerates when the nuclei are brought together, as well as by the atomic orbital (or combination of such) which it becomes when the nuclei are separated.

As an example of this procedure let us consider the hydrogen molecular ion $H_2{}^+$. In this molecule just one electron is moving in the potential field of the two nuclei. We may get a rough description of the lowest orbital of this molecule by considering it as a linear combination of the $1s$ orbitals of the two hydrogen atoms. Let us designate the nuclei by the letters a and b, the $1s$ orbital of an electron in the field of nucleus a alone by ψ_a, and the $1s$ orbital of an electron in the field of nucleus b alone by ψ_b. Analytically (in atomic units)

$$\psi_a = \frac{1}{\sqrt{\pi}} e^{-R_a}$$

$$\psi_b = \frac{1}{\sqrt{\pi}} e^{-R_b}$$

11·17

If we put

$$S = \int \psi_a \psi_b \, d\tau \qquad H_{bb} = \int \psi_b \mathbf{H} \psi_b \, d\tau$$

$$H_{aa} = \int \psi_a \mathbf{H} \psi_a \, d\tau \qquad H_{ab} = \int \psi_a \mathbf{H} \psi_b \, d\tau = H_{ba}$$

11·18

the determination of the coefficients in the linear combination

$$\psi = c_a \psi_a + c_b \psi_b \qquad\qquad 11·19$$

leads to the following secular determinant for the energy

$$\begin{vmatrix} H_{aa} - E & H_{ab} - SE \\ H_{ab} - SE & H_{bb} - E \end{vmatrix} = 0 \qquad\qquad 11·20$$

From the symmetry of the problem it is evident that $H_{aa} = H_{bb}$. Using this relation, the roots of the determinant are found to be

$$H_{aa} - E = \mp (H_{ab} - SE)$$

or

$$E_1 = \frac{H_{aa} + H_{ab}}{1 + S}; \quad E_2 = \frac{H_{aa} - H_{ab}}{1 - S} \qquad 11·21$$

The first root gives the following set of simultaneous equations for the coefficients in 11·19

$$\pm [(H_{aa}S - H_{ab})c_a + (H_{ab} - SH_{aa})c_b] = 0 \qquad 11·22$$

Equations 11·22 are satisfied only if $c_a = c_b$. In order that the eigenfunction 11·19 be normalized, we must have

$$c_a^2 + c_b^2 + 2c_a c_b S = 1$$

so that

$$c_a = c_b = \frac{1}{\sqrt{2 + 2S}}$$

Similarly, the second root gives

$$c_a = -c_b = \frac{1}{\sqrt{2 - 2S}}$$

The wave functions and their associated energies are therefore

$$\psi_1 = \frac{\psi_a + \psi_b}{\sqrt{2 + 2S}} \qquad E_1 = \frac{H_{aa} + H_{ab}}{1 + S}$$

$$\psi_2 = \frac{\psi_a - \psi_b}{\sqrt{2 - 2S}} \qquad E_2 = \frac{H_{aa} - H_{ab}}{1 - S}$$

11·23

The integrals S, H_{aa}, and H_{ab} may all be evaluated exactly. In atomic units the Hamiltonian is

$$\mathbf{H} = -\left(\tfrac{1}{2}\nabla^2 + \frac{1}{R_a} + \frac{1}{R_b} - \frac{1}{R}\right)$$

11·24

where R is the internuclear distance in units of a_0. Since

$$\mathbf{H}\psi_a = \left(E_{\mathrm{H}} - \frac{1}{R_b} + \frac{1}{R}\right)\psi_a$$

where E_{H} is the energy of the ground state of hydrogen, the matrix elements for the energy become

$$H_{aa} = E_{\mathrm{H}} + \frac{1}{R} - \epsilon_{aa}; \qquad \epsilon_{aa} = \int \frac{\psi_a^2}{R_b} d\tau$$

$$H_{ab} = \left(E_{\mathrm{H}} + \frac{1}{R}\right)S - \epsilon_{ab}; \qquad \epsilon_{ab} = \int \frac{\psi_a \psi_b}{R_a} d\tau$$

11·25

so that the energy levels are

$$E_1 = E_{\mathrm{H}} + \frac{1}{R} - \frac{\epsilon_{aa} + \epsilon_{ab}}{1 + S}$$

$$E_2 = E_{\mathrm{H}} + \frac{1}{R} - \frac{\epsilon_{aa} - \epsilon_{ab}}{1 - S}$$

11·26

In order to evaluate the integrals involved in 11·25 and 11·26, it is convenient to transform to elliptical coordinates (Appendix III)

$$\mu = \frac{R_a + R_b}{R}; \quad \nu = \frac{R_a - R_b}{R}; \quad \varphi$$

$$d\tau = \frac{R^3}{8}(\mu^2 - \nu^2)\, d\mu\, d\nu\, d\varphi$$

$$1 \leq \mu \leq \infty; \quad -1 \leq \nu \leq 1; \quad 0 \leq \varphi \leq 2\pi$$

For the " overlap " integral S we have

$$S = \int \psi_a \psi_b \, d\tau = \frac{1}{\pi} \int e^{-(R_a + R_b)} \, d\tau$$

$$= \frac{R^3}{8\pi} \int_1^\infty e^{-R\mu} \, d\mu \int_{-1}^1 (\mu^2 - \nu^2) \, d\nu \int_0^{2\pi} d\varphi$$

$$= \frac{R^3}{2} \int_1^\infty \mu^2 e^{-R\mu} \, d\mu - \frac{R^3}{6} \int_1^\infty e^{-R\mu} \, d\mu \qquad 11\cdot27$$

The integrals involved are special cases of the general integral (Appendix VIII).

$$\int_1^\infty x^n e^{-ax} \, dx = \frac{n! e^{-a}}{a^{n+1}} \sum_{k=0}^n \frac{a^k}{k!} = A_n(a) \qquad 11\cdot28$$

so that S is readily found to be

$$S = e^{-R} \left(1 + R + \frac{R^2}{3} \right) \qquad 11\cdot29$$

The integral ϵ_{aa} is

$$\epsilon_{aa} = \frac{1}{\pi} \int \frac{e^{-2R_a}}{R_b} \, d\tau = \frac{1}{\pi} \frac{2}{R} \int \frac{e^{-R(\mu+\nu)}}{\mu - \nu} \, d\tau$$

$$= \frac{R^2}{2} \left\{ \int_1^\infty \mu e^{-R\mu} \, d\mu \int_{-1}^1 e^{-R\nu} \, d\nu + \int_1^\infty e^{-R\mu} \, d\mu \int_{-1}^1 \nu e^{-R\nu} \, d\nu \right\} \qquad 11\cdot30$$

The integrals in ν are special cases of the integral

$$\int_{-1}^1 x^n e^{-ax} \, dx = (-1)^{n+1} A_n(-a) - A_n(a) \qquad 11\cdot31$$

Inserting the proper values for the integrals gives

$$\epsilon_{aa} = \frac{1}{R} \{ 1 - e^{-2R}(1 + R) \} \qquad 11\cdot32$$

In the same way, we find for ϵ_{ab}:

$$\epsilon_{ab} = e^{-R}(1 + R) \qquad 11\cdot33$$

For large values of R we see that $S = 0$, $H_{aa} = E_H$, $H_{ab} = 0$, so that $E_1 = E_2 = E_H$, that is, just the energy of a normal hydrogen atom, as of course it should be. For $R = 0$, $S = 1$, $H_{aa} = E_H - 1 + \frac{1}{R}$, $H_{ab} = H_{aa}$. Neglecting the nuclear repulsion term $\frac{1}{R}$ for the time being, we see that the electronic energies are $E_1' = 3E_H$, $E_2' = 0$.

When $R = 0$, the lowest molecular orbital should become the $1s$ atomic orbital of He, with an energy $4E_H$. Our approximation is therefore in error by an amount E_H for $R = 0$, although it is correct for large R. The reason for this is clear. For large R the orbital ψ_1 is the correct orbital for a hydrogen atom, but for $R = 0$ it is again a hydrogen orbital, but surrounding a nucleus whose charge is two instead of one. In order to get a good approximation for small R we should take a number of orbitals for each atom.

Referring to 11·26, and for simplicity neglecting S as compared with unity, we see that the difference in energy between the two states, to this approximation, is just $2\epsilon_{ab}$. Also, to this approximation, state ψ_2 is unstable with respect to a hydrogen atom and a proton by an amount $(1 + R)(e^{-R} + e^{-2R})$ while state ψ_1 is stable by an amount $(1 + R)(e^{-R} - e^{-2R})$. That this should be so may be seen qualitatively in the following manner. For state ψ_1, the electron density is

$$\rho_1 = \psi_1^* \psi_1 = \frac{1}{2 + 2S} (\psi_a^2 + \psi_b^2 + 2\psi_a \psi_b)$$

While for state ψ_2 it is

$$\rho_2 = \psi_2^* \psi_2 = \frac{1}{2 - 2S} (\psi_a^2 + \psi_b^2 - 2\psi_a \psi_b)$$

At a point midway between the two nuclei, we have

$$\rho_1 = \frac{4}{2 + 2S} \psi_a^2; \quad \rho_2 = 0$$

State ψ_1 thus has a much greater accumulation of charge between the two nuclei than state ψ_2; the attraction between this accumulation of charge and the two protons may be considered as producing the stability of state ψ_1.

It is of some interest to look at this problem from the following viewpoint. The wave functions, including the time-dependent term, are, if we neglect S as compared with unity,

$$\Psi_1 = \psi_1 e^{-i\frac{E_1}{\hbar}t} = \frac{1}{\sqrt{2}} (\psi_a + \psi_b)e^{-i\frac{E_1}{\hbar}t}$$

$$\Psi_2 = \psi_2 e^{-i\frac{E_2}{\hbar}t} = \frac{1}{\sqrt{2}} (\psi_a - \psi_b)e^{-i\frac{E_2}{\hbar}t}$$

Any linear combination of these two solutions will represent some particular distribution of electron density. Let us consider the combination $\Psi = \frac{1}{\sqrt{2}} (\Psi_1 + \Psi_2)$. The electron density corresponding to this state is

$$\rho = \frac{1}{2}\left(\psi_1^2 + \psi_1\psi_2\left[e^{i\frac{(E_1-E_2)}{\hbar}t} + e^{-i\frac{(E_1-E_2)}{\hbar}t}\right] + \psi_2^2\right)$$

For $t = 0$, $\rho = \frac{1}{2}(\psi_1 + \psi_2)^2 = \psi_a^2$, so that the electron is on nucleus a.

For $t = \dfrac{\pi\hbar}{E_1 - E_2}$,

$$\rho = \tfrac{1}{2}(\psi_1 - \psi_2)^2 = \psi_b^2$$

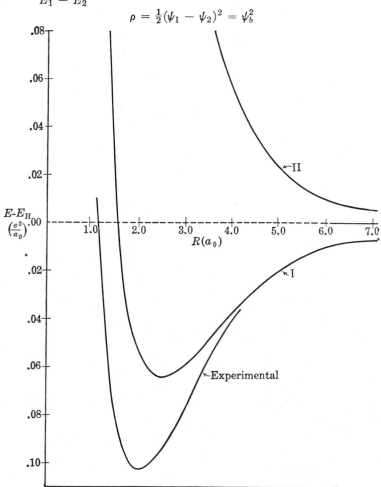

FIG. 11·1.   Binding energy of H₂⁺ as a function of the internuclear distance.

so that the electron is on nucleus b.   From this viewpoint (which should not be taken too literally), the electron oscillates between a and b, the frequency of the oscillation being $\nu = \dfrac{E_1 - E_2}{h}$.   We thus have the result $\Delta E = h\nu$, where ν is the frequency of the oscillation between the two states and ΔE is the difference in energy between these two states.

In Figure 11·1 the energy levels for these two states are plotted as a function of the internuclear distance R, along with the experimental curve as determined from spectroscopic data.   In Figure 11·2 the dis-

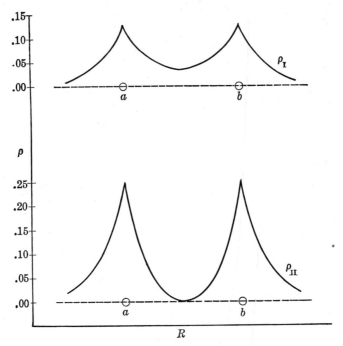

FIG. 11·2.   Electron density distribution in H_2^+.

tribution of charge along the internuclear axis is shown.   It is seen that this approximation gives qualitatively correct results, although quantitatively the treatment is not very satisfactory.   The results can be somewhat improved by taking more complicated zero-order functions.

A simple method of improving the agreement would be to introduce a parameter into ψ_a and ψ_b; for example, we might take

$$\psi_a = \left(\frac{\alpha^3}{\pi}\right)^{\frac{1}{2}} e^{-\alpha R_a}; \quad \psi_b = \left(\frac{\alpha^3}{\pi}\right)^{\frac{1}{2}} e^{-\alpha R_b}$$

and then vary α so that the energy is minimized.   We should then get agreement at $R = 0$ as well as at $R = \infty$.   The energy may be further improved by including in the secular equation the $2p$ orbitals of the hydrogen atoms. The inclusion of these terms partly takes into account the polarization of the hydrogen atom by the other nucleus.

We shall see in Chapter XIV how the depth D_e, the internuclear distance r_e, and the curvature of the energy curve at the minimum may be determined from spectroscopic data. For H_2^+ the band spectra indicate the values $D_e = 2.791$ e.v. and $r_e = 1.06$ Å. The simple theory as described above gives $D_e = 1.76$ e.v. and $r_e = 1.32$ Å. Introduction of the parameter α improves these results to $D_e = 2.25$ e.v. and $r_e = 1.06$ Å,[1] and inclusion of the $2p$ orbitals gives $D_e = 2.71$ e.v., $r_e = 1.06$ A.[2] The value of D_e could, of course, be improved by adding more and more hydrogen orbitals.

The best orbitals which have been obtained were found by a different method of approach. This method is similar to that used in the variational treatment of the helium atom; hydrogenlike orbitals are given up completely. For the H_2^+ ion, the natural coordinates to use are the elliptical coordinates μ, ν, φ. James[3] found that a good approximation to the lowest orbital of this molecule is

$$\psi = e^{-\delta\mu}(1 + c\nu^2)$$

where δ and c are parameters. For the observed internuclear distance 1.06 Å, the best values of the parameters give $D_e = 2.772$ e.v., which is quite close to the experimental value. Even better results may be obtained, however, since the wave equation is separable in these coordinates and may be solved by numerical integration. We shall discuss the results in detail in the following section.

11c. The Electronic States of the H_2^+ Ion. In the theory of the electronic states of molecules, particularly of diatomic molecules, the simplest example, H_2^+, plays a role of importance equal to that of the hydrogen atom in the problem of the electronic structure of complex atoms. We wish at this point, therefore, to present a general discussion of the possible states of this molecule and its exact energy levels before proceeding to the description of more complicated diatomic molecules.

The wave equation for the hydrogen molecule ion may be written as

$$\nabla^2\psi + \frac{2m}{\hbar^2}\left(E + \frac{e^2}{r_a} + \frac{e^2}{r_b} - \frac{e^2}{r_{ab}}\right)\psi = 0 \qquad 11\cdot34$$

[1] B. Finkelstein and G. Horowitz, *Z. Physik*, **48**, 118 (1928).
[2] B. Dickinson, *J. Chem. Phys.*, **1**, 317 (1933).
[3] H. M. James, *J. Chem. Phys.*, **3**, 7 (1935).

We now transform to the elliptical coordinates

$$\mu = \frac{r_a + r_b}{r_{ab}} ; \quad \nu = \frac{r_a - r_b}{r_{ab}} ; \quad \varphi$$

In this coordinate system, the Laplacian operator ∇^2 is (Appendix III)

$$\nabla^2 = \frac{4}{r_{ab}^2(\mu^2 - \nu^2)} \times$$

$$\left\{ \frac{\partial}{\partial \mu}\left[(\mu^2 - 1)\frac{\partial}{\partial \mu} \right] + \frac{\partial}{\partial \nu}\left[(1 - \nu^2)\frac{\partial}{\partial \nu} \right] + \frac{\mu^2 - \nu^2}{(\mu^2 - 1)(1 - \nu^2)}\frac{\partial^2}{\partial \varphi^2} \right\}$$

Equation 11·34, in the new coordinate system, is then

$$\frac{\partial}{\partial \mu}\left[(\mu^2 - 1)\frac{\partial \psi}{\partial \mu} \right] + \frac{\partial}{\partial \nu}\left[(1 - \nu^2)\frac{\partial \psi}{\partial \nu} \right] + \frac{\mu^2 - \nu^2}{(\mu^2 - 1)(1 - \nu^2)}\frac{\partial^2 \psi}{\partial \varphi^2}$$
$$+ \{-(\mu^2 - \nu^2)\epsilon + 2\mu R\}\psi = 0 \quad 11·35$$

where

$$\epsilon = -\frac{mr_{ab}^2}{2\hbar^2}\left(E - \frac{e^2}{r_{ab}} \right); \quad R = \frac{me^2}{\hbar^2}r_{ab} = \frac{r_{ab}}{a_0}$$

We now try to find a solution of the form

$$\psi = M(\mu)N(\nu)\Phi(\varphi) \qquad\qquad 11·36$$

Since φ enters equation 11·35 only in the term $\dfrac{\partial^2}{\partial \varphi^2}$, it is at once apparent that this equation can be separated into a part dependent on φ alone and a part dependent on μ and ν. We call the first separational parameter $-\lambda^2$, so that $\Phi(\varphi)$ satisfies the equation

$$\frac{d^2\Phi}{d\varphi^2} = -\lambda^2\varphi \qquad\qquad 11·37$$

Equation 11·35 is thus reduced to

$$\frac{1}{M}\frac{\partial}{\partial \mu}(\mu^2 - 1)\frac{\partial M}{\partial \mu} - \frac{\lambda^2}{\mu^2 - 1} - \mu^2\epsilon + 2R\mu$$
$$= -\frac{1}{N}\frac{\partial}{\partial \nu}(1 - \nu^2)\frac{\partial N}{\partial \nu} + \frac{\lambda^2}{1 - \nu^2} - \nu^2\epsilon \quad 11·38$$

We set both sides of this equation equal to $-\tau$ and thus obtain the final differential equations for $M(\mu)$ and $N(\nu)$.

$$\frac{d}{d\mu}\left[(\mu^2 - 1)\frac{dM}{d\mu} \right] + \left(-\frac{\lambda^2}{\mu^2 - 1} - \mu^2\epsilon + 2\mu R + \tau \right) M = 0 \quad 11·39$$

$$\frac{d}{d\nu}(1 - \nu^2)\frac{dN}{d\nu} + \left(-\frac{\lambda^2}{1 - \nu^2} + \nu^2\epsilon - \tau\right)N = 0 \qquad 11 \cdot 40$$

The set of equations 11·37, 11·39, 11·40 will possess satisfactory solutions only if the parameters λ, τ, and ϵ have certain definite values. The set of simultaneous equations has been solved by Teller,[4] and, for the ground state, by Burrau,[5] Hylleraas,[6] and Jaffe,[7] leading to results in complete agreement with experiment. The solution of the φ equation leads to the familiar result

$$\Phi(\varphi) = \frac{1}{\sqrt{2\pi}} e^{i\lambda\varphi}$$

where λ takes on positive or negative integral values. The energy depends on λ through $|\lambda|$, since only λ^2 occurs in the equations which determine the energy parameter ϵ. For $r_{ab} = 0$, the wave equation is the same as that for He^+, except for the difference in nuclear mass. The quantum number λ is a " good " quantum number at all internuclear distances, since the equation in φ can always be separated from the remainder of the wave equation. For $r_{ab} = 0$, that is, for the united atom, λ becomes equivalent to the atomic quantum number m. In describing the molecular orbital, it is therefore characterized by the designation of the state of the united atom to which it reduces, $2s$, $2p$, etc., plus the designation of the λ value; the symbols σ, π, $\delta \cdots$ denote $|\lambda| = 0$, 1, $2 \cdots$. Since, for the united atom, $m = l$, $l - 1 \cdots -l$, the possible molecular orbitals are $1s\sigma$, $2s\sigma$, $2p\sigma$, $2p\pi$, $3s\sigma$, $3p\sigma$, $3p\pi$, $3d\sigma$, $3d\pi$, $3d\delta \cdots$. The σ states are non-degenerate, the π, δ, etc., states are doubly degenerate because of the equivalence of the two values $\pm\lambda$. In Figure 11·3 the electronic energies of several of the lowest states of H_2^+ are plotted; in Figure 11·4 the total energy for the $1s\sigma$ and $2p\sigma$ states are plotted as a function of the internuclear distance.[4] It will be noted that the state $1s\sigma$ corresponds to the state $\{\psi_a(1s) + \psi_b(1s)\}$ of our earlier treatment; the state $2p\sigma$ corresponds to $\{\psi_a(1s) - \psi_b(1s)\}$.

11d. Homonuclear Diatomic Molecules. At this point it is of value to consider, on the basis of group theory, the possible states of a homonuclear diatomic molecule. Such molecules belong to the symmetry group $D_{\infty h}$; the characteristics of the possible states, including their degeneracies, are determined directly from the character table

[4] E. Teller, *Z. Physik*, **61**, 458 (1930).
[5] O. Burrau, *Kgl. Danske Videnskab. Selskab.*, **7**, 1 (1927).
[6] E. Hylleraas, *Z. Physik*, **71**, 739 (1931).
[7] G. Jaffe, *Z. Physik*, **87**, 535 (1934).

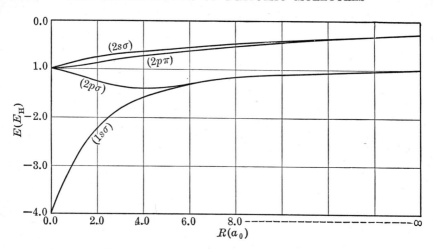

Fig. 11·3.   Calculated electronic energy of H_2^+.

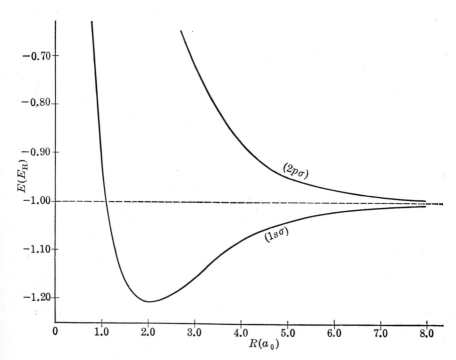

Fig. 11·4.   Calculated total energy of H_2^+.

of the irreducible representations of this group. This character table is shown below. The symbols in the first column are those used to describe the electronic states of homonuclear diatomic molecules.

	E	$2C_\varphi$	σ_v	iE	$2iC_\varphi$	$i\sigma_v$
Σ_g^+	1	1	1	1	1	1
Σ_u^+	1	1	1	-1	-1	-1
Σ_g^-	1	1	-1	1	1	-1
Σ_u^-	1	1	-1	-1	-1	1
Π_g	2	$2\cos\varphi$	0	2	$2\cos\varphi$	0
Π_u	2	$2\cos\varphi$	0	-2	$-2\cos\varphi$	0
Δ_g	2	$2\cos 2\varphi$	0	2	$2\cos 2\varphi$	0
Δ_u	2	$2\cos 2\varphi$	0	-2	$-2\cos 2\varphi$	0

States which are invariant under rotation about the symmetry axis are called Σ states. If only one electron is present, these are the states for which $\lambda = 0$; if more than one electron is present, these are the states for which $\Lambda = \sum_i \lambda_i = 0$. Π states are those for which $\Lambda = 1$; Δ states those for which $\Lambda = 2$, etc. If only one electron is present, these are equivalent to the π and δ states discussed above. In addition, the Σ states are characterized by the designation $+$ or $-$ according to the manner in which they behave when subjected to the operation σ_v, which is a reflection in a plane in which the symmetry axis lies. All states are further characterized by the symbols g ("gerade") and u ("ungerade"). These symbols tell whether the wave function remains invariant or changes sign upon inversion at the center of symmetry. For the special case of the H_2^+ ion, we readily see that σ orbitals give Σ^+ states, π orbitals give Π states, etc. The g or u property is independent of the internuclear distance. If the molecular orbital is written as a linear combination of atomic orbitals, then we immediately see that combinations of the type $\{\psi_a + \psi_b\}$ are g, those of the type $\{\psi_a - \psi_b\}$ are u. For the united atom, the center of symmetry becomes the atomic nucleus; a molecular orbital thus has the same g or u property as the atomic orbital to which it reduces. For a one-electron atom, the wave function is g or u according as l is even or odd; for a many-electron atom, the atomic wave function is g or u according as $\sum_i l_i$ is even or odd. We thus see that a $2s\sigma$ orbital gives a Σ_g^+ state, a $2p\sigma$ orbital gives a Σ_u^+ state, and a $2p\pi$ orbital gives a Π_u state. Referring to Figure 11·4, we note that in H_2^+ the Σ_g^+ state is stable, the Σ_u^+ state is unstable.

It is possible to make a unique correlation between the states of the united atoms and the states of the separated atom by means of the theorem which says that two levels with the same symmetry properties cannot cross as the internuclear distance is varied. The following proof of this theorem is that given by Neumann and Wigner[8] as modified by Teller.[9] Suppose that we know all the electronic wave functions except two. These two may be written as linear combinations of the functions ψ_1 and ψ_2, which have been chosen to be mutually orthogonal and orthogonal to all the remaining wave functions. The energy levels are given by the solutions of the equation

$$\begin{vmatrix} H_{11} - E & H_{12} \\ H_{12} & H_{22} - E \end{vmatrix} = 0$$

In order that the two roots be equal, the conditions $H_{11} = H_{22}$, $H_{12} = 0$ must be satisfied simultaneously. If ψ_1 and ψ_2 have different symmetry properties, then H_{12} is identically zero. Since H_{11} and H_{22} are functions of the internuclear distance, it is possible for the two to be equal at some distance; when this is true, the two energy levels are equal, and crossing can occur. If ψ_1 and ψ_2 have the same symmetry, H_{12} will not be zero. It will not, in general, be possible to satisfy the two conditions by varying one parameter, hence the two energy levels can never be equal, and crossing is impossible.

Since λ is a good quantum number at all times, and since the g and u properties must be preserved as the internuclear distance is varied, the correlation between the states of the united atom and those of the separated atom must be $\sigma_g \to \sigma_g$, $\sigma_u \to \sigma_u$, $\pi_g \to \pi_g$, etc. Further, two σ_g orbitals cannot cross; neither can two σ_u orbitals, etc. In Figure 11·5, we have on the left the various states of the united atom and the possible molecular orbitals into which they can split; on the right we have the various states of the separated atoms and the symmetry properties of the molecular orbitals which can be formed by taking linear combinations of the atomic orbitals. The correlation between the two sets of states is given by the connecting lines which were drawn in accordance with the above rules. It will be noted that this schematic representation corresponds exactly (as of course it must) with the exact energy level diagram for H_2^+ (Figure 11·3).

In determining the electron configurations of complex atoms, we added the electrons to hydrogenlike orbitals, placing the electrons into the lowest orbitals allowed by the exclusion principle. Similarly, for

[8] J. v. Neumann and E. Wigner, *Physik. Z.*, **30**, 467 (1929).

[9] E. Teller, *J. Chem. Phys.*, **41**, 109 (1936).

complex homonuclear diatomic molecules, we add the electrons to the lowest allowed H_2^+-like molecular orbitals. Taking account of electron spin, the exclusion principle allows us to place two electrons in σ orbitals, and four electrons in π, $\delta \cdots$ orbitals, because of the two possible values of λ in the latter. This procedure gives us the electron configuration of the lowest state, which will then be characterized by the values of $\Lambda = \sum_i \lambda_i$ and $S = \sum_i s_i$. States with $S = 0$, $\frac{1}{2}$, $1 \cdots$ are called singlet, doublet, triplet, $\cdots$ states, just as for atoms.

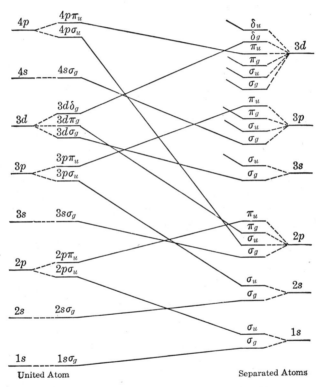

FIG. 11·5. Correlation diagram for like nuclei.

This procedure will be perhaps clarified by several examples. For the simplest homonuclear diatomic molecule, H_2^+, the electron configuration is $(\sigma_g 1s)$, the notation referring to the states of the separated atoms, which gives $\Lambda = 0$, $S = \frac{1}{2}$, so that the state is $^2\Sigma_g^+$. (σ orbitals can, of course, give only $+$ states; π, $\delta \cdots$ orbitals can lead to either $+$

or $-$ states. If the number of electrons in u orbitals is even, the resulting states will be g; if the number of electrons in u orbitals is odd, the resulting states will be u.) For H_2, the electron configuration is $(\sigma_g 1s)^2$, so that $\Lambda = 0$, $S = 0$ (because of the exclusion principle), and the ground state is $^1\Sigma_g^+$. For Li_2, the electron configuration is $(\sigma_g 1s)^2(\sigma_u 1s)^2(\sigma_g 2s)^2$; the corresponding state is $^1\Sigma_g^+$. For more complex molecules, there is a possible ambiguity in the order of the orbitals, as this order sometimes changes as the internuclear distance is varied. For these molecules it is necessary to resort to experimental evidence to determine the electron configuration of the ground state. For example, the electron configuration of N_2 is found to be $(\sigma_g 1s)^2(\sigma_u 1s)^2(\sigma_g 2s)^2(\sigma_u 2s)^2(\pi_u 2p)^4(\sigma_g 2p)^2$. Only closed shells of electrons are involved, so that the state represented by this configuration is $^1\Sigma_g^+$. In O_2, the two additional electrons go into the $(\pi_g 2p)$ orbital. The quantum number Λ can be either 0 or 2, depending on whether or not the λ's are directed oppositely or are parallel. If Λ is 2 the spins must be opposed; if 0 they may be either parallel or opposed. The configuration $\cdots (\pi_g 2p)^2$ thus leads to $^1\Sigma$, $^3\Sigma$, and $^1\Delta$ states. All states are, of course, g; the detailed theory[10] shows that they are in fact $^1\Sigma_g^+$, $^3\Sigma_g^-$, and $^1\Delta_g$. The lowest state of O_2 is found experimentally to be the $^3\Sigma_g^-$ state; as a result, O_2 is paramagnetic (Chapter XVII).

An interesting interpretation of the character of the chemical bond in diatomic molecules can be given in terms of the above considerations. If an orbital maintains the same principal quantum number as the transition is made from the separated atoms to the united atom, it is said to be a "bonding orbital." If the principal quantum number increases, it is said to be an "anti-bonding orbtial," and an electron in an orbital of this type is said to have been "promoted." As may be seen in Figure 11·4, occupied bonding orbitals will tend to form stable states; occupied anti-bonding orbitals will tend to form unstable states. The difference between the number of pairs of electrons in bonding orbitals and the number of pairs in anti-bonding orbitals may be regarded as the effective number of "electron pair" bonds. For Li_2, O_2, and N_2 this difference is seen to be 1, 2, and 3, respectively, which corresponds to the usual designation of the bonds in these molecules as single, double, and triple.

11e. Heteronuclear Diatomic Molecules. For heteronuclear diatomic molecules we no longer have the center of symmetry which was present in the homonuclear diatomic molecules. Heteronuclear diatomic molecules belong to the symmetry group $C_{\infty v}$, for which the

---

[10] E. Wigner and E. Witmer, Z. Physik, **51**, 859 (1928).

character table is

	E	$2C_\varphi$	σ_v
Σ^+	1	1	1
Σ^-	1	1	-1
Π	2	$2\cos\varphi$	0
Δ	2	$2\cos 2\varphi$	0
...	..	......	: : :

We note that we have the same types of possible states as for the group $D_{\infty h}$, except that the g and u property has been lost. In drawing the correlation diagram analogous to Figure 11·5, we must take into account the fact that there are now, for example, two 1s states for the separated atoms, since, if we designate the atoms by a and b, the atomic orbitals $\psi_a(1s)$ and $\psi_b(1s)$ will have different energies because of their different nuclear charges. Let us suppose that we again write the molecular orbital as a linear combination of atomic orbitals, for example

$$\psi = c_a\psi_a(1s) + c_b\psi_b(1s) \qquad 11\cdot41$$

The secular equation is

$$\begin{vmatrix} H_{aa} - E & H_{ab} - SE \\ H_{ab} - SE & H_{bb} - E \end{vmatrix} = 0 \qquad 11\cdot42$$

where the symbols have their usual meaning. We now wish to investigate the values of the coefficients c_a and c_b. We imagine the internuclear distance to be sufficiently large so that the overlap integral S may be taken equal to zero. We further assume that a has the greater nuclear charge, so that $H_{aa} > H_{bb}$. The energy eigenvalues, given by the solution of 11·42, are

$$E = \tfrac{1}{2}\{(H_{aa} + H_{bb}) \pm \sqrt{(H_{aa} - H_{bb})^2 + 4H_{ab}^2}\} \qquad 11\cdot43$$

For $H_{aa} = H_{bb}$, the upper sign gives $c_a = c_b$; the lower sign gives $c_a = -c_b$. For $H_{aa} > H_{bb}$ we may therefore conclude that the upper sign corresponds to the case where c_a and c_b have the same sign; the lower sign corresponds to the case where c_a and c_b have opposite signs. Further, for the limiting case where $H_{ab} = 0$, the upper sign gives $E = H_{aa}$, $c_a^2 = 1$, $c_b^2 = 0$; the lower sign gives $E = H_{bb}$, $c_a^2 = 0$, $c_b^2 = 1$. For any internuclear distance we therefore conclude that the proper linear combinations of atomic orbitals are

$$\psi_{\rm I} = c_a'\psi_a(1s) + c_b'\psi_b(1s)$$
$$\psi_{\rm II} = c_a''\psi_a(1s) - c_b''\psi_b(1s) \qquad 11\cdot44$$

where $c_a' > c_b'$; $c_b'' > c_a''$. Using the correlations $\sigma \rightarrow \sigma$, $\pi \rightarrow \pi$, etc., and noting that two σ or two π orbitals cannot cross, we obtain the correlation diagram for heteronuclear diatomic molecules given in Figure 11·6, where atom a is considered to have the greater nuclear charge. The method of determining the electron configuration for the ground state is identical with that applied previously. For example, LiH should have the electron configuration $(1s\sigma)^2(2s\sigma)^2$ if we use the united atom notation, which leads to the ground state $^1\Sigma^+$.

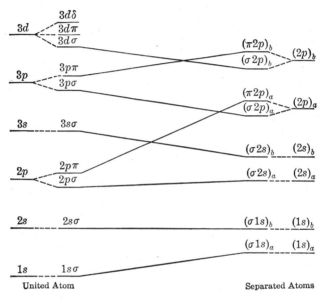

FIG. 11·6.   Correlation diagram for unlike nuclei.

If we consider the molecule $(\text{LiH})^{++}$, we see that the electron configuration for the ground state is $(1s\sigma)^2$. Upon separation of the nuclei, Figure 11·6 tells us that we obtain Li^+ and H^+; that is, both electrons remain on the Li nucleus, which is in accord with our conclusion that $c_a' > c_b'$. However, if we separate the nuclei in LiH, the correlation diagram states that we would obtain Li^+ and H^-. Actually we would obtain Li and H. These considerations suggest that we would obtain better molecular orbitals by the following procedure. We consider that the $1s$ electrons of Li are unaffected by the formation of the molecule, and we form molecular orbitals, not between Li^{+++} and H^+, but between Li^+ and H^+. The problem then becomes quite similar to that of the hydrogen molecule; we take as the molecular orbital which leads to a stable molecule the linear combination

$$\psi = a\psi_{\text{Li}}(2s) + b\psi_{\text{H}}(1s) \qquad\qquad 11\cdot45$$

This orbital can, of course, be occupied by two electrons, provided that their spins are antiparallel.

The above considerations have enabled us to determine the types of states that may arise in diatomic molecules and have shown us how to write approximate orbitals to describe these states. It cannot be expected that the use of these simple orbitals will give quantitatively correct results. In the next chapter we shall see what results can be expected in the simpler cases, and, on the basis of these results and the above considerations, we shall attempt to develop a satisfactory qualitative theory of valence.

CHAPTER XII

THE COVALENT BOND

12a. The Hydrogen Molecule. For the hydrogen molecule, the Hamiltonian operator, in atomic units, is

$$\mathbf{H} = -\left\{\frac{1}{2}\nabla_1^2 + \frac{1}{2}\nabla_2^2 + \frac{1}{R_{a1}} + \frac{1}{R_{a2}} + \frac{1}{R_{b1}} + \frac{1}{R_{b2}} - \frac{1}{R_{12}} - \frac{1}{R_{ab}}\right\} \quad 12\cdot1$$

where the subscripts 1 and 2 refer to the electrons and the subscripts a and b refer to the nuclei. According to the results given in the previous chapter, the lowest molecular orbital, expressed as a linear combination of the atomic orbitals of hydrogen, is

$$\psi_{1s\sigma} = \psi_a(1s) + \psi_b(1s) \quad 12\cdot2$$

We can, according to the exclusion principle, place two electrons in this orbital, with their spins opposed. If we designate the electrons by 1 and 2, the unnormalized wave function for the ground state of the hydrogen molecule would then be, to this approximation,

$$\psi = \{\psi_a(1) + \psi_b(1)\}\{\psi_a(2) + \psi_b(2)\} \quad 12\cdot3$$

where

$$\psi_a(1) = \frac{1}{\sqrt{\pi}}\,e^{-R_{a1}}; \quad \psi_b(1) = \frac{1}{\sqrt{\pi}}\,e^{-R_{b1}}; \quad \text{etc.}$$

The energy $E = \dfrac{\displaystyle\int \psi \mathbf{H} \psi \, d\tau}{\displaystyle\int \psi\psi \, d\tau}$ of the ground state of hydrogen as given

by this wave function has been calculated approximately by Hellmann.[1] He finds the equilibrium distance to be $R \sim 1.6a_0$; the dissociation energy to be ~2.65 e.v. — values which are not at all in agreement with the experimental values $R = 1.40a_0$; $D = 4.72$ e.v. One reason for this disagreement may be seen immediately from the following argument. If we multiply out equation 12·3, we obtain

$$\psi = \psi_a(1)\psi_a(2) + \psi_a(1)\psi_b(2) + \psi_b(1)\psi_a(2) + \psi_b(1)\psi_b(2) \quad 12\cdot4$$

---

[1] H. Hellmann, *Einführung in die Quantenchemie*, p. 133, Franz Deuticke, 1937.

The first and last terms in this expression represent electron density distributions in which both electrons are on the same hydrogen nucleus; that is, they represent ionic states such as H^+H^-. Since it is known that the electron affinity of hydrogen is very much less than the ionization potential of hydrogen, we would expect that such states are not very stable, and hence that we might obtain a better representation of the ground state of the hydrogen molecule by dropping these terms. This leads us to the function used by Heitler and London[2] in the first successful attack on the problem of chemical valence.   These authors wrote

$$\psi = \psi_a(1)\psi_b(2) + \psi_b(1)\psi_a(2) \qquad 12\cdot5$$

as the function representing the ground state of the hydrogen molecule. The energy corresponding to this function may be written as

$$E = \frac{J' + K'}{1 + S^2} \qquad 12\cdot6$$

where

$$J' = \int \psi_a(1)\psi_b(2)\mathbf{H}\psi_a(1)\psi_b(2)\ d\tau_1\ d\tau_2$$

$$K' = \int \psi_a(1)\psi_b(2)\mathbf{H}\psi_a(2)\psi_b(1)\ d\tau_1\ d\tau_2$$

$$S^2 = \int \psi_a(1)\psi_b(2)\psi_a(2)\psi_b(1)\ d\tau_1\ d\tau_2$$

From the form of $\mathbf{H}$ and the functions $\psi_a(1)$, etc., it is readily seen that the energy may be written as

$$E = 2E_{1s}(\mathrm{H}) + Q + \alpha \qquad 12\cdot7$$

where

$$Q = \frac{J}{1 + S^2}\ ;\quad \alpha = \frac{K}{1 + S^2} \qquad 12\cdot8$$

$$J = \int \psi_a(1)\psi_b(2)\left\{-\frac{1}{R_{b1}} - \frac{1}{R_{a2}} + \frac{1}{R_{12}} + \frac{1}{R_{ab}}\right\}\psi_a(1)\psi_b(2)\ d\tau_1\ d\tau_2$$

$$= -2\epsilon_{aa} + \frac{1}{R_{ab}} + \int \frac{\{\psi_a(1)\}^2\{\psi_b(2)\}^2}{R_{12}}\ d\tau_1\ d\tau_2 \qquad 12\cdot9$$

$$K = \int \psi_a(1)\psi_b(2)\left\{-\frac{1}{R_{a1}} - \frac{1}{R_{b2}} + \frac{1}{R_{12}} + \frac{1}{R_{ab}}\right\}\psi_a(2)\psi_b(1)\ d\tau_1\ d\tau_2$$

$$= \frac{S^2}{R_{ab}} - 2S\epsilon_{ab} + \int \frac{\psi_a(1)\psi_b(2)\psi_a(2)\psi_b(1)}{R_{12}}\ d\tau_1\ d\tau_2 \qquad 12\cdot10$$

[2] W. Heitler and F. London, Z. Physik, 44, 455 (1927).

The integrals S, ϵ_{aa}, ϵ_{ab} have been evaluated in section 11b. The remaining integrals have been evaluated by Heitler and London[2] and by Sugiura.[3] The results gave for the internuclear distance and the dissociation energy the values $R = 1.64a_0$, $D = 3.14$ e.v. Although this value of the dissociation energy is only slightly better than that obtained from the strict molecular orbital treatment, the Heitler-London method is somewhat easier to handle than the molecular orbital method, and we shall make considerable use of this method of writing approximate wave functions in the following pages.

It is of interest to investigate the state of the hydrogen molecule that arises when one electron is placed in the $1s\sigma$ orbital and the other in the $2p\sigma$ orbital. The wave function is then

$$\psi = \{\psi_a(1) + \psi_b(1)\}\{\psi_a(2) - \psi_b(2)\} \qquad 12\cdot11$$

which, if we drop the ionic terms as in the Heitler-London approximation, may be written as

$$\psi = \psi_a(1)\psi_b(2) - \psi_a(2)\psi_b(1) \qquad 12\cdot12$$

For this state, the energy is

$$E = 2E_{1s}(\text{H}) + Q' - \alpha' \qquad 12\cdot13$$

where

$$Q' = \frac{J}{1 - S^2}; \quad \alpha' = \frac{K}{1 - S^2}$$

and where the remaining symbols have the same significance as before. The quantities Q and α are called the " coulombic " and " exchange " energies, respectively; the integrals J and K are called the coulombic and exchange integrals. The state represented by $12\cdot12$ is unstable. It is noted that the stability of $12\cdot5$ relative to $12\cdot12$ is due essentially to the difference in sign of the exchange energy, the binding energy of $12\cdot5$ being $Q + \alpha$, and of $12\cdot12$ being $Q' - \alpha'$. In Figure $12\cdot1$ the coulombic energy and the total energy, as calculated from the above equations, are plotted as a function of the internuclear distance. It is observed that the greater part of the binding energy arises from the exchange term, the coulombic energy being only about 10–15 per cent of the total. We further note from equation $12\cdot10$ that the exchange integral K will be at least roughly proportional to the overlap integral S, so that if two orbitals overlap only slightly the exchange integral will be small, and hence the binding energy of the two orbitals will be small. This result will later become of great importance.

[3] Y. Sugiura, Z. Physik, **45**, 484 (1937).

We have as yet made no explicit mention of electron spin. To the approximation that we have been using, the Hamiltonian operator contains no terms dependent on spin, so that the spin wave functions and the orbital wave functions are separable. As before, we designate by α the spin eigenfunction which has the eigenvalue $+\frac{1}{2}$, and by β

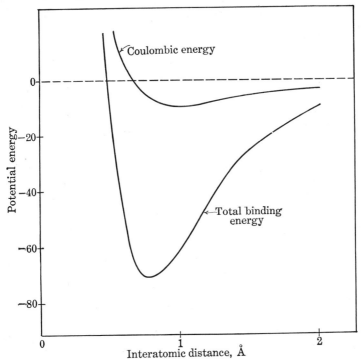

Fig. 12·1. Calculated coulombic and total energies of H_2 as functions of the interatomic distance.

the spin eigenfunction which has the eigenvalue $-\frac{1}{2}$. If we have two electrons, we can form one spin eigenfunction

$$\{\alpha(1)\beta(2) - \alpha(2)\beta(1)\}$$

which is antisymmetric in the electrons, and three spin eigenfunctions

$$\{\alpha(1)\alpha(2)\}$$
$$\{\beta(1)\beta(2)\}$$
$$\{\alpha(1)\beta(2) + \alpha(2)\beta(1)\}$$

which are symmetric in the electrons. Of the orbital wave functions which we have thus far considered for the hydrogen molecule, 12·5 is symmetric in the electrons and 12·12 is antisymmetric in the electrons. According to the exclusion principle, the complete wave function for a system must change sign if two electrons are interchanged; in order to form acceptable wave functions of the above type we must therefore combine a symmetrical orbital with an antisymmetrical spin function, and conversely.   We thus obtain the complete wave functions

$$\psi_{1\Sigma_g^+} = \{\psi_a(1)\psi_b(2) + \psi_a(2)\psi_b(1)\}\{\alpha(1)\beta(2) - \alpha(2)\beta(1)\} \qquad 12·14$$

$$\psi_{3\Sigma_u^+} = \{\psi_a(1)\psi_b(2) - \psi_a(2)\psi_b(1)\} \left[\begin{array}{c} \{\alpha(1)\alpha(2)\} \\ \{\alpha(1)\beta(2) + \alpha(2)\beta(1)\} \\ \{\beta(1)\beta(2)\} \end{array} \right] \qquad 12·15$$

We note that in the stable state $^1\Sigma_g^+$ the spins are opposed; in the unstable state $^3\Sigma_u^+$ they are parallel.   The general theory of valence will be based almost entirely upon the material thus far presented in this and the preceding chapter.   Before beginning this general discussion, we shall see how the above method of approach should be modified in order to obtain better quantitative agreement with experiment.

Several simple modifications of the function 12·5 have been made. A considerable improvement in the calculated dissociation energy is obtained by introducing an effective nuclear charge as a variational parameter, that is, writing

$$\psi_a(1) = \left(\frac{\alpha^3}{\pi}\right)^{1/2} e^{-\alpha R_{a1}}, \text{ etc.}$$

This function, with $\alpha = 1.17$, gives $D = 3.76$ e.v.[4]   A more general function is obtained by writing the unnormalized function as

$$\psi_{a1} = (1 + c_1 z_{a1})e^{-\alpha R_{a1}}$$

where the nuclei lie along the z axis, that is, including the $2p_z$ hydrogen orbital in the variational function in order to take account of the fact that one hydrogen atom will polarize the other.   With $\alpha = 1.17$, $c_1 = 0.10$, a value $D = 4.02$ e.v. is obtained for the dissociation energy.[5] If in addition the ionic terms in 12·4 are included, multiplied by a parameter c_2, then, with $\alpha = 1.19$, $c_1 = 0.07$, $c_2 = 0.175$, the dissociation energy is calculated[6] to be $D = 4.10$ e.v. as compared with the experimental value $D = 4.72$ e.v.   This small value for c_2 is further confirmation of the fact that, for the hydrogen molecule at least, the

[4] S. Wang, *Phys. Rev.*, **31**, 579 (1928).
[5] N. Rosen, *Phys. Rev.*, **38**, 2099 (1931).
[6] S. Weinbaum, *J. Chem. Phys.*, **1**, 317 (1933).

Heitler-London or " valence-bond " method is superior to the method of molecular orbitals.

As for H_2^+, it is again found that an accurate value of the binding energy can be obtained only by a method of approach which is not based upon the use of one-electron approximate wave functions. James and Coolidge[7] used a variation function which was written as a function of elliptic coordinates and which included the interelectron distances R_{12} explicitly. These authors investigated the function

$$\psi = e^{-\delta(\mu_1 + \mu_2)} \sum_{klmnp} c_{klmnp} \{\mu_1^k \mu_2^l \nu_1^m \nu_2^n u^p + \mu_1^l \mu_2^k \nu_1^n \nu_2^m u^p\} \qquad 12 \cdot 16$$

where

$$\mu_1 = \frac{R_{a1} + R_{b1}}{R_{ab}}; \quad \mu_2 = \frac{R_{a2} + R_{b2}}{R_{ab}}$$

$$\nu_1 = \frac{R_{a1} - R_{b1}}{R_{ab}}; \quad \nu_2 = \frac{R_{a2} - R_{b2}}{R_{ab}}; \quad u = \frac{2R_{12}}{R_{ab}}$$

The form of the function is such that it is symmetric in regard to interchange of electrons. In order that it may also be symmetric in the coordinates of the nuclei, only those terms which have $(m + n)$ an even interger were included; the indices were taken to be positive integers or zero. With $\delta = 0.75$, the calculations, for a thirteen-term function, gave $R_{ab} = 1.40 \ a_0$ and $D = 4.698$ e.v., in essentially complete agreement with experiment. The accuracy could no doubt be further improved by the inclusion of additional terms. We have had several examples (He, H_2^+, H_2) of the exact results which can be obtained by means of the variational method with a wisely chosen variation function. However, the labor involved in these calculations is so great even for these simple systems that it does not appear to be a profitable method of attack on molecular problems in general. Because of the mathematical difficulties involved, we are forced to use much less accurate approximations; usually we are forced to write the wave function as some linear combination of one-electron wave functions. Although these will not give satisfactory quantitative results, they should in general be qualitatively correct, and should enable us to correlate experimental chemical facts. It is to be noted that the James and Coolidge treatment of H_2 contains nothing corresponding to the separation of the binding energy into a coulombic part and an exchange part which appeared in the Heitler-London treatment. This separation is a mathematical result of the use of one-electron orbitals in forming the valence-bond function. Thus, though we shall

[7] H. James and A. Coolidge, *J. Chem. Phys.*, **1**, 825 (1933).

continually use the terms " coulombic energy " and " exchange energy," the reader should remember that these terms have more of a mathematical than a physical significance. It might be added, however, that in principle any wave function can be written in the form

$$\psi = \sum_{\nu} (-1)^{\nu} P_{\nu} \{f(a_1^1, a_2^2, a_3^3, \cdots a_n^n)\}$$

where P_{ν} is the operator which interchanges the subscripts of the sets of quantum numbers a_1^1, etc., this form of function being that which has the proper symmetry in regard to the interchange of like particles. The associated energy will then be a sum of integrals. Certain of these integrals will be of the type

$$\int f(a_1^1,\ a_2^2, \cdots a_n^n) \mathbf{H} f(a_1^1, a_2^2, \cdots a_n^n)$$

which may be called coulombic integrals; others will be of the type

$$\int f(a_1^1, a_2^2, \cdots a_n^n) \mathbf{H} f(a_2^1, a_1^2, \cdots a_n^n),\ \ \text{etc.}$$

which may be called exchange integrals.

12b. The Covalent or Electron-Pair Bond.[8] According to the Heitler-London theory, which gives a satisfactory qualitative description of the hydrogen molecule, the covalent bond in this molecule is represented by the orbital wave function

$$\{\psi_a(1)\psi_b(2) + \psi_a(2)\psi_b(1)\} \qquad 12 \cdot 17$$

where the functions $\psi_a(1)$, etc., have the significance previously stated. This orbital wave function must be combined with the spin wave function

$$\{\alpha(1)\beta(2) - \alpha(2)\beta(1)\}$$

representing oppositely directed spins, in order that the complete wave function be antisymmetric in the electrons. Parallel spins lead, as we have seen, to unstable states. The valence bond in LiH, according to the discussion in the last chapter, will be represented, in the molecular orbital method, by the function

$$\{a\psi_{\text{Li}}(1) + b\psi_{\text{H}}(1)\}\{a\psi_{\text{Li}}(2) + b\psi_{\text{H}}(2)\} \qquad 12 \cdot 18$$

or, in the Heitler-London method, by the function

$$\{\psi_{\text{Li}}(1)\psi_{\text{H}}(2) + \psi_{\text{Li}}(2)\psi_{\text{H}}(1)\} \qquad 12 \cdot 19$$

---

[8] The methods employed in this section are essentially those employed by Pauling. See L. Pauling, *Nature of the Chemical Bond*, Cornell University Press, 1940.

where ψ_{Li} is the $2s$ wave function of Li and ψ_H is the $1s$ wave function of H. The mathematical treatment follows the same lines as for H_2; the function 12·19, which must be combined with an antisymmetric spin function representing oppositely directed spins, leads to a stable molecule.

The Heitler-London method is obviously not limited to the treatment of the formation of the bonds in diatomic molecules. In CH_4, for example, if we let ψ_{C1}, ψ_{C2}, ψ_{C3}, ψ_{C4} be the orbitals occupied by four of the electrons of the carbon atom, and ψ_{H1}, ψ_{H2}, ψ_{H3}, ψ_{H4} be the $1s$ orbitals of the four hydrogen atoms, then the set of functions

$$\{\psi_{C1}(1)\psi_{H1}(2) + \psi_{C1}(2)\psi_{H1}(1)\}$$
$$\{\psi_{C2}(3)\psi_{H2}(4) + \psi_{C2}(4)\psi_{H2}(3)\}$$
$$\{\psi_{C3}(5)\psi_{H3}(6) + \psi_{C3}(6)\psi_{H3}(5)\}$$
$$\{\psi_{C4}(7)\psi_{H4}(8) + \psi_{C4}(8)\psi_{H4}(7)\}$$

12·20

would represent four covalent bonds formed by eight electrons. Without at this time further specifying the nature of the four carbon orbitals, we can state that they will be orbitals with the principal quantum number n equal to 2. The remaining two electrons of carbon will be in the $1s$ orbital and will have their spins paired; as each of the four valence electrons has its spin paired with an electron from a hydrogen atom, we see that all electron spins in the molecule are paired, so that the resultant spin S of the molecule is zero. Similarly in LiH and in H_2 all the electron spins are paired. The experimental fact that stable molecules (with a very few exceptions) are non-paramagnetic (see Chapter XVII) is a confirmation of the above-derived results that the resultant spin should be zero for molecules in their ground states.

An electron which has its spin paired with another electron from the same atom obviously cannot take part in the formation of a covalent bond, so that the covalency of an atom is equal to the number of electrons with unpaired spins possessed by the atom. The results of this rule have been mentioned in Chapter IX; we shall not repeat that discussion at this point but shall consider a number of examples in greater detail.

The electron configuration of the ground state of the nitrogen atom is $(1s)^2(2s)^2(2p)^3$; the lowest term is ^4S, indicating that the spins of the three $2p$ electrons are parallel. Nitrogen should thus have a covalence of 3, in accordance with experimental facts. The three valence orbitals may be written as ψ_{2p_x}, ψ_{2p_y}, ψ_{2p_z}; if we were to carry out actual numerical calculations, we would use, for example, Slater-type eigenfunctions with the effective nuclear charge appropriate for the $2p$ orbitals of nitrogen. If we wished to describe the valence bonds in NH_3, then, according to the Heitler-London theory, we would write

$$\{\psi_{2p_x}(1)\psi_H(2) + \psi_{2p_x}(2)\psi_H(1)\} \qquad 12 \cdot 21$$

with analogous expressions for the two remaining bonds. According to the results of the similar calculation for H_2, the energy of the bond represented by 12·21 is determined largely by the value of the exchange integral between ψ_{2p_x} and ψ_H. This exchange integral is, as we have seen, proportional to the overlap integral between ψ_{2p_x} and ψ_H. Now ψ_{2p_x} has its maximum value along the x axis. Consequently the overlap integral and hence the exchange integral will have their maximum values when the hydrogen atom lies along the x axis; that is, this particular N—H bond will be stronger when the hydrogen atom is on the x axis. The same argument can be carried out for the other bonds; the stable configuration for the ammonia molecule is thus that in which the three hydrogen atoms lie along the x, y, and z axes, respectively. Since the three bonds are equivalent except for orientation in space, this simple theory of directed valence predicts that the ammonia molecule should be a triangular pyramid, with all H—N—H angles equal to 90°. The experimental value is about 108°; the manner in which the simple theory must be modified will be discussed later.

The oxygen atom has the electron configuration $(1s)^2(2s)^2(2p)^4$ the lowest term being ^3P. Since there are four electrons to be placed in the three $2p$ orbitals, one of the orbitals, which we may take to be the $2p_z$ orbital, must be occupied by two electrons with their spins paired. The two valence orbitals are then ψ_{2p_x} and ψ_{2p_y}; the arguments used above for NH_3 lead us to expect that the H—O—H angle in H_2O would be 90°. The actual angle is 105°, indicating that the simple picture of the oxygen valence also requires some modification.

The description of the covalent bonds formed by the carbon atom is less simple than the description given above for nitrogen and oxygen, and it requires a new concept: that of the formation of valence orbitals by the "hybridization" of the simple atomic orbitals. The lowest electron configuration of carbon is $(1s)^2(2s)^2(2p)^2$; the lowest term is ^3P. If this electron configuration represented the valence state of carbon, it would be divalent, with the spatial distribution of the bonds similar to that of oxygen, in complete contradiction to experimental facts. However, the first excited electron configuration of carbon is $(1s)^2(2s)(2p)^3$; the lowest term arising from this electron configuration is ^5S; carbon in this state had four electrons with unpaired spins and hence has a valence of 4. This excited state, arising from the " promotion " of a $2s$ electron into the $2p$ level, has not been definitely located experimentally, but according to calculations by the Hartree method, as well as certain indirect experimental evidence, the ^5S term lies about 3–4 e.v. above the ground state.[9] There is probably no very close correlation between this energy difference in the carbon atom itself and the energy required to " promote " a $2s$ electron when a compound such as CH_4 is formed, since the perturbation of the energy levels of carbon by the hydrogen atoms will be exceedingly large. This promotional energy would be more than compensated for by the energy furnished during the formation of the two additional covalent bonds. It may therefore be regarded as a reasonable assumption that quadricovalent carbon is represented by the electronic state $(1s)^2(2s)(2p)^3$, ^5S.

The four valence orbitals of carbon could then be written as ψ_{2s}, ψ_{2p_x}, ψ_{2p_y}, ψ_{2p_z}. However, we need not limit ourselves to this particular set of four valence orbitals but may use linear combinations of them. We will therefore take as our valence orbitals the set of linear combinations ψ_1, ψ_2, ψ_3, ψ_4, the combinations being formed in such a way that they fulfill the necessary requirements of being normalized and mutually orthogonal. In addition, we will require the four valence orbitals to have the maximum possible bond-forming power. According to our previous discussion regarding exchange and overlap integrals, this means that we want ψ_1, for example, to be that linear combination of ψ_{2s}, ψ_{2p_x}, ψ_{2p_y}, ψ_{2p_z} which has the largest possible magnitude along some arbitrary direction in space, subject, of course, to the condition that it be normalized. The functions ψ_{2s}, ψ_{2p_x}, ψ_{2p_y}, ψ_{2p_z} may be written

$$\psi_{2s} = R_{2s}(r)$$
$$\psi_{2p_x} = R_{2p}(r) \sin \theta \cos \varphi$$
$$\psi_{2p_y} = R_{2p}(r) \sin \theta \sin \varphi \qquad 12 \cdot 22$$
$$\psi_{2p_z} = R_{2p}(r) \cos \theta$$

The radial functions $R_{2s}(r)$ and $R_{2p}(r)$ will not differ greatly; if we use Slater-type eigenfunctions the two are identical. Assuming the radial functions to be identical, and writing only the angular parts of the wave functions, we have

$$\psi_{2s} = 1 \qquad\qquad \psi_{2p_y} = \sqrt{3} \sin \theta \sin \varphi$$
$$\psi_{2p_x} = \sqrt{3} \sin \theta \cos \varphi \qquad \psi_{2p_z} = \sqrt{3} \cos \theta \qquad 12 \cdot 23$$

where the angular parts of the wave functions are normalized to 4π.

[9] C. W. Ufford, *Phys. Rev.*, **53**, 568 (1938).

In accordance with the result that the strength of the bond formed by two valence orbitals will be proportional to the overlap of the two orbitals, Pauling[10] has defined the bond-forming strengths of the above orbitals to be 1 for ψ_{2s} and $\sqrt{3}$ for ψ_{2p_x}, ψ_{2p_y}, and ψ_{2p_z}, these being the maximum values possessed by the angular parts of the wave functions.

We now write

$$\psi_1 = a\psi_{2s} + b\psi_{2p_x} + c\psi_{2p_y} + d\psi_{2p_z} \qquad 12{\cdot}24$$

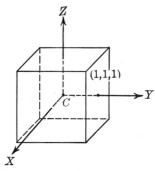

Fig. 12·2. Coordinate system for tetrahedral carbon orbitals.

where the possible values of the coefficients are restricted by the normalization condition $a^2 + b^2 + c^2 + d^2 = 1$. The direction in space in which this first orbital has its maximum value is arbitrary. We choose this direction to be along the $(1, 1, 1)$ diagonal of a cube with the carbon atom at its center and with the x, y, and z axes parallel to edges of the cube, as illustrated in Figure 12·2. This choice of direction requires the coefficients b, c, and d to be equal, so that ψ_1 may be written as

$$\psi_1 = a\psi_{2s} + b(\psi_{2p_x} + \psi_{2p_y} + \psi_{2p_z}) \qquad 12{\cdot}25$$

with the normalization condition $a^2 + 3b^2 = 1$. Along the $(1, 1, 1)$ diagonal, $\sin\varphi = \cos\varphi = \dfrac{1}{\sqrt{2}}$, $\cos\theta = \dfrac{1}{\sqrt{3}}$, $\sin\theta = \dfrac{\sqrt{2}}{\sqrt{3}}$, so that $\psi_{2p_x} = \psi_{2p_y} = \psi_{2p_z} = 1$ along this diagonal. The bond-forming strength of ψ_1 is thus $(a + 3b)$, or, by use of the normalization condition $(a + \sqrt{3}\sqrt{1 - a^2})$. The condition that the bond strength be a maximum gives us the relation

$$\frac{d}{da}\left(a + \sqrt{3}\sqrt{1 - a^2}\right) = 0$$

so that $a = \tfrac{1}{2}$. The condition $a^2 + 3b^2 = 1$ gives $b = \tfrac{1}{2}$; the valence orbital ψ_1 is thus

$$\psi_1 = \tfrac{1}{2}(\psi_{2s} + \psi_{2p_x} + \psi_{2p_y} + \psi_{2p_z}) \qquad 12{\cdot}26$$

This valence orbital, which has the bond-forming strength 2.00, has the maximum strength which can be obtained from any linear combination of $2s$ and $2p$ orbitals.

[10] See page 78 of reference 8.

If we form the set of valence orbitals

$$\psi(1, 1, 1) = \tfrac{1}{2}(\psi_{2s} + \psi_{2p_x} + \psi_{2p_y} + \psi_{2p_z})$$
$$\psi(1, -1, -1) = \tfrac{1}{2}(\psi_{2s} + \psi_{2p_x} - \psi_{2p_y} - \psi_{2p_z})$$
$$\psi(-1, 1, -1) = \tfrac{1}{2}(\psi_{2s} - \psi_{2p_x} + \psi_{2p_y} - \psi_{2p_z})$$
$$\psi(-1, -1, 1) = \tfrac{1}{2}(\psi_{2s} - \psi_{2p_x} - \psi_{2p_y} + \psi_{2p_z})$$

12·27

we note that these functions are normalized and mutually orthogonal, each function having a bond-forming strength of 2.00 (the maximum possible value for $2s$ and $2p$ functions), with the maximum density along the diagonal of the cube indicated. All members of the set are equivalent except for orientation in space. Each member of the set has its maximum value along one of the lines from the carbon atom to a corner of a regular tetrahedron with the carbon atom at its center. This set of orbitals, determined by the condition that their bond-forming power should be a maximum, thus gives a description of the valence of carbon in complete accord with the experimental facts.

It seems probable that promotion of a $2s$ electron also takes place to a certain extent in nitrogen and oxygen. Since the strongest possible bonds that can be formed from a combination of $2s$ and $2p$ orbitals are the tetrahedral type with the coefficient of ψ_{2s} equal to $\tfrac{1}{2}$, we would expect sufficient promotion in nitrogen and oxygen to make the bond angles tetrahedral in NH_3 and H_2O, provided that bond strength were the only criterion for the type of bond formed. However, the necessary promotional energy increases as we go along the series, C, N, O; in addition, promotion does not increase the valence of nitrogen and oxygen. The experimental facts indicate that a compromise is reached in N and O; the angles are slightly less than tetrahedral, showing that promotion takes place to a lesser extent than would be necessary to give pure tetrahedral bonds.

Actual calculations made with these valence bond functions cannot be expected to lead to accurate values of bond energies, nor could they be expected to lead to any results not given by the above qualitative procedure. The above procedure must be looked upon as a quantum-mechanical description of covalent bond formation based largely on a previous knowledge of experimental fact. In the next chapter we will find that it is possible to treat many problems in a more quantitative manner; we will here largely limit ourselves to this descriptive method.

The carbon-carbon double bond, such as that in ethylene, may be described as follows. From ψ_{2s}, and two of the $2p$ orbitals, which we may take to be ψ_{2p_x} and ψ_{2p_y}, we form three equivalent bond orbitals, which will have their maximum values in the xy plane and will be separated by angles of 120°. Taking one bond direction to be the x direction, these bond orbitals are

$$\psi_1 = \frac{1}{\sqrt{3}}\psi_{2s} + \frac{\sqrt{2}}{\sqrt{3}}\psi_{2p_x}$$

$$\psi_2 = \frac{1}{\sqrt{3}}\psi_{2s} - \frac{1}{\sqrt{6}}\psi_{2p_x} + \frac{1}{\sqrt{2}}\psi_{2p_y} \qquad 12\cdot28$$

$$\psi_3 = \frac{1}{\sqrt{3}}\psi_{2s} - \frac{1}{\sqrt{6}}\psi_{2p_x} - \frac{1}{\sqrt{2}}\psi_{2p_y}$$

The remaining carbon valence orbital is $\psi_4 = \psi_{2p_z}$. Using the first three valence orbitals, the carbon atom can form two C—H bonds and a single C—C bond. With the fourth orbital, an additional carbon-carbon bond can be formed with the corresponding orbital of the second carbon atom. The bond formed by orbitals of the type ψ_1 is called a σ bond; that formed by orbitals of the type ψ_4 is called a π bond. Let us denote the coordinate system of the first carbon atom by x, y, z; that of the second, by x', y', z'. The strongest π bond will be formed when the relative orientation of the two carbon atoms is such that ψ_{2p_z} and $\psi_{2p_{z'}}$ overlap as much as possible, that is, when z and z' are parallel. The stable configuration should thus be a planar configuration, with the H—C—C and H—C—H angles equal

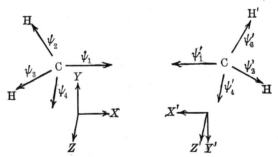

Fig. 12·3. Stable configuration of C_2H_4.

to 120°, as illustrated in Figure 12·3 (the z directions are upward, perpendicular to the plane of the paper). This is in agreement with the experimental facts for ethylene. It also gives a reason for the rigidity of the double bond; if we were to rotate one end of the molecule relative to the other, we would have to supply energy to compensate for the weakening of the π bond caused by this rotation. Since the carbon-carbon σ bond is not equivalent to the C—H bonds, we would not have been required to make ψ_2 and ψ_3 equivalent to ψ_1; in other words, the H—C—C angle could have been made unequal to the H—C—H angle. The angles in ethylene are as indicated; these angles may not persist in substituted ethylenes.

In acetylene, we may describe the carbon-carbon triple bond as consisting of one σ bond and two π bonds of the type given above. This valence form would give acetylene the known linear configuration. Since the $2p$ orbitals in a π bond overlap less than the orbitals in a σ bond, we expect a π bond to be weaker than a σ bond, and hence expect a C=C bond to be less than twice as strong as a C—C bond. The experimentally observed bond strengths are C—C, 59 kcal.; C=C, 100 kcal.; C≡C, 123 kcal., in agreement with this expectation.

When we come to second-row atoms, there are available for the formation of valence orbitals not only the $3s$ and $3p$ orbitals, but also the $3d$ orbitals, five in number. It is thus possible to have a covalence greater than 4. Rather than discuss the many individual cases by the methods used above, we shall later present the general theory of directed valence and show how it is possible to predict, by application of group theory, the types of bonds formed by any combination of s, p, and d orbitals. First, however, it is of interest to see to what extent the above qualitative conclusions can be justified by approximate calculations; as an example, we consider the H₂O molecule.

12c. The Quantitative Treatment of H₂O.[11]   In the valence bond method, the valence orbitals of the oxygen atom may be taken to be $\psi_{2p_x}(O)$ and $\psi_{2p_y}(O)$, those of the hydrogen atoms to be $\psi_{1s}(H)$. We first investigate the energy of the valence structure shown in Figure 12·4, where φ is the angle between the O—H bond and the x axis. For a particular valence structure, the energy may be written as

$$E = Q + \alpha \qquad 12·29$$

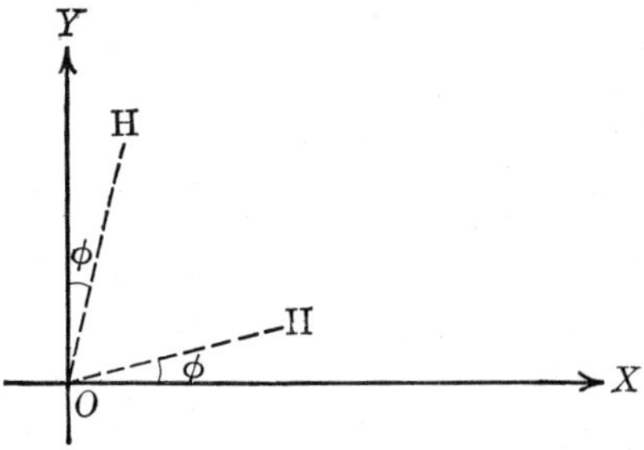

Fig. 12·4.

where Q is the coulombic and α is the exchange energy. According to equation 13·30 of the next chapter, the exchange energy for this case will be

$$\alpha = K_{13} + K_{24} - \tfrac{1}{2}(K_{14} + K_{23} + K_{12} + K_{34}) \qquad 12·30$$

where the K's are integrals of the type 12·10. The oxygen $2p_x$ orbital

[11] J. Van Vleck and A. Sherman, *Rev. Modern Phys.*, **7**, 200 (1935).

can be expressed as

$$\psi_{2p_x} = \psi_{2p\sigma} \cos \varphi + \psi_{2p\pi} \sin \varphi \qquad 12\cdot31$$

where $\psi_{2p\sigma}$ is an oxygen $2p$ orbital with its axis along the O—H bond and $\psi_{2p\pi}$ is an oxygen $2p$ orbital with its axis perpendicular to the bond direction. We may therefore write K_{13} as

$$K_{13} = \int \psi_{2p_x}(1)\psi_{1s}(2)\mathbf{H}\psi_{2p_x}(2)\psi_{1s}(1) \, d\tau_1 \, d\tau_2$$

$$= K_{\sigma\sigma} \cos^2 \varphi + K_{\pi\pi} \sin^2 \varphi + 2K_{\pi\sigma} \sin \varphi \cos \varphi \qquad 12\cdot32$$

where

$$K_{\sigma\sigma} = \int \psi_{2p\sigma}(1)\psi_{1s}(2)\mathbf{H}\psi_{2p\sigma}(2)\psi_{1s}(1) \, d\tau_1 \, d\tau_2$$

with similar expressions for the other exchange integrals between oxygen and hydrogen orbitals. The integral K_{12} is independent of φ. If we neglect the hydrogen-hydrogen exchange energy, the part of the exchange energy that depends on the angle φ will be

$$K_{\sigma\sigma}(2 \cos^2 \varphi - \sin^2 \varphi) + K_{\pi\pi}(2 \sin^2 \varphi - \cos^2 \varphi)$$

$$+ 2K_{\pi\sigma} \cos \varphi \sin \varphi \qquad 12\cdot33$$

The integrals $K_{\pi\sigma}$ are of the form

$$\int R_{2p}(r_1)R_{1s}(r_2)\mathbf{H}R_{2p}(r_2)R_{1s}(r_1)x'z' \, d\tau_1 \, d\tau_2$$

where the z' axis is along the O—H bond direction and R_{1s} is the radial part of ψ_{1s}, etc. The integrals $K_{\pi\sigma}$ are therefore zero, since they involve odd powers of x'. The orbitals $\psi_{2p\pi}$ and ψ_{1s} are orthogonal; the integral $K_{\pi\pi}$ thus contains only the electron repulsion term, so that this integral is positive. The orbitals $\psi_{2p\sigma}$ and ψ_{1s} are not orthogonal; the integral $K_{\sigma\sigma}$ is therefore similar to the analogous integral in the H_2 problem and is negative (corresponding to attraction). The value of φ which gives α the greatest negative value is therefore $90°$. On the basis of the exchange energy alone, and without considering the effect of hydrogen-hydrogen repulsions, this calculation gives the same results as our previous qualitative investigation. The coulombic energy for this structure is

$$Q = J_{13} + J_{24} + J_{14} + J_{23} + J_{12} + J_{34} \qquad 12\cdot34$$

J_{12} and J_{34} being neglected, the coulombic energy becomes

$$Q = 2J_{\sigma\sigma} + 2J_{\pi\pi}$$

where

$$J_{\sigma\sigma} = \int \psi_{2p\sigma}(1)\psi_{1s}(2)\mathbf{H}\psi_{2p\sigma}(1)\psi_{1s}(2) \, d\tau_1 \, d\tau_2$$

The coulombic energy is thus independent of φ, so that only the exchange energy is effective in giving directional properties to the valence bonds in H_2O. Inclusion of the hydrogen repulsions would, of course, tend to increase the bond angle, as would the use of s-p hybrid orbitals for the oxygen atom.

12d. The General Theory of Directed Valence.[12] In discussing the valence of the carbon atom, we found that it was possible to construct four equivalent valence orbitals from the four atomic orbitals ψ_{2s}, ψ_{2p_x}, ψ_{2p_y}, ψ_{2p_z}, these valence orbitals having their maximum values in the directions of the corners of a regular tetrahedron. Similarly, from the orbitals ψ_{2s}, ψ_{2p_x}, ψ_{2p_y} we found that it was possible to construct three equivalent valence orbitals in the xy plane, separated by angles of 120°. We now wish to investigate the possible sets of equivalent valence orbitals which can be formed from any combination of s, p, and d atomic orbitals, that is, from any combination of some or all of the atomic orbitals s, p_x, p_y, p_z, d_{z^2}, d_{xz}, d_{yz}, d_{xy}, $d_{x^2-y^2}$. These sets of equivalent valence orbitals can be most easily found by means of group theory. Any set of such orbitals has a characteristic symmetry group. The set will form a basis for a representation of the group which will in general be reducible, but which can be expressed in terms of the irreducible representations of the group by means of the group character table. The s, p, and d orbitals of the atom will also form representations of the group. By comparing the component irreducible representations of the set of valence orbitals with those of the atomic orbitals it will be possible to tell which combination of atomic orbitals will lead to a set of valence orbitals of the required symmetry. The general procedure can be best described by an example; we will discuss the possibilities of forming three equivalent coplanar bonds, separated by angles of 120°.

This set of valence orbitals has the symmetry D_{3h}; the character table for this group is reproduced in Table 12·1. The table also includes the transformation properties of the coordinates and the pertinent combinations of the coordinates. The atomic orbitals are functions of r multiplied by the function written as subscript. Hence they transform under the operations of the group in the same way as their subscripts. The atomic orbitals therefore form bases for representations of the group as given in the table. It is now necessary

[12] G. Kimball, *J. Chem. Phys.*, **8**, 188 (1940).   J. H. Van Vleck and A. Sherman. *Rev. Modern Phys.*, **7**, 174 (1935).

to investigate the transformation properties of the set of valence orbitals. These are represented schematically in Figure 12·5. Applying the operation E leaves the three orbitals unchanged; the character of the representation for the operation E, applied to this set of orbitals which we denote by σ, is consequently 3. The operation σ_h, reflection in the xy plane, likewise leaves the orbitals unchanged; the character for this operation is thus 3. The operation C_3, a rotation

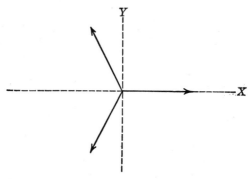

Fig. 12·5.　Valence orbitals with symmetry D_{3h}.

by 120° about the z axis, changes the position of all orbitals, and thus has the character zero. The operation S_3, a rotation by 120° followed by a reflection in the xy plane, likewise has the character zero. The operation C_2', a rotation by 180° about an axis which we may take to be the x axis, interchanges orbitals 2 and 3 and leaves orbital 1 unchanged, and hence has the character 1. Similarly, the operation σ_v, which we may take to be a reflection in the xz plane, is seen to have the character 1. The character of the representation σ is given in the table. Either by inspection or by applying equation 10·31, we see that this representation may be broken up into the sum of irreducible representations

$$\sigma = A_1' + E' \qquad 12\cdot35$$

The set of valence orbitals σ can therefore be made up of any of the combinations

$$\sigma = s + p_x + p_y$$
$$\sigma = d_z + p_x + p_y$$
$$\sigma = s + d_{xy} + d_{x^2-y^2} \qquad 12\cdot36$$
$$\sigma = d_z + d_{xy} + d_{x^2-y^2}$$

that is, it is possible to form the set of three equivalent valence orbitals from any of the electron configurations sp^2, sd^2, dp^2, d^3.

TABLE 12·1

CHARACTER TABLE FOR TRIGONAL ORBITALS

			E	σ_h	$2C_3$	$2S_3$	$3C_2'$	$3\sigma_v$
s, d_{z^2}	$1, x^2 + y^2, z^2$	A_1'	1	1	1	1	1	1
		A_2'	1	1	1	1	-1	-1
		A_1''	1	-1	1	-1	1	-1
p	z	A_2''	1	-1	1	-1	-1	1
$\begin{Bmatrix} p_x, p_y \\ d_{xy}, d_{x^2-y^2} \end{Bmatrix}$	$(x^2 - y^2, xy)(x, y)$	E'	2	2	-1	-1	0	0
d_{xz}, d_{yz}	(xz, yz)	E''	2	-2	-1	1	0	0
		σ	3	3	0	0	1	1
		π	6	0	0	0	-2	0

The possibility of double bond formation can be discussed in a similar fashion. In describing the valence bonds in ethylene, we stated that a double bond can be considered as a σ bond, with valence orbitals of the type discussed above, plus a π bond formed by the interaction of two p electrons in orbitals which have their axis perpendicular to that of the

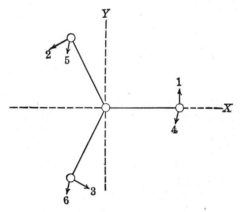

FIG. 12·6. Double bond formation for group D_{3h}.

σ bond. In a polyatomic molecule, consisting of a central atom with a number of external atoms bound to it, bonds of this type can also be formed; as far as the external atoms are concerned, the condition for the formation of π bonds is the presence of p orbitals at right angles to the bond axes. Since there can be two such p orbitals per external atom, the configuration of these p orbitals can be represented by the arrows in Figure 12·6, where orbitals 1, 2, 3 are in the xy plane and orbitals 4, 5, 6 are parallel to the z axis. Designating this set of orbitals by the symbol π, we proceed to find the character of the π representation in the same manner as for the σ representation. We have:

E: all orbitals unchanged; character 6.

σ_h: 1, 2, 3 unchanged; 4, 5, 6 changed in sign; character 0.

C_3: all orbitals changed in position; character 0.

S_3: all orbitals changed in position; character 0.

C_2' (considered as rotation about the x axis): orbitals 2, 3, 5, 6 changed in position; orbitals 1 and 4 changed in sign; character -2.

σ_v (considered as reflection in the xz plane): orbitals 2, 3, 5, 6 changed in position; orbital 4 unchanged; orbital 1 changed in sign; character 0.

The character of the π representation is given in the table.

Breaking the π representation down into its irreducible components, we have

$$\pi = A_2' + A_2'' + E' + E'' \qquad 12\cdot37$$

In order that π bonds may be formed, the central atom must have available orbitals which transform in the same manner as the p orbitals of the external atoms, so that any orbital of the central atom which belongs to one of the irreducible representations in 12·37 may be used in double bond formation. Consequently the orbitals available for the formation of π bonds are the p orbital belonging to A_2'' (p_z), the d orbitals belonging to E'' (d_{xz}, d_{yz}), and the two orbitals belonging to E' which are not used in forming the original σ bonds. The original σ orbitals probably contain a mixture of both the p and the d, E' orbitals, so that the π orbitals formed from these orbitals are probably weaker than those formed from the A_2'' and E'' orbitals. We may divide π bonds into two classes, calling them " strong " if they belong to representations not used in σ bond formation, and " weak " otherwise.

The results of such calculations for a central atom surrounded by two to eight external atoms are shown in Table 12·2. The columns give the coordination number, the configuration of electrons used in the formation of σ orbitals, the arrangement of the bonds obtained from this electron configuration, the orbitals available for the formation of the strong and weak π orbitals, in this order. Where there is a choice of two or more orbitals when only one can be used, the orbitals are enclosed in parentheses.

It should be noted that this method does not predict directly the type of bond arrangement formed from any given electron configuration; it merely tells whether or not a given arrangement is possible. If, as often happens, it is found that several arrangements of the bonds are possible for a single configuration of electrons, the relative stability of the various arrangements must be decided by other methods, such as Pauling's strength criterion discussed earlier in this chapter, or considerations of the repulsions between non-bonded atoms.

TABLE 12·2

STABLE BOND ARRANGEMENTS AND MULTIPLE BOND POSSIBILITIES

I	II	III	IV	V
2	sp	Linear	p^2d^2	—
	dp	Linear	p^2d^2	—
	p^2	Angular	$d(pd)$	$d(sd)$
	ds	Angular	$d(pd)$	$p(pd)$
	d^2	Angular	$d(pd)$	$p(spd)$
3	sp^2	Trigonal plane	pd^2	d^2
	dp^2	Trigonal plane	pd^2	d^2
	ds^2	Trigonal plane	pd^2	p^2
	d^3	Trigonal plane	pd^2	p^2
	dsp	Unsymmetrical plane	pd^2	$(pd)d$
	p^3	Trigonal pyramid	—	$(sd)d^4$
	d^2p	Trigonal pyramid	—	$(sd)p^2d^2$
4	sp^3	Tetrahedral	d^2	d^3
	d^3s	Tetrahedral	d^2	p^3
	dsp^2	Tetragonal plane	d^3p	—
	d^2p^2	Tetragonal plane	d^3p	—
	d^2sp	Irregular tetrahedron	—	d
	dp^3	Irregular tetrahedron	—	s
	d^3p	Irregular tetrahedron	—	s
	d^4	Tetragonal pyramid	d	$(sp)p$
5	dsp^3	Bipyramid	d^2	d^2
	d^3sp	Bipyramid	d^2	p^2
	d^2sp^2	Tetragonal pyramid	d	pd^2
	d^4s	Tetragonal pyramid	d	p^3
	d^2p^3	Tetragonal pyramid	d	sd^2
	d^4p	Tetragonal pyramid	d	sp^2
	d^3p^2	Pentagonal plane	pd^2	—
	d^5	Pentagonal pyramid	—	$(sp)p^2$
6	d^2sp^3	Octahedron	d^3	—
	d^4sp	Trigonal prism	—	p^2d
	d^5p	Trigonal prism	—	p^2s
	d^3p^3	Trigonal antiprism	—	sd
	d^3sp^2	Mixed	—	—
	d^5s	Mixed	—	—
	d^4p^2	Mixed	—	—
7	d^3sp^3	ZrF_7^{-3}	—	d^2
	d^5sp	ZrF_7^{-3}	—	p^2
	d^4sp^2	TaF_7^{-2}	—	dp
	d^4p^3	TaF_7^{-2}	—	ds
	d^5p^2	TaF_7^{-2}	—	ps
8	d^4sp^3	Dodecahedron	d	—
	d^5p^3	Antiprism	—	s
	d^5sp^2	Face-centered prism	p	—

CHAPTER XIII

RESONANCE AND THE STRUCTURE OF COMPLEX MOLECULES

13a. Spin Theory and Bond Eigenfunctions. We will now develop the methods which will enable us to give an approximate quantitative treatment of many-electron molecules. Because of the complexity of the problem, we again use products of one-electron eigenfunctions as the basis for a perturbation calculation. For a system of n atoms, each with one valence electron, we denote the eigenfunctions of the valence orbitals of the atoms by $a(x, y, z)$, $b(x, y, z)$, $c(x, y, z) \cdots n(x, y, z)$. Let the coordinates of the ith electron be (x_i, y_i, z_i). Then a possible eigenfunction for the n electrons, with spin neglected, will be $a(1)b(2)c(3) \cdots n(n)$, where $a(x_1, y_1, z_1)$ has been abbreviated to $a(1)$, etc. Any function which may be obtained from this by permutation of the numbers $1, 2 \cdots n$ is an equally good eigenfunction. To be complete, each of the above orbital eigenfunctions must be multiplied by a spin function of the type $\alpha(1)\alpha(2)\beta(3) \cdots \alpha(n)$. According to the exclusion principle, only those functions are allowed which are antisymmetric with regard to electron interchange. As for the atom, our zero-order eigenfunctions are therefore the linear combinations

$$\varphi = \frac{1}{\sqrt{n!}} \begin{vmatrix} (a\alpha)_1 & (b\alpha)_1 & (c\beta)_1 & \cdots & (n\alpha)_1 \\ (a\alpha)_2 & (b\alpha)_2 & (c\beta)_2 & \cdots & (n\alpha)_2 \\ \cdot & & & & \\ \cdot & & & & \\ \cdot & & & & \\ (a\alpha)_n & (b\alpha)_n & (c\beta)_n & \cdots & (n\alpha)_n \end{vmatrix} \qquad 13 \cdot 1$$

where $(a\alpha)_1 = a(1)\alpha(1)$, etc. There are 2^n such determinants, since each column may contain either α or β. We will denote the above eigenfunction by

$$\varphi = \begin{pmatrix} a & b & c & \cdots & n \\ \alpha & \alpha & \beta & \cdots & \alpha \end{pmatrix}$$

The energy, to the first order, is given by the roots of the secular equation

$$\left| H_{ij} - S_{ij}E \right| = 0$$

where

$$H_{ij} = \int \varphi_i^* \mathbf{H} \varphi_j \, d\tau; \quad S_{ij} = \int \varphi_i^* \varphi_j \, d\tau$$

For the n-electron problem, the order of this equation is 2^n, so that the problem will be tractable only if we can break the secular determinant down into a product of determinants of lower order. In the atomic problem this was done by means of the operators $\mathbf{M}^2$, $\mathbf{M}_z$, $\mathbf{S}^2$, $\mathbf{S}_z$, all of which commuted with the Hamiltonian. Owing to the lack of spherical symmetry of most molecular systems, the operators $\mathbf{M}^2$ and $\mathbf{M}_z$ will no longer commute with the Hamiltonian, and so they lose their usefulness. To the approximation we are considering, in which spin interactions are neglected, the operators $\mathbf{S}^2$ and $\mathbf{S}_z$ commute with the Hamiltonian and may be used to reduce the order of the secular determinant. Each of the eigenfunctions φ is already an eigenfunction of $\mathbf{S}_z$, since each term in the expansion of the determinant of φ is an eigenfunction of $\mathbf{S}_z$ with the same eigenvalue. The eigenvalue of any φ for S_z is found from the relation

$$\mathbf{S}_z \varphi = (n_\alpha - n_\beta) \frac{h}{4\pi} \varphi$$

where n_α is the number of columns of α's and n_β is the number of columns β's. For $n = 6$, we have $2^6 = 64$ eigenfunctions φ. Classifying these according to their eigenvalues of $\mathbf{S}_z$, we have:

Eigenvalue of $\mathbf{S}_z$ (units of $\dfrac{h}{2\pi}$)	3	2	1	0	-1	-2	-3
Number of eigenfunctions	1	6	15	20	15	6	1

Since $H_{ij} = S_{ij} = 0$ if φ_i and φ_j have different eigenvalues for $\mathbf{S}_z$, this classification results in a considerable simplification of the secular equation. Further simplification is possible if the φ's are combined into linear combinations which are eigenfunctions of $\mathbf{S}^2$ as well as of $\mathbf{S}_z$.

Let us imagine the n atoms to be divided into pairs (a, b) (c, d), etc., with each pair at a great distance from all the other pairs. The system will be most stable if there is a bond between a and b, one between c and d, etc. According to our previous discussion, a and b will have a stable bond between them only if the spins of the corresponding electrons are paired; the same condition holds for each of the other pairs. Such a distribution of spins corresponds to the condition $\mathbf{S}_z \varphi = 0$. Even if the atoms are not separated, it would seem reasonable to assume that the most stable configuration would be that corresponding to the maximum number of bonds. We will therefore focus our attention on the determinants containing only the φ's which have the eigenvalue for the operator S_z equal to zero; that is, in the six-electron case for example, we assume that the ground state of the molecule is given by one of the roots of the twenty-row secular determinant. The eigenfunctions φ are not in general eigenfunctions of S^2, but we can form linear combinations of the φ's which are. Rather than treat the general case, let us consider the system of four electrons. The eigenfunctions φ which have the eigenvalue zero for S_z are

	a	b	c	d
φ_1	α	α	β	β
φ_2	α	β	α	β
φ_3	β	α	α	β
φ_4	α	β	β	α
φ_5	β	α	β	α
φ_6	β	β	α	α

We will now form a linear combination of the φ's which corresponds to a bond between a and b and one between c and d. This requires a and b to have opposite spins, so that we are limited to the functions φ_2, φ_3, φ_4, and φ_5. The combination will therefore be of the form

$$\psi_{ab,\ cd} = a_2\varphi_2 + a_3\varphi_3 + a_4\varphi_4 + a_5\varphi_5 \qquad 13\cdot2$$

If we interchange the spins on a and b, the function $\psi_{ab,\ cd}$ must change sign, since the spin function associated with a stable bond is antisymmetric in the electrons. We therefore obtain

$$\psi_{ab,\ cd} = -a_2\varphi_3 - a_3\varphi_2 - a_4\varphi_5 - a_5\varphi_4 \qquad 13\cdot3$$

Performing the same operation with the spins on c and d, we have

$$\psi_{ab,\ cd} = -a_2\varphi_4 - a_3\varphi_5 - a_4\varphi_2 - a_5\varphi_3 \qquad 13\cdot4$$

The above equations are consistent only if $a_5 = a_2$, $a_3 = a_4 = -a_2$. We have, therefore, for the (unnormalized) function representing the two bonds a–b, c–d, the *bond eigenfunction*

$$\psi_{ab,\ cd} = \varphi_2 - \varphi_3 - \varphi_4 + \varphi_5 \qquad 13\cdot5$$

In a similar manner, we find the bond eigenfunctions

$$\psi_{ad,\ bc} = \varphi_1 - \varphi_2 - \varphi_5 + \varphi_6 \qquad 13\cdot6$$

$$\psi_{ac,\ bd} = \varphi_1 - \varphi_3 - \varphi_4 + \varphi_6 \qquad 13\cdot7$$

We note that these bond eigenfunctions can be written as

$$\psi_{ij,\ kl} = \sum_{n=1}^{6} \delta_{ij}(n)\ \delta_{kl}(n)\varphi_n \qquad 13\cdot8$$

where $\delta_{ij}(n)$ is 1 if i has the spin α and j has the spin β; $\delta_{ij}(n)$ is -1 if i has the spin β and j the spin α; $\delta_{ij}(n) = 0$ if i and j have the same spin. This expression can readily be generalized.

If we want the bond eigenfunction corresponding to a bond between a and b, but none between c and d, we proceed in an analogous manner. Only φ_2, φ_3, φ_4, φ_5 can be used, as they are the only functions in which a and b have opposite spins. This function must be antisymmetric with respect to exchange of the spins on a and b but symmetric with respect to the exchange of the spins on c and d. We readily find the appropriate bond eigenfunction to be

$$\psi_{ab} = \varphi_2 - \varphi_3 + \varphi_4 - \varphi_5 = \sum_{n=1}^{6} \delta_{ab}(n)\varphi_n \qquad 13 \cdot 9$$

The other one-bond eigenfunctions are

$$\psi_{bc} = \varphi_1 - \varphi_2 + \varphi_5 - \varphi_6$$

$$\psi_{cd} = \varphi_2 + \varphi_3 - \varphi_4 - \varphi_5$$

$$\psi_{ad} = \varphi_1 + \varphi_2 - \varphi_5 - \varphi_6 \qquad 13 \cdot 10$$

$$\psi_{ac} = \varphi_1 - \varphi_3 + \varphi_4 - \varphi_6$$

$$\psi_{bd} = \varphi_1 + \varphi_3 - \varphi_4 - \varphi_6$$

The bond eigenfunction corresponding to no bonds is obviously

$$\psi = \varphi_1 + \varphi_2 + \varphi_3 + \varphi_4 + \varphi_5 + \varphi_6 \qquad 13 \cdot 11$$

This eigenfunction is symmetric with respect to exchange of the spins on any pair.

Not all the above bond eigenfunctions are independent. As our independent set we take the bond eigenfunctions $\psi_{ab,\ cd}$, $\psi_{ad,\ bc}$, ψ_{ab}, ψ_{bc}, ψ_{cd}, ψ. The remaining bond eigenfunctions can be expressed in terms of these as

$$\psi_{ac,\ bd} = \psi_{ab,\ cd} + \psi_{ad,\ bc}$$

$$\psi_{ad} = \psi_{ab} + \psi_{bc} + \psi_{cd}$$

$$\psi_{ac} = \psi_{ab} + \psi_{bc} \qquad 13 \cdot 12$$

$$\psi_{bd} = \psi_{bc} + \psi_{cd}$$

We will now show that the bond eigenfunctions derived above are eigenfunctions of $\mathbf{S}^2$, and further, that bond eigenfunctions corresponding to different numbers of bonds have different eigenvalues for $\mathbf{S}^2$. According to equation 9·3, the spin operators $\mathbf{S}_x$, $\mathbf{S}_y$ and the spin eigenfunctions

α and β obey the relations

$$(S_{x1} + iS_{y1})\alpha(1) = 0 \qquad\qquad (S_x + iS_y) = \sum_n (S_{xn} + iS_{yn})$$

$$(S_{x1} + iS_{y1})\beta(1) = \frac{h}{2\pi}\,\alpha(1)$$

$$(S_{x1} - iS_{y1})\alpha(1) = \frac{h}{2\pi}\,\beta(1)$$

13·13

$$(S_{x1} - iS_{y1})\beta(1) = 0 \qquad\qquad (S_x - iS_y) = \sum_n (S_{xn} - iS_{yn})$$

where S_{x1} is the operator for the x component of the spin of electron (1), etc. Denoting the φ eigenfunctions by the abbreviated notation $(\alpha\beta\alpha\beta)$, etc., we have

$$(S_x + iS_y)(\alpha\alpha\beta\beta) = \frac{h}{2\pi}\,\{(\alpha\alpha\alpha\beta) + (\alpha\alpha\beta\alpha)\}$$

$$(S_x + iS_y)(\alpha\beta\alpha\beta) = \frac{h}{2\pi}\,\{(\alpha\alpha\alpha\beta) + (\alpha\beta\alpha\alpha)\}$$

$$(S_x + iS_y)(\beta\alpha\alpha\beta) = \frac{h}{2\pi}\,\{(\alpha\alpha\alpha\beta) + (\beta\alpha\alpha\alpha)\}$$

$$(S_x + iS_y)(\alpha\beta\beta\alpha) = \frac{h}{2\pi}\,\{(\alpha\alpha\beta\alpha) + (\alpha\beta\alpha\alpha)\}$$

$$(S_x + iS_y)(\beta\alpha\beta\alpha) = \frac{h}{2\pi}\,\{(\alpha\alpha\beta\alpha) + (\beta\alpha\alpha\alpha)\}$$

$$(S_x + iS_y)(\beta\beta\alpha\alpha) = \frac{h}{2\pi}\,\{(\alpha\beta\alpha\alpha) + (\beta\alpha\alpha\alpha)\}$$

$$(S_x - iS_y)(\alpha\alpha\beta\beta) = \frac{h}{2\pi}\,\{(\beta\alpha\beta\beta) + (\alpha\beta\beta\beta)\} \qquad 13\cdot14$$

$$(S_x - iS_y)(\alpha\beta\alpha\beta) = \frac{h}{2\pi}\,\{(\beta\beta\alpha\beta) + (\alpha\beta\beta\beta)\}$$

$$(S_x - iS_y)(\beta\alpha\alpha\beta) = \frac{h}{2\pi}\,\{(\beta\beta\alpha\beta) + (\beta\alpha\beta\beta)\}$$

$$(S_x - iS_y)(\alpha\beta\beta\alpha) = \frac{h}{2\pi}\,\{(\beta\beta\beta\alpha) + (\alpha\beta\beta\beta)\}$$

$$(S_x - iS_y)(\beta\alpha\beta\alpha) = \frac{h}{2\pi}\,\{(\beta\beta\beta\alpha) + (\beta\alpha\beta\beta)\}$$

$$(S_x - iS_y)(\beta\beta\alpha\alpha) = \frac{h}{2\pi}\,\{(\beta\beta\beta\alpha) + (\beta\beta\alpha\beta)\}$$

Operating on the bond eigenfunctions we therefore obtain

$$(\mathbf{S}_x + i\mathbf{S}_y)\psi_{ab,\ cd} = 0$$

$$(\mathbf{S}_x + i\mathbf{S}_y)\psi_{ad,\ bc} = 0$$

13·15

Since

$$\mathbf{S}^2 = (\mathbf{S}_x - i\mathbf{S}_y)(\mathbf{S}_x + i\mathbf{S}_y) + \frac{h}{2\pi}\,\mathbf{S}_z + \mathbf{S}_z^2$$

and since the eigenvalues of the bond eigenfunctions for the operator $\mathbf{S}_z$ are zero, we see that the bond eigenfunctions representing two bonds are eigenfunctions of $\mathbf{S}^2$ with the eigenvalue zero.

Operating on ψ_{ab}, we obtain

$$(\mathbf{S}_x + i\mathbf{S}_y)\psi_{ab} = \frac{h}{2\pi}\left\{ \begin{matrix} (\alpha\alpha\alpha\beta) + (\alpha\beta\alpha\alpha) - (\alpha\alpha\alpha\beta) - (\beta\alpha\alpha\alpha) \\ + (\alpha\alpha\beta\alpha) + (\alpha\beta\alpha\alpha) - (\alpha\alpha\beta\alpha) - (\beta\alpha\alpha\alpha) \end{matrix} \right\} \quad 13·16$$

$$= 2\,\frac{h}{2\pi}\left\{ (\alpha\beta\alpha\alpha) - (\beta\alpha\alpha\alpha) \right\}$$

$$(\mathbf{S}_x - i\mathbf{S}_y)(\mathbf{S}_x + i\mathbf{S}_y)\psi_{ab} = 2\,\frac{h^2}{4\pi^2}\left\{ \begin{matrix} (\beta\beta\alpha\alpha) + (\alpha\beta\beta\alpha) + (\alpha\beta\alpha\beta) \\ - (\beta\beta\alpha\alpha) - (\beta\alpha\beta\alpha) - (\beta\alpha\alpha\beta) \end{matrix} \right\}$$

$$= 2\,\frac{h^2}{4\pi^2}\left\{ \varphi_2 - \varphi_3 + \varphi_4 - \varphi_5 \right\} = 2\,\frac{h^2}{4\pi^2}\,\psi_{ab}$$

ψ_{ab} is therefore an eigenfunction of $\mathbf{S}^2$ with the eigenvalue $1(1 + 1)\,\dfrac{h^2}{4\pi^2}$.

In the same way we find that ψ_{bc} and ψ_{cd} are eigenfunctions of $\mathbf{S}^2$ with the eigenvalues $1(1 + 1)\,\dfrac{h^2}{4\pi^2}$; and that ψ is an eigenfunction of $\mathbf{S}^2$ with the eigenvalue $2(2 + 1)\,\dfrac{h^2}{4\pi^2}$. Since matrix elements between functions with different values of their eigenvalue for $\mathbf{S}^2$ vanish, the six-row secular determinant for the four-electron problem is thus reduced to one three-row, one two-row, and one one-row determinant. The energy of the ground state of the system should be given by one of the roots of the two-row determinant, since the bond eigenfunctions involved in this secular determinant correspond to the maximum number of bonds. This is further confirmed by the observation that the ground state of most molecules is non-paramagnetic, indicating zero spin.

The above results are readily generalized for more than four electrons. To summarize the procedure when we are interested in the ground state of a complex molecule, we first form the zero-order eigenfunctions φ in determinantal form. These functions are eigenfunctions of S_z; we consider only those for which $S_z \varphi = 0$. From these functions φ we form the bond eigenfunctions ψ by the rule

$$\psi_{ij,\ kl,\ mn\ldots} = \sum_{\nu} \delta_{ij}(\nu)\ \delta_{kl}(\nu)\ \delta_{mn}(\nu)\cdots\varphi_\nu \qquad 13\cdot17$$

Bond eigenfunctions corresponding to different numbers of bonds have different eigenvalues for S^2; we consider only those corresponding to the maximum number of bonds, which have the eigenvalue zero for S^2.

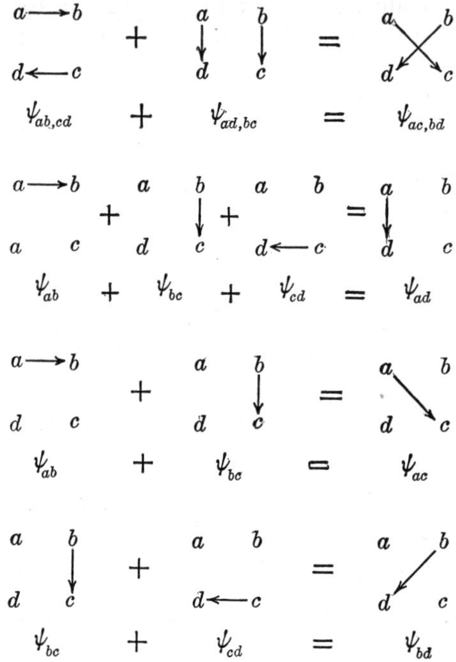

FIG. 13·1. Bond eigenfunctions for four electrons.

The energy of the ground state is then given by the solution of the secular equation $|H_{ij} - S_{ij}E| = 0$. (In the above discussion, we implicitly assumed the number of electrons to be even. For an odd number of electrons, the problem is first solved for the next higher even number, and then all integrals in the secular equation which involve the extra electron are placed equal to zero.) In the general case, no further reduction of the secular determinant can be made. If the molecule possesses external symmetry, a further reduction is possible, as will be shown later.

The possible bond eigenfunctions for the four-electron problem and the relations between them are illustrated graphically in Figure 13·1 (from equations 13·12). We note that a kind of vector addition law holds for the bond eigenfunctions. Usually we are interested only in bond eigenfunctions corresponding to the maximum number of bonds. Figure 13·1 tells us how to determine the number of independent bond eigenfunctions for any number of electrons. We arrange the symbols for the orbitals

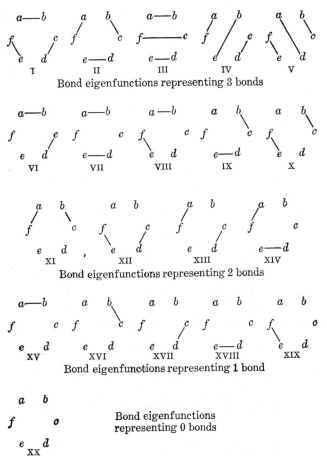

Bond eigenfunctions representing 3 bonds

Bond eigenfunctions representing 2 bonds

Bond eigenfunctions representing 1 bond

Bond eigenfunctions representing 0 bonds

FIG. 13·2. Bond eigenfunctions for six electrons.

in a circle, which, of course, need have no correlation with the actual structure of the molecule. We then draw the bonds in all possible ways. Some of these will involve bonds which cross, such as $\psi_{ac,\,bd}$. Any two bonds which cross can be uncrossed by the application of equations of the type

$$\psi_{ac,\,bd} = \psi_{ab,\,cd} + \psi_{ad,\,bc} \qquad\qquad 13\cdot18$$

This procedure can be continued until the original bond eigenfunction has been expanded into a linear combination of bond eigenfunctions which do not involve crossed bonds. Conversely, any eigenfunction can be built up from eigenfunctions which do not involve crossed bonds. We thus have the theorem due to Rumer:[1] arrange the orbitals in a circle, draw all the structures which contain the maximum number of bonds, but draw only those which contain no crossed bonds. The eigenfunctions corresponding to these structures are linearly independent, and, as all other bond eigenfunctions representing the maximum number of bonds can be expressed in terms of them, they form a complete set.

In order to form the bond eigenfunctions with the eigenvalue of S_z equal to zero, but representing less than the maximum possible number of bonds, we proceed in an analogous manner, including only those bond structures which are not derivable from others by the rule of vector addition. For six electrons, for example, we have the bond eigenfunctions as given in Figure 13·2. There is a total of twenty, as this is the number of φ's with the eigenvalue zero for the operator S_z. The determination of the energy of the ground state for a six-electron problem would thus involve the solution of a five-row determinant.

13b. Evaluation of the Integrals. In order to complete the solution of the problem, we need the values of the integrals of the type

$$H_{AB} = \int \psi_A^* H \psi_B \, d\tau \quad \text{and} \quad S_{AB} = \int \psi_A^* \psi_B \, d\tau$$

Since the ψ's are expressed as linear combinations of the φ's, we will first focus our attention on the integrals of the type $\int \varphi_i^* H \varphi_j \, d\tau$. Returning to the four-electron case, we consider the eigenfunctions

$$\varphi_1 = \frac{1}{\sqrt{4!}} \sum_\nu (-1)^\nu P_\nu^1 \{ (a\alpha)_1 (b\alpha)_2 (c\beta)_3 (d\beta)_4 \}$$

$$\varphi_2 = \frac{1}{\sqrt{4!}} \sum_{\nu'} (-1)^{\nu'} P_{\nu'}^2 \{ (a\alpha)_1 (b\beta)_2 (c\alpha)_3 (d\beta)_4 \}$$

The integral $\int \varphi_1^* H \varphi_2 \, d\tau$ is therefore

$$H_{12} = \frac{1}{4!} \int [\sum_\nu (-1)^\nu P_\nu^1 \{ (a\alpha)_1 (b\alpha)_2 (c\beta)_3 (d\beta)_4 \}]^*$$
$$H[\sum_{\nu'} (-1)^{\nu'} P_{\nu'}^2 \{ (a\alpha)_1 (b\beta)_2 (c\alpha)_3 (d\beta)_4 \}] d\tau \quad \text{13-19}$$

[1] G. Rumer, *Göttingen Nachr.*, **1932**, 377.

If the operator P_ν^1 is multiplied by another permutation operator, the result will be unchanged, since the integral already contains all possible terms. As in dealing with the atom, we therefore multiply by the inverse operator $(-1)^\nu [P_\nu^1]^{-1}$, obtaining for the first summation

$$\sum_\nu P_\nu^1 [P_\nu^1]^{-1} \{ (a\alpha)_1 (b\alpha)_2 (c\beta)_3 (d\beta)_4 \} = 4! \{ (a\alpha)_1 (b\beta)_2 (c\beta)_3 (d\beta)_4 \}$$

since there are 4! identical terms in this summation. The integral is thus reduced to

$$H_{12} = \int \{ (a\alpha)_1 (b\alpha)_2 (c\beta)_3 (d\beta)_4 \}$$
$$\mathbf{H}[\sum_{\nu''} (-1)^{\nu''} P_{\nu''} \{ (a\alpha)_1 (b\beta)_2 (c\alpha)_3 (d\beta)_4 \}] \, d\tau \quad 13\cdot20$$

Because of the orthogonality of the spin functions, all the terms in 13·20 will vanish except those for which the spins match identically. Integrating over the spins, we therefore have

$$H_{12} = -(abcd|\mathbf{H}|acbd) + (abcd|\mathbf{H}|acdb)$$
$$+ (abcd|\mathbf{H}|cabd) - (abcd|\mathbf{H}|cadb) \qquad 13\cdot21$$

where

$$(abcd|\mathbf{H}|acbd) = \int (a_1 b_2 c_3 d_4) \mathbf{H} (a_1 c_2 b_3 d_4) \, d\tau, \quad \text{etc.}$$

If we now assume that the one-electron functions a, b, etc., are mutually orthogonal (or are willing to set all integrals involving multiple exchanges of electrons equal to zero), all the above integrals with the exception of the first are equal to zero; this integral will be further abbreviated to (bc). We thus have the result

$$H_{12} = -(bc) \qquad 13\cdot22$$

This result is perfectly general: *The matrix element H_{ij} between two different φ functions is zero unless the functions differ only in the spins of two orbitals; then it is the negative of the corresponding exchange integral.*
    For the integral H_{11} we obtain the result

$$H_{11} = \int \{ (a\alpha)_1 (b\alpha)_2 (c\beta)_3 (d\beta)_4 \} \mathbf{H}[(-1)^{\nu''} P_{\nu''} \{ (a\alpha)_1 (b\alpha)_2 (c\beta)_3 (d\beta)_4 \}] \, d\tau$$

$$= (abcd|\mathbf{H}|abcd) - (abcd|\mathbf{H}|abdc) - (abcd|\mathbf{H}|bacd)$$

$$= Q - (cd) - (ab) \qquad 13\cdot23$$

That is: *The matrix element H_{ij} between a φ function and itself is the coulombic integral Q minus the sum of all exchange integrals between orbitals having the same spin.*

Continuing with the four-electron problem, and denoting $\psi_{ab,\,cd}$ by ψ_A and $\psi_{ad,\,bc}$ by ψ_B, we require the matrix elements H_{AA}, H_{BB}, H_{AB}. In terms of the integrals H_{12}, etc., we obtain from 13·5 and 13·6 the results

$$H_{AA} = H_{22} + H_{33} + H_{44} + H_{55}$$
$$+ 2(H_{25} + H_{34} - H_{23} - H_{24} - H_{35} - H_{45})$$

$$H_{BB} = H_{11} + H_{22} + H_{55} + H_{66}$$
$$+ 2(-H_{12} - H_{15} + H_{16} - H_{26} + H_{25} - H_{56})$$

$$H_{AB} = H_{12} - H_{13} - H_{14} + H_{15} - H_{22} + H_{23} + H_{24} - 2H_{25}$$
$$+ H_{35} + H_{45} - H_{55} + H_{26} - H_{36} - H_{46} + H_{56}$$

The necessary matrix elements H_{ij} are readily found by application of the rules given above; we have

$H_{11} = Q - (ab) - (cd)$	$H_{12} = -(bc)$	$H_{25} = 0$
$H_{22} = Q - (ac) - (bd)$	$H_{13} = -(ac)$	$H_{26} = -(ad)$
$H_{33} = Q - (ad) - (bc)$	$H_{14} = -(bd)$	$H_{34} = 0$
$H_{44} = Q - (ad) - (bc)$	$H_{15} = -(ad)$	$H_{35} = -(cd)$
$H_{55} = Q - (ac) - (bd)$	$H_{16} = 0$	$H_{36} = -(bd)$
$H_{66} = Q - (ab) - (cd)$	$H_{23} = -(ab)$	$H_{45} = -(ab)$
	$H_{24} = -(cd)$	$H_{46} = -(ac)$
		$H_{56} = -(bc)$

Therefore

$$H_{AA} = \quad 4Q - 2\{(ac) + (ad) + (bc) + (bd)\} + 4\{(ab) + (cd)\}$$
$$H_{BB} = \quad 4Q - 2\{(ab) + (ac) + (cd) + (bd)\} + 4\{(ad) + (bc)\} \quad 13\cdot24$$
$$H_{AB} = -2Q + 4\{(ac) + (bd)\} - 2\{(ab) + (ad) + (bc) + (cd)\}$$

Since $\int \varphi_i^* \varphi_j \, d\tau = \delta_{ij}$, we have the results $S_{AA} = S_{BB} = 4$; $S_{AB} = -2$. In general, S_{AB} will be equal to the coefficient of Q in H_{AB}.

The above procedure, although straightforward, becomes rather tedious for more than four electrons. By an extension of arguments of the above type, the following general formulation can be made.

To find the matrix element of **H** between two bond eigenfunctions, say (1) $\psi_{ab,\,cd,\,ef,\,gh}$ and (2) $\psi_{ac,\,bd,\,eg,\,fh}$, we note that the two electrons in any bond must have opposite spins. If we let the spin of a be α, that of b must be β from (1); according to (2) the spin of c must be β and that of d must be α. The spin of e can now be chosen arbitrarily; for a given choice of the spin of e the remaining spins are fixed. We say that

a, b, c, d form a cycle and e, f, g, h another. Let us assign the spin α to e. This situation is denoted by

$$\left(\frac{ad}{bc}\right)\left(\frac{eh}{fg}\right)$$

where the orbitals associated with α's are written above the line and those associated with β's are written below the line. The matrix element of **H** for the bond eigenfunctions (1) and (2) is then, where x is the number of cycles, and ν is the number of interchanges of orbitals which are assigned different spins in the diagram in ψ_2 required to make it equal to ψ_1.

$H_{12} = (-1)^\nu 2^x \{Q + \frac{3}{2}[\sum(\text{single exchange integrals between}$
  orbitals in the same cycle with opposite spins) $- \sum(\text{single}$
  exchange integrals between orbitals in the same cycle with
  the same spin)] $- \frac{1}{2}\sum(\text{all single exchange integrals})\}$ 13·25

Equation 13·25 is perfectly general; the proof goes as follows. Let us consider the matrix component of **H** between the two functions

$$\psi_A = \psi_{ab,\, cd,\, ef,\, gh} \qquad \text{and} \qquad \psi_B = \psi_{ac,\, be,\, dh,\, fg}$$

for which the diagram is $\left(\dfrac{aegd}{bfhc}\right)$. This integral will be expressed as a sum

of integrals involving φ functions, of the type $\int \varphi_i^* \mathbf{H} \varphi_j \, d\tau$. There are

three possibilities:

1. $\varphi_i \equiv \varphi_j$; according to 13·17, the sign of the integral is $(-1)^\nu$. This gives a contribution to H_{AB}, according to equation 13·22, equal to

$$(-1)^\nu \{2(Q - \sum[(ae)\text{-type}])\}$$

the factor 2 arising from the fact that either α or β could be assigned to a.

2. The two φ functions differ in the spins assigned to, say, a and b. This integral is multiplied by -1, relative to the coefficient of Q, as can be seen from 13·17, and therefore, according to 13·22, gives a contribution $+(ab)$. Since there are two such integrals, and since the spins of any pair of this type could have been interchanged, the total contribution to H_{AB} arising from integrals of this type is

$$(-1)^\nu \{+2\sum[(ab)\text{-type}]\}$$

3. The two φ functions differ in the spins assigned to, say, a and d. This integral has the coefficient $+1$, relative to the coefficient of Q, so that the total contribution to H_{AB} arising from integrals of this type is

$$(-1)^\nu \{-2\sum[(ad)\text{-type}]\}$$

and the integral H_{AB} is

$$H_{AB} = (-1)^{\nu} 2\{Q + \sum[(ab)\text{-type}] - 2\sum[(ad)\text{-type}]\}$$

in agreement with equation 13·25.

For the functions $\psi_C = \psi_{ab,\,cd,\,ef,\,gh}$ and $\psi_D = \psi_{ac,\,bd,\,eg,\,fh}$ we have the diagram $\left(\dfrac{ad}{bc}\right)\left(\dfrac{eh}{fg}\right)$. Again there are three cases.

1. The two φ's are identical. There are then four different ways of assigning spins to a and e:

$a \sim \alpha,\ e \sim \alpha$, gives $(-1)^{\nu}\{Q - \sum[(ad)\text{-type}] - \sum[(ae)\text{-type}]\}$
$a \sim \alpha,\ e \sim \beta$, gives $(-1)^{\nu}\{Q - \sum[(ad)\text{-type}] - \sum[(af)\text{-type}]\}$
$a \sim \beta,\ e \sim \alpha$, gives $(-1)^{\nu}\{Q - \sum[(ad)\text{-type}] - \sum[(af)\text{-type}]\}$
$a \sim \beta,\ e \sim \beta$, gives $(-1)^{\nu}\{Q - \sum[(ad)\text{-type}] - \sum[(ae)\text{-type}]\}$

Cases 2 and 3 are identical with the similar cases above, except that the numerical factor is 4. Since it is impossible to change the spin on only one orbital in a given cycle, there are no integrals of this type in which the two functions differ in the spins of a and e, etc. We therefore have the result

$$H_{CD} = (-1)^{\nu} 4\{Q - 2\sum[(ad)\text{-type}] + \sum[(ab)\text{-type}]$$
$$- \tfrac{1}{2}\sum[(ae)\text{- and } (af)\text{-types}]$$

which is equivalent to the general expression 13·25. The proof can readily be extended to more general cases.

Returning to the four-electron case, for H_{AA} we have the diagram $\left(\dfrac{a}{b}\right)\left(\dfrac{c}{d}\right)$. The matrix component of $\mathbf{H}$ is therefore

$$H_{AA} = 2^2\{Q + \tfrac{3}{2}[(ab) + (cd)]$$
$$- \tfrac{1}{2}[(ab) + (ac) + (ad) + (bc) + (bd) + (cd)]$$
$$= 4Q - 2[(ac) + (ad) + (bc) + (bd)] + 4[(ab) + (cd)]$$

in agreement with the previous calculation. For H_{AB} we have the diagram $\left(\dfrac{ac}{bd}\right)$, so that

$$H_{AB} = (-1)2\{Q + \tfrac{3}{2}[(ab) + (ad) + (bc) + (cd)] - \tfrac{3}{2}[(ac) + (bd)]$$
$$- \tfrac{1}{2}[(ab) + (ac) + (ad) + (bc) + (bd) + (cd)]\}$$
$$= -2Q + 4[(ac) + (bd)] - 2[(ab) + (ad) + (bc) + (cd)]$$

13c. The Two-Electron Problem. Although the two-electron problem has previously been treated in detail, it is of interest to consider at this point the results obtained by the above method.   Denoting the orbitals by a and b, there are four possible φ functions:

	a	b
φ_1	α	β
φ_2	β	α
φ_3	α	α
φ_4	β	β

Of these four functions, φ_1 and φ_2 have the eigenvalue zero for $\mathbf{S}_z$.   The linear combination having the eigenvalue zero for $\mathbf{S}^2$ is the bond eigenfunction

$$\psi_A = \psi_{ab} = \varphi_1 - \varphi_2$$

The energy of the ground state is therefore given by the solution of the one-row secular determinant

$$H_{AA} - S_{AA}E = 0$$

According to the rules developed above,

$$H_{AA} = 2[Q + (ab)], \quad S_{AA} = 2$$

so that the energy is

$$E = Q + (ab) \qquad\qquad 13.26$$

Comparing this with the result given by equation 12·7, we see that they become identical if the overlap integral $S = \int \psi_a \psi_b \, d\tau$ in 12·7 is placed equal to zero, as it has been assumed to be in the present method. Although this discrepancy may appear to be quite serious, in actual practice a compensation is made, as will become evident later.

13d. The Four-Electron Problem.   The matrix elements have already been determined.   Inserting these in the secular determinant

$$\begin{vmatrix} H_{AA} - S_{AA}E & H_{AB} - S_{AB}E \\ H_{AB} - S_{AB}E & H_{BB} - S_{BB}E \end{vmatrix} = 0$$

we obtain

$$\begin{vmatrix} \tfrac{3}{2}(\alpha_1+\alpha_2)-W & -\tfrac{3}{4}(\alpha_1+\alpha_2+\beta_1+\beta_2-\gamma_1-\gamma_2)+\tfrac{1}{2}W \\ -\tfrac{3}{4}(\alpha_1+\alpha_2+\beta_1+\beta_2-\gamma_1-\gamma_2)+\tfrac{1}{2}W & \tfrac{3}{2}(\beta_1+\beta_2)-W \end{vmatrix} = 0 \qquad 13.26$$

where the common factor 4 has been removed from each term, (ab), (cd), (ad), (bc), (ac), (bd) have been replaced by α_1, α_2, β_1, β_2, γ_1, γ_2, respectively, and

$$W = E - Q + \tfrac{1}{2}(\alpha_1 + \alpha_2 + \beta_1 + \beta_2 + \gamma_1 + \gamma_2)$$

Writing $\alpha = \alpha_1 + \alpha_2$, $\beta = \beta_1 + \beta_2$, $\gamma = \gamma_1 + \gamma_2$, 13·26 reduces to

$$W^2 - (\alpha + \beta + \gamma)W - \tfrac{3}{4}(\alpha + \beta - \gamma)^2 + 3\alpha\beta = 0$$

so that

$$W = \frac{\alpha + \beta + \gamma}{2} \pm \tfrac{1}{2}\sqrt{(\alpha + \beta + \gamma)^2 + 3(\alpha + \beta - \gamma)^2 - 12\alpha\beta}$$

or

$$E = Q \pm \sqrt{\alpha^2 + \beta^2 + \gamma^2 - \alpha\beta - \alpha\gamma - \beta\gamma} \qquad 13\cdot27$$

Of these two solutions the one with the negative sign represents the more stable state; this may be written as

$$E = Q - \sqrt{\tfrac{1}{2}\{(\alpha - \beta)^2 + (\beta - \gamma)^2 + (\gamma - \alpha)^2\}} \qquad 13\cdot28$$

a result first obtained by London.[2]

If we now remove the electrons c and d to infinity, equation 13·28 reduces to

$$E_{ab} = Q_{ab} + \alpha_1 \qquad 13\cdot29$$

(the sign of α_1 is taken to be $+$ since α_1 is a negative quantity; equation 13·29 therefore represents the lowest state of the system), which is identical with 13·26, as of course it should be. This result forms the basis for the " semi-empirical " method of treating complex molecules. We assume that the energy of any electron pair bond a–b can be represented by an equation of the form $E_{ab} = Q_{ab} + \alpha_{ab}$. The energy of this bond is obtained from the experimental data on some simple system, usually the data on the corresponding diatomic molecule. Some assumed ratio for $\dfrac{Q_{ab}}{\alpha_{ab}}$ being taken, each of these quantities can be determined independently. It is then further assumed that the quantities α_1, etc., which appear in the energy equation for a many-electron system, are identical with the corresponding quantities for the two-electron system, and that Q for the many-electron system is equal to $\sum_{ij} Q_{ij}$, where Q_{ij} is the coulombic energy for the two-electron system $i - j$. For example, if we had the problem of four atoms A, B, C, D with the corresponding orbitals a, b, c, d, the various terms in 13·28 are obtained as follows. We draw the diagram illustrating the various energy terms (Figure 13·3). From experimental data on the diatomic molecules AB, CD, AC, BD, CB, AD we determine the energies E_{ab}, E_{cd}, E_{ac}, E_{bd}, E_{cb}, E_{ad}. These energies may be expressed as functions

[2] F. London, Z. Elektrochem., **35**, 552 (1929).

of the corresponding interatomic distances by means of an empirical equation such as the Morse function (equation 14·31). We now assume some value for the ratios $\dfrac{Q_{ab}}{\alpha_1}$, etc., and thus calculate the individual quantities. These values of α_1, etc., as obtained from the diatomic molecules, are now used directly in 13·28. Q in this equation is assumed to be given by

$$Q = Q_{ab} + Q_{cd} + Q_{ac} + Q_{bd} + Q_{cb} + Q_{ad}$$

It will be observed that this procedure is actually an extrapolation of the binding energy between atoms from the diatomic to the polyatomic problem. Some such extrapolation is necessary if any treatment of polyatomic molecules is to be made, since actual evaluation of the integrals, even if a satisfactory set of zero-order functions were known, is completely out of the question. Since the above method of treatment involves the same type of approximation for both the diatomic and the polyatomic problem, we would expect the defects arising from these approximations to be at least partially compensated for by the method of determining the integrals from experimental data. Actually it

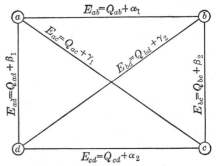

FIG. 13·3. Coulombic and exchange energies for a four-atom system.

must be recognized that this is an empirical method, and its validity must be determined largely by the results obtained.

In determining Q_{ab} and α_1 from E_{ab}, it is necessary to assume some definite ratio for the two integrals. In the Heitler-London treatment of the hydrogen molecule, where the corresponding integrals can be evaluated, the total binding energy is about 10–15 per cent coulombic. In actual practice satisfactory results are usually obtained if the coulombic energy is assumed to be about 14 per cent of the total binding energy for a given electron pair.

We may summarize the situation with regard to quantum-mechanical calculations involving polyatomic molecules as follows. The correct wave function for a system of n electrons would be a complicated function of the $3n$ coordinates. Judging from the results on H_2, a satisfactory wave function should contain the interelectron distances r_{ij} explicitly. However, with such a wave function, the n-electron problem becomes completely intractable; we are forced to make drastic

simplifications.   The first approximation that is made is to assume that
the eigenfunction for the system can be written as a product of one-
electron functions.   Even in the simple case of H_2, these wave functions
will not give very accurate results.   Using these functions as a basis,
we carry out a first-order perturbation calculation in which the further
approximation that the one-electron functions are orthogonal is made.
The energy of the system is then obtained as a function of certain coulombic and exchange integrals.   These particular integrals arise from
the method of writing the zero-order wave function and might not appear
in this particular form in a more accurate formulation of the problem.
These integrals are in general evaluated, not by direct calculation, but
from experimental data on simple systems.   In spite of the approximations, these calculations usually give results of considerable value in the
interpretation of chemical phenomena.

13e.   The Concept of Resonance.   We have seen that, for a system
involving many electrons, it is possible to write a number of bond eigenfunctions representing various ways of pairing the electrons to form
two-electron bonds;   the energy of the system is then given by the
solution of a secular determinant of high degree.   In many cases only
one of these bond eigenfunctions will be of importance in determining
the energy of the ground state of the molecule;   we say then that the
electrons are localized in particular bonds.   If we assume that the ground
state of a given molecule can be represented with sufficient accuracy
by one bond eigenfunction ψ_A, the energy of the ground state is given by

$E = \dfrac{H_{AA}}{S_{AA}}$.   From equation 13·25, we have

$$E = Q + \sum(\text{exchange integrals between bonded orbitals})$$
$$- \tfrac{1}{2}\sum(\text{exchange integrals between non-bonded orbitals})\quad 13\cdot30$$

This equation has been used in section 12c in the discussion of the water
molecule, where it was assumed that the bonds could be drawn in a
unique way.   In many molecules there does not appear to be any single
way of drawing the bonds which is a better representation of the actual
state of the molecule than other possible ways of drawing the bonds; in
this event the complete problem must be solved by the above methods.
We then say that the molecule " resonates " among the various states
represented by the individual bond eigenfunctions;   the difference in
energy between the actual molecule and the energy of the most stable
bond eigenfunction is called the " resonance energy."   This concept of
resonance has been applied, especially by Pauling,[3] to the elucidation of

---

[3] See L. Pauling, *The Nature of the Chemical Bond*, Cornell University Press, 1940.

many problems in molecular structure. As an example of this concept and of the methods derived in this chapter, we calculate the resonance energy of benzene.

13f. The Resonance Energy of Benzene.[4] Experimental evidence shows that benzene is a planar molecule, with the carbon atoms at the corners of a regular hexagon, and with all C—C—C and C—C—H angles equal to 120°. Taking the plane of the molecule to be the xy plane, we can form three carbon valence bonds with bond angles equal to 120° from the proper linear combination of the s, p_x, and p_y carbon orbitals. This leaves the six p_z orbitals, one on each carbon atom. The valence structure is thus similar to that of ethylene. In benzene, however, there is no unique way of pairing the spins of the p_z electrons to form π bonds. We shall not attempt to solve the benzene molecule completely, but shall assume the s, p_x, and p_y carbon electrons and the hydrogen electrons to be localized in σ bonds, and shall limit ourselves to the calculation of the binding energy arising from the interaction of the p_z electrons. This is a six-electron problem; if we denote the p_z orbitals on the various carbon atoms by a, b, c, d, e, f, the five independent bond eigenfunctions corresponding to the maximum number of bonds are

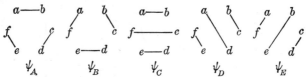

We note that, owing to the symmetry of benzene, the following relations hold between the matrix elements:

$$H_{AA} = H_{BB}; \quad H_{CC} = H_{DD} = H_{EE}$$
$$H_{AC} = H_{AD} = H_{AE} = H_{BC} = H_{BD} = H_{BE}$$
$$H_{CD} = H_{DE} = H_{CE}$$

We need calculate only the matrix elements H_{AA}, H_{AB}, H_{AC}, H_{CD}, H_{CC}, which is readily done by use of equation 13·25. For H_{AA} we have the diagram $\left(\dfrac{a}{b}\right)\left(\dfrac{c}{d}\right)\left(\dfrac{e}{f}\right)$, so that ·

$$H_{AA} = 2^3\{Q + \tfrac{3}{2}[(ab) + (cd) + (ef)] - \tfrac{1}{2}\Sigma \,(\text{all exchange integrals})\}$$
$$= 2^3\{Q + \tfrac{3}{2}[(ab) + (cd) + (ef)]$$
$$- \tfrac{1}{2}[(ab) + (bc) + (cd) + (de) + (ef) + (af)]$$
$$- \tfrac{1}{2}[(ac) + (bd) + (ce) + (df) + (ae) + (bf)]$$
$$- \tfrac{1}{2}[(ad) + (be) + (cf)]\}$$

Again, owing to the symmetry of benzene, there are only three different

[4] L. Pauling and G. W. Wheland, *J. Chem. Phys.*, **1**, 362 (1933).

exchange integrals: the type (ab), the type (ac), and the type (ad). We denote these types by α, β, γ, respectively, so that

$$H_{AA} = 2^3\{Q + \tfrac{3}{2}\alpha - 3\beta - \tfrac{3}{2}\gamma\}$$

Since exchange integrals will decrease rather rapidly as the distance between the atoms increases, we now make the approximation that β and γ can be neglected in comparison to α, and write

$$H_{AA} = 2^3\{Q + \tfrac{3}{2}\alpha\}$$

In the same way we find for the other necessary matrix elements the values

$$H_{CC} = 2^3\{Q\}$$
$$H_{AB} = 2\{Q + 6\alpha\}$$
$$H_{AC} = -2^2\{Q + 3\alpha\}$$
$$H_{CD} = 2\{Q + 6\alpha\}$$

The secular determinant, after the common factor 2^3 is removed, is therefore

$$\begin{vmatrix} (x+y) & \left(\dfrac{x}{4}+y\right) & -\left(\dfrac{x}{2}+y\right) & -\left(\dfrac{x}{2}+y\right) & -\left(\dfrac{x}{2}+y\right) \\[2mm] \left(\dfrac{x}{4}+y\right) & (x+y) & -\left(\dfrac{x}{2}+y\right) & -\left(\dfrac{x}{2}+y\right) & -\left(\dfrac{x}{2}+y\right) \\[2mm] -\left(\dfrac{x}{2}+y\right) & -\left(\dfrac{x}{2}+y\right) & x & \left(\dfrac{x}{4}+y\right) & \left(\dfrac{x}{4}+y\right) \\[2mm] -\left(\dfrac{x}{2}+y\right) & -\left(\dfrac{x}{2}+y\right) & \left(\dfrac{x}{4}+y\right) & x & \left(\dfrac{x}{4}+y\right) \\[2mm] -\left(\dfrac{x}{2}+y\right) & -\left(\dfrac{x}{2}+y\right) & \left(\dfrac{x}{4}+y\right) & \left(\dfrac{x}{4}+y\right) & x \end{vmatrix} = 0$$

where $x = Q - E$ and $y = \tfrac{3}{2}\alpha$. After a slight manipulation, this determinant reduces to

$$\begin{vmatrix} \tfrac{3}{2}x & 0 & 0 & 0 & 0 \\[2mm] 0 & (\tfrac{5}{8}x+y) & -\left(\dfrac{x}{2}+y\right) & 0 & 0 \\[2mm] 0 & -\left(\dfrac{x}{2}+y\right) & \left(\dfrac{x}{2}+\tfrac{2}{3}y\right) & 0 & 0 \\[2mm] 0 & 0 & 0 & (\tfrac{9}{8}x-\tfrac{3}{2}y) & 0 \\[2mm] 0 & 0 & 0 & 0 & (\tfrac{3}{2}x-2y) \end{vmatrix} = 0$$

The roots of the secular equation are therefore

$$x = 0, \quad \tfrac{4}{3}y, \quad \tfrac{4}{3}y, \quad \tfrac{2}{3}(1 + \sqrt{13})y, \quad \tfrac{2}{3}(1 - \sqrt{13})y$$

so that the energy levels are

$$
\begin{aligned}
E &= Q & E &= Q - (1 + \sqrt{13})\alpha \\
E &= Q - 2\alpha & E &= Q - (1 - \sqrt{13})\alpha \\
E &= Q - 2\alpha
\end{aligned}
$$

α is a negative quantity, so that the energy of the ground state is

$$E = Q - (1 - \sqrt{13})\alpha = Q + 2.61\alpha$$

In determining the coefficients in the expression

$$\psi = c_A\psi_A + c_B\psi_B + c_C\psi_C + c_D\psi_D + c_E\psi_E$$

for the wave function of the ground state of benzene, we note that, owing to the symmetry of the problem, $c_A = c_B$, $c_C = c_D = c_E$. (It is not necessary to make this assumption; the solution of the five simultaneous equations will give the same result.) From the first equation in the set which determines the coefficients, we thus obtain the ratio

$$\frac{c_C}{c_A} = \frac{5\sqrt{13} - 17}{24 - 6\sqrt{13}} = 0.434$$

so that the unnormalized wave function for the ground state of benzene is

$$\psi = \psi_A + \psi_B + 0.434(\psi_C + \psi_D + \psi_E)$$

Had we assumed that the ground state of the benzene molecule was represented by one of the Kekulé structures, say ψ_A, the calculated energy would have been $E' = Q + 1.50\alpha$. According to the above calculation, the actual benzene molecule is more stable than this hypothetical molecule by the amount 1.11α. The resonance energy of benzene is therefore 1.11α. Had we based our calculation on the two Kekulé structures alone, we would have obtained the secular determinant

$$
\begin{vmatrix}
(x + y) & \left(\dfrac{x}{4} + y\right) \\[2mm]
\left(\dfrac{x}{4} + y\right) & (x + y)
\end{vmatrix} = 0
$$

with the roots $x = 0$, $x = -\tfrac{8}{5}y$, corresponding to the energy values $E = Q$, $E = Q + 2.40\alpha$. The resonance energy here is $2.40\alpha - 1.50\alpha = 0.90\alpha$. We therefore see that the greater part of the resonance energy arises from resonance between the two Kekulé structures.

The factorization of the secular determinant is not accidental. In the general six-electron problem the determinant would not be further reducible; however, on account of the presence of symmetry in the benzene molecule we may reduce the determinant by the aid of group theory. Benzene belongs to the symmetry group D_{6h}; in this particular problem the operation i gives no new results, so that we may use the group D_6. In Table 13·1 we present the results of the application of the

TABLE 13·1

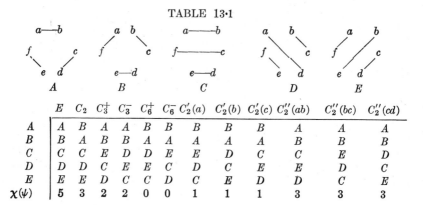

	E	C_2	C_3^+	C_3^-	C_6^+	C_6^-	$C_2'(a)$	$C_2'(b)$	$C_2'(c)$	$C_2''(ab)$	$C_2''(bc)$	$C_2''(cd)$
A	A	B	A	A	B	B	B	B	B	A	A	A
B	B	A	B	B	A	A	A	A	A	B	B	B
C	C	C	E	D	D	E	E	D	C	C	E	D
D	D	D	C	E	E	C	D	C	E	E	D	C
E	E	E	D	C	C	D	C	E	D	D	C	E
$\chi(\psi)$	5	3	2	2	0	0	1	1	1	3	3	3

TABLE 13·2

CHARACTER TABLE FOR D_6

		E	C_2	$2C_3$	$2C_6$	$3C_2'$	$3C_2''$
Γ_1	A_1	1	1	1	1	1	1
Γ_2	A_2	1	1	1	1	-1	-1
Γ_3	B_1	1	-1	1	-1	1	-1
Γ_4	B_2	1	-1	1	-1	-1	1
Γ_5	E_1	2	2	-1	-1	0	0
Γ_6	E_2	2	-2	-1	1	0	0
	ψ	5	3	2	0	1	3

operations of this group to the five bond eigenfunctions, which have been denoted by the letters A, B, C, D, and F rather than by ψ_A, etc. In this table, C_3^+ means a rotation by $+120°$, etc.; $c_2'(a)$ is a rotation about the symmetry axis through atom a; $c_2''(ab)$ is a rotation about the symmetry axis perpendicular to the bond a—b, etc. The character of the representation which has this set of bond eigenfunctions as its basis is given in Table 13·2, which contains the characters of the irreducible representations of the group. $\chi(\psi)$ was determined directly from the results given in Table 13·1. $\Gamma(\psi)$ can now be expressed in terms of the irreducible representations of the group as

$$\Gamma(\psi) = 2\Gamma_1 + \Gamma_4 + \Gamma_5$$

By means of equation 10·45 we now find the proper linear combinations of the original set which are the bases for these irreducible representations. The various sums $\sum_R \chi_i(R)RA$, etc., of interest are given in Table 13·3. From the three combinations denoted by (1), (2), (3), we

TABLE 13·3

$$\sum_R \chi_1(R)RA = 6(A + B) \qquad\qquad \sum_R \chi_4(R)RA = 6(A - B)$$

$$\sum_R \chi_1(R)RB = 6(A + B) \qquad\qquad \sum_R \chi_4(R)RB = -6(A - B)$$

$$\sum_R \chi_1(R)RC = 4(C + D + E) \qquad\qquad \sum_R \chi_4(R)RC = 0$$

$$\sum_R \chi_1(R)RD = 4(C + D + E) \qquad\qquad \sum_R \chi_4(R)RD = 0$$

$$\sum_R \chi_1(R)RE = 4(C + D + E) \qquad\qquad \sum_R \chi_4(R)RE = 0$$

$$\sum_R \chi_5(R)RA = 0$$

$$\sum_R \chi_5(R)RB = 0$$

$$\sum_R \chi_5(R)RC = 4C - 2E - 2D \qquad (1)$$

$$\sum_R \chi_5(R)RD = 4D - 2C - 2E \qquad (2)$$

$$\sum_R \chi_5(R)RE = 4E - 2D - 2C \qquad (3)$$

can form the independent linear combinations $(2) - (3) = 6(D - E)$ and $(1) - (2) = 6(C - D)$, so that the linear combinations which are bases for irreducible representations of the group are

$$\left.\begin{array}{l} \psi_1 = \psi_A + \psi_B \\ \psi_2 = \psi_C + \psi_D + \psi_E \end{array}\right\} \Gamma_1 \qquad\qquad \left.\begin{array}{l} \psi_4 = \psi_C - \psi_D \\ \psi_5 = \psi_D - \psi_E \end{array}\right\} \Gamma_5$$

$$\psi_3 = \psi_A - \psi_B \} \; \Gamma_4$$

Since matrix elements between eigenfunctions belonging to different irreducible representations of the group vanish identically, our problem is reduced by this method to the solution of two two-row and one one-row determinants. These are:

$$\begin{vmatrix} H_{11} - S_{11}E & H_{12} - S_{12}E \\ H_{12} - S_{12}E & H_{22} - S_{22}E \end{vmatrix} = \begin{vmatrix} (\tfrac{5}{2}x + 4y) & -(3x + 6y) \\ -(3x + 6y) & (\tfrac{9}{2}x + 6y) \end{vmatrix} = 0 \quad (1)$$

$$(H_{33} - S_{33}E) = \tfrac{5}{2}x = 0 \tag{2}$$

$$\begin{vmatrix} H_{44} - S_{44}E & H_{45} - S_{45}E \\ H_{45} - S_{45}E & H_{55} - S_{55}E \end{vmatrix} = \begin{vmatrix} (\tfrac{3}{2}x - 2y) & (-\tfrac{3}{4}x + y) \\ (-\tfrac{3}{4}x + y) & (\tfrac{3}{2}x - 2y) \end{vmatrix} = 0 \quad (3)$$

where the notation is the same as above. The matrix elements H_{12}, etc., are easily found from the previously derived matrix elements H_{AB}, etc. The roots of (1) are

$$x = \tfrac{2}{3}(1 + \sqrt{13})y, \quad x = \tfrac{2}{3}(1 - \sqrt{13})y$$

For the coefficients in the expression $\psi = c_1\psi_1 + c_2\psi_2$ we obtain, for the root $x = \tfrac{2}{3}(1 - \sqrt{13})y$, the ratio $\dfrac{c_2}{c_1} = 0.434$, which is identical with the previous result. From (2) we have $x = 0$; from (3) we have $x = \tfrac{4}{3}y$, $x = \tfrac{4}{3}y$, so that the results are in accord with our previous findings, as of course they must be. Determinant (3) can be reduced further, since the two roots are known to be equal from the fact that the functions ψ_4 and ψ_5 belong to a doubly degenerate representation.

The calculated resonance energy of benzene has been found to be 1.11α, where α is the exchange integral between the orbitals on adjacent carbon atoms. It would be of little value to attempt to calculate this integral directly; we may estimate its value in the following manner. From thermochemical data, Pauling finds that the strength of the C—C bond is 59 kcal., that of the C=C bond is 100 kcal. From our previous discussion of ethylene, we see that the difference between these values, 41 kcal., should be approximately equal to the strength of the π bond between the p_z orbitals. Since the energy of a bond is largely exchange energy, we would therefore estimate the value of the integral α to be about 40 kcal. (Since the carbon-carbon distance in benzene is greater than that in ethylene, this estimate should be a maximum.) We would therefore expect the resonance energy in benzene to be of the order of 40 kcal. From thermochemical data, it is found that 1039 kcal. is required to break all the bonds in benzene, while only 1000 kcal. would be required to break three C—C bonds, three C=C bonds, and six C—H bonds; that is, the experimental resonance energy is 39 kcal. This agreement is perhaps better than should reasonably be expected, although we shall see later that this method gives internally consistent results for benzene and the other condensed ring systems. First, we wish to treat the resonance energy in benzene by the molecular orbitals method.

13g. The Resonance Energy of Benzene — Molecular Orbitals Method.[5] In the molecular orbitals method, we do not attempt to find a set of functions with the significance of the bond eigenfunctions used above. Rather, we form molecular orbitals which are linear combinations of the atomic orbitals on the six carbon atoms. From the six

[5] E. Hückel, *Z. Physik*, **70**, 204 (1931); **72**, 310 (1931); **76**, 628 (1932).

atomic orbitals, we can form six independent molecular orbitals. Two electrons can then be placed in each of the three most stable molecular orbitals, giving the state of lowest energy. We denote the six orbitals on the six carbon atoms by ψ_a, ψ_b, ψ_c, ψ_d, ψ_e, and ψ_f. These are considered to be the solutions of a Hartree-type calculation, although we shall not specify them further. The molecular orbitals are then of the form

$$\psi = c_a\psi_a + c_b\psi_b + c_c\psi_c + c_d\psi_d + c_e\psi_e + c_f\psi_f$$

Carrying out the usual first-order perturbation calculation, we are led to the secular equation

$$\begin{vmatrix} W & \beta & 0 & 0 & 0 & \beta \\ \beta & W & \beta & 0 & 0 & 0 \\ 0 & \beta & W & \beta & 0 & 0 \\ 0 & 0 & \beta & W & \beta & 0 \\ 0 & 0 & 0 & \beta & W & \beta \\ \beta & 0 & 0 & 0 & \beta & W \end{vmatrix} = 0 \qquad 13\cdot31$$

where $W = Q - E$, $H_{ii} = Q$, $H_{ij} = \beta$ if $i = j \pm 1$, $H_{ij} = 0$ otherwise; that is, the ψ_a's are assumed to be normalized and mutually orthogonal, and the integrals of $\mathbf{H}$ between non-adjacent carbon atoms are placed equal to zero. The roots of this equation can be shown by an algebraic method to be

$$W = 2\beta \cos \frac{2\pi k}{6} \qquad k = 0, 1, 2, 3, 4, 5 \qquad 13\cdot32$$

or

$$W - 2\beta, \beta, -\beta, -2\beta, -\beta, \beta \qquad 13\cdot33$$

We shall later obtain these roots by a different method. The integral β is presumably negative, representing attraction, so that the three lowest levels are those for which $W = -2\beta, -\beta, -\beta$, or

$$E_1 = Q + 2\beta, \quad E_2 = Q + \beta, \quad E_3 = Q + \beta$$

If we place two electrons in each of these levels, we find the energy of the six p_z electrons in benzene to be $E = 6Q + 8\beta$. For one of the Kekulé structures, we have the corresponding secular equation

$$\begin{vmatrix} W & \beta & 0 & 0 & 0 & 0 \\ \beta & W & 0 & 0 & 0 & 0 \\ 0 & 0 & W & \beta & 0 & 0 \\ 0 & 0 & \beta & W & 0 & 0 \\ 0 & 0 & 0 & 0 & W & \beta \\ 0 & 0 & 0 & 0 & \beta & W \end{vmatrix} = 0$$

with the triply degenerate lowest root $W = -\beta$. For this structure the energy is therefore $E = 6Q + 6\beta$, so that the resonance energy of benzene, on the basis of this treatment, is 2.00β. It does not seem possible to estimate the value of β directly; we may test the theory as follows. The resonance energy of the series of compounds benzene, naphthalene, anthracene, and phenanthrene is calculated by this method. The resonance energies will be functions of the parameter β. If the values obtained by comparison with experimental data agree, we may assume that our description of the structure of benzene is substantially correct. The same test can be applied to the method of bond eigenfunctions. The results obtained are tabulated in Table 13·4.[6]

TABLE 13·4

	A	B	C	D	E
Benzene	39	1.11α	35	2.00β	20
Naphthalene	75	2.04α	37	3.68β	20
Anthracene	105	3.09α	34	5.32β	20
Phenanthrene	110	3.15α	35	5.45β	20

A = experimental resonance energy.
B, D = calculated resonance energies.
C, E = calculated values of α and β.

It is seen that both theories give consistent values for the parameters; the molecular orbital method seems slightly better here. In general, it appears that both methods give about the same results;[7] sometimes the method of bond eigenfunctions is slightly superior to the molecular orbitals method, as it was for H_2.

By means of group theory, we can find directly the molecular orbitals which form bases for irreducible representations of the symmetry group of the benzene molecule. The procedure is identical with that followed in finding the proper linear combinations of bond eigenfunctions. In place of the set of five bond eigenfunctions we use the set of six atomic orbitals as the basis for the reducible representation. The character of this representation is

$$\begin{array}{ccccccc}
 & E & C_2 & 2C_3 & 2C_6 & 3C_2' & 3C_2'' \\
\chi(\psi) = & 6 & 0 & 0 & 0 & 2 & 0
\end{array}$$

which, in terms of the irreducible representations gives

$$\Gamma(\psi) = \Gamma_1 + \Gamma_3 + \Gamma_5 + \Gamma_6$$

Proceeding as above, we find the linear combinations which are the bases

[6] E. Hückel, Reference 5. L. Pauling and G. Wheland, *J. Chem. Phys.*, **1**, 362 (1933); G. Wheland, *ibid.*, **3**, 356 (1935).

[7] G. W. Wheland, *J. Chem. Phys.*, **2**, 474 (1934).

of these irreducible representations to be

$$\psi_1 = \frac{1}{\sqrt{6}} \{\psi_a + \psi_b + \psi_c + \psi_d + \psi_e + \psi_f\} \quad (\Gamma_1)$$

$$\psi_2 = \frac{1}{\sqrt{6}} \{\psi_a - \psi_b + \psi_c - \psi_d + \psi_e - \psi_f\} \quad (\Gamma_3)$$

$$\psi_3 = \frac{1}{\sqrt{12}} \{2\psi_a - \psi_b - \psi_c + 2\psi_d - \psi_e - \psi_f\}$$

$$\psi_4 = \frac{1}{\sqrt{12}} \{\psi_a - 2\psi_b + \psi_c + \psi_d - 2\psi_e + \psi_f\} \qquad (\Gamma_5) \qquad 13 \cdot 34$$

$$\psi_5 = \frac{1}{\sqrt{12}} \{2\psi_a + \psi_b - \psi_c - 2\psi_d - \psi_e + \psi_f\}$$

$$\psi_6 = \frac{1}{\sqrt{12}} \{\psi_a + 2\psi_b + \psi_c - \psi_d - 2\psi_e - \psi_f\} \qquad (\Gamma_6)$$

From these linear combinations, we can immediately write down the pertinent matrix elements of **H**. These are

$$
\begin{array}{ll}
H_{11} = Q + 2\beta & H_{34} = \frac{1}{2}(Q - \beta) \\
H_{22} = Q - 2\beta & H_{55} = Q + \beta \\
H_{33} = Q - \beta & H_{66} = Q + \beta \\
H_{44} = Q - \beta & H_{56} = \frac{1}{2}(Q + \beta)
\end{array}
\qquad 13 \cdot 35
$$

The solution of the one- and two-row determinants now gives us the energy levels:

$$
\begin{array}{ll}
E = Q + 2\beta \quad (\Gamma_1) & E = Q - \beta \quad (\Gamma_5) \\
E = Q - 2\beta \quad (\Gamma_3) & E = Q + \beta \quad (\Gamma_6)
\end{array}
\qquad 13 \cdot 36
$$

The six electrons go into the lowest three molecular orbitals ψ_1, ψ_5, ψ_6. The molecular orbital with the lowest energy, ψ_1, represents a charge distribution in which the electrons are distributed symmetrically about the ring. The second level, which is degenerate, has associated with it an unsymmetrical charge distribution. ψ_5, for example, represents a charge distribution in which the electron density on atoms a and d is four times greater than the density on any of the other atoms. This does not mean that the resultant electron distribution is unsymmetrical. If we take the normalized linear combinations

$$\psi_5' = \frac{1}{\sqrt{3}} (\psi_5 + \psi_6) = \frac{1}{\sqrt{4}} (\psi_a + \psi_b - \psi_d - \psi_e)$$

$$\psi_6' = (\psi_5 - \psi_6) = \frac{1}{\sqrt{12}} (\psi_a - \psi_b + 2\psi_c - \psi_d + \psi_e - 2\psi_f) \qquad 13 \cdot 37$$

we see that we have a symmetrical distribution of charge if both ψ_5' and ψ_6' are occupied by electrons.

CHAPTER XIV

THE PRINCIPLES OF MOLECULAR SPECTROSCOPY

In the preceding chapters we have discussed the energy levels and electronic wave functions for molecules in which the nuclei were assumed to be at rest. For a diatomic molecule the electronic energy levels were given by the solution of the equation

$$\{H_0 - E_0(r)\}\psi = 0 \qquad 14 \cdot 1$$

where the electronic energy $E_0(r)$ was a function of the internuclear distance r, the stable position for the nuclei being that which made $E_0(r)$ a minimum. We wish in this chapter to drop the restriction that the nuclei remain in fixed positions, and to consider the possible wave functions and energy levels for actual molecules in which the nuclei may move relative to one another or relative to a set of axes fixed in space.

14a. Diatomic Molecules (Spin Neglected). For the discussion of diatomic molecules we will use the following coordinate system. Let x', y', and z' be the axes of a rectangular coordinate system fixed in space, and let x, y, and z be the axes of a similar movable system with the same origin. The orientation of the movable system relative to the stationary system will be defined by the Eulerian angles θ, χ, φ, as illustrated in Figure 14·1. The equations giving the relation between x, y, z and x', y', z' are:

$$x' = x(\cos\varphi\cos\chi - \cos\theta\sin\varphi\sin\chi)$$
$$\qquad - y(\sin\varphi\cos\chi + \cos\theta\cos\varphi\sin\chi) + z\sin\theta\sin\chi$$

$$y' = x(\cos\varphi\sin\chi + \cos\theta\sin\varphi\cos\chi) \qquad 14 \cdot 2$$
$$\qquad - y(\sin\varphi\sin\chi - \cos\theta\cos\varphi\cos\chi) - z\sin\theta\cos\chi$$

$$z' = x\sin\theta\sin\varphi + y\sin\theta\cos\varphi + z\cos\theta$$

The concept of a molecule possessing electronic, vibrational, and rotational energy levels is quite familiar. Similarly, several investigations along the lines indicated in section 11a have shown that the complete wave equation for a diatomic molecule can be separated into parts corresponding to electronic, vibrational, and rotational motion, the terms which must be neglected in order to make this separation being in general

258

very small.[1] The results of these investigations show that if the complete wave function ψ is written as

$$\psi = F(x, y, z, r)R(r)U(\theta, \chi) \qquad 14\cdot3$$

then the component wave functions satisfy the equations

$$\{\mathbf{H}_0(x, y, z, r) - E_0(r)\}F(x, y, z, r) = 0 \qquad 14\cdot4$$

$$\left\{\frac{h^2}{8\pi^2\mu r^2}\frac{\partial}{\partial r}\left(r^2\frac{\partial}{\partial r}\right) + E - E_0(r) - E'(r)\right\}R(r) = 0 \qquad 14\cdot5$$

$$\left\{\frac{1}{\sin\theta}\frac{\partial}{\partial\theta}\left(\sin\theta\frac{\partial}{\partial\theta}\right) + \frac{1}{\sin^2\theta}\left(\frac{\partial}{\partial\chi} - i\lambda\cos\theta\right)^2 + \frac{8^2\pi\mu r^2}{h^2}E'(r)\right\} \times$$
$$U(\theta, \chi) = 0 \qquad 14\cdot6$$

In these equations E is the total energy of the system, r is the internuclear distance, μ is the reduced mass, and $\lambda\dfrac{h}{2\pi}$ is the angular momentum about the z axis associated with the electronic wave function $F(x, y, z, r)$. $R(r)$ and $U(\theta, \chi)$ are the vibrational and rotational wave functions, respectively; we see that the rotational and electronic energies enter the vibrational wave equation as effective potential energies. We shall first investigate the possible states of the system and the symmetry properties of these states before we consider the energy levels in detail.

Equation 14·4 is just the equation for the electronic energy which was discussed in Chapter XI. The electronic wave functions $F(x, y, z, r)$ therefore have the symmetry properties of the various irreducible representations of the groups $D_{\infty h}$ or $C_{\infty v}$ according as the nuclei are identical or different. The vibrational wave function $R(r)$ depends only on the distance between the two nuclei and therefore belongs to the totally symmetrical representation. The complete wave function will thus have the symmetry properties of the product $F(x, y, z, r)U(\theta, \chi)$. In order to discuss the nature of the solutions of 14·6 it will be convenient to consider first the wave equation for a symmetrical top,

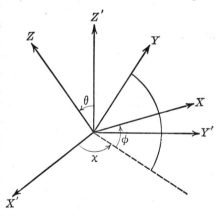

FIG. 14·1. Rotating coordinate system

that is, a rigid body with rotational symmetry about one axis. Using the coordinate system of Figure 14·1, with the symmetry axis of the rigid

[1] M. Born and E. Oppenheimer, *Ann. Physik*, **84**, 457 (1927). R. Kronig, *Z. Physik*, **46**, 814; **50**, 347 (1928). J. Van Vleck, *Phys. Rev.*, **33**, 467 (1929).

body along the z axis, the wave equation[2] for the system is

$$\frac{1}{\sin \theta} \frac{\partial}{\partial \theta} \left(\sin \theta \frac{\partial \psi}{\partial \theta} \right) + \frac{1}{\sin^2 \theta} \frac{\partial^2 \psi}{\partial \chi^2} + \left(\frac{\cos^2 \theta}{\sin^2 \theta} + \frac{A}{C} \right) \frac{\partial^2 \psi}{\partial \varphi^2}$$
$$- \frac{2 \cos \theta}{\sin^2 \theta} \frac{\partial^2 \psi}{\partial \chi \, \partial \varphi} + \frac{8\pi^2 A}{h^2} E\psi = 0 \quad 14 \cdot 7$$

where C is the moment of inertia about the symmetry axis and A is the moment of inertia about an axis perpendicular to the symmetry axis. If we now set

$$\psi = \Theta(\theta) e^{iK\varphi} e^{iM\chi}$$

we obtain the equation

$$\frac{1}{\sin \theta} \frac{d}{d\theta} \left(\sin \theta \frac{d\Theta}{d\theta} \right) - \left\{ \frac{M^2}{\sin^2 \theta} + \left(\frac{\cos^2 \theta}{\sin^2 \theta} + \frac{A}{C} \right) K^2 \right.$$
$$\left. - \frac{2 \cos \theta}{\sin^2 \theta} KM - \frac{8\pi^2 A}{h^2} E \right\} \Theta = 0 \quad 14 \cdot 8$$

For the special case in which $K = 0$, this equation reduces to

$$\frac{1}{\sin \theta} \frac{d}{d\theta} \left(\sin \theta \frac{d\Theta}{d\theta} \right) - \left\{ \frac{M^2}{\sin^2 \theta} - \frac{8\pi^2 A}{h^2} E \right\} \Theta = 0 \quad 14 \cdot 9$$

which is identical with the equation discussed in section 5c. The energy levels are therefore

$$E_{J, \, 0, \, M} = \frac{h^2}{8\pi^2 A} J(J + 1) \quad 14 \cdot 10$$

and the wave functions are

$$\Theta_{J, \, 0, \, M} = P_J^{|M|} (\cos \theta) \quad 14 \cdot 11$$

For $K \neq 0$, the solutions of 14·8 are quite complex, and we shall give here only those results which are significant for our discussion. The energy levels in this case are

$$E_{J, \, K, \, M} = \frac{h^2}{8\pi^2} \left\{ \frac{J(J + 1)}{A} + K^2 \left(\frac{1}{C} - \frac{1}{A} \right) \right\} \quad 14 \cdot 12$$

where $J \geq |K|$, and the solutions $\Theta_{J, \, K, \, M}$ have the property that

$$\Theta_{J, \, K, \, M}(\pi - \theta) = (-1)^{J-K-M} \Theta_{J, \, -K, \, M} (\theta) \quad 14 \cdot 13$$

Returning now to equation 14·6, we see that if we write

$$U(\theta, \chi) = \Theta'(\theta) e^{iM\chi}$$

[2] F. Reiche and H. Rademacher, Z. Physik, **39**, 444; **41**, 453 (1927).   R. Kronig and I. Rabi, Phys. Rev., **29**, 262 (1927).   D. Dennison, Rev. Modern Phys., **3**, 280 (1931):

we obtain the equation

$$\frac{1}{\sin\theta}\frac{d}{d\theta}\left(\sin\theta\frac{d\Theta'}{d\theta}\right) - \left\{\frac{M^2}{\sin^2\theta} + \frac{\cos^2\theta}{\sin^2\theta}\lambda^2 - \frac{2\cos\theta}{\sin^2\theta}M\lambda - \frac{8\pi^2\mu r^2}{h^2}E'\right\}\Theta'$$

$$= 0 \qquad 14\cdot14$$

This is identical with equation 14·8, provided that we replace K by λ, A by μr^2, and put $\dfrac{1}{C}$ equal to zero in equation 14·8, so that

$$\Theta'(\theta) = \Theta_{J,\,K,\,M}(\theta)$$

14b. Symmetry Properties of the Wave Functions.[3] If all the particles of the system are subjected to an inversion through the origin of coordinates, the transformation is equivalent to changing from a right-handed to a left-handed coordinate system. The Hamiltonian operator is invariant under such a transformation, so that the complete wave function must either remain unchanged or must change only in sign. This inversion at the origin is equivalent to a rotation of 180° about an axis perpendicular to the z axis, which we may take to be the y axis, followed by a reflection in the xz plane. If the transformed angles are denoted by the superscript t, then $\theta^t = \pi - \theta, \varphi^t = 2\pi - \varphi, \chi^t = \pi + \chi.$ If $\psi^t = \psi$, the wave function is said to be positive; if $\psi^t = -\psi$, the wave function is said to be negative (the superscript t denotes the transformed wave function). The rotation about the y axis cannot change the electronic wave function since it leaves the relative positions of electrons and nuclei unaltered; the reflection in the xz plane is equivalent to the operation σ_v. Σ^+ states are unchanged by the operation σ_v; for Σ^- states, the operation σ_v changes the sign of the wave function. For the Σ states we thus have the result that $(\Sigma^+)^t = \Sigma^+$, $(\Sigma^-)^t = -\Sigma^-$. For $\lambda \neq 0$, we have the doubly degenerate states Π, Δ, etc. For these states the electronic wave functions $F_{\pm\lambda}$ will be of the form $F_{\pm\lambda} = f_{\pm\lambda}e^{\pm i\lambda\varphi}$, where $f_{\pm\lambda}$ is a function independent of φ. Since $e^{\pm i\lambda(2\pi-\varphi)} = e^{\mp i\lambda\varphi}$ we conclude that $F^t_{+\lambda} = F_{-\lambda}$, $F^t_{-\lambda} = F_{+\lambda}$. From 14·13, we see that $\Theta^t_{J,\,\lambda,\,M} = (-1)^{J-\lambda-M}\Theta_{J,\,-\lambda,\,M}$. Since $e^{iM(\pi+\chi)} = (-1)^M e^{iM\chi}$, we have, for the transformed value of $U(\theta,\chi)$, the result $U^t_{J,\,\lambda,\,M} = (-1)^{J-\lambda}U_{J,\,-\lambda,\,M}$. The complete wave function will transform in the same way as the product of F and U. For $\lambda = 0$, we therefore have the following relations:

1. If the electronic state is Σ^+, then $\psi^t = (-1)^J\psi$, so that a rotational state is positive for even J and negative for odd J.

2. If the electronic state is Σ^-, then $\psi^t = (-1)^{J+1}\psi$, so that a rotational state is negative for even J and positive for odd J.

[3] E. Wigner and E. Witmer, *Z. Physik*, **51**, 859 (1928).

When $\lambda \neq 0$, we can form two linear combinations of the functions such that $\psi_1^t = \psi_1$, $\psi_2^t = -\psi_2$; these combinations are

$$\psi_1 = U_{J,\,\lambda,\,Mf+\lambda} e^{i\lambda\varphi} + (-1)^{J-\lambda} U_{J,\,-\lambda,\,Mf-\lambda} e^{-i\lambda\varphi}$$
$$\psi_2 = U_{J,\,\lambda,\,Mf+\lambda} e^{i\lambda\varphi} - (-1)^{J-\lambda} U_{J,\,-\lambda,\,Mf-\lambda} e^{-i\lambda\varphi}$$

14·15

For $\lambda \neq 0$, we thus have both a positive and a negative state for each value of J.

The positive or negative character of the wave functions is independent of the nature of the nuclei. For identical nuclei we have in addition the g or u property; the electronic wave function either remains the same or changes sign upon inversion at the origin. Since an interchange of the nuclei does not affect the Hamiltonian, the complete wave function must either remain unchanged or must change sign when the nuclei are interchanged. Wave functions of the type that remain unchanged are called symmetric in the nuclei; those that change sign are called anti-symmetric. Interchange of the nuclei is equivalent to an inversion of all particles through the origin, followed by an inversion of the electrons only. Under the first operation the wave functions transform according to their positive or negative character; under the second they transform according to the g or u property of the electronic wave function. We therefore have the following relations:

1. For molecules in g states, positive terms are symmetrical in the nuclei, negative terms are antisymmetrical in the nuclei.

2. For molecules in u states, positive terms are antisymmetrical in the nuclei, negative terms are symmetrical in the nuclei. In Tables 14·1 and 14·2 we give the symmetry properties of the various allowed states for diatomic molecules,[3] where the positive and negative property is designated by the symbols $+$ and $-$, the symmetric-antisymmetric property by s and a.

14c. Selection Rules for Optical Transitions in Diatomic Molecules. According to the results derived in Chapter VIII, a transition between two states ψ_1 and ψ_2, resulting in the emission or absorption of radiation, is possible only if the integral $\int \psi_1^* x' \psi_2 \, d\tau$ is different from zero (x' represents x', y', or z'). Using the symmetry properties of the wave functions we can immediately derive several selection rules for transitions in diatomic molecules. Since x' changes sign upon inversion, the integral $\int \psi_1^* x' \psi_2 \, d\tau$ will be different from zero only if $\psi_1^* \psi_2$ changes sign upon inversion. We thus have the selection rule:

1. Positive terms combine only with negative terms.

Since interchange of the nuclei does not affect the electric moment integral for molecules with like nuclei, and since x' is unaffected by this interchange, the integral $\int \psi_1^* x' \psi_2 \, d\tau$ will be different from zero only if the product $\psi_1^* \psi_2$ does not change sign under this operation. This gives the additional selection rules for homonuclear molecules:

2. Symmetric terms combine only with symmetric terms.

3. Antisymmetric terms combine only with antisymmetric terms.

We need in addition the selection rules for changes in J, λ, and M.

TABLE 14·1

SYMMETRY OF ROTATIONAL STATES FOR HOMONUCLEAR DIATOMIC MOLECULES

	$J = 0$	1	2	3	4
Σ_g^+	+	−	+	−	+
	s	a	s	a	s
Σ_u^+	+	−	+	−	+
	a	s	a	s	a
Σ_g^-	−	+	−	+	−
	a	s	a	s	a
Σ_u^-	−	+	−	+	−
	s	a	s	a	s
Π_g		+ −	+ −	+ −	+ −
		s a	s a	s a	s a
Π_u		+ −	+ −	+ −	+ −
		a s	a s	a s	a s
Δ_g			+ −	+ −	+ −
			s a	s a	s a
Δ_u			+ −	+ −	+ −
			a s	a s	a s

TABLE 14·2

SYMMETRY OF ROTATIONAL STATES FOR HETERONUCLEAR DIATOMIC MOLECULES

	$J = 0$	1	2	3	4
Σ^+	+	−	+	−	+
Σ^-	−	+	−	+	−
Π		+−	+−	+ −	+−
Δ			+−	+ −	+−

(Since the energy does not depend on M in the absence of a magnetic field the selection rule for ΔM is of little significance.) Using the transformations 14·1 for x, y, and z, we will obtain a series of integrals, each of which may be written as the product of two integrals, the first involving the functions $F_{\pm\lambda}$, $R(r)$, and the coordinates x, y, z; the second involving the functions $U_{J, \lambda, M}(\theta, \chi)e^{\pm i\lambda\varphi}$ and the angular coordinates

θ, χ, φ. Since $R(r)$ is totally symmetric, the first of these integrals will be non-zero if the product of the electronic wave functions transforms under the operations of the group in the same manner as one of the coordinates.

We consider first the transitions between two Σ states. For molecules with unlike nuclei, belonging to the group $C_{\infty v}$, the possible direct products of the irreducible representations are

$$\Sigma^+\Sigma^+ = \Sigma^+; \quad \Sigma^-\Sigma^- = \Sigma^+; \quad \Sigma^+\Sigma^- = \Sigma^-$$

The only coordinate which transforms like any of these products is z, which belongs to the representation Σ^+. The possible transitions are therefore

$$\Sigma^+ \leftrightarrow \Sigma^+ \qquad \Sigma^- \leftrightarrow \Sigma^-$$

For these transitions the electric moment is along the z axis; the band spectra corresponding to such transitions are known as parallel bands. For molecules with like nuclei, belonging to the group $D_{\infty h}$, the possible direct products are

$$\Sigma_g^+\Sigma_g^+ = \Sigma_g^+ \qquad \Sigma_g^+\Sigma_g^- = \Sigma_g^- \qquad \Sigma_g^-\Sigma_u^- = \Sigma_u^+$$
$$\Sigma_g^-\Sigma_g^- = \Sigma_g^+ \qquad \Sigma_u^+\Sigma_u^- = \Sigma_g^- \qquad \Sigma_g^+\Sigma_u^- = \Sigma_u^-$$
$$\Sigma_u^+\Sigma_u^+ = \Sigma_g^+ \qquad \Sigma_g^+\Sigma_u^+ = \Sigma_u^+ \qquad \Sigma_g^-\Sigma_u^+ = \Sigma_u^-$$
$$\Sigma_u^-\Sigma_u^- = \Sigma_g^+$$

Again the only coordinate which transforms like a Σ state is z, which belongs to the representation Σ_u^+. The possible transitions are therefore

$$\Sigma_g^+ \leftrightarrow \Sigma_u^+ \qquad \Sigma_g^- \leftrightarrow \Sigma_u^-$$

The integrals over the angular functions associated with the integrals over z are the same as those involved in determining the selection rules for the hydrogen atom, where it was shown that the integrals vanish unless

$$\Delta J = \pm 1, \quad \Delta M = 0, \pm 1$$

From Tables 14·1 and 14·2 it can readily be seen that the selection rule $\Delta J = \pm 1$, together with the selection rules $+ \leftrightarrow -$, $s \leftrightarrow s$, $a \leftrightarrow a$, give the same results for the allowed transitions between Σ states as the above considerations based on group theory.

When one or more of the states has $\lambda \neq 0$, then the integrals over the angles give the following allowed transitions:

x, y integrals $\neq 0$ $\qquad \Delta J = 0, \pm 1; \quad \Delta\lambda = \pm 1, \quad \Delta M = 0, \pm 1$
(perpendicular bands)

z integral $\neq 0$ $\qquad \Delta J = 0, \pm 1; \quad \Delta\lambda = 0, \quad \Delta M = 0, \pm 1$
(parallel bands)

These restrictions on J and λ, plus the selection rules $+ \leftrightarrow -$, $s \leftrightarrow s$, $a \leftrightarrow a$, are sufficient to determine the selection rules for such transitions. All allowed transitions for diatomic molecules[3] are listed in Table 14·3.

We note that, for homonuclear molecules, all allowed transitions require a change in the electronic state; that is, pure rotation or rotation-vibration spectra are forbidden.

TABLE 14·3

ALLOWED TRANSITIONS IN DIATOMIC MOLECULES

$C_{\infty v}$	$D_{\infty h}$	
$\Sigma^+ \leftrightarrow \Sigma^+$	$\Sigma_g^+ \leftrightarrow \Sigma_u^+$	
$\Sigma^- \leftrightarrow \Sigma^-$	$\Sigma_g^- \leftrightarrow \Sigma_u^-$	
$\Pi \leftrightarrow \Sigma^+$	$\Pi_g \leftrightarrow \Sigma_u^+$	$\Pi_u \leftrightarrow \Sigma_g^+$
$\Pi \leftrightarrow \Sigma^-$	$\Pi_g \leftrightarrow \Sigma_u^-$	$\Pi_u \leftrightarrow \Sigma_g^-$
$\Pi \leftrightarrow \Pi$	$\Pi_g \leftrightarrow \Pi_u$	
$\Delta \leftrightarrow \Pi$	$\Pi_g \leftrightarrow \Delta_u$	$\Pi_u \leftrightarrow \Delta_g$
$\Delta \leftrightarrow \Delta$	$\Delta_g \leftrightarrow \Delta_u$	

So far in this chapter we have not included the effect of electron spin. As mentioned in Chapter XI, molecules may possess singlet, doublet, triplet states, etc., according as the total spin angular momentum quantum number S is equal to $0, \frac{1}{2}, 1, \cdots$. For molecules, just as for atoms, the selection rule is $\Delta S = 0$; this rule must be considered in applying the results given in Table 14·3. Tables 14·1 and 14·2 are correct only for singlet states, which are by far the most important. For a detailed account of the way the states are modified when $S \neq 0$, the reader is referred to a textbook on molecular spectroscopy.[4]

14d. The Influence of Nuclear Spin. Since it is known that an atomic nucleus has spin angular momentum as well as mass and charge, we will have obtained an exact wave function for a molecule only when the wave functions discussed above are multiplied by a nuclear spin wave function φ. Designating the total wave function by ψ_t, we have $\psi_t = \psi\varphi$, where ψ is the wave function previously discussed. We have previously stated that a wave function must be antisymmetric in electrons; the wave function must change sign when two electrons are interchanged. It has been found that the total wave function ψ_t must be chosen so that it changes sign whenever any two like particles are interchanged; the behavior of ψ_t for the interchange of two protons or two neutrons is the same as for the interchange of two electrons. If, in a homonuclear molecule, the two nuclei are interchanged, the total wave function will change sign if the number of particles (and hence the

---

[4] G. Herzberg, *Molecular Spectra and Molecular Structure*, 1, 231, Prentice-Hall, 1939.

atomic weight) is odd, and will remain unchanged if the number of particles is even. We thus have the following rules for homonuclear molecules:

1. If the atomic weight is even, the combinations $\psi(s)\varphi(s)$ and $\psi(a)\varphi(a)$ are possible wave functions.

2. If the atomic weight is odd, the combinations $\psi(s)\varphi(a)$ and $\psi(a)\varphi(s)$ are possible wave functions.

The symbols s and a denote functions which are symmetric and anti-symmetric in the nuclei, respectively. Since it is known that protons and neutrons, as well as electrons, have spin $\frac{1}{2}$, the resultant nuclear spin is integral for even atomic weight and half-integral for odd atomic weight. For atoms with nuclear spin equal to zero, we can construct only one nuclear spin wave function $\psi_0(1)\psi_0(2)$, where $\psi_0(1)$ means that nucleus (1) has zero spin, etc. This wave function is symmetrical in the nuclei. Since zero spin can occur only for even atomic weight, we have the following corollary to the above rules:

3. For atoms with nuclear spin zero, only those states with wave functions $\psi(s)$ are possible.

When we construct nuclear spin wave functions as indicated below, we find that, if the nuclear spin is I, then

$$\frac{\text{Number of functions } \varphi(s)}{\text{Number of functions } \varphi(a)} = \frac{I+1}{I} = \frac{\text{Number of `` ortho '' states}}{\text{Number of `` para '' states}}$$

For molecules in Σ states this will result in alternating statistical weights for the alternating J values, giving alternating intensities of ratio $\frac{I+1}{I}$ to the lines in the rotational bands resulting from transitions between these states.

We discuss first ortho- and parahydrogen. Since the proton has spin $\frac{1}{2}$, the possible nuclear spin wave functions are $\varphi_{+\frac{1}{2}}$ and $\varphi_{-\frac{1}{2}}$, corresponding to the spin wave functions α and β for an electron. We can therefore construct three symmetrical wave functions

$$\varphi_{+\frac{1}{2}}(1)\varphi_{+\frac{1}{2}}(2)$$
$$\varphi_{+\frac{1}{2}}(1)\varphi_{-\frac{1}{2}}(2) + \varphi_{-\frac{1}{2}}(1)\varphi_{+\frac{1}{2}}(2)$$
$$\varphi_{-\frac{1}{2}}(1)\varphi_{-\frac{1}{2}}(2)$$

and one antisymmetric wave function

$$\varphi_{+\frac{1}{2}}(1)\varphi_{-\frac{1}{2}}(2) - \varphi_{-\frac{1}{2}}(1)\varphi_{+\frac{1}{2}}(2)$$

giving a ratio of symmetric to antisymmetric functions equal to $3 = \frac{\frac{1}{2}+1}{\frac{1}{2}}$. The ground state of hydrogen is $^1\Sigma_g^+$. As hydrogen belongs to case 2, we see that the function ψ must be combined with antisymmetric nuclear spin wave functions for even values of J, and with symmetric nuclear spin wave functions for odd values of J. Since the forces acting on nuclear spins are very small, there is little possibility of a transition from a symmetrical nuclear state to an antisymmetrical one, hence hydrogen exists in two quite distinct species: orthohydrogen, with only odd J values allowed, and with nuclear spin statistical weight 3; and parahydrogen, with only even J values allowed, and with nuclear spin statistical weight equal to 1. In hydrogen gas under ordinary conditions the two species are thus present in the ratio 3 : 1. A possible electronic transition for hydrogen is from the ground state $^1\Sigma_g^+$ to an excited state $^1\Sigma_u^+$. The symmetry properties of these states are given in Table 14·4, with the possible transitions indicated by full and broken lines. We see from this table that transitions involving odd values of J in the ground state will be three times as intense as those involving even values of J.

Deuterium has a nuclear spin of unity, so that the possible nuclear spin wave functions are $\varphi_{+1}, \varphi_0, \varphi_{-1}$. With these functions we can form six symmetrical combinations

$$\varphi_{+1}(1)\varphi_{+1}(2) \qquad \varphi_{+1}(1)\varphi_0(2) + \varphi_{+1}(2)\varphi_0(1)$$
$$\varphi_0(1)\varphi_0(2) \qquad \varphi_{+1}(1)\varphi_{-1}(2) + \varphi_{+1}(2)\varphi_{-1}(1)$$
$$\varphi_{-1}(1)\varphi_{-1}(2) \qquad \varphi_0(1)\varphi_{-1}(2) + \varphi_0(2)\varphi_{-1}(1)$$

and three antisymmetrical combinations

$$\varphi_{+1}(1)\varphi_0(2) - \varphi_{+1}(2)\varphi_0(1)$$
$$\varphi_{+1}(1)\varphi_{-1}(2) - \varphi_{+1}(2)\varphi_{-1}(1)$$
$$\varphi_0(1)\varphi_{-1}(2) - \varphi_0(2)\varphi_{-1}(1)$$

TABLE 14·4

$$^1\Sigma_u^+ \rightarrow {}^1\Sigma_g^+ \quad \text{in} \quad H_2$$

Excited State $(^1\Sigma_u^+)$

$J =$	0	1	2	3	4	5
ψ	$\overset{+}{a}$	$\overset{-}{s}$	$\overset{+}{a}$	$\overset{-}{s}$	$\overset{+}{a}$	$\overset{-}{s}$
ϕ	s	a	s	a	s	a
Nuclear Spin Statistical Weight	3	1	3	1	3	1

Ground State $(^1\Sigma_g^+)$

$J =$	0	1	2	3	4	5
ψ	$\overset{+}{s}$	$\overset{-}{a}$	$\overset{+}{s}$	$\overset{-}{a}$	$\overset{+}{s}$	$\overset{-}{a}$
ϕ	a	s	a	s	a	s
Nuclear Spin Statistical Weight	1	3	1	3	1	3

Deuterium has the ground state $^1\Sigma_g^+$ and belongs to case 1, so that ortho-deuterium has even J values, paradeuterium has odd J values; the ortho-para ratio is 2 : 1. For a transition such as that illustrated for hydrogen in Table 14·4, transitions involving even values of J in the ground state are twice as intense as those involving odd J values.

The ground state of O_2^{16} is $^3\Sigma_g^-$. O^{16} has zero nuclear spin and therefore belongs to case 3. In the ground state, only even J values are allowed.

14e. The Vibrational and Rotational Energy Levels of Diatomic Molecules. The radial wave function $R(r)$ satisfies the equation

$$\left\{\frac{h^2}{8\pi^2\mu r^2}\frac{d}{dr}\left(r^2\frac{d}{dr}\right) + E - E_0(r) - E'(r)\right\}R(r) = 0 \qquad 14\cdot16$$

where E is the total energy, $E_0(r)$ is the electronic energy, and $E'(r)$, the solution of 14·5, is, according to 14·12 and 14·14, given by the expression

$$E'(r) = \frac{h^2}{8\pi^2\mu r^2}\{J(J+1) - \lambda^2\} \qquad 14\cdot17$$

The electronic energy $E_0(r)$, according to the results of Chapter XI, has the following qualitative behavior. For $r = \infty$, it has the value zero, corresponding to dissociation of the molecule. For some value $r = r_e$, the equilibrium distance, it has the minimum value $E_0(r_e)$. For $r \to 0$, $E_0(r) \to \infty$. Regardless of the exact form of $E_0(r)$, it can be expanded in a Taylor's series about the position $r = r_e$ as

$$E_0(r) = E_0(r_e) + (r - r_e)\left(\frac{\partial E_0(r)}{\partial r}\right)_{r=r_e}$$

$$+ \frac{(r - r_e)^2}{2!}\left(\frac{\partial^2 E_0(r)}{\partial r^2}\right)_{r=r_e} + \cdots \qquad 14\cdot18$$

Since $r = r_e$ is a position of equilibrium,

$$\left(\frac{\partial E_0(r)}{\partial r}\right)_{r=r_e} = 0$$

Equation 14·16 may then be written as

$$\left\{\frac{h^2}{8\pi^2\mu r^2}\frac{d}{dr}\left(r^2\frac{d}{dr}\right) + \epsilon - V(r) - \frac{h^2 A}{8\pi^2\mu r^2}\right\}R(r) = 0$$

or

$$\frac{1}{r^2}\frac{d}{dr}\left(r^2\frac{dR}{dr}\right) + \left\{-\frac{A}{r^2} + \frac{8\pi^2\mu}{h^2}(\epsilon - V(r))\right\}R = 0 \qquad 14\cdot19$$

where

$$\epsilon = E - E_0(r_e)$$
$$V(r) = E_0(r) - E_0(r_e)$$
$$A = J(J + 1) - \lambda^2$$

The function $V(r)$ acts in this equation as a potential energy; the energy origin has been shifted so that $V(r) = 0$ for $r = r_e$. The energy ϵ now represents the energy of vibration and rotation of the molecule. If we now let $R(r) = \dfrac{1}{r} S(r)$, the function $S(r)$ satisfies the equation

$$\frac{d^2 S}{dr^2} + \left\{ -\frac{A}{r^2} + \frac{8\pi^2\mu}{h^2}(\epsilon - V(r)) \right\} S = 0 \qquad 14\cdot20$$

To a first approximation, we may write

$$V(r) = \tfrac{1}{2}(r - r_e)^2 \left(\frac{\partial^2 E_0(r)}{\partial r^2} \right)_{r=r_e} = \tfrac{1}{2}k(r - r_e)^2$$

that is, the potential energy curve, to this approximation, is that of a harmonic oscillator. Using this value for the potential, the equation for S becomes

$$\frac{d^2 S}{dr^2} + \left\{ -\frac{A}{r^2} + \frac{8\pi^2\mu}{h^2}(\epsilon - \tfrac{1}{2}k(r - r_e)^2) \right\} S = 0 \qquad 14\cdot21$$

Let us treat the term $\dfrac{h^2}{8\pi^2\mu}\dfrac{A}{r^2}$ as a perturbation. Then, if we let $x = r - r_e$, the equation for S is

$$\frac{d^2 S}{dx^2} + \frac{8\pi^2\mu}{h^2}\{\epsilon - \tfrac{1}{2}kx^2\} S = 0 \qquad 14\cdot22$$

The boundary conditions for this problem require that $R = 0$ for $r = 0$, $r = +\infty$, which is equivalent to the conditions that $S = 0$ for $r = 0$, $r = +\infty$; or $S = 0$ for $x = -r_e$, $x = \infty$. At $x = -r_e$, the potential energy is $V(r) = \tfrac{1}{2}kr_e^2$. For those states for which $\epsilon \ll \tfrac{1}{2}kr_e^2$, the wave function will be quite small in the region $x = -r_e$ from these energy considerations alone. It will therefore be a valid approximation for small values of ϵ to replace the boundary condition $S = 0$ for $x = -r_e$ by the condition $S = 0$ for $r = -\infty$. Equation 14·22 thus has the same form and the same boundary conditions as the equation for the harmonic oscillator problem; the solutions are

$$S_n(x) = \left\{ \left(\frac{\alpha}{\pi}\right)^{\frac{1}{2}} \frac{1}{2^n n!} \right\}^{\frac{1}{2}} e^{-\frac{\alpha}{2}x^2} H_n(\sqrt{\alpha}\, x) \qquad 14\cdot23$$

where

$$\alpha = \frac{4\pi^2 \mu \nu_e}{h}, \quad \nu_e = \frac{1}{2\pi}\sqrt{\frac{k}{\mu}}$$

and the energy levels are $\epsilon_n = (n + \tfrac{1}{2})h\nu_e$.

The first-order correction to the energy will be

$$\epsilon'_n = \frac{h^2 A}{8\pi^2 \mu} \int_{-\infty}^{\infty} S_n^*(x) \left\{\frac{1}{(x + r_e)^2}\right\} S_n(x)\, dx \qquad 14\cdot24$$

The term $\dfrac{1}{(x + r_e)^2}$ may be expanded in terms of $\dfrac{x}{r_e}$ as

$$\frac{1}{(x + r_e)^2} = \frac{1}{r_e^2 \left(1 + \dfrac{x}{r_e}\right)^2} = \frac{1}{r_e^2}\left(1 - 2\frac{x}{r_e} + 3\frac{x^2}{r_e^2} + \cdots\right) \qquad 14\cdot25$$

Only the first three terms in this expression being kept, the perturbation energy is

$$\epsilon'_n = \frac{h^2 A}{8\pi^2 \mu r_e^2} \int_{-\infty}^{\infty} S_n^*(x) \left\{1 - 2\frac{x}{r_e} + 3\frac{x^2}{r_e^2}\right\} S_n(x)\, dx \qquad 14\cdot26$$

The first integral is equal to unity. Using the recursion formulas for the harmonic oscillator (equation 4·99), we find that the second integral is zero, the third is equal to $\dfrac{3}{r\alpha_e^2}(n + \tfrac{1}{2})$, so that the first-order perturbation energy is

$$\epsilon'_n = B'_n A, \quad B'_n = B'_e - \alpha'_e(n + \tfrac{1}{2}), \quad B'_e = \frac{h^2}{8\pi^2 \mu r_e^2},$$

$$\alpha'_e = -\frac{3}{\alpha r_e^2} = -\frac{6B'_e}{h\nu_e} \qquad 14\cdot27$$

Of equal importance to the term in α'_e is the contribution to the second-order perturbation energy arising from the term $-\dfrac{2x}{r_e^2} B'_e A$. This gives a contribution

$$\epsilon''_n = \frac{|H'_{n,\,n-1}|^2}{\epsilon_n - \epsilon_{n-1}} + \frac{|H'_{n,\,n+1}|^2}{\epsilon_n - \epsilon_{n+1}} = \frac{|H'_{n,\,n-1}|^2 - |H'_{n,\,n+1}|^2}{h\nu_e} \qquad 14\cdot28$$

Using the results

$$(n|x|n + 1) = \sqrt{\frac{n + 1}{2\alpha}}; \quad (n|x|n - 1) = \sqrt{\frac{n}{2\alpha}}$$

of equations 8·48 and 8·49, this becomes

$$\epsilon_n'' = -\frac{2B_e'^2 A^2}{4\pi^2 \nu_e^2 r_e^2} = -D'A^2; \quad D' = \frac{4B_e'^3}{h^2 \nu_e^2} \qquad 14\cdot29$$

The coefficient of A in the energy expression is $\dfrac{h^2}{8\pi^2\mu}\overline{\left(\dfrac{1}{r^2}\right)}$. For the

harmonic oscillator, $\overline{\left(\dfrac{1}{r^2}\right)}$ is greater than $\dfrac{1}{r_e^2}$, so that α_e' is negative. For

actual potential energy curves, the curve is flatter in the direction of

greater r than in the other direction; as a result, $\overline{\left(\dfrac{1}{r^2}\right)}$ is less than $\dfrac{1}{r_e^2}$

and α_e' is positive for actual molecules. The part of the vibration-rotation energy which is a function of A, or, as λ is usually zero, of $J(J+1)$, is usually written, in analogy with the above results, as

$$\frac{E_{\text{rot}}}{hc} = B_n J(J+1) - D_n[J(J+1)]^2 \qquad 14\cdot30$$

where

$$B_n = B_e - \alpha_e(n + \tfrac{1}{2}) \qquad B_e = \frac{h}{8\pi^2 c\mu r_e^2} = \frac{h}{8\pi^2 cI_e}$$

$$D_n = D_e + \beta_e(n + \tfrac{1}{2})$$

When the molecule is in the vibrationless state $n = 0$, its effective moment of inertia can be found from the equation

$$B_0 = B_e - \tfrac{1}{2}\alpha_e$$

In general, α_e will be positive; therefore $B_0 < B_e$ and thus $r_0 > r_e$; that is, the average value of r, due to the zero-point vibrational energy, is greater than the distance r_e corresponding to the minimum in the potential energy curve. For example, in HCl the values of the constants are $B_e = 10.5909$, $\alpha_e = 0.3019$, giving $r_e = 1.2747$ Å, $r_0 = 1.2839$ Å.[5] The quantities α_e, D_e, β_e will usually be quite small in comparison to B_e; their exact analytical form depends upon the exact form of the potential energy curve.

The above results are based upon a harmonic oscillator potential energy curve, which of course does not give a particularly good representation of the potential energy curves for actual molecules. We could include additional terms of 14·18 in the expression for the potential energy; a more satisfactory procedure is to assume some appropriate

[5] Reference 4, p. 488.

analytical expression for the potential energy curve.   Morse[6] has written the potential energy as

$$V(r) = D_e\{1 - e^{-a(r-r_e)}\}^2 \qquad 14\cdot31$$

which has the correct qualitative form; the constant D_e (not to be confused with the constant used above) is equal to the depth of the potential energy curve at $r = r_e$. Using this value for $V(r)$, the equation for $S(r)$ becomes

$$\frac{d^2S}{dr^2} + \left\{-\frac{A}{r^2} + \frac{8\pi^2\mu}{h^2}\left(\epsilon - D_e\{1 - e^{-a(r-r_e)}\}^2\right)\right\}S = 0 \qquad 14\cdot32$$

or, if $\dfrac{h^2A}{8\pi^2\mu r^2}$ is to be treated as a perturbation

$$\frac{d^2S}{dr^2} + \frac{8\pi^2\mu}{h^2}\left(\epsilon - D_e\{1 - e^{-a(r-r_e)}\}^2\right)S = 0 \qquad 14\cdot33$$

If we now make the substitution $x = e^{-a(r-r_e)}$, equation 14·33 reduces to

$$\frac{d^2S}{dx^2} + \frac{1}{x}\frac{dS}{dx} + \frac{8\pi^2\mu}{a^2h^2}\left(\frac{\epsilon - D_e}{x^2} + \frac{2D_e}{x} - D_e\right)S = 0 \qquad 14\cdot34$$

Making the further substitution

$$S(x) = e^{\frac{-y}{2}}y^{\frac{b}{2}}L(y) \qquad 14\cdot35$$

where

$$y = \frac{4\pi}{ah}\sqrt{2\mu D_e}\,x$$

$$b = \frac{4\pi}{ah}\sqrt{2\mu(D_e - \epsilon)}$$

we obtain as the equation satisfied by $L(y)$ the result

$$\frac{d^2L}{dy^2} + \left(\frac{b+1}{y} - 1\right)\frac{dL}{dy} + \frac{\left(\dfrac{2\pi}{ah}\sqrt{2\mu D_e} - \dfrac{b+1}{2}\right)}{y}L = 0 \qquad 14\cdot36$$

The associated Laguerre polynomials L_{m+l}^{2l+1} satisfy the equation

$$\frac{d^2L_{m+l}^{2l+1}}{dy^2} + \left(\frac{2(l+1)}{y} - 1\right)\frac{dL_{m+l}^{2l+1}}{dy} + \frac{m-l-1}{y}L_{m+l}^{2l+1} = 0 \qquad 14\cdot37$$

Equations 14·36 and 14·37 will be identical if we set $b + 1 = 2(l + 1)$ and the quantity $\left\{\dfrac{2\pi}{ah}\sqrt{2\mu D_e} - \dfrac{b+1}{2}\right\}$ equal to some integer n.   This

[6] P. Morse, *Phys. Rev.*, **34**, 57 (1929).

last step gives an equation which will determine the energy.   We have

$$\left\{ \frac{2\pi}{ah} \sqrt{2\mu D_e} - n + \tfrac{1}{2} \right\} = \frac{b}{2} = \frac{2\pi}{ah} \sqrt{2\mu(D_e - \epsilon)} \qquad 14\cdot38$$

from which

$$\frac{\epsilon_{\text{vib.}}}{hc} = \omega_e(n + \tfrac{1}{2}) - x_e\omega_e(n + \tfrac{1}{2})^2$$

where

$$\omega_e = \frac{a}{\pi c} \sqrt{\frac{D_e}{2\mu}} \;;\quad x_e = \frac{hc}{4D_e}\omega_e \qquad 14\cdot39$$

According to the results of 14·39 and 14·30, we should expect the vibrational-rotational energy levels to be expressible by a function of the form

$$\frac{\epsilon_{v,\,r}}{hc} = \omega_e(n + \tfrac{1}{2}) - x_e\omega_e(n + \tfrac{1}{2})^2$$
$$+ B_nJ(J + 1) - D_n[J(J + 1)]^2 \quad 14\cdot40$$

For example, the energy levels of HCl (in the ground electronic state) can be very accurately reproduced by the equation[7]

$$\frac{\epsilon}{hc} = 2988.95(n + \tfrac{1}{2}) - 51.65(n + \tfrac{1}{2})^2$$
$$+[10.5909 - 0.3019(n + \tfrac{1}{2})]J(J + 1) - 0.0004[J(J + 1)]^2$$

The values of the constants D_e and a in the Morse curve can be determined from the experimental values of ω_e and $x_e\omega_e$; however, the values of the dissociation energy $D_0 = D_e - \tfrac{1}{2}h\nu_e$ as determined in this manner will usually be in disagreement with the values determined by more direct methods.

14f.   The Vibrational Spectra of Polyatomic Molecules.   If we consider a molecule as a system of point masses (the atomic nuclei), then, according to section 2d, the kinetic and potential energies of the molecule can be written in the form

$$T = \tfrac{1}{2} \sum_{k=1}^{3N} \left(\frac{dQ_k}{dt}\right)^2, \quad V = \tfrac{1}{2} \sum_{k=1}^{3N} \lambda_k Q_k^2 \qquad 14\cdot41$$

where N is the number of atoms in the molecule.   Most of the simpler molecules will have certain elements of symmetry; they will belong to one of the symmetry groups of Appendix VII.   Since subjecting a molecule to a symmetry operation cannot change the potential or kinetic energy of a molecule, the normal coordinates must transform in the

[7] Reference 4, p. 121.

following manner. If Q_k is non-degenerate, that is, if no other λ is equal to λ_k, then the symmetry operation R acting on Q_k must change it either into itself or its negative, so that $RQ_k = \pm 1 Q_k$. If Q_k is degenerate, for example if $\lambda_l = \lambda_k$, then the symmetry operation may change Q_k into a linear combination of Q_k and Q_l. In general we would have

$$RQ_{ik} = \sum_{l=1}^{f_i} a_{lk}Q_{il}$$

where the summation is over the f_i values of λ for which $\lambda_{il} = \lambda_{ik}$. If S is another symmetry operation, then

$$SRQ_{ik} = \sum_{l=1}^{f_i} a_{lk}SQ_{il} = \sum_{l=1}^{f_i} \sum_{m=1}^{f_i} a_{lk}b_{ml}Q_{im}$$

and if T is the resultant of the successive application of the two operations R and S, $T = SR$, we have

$$TQ_{ik} = \sum_{m=1}^{f_i} c_{mk}Q_{im}$$

The coefficients therefore obey the relation

$$c_{mk} = \sum_{l=1}^{f_i} b_{ml}a_{lk}$$

We thus see that the normal coordinates form bases for irreducible representations of the symmetry group of the molecule in exactly the same way as do the eigenfunctions of $\mathbf{H}$. If we form a reducible representation of the group based upon any arbitrary set of $3N$ coordinates, and then find the irreducible representations of which it is composed, there will be as many distinct values of λ (except for accidental degeneracy) as there are irreducible representations in the reducible representation. The degeneracy of a given λ, that is, the number of normal coordinates which have this value of λ as their coefficient in the potential energy expression, will be equal to the dimension of the corresponding irreducible representation. Further, these normal coordinates will transform in the manner indicated by the matrices of the corresponding irreducible representations.

If we express the kinetic and potential energies in terms of an arbitrary coordinate system as

$$T = \tfrac{1}{2}\sum_{ij}a_{ij}\frac{dQ_i'}{dt}\frac{dQ_j'}{dt} \qquad V = \tfrac{1}{2}\sum_{ij}b_{ij}Q_i'Q_j'$$

then, according to 2·55, the values of λ in equation 14·41 are given by the roots of the determinantal equation

$$\begin{vmatrix} a_{11}\lambda - b_{11} & a_{12}\lambda - b_{12} & \cdots & a_{1,3N}\lambda - b_{1,3N} \\ \cdot & & & \\ \cdot & & & \\ \cdot & & & \\ a_{3N,1}\lambda - b_{3N,1} & \cdots & \cdots & a_{3N,3N}\lambda - b_{3N,3N} \end{vmatrix} = 0$$

If, however, we use a set of coordinates (which are not necessarily normal coordinates) that transform under the symmetry operations of the group to which the molecule belongs in the manner indicated by the matrices of the irreducible representations, then all cross products of the type $Q_i'Q_j'$, where Q_i' and Q_j' belong to different irreducible representations, will vanish; this choice of coordinates will thus greatly simplify the solution of equation 2·55. We shall return to this point briefly a little later; first we wish to derive the selection rules for optical transitions between the various possible vibrational states of polyatomic molecules.

Using equations 14·41 for the kinetic and potential energies of a molecule, the vibrational wave function is found to be

$$\sum_{i=1}^{3N} \frac{\partial^2 \psi}{\partial Q_i^2} + \frac{8\pi^2}{h^2} (E - \tfrac{1}{2} \sum_{i=1}^{3N} \lambda_i Q_i^2)\psi = 0 \qquad 14\cdot42$$

Making the substitutions

$$\psi = \prod_{i=1}^{3N} \psi_i(Q_i); \quad E = \sum_{i=1}^{3N} E_i$$

we obtain the set of $3N$ equations

$$\frac{d^2\psi_i}{dQ_i^2} + \frac{8\pi^2}{h^2} (E_i - \tfrac{1}{2}\lambda_i Q_i^2)\psi_i = 0 \qquad 14\cdot43$$

each of which is the equation for a one-dimensional harmonic oscillator. Some of the λ_i's may, of course, be equal; the vibrational wave function, aside from a normalizing factor, may be written as

$$\psi_{n_1, n_2, n_3 \cdots n_{3N}} = e^{-\frac{1}{2}\sum_i \alpha_i Q_i^2}\prod_i H_{n_i}(\sqrt{\alpha_i}\, Q_i)$$

where H_{n_i} is the Hermitian polynomial of degree n_i in $(\sqrt{\alpha_i}\, Q_i)$.

According to the discussion in Chapter VIII, a transition from the state $\psi_{n_1, n_2 \cdots n_{3N}}$ to the state $\psi_{n_1', n_2' \cdots n_{3N}'}$ is possible only if

$$\int \psi^*_{n_1, n_2, \cdots n_{3N}} x \psi_{n_1', n_2', \cdots n_{3N}'}\, d\tau \neq 0$$

(in this general discussion, $x = x$, y, or z). But, according to section 10d, this integral will be zero unless the direct product $\Gamma(\psi_{n_1}...n_{3N})\ \Gamma(\psi_{n_1'}...n_{3N}')$ is identical with $\Gamma(x)$. This is a general statement of the selection rule for vibrational transitions in polyatomic molecules; all the selection rules for the appearance of fundamentals, overtones, or combinations can be derived from it. Here, however, we shall be interested only in the selection rules for the fundamental frequencies, that is, for transitions of the type

$$\psi_{0_1,\ 0_2,\ \cdots 0_{3N}} \rightarrow \psi_{0_1,\ 0_2,\ \cdots 1_i,\ \cdots 0_{3N}}$$

The exponent in $\psi_{n_1} \ldots n_{3N}$ has the same form as the potential energy, and hence is invariant with respect to every symmetry operation. The function ψ will thus belong to the same representation as the product of the Hermite polynomials. We therefore have the results

$$\Gamma(\psi_{0_1,\ 0_2,\ \cdots 0_{3N}}) = \Gamma_1 \quad \text{(the totally symmetrical representation)}$$
$$\Gamma(\psi_{0_1,\ 0_2,\ \cdots 1_i,\ \cdots 0_{3N}}) = \Gamma(Q_i)$$

so that the selection rule for the appearance of fundamentals in the infrared is: *The frequency ν_i is infra-red active if $\Gamma(Q_i) = \Gamma(x)$, $\Gamma(y)$, or $\Gamma(z)$, where $\Gamma(Q_i)$ is the irreducible representation to which the corresponding normal coordinate Q_i belongs.*

According to section 8g, a frequency ν_{ab} is Raman active if one of the matrix elements of the type $(a|xy|b)$ is different from zero. Proceeding as above, we therefore have the selection rule for the appearance of fundamentals in the Raman effect: *The frequency ν_i is Raman active if $\Gamma(Q_i) = \Gamma(x^2)$, $\Gamma(y^2)$, $\Gamma(z^2)$, $\Gamma(xy)$, $\Gamma(xz)$, or $\Gamma(yz)$, where $\Gamma(Q_i)$ is the irreducible representation to which the corresponding normal coordinate Q_i belongs.*

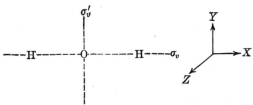

Fig. 14·2. Symmetry properties of the H_2O molecule.

We shall now proceed to the discussion of several examples.

EXAMPLE 1: H_2O. H_2O belongs to the symmetry group C_{2v}; the symmetry elements are the identity E, C_2 (rotation about the z axis by 180°, the xz plane is taken to be the H—O—H plane, the z axis goes through the O atom), σ_v (reflection in the xz plane), σ_v' (reflection in the yz plane); in Figure 14·2, the O atom is above the plane of the paper, the hydrogen atoms are in the plane of the paper. The character table for this group is reproduced in Table 14·5; the character of the representation generated by the possible motions of the molecule is included in this table. The character of this representation is found as follows.

TABLE 14·5

$C_{2v}(H_2O)$

				E	C_2	σ_v	σ_v'
x^2, y^2, z^2		z	A_1	1	1	1	1
xy	R_z		A_2	1	1	−1	−1
xz	R_y	x	B_1	1	−1	1	−1
yz	R_x	y	B_2	1	−1	−1	1
			Γ_m	9	−1	3	1

Each atom can move in any direction. We therefore imagine vectors x_i, y_i, z_i attached to each atom i, these vectors representing the displacements of this atom from its equilibrium position, and see how these vectors transform under the operations of the group. The operation E leaves each vector unchanged; therefore $\chi(E) = 9$. The operation C_2 interchanges the hydrogen atoms, so that the contribution to $\chi(C_2)$ from these atoms is zero. For the oxygen atom, $z \to z$, $y \to -y$, $x \to -x$ under this operation, so that $\chi(C_2) = -1$. σ_v' interchanges the hydrogen atoms, for the oxygen atom $z \to z$, $y \to y$, $x \to -x$, so that $\chi(\sigma_v') = 1$. For σ_v $z \to z$, $y \to -y$, $x \to x$ for each atom, so that $\chi(\sigma_v) = 3$. Breaking the reducible representation down into its irreducible components, we have

$$\Gamma_m = 3A_1 + A_2 + 3B_1 + 2B_2$$

Certain of the normal coordinates which belong to these irreducible representations represent translational and rotational motion. Since the vectors representing translational motion transform in the same way as the coordinates x, y, and z, and the vectors representing rotational motion transform in the manner given in the table, we have for the representation which has these motions as its basis

$$\Gamma_{t, r} = A_1 + A_2 + 2B_1 + 2B_2$$

Subtracting $\Gamma_{t, r}$ from Γ_m, we obtain

$$\Gamma_{\text{vib}} = 2A_1 + B_1$$

as the representation which has the vibrational motions as its basis. There are therefore three distinct vibrational frequencies for H_2O. Two of the normal coordinates associated with these frequencies belong to the totally symmetric representation A_1; one belongs to B_1, and this normal coordinate changes sign when the hydrogen atoms are interchanged. In order to find the actual normal coordinates we would have to solve the secular equation with some assumed form of the potential energy. We can, however, find by inspection certain coordinates which have the necessary symmetry properties. If, for simplicity, we assume that the mass of the oxygen atom is infinite, a possible set of such coordinates would be

$$Q_1' = a'\varphi + b'(r_1 + r_2)$$
$$Q_2' = c'\varphi + d'(r_1 + r_2)$$
$$Q_3' = e'(r_1 - r_2)$$

where φ is the H—O—H angle and r_1 and r_2 are the O—H distances. (Coordinates of this type must always be chosen in such a way that they do not introduce any translational or rotational motion.) With these coordinates, the secular determinant, which would in general be a three-row determinant for H_2O, is broken down into the product of a two-row and a one-row determinant, since the products $Q_1'Q_3'$ and $Q_2'Q_3'$ may not appear in either the kinetic or potential energies. Solution of the determinant, with an assumed potential energy, would then lead to the proper linear combinations of Q_1' and Q_2' which are the actual normal coordinates. When this is carried out, it is found that one of the normal coordinates belonging to A_1 represents (approximately) a stretching of the O—H bond; the other represents a bending of the O—H bond. The normal coordinates are thus approximately

$$Q_1 = a\varphi \qquad Q_2 = b(r_1 + r_2) \qquad Q_3 = c(r_1 - r_2)$$

The modes of vibration associated with these normal coordinates are illustrated in Figure 14·3. Actual calculations involving the solution

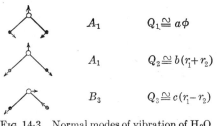

$$A_1 \qquad Q_1 \cong a\phi$$

$$A_1 \qquad Q_2 \cong b(r_1 + r_2)$$

$$B_3 \qquad Q_3 \cong c(r_1 - r_2)$$

Fig. 14·3. Normal modes of vibration of H_2O.

of the secular determinant are rather difficult and are carried out only if one wishes to find the force constants in some assumed potential energy expression. By inspection, diagrams of the type in Figure 14·3 can usually be drawn. These will not in general represent normal coordinates but merely coordinates with the proper symmetry.

From the selection rules for the infra-red transitions and Raman scattering, and the transformation properties of the coordinates and products of the coordinates, we see that in H_2O all fundamentals are allowed in both spectra.

In studies of the Raman effect, the degree of polarization of the Raman lines is usually measured; this information often aids in assigning the observed frequencies to particular modes of vibration of the molecule. If the incident light is traveling in the $-y$ direction and the scattered light is observed in the x direction, then, if the incident light was polarized in the z direction, the degree of depolarization is defined by the equation $\rho = \dfrac{I(y)}{I(z)}$, where $I(y)$ and $I(z)$ are the observed intensities of light polarized in the y and z directions, respectively. The theory of the polarization of Raman lines is given by Kohlrausch.[8] If the incident light is unpolarized, then the degree of depolarization ρ_n of the scattered light is given by $\rho_n = \dfrac{2\rho}{1 + \rho}$. The degrees of depolarization are given by the following rules:

1. If the matrix elements of x^2, y^2, z^2 are all zero, then

$$\rho = \tfrac{3}{4}, \quad \rho_n = \tfrac{6}{7}$$

2. If not all the matrix elements of x^2, y^2, z^2 are zero, then

$$0 \leq \rho \leq \tfrac{3}{4}, \quad 0 \leq \rho_n \leq \tfrac{6}{7}$$

For H_2O, we see that the frequencies belonging to A_1 have $\rho_n \leq \tfrac{6}{7}$; the frequency belonging to B_1 has $\rho_n = \tfrac{6}{7}$.

EXAMPLE 2: Acetylene. In Table 14·6 we have reproduced the character table for the group $D_{\infty h}$, to which acetylene belongs, and have

TABLE 14·6

$D_{\infty h}(C_2H_2)$

					E	$2C_\varphi$	C_2	iE	$2iC_\varphi$	iC_2
$x^2 + y^2, z^2$				A_{1g}	1	1	1	1	1	1
				A_{1u}	1	1	1	-1	-1	-1
				A_{2g}	1	1	-1	1	1	-1
		z		A_{2u}	1	1	-1	-1	-1	1
(xz, yz)	(R_x, R_y)			E_{1g}	2	$2\cos\varphi$	0	2	$2\cos\varphi$	0
		(x, y)		E_{1u}	2	$2\cos\varphi$	0	-2	$-2\cos\varphi$	0
$(x^2 - y^2, xy)$				E_{2g}	2	$2\cos 2\varphi$	0	2	$2\cos 2\varphi$	0
				E_{2u}	2	$2\cos 2\varphi$	0	-2	$-2\cos 2\varphi$	0
				· · · ·						
				Γ_m	12	$4 + 8\cos\varphi$	0	0	0	4

[8] K. Kohlrausch, *Der Smekal-Raman Effekt*, p. 27, Springer, Berlin, 1938.

included in this table the character of the representation which has all possible motions of the molecule as its basis. For the operation C_φ, all z coordinates are unchanged, giving a contribution 4 to $\chi(C_\varphi)$. The matrix of this transformation for the x and y coordinates has the character $2 \cos \varphi$, so that these coordinates give a contribution $8 \cos \varphi$ to $\chi(C_\varphi)$. The characters for the other operations are found in a straightforward manner. Breaking the reducible representation down into its irreducible components, we have

$$\Gamma_m = 2A_{1g} + 2A_{2u} + 2E_{1g} + 2E_{1u}$$

Subtracting the representations for the external motions leaves

$$\Gamma_{\text{vib}} = 2A_{1g} + A_{2u} + E_{1g} + E_{1u}$$

so that there are two non-degenerate modes of vibration belonging to the totally symmetric representation A_{1g}, one non-degenerate mode which is antisymmetric to inversion, and two doubly degenerate modes. In

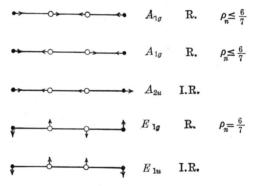

FIG. 14·4.   Normal modes of vibration of C_2H_2.

Figure 14·4 we present a schematic representation of possible coordinates having the required symmetry, as well as the selection rules for the corresponding frequencies.

EXAMPLE 3.   Benzene.   The results of a similar calculation for benzene are given in Table 14·7.   In determining the characters of the reducible representation for the operations C_2' and C_2'' it is convenient to let the axis of rotation be one of the coordinate axes x or y.   Benzene is seen to have twenty frequencies, of which ten are doubly degenerate. Of these frequencies, those associated with the representations E_{1u} and A_{2u} are infra-red active, so that the infra-red spectrum should contain three degenerate frequencies and one non-degenerate frequency. The frequencies associated with E_{1g}, E_{2g}, and A_{1g} are Raman active, so that the Raman spectrum should contain five degenerate and two non-degenerate frequencies. The other frequencies do not appear (as fundamentals) in either case.

TABLE 14·7

D_{6h} (C_6H_6)

			E	C_2	$2C_3$	$2C_6$	$3C_2'$	$3C_2''$	iE	iC_2	$2iC_3$	$2iC_6$	$3iC_2'$	$3iC_2''$
$x^2 + y^2, z^2$		A_{1g}	1	1	1	1	1	1	1	1	1	1	1	1
		A_{1u}	1	1	1	1	1	1	−1	−1	−1	−1	−1	−1
	R_z	A_{2g}	1	1	1	1	−1	−1	1	1	1	1	−1	−1
	z	A_{2u}	1	1	1	1	−1	−1	−1	−1	−1	−1	1	1
		B_{1g}	1	−1	1	−1	1	−1	1	−1	1	−1	1	−1
		B_{1u}	1	−1	1	−1	1	−1	−1	1	−1	1	−1	1
		B_{2g}	1	−1	1	−1	−1	1	1	−1	1	−1	−1	1
		B_{2u}	1	−1	1	−1	−1	1	−1	1	−1	1	1	−1
$(x^2 - y^2, xy)$		E_{2g}	2	2	−1	−1	0	0	2	2	−1	−1	0	0
		E_{2u}	2	2	−1	−1	0	0	−2	−2	1	1	0	0
(xz, yz)	(R_x, R_y)	E_{1g}	2	−2	−1	1	0	0	2	−2	−1	1	0	0
	(x, y)	E_{1u}	2	−2	−1	1	0	0	−2	2	1	−1	0	0
		Γ_m	36	0	0	0	−4	0	0	12	0	0	0	4

$$\Gamma_m = 2A_{1g} + 2A_{2g} + 2A_{2u} + 2B_{1u} + 2B_{2g} + 2B_{2u}$$
$$+ 4E_{2g} + 2E_{2u} + 2E_{1g} + 4E_{1u}$$
$$\Gamma_{vib} = 2A_{1g} + A_{2g} + A_{2u} + 2B_{1u} + 2B_{2g} + 2B_{2u}$$
$$+ 4E_{2g} + 2E_{2u} + E_{1g} + 3E_{1u}$$

If the molecule has a center of symmetry, then x, y, and z belong to u representations while their products belong to g representations. In such molecules, therefore, a frequency cannot appear as a fundamental in both the infra-red and the Raman spectrum.

CHAPTER XV

ELEMENTS OF QUANTUM STATISTICAL MECHANICS

Our study has thus far been limited to the discussion of the structure and properties of individual atoms and molecules. The determination of the properties of a system of atoms or molecules (" particles ") from a knowledge of the properties of the individual particles requires the use of the methods of statistical mechanics. We do not intend to treat this subject in any great detail; but it is of interest at this point to see how the connection between the properties of individual particles and the properties of systems of these particles is made.

Let us consider a system of n particles, all of the same kind. We represent the coordinates of the n particles by the symbols $q_1, q_2, q_3 \cdots q_n$, where q_i represents all the coordinates necessary to specify the state of the ith particle. We assume that the Hamiltonian operator $\mathbf{H}$ of the system can be expressed in the form

$$\mathbf{H} = \mathbf{H}(q_1) + \mathbf{H}(q_2) + \cdots + \mathbf{H}(q_n) \qquad 15 \cdot 1$$

If we represent the wave function for the system by ψ_n, then the energy levels E_n of the system are given by the solutions of the equation

$$\mathbf{H}\psi_n = E_n\psi_n \qquad 15 \cdot 2$$

Because of the assumed form of $\mathbf{H}$, this equation may be separated into the n equations

$$\mathbf{H}(q_1)\varphi_a(q_1) = \epsilon_a\varphi_a(q_1)$$
$$\mathbf{H}(q_2)\varphi_b(q_2) = \epsilon_b\varphi_b(q_2)$$
$$\cdot$$
$$\cdot \qquad\qquad 15 \cdot 3$$
$$\cdot$$
$$\mathbf{H}(q_n)\varphi_m(q_n) = \epsilon_m\varphi_m(q_n)$$

The function ψ will be expressible in terms of the φ's; we must, however, take a combination of the φ's which will give ψ the proper symmetry. These symmetry requirements lead to three possible cases, which we now discuss.

15a. The Maxwell-Boltzmann Statistics. We consider first the classical case, where our system contains n distinguishable particles. In this case there are no symmetry restrictions on ψ; any combination of the φ's such as

$$\psi_n = \varphi_a(q_1)\varphi_b(q_2) \cdots \varphi_m(q_n) \qquad 15\cdot4$$

will be an acceptable wave function for the system. Since the particles are distinguishable, any interchange of particles among the occupied states $\varphi_a, \varphi_b \cdots \varphi_m$ will lead to a new state for the system.

Let us now divide the φ's into the groups $1, 2 \cdots k \cdots$ so that the eigenvalues for all the φ's in the kth group lie between the limits ϵ_k and $\epsilon_k + d\epsilon_k$, and let us suppose that there are $g_k \varphi$'s in the kth such group. We now ask the question: How many ψ's correspond to a distribution of the n particles such that there are n_1 in the energy region corresponding to group 1, n_2 in the energy region corresponding to group 2, etc.? (If a particle is in the kth energy region, it may be considered to have the energy ϵ_k.) In order to answer this question, let us calculate the number of different ways in which we can distribute the n particles among the various regions so that there are n_1 particles in region 1, etc. For simplicity, let us consider that we have only two such regions. We readily obtain the following table:

n	n_1	n_2	N
1	0	1	1
	1	0	1
2	0	2	1
	1	1	2
	2	0	1
3	0	3	1
	1	2	3
	2	1	3
	3	0	1
4	0	4	1
	1	3	4
	2	2	6
	3	1	4
	4	0	1

(N = number of ways of obtaining the given distribution.) In order to see how this table was formed, consider the case where $n = 4$, $n_1 = 2$, $n_2 = 2$. If the particles are numbered from 1 to 4, the six possible distributions are:

REGION 1	REGION 2
1 2	3 4
1 3	2 4
1 4	2 3
2 3	1 4
2 4	1 3
3 4	1 2

Since the order in which we select the particles which we are going to put into a given region is immaterial, the designations 1 2 and 2 1 are equivalent and are counted only once. It is to be noted that, in each of the cases listed, $N_{n, n_1, n_2} = \dfrac{n!}{n_1!n_2!}$ (0! defined to be 1). If the above table is extended to include more particles or more regions, we find that the same expression holds. The number of ways of distributing the particles among the different regions will therefore be

$$N_{n, n_1, n_2 \cdots n_k \cdots} = \frac{n!}{n_1!n_2! \cdots n_k! \cdots} \qquad 15 \cdot 5$$

We now wish to calculate the number of ψ's corresponding to the above distribution. We denote this number by $G_{n, n_1, n_2 \cdots n_k \cdots}$. Since there are g_k φ's in the kth region, each of the n_k particles can be in any one of the g_k different φ's, since there is no restriction regarding the number of particles that can occupy a given φ. The n_k particles can thus be put into the g_k states in $g_k^{n_k}$ different ways, each corresponding to a new ψ. This gives us the relation

$$G_{n, n_1, n_2 \cdots n_k \cdots} = g_1^{n_1} g_2^{n_2} \cdots g_k^{n_k} \cdots N_{n, n_1, n_2 \cdots n_k \cdots} \qquad 15 \cdot 6$$

or

$$G_{n, n_1, n_2 \cdots n_k \cdots} = \prod_k \frac{n! g_k^{n_k}}{n_k!} \qquad 15 \cdot 7$$

This is the answer to our first question. We now ask the additional question: If our system contains a fixed number of particles n, and a fixed total energy E, what distribution is the most probable? In order to answer this question, statistical mechanics makes the following assumption: Each state of the system which is consistent with the requirements that $n = $ constant and $E = $ constant has the same *a priori* probability; that is, any two such states have equal chances of occurring. It therefore follows that the probability of the occurrence of a given distribution is directly proportional to the number of states representing such a distribution; if we call this probability $P_{n, n_1, n_2 \cdots n_k \cdots}$, then

$$P_{n, n_1, n_2 \cdots n_k \cdots} = CG_{n, n_1, n_2 \cdots n_k \cdots} \qquad 15 \cdot 8$$

where C is a constant. If we consider P to be a function of the n_k's, then the most probable distribution will be that for which P is a maximum, or that for which $\delta P = 0$ (where the variation is with respect to the n_k's), subject, of course, to the restriction that $\delta n = 0$ and $\delta E = 0$. Since log x is a maximum when x is a maximum, it will be equally valid and more convenient to determine the distribution for which $\delta \log P = 0$. According to 15·7 and 15·8,

$$\log P_{n,\,n_1\ldots} = \log C + \log n! + \sum_k n_k \log g_k - \sum_k \log n_k! \qquad 15·9$$

For x sufficiently large, Stirling's formula states that $\log x! = x \log x - x$. Using this relation, the condition $\delta \log P = 0$ gives

$$\sum_k \log \frac{n_k}{g_k}\, \delta n_k = 0 \qquad 15·10$$

Equation 15·10 must be solved subject to the restrictions

$$\delta n = \sum_k \delta n_k = 0 \qquad 15·11$$

$$\delta E = \sum_k \epsilon_k \delta n_k = 0 \qquad 15·12$$

The desired solution can be obtained by the method of Lagrangian multipliers; we multiply 15·11 by the parameter α, 15·12 by the parameter β, and add the three equations, obtaining

$$\sum_k \left(\log \frac{n_k}{g_k} + \alpha + \beta \epsilon_k \right) \delta n_k = 0 \qquad 15·13$$

The variations δn_k may now be considered to be arbitrary; therefore equation 15·13 can hold only if

$$\log \frac{n_k}{g_k} + \alpha + \beta \epsilon_k = 0 \qquad 15·14$$

for all values of k. The most probable distribution will thus be that for which each n_k satisfies the equation

$$n_k = g_k e^{-\alpha} e^{-\beta \epsilon_k} \qquad 15·15$$

Equation 15·15 is correct only when each n_k is large enough so that the Stirling formula does not introduce any error. When this approximation cannot be used, the most probable distribution would have to be computed directly from 15·9. The systems ordinarily considered in chemistry contain a sufficiently large number of particles to make the Stirling formula adequate.

15b. The Fermi–Dirac Statistics. If our system contains n indistinguishable particles, and we require that the total wave function ψ be antisymmetric with regard to interchange of two particles, we are led to the Fermi–Dirac statistics. As we saw in Chapter IX, an antisymmetric wave function can be represented by a determinant, or by the expression

$$\psi = \sum (-1)^{\nu} P^{\nu} \{\varphi_a(q_1)\varphi_b(q_2) \cdots \varphi_m(q_n)\} \qquad 15\cdot16$$

This method of writing ψ is equivalent to stating that no state φ may contain more than one particle. Since the particles are indistinguishable, it does not matter which particle we choose to occupy a given state; the number of ψ's corresponding to a given distribution will be equal to the number of ways in which we can select occupied φ's for this distribution. As before, we divide the φ's into groups of essentially equal energy. If there are g_k φ's in the kth group, then the number of ways N_{g_k, n_k} in which we can select n_k occupied φ's is illustrated by the following table:

g_k	n_k	N_{g_k, n_k}
2	0	1
	1	2
	2	1
3	0	1
	1	$2 + 1 = 3$
	2	$1 + 2 = 3$
	3	1
4	0	1
	1	$3 + 1 = 4$
	2	$3 + 3 = 6$
	3	$1 + 3 = 4$
	4	1
5	0	1
	1	$4 + 1 = 5$
	2	$6 + 4 = 10$
	3	$4 + 6 = 10$
	4	$1 + 4 = 5$
	5	1

Since a given φ can be occupied by not more than 1 particle, $n_k \leq g_k$. The method of forming the above table can be illustrated by the case $g_k = 5$, $n_k = 2$. If the first φ is empty we have 2 particles to be divided among 4 states, which, according to an earlier section of the table, can be done in 6 ways. If the first φ is occupied, we have 1 particle to be distributed among 4 states, which can be done in 4 ways, so that, for $g_k = 5$, $n_k = 2$; $N_{g_k, n_k} = 6 + 4 = 10$. In a similar manner, each line of the table can be obtained from some preceding lines, so that the entire table can be built up from the trivial case $g_k = 2$. It is to be noted that in every case

$$N_{g_k, n_k} = \frac{g_k!}{n_k!(g_k - n_k)!} \qquad 15\cdot17$$

a result which is perfectly general. The number of ways in which a given distribution can occur will evidently be equal to the product of the number of different ways that we can select occupied states in the various regions, that is,

$$G_{n, n_1, n_2 \cdots n_k \cdots} = \prod_k N_{g_k, n_k} = \prod_k \frac{g_k!}{n_k!(g_k - n_k)!} \qquad 15 \cdot 18$$

The remainder of the analysis for the Fermi-Dirac statistics is identical with that for the Maxwell-Boltzmann case. We find that the most probable distribution is that for which

$$n_k = \frac{g_k}{e^\alpha e^{\beta \epsilon_k} + 1} \qquad 15 \cdot 19$$

15c. The Bose-Einstein Statistics. If our system contains n indistinguishable particles, and we require that the total wave function ψ be symmetrical with respect to the interchange of two particles, we obtain the Bose-Einstein statistics. A symmetric wave function may be represented by the linear combination

$$\psi = \sum_\nu P^\nu \{ \varphi_a(q_1) \varphi_b(q_2) \cdots \varphi_m(q_n) \} \qquad 15 \cdot 20$$

For this case of symmetric wave functions, there is no limitation on the number of particles which we can put in a given state φ. Aside from this difference, the procedure is identical with that followed in the Fermi-Dirac statistics. The analogous table is:

g_k	n_k	N_{g_k, n_k}
2	0	1
	1	2
	2	3
	3	4
	4	5
	$\cdots$	$\cdots$
3	0	1
	1	$1 + 2 = 3$
	2	$1 + 2 + 3 = 6$
	3	$1 + 2 + 3 + 4 = 10$
	4	$1 + 2 + 3 + 4 + 5 = 15$
	$\cdots$	$\cdots\cdots\cdots\cdots\cdots\cdots\cdots$
4	0	1
	1	$1 + 3 = 4$
	2	$1 + 3 + 6 = 10$
	3	$1 + 3 + 6 + 10 = 20$
	4	$1 + 3 + 6 + 10 + 15 = 35$
	$\cdots$	$\cdots\cdots\cdots\cdots\cdots\cdots\cdots$

For $g_k = 2$, $n_k = 2$, the first state can contain either 0, 1, or 2 particles, the remainder being in the second state, giving $N_{2,2} = 3$, etc. The section of the table for $g_k = 3$ can be obtained from that for $g_k = 2$ as follows. For $g_k = 3$, $n_k = 4$, the first state can have either 4, 3, 2, 1, or 0 particles in it. If the first state has 4, the remaining 0 particles can be distributed among the remaining 2 states in 1 way; if the first state has 3, the remaining particle can be distributed among the remaining 2 states in 2 ways; if the first state has 2, the remaining 2 particles can be distributed among the remaining 2 states in 3 ways; etc., so that

$$N_{3,4} = 1 + 2 + 3 + 4 + 5 = 15 = \sum_{i=0}^{4} N_{2,i}$$

In each case

$$N_{g_k, n_k} = \frac{(n_k + g_k - 1)!}{n_k!(g_k - 1)!} \qquad 15 \cdot 21$$

so that

$$G_{n, n_1, n_2 \cdots n_k \cdots} = \prod_k \frac{(n_k + g_k - 1)!}{n_k!(g_k - 1)!} \qquad 15 \cdot 22$$

The completion of the analysis shows that, for Bose-Einstein statistics the most probable distribution is that for which

$$n_k = \frac{g_k}{e^\alpha e^{\beta \epsilon_k} - 1} \qquad 15 \cdot 23$$

The expressions for n_k (15·15, 15·19, 15·23) contain two parameters, α and β. The value of α may be determined by means of the requirement that

$$\sum_k n_k = n \qquad 15 \cdot 24$$

The parameter β may be evaluated by calculating some property of the system, such as, for example, the pressure if our system is a perfect gas, and comparing the calculated with the observed value. In this way it is found that, for each of the three statistics, $\beta = \dfrac{1}{kT}$, where k is the Boltzmann constant and T is the absolute temperature. For all actual systems (except electrons in metals and gases at temperatures very close to the absolute zero), $e^\alpha e^{\beta \epsilon_k} \gg 1$. The term ± 1 in the denominators of 15·19 and 15·23 may thus be neglected; the three statistics then give the same result

$$n_k = g_k e^{-\alpha} e^{-\beta \epsilon_k} = g_k e^{-\alpha} e^{-\frac{\epsilon_k}{kT}} \qquad 15 \cdot 25$$

Since

$$\sum_k n_k = e^{-\alpha}\sum_k g_k e^{-\frac{\epsilon_k}{kT}} = n$$

we have

$$\frac{n_k}{n} = \frac{g_k e^{-\frac{\epsilon_k}{kT}}}{\sum_k g_k e^{-\frac{\epsilon_k}{kT}}}$$ 15·26

as the general expression defining the most probable distribution. Equation 15·26 may with equal validity be regarded as the probability that a given particle will be in the state with energy ϵ_k.

15d. The Relation of Statistical Mechanics to Thermodynamics. The relation between the energy levels of a system and its thermodynamic properties may be simply derived by the following argument. Let us regard the " particle " in the above discussion not as a single atom or molecule but as, let us say, a mole of any chemical substance; that is, we now regard our " system " as a " particle."   An analysis identical with that presented above then leads to the result that the probability that the system be in the state with energy E_i is equal to $\dfrac{e^{-\frac{E_i}{kT}}}{\sum_i e^{-\frac{E_i}{kT}}}$.   The average energy of the system, the thermodynamic internal energy E, is therefore given by the expression

$$E = \frac{\sum_i E_i e^{-\frac{E_i}{kT}}}{\sum_i e^{-\frac{E_i}{kT}}} = kT^2\left(\frac{\partial}{\partial T}\log\left\{\sum_i e^{-\frac{E_i}{kT}}\right\}\right)_v$$ 15·27

and the specific heat at constant volume will be

$$C_v = \left(\frac{\partial E}{\partial T}\right)_v = \frac{\partial}{\partial T}\left[kT^2\left(\frac{\partial}{\partial T}\log\left\{\sum_i e^{-\frac{E_i}{kT}}\right\}\right)_v\right]$$ 15·28

If we now calculate the entropy of this system, we have

$$S - S_0 = \int_0^T \frac{C_v}{T}dT = \int_0^T \frac{1}{T}\frac{\partial}{\partial T}\left[kT^2\left(\frac{\partial}{\partial T}\log\left\{\sum_i e^{-\frac{E_i}{kT}}\right\}\right)_v\right]dT$$ 15·29

By integrating by parts, we obtain

$$S - S_0 = \frac{1}{T}kT^2\left(\frac{\partial}{\partial T}\log\left\{\sum_i e^{-\frac{E_i}{kT}}\right\}\right)_v + k\int_0^T\left(\frac{\partial}{\partial T}\log\left\{\sum_i e^{-\frac{E_i}{kT}}\right\}\right)dT$$

$$= \frac{E}{T} + k\log\left\{\sum_i e^{-\frac{E_i}{kT}}\right\} - k\left(\log\left\{\sum_i e^{-\frac{E_i}{kT}}\right\}\right)_{T=0}$$ 15·30

The constant term may be identified with S_0; we note that $S_0 = k \log g_0$, where g_0 is the "statistical weight" of the ground state, that is, the number of eigenfunctions corresponding to this state. This is the statistical-mechanical formulation of the third law of thermodynamics. If, as is usually true, the ground state of a system is non-degenerate, then $S_0 = 0$. Since $S = \dfrac{E}{T} - \dfrac{A}{T}$, we have the final result

$$A = -kT \log Z \qquad\qquad 15\cdot31$$

where

$$Z = \sum_n e^{-\frac{E_n}{kT}}$$

and the summation is over all energy levels E_n corresponding to the allowed eigenfunctions ψ_n of the system. The effect of phase transitions is the addition of the same term to TS and E; equation $15\cdot31$ is thus perfectly general. The quantity Z is known as the "sum-over-states" or "partition function" for the complete system.

Where it is possible to express the energy E_n as a sum of terms each of which depends on one particle only, it is convenient to write Z as a function of the partition functions of the individual particles. If ψ_n is

$$\psi_n = \varphi_a(q_1)\varphi_b(q_2) \cdots \varphi_m(q_n) \qquad\qquad 15\cdot32$$

then

$$E_n = \epsilon_a(1) + \epsilon_b(2) + \cdots + \epsilon_m(n) \qquad\qquad 15\cdot33$$

where $\epsilon_a(1)$ signifies that particle (1) has the energy ϵ_a. We now consider a system where the available number of states φ is much greater than the number of particles n — a condition which is well satisfied for most systems of chemical interest. It will then be extremely unlikely that a given φ will be occupied by more than one particle, and the possibility of the occurrence of such states can be neglected. From $15\cdot33$ we note that a given value of E_n can then be obtained in $n!$ different ways which differ only in the numbering of the particles. For the Maxwell-Boltzmann statistics, each of these $n!$ ways of obtaining E_n corresponds to a different function ψ, since the particles are distinguishable. For this case, therefore, we may write

$$\sum_n e^{-\frac{E_n}{kT}} = \sum_{\epsilon_i(1),\epsilon_i(2)\cdots} e^{-\frac{\epsilon_i(1)+\epsilon_i(2)+\cdots+\epsilon_i(n)}{kT}} \qquad 15\cdot34$$

where the second summation is over all possible values of $\epsilon_i(1)$, $\epsilon_i(2)$, etc. For the Fermi-Dirac or Bose-Einstein statistics, where the particles are indistinguishable, the $n!$ ways of obtaining E_n according to 15·33 represent only one wave function ψ. If we were to form a sum of the type 15·34 for these cases, we would have, corresponding to a given value of E_n, $n!$ terms in the summation on the right which differ only in the numbering of the particles. Since our summation is to contain only one term for each distinct ψ, a summation of the type 15·34 is thus too large by a factor $n!$. The correct expression for indistinguishable particles is therefore

$$\sum_n e^{-\frac{E_n}{kT}} = \frac{1}{n!} \sum_{\epsilon_i(1),\,\epsilon_i(2)\,\cdots} e^{-\frac{\epsilon_i(1)+\epsilon_i(2)+\cdots+\epsilon_i(n)}{kT}} \qquad 15\cdot35$$

If the particles are all alike, as we have assumed them to be in this discussion, then

$$\sum_{\epsilon_i(1),\,\epsilon_i(2),\,\cdots} e^{-\frac{\epsilon_i(1)+\epsilon_i(2)+\cdots+\epsilon_i(n)}{kT}} = \left(\sum_i e^{-\frac{\epsilon_i}{kT}}\right)^n = f^n \qquad 15\cdot36$$

where f is the partition function per particle. We have as our final results:

$$\text{For distinguishable particles} \quad Z = f^n \qquad 15\cdot37$$

$$\text{For indistinguishable particles} \quad Z = \frac{1}{n!}f^n \qquad 15\cdot38$$

If our system is a perfect gas, the particles are obviously indistinguishable, and the correct partition function for the system is given by 15·38. If our system is a perfect crystal, the particles are distinguishable because of their fixed positions in space, and the correct partition function for the system is given by 15·37. Intermediate systems such as an imperfect gas or, more important, a liquid, introduce considerable difficulty. In the first place, it will not in general be very exact to write the Hamiltonian in the form 15·1. If we make the approximation that the interactions of the neighboring particles with a given particle can be represented by some average potential field, this separation of the Hamiltonian can be achieved; the question then arises whether we should use 15·37 or 15·38. Since the particles are actually indistinguishable, and since they have a certain amount of mobility, it would appear that the correct partition function would be $Z = \frac{1}{N}f^n$, where $1 \leq N \leq n!$. It seems likely, however, that any exact treatment of such systems must be based upon the use of a Hamiltonian which contains terms involving the coordinates of more than one particle.

15e. Approximate Molecular Partition Functions. The partition function for a single molecule, as defined above, is given by the relation

$$f = \sum_j e^{-\frac{\epsilon_j}{kT}} \qquad 15\cdot39$$

where the summation is over all the allowed energy levels of the molecule. Equation 15·39 may alternatively be written

$$f = \sum_i g_i e^{-\frac{\epsilon_i}{kT}} \qquad 15\cdot40$$

where g_i is the degeneracy or statistical weight of the ith level. To a good approximation, ϵ_i may be expressed as the sum

$$\epsilon_i = \epsilon_i(t) + \epsilon_i(v) + \epsilon_i(r) + \epsilon_i(e) + \epsilon_i(n) \qquad 15\cdot41$$

where $\epsilon_i(t)$, $\epsilon_i(v)$, $\epsilon_i(r)$, $\epsilon_i(e)$, $\epsilon_i(n)$ are the energy levels associated with translational, vibrational, rotational, electronic, and nuclear motions, respectively. To this approximation, the partition function for the molecule becomes

$$f = f_t f_v f_r f_e f_n \qquad 15\cdot42$$

where

$$f_t = \sum_i g_i(t) e^{-\frac{\epsilon_i(t)}{kT}}, \qquad f_v = \sum_i g_i(v) e^{-\frac{\epsilon_i(v)}{kT}}, \quad \text{etc.} \qquad 15\cdot43$$

We now consider these terms separately. As far as nuclear energy is concerned, it may be taken equal to zero. The nuclear partition function then becomes $f_n = g_{ns}$, where g_{ns} is the nuclear spin statistical weight. Since the allowed rotational levels are dependent upon the nuclear spin wave functions, as we have seen in section 14c, it is convenient to combine the nuclear spin statistical weight with the rotational partition function, and write

$$f_R = f_r f_n = \sum_i g_{ns}(i) g_i(r) e^{-\frac{\epsilon_i(r)}{kT}} \qquad 15\cdot44$$

The partition function for electronic energy cannot be further simplified; however, the first excited electronic state is usually so high above the ground electronic state that the term $e^{-\frac{\epsilon_1(e)}{kt}}$ may be neglected in comparison with unity. Then the electronic partition function is $g_0(e)$, where $g_0(e)$ is the degeneracy of the ground state.

According to section 14e, the vibrational energy of a polyatomic molecule, to the harmonic oscillator approximation, is

$$\epsilon(v) = (n_1 + \tfrac{1}{2})h\nu_1 + \cdots + (n_i + \tfrac{1}{2})h\nu_i + \cdots + (n_k + \tfrac{1}{2})h\nu_k$$
$$n_i = 0, 1, 2, 3 \cdots \qquad 15\cdot45$$

where ν_i is the fundamental frequency of the ith vibrational degree of freedom and there are k vibrational degrees of freedom. Now

$$\sum_{n=0}^{\infty} e^{-\frac{(n+\frac{1}{2})h\nu}{kT}} = e^{-\frac{h\nu}{2kT}} \sum_{n=0}^{\infty} e^{-\frac{nh\nu}{kT}}$$

$$= e^{-\frac{h\nu}{2kT}} \left\{ 1 + e^{-\frac{h\nu}{kT}} + \left(e^{-\frac{h\nu}{kT}} \right)^2 + \left(e^{-\frac{h\nu}{kT}} \right)^3 + \cdots \right\} \quad 15\cdot46$$

$$= e^{-\frac{h\nu}{2kT}} \left\{ \frac{1}{1 - e^{-\frac{h\nu}{kT}}} \right\}$$

so that the vibrational partition function for a polyatomic molecule, to the harmonic oscillator approximation, is

$$f_v = \prod_{i=1}^{i=k} \left\{ \frac{e^{-\frac{h\nu_i}{2kT}}}{1 - e^{-\frac{h\nu_i}{kT}}} \right\} \quad\quad 15\cdot47$$

The translational energy levels of a molecule are given by the solution of the wave equation for a particle in a box (section 5b). If the mass of the molecule is m, and if it is constrained to move in a rectangular box of edges a, b, and c and volume $V = abc$, the translational energy levels are

$$E = \frac{h^2}{8m} \left(\frac{n_x^2}{a^2} + \frac{n_y^2}{b^2} + \frac{n_z^2}{c^2} \right)$$

$$n_x, n_y, n_z = 1, 2, 3, 4 \cdots \quad\quad 15\cdot48$$

The translational partition function is therefore

$$f_t = \sum_{n_x=1}^{\infty} e^{-\frac{h^2 n_x^2}{8ma^2kT}} \sum_{n_y=1}^{\infty} e^{-\frac{h^2 n_y^2}{8mb^2kT}} \sum_{n_z=1}^{\infty} e^{-\frac{h^2 n_z^2}{8mc^2kT}} \quad 15\cdot49$$

Now the quantity $\dfrac{h^2}{8ma^2kT}$ is very much less than unity for ordinary temperatures and reasonable values of a, so that $\dfrac{h^2 n_x^2}{8ma^2kT}$ changes only slightly as we vary n_x. For this reason it is permissible to replace the summations by integrations, and write

$$f_t = \int^{\infty} e^{-\frac{h^2 n_x^2}{8ma^2kT}} dn_x \int_0^{\infty} e^{-\frac{h^2 n_y^2}{8mb^2kT}} dn_y \int_0^{\infty} e^{-\frac{h^2 n_z^2}{8mc^2kT}} dn_z \quad 15\cdot50$$

according to Appendix VIII,

$$\int_0^{\infty} e^{-\frac{h^2 n_x^2}{8ma^2kT}} dn_x = \frac{(2\pi mkT)^{\frac{1}{2}}}{h} a \quad\quad 15\cdot51$$

so that the translational partition function becomes

$$f_t = \frac{(2\pi mkT)^{3/2}}{h^3} \, abc = \frac{(2\pi mkT)^{3/2}}{h^3} \, V \qquad 15\cdot52$$

Classically, the energy of a system is given by the equation $H(p, q) = E$. The classical analogue of equation 15·40 is therefore

$$f = \frac{1}{h^n} \int e^{-\frac{H(p,\, q)}{kT}} \, dp_1 \cdots dp_n \, dq_1 \cdots dq_n \qquad 15\cdot53$$

where the factor $\dfrac{1}{h^n}$ has been introduced so that f may be non-dimensional.   The introduction of this specific factor may be further justified as follows.   For a particle of mass m moving under the influence of no forces, the Hamiltonian function is

$$H = \frac{1}{2m} \, (p_x^2 + p_y^2 + p_z^2) \qquad 15\cdot54$$

so that equation 15·53 gives for the translational partition function the result

$$f_t = \frac{1}{h^3} \int\!\!\int\!\!\int_{-\infty}^{\infty} e^{-\frac{(p_x^2+p_y^2+p_z^2)}{2mkT}} \, dp_x \, dp_y \, dp_z \int\!\!\int\!\!\int dx \, dy \, dz \qquad 15\cdot55$$

If the particle is constrained to move in a volume V, then

$$\int\!\!\int\!\!\int dx \, dy \, dz = V$$

Integrating over the momenta, we obtain

$$f_t = \frac{(2\pi mkT)^{3/2}V}{h^3} \qquad 15\cdot56$$

which is identical with 15·52.

We next consider the rotational partition functions for diatomic molecules. According to section 14c, there is no restriction on the allowed values of the rotational quantum number J if the nuclei are different. If the two nuclei have spins s_1 and s_2 the nuclear spin statistical weight is $(2s_1 + 1)(2s_2 + 1)$. The rotational energy levels are

$$E_J = \frac{h^2}{8\pi^2 I} \, J(J + 1) \qquad 15\cdot57$$

where I is the moment of inertia, and each level is $(2J + 1)$-fold degenerate.   The rotational partition function f_R is thus

$$f_R = (2s_1 + 1)(2s_2 + 1) \sum_{J=0}^{\infty} (2J + 1)e^{-\frac{h^2 J(J+1)}{8\pi^2 I k T}} \qquad 15\cdot 58$$

For large values of I and T, we may replace the summation by an integration, and obtain

$$f_R = (2s_1 + 1)(2s_2 + 1) \int_0^{\infty} e^{-\frac{h^2 J(J+1)}{8\pi\cdot I k T}} (2J + 1) \, dJ$$

$$= (2s_1 + 1)(2s_2 + 1) \frac{8\pi^2 I k T}{h^2} \qquad 15\cdot 59$$

When the nuclei are identical, there is a restriction on the allowed J values.   For hydrogen in the ground electronic state, even J values are allowed for parahydrogen, with nuclear spin weight unity; odd J values are allowed for orthohydrogen, with nuclear spin weight three. If we consider hydrogen as being a single species, which is legitimate at high temperatures, we have the rotational partition function

$$f_R = 3 \sum_{J \text{ odd}} (2J + 1)e^{-\frac{h^2 J(J+1)}{8\pi^2 I k T}} + 1 \sum_{J \text{ even}} (2J + 1)e^{-\frac{h^2 J(J+1)}{8\pi^2 I k T}} \qquad 15\cdot 60$$

If we replace the summations by integrations, then, since the summations contain only one-half the possible terms, we obtain, according to 15·59, the result

$$f_R = (3 + 1) \frac{8\pi^2 I k T}{2h^2}$$

In any homonuclear diatomic molecule, with nuclear spin s, the statistical weight of the ortho states is $(s + 1)(2s + 1)$; that of the para states is $s(2s + 1)$.   The rotational partition function will thus in general be

$$\{(s + 1)(2s + 1) + s(2s + 1)\} \frac{8\pi^2 I k T}{2h^2} = (2s + 1)^2 \frac{8\pi^2 I k T}{2h^2} \qquad 15\cdot 61$$

For all diatomic molecules, we may therefore write the rotational partition function as

$$f_R = (2s_1 + 1)(2s_2 + 1) \frac{8\pi^2 I k T}{\sigma h^2} \qquad 15\cdot 62$$

where σ, the "symmetry number," is 1 for heteronuclear and 2 for homonuclear diatomic molecules; that is, σ is the number of indistinguishable ways of orienting the molecule in space.

For polyatomic molecules, the analysis is similar to that given above. For high temperature, the result is

$$f_R = \frac{8\pi^2 (8\pi^3 ABC)^{\frac{1}{2}} (kT)^{\frac{3}{2}}}{\sigma h^3} \prod_i (2s_i + 1) \qquad 15\cdot63$$

where A, B, C are the principal moments of inertia and where the symmetry number σ is again equal to the number of indistinguishable ways of orienting the molecule in space; for example, $\sigma = 2$ for H_2O; $\sigma = 3$ for NH_3; $\sigma = 12$ for CH_4 and C_6H_6. The origin of the symmetry number is the same as in the diatomic case; if there are n equivalent orientations of the molecule in space, then only $\frac{1}{n}$ of the possible energy levels are allowed by the symmetry restrictions on the wave functions.

15f. An Alternative Formulation of the Distribution Law.[1] Consider some definite atomic or molecular system A which is in thermal equilibrium with a system B composed of s harmonic oscillators. Suppose that the combined system $A + B$ possesses a total energy E. What will then be the probability that the system A has an amount of energy ϵ distributed in some one exactly specified way among the various degrees of freedom of A?

In order to perform this calculation we make the usual assumption of statistical mechanics: *Any exactly specified way of distributing the energy E in the system $A + B$ is as probable as any other exactly specified way of distributing the same total energy.* The probability of a partially specified distribution is consequently proportional to the number of exactly specified distributions which are compatible with it. Thus the probability of A having the energy ϵ in some exactly specified way is proportional to the number of exactly specified ways of distributing the remaining energy $(E - \epsilon)$ among the s oscillators of the system B. But this is just the number of ways of distributing $n = \dfrac{(E - \epsilon)}{h\nu}$ quanta of energy among s oscillators, where $h\nu$ is the energy per quanta. Since the quanta are indistinguishable, and since there is no restriction on the number of quanta in a given oscillator, the problem is similar to that already met in the discussion of the Bose-Einstein statistics. The number of ways $N_{n,s}$ of distributing n quanta among the s oscillators is, analogous to Equation 15·21,

$$N_{n,s} = \frac{(n + s - 1)!}{n!(s - 1)!} \qquad 15\cdot64$$

This result can be derived quite simply in the following way. We count

[1] See E. U. Condon, *Phys. Rev.*, **54**, 937 (1938).

the number of different ways in which n quanta and s oscillators can be arranged in a line so that there is always at least one oscillator on the extreme right; all quanta which are placed between two oscillators are considered as belonging to the oscillator to the right. There are $(n + s - 1)!$ such arrangements. Eliminating arrangements which have been counted more than once then leads directly to 15·64.

Equation 15·64 is an exact answer to our problem but can be simplified when n and s are very large numbers. Using Sterling's approximation

$$x! = (2\pi x)^{\frac{1}{2}} x^x e^{-x} \qquad 15\cdot 65$$

which is valid for large values of x, equation 15·64 becomes:

$$N_{n,\,s} = (2\pi)^{-\frac{1}{2}} \left(\frac{n+s-1}{n}\right)^{n+\frac{1}{2}} \frac{(n+s-1)^{s-1}}{(s-1)^{s-\frac{1}{2}}} \qquad 15\cdot 66$$

If $n \gg s$ we have

$$\left(\frac{n+s-1}{n}\right)^{n+\frac{1}{2}} = \left(1 + \frac{s-1}{n}\right)^{\frac{1}{2}} \left(1 + \frac{s-1}{n}\right)^n$$

$$= \left(1 + \frac{s-1}{n}\right)^{\frac{1}{2}} \left\{ 1 + n\left(\frac{s-1}{n}\right) + \frac{n(n-1)}{2!}\left(\frac{s-1}{n}\right)^2 \right.$$

$$\left. + \frac{n(n-1)(n-2)}{3!}\left(\frac{s-1}{n}\right)^3 + \cdots \right\}$$

$$\cong e^{s-1}$$

a result which becomes strictly correct as $n \to \infty$. Also,

$$(n+s-1)^{s-1} = \left(\frac{E-\epsilon}{h\nu} + s - 1\right)^{s-1} = \left(\frac{E + (s-1)h\nu}{h\nu}\right)^{s-1}$$

$$\left\{ 1 - \frac{\epsilon}{E + (s-1)h\nu} \right\}^{s-1}$$

If the average energy per oscillator is γ, we can write

$$E + (s-1)h\nu = s\gamma + g$$

where g will be much smaller than $s\gamma$ provided that n is large compared with s and ϵ is much smaller than E. In this case

$$(n+s-1)^{s-1} = \left(\frac{E + (s-1)h\nu}{h\nu}\right)^{s-1} \left(1 - \frac{\epsilon}{s\gamma + g}\right)^{s-1}$$

$$= \left(\frac{E + (s-1)h\nu}{h\nu}\right)^{s-1}$$

$$\left\{ 1 - (s-1)\left(\frac{\epsilon}{s\gamma + g}\right) + \frac{(s-1)(s-2)}{2!}\left(\frac{\epsilon}{s\gamma + g}\right)^2 \cdots \right\}$$

$$\cong \left(\frac{E + (s-1)h\nu}{h\nu}\right)^{s-1} \left\{1 - \frac{\epsilon}{\gamma} + \frac{\epsilon^2}{2!\gamma^2} - \frac{\epsilon^3}{3!\gamma^3} + \cdots\right\}$$

$$\cong \left(\frac{E + (s-1)h\nu}{h\nu}\right)^{s-1} e^{-\frac{\epsilon}{\gamma}}$$

Therefore

$$N_{n,\,s} \cong (2\pi)^{-\frac{1}{2}} \frac{e^{s-1}}{(s-1)^{s-\frac{1}{2}}} \left(\frac{E + (s-1)h\nu}{h\nu}\right)^{s-1} e^{-\frac{\epsilon}{\gamma}} = Ce^{-\frac{\epsilon}{\gamma}} \qquad 15\cdot67$$

where C is a constant independent of ϵ. But, according to our original postulate, $N_{n,\,s}$ is just proportional to the probability $P(\epsilon)$ that the system A have the energy ϵ in an exactly specified way. Therefore, we have

$$P(\epsilon) = Ce^{-\frac{\epsilon}{\gamma}} \qquad 15\cdot68$$

The constant γ in 15·68 (which is the reciprocal of the β in our earlier discussion) can be evaluated by calculating some property of the system A (such as the pressure if we let A be a perfect gas) and comparing with the experimental results. As mentioned before, such an analysis gives the value $\gamma = kT$, where k is Boltzmann's constant and T is the absolute temperature.

CHAPTER XVI

THE QUANTUM-MECHANICAL THEORY OF REACTION RATES

16a. Formulation of the General Theory. In previous chapters we were largely interested in the application of the principles of quantum mechanics and statistical mechanics to the study of those properties of chemical systems which are independent of time, that is, to the study of structural chemistry. These same principles can be applied successfully to the problem of the calculation of rates of chemical reactions. As the first step toward the solution of this problem it will be profitable to consider the method of representing reactions and changes in the state of a system generally by means of a geometrical picture.

The state of any system is described in quantum mechanics by its eigenfunction $\Psi(q, t)$, where t is the time and q represents all the coordinates which would be necessary, in classical mechanics, to specify the positions of all the particles in the system completely. With some reservations, these positional coordinates will be termed " degrees of freedom," although this notion is not so precise in quantum mechanics as in classical mechanics. (Since the observable properties of a mechanical system are completely determined by the energy of the system, it might be said to have only one degree of freedom, even though it consisted of many interacting particles. In the following discussion we shall use the term only in the sense of classical degrees of freedom.) Given the eigenfunction Ψ, we can calculate all the physical properties of the system; if **R** is the operator which corresponds to the property in question, then

$$\bar{R} = \frac{\displaystyle\int \Psi^* R \Psi \, d\tau}{\displaystyle\int \Psi^* \psi \, d\tau} \qquad 16 \cdot 1$$

is the expectation value of the property, that is, the average value of a large number of measurements of the property. If Ψ does not represent a stationary state, that is, if $\Psi^*\Psi$ is a function of the time, these expectation values will be functions of the time.

The reaction between a hydrogen molecule and a hydrogen atom, such as occurs in ortho-para hydrogen conversion, constitutes a transition in a three-atom system.   The properties of this system are completely determined by the Schrödinger equation governing it, that is, by its eigenfunctions.   The system itself may be represented by a point in four-dimensional space: three dimensions are required to specify the relative positions of the nuclei, one additional dimension is required to specify the energy.   (We assume here that the motion of the electrons is so rapid that the electrons form a static field for the slower nuclear motions.)   The three internuclear distances r_{12}, r_{23}, r_{13} can be conveniently used to specify the configuration of the system.   At some time t_0 this system is found in a configuration in which, say, r_{12} is much smaller than either r_{23} or r_{13}; that is, atoms 1 and 2 form a molecule.   The reaction in question is represented by a transition from this configuration to one in which, say, r_{23} is much smaller than either r_{13} or r_{12}.   The probability of such a transition will be denoted by κ.

As the internuclear distances change in such a transition, the total binding energy of the system, that is, the electronic energy of the ground state of the system, will also change.   The problem of determining the binding energy for any given values of the positional coordinates is identical with the problem of the calculation of the binding energy of stable molecules and is subject to the same limitations.   The surface which represents the binding energy of the system as a function of the positional coordinates is known as the potential energy surface for the system; its determination is usually the first step in the theoretical discussion of the rate of a chemical reaction.   The general features of potential energy surfaces may be illustrated by the surface for the reaction $H + H_2$.   For simplicity we assume the three hydrogen atoms to be collinear; the system is then completely specified by the two coordinates r_{12} and r_{23}.   If the calculation of the binding energy is made by use of the London formula (equation 13·28), assuming the coulombic energy to be 14 per cent we obtain the surface illustrated in Fig. 16·1,[1] where the lines of constant energy have been plotted as contour lines.   The coordinate axes are inclined at an angle of 60° rather than 90°, since for this particular system this choice of axes diagonalizes the kinetic energy; that is, the kinetic energy is expressible as[2]

$$T = \tfrac{1}{2}\mu \left[\left(\frac{dx}{dt}\right)^2 + \left(\frac{dy}{dt}\right)^2 \right]; \quad \mu = \tfrac{2}{3}m \qquad 16\cdot2$$

where m is the mass of a hydrogen atom.   The equations of motion of the system, from the classical viewpoint, therefore represent the friction,

---

[1] H. Eyring, H. Gershinowitz, and C. E. Sun, *J. Chem. Phys.*, **3**, 786 (1935).

[2] S. Glasstone, K. Laidler, and H. Eyring, *The Theory of Rate Processes*, p. 100, McGraw-Hill Book Company, 1941.

less sliding of a mass point of mass μ on the surface of potential energy. (Strictly speaking, the analogy is not exact, since the motion of a mass point on a gravitational potential surface takes place in three dimensions; the discrepancy is not serious for our purposes.) We note that the potential energy surface is made up of two long narrow valleys, representing the stable H_2 molecules, connected by a region of higher energy and separated by regions of still higher energy. The potential energy surfaces for more complicated reactions are similar. The regions corre-

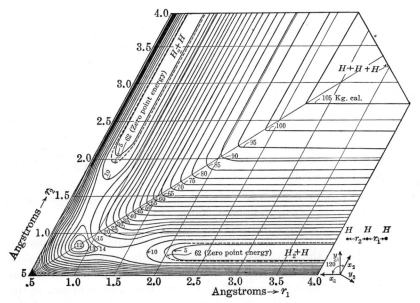

Fig. 16·1. Potential energy surface for three hydrogen atoms (after Eyring, Gershinowitz, and Sun).

sponding to the configuration of the reactants (the initial state) will usually be separated from the regions corresponding to the configuration of the products (the final state) by a region of higher energy, in which event the reaction has an *activation energy*. Classical mechanics predicts that, if the height of the barrier is V_0, no systems with energy $E < V_0$ can react, and all systems with energy $E > V_0$ which approach the top of the barrier proceed to cross it and lead to reaction. If, as in the $H + H_2$ example, there is a shallow basin with a second pass just beyond the first barrier, a system may move into this basin and be reflected into the valley from which it came. Figure 16·2,[3] illustrating the classical motion of a system entering this basin, is interesting in that

[3] J. Hirschfelder, H. Eyring, and B. Topley, *J. Chem. Phys.*, **4**, 170 (1936).

it shows that the motion of a particle in the basin tends to become completely random, and thus has an equal chance of leaving by either pass. In this case only about one-half of the systems which enter the basin will leave it through the pass into the valley corresponding to the con-

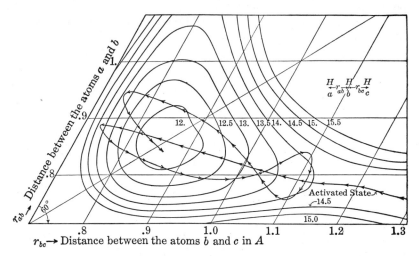

FIG. 16·2.   Path of representative point on H—H—H potential energy surface (after Hirschfelder, Eyring, and Topley).

figuration of the products.   These predictions of classical mechanics are modified when the problem is considered from the quantum-mechanical viewpoint.   In the first place, there is a finite probability that a system in the initial state with energy $E < V_0$ may nevertheless appear in the final state at a later time.   This phenomenon of " leakage " through the potential energy barrier is important in the decay of radioactive nuclei

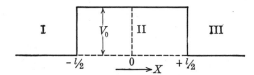

FIG. 16·3.   One-dimensional potential energy barrier.

and in reactions involving only the transfer of electrons.   In the second place, even if $E > V_0$, there is a finite probability that the system will be reflected in the region of the barrier and will hence not proceed to the final state.

The method of calculating these probabilities may be illustrated for motion in one dimension in the potential field of Fig. 16·3.   The potential energy is

$$V(x) = 0 \qquad -\infty < x < -\frac{l}{2}$$

$$V(x) = V_0 \qquad -\frac{l}{2} \leq x \leq \frac{l}{2} \qquad 16\text{·}3$$

$$V(x) = 0 \qquad \frac{l}{2} < x < +\infty$$

The Schrödinger equation for the system is

$$\frac{d^2\psi}{dx^2} + \frac{8\pi^2 m}{h^2}[(E - V(x)]\psi = 0 \qquad 16\text{·}4$$

In region I, where $V(x) = 0$, ψ has the form of a plane wave (section 5·1), the two independent solutions corresponding to motion toward the barrier and away from the barrier. The general solution in this region is then

$$\psi_\mathrm{I} = Ae^{i\alpha x} + Be^{-i\alpha x} \qquad 16\text{·}5$$

where $\alpha = \dfrac{2\pi}{h}\sqrt{2mE}$, and E is the total energy of the system. In region II, where $V(x) = V_0$, the solution is of the same form if α is replaced by $\beta = \dfrac{2\pi}{h}\sqrt{2m(E - V_0)}$. When $E < V_0$, β is imaginary, and ψ_II corresponds to an exponentially decreasing probability of finding the system in the region inside the barrier. In region III, ψ_III has the same form as ψ_I, and so we have

$$\psi_\mathrm{II} = Ce^{i\beta x} + De^{-i\beta x} \qquad 16\text{·}6$$

$$\psi_\mathrm{III} = Fe^{i\alpha x} + Ge^{-i\alpha x} \qquad 16\text{·}7$$

The eigenfunction for the entire region must be continuous and have a continuous first derivative; therefore the following conditions must be fulfilled:

$$\psi_\mathrm{I} = \psi_\mathrm{II}, \quad \frac{\partial\psi_\mathrm{I}}{\partial x} = \frac{\partial\psi_\mathrm{II}}{\partial x} \quad \text{when} \quad x = -\frac{l}{2} \qquad 16\text{·}8$$

$$\psi_\mathrm{II} = \psi_\mathrm{III}, \quad \frac{\partial\psi_\mathrm{II}}{\partial x} = \frac{\partial\psi_\mathrm{III}}{\partial x} \quad \text{when} \quad x = +\frac{l}{2} \qquad 16\text{·}9$$

These four conditions enable us to determine the constants B, C, D, and

F in terms of the constants A and G. The set of simultaneous equations is readily found to be

$$Be^{i\alpha\frac{l}{2}} - Ce^{-i\beta\frac{l}{2}} - De^{i\beta\frac{l}{2}} = -Ae^{-i\alpha\frac{l}{2}}$$

$$-\alpha Be^{i\alpha\frac{l}{2}} - \beta Ce^{-i\beta\frac{l}{2}} + \beta De^{i\beta\frac{l}{2}} = -\alpha Ae^{-i\alpha\frac{l}{2}}$$

$$Ce^{i\beta\frac{l}{2}} + De^{-i\beta\frac{l}{2}} - Fe^{i\alpha\frac{l}{2}} = Ge^{-i\alpha\frac{l}{2}}$$

$$\beta Ce^{i\beta\frac{l}{2}} - \beta De^{-i\beta\frac{l}{2}} - \alpha Fe^{i\alpha\frac{l}{2}} = -\alpha Ge^{-i\alpha\frac{l}{2}}$$

16·10

whence

$$B = \frac{\begin{vmatrix} -Ae^{-i\alpha\frac{l}{2}} & -e^{-i\beta\frac{l}{2}} & -e^{i\beta\frac{l}{2}} & 0 \\ -\alpha Ae^{-i\alpha\frac{l}{2}} & -\beta e^{-i\beta\frac{l}{2}} & \beta e^{i\beta\frac{l}{2}} & 0 \\ Ge^{-i\alpha\frac{l}{2}} & e^{i\beta\frac{l}{2}} & e^{-i\beta\frac{l}{2}} & -e^{i\alpha\frac{l}{2}} \\ -\alpha Ge^{-i\alpha\frac{l}{2}} & \beta e^{i\beta\frac{l}{2}} & -\beta e^{-i\beta\frac{l}{2}} & -\alpha e^{i\alpha\frac{l}{2}} \end{vmatrix}}{\begin{vmatrix} e^{i\alpha\frac{l}{2}} & -e^{-i\beta\frac{l}{2}} & -e^{i\beta\frac{l}{2}} & 0 \\ -\alpha e^{i\alpha\frac{l}{2}} & -\beta e^{-i\beta\frac{l}{2}} & \beta e^{i\beta\frac{l}{2}} & 0 \\ 0 & e^{i\beta\frac{l}{2}} & e^{-i\beta\frac{l}{2}} & -e^{i\alpha\frac{l}{2}} \\ 0 & \beta e^{i\beta\frac{l}{2}} & -\beta e^{-i\beta\frac{l}{2}} & -\alpha e^{i\alpha\frac{l}{2}} \end{vmatrix}}$$

16·11

with the analogous expressions for C, D, and F.

Let us suppose that there are no systems returning from the final state; that is, there are no systems in region III with negative momentum. In this case $G = 0$. Let the probability of finding a system in region I with positive momentum be unity; that is, let $A = 1$. Then $|F|^2$ gives the chance that it be transmitted into region III and $|B|^2$ gives the chance that it be reflected back into region I. For $E > V_0$, it is seen that the *transmission coefficient* $|F|^2$ is small but finite. Moreover, it is a function of the variable $\theta = \beta l$; that is, it varies with the original momentum of the particle, the height of the barrier, and the width of the barrier. When $E > V_0$, the transmission coefficient oscillates with these variables. Thus, for a fixed barrier height and width, particles of certain energies will be completely transmitted, while those of slightly different energies will be less likely to cross the barrier, even though they have enough energy.

The energy surface for an actual chemical reaction is always at least two-dimensional and is usually many-dimensional, since it must include a dimension for every internuclear distance for all the nuclei involved in the reaction. In every case, however, there will be some initial configuration in which the eigenfunction for the system can be well approximated in one dimension by a plane wave traveling toward the region of configuration space which connects with the region of the products. Also, there will be a region where the eigenfunction for the configuration of the system representing products can be well approximated in one dimension by a traveling plane wave. Thus it will always be possible to expand the exact eigenfunction for the system so that it will represent, asymptotically at least, a plane wave which we shall call the transmitted wave, traveling away from the activated state down the valley representing products. Then this representation will, in general, reduce asymptotically in the reactants valley to the superposition of plane waves traveling to and from the activated state, that is, an incident and a reflected wave. The ratio of the amplitude of the transmitted wave to that of the incident wave defines the transmission coefficient. Similarly, the ratio of the amplitude of the reflected wave to that of the incident wave defines the reflection coefficient.

It often happens that motion in degrees of freedom orthogonal to that in which the reaction takes place is quantized, and the system exists in discrete energy levels corresponding to vibrations of the reactants or products. These vibrational quantum numbers may or may not change during the course of a reaction. A change in the energy of some quantized degree of freedom requires a corresponding change in the energy of some other degree of freedom. Thus, reflection or transmission at a barrier in the energy surface may induce a transfer of energy between the various degrees of freedom of the system. Let ψ_n represent the eigenfunction of the incident wave, where n denotes the set of quantum numbers specifying its vibrational state. Let p_n be the translational momentum of a wave in the vibrational state n. The reflected wave may have any vibrational state consistent with the available total energy. Let the eigenfunction of that fraction of incident systems initially in the vibrational state n which are reflected in state m be $R_{nm}\psi_m$. Their momentum will be p_m. Similarly, let $T_{nm}\psi_m$ be the eigenfunction of the wave transmitted with change in vibrational state from n to m. Then $|\psi_n|^2$ is the density of incident systems and $\frac{p_n}{M}$ their velocity. (M is their mass.) Since all systems are either reflected or transmitted, and since there is no piling up in the region of the barrier, we have the relation

$$|\psi_n|^2 \frac{p_n}{M} = \sum_m |R_{nm}|^2 |\psi_m|^2 \frac{p_m}{M} + \sum_k |T_{nk}|^2 |\psi_k|^2 \frac{p_k}{M} \qquad 16\cdot12$$

where the sums are over all values of m and k which are consistent with the total energy of the system. When the ψ's are normalized to unity, the ratio $|R_{nm}|^2 \frac{p_m}{p_n} = \rho_{nm}$ is defined as the *reflection coefficient*, and the

ratio $|T_{nk}|^2 \frac{p_k}{p_n} = \kappa_{nk}$ is defined as the *transmission coefficient* for the transition from level n to level k.

Let us now formulate the rate of a chemical reaction in terms of these coefficients. We consider a region in the reactant valley which is far removed from the potential energy barrier. Let $C_n(p)$ be the number of systems in length of path dx in this region which have momentum between p and $p + dp$ along the reaction coordinate and energy E_n in the other degrees of freedom. The number of such systems which pass a given point in the reaction path per second moving toward the barrier will be $\frac{C_n(p)}{dx} \frac{p}{m}$, since $\frac{p}{m}$ is the velocity of these systems, where p is considered to have only positive values. The fraction of these systems which react will be

$$\sum_k \kappa_{nk}(p) \frac{C_n(p)}{dx} \frac{p}{m} \qquad 16\cdot13$$

where $\kappa_{nk}(p)$ is the transmission coefficient as defined above. Assuming an equilibrium distribution in this region, the concentration $C_n(p)$ will be

$$C_n(p) = \frac{(A_1)(A_2) \cdots}{F_1 F_2 \cdots} \omega_n e^{-\frac{E_n}{kT}} e^{-\frac{p^2}{2mkT}} \frac{dx\, dp}{h} \qquad 16\cdot14$$

where (A_1), (A_2), $\cdots$ are the concentrations of the reactants, $F_1, F_2, \cdots$ are the partition functions for the reactants, and ω_n is the statistical weight of the level with energy E_n. The net rate is obtained by summing 16·13 over n and integrating over the momentum p. The general expression for the rate of a chemical reaction is therefore

$$k = \frac{(A_1)(A_2) \cdots}{F_1 F_2 \cdots} \int_0^\infty \sum_k \sum_n \kappa_{nk}(p) \omega_n e^{-\frac{E_n}{kT}} e^{-\frac{p^2}{2mkT}} \frac{p\, dp}{mh} \qquad 16\cdot15$$

This expression cannot be further reduced unless certain simplifying assumptions are made. We obtain an approximation to the classical case if we assume $\kappa_{nk}(p) = 0$ for $\dfrac{p^2}{2m} \le V_0$, $\kappa_{nk}(p)$ equal to some average value κ for $\dfrac{p^2}{2m} > V_0$. Equation 16·15 then becomes

$$
\begin{aligned}
k &= \frac{(A_1)(A_2)\cdots}{F_1 F_2 \cdots} \kappa \sum_n \omega_n e^{-\frac{E_n}{kT}} \int_{\sqrt{2mV_0}}^{\infty} e^{-\frac{p^2}{2mkT}} \frac{p\,dp}{mh} \\
&= \frac{(A_1)(A_2)\cdots}{F_1 F_2 \cdots} \kappa \sum_n \omega_n e^{-\frac{E_n}{kT}} \frac{kT}{h} e^{-\frac{V_0}{kT}}
\end{aligned}
\qquad 16\cdot16
$$

The quantity $\sum_n \omega_n e^{-\frac{E_n}{kT}}$ has the general form of a partition function and may be denoted by $F^{\ddagger}$. We therefore have for the specific reaction rate, to this approximation, the result

$$
k' = \kappa \frac{F^{\ddagger}}{F_1 F_2 \cdots} \frac{kT}{h} e^{-\frac{V_0}{kT}}
\qquad 16\cdot17
$$

This is the familiar equation originally derived by Eyring,[4] using a slightly different method of approach, and is a generalization of the results obtained by Pelzer and Wigner[5] in their study of the H + H$_2$ reaction. In the derivation by Eyring's method, it was shown that $F^{\ddagger}$ is the partition function for the activated complex (not including the degree of freedom along the reaction path). The investigation of the specifically quantum-mechanical effects in chemical reactions, as discussed later in this chapter, have confirmed the validity of equation 16·17 for most cases of interest. Most of the applications of the theory of absolute reaction rates have been based directly on equation 16·17; the results are discussed in detail in the recent textbook by Glasstone, Laidler, and Eyring.[2]

It will be noted that in equation 16·15 all explicit reference to the nature of the potential energy surface in the region of the barrier has disappeared; the effect of the barrier is contained implicitly in the transmission coefficients $\kappa_{nk}(p)$. In this formulation of the theory there is no assumption of equilibrium between the initial and activated states. It is necessary to assume equilibrium between the various vibrational states of the initial configuration, which appears always justifiable, since the initial configuration can be chosen in such a way that the interactions between the reactant molecules are as small as desired. When reaction

[4] H. Eyring, *J. Chem. Phys.*, **3**, 107 (1935).
[5] H. Pelzer and E. Wigner, *Z. physik. Chem.*, **B15**, 445 (1932).

induces transfer of energy from translational to vibrational degrees of freedom in the system, there will be, as we have seen, a different $\kappa_{nk}(p)$ and hence a different rate for each vibrational level in the *final* state. In general, the distribution of systems over the vibrational levels in the final state will not be the equilibrium distribution, but is given automatically by adding the rates of reaction for each level. Thus there will be a rate k'_m for reaction in which the products are in the vibrational level m given by

$$k'_m = \frac{1}{F_1 F_2 \cdots} \int_0^\infty \sum_n \kappa_{nm}(p)\omega_n e^{-\frac{E_n}{kT}} e^{-\frac{p^2}{2mkT}} \frac{p\, dp}{mh} \qquad 16\cdot18$$

Integrating this expression with respect to time will give the concentration of products in the mth vibrational state (disregarding changes *after* reaction). This will be the equilibrium value only for special forms of κ.

The above formulation is completely general and applies immediately to bimolecular and higher-order reactions. Unimolecular reactions require further consideration. They are usually considered to involve two steps, an activation by collision followed by a decomposition of the activated molecule. The first step, activation by collision, can be treated in principle by the method given above. Here we are interested in the calculation of the probability that systems approaching the barrier will be reflected with a change in vibrational energy. Analogously to equation 16·18, we have for the rate of formation of molecules in vibrational state l the result

$$k'_l = \frac{1}{F_1 F_2 \cdots} \int_0^\infty \sum_n \rho_{nl}(p)\omega_n e^{-\frac{E_n}{kT}} e^{-\frac{p^2}{2mkT}} \frac{p\, dp}{mh} \qquad 16\cdot19$$

where $\rho_{nl}(p)$ is the reflection coefficient. The rate of deactivation by collision is given by an analogous equation. Activated molecules can disappear either by decomposition into the products or by deactivation by collision. The usual theory of unimolecular reactions, as developed by Lindemann, Hinshelwood, Kassel, Rice, Ramsperger, and others,[6] assumes that the concentration of activated molecules is constant. This steady-state assumption leads to the equation

$$k_1(A)(N) = k_2(A)(N^*) + k_3(N^*)$$

where (N) is the concentration of normal reacting molecules, (N^*) is the concentration of activated molecules, (A) is the total concentration

[6] L. S. Kassel, *Kinematics of Homogeneous Gas Reaction*, p. 93, The Chemical Catalog Co., New York, 1932. C. N. Hinshelwood, *The Kinetics of Chemical Change*, Oxford Clarendon Press, 1940.

of molecules which can cause activation or deactivation by collisions. k_1 and k_2 are the specific rates for activation and deactivation by collision, respectively, and k_3 is the specific rate for reaction of the activated molecule. The actual rate of production of the products will be

$$k' = \kappa_3(N^*) = \frac{k_1 k_3 (A)(N)}{k_2(A) + k_3}$$

or, in the high-pressure limit

$$k' = \frac{k_1 k_3}{k_2}(N)$$

The rate constants k_1 and k_2 are calculable by the equation given above; however, in the high-pressure region, where only a negligible fraction of activated molecules disappear by reaction, we may write

$$\frac{k_1}{k_2} = \frac{(N^*)}{(N)} = \frac{F_{N*}}{F_N}$$

where F_{N*} is the partition function for activated molecules and F_N is the partition function for normal molecules. According to equation 16·17, k_3 may be written as

$$k_3 = \kappa \frac{kT}{h} \frac{F_{N\ddagger}}{F_{N*}}$$

where $F_{N\ddagger}$ is the partition function for the activated complex of the reaction $N^* \rightarrow$ products. (In $F_{N\ddagger}$ and F_{N*} the zero of energy is taken to be the ground state of the normal N molecules.) The high-pressure rate is therefore

$$k' = \frac{k_1 k_3}{k_2}(N) = \frac{F_{N*}}{F_N} \kappa \frac{kT}{h} \frac{F_{N\ddagger}}{F_{N*}}(N) = \kappa \frac{kT}{h} \frac{F_{N\ddagger}}{F_N}(N)$$

that is, all explicit reference to the activated molecules N^* has disappeared, and we are back to our familiar rate equation.

There are two alternative ways of formulating the reaction rate problem which are more useful for some purposes. In practice it is not possible to obtain the exact eigenfunctions for an n-body system when n is greater than 2 because of the fact that the equations of motion are not separable. They can be computed approximately, however, by first calculating the eigenfunctions for an approximate Schrödinger equation which is separable and then treating the terms which were neglected in order to make the separation as a perturbation on these approximate solutions. It is then found that the density of systems in any particular unperturbed level is a periodic function of the time. The perturbation induces transitions from one approximate level to another. For unimolecular decompositions the approximate levels are those of the molecule which is decomposing, and the lifetime of an energy-rich molecule is determined by the probability with which transitions to continuous levels (corresponding to dissociation) are induced. Rosen[7] has used this method to calculate the mean life of a linear triatomic molecule. For more complicated molecules, even the separable problem is difficult to solve. Kimball[8] has treated the question classically by calculating the time elapsed before the amplitude of harmonic oscillations exceeds a critical value such that the energy of the oscillation is equal to the dissociation energy of the molecule.

A third method which is often useful in treating problems where the rate is determined primarily by leakage through an energy barrier may be called the method of beats. If two single minimum potentials are connected by an energy barrier, it is found that the energy levels which lie below the top of the barrier split into two levels of slightly different energy as the width of the barrier is decreased. The amount of splitting is small compared to the energy difference between pairs of levels. The corresponding eigenfunctions have different symmetry with respect to inversion in the origin. The one corresponding to the lowest level of any pair is antisymmetric, that is, it changes sign when the coordinate changes sign; the other eigenfunction is symmetric with regard to inversion. We then see that the function $|\psi_a + \psi_s|^2$ is located almost entirely on the left side of the barrier; the function $|\psi_a - \psi_s|^2$ is located almost entirely on the right side of the barrier. The subscripts s and a refer to the symmetric and antisymmetric eigenfunctions, respectively. We therefore represent a system moving from one side of the barrier to the other by the eigenfunction

$$\Psi = \psi_a e^{-\frac{2\pi i}{h} E_a t} + \psi_s e^{-\frac{2\pi i}{h} E_s t} \qquad 16 \cdot 20$$

The density is given by

$$\Psi^* \Psi = \psi_a^* \psi_a + \psi_s^* \psi_s + \psi_a^* \psi_s e^{-\frac{2\pi i}{h}(E_s - E_a)t} + \psi_a \psi_s^* e^{\frac{2\pi i}{h}(E_s - E_a)t}$$

When $t = 0$,

$$\Psi^* \Psi = |\psi_a + \psi_s|^2$$

and the system is on the left side of the barrier; when $t = \dfrac{h}{2(E_s - E_a)}$,

$$\Psi^* \Psi = |\psi_a - \psi_s|^2$$

[7] N. Rosen, *J. Chem. Phys.*, **1**, 319 (1933).
[8] G. E. Kimball, *J. Chem. Phys.*, **5**, 310 (1937).

and the system is on the right side of the barrier. The frequency

$$\nu = \frac{1}{\tau} = \frac{2(E_s - E_a)}{h}$$

is therefore the rate of penetration of the barrier. As the barrier width increases, $(E_s - E_a)$ decreases and ν decreases. This method is applicable only for small splitting of the energy levels and thus cannot be used to determine the rate of passing *over* the barrier. Of the three methods presented, the method of transmission coefficients, leading to equation 16·15 for the rate, is the most satisfactory from the theoretical viewpoint. The applications of the approximate equation 16·17 have been adequately discussed elsewhere; we wish at this point to investigate the behavior of the transmission coefficients $\kappa_{nk}(p)$ more closely.

16b. General Behavior of the Transmission Coefficient. The transmission coefficients for a number of special types of energy barriers can be calculated exactly; this calculation has already been carried through for a sharp rectangular barrier. A less drastically idealized case has been considered by Eckart.[9] The Eckart potential is

$$V(x) = -\frac{A\xi}{1 - \xi} - \frac{B\xi}{(1 - \xi)^2}; \quad \xi = -e^{-\frac{2\pi x}{l}} \qquad 16\cdot21$$

and the corresponding Schrödinger equation has exact solutions in terms of hypergeometric series. This potential is a step function of the coordinate x; its exact shape is fixed by specifying the constants A, B, and l. We have

$$V(-\infty) = 0, \quad V(+\infty) = A \qquad 16\cdot22$$

For $0 < |B| < |A|$, the potential has a maximum whose height is

$$V_{\max} = \frac{(A + B)^2}{4B} \qquad 16\cdot23$$

The rise in potential is accomplished practically in the distance $2l$. The Schrödinger equation with this potential is

$$\frac{d^2\psi}{dx^2} + \frac{8\pi^2 m}{h^2}\left\{\frac{A\xi}{1 - \xi} + \frac{B\xi}{(1 - \xi)^2} + E\right\}\psi = 0 \qquad 16\cdot24$$

Changing variable from x to ξ gives

$$\xi^2 \frac{d^2\psi}{d\xi^2} + \xi \frac{d\psi}{d\xi} + \frac{2ml^2}{h^2}\left\{\frac{A\xi}{1 - \xi} + \frac{B\xi}{(1 - \xi)^2} + E\right\}\psi = 0 \qquad 16\cdot25$$

[9] C. Eckart, *Phys. Rev.*, **35**, 1303 (1930).

This equation is of the hypergeometric type and has solutions in the form

$$F(a, b, c, y) = 1 + \frac{a \cdot b}{1 \cdot c} y + \frac{a(a+1) \cdot b(b+1)}{1 \cdot 2 \cdot c(c+1)} y^2 + \cdots \qquad 16 \cdot 26$$

Since for large positive or large negative values of x, the potential $16 \cdot 23$ reduces to a constant, the solutions $16 \cdot 26$ should be asymptotic to plane waves with wavelength

$$\lambda = \frac{h}{\sqrt{2mE}} \qquad \text{for } x \to -\infty$$

and

$$\lambda' = \frac{h}{\sqrt{2m(E-A)}} \qquad \text{for } x \to +\infty$$

At $x = +\infty$ there will be a single transmitted wave:

$$e^{\frac{2\pi i x}{\lambda'}} = (-\xi)^{i \frac{l}{\lambda'}} \qquad\qquad 16 \cdot 27$$

At $x = -\infty$ there will be an incident and a reflected wave:

$$a_1 e^{\frac{2\pi i x}{\lambda}} + a_2 e^{-\frac{2\pi i x}{\lambda}} = a_1 (-\xi)^{i \frac{l}{\lambda}} + a_2 (-\xi)^{-i \frac{l}{\lambda}} \qquad 16 \cdot 28$$

The requirement that the exact solution reduce asymptotically to the forms $16 \cdot 27$ and $16 \cdot 28$ determines it uniquely and also determines the coefficients a_1 and a_2. The reflection coefficient is then $\rho = \left|\dfrac{a_2}{a_1}\right|^2$.

A solution of $16 \cdot 25$ which converges for large values of $\xi (x > 1)$ and reduces asymptotically to $(-\xi)^{i\frac{l}{\lambda'}}$ as $|\xi|$ becomes very large is given by

$$\psi = (1-\xi)^{i\beta} \left(\frac{\xi}{\xi-1}\right)^{i\alpha} F\left\{\frac{1}{2} + i(\alpha - \beta + \delta),\right.$$

$$\left. -\frac{1}{2} + i(\alpha - \beta - \delta), \quad 1 - 2i\beta, \quad \frac{1}{1-\xi}\right\} \qquad 16 \cdot 29$$

where

$$\alpha = \frac{l}{\lambda} = \frac{1}{2}\sqrt{\frac{E}{C}}, \quad \beta = \frac{l}{\lambda'} = \frac{1}{2}\sqrt{\frac{E-A}{C}}$$

$$\delta = \frac{1}{2}\sqrt{\frac{B-C}{C}}; \quad C = \frac{h^2}{8ml^2} \qquad 16 \cdot 30$$

That this reduces to $(-\xi)^{i\beta}$ for large ξ is evident since $F(a, b, c, 0) = 1$. Its value for small ξ cannot be determined immediately, however, since $F(a, b, c, 1)$ does not converge. But it is possible to express $16 \cdot 29$ as the sum of two series which do converge for small values of ξ.   We thus find the analytic extension of ψ in the region where its representation by 16·29 does not converge.

Using the known formula, we get

$$\psi = a_1 \left(\frac{\xi}{\xi - 1}\right)^{i\alpha} (1 - \xi)^{i\beta} F \left\{\tfrac{1}{2} + i(\alpha - \beta + \delta),\right.$$

$$\left. -\tfrac{1}{2} + i(\alpha - \beta - \delta),\quad 1 + 2i\alpha,\quad \frac{\xi}{\xi - 1}\right\}$$

$$+ a_2 \left(\frac{\xi}{\xi - 1}\right)^{-i\alpha} (1 - \xi)^{i\beta} F \left\{\tfrac{1}{2} + i(-\alpha - \beta + \delta),\right.$$

$$\left. -\tfrac{1}{2} + i(-\alpha - \beta - \delta),\quad 1 - 2i\alpha,\quad \frac{\xi}{\xi - 1}\right\} \qquad 16\cdot31$$

where

$$a_1 = \frac{\Gamma(1 - 2i\beta)\,\Gamma(-2i\alpha)}{\Gamma\{\tfrac{1}{2} + i(-\alpha - \beta - \delta)\}\,\Gamma\{\tfrac{1}{2} + i(-\alpha - \beta + \delta)\}}$$

$$a_2 = \frac{\Gamma(1 - 2i\beta)\,\Gamma(+2i\alpha)}{\Gamma\{\tfrac{1}{2} + i(\alpha - \beta - \delta)\}\,\Gamma\{\tfrac{1}{2} + i(\alpha - \beta + \delta)\}} \qquad 16\cdot32$$

For small values of ξ, equation 16·31 reduces to equation 16·28 with the values 16·32 for a_1 and a_2.   The reflection coefficient is then given by

$$\rho = \left|\frac{a_2}{a_1}\right|^2 = \left|\frac{\Gamma\{\tfrac{1}{2} + i(\delta - \beta - \alpha)\}\,\Gamma\{\tfrac{1}{2} + i(-\delta - \beta - \alpha)\}}{\Gamma\{\tfrac{1}{2} + i(\delta - \beta + \alpha)\}\,\Gamma\{\tfrac{1}{2} + i(-\delta - \beta + \alpha)\}}\right|^2 \qquad 16\cdot33$$

When the constant C is small, δ is real and applies when the wavelength of the incident particle is short compared to the region where potential is changing.   If the wavelength is long compared to the length l, C will be large and δ will be imaginary.   The expression for ρ is expressed differently in the two cases.   For δ real, we have

$$\rho = \frac{\cosh 2\pi(\alpha - \beta) + \cosh 2\pi\delta}{\cosh 2\pi(\alpha + \beta) + \cosh 2\pi\delta} \qquad 16\cdot34$$

For δ imaginary,

$$\rho = \frac{\cosh 2\pi(\alpha - \beta) + \cos 2\pi|\delta|}{\cosh 2\pi(\alpha + \beta) + \cos 2\pi|\delta|} \qquad 16\cdot35$$

The transmission coefficient is given by $\kappa = 1 - \rho$.

This value of ρ or κ may be used for any potential barrier which is sufficiently well represented by equation 16·23.   The general method, of course, is applicable whenever the exact solutions of the Schrödinger equation corresponding to the given potential are known.   However, many barriers are flatter than that represented by equation 16·23. The question then arises: Under what conditions is it permissible to treat the rising side and the falling side of the potential as independent changes, each having a reflection coefficient given by 16·34 or 16·35? This question has been investigated by Hirschfelder and Wigner.[10] Any irregularity in the potential surface, besides inducing transitions in the reflected and transmitted waves, also sets up non-propagating " diffraction patterns " which may be considered to be exponentially damped standing waves in the vicinity of the irregularity of the potential. If the top of the barrier is wide enough so that these diffraction patterns do not overlap, the transmission coefficients at the two edges may be considered independent. The progressive wave representing the reacting system on the top of the barrier then loses all traces of the effects of one edge before it reaches the other. It then exists in a fairly well-defined quasi-stationary state while it is on the top of the barrier. Under these conditions, it will be permissible to treat the activated complex as a definite molecule with properties which can be calculated from the shape of the potential at the top of the barrier. The potential surface must be flat enough so that the density of reaction complexes, as given by the Boltzmann factor, is sensibly uniform over it, and the flat portion must be wide enough so that the uncertainty in the velocity due to the relationship $\Delta p \, \Delta x \sim h$ is negligibly small. If the potential along the reaction path through the activated state is approximated by the parabola

$$V = V_0 - ax^2$$

these conditions may be expressed in the inequality:

$$h\nu_0 = \frac{h}{2\pi} \sqrt{\frac{a}{M}} \ll kT \qquad 16\cdot36$$

where M is the mass of the complex. It appears very probable that most reactions satisfy this criterion, and it is consequently justifiable to treat the transmission coefficients at the two ends of the activated state as independent.

We may suppose that there is a probability ρ_i that a system entering the activated state will be reflected and a second probability ρ_f that a system leaving the activated state will be reflected. The transmission coefficient κ is the fraction of those systems in the activated state moving from the initial to the final state at thermal equilibrium which originally came from the initial state and which will proceed directly to the final state without returning to the activated state. At thermal equilibrium,

[10] J. Hirschfelder and E. Wigner, *J. Chem. Phys.*, **7**, 616 (1939).

let there be N systems in the activated state, A of which arrive in unit time from the initial state, $N - A = B$ of which arrive from the final state. Of the A systems, $A\rho_f$ will be reflected at the boundary of the activated state and $A(1 - \rho_f)$ will be transmitted. Of those reflected, $A\rho_i\rho_f$ will be reflected at the other edge of the activated state and will

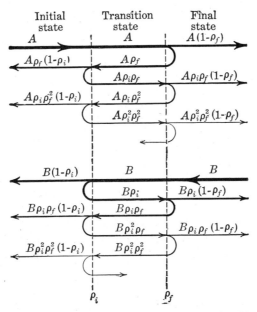

FIG. 16·4. Calculation of transmission coefficients (after Hirschfelder and Wigner).

recross it toward the final state. Figure 16·4 illustrates the flux of systems of various types. Adding up the number of systems crossing from left to right, we find the total number to be

$$N_{l\to r} = A(1 + \rho_i\rho_f + \rho_i^2\rho_f^2 + \cdots) + B\rho_i(1 + \rho_i\rho_f + \rho_i^2\rho_f^2 + \cdots)$$
$$= (A + B\rho_i)(1 - \rho_i\rho_f)^{-1} \qquad 16\cdot37$$

Similarly, the number crossing from right to left is

$$N_{r\to l} = (A\rho_f + B)(1 - \rho_i\rho_f)^{-1} \qquad 16\cdot38$$

At equilibrium, equal numbers of systems will be moving in each direction, that is, $N_{l\to r} = N_{r\to l}$, so that

$$B = \frac{A(1 - \rho_f)}{(1 - \rho_i)} \qquad 16\cdot39$$

Substituting this expression into 16·37 gives

$$N_{l \to r} = \frac{A}{(1 - \rho_i)} \qquad 16\cdot40$$

But the number of systems originating in the initial state which proceed to the final state is, by addition,

$$N_{i \to f} = \frac{A(1 - \rho_f)}{(1 - \rho_i \rho_f)} \qquad 16\cdot41$$

and the transmission coefficient is the ratio

$$\kappa = \frac{N_{i \to f}}{N_{l \to r}} = \frac{(1 - \rho_i)(1 - \rho_f)}{(1 - \rho_i \rho_f)} \qquad 16\cdot42$$

This expression for κ is the average for a great many systems in thermal equilibrium, whose energies consequently differ slightly. The transmission of a single quantum state will depend critically upon the energy of the system, as we shall see, but averaging over a range of energies gives an average transmission coefficient which agrees with equation 16·42.

We can complete the calculation of κ for the Eckart potential. Taking $B = 0$ reduces the barrier to a simple step of energy A with no maximum in V. For this special case the reflection coefficient is

$$\rho = \left[\frac{e^{\frac{2\pi l}{h}(p-q)} - 1}{e^{\frac{2\pi l}{h}(p+q)} - 1} \right]^2 e^{\frac{4\pi l}{h} q} \qquad 16\cdot43$$

where $p = \sqrt{2mE}$ and $q = \sqrt{2m(E - A)}$ are the momenta in the initial (or final) and activated states, respectively. For an abrupt energy change, $l = 0$, and the transmission coefficient becomes

$$\bar{\kappa} = \frac{4qp_i p_f}{(q^2 + p_i p_f)(p_i + p_f)} \qquad 16\cdot44$$

where p_i, q, and p_f are the momenta of the system in the initial, activated, and final states, respectively. This value for $\bar{\kappa}$ may be compared with the exact result for a rectangular barrier, as determined earlier in this chapter. If we take the expression analogous to 16·11 and reduce the determinants, we find for the transmission coefficient the result

$$\kappa = \frac{4q^2 p_i p_f}{q^2(p_i + p_f)^2 \cos^2 \varphi + (q^2 + p_i p_f)^2 \sin^2 \varphi}; \quad \varphi = \frac{2\pi q}{h} d \qquad 16\cdot45$$

where d is the barrier width. If this equation is averaged over φ, that is, over a range of momenta in the activated state, the result is identical with equation 16·44 for $\bar{\kappa}$. κ covers a cycle in its oscillation as φ goes from 0 to 2π or as q goes from 0 to $\dfrac{h}{d}$. Thus, for wide barriers, the oscillation in κ as the momentum in the activated state is increased becomes more rapid, and averaging over a small range of momenta smooths out the oscillations more completely. Thus the treatment of p_i and p_f as independent is justified in a statistical sense as giving the average transmission coefficient over a band of energies when the barrier is sufficiently wide.

In an n-atom system a decrease in momentum as the system passes from the initial to the activated state means that some of the initial translational energy has been converted to vibrational energy. To consider such a possibility, we must treat the problem in more dimensions. An abrupt increase in potential in a straight channel of parabolic cross section will illustrate the essential features of the two-dimensional case. Let us designate by X the coordinate along the channel, and that perpendicular to the bottom of the channel by x. We consider an abrupt change in the potential at $X = 0$, i.e., for $X < 0$, let $V_i = A + a_i x^2$; for $X > 0$, let $V_f = a_f x^2$. In the left-hand region, the Schrödinger equation

$$\mathbf{H}_i \psi_k = I_k \psi_k$$

with potential V_i, must be satisfied. On the right side of the potential drop, the equation to be satisfied is

$$\mathbf{H}_f \varphi_k = F_k \varphi_k$$

with potential V_f. The φ's may be expanded in terms of the ψ's as

$$\varphi_k(x) = \sum u_{lk} \psi_l(x) \qquad 16\text{·}46$$

An incident wave from the left has the form $\psi_l(x) e^{\frac{2\pi i}{h} q_l X}$ and gives rise to a reflected beam in which the systems have all possible quantum numbers m for their motion in the x direction. Thus the wave function for $X < 0$ is

$$\psi_l e^{\frac{2\pi i}{h} q_l X} + \sum_{m=0}^{\infty} R_{lm} \psi_m e^{-\frac{2\pi i}{h} q_m X} \qquad 16\text{·}47$$

and the total energy of the system is given by

$$E = \frac{q_l^2}{2M} + I_l \qquad 16\text{·}48$$

For $X > 0$, there is only an outgoing wave

$$\sum_{k=0}^{\infty} T_{lk}\varphi_k e^{\frac{2\pi i}{h}p_k X} = \sum_{k, m} T_{lk}u_{km}\psi_m e^{\frac{2\pi i}{h}p_k X} \qquad 16\cdot49$$

and the energy is

$$E = \frac{p_k^2}{2M} + F_k \qquad 16\cdot50$$

For high quantum numbers, the momenta p_k and q_k are imaginary, and the corresponding wave function represents a local non-propagating disturbance in the neighborhood of the discontinuity. These imaginary momenta, when divided by i, must be positive to represent exponentially decreasing disturbances.

Both the wave function and its derivative must be continuous at $X = 0$. Equating 16·47 and 16·49 and their derivatives with respect to X at $X = 0$, and comparing coefficients of ψ_m, gives

$$\delta_{lm} + R_{lm} = \sum_k T_{lk}u_{km}$$

$$\delta_{lm}q_l - R_{lm}q_m = \sum_k T_{lk}u_{km}p_k \qquad 16\cdot51$$

These equations may be solved for R_{lm} and T_{lk} by the methods of matrix algebra. The results are

$$R = (\xi - 1)(\xi + 1)^{-1}$$
$$T = 2\xi(\xi + 1)^{-1}u^{-1} \qquad 16\cdot52$$

where ξ is the infinite square matrix $\xi = qu^{-1}p^{-1}u$. From the wave function 16·47 we see that the number of systems with quantum number l which are incident in unit time is $\dfrac{q_l}{M}$, that is, density times velocity.

Similarly the number reflected with quantum number m is $\left|R_{lm}\right|^2 \dfrac{q_m}{M}$, so that the probability of reflection with quantum number m is $\left|R_{lm}\right|^2 \dfrac{q_m}{q_l}$. In the same way we see that the probability of transmission with quantum number k is $\left|T_{lk}\right|^2 \dfrac{p_k}{q_l}$.

Equations 16·52 are only a formal solution, since we have not evaluated the matrix elements of ξ. This can be done for the case where the total energy E is much greater than the energy of the highest vibrational state F_k to which there is likely to be a transition. This means that the translational energy in the final state will be large compared with the vibrational energy, though this need not have been true in the initial state.   The results of this calculation show that the reflection coefficients for no change in vibrational quantum number are slightly smaller than those calculated for one dimension, owing to the possibility

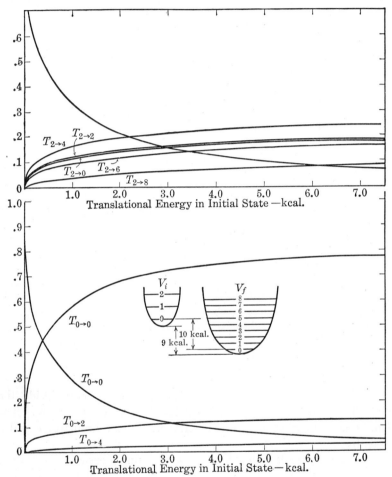

FIG. 16·5.   Probabilities of reflection and transmission at abrupt drop of 9 kcal. in potential energy when vibrational frequency changes simultaneously from $h\nu_i = 4$ kcal. to $h\nu_f = 2$ kcal. (after Hirschfelder and Wigner).

for reflection with simultaneous change in vibrational quantum number. To the approximations made, such changes can be either 0 or ± 2 for the reflected wave; the transmitted wave may have any quantum number differing by an even integer from that of the initial state.

In Figure 16·5 the calculated transmission and reflection probabilities are plotted.   It is evident that the probability of a vibrational transition is not large and that it decreases with increasing initial translational energy.   It thus appears that the interchange of translational and vibrational energy has little effect on the transmission coefficient, at least as long as the translational energy is large in the final state.

The effect of curvature of the reaction path on the transmission probability may be investigated in the same manner.   A convenient energy surface to consider is that formed by the channel between two

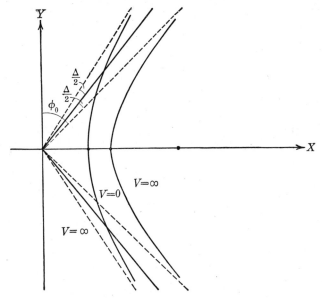

Fig. 16·6.   Hyperbolic reaction path.

confocal hyperbolas, Figure 16·6.   The potential energy inside the channel is taken to be $V = 0$; outside the channel, $V = \infty$.   The Schrödinger equation is separable in the elliptic coordinates μ and φ given by

$$x = R \cosh \mu \sin \varphi \qquad y = R \sinh \mu \cos \varphi \qquad 16\cdot53$$

into two equations: the equation in μ describes the motion parallel to the reaction path, and the equation in φ describes motion perpendicular to the reaction path.   These equations are

$$\frac{d^2 U}{d\mu^2} + \frac{8\pi^2 M R^2}{h^2} \left(\frac{E}{2}\cosh 2\mu - \lambda\right) U = 0 \qquad 16\cdot54$$

$$\frac{d^2 \Phi}{d\varphi^2} + \frac{8\pi^2 M R^2}{h^2} \left(\frac{E}{2}\cos 2\varphi + \lambda\right) \Phi = 0 \qquad 16\cdot55$$

where R is the focal length of the hyperbolas, E is the total energy of the system, and λ is the separation parameter to be determined by the boundary conditions. The lines $\varphi = \varphi_0$ are the hyperbolas

$$\frac{x^2}{\sin^2 \varphi_0} - \frac{y^2}{\cos^2 \varphi_0} = R^2 \qquad 16\cdot56$$

whose asymptotes have the slope $\dfrac{dy}{dx} = \cot \varphi_0$, so that φ_0 is the angle between the asymptote and the y axis. If the angle between the asymptotes of the two bounding hyperbolas is denoted by Δ, the boundary condition is that $\Phi = 0$ on the two hyperbolas whose asymptotes are given by $\varphi = \varphi_0 + \dfrac{\Delta}{2}$ and $\varphi = \varphi_0 - \dfrac{\Delta}{2}$.

Equation 16·55 is now solved for Φ, and the allowed values of λ are determined. When these values are substituted into equation 16·54 it becomes a one-dimensional equation for the translational motion of the system through the channel. For low values of E and for $\Delta < 30°$, the characteristic values for λ may be developed in a power series in Δ.[11] Up to terms in Δ^2, the allowed values of λ are

$$\lambda = \frac{h^2 n^2}{8MW^2} \cos^2 \varphi_0 - \frac{E}{2} \cos 2\varphi_0 \qquad 16\cdot57$$

where W is the width of the channel at its narrowest point. With this value of λ, equation 16·54 is a one-dimensional equation for motion parallel to the reaction path φ_0. It is not in the usual form, since the energy E is multiplied by a function of the coordinates. Making the transformation

$$\chi = U\sqrt[4]{\sinh^2 \mu + \cos^2 \varphi_0}$$

$$s = R \int_0^\mu \sqrt{\sinh^2 \mu + \cos^2 \varphi_0}\, d\mu \qquad 16\cdot58$$

equation 16·54 becomes

$$\frac{d^2\chi}{ds^2} + \frac{8\pi^2 M}{h^2}(E - V_{\varphi_0} - V_\lambda)\chi = 0 \qquad 16\cdot59$$

where

$$V_{\varphi_0} = \frac{h^2}{8\pi^2 MR^2} \left[\frac{\frac{3}{2} - \frac{1}{2}\cosh^2 2\mu + 2\cosh 2\mu \cos 2\varphi_0}{(\cosh 2\mu + \cos 2\varphi_0)^3} \right]$$

[11] R. Langer, *Trans. Am. Math. Soc.*, **36**, 637 (1934).

$$V_\lambda = \frac{h^2 n^2 \cos^2 \varphi_0}{8MW^2 \cdot \frac{1}{2} (\cosh 2\mu + \cos 2\varphi_0)}$$

The coordinate s is measured along the reaction path with $s = 0$ at the narrowest point of the channel.

Classically, every system which began the journey through the hyperbolic channel would get through. However, equation 16·59 shows that the quantum-mechanical wave packet encounters an effective barrier. This barrier may be ascribed to two causes. The largest part of it is V_λ, which arises from the increasing zero-point energy of vibration as the channel narrows. In order to get through the neck of the channel, the system must have sufficient translational energy initially to overcome the increased zero-point energy of vibration in the narrow neck. The second part of the effective barrier is much smaller, of the order of 0.3 kcal. per mole at most. At large distances, the potential V_{φ_0} is attractive, but it goes through a maximum at the activated state, adding to the effect of V_λ. It arises from the transformation of coordinates made in equation 16·54 and may be considered analogous to the centrifugal potential which appears in discussions of the motion of a particle which is constrained to move in a circular orbit. From the wave viewpoint, the attractive minimum corresponds to a focusing effect similar to that observed with light reflected from concave mirrors. In regions where V_{φ_0} is low there is a concentration of systems, due to the Boltzmann distribution, similar to the concentration of light intensity at some points in front of a curved mirror.

We may conclude from this example that the effect of curvature of the reaction path is to introduce a virtual potential barrier at which there will be a reflection probability given by equation 16·44 or 16·45. However, it is important to note that for a hyperbolic channel there can be no interaction of vibration and translation, since the Schrödinger equation is exactly separable in the coordinates corresponding to these motions. This, as we have seen, is never completely realized in actual reactions, although for many reactions it may be a good approximation.

The transmission coefficient for a surface where vibrational transitions do take place may be calculated for a channel having vertical parallel walls which makes a 90° turn. Here, as in dealing with the straight parabolic channel, it is necessary to join solutions of the Schrödinger equation for each of the three regions shown in Figure 16·7. If the width of the channel is l and the origin of coordinates is at the outside corner, then, for $x > l$, $0 \leq y \leq l$, there is an incident wave moving to the left on which is superposed a number of reflected waves moving to the right, so that the wave function is

$$\psi_k^I = e^{-\frac{2\pi i}{h}p_{kx}} \sin \frac{\pi k}{l} y + \sum_{j=0}^{\infty} R_{kj} e^{\frac{2\pi i}{h}p_{jx}} \sin \frac{\pi j}{l} y \qquad 16 \cdot 60$$

For $0 \le x \le l, 0 \le y \le l$, the wave function must satisfy the boundary conditions

$$\psi(x, 0) = \psi(0, y) = \psi(l, l) = 0$$

Such a function is

$$\psi_k^{II} = \sum_j \left[A_{kj} \sin \frac{2\pi p_j}{h} x \sin \frac{\pi j}{l} y + B_{kj} \sin \frac{\pi j}{l} x \sin \frac{2\pi p_j}{h} y \right] \qquad 16 \cdot 61$$

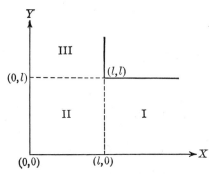

FIG. 16·7. Reaction path with 90° turn.

In region III, where $y > l, 0 \le x \le l$, there are only the outgoing waves

$$\psi_k^{III} = \sum_j T_{kj} e^{\frac{2\pi i}{h}p_{jy}} \sin \frac{\pi j}{l} x \qquad 16 \cdot 62$$

At $x = l$ we must have

$$\psi_k^I(l, y) = \psi_k^{II}(l, y); \quad \frac{\partial \psi_k^I}{\partial x}\bigg]_{x=l} = \frac{\partial \psi_k^{II}}{\partial x}\bigg]_{x=l} \qquad 16 \cdot 63$$

Similarly, at $y = l$ we must have

$$\psi_k^{II}(x, l) = \psi_k^{III}(x, l); \quad \frac{\partial \psi_k^{II}}{\partial y}\bigg]_{y=l} = \frac{\partial \psi_k^{III}}{\partial y}\bigg]_{y=l} \qquad 16 \cdot 64$$

If we expand $\sin \frac{2\pi p_j}{h} x$ in terms of $\sin \frac{\pi j}{l} x$, we can write down the four

equations indicated above and compare coefficients of $\sin \frac{\pi j}{l} x$. This gives

$$R_{kj} = \left[A_{kj} \sin \frac{2\pi p_j}{h} l - e^{-\frac{2\pi i}{h} p_j l} \delta_{kj} \right] e^{-\frac{2\pi i}{h} p_j l}$$

$$\frac{2\pi i}{h} p_j \left[R_{kj} e^{\frac{2\pi i}{h} p_j l} - e^{-\frac{2\pi i}{h} p_j l} \delta_{kj} \right]$$

$$= A_{kj} \frac{2\pi}{h} p_j \cos \frac{2\pi p_j}{h} l + \sum_n (-1)^n \frac{\pi n}{l} B_{kn} C_{nj}$$

$$T_{kj} = B_{kj} \sin \frac{2\pi p_j}{h} l e^{-\frac{2\pi i}{h} p_j l} \qquad 16\cdot 65$$

$$\frac{2\pi i}{h} p_j T_{kj} e^{\frac{2\pi i}{h} p_j l} = B_{kj} \frac{2\pi}{h} p_j \cos \frac{2\pi p_j}{h} l + \sum_n (-1)^n \frac{\pi n}{l} A_{kn} C_{nj}$$

where

$$C_{nj} = \frac{2}{l} \int_0^l \sin \frac{2\pi p_j}{h} x \sin \frac{\pi j}{l} x \, dx$$

The solution of these equations gives for the matrices of the coefficients A_{kj} and B_{kj} the results

$$A = -2i(1 - G^2)^{-1}$$

$$B = -2i(1 - G^2)^{-1} G \qquad 16\cdot 66$$

where G is a matrix with elements given by

$$G_{kj} = \frac{(-1)^{k+j} 2\pi^2 kj \sin \frac{2\pi}{h} p_{kl} e^{-\frac{2\pi i}{h} p_j}}{\frac{2\pi}{h} p_j l \left[\left(\frac{2\pi}{h} p_k l \right)^2 - \pi^2 j^2 \right]} \qquad 16\cdot 67$$

For a given total energy p_k can be calculated for different values of k and the matrix elements evaluated. Equations 16·65 then give the amplitudes of the reflected and transmitted waves.

Inspection of equation 16·67 shows that, if $\frac{p_j l}{h}$ is equal to some integer n, there is no transmission. Such energies correspond to resonant frequencies for region II. The transmission coefficient is consequently an oscillating function of the energy of the system, as it is for a one-dimensional barrier. Figure 16·8 shows the density of transmitted systems in the first and second vibrational states if the incident wave is in the lowest vibrational state. In contrast to the results for a straight channel, it is seen that the probability of a vibrational transition upon turning the corner is quite high. That this is not a peculiarity of the sharpness of the corner is evident from the classical consideration of two straight channels joined by a circular section, as in Figure 16·9. Let

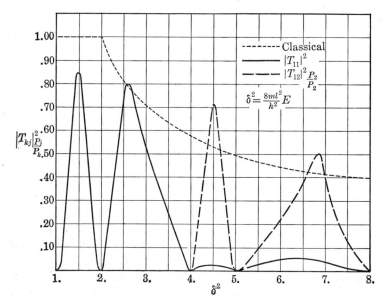

FIG. 16·8. Density of transmitted systems for 90° turn.

the last collision with the walls of the straight section be just at the point where the circular section begins. Inspection of the geometry of the figure shows that, unless the circular channel has a certain very definite length, the component of velocity perpendicular to the reaction path will be altered in passing around the corner. This is equivalent to a change in the vibrational quantum state of the system.

From these results, we are led to the conclusion that, though a barrier does not very often cause a vibrational transition in the reacting system, a bend in the reaction path nearly always induces transitions to the highest vibrational state consistent with the total energy of the system. A system moving slowly in the initial state has less chance of surmounting the barrier but more of turning a corner than one with a high initial velocity. Actually, it is seldom

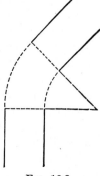

FIG. 16·9.

that the sharpest bend in the reaction path occurs just at the activated state; usually it occurs just after the system has passed through the activated state and consequently is moving slowly. It thus seems unlikely that large reflections due to a bend occur in practice.

It will be noted that the energy unit in Figure 16·8 is inversely proportional to the effective mass of the reacting system. Consequently it will be different for different isotopic compounds. Thus if $\delta^2 = 3$ for the complex H + HCl, it will be 6 for D + HCl. The transmission coefficients are markedly different. The extent to which this difference is realized in practice depends upon the degree to which the maxima in the transmission coefficient average out as the result of the thermal energy distribution. For reactions involving light atoms, the zero-point energy is so high that averaging over the thermal spread may not affect the peaks to any great extent. However, the potential used in calculating Figure 16·8 is highly idealized. If the incoming channel is narrower than the outgoing the width of the peaks is much diminished. Furthermore, any smoothing of the sharp corner ought to increase the rapidity of oscillation of the transmission coefficient, so that it appears that only exceptionally should there be any noticeable experimental result from these peaks. In reactions involving isotope separations, the slight differences in transmission coefficient of the isotopes may well be important. It should also be observed that the classical transmission coefficient rapidly becomes equal to the average of the quantum-mechanical transmission coefficient. For all ordinary cases it thus appears justifiable to calculate the transmission coefficients on a classical basis.

16c. Transition Probability in Non-Adiabatic Reactions.[12,13] We have considered so far only those reactions which proceed on one energy surface. Frequently, however, two such surfaces come very close together or, in fact, appear to cross each other. Actually, at the point of the apparent crossing the system is degenerate, since the two different electronic configurations have the same energy. This introduces a resonance energy which separates the surfaces slightly so that they never actually intersect but only approach each other closely, as has been explained in section 11d. This state of affairs is typified by a diatomic molecule which has both homopolar and ionic states. Figure 16·10 is a plot of the energy as a function of the interatomic distance for such a molecule. The electronic eigenfunctions are ψ_1 and ψ_2. For $r \gg r_0$, ψ_1 is ionic in nature and ψ_2 is homopolar; for $r \ll r_0$, the roles are reversed. If the molecule is initially in state ψ_2 (homopolar) and the internuclear distance r increases infinitely slowly, the molecule will remain in state ψ_2 for $r \gg r_0$. But if r changes with a finite velocity, there will be a finite probability that the molecule will change from

[12] C. Zener, *Proc. Roy. Soc., London*, **A137**, 696; **A140**, 660 (1933).
[13] L. Landau, *Physik. Z. Sowjetunion*, **2**, 46 (1932).

ψ_2 to ψ_1 as it passes $r = r_0$ so that its final electronic state will be represented by a linear combination

$$\psi = A_1(r)\psi_1 + A_2(r)\psi_2 \qquad 16\cdot68$$

For convenience in calculating A_1 and A_2, however, we shall express ψ_1 and ψ_2 in terms of two other wave functions φ_1 and φ_2, defined so that

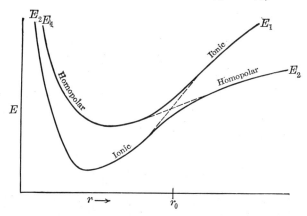

FIG. 16·10.   " Crossing " of energy surfaces (schematic).

φ_1 is equal to ψ_1 for $r \gg r_0$, that is, ionic in this example, but φ_1 remains ionic in character for all r.   Similarly, φ_2 is equal to ψ_2 for large r (homopolar) and remains homopolar in character for all r.   The energies ϵ_1

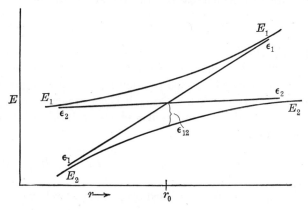

FIG. 16·11.   Energy relations at point of " crossing."

and ϵ_2 corresponding to φ_1 and φ_2 intersect when plotted as functions of the internuclear distance r (Figure 16·11).   Consequently φ_1 and φ_2 are not exact eigenfunctions of the complete Hamiltonian for the system, and their eigenvalues ϵ_1 and ϵ_2 are only approximate; actually they are eigenvalues for the Hamiltonian which does not include the interaction energy ϵ_{12} between the two states φ_1 and φ_2. At the point of crossing we have $E_1 = \epsilon_1 - \epsilon_{12}$ and $E_2 = \epsilon_2 + \epsilon_{12}$, where ϵ_{12} is the difference between the exact eigenvalues E_1 and E_2 and the approximate eigenvalues ϵ_1 and ϵ_2. If we choose φ_1, φ_2, ψ_1, ψ_2 to be normalized and orthogonal we must have

$$\psi_1 = \frac{1}{\sqrt{2}}(\varphi_1 + \varphi_2); \quad \psi_2 = \frac{1}{\sqrt{2}}(\varphi_1 - \varphi_2) \qquad 16\cdot69$$

Then, since

$$\mathbf{H}\psi_1 = E_1\psi_1; \quad \mathbf{H}\psi_2 = E_2\psi_2 \qquad 16\cdot70$$

we readily see that

$$\mathbf{H}\varphi_1 = \epsilon_1\varphi_1 - \epsilon_{12}\varphi_2$$
$$\mathbf{H}\varphi_2 = \epsilon_2\varphi_2 - \epsilon_{12}\varphi_1 \qquad 16\cdot71$$

We now consider the state of the system in terms of φ_1 and φ_2 as it passes through $r = r_0$. Suppose that initially it is in the state ψ_2. The final state will be given by equation 16·68. But this can also be expressed in terms of φ_1 and φ_2, if we consider the state of the system to vary with the time rather than with the internuclear distance. φ_1 and φ_2 are not functions of t; they do not, however, represent steady states, since systems are jumping from φ_1 to φ_2 at the crossing. We must therefore write for the final state of the system the expression

$$\psi = c_1(t)e^{\frac{2\pi i}{h}\epsilon_1 t}\varphi_1(r) + c_2(t)e^{\frac{2\pi i}{h}\epsilon_2 t}\varphi_2(r) \qquad 16\cdot72$$

At any time t_0, there are $|c_1(t_0)|^2$ systems in the state φ_1 and $|c_2(t_0)|^2$ in the state φ_2. It is thus necessary to consider the time rate of change of c_1 and c_2 at any convenient fixed position r_1. Since we know the relation of φ_1 to ψ_1 and φ_2 to ψ_2 for $r \gg r_0$, it is convenient to take r_1 at ∞. We now study the time variation of ψ given by 16·72, using the time-dependent Schrödinger equation:

$$\left(\mathbf{H} - \frac{h}{2\pi i}\frac{\partial}{\partial t}\right)\left\{c_1(t)e^{\frac{2\pi i}{h}\epsilon_1 t}\varphi_1(r) + c_2(t)e^{\frac{2\pi i}{h}\epsilon_2 t}\varphi_2(r)\right\} = 0 \qquad 16\cdot73$$

Substituting equation 16·71, satisfied by φ_1 and φ_2, we have

$$\frac{h}{2\pi i}\frac{\partial c_1}{\partial t} = \epsilon_{12}e^{-\frac{2\pi i}{h}(\epsilon_1 - \epsilon_2)t}c_2$$
$$\frac{h}{2\pi i}\frac{\partial c_2}{\partial t} = \epsilon_{12}e^{\frac{2\pi i}{h}(\epsilon_1 - \epsilon_2)t}c_1 \qquad 16\cdot74$$

These equations must be solved simultaneously subject to the boundary conditions

$$c_1(-\infty) = 0 \qquad |c_2(-\infty)| = 1 \qquad \text{16·75}$$

which correspond to our knowledge that initially, $t = -\infty$, for $r \gg r_0$, the system is in the state φ_2, equivalent to ψ_2. The probability of a non-adiabatic transition is $|A_1(r \gg r_0)|^2$ in equation 16·68. Denoting this by P, we have

$$P = |A_1(r \gg r_0)|^2 = |c_2(\infty)|^2 = 1 - |c_1(\infty)|^2 \qquad \text{16·76}$$

Equations 16·74 need be solved only for their asymptotic values of c_1 and c_2. Eliminating c_2 from 16·74 gives

$$\frac{d^2 c_1}{dt^2} + \left\{ \frac{2\pi i}{h} (\epsilon_1 - \epsilon_2) - \frac{1}{\epsilon_{12}} \frac{\partial \epsilon_{12}}{\partial t} \right\} \frac{dc_1}{dt} + \left(\frac{2\pi \epsilon_{12}}{h} \right)^2 c_1 = 0 \qquad \text{16·77}$$

We now simplify this equation by means of the following assumptions.

(a) $\epsilon_{12}(r_0) \ll$ the relative kinetic energy of the two systems. When this is true, the motion of the centers of gravity of the two atoms is so fast that this motion will have a negligible effect on ϵ_{12} during a crossing.

(b) The transition region is so small that we may regard $\epsilon_1 - \epsilon_2$ as a linear function of the time, and ϵ_{12}, φ_1, and φ_2 as independent of the time. This is true if ϵ_{12} is sufficiently small.

We therefore write

$$\frac{2\pi}{h} (\epsilon_1 - \epsilon_2) = \alpha t$$

$$\frac{\partial \epsilon_{12}}{\partial t} = \frac{\partial \varphi_1}{\partial t} = \frac{\partial \varphi_2}{\partial t} = 0 \qquad \text{16·78}$$

This means that $\epsilon_1(r)$ and $\epsilon_2(r)$ are the asymptotes to the curves $E_1(r)$ and $E_2(r)$ in the region of the crossing. The smallest separation of E_1 and E_2 is $E_1(r_0) - E_2(r_0) = 2\epsilon_{12}(r_0)$.

The assumptions 16·78, together with the substitutions

$$f = \frac{2\pi \epsilon_{12}}{h}; \quad c_1 = e^{-\frac{\pi i}{h}(\epsilon_1 - \epsilon_2)t} U_1 \qquad \text{16·79}$$

reduce equation 16·77 to the form

$$\frac{d^2 U_1}{dt^2} + \left(f^2 - \frac{i\alpha}{2} + \frac{\alpha^2 t^2}{4} \right) U_1 = 0 \qquad \text{16·80}$$

The solution of this differential equation, subject to the boundary conditions 16·75, gives for the asymptotic value of $|c_1(\infty)|^2$ the result

$$|c_1(\infty)|^2 = 1 - e^{-2\pi \gamma} \qquad \text{16·81}$$

where

$$\gamma = \frac{2\pi}{h} \frac{\epsilon_{12}^2}{\left|\frac{d}{dt}(\epsilon_1 - \epsilon_2)\right|^2} \qquad 16\cdot82$$

Therefore

$$P = e^{-2\pi\gamma} \qquad 16\cdot83$$

The denominator in 16·82 can be expressed as

$$\left|\frac{d}{dt}(\epsilon_1 - \epsilon_2)\right| = V\left|\frac{\partial\epsilon_1}{\partial r} - \frac{\partial\epsilon_2}{\partial r}\right| = V|s_1 - s_2| \qquad 16\cdot84$$

where $V = \dfrac{dr}{dt}$ is the velocity with which a system crosses $r = r_0$ and $|s_1 - s_2|$ is the difference of the slopes of the two crossing potential surfaces at $r = r_0$. We have

$$P = e^{-\frac{4\pi^2\epsilon_{12}^2}{hV|s_1 - s_2|}} \qquad 16\cdot85$$

for the probability of a transition, that is, of " non-adiabatic " behavior. The probability that a system stay on the initial energy surface is then

$$P' = 1 - e^{-\frac{4\pi^2\epsilon_{12}^2}{hV|s_1 - s_2|}} \qquad 16\cdot86$$

16d. Thermodynamics of Reaction Rates and the Effect of Applied External Forces. Returning to equation 16·17, we may formally write it

$$k' = \kappa \frac{kT}{h} \frac{F^{\ddagger}}{F_1 F_2 \cdots} e^{-\frac{V_0}{kT}} = \kappa \frac{kT}{h} K^{\ddagger} \qquad 16\cdot87$$

where $K^{\ddagger}$ is the constant for the equilibrium between the activated complex and the reactant molecules. Using the thermodynamic relation $-\Delta F = RT \log K$, we may write 16·87 as

$$k' = \kappa \frac{kT}{h} e^{-\frac{\Delta F^{\ddagger}}{RT}} \qquad 16\cdot88$$

where $\Delta F^{\ddagger}$ is the difference in free energy between the activated and normal states and is called the " free energy of activation." Since $\Delta F = \Delta H - T\Delta S$, we also have

$$k' = \kappa \frac{kT}{h} e^{-\frac{\Delta H^{\ddagger}}{RT}} e^{\frac{\Delta S^{\ddagger}}{R}} \qquad 16\cdot89$$

Equations 16·88 and 16·89 have proved to be very useful in the interpretation and correlation of experimental data.[2, 14, 15]

Equation 16·88 may readily be extended to include the effect of an applied external force. Let $\Delta F^{\ddagger}$ be the free energy of activation for a given process in the absence of the external force. Then if an applied force has a component f along the reaction path, and if this force acts through a distance $\frac{x}{2}$ from the normal to the activated state, the free energy of activation will be decreased by an amount $\frac{fx}{2}$. The specific forward rate in the presence of the external force will thus be

$$k_f = \kappa \frac{kT}{h} e^{-\frac{\left(\Delta F^{\ddagger} - \frac{Nfx}{2}\right)}{RT}} = k_0 e^{\frac{fx}{2kT}} \qquad 16\cdot 90$$

where k_0 is the rate in the absence of the external force and N is Avogadro's number.

In the same way there is a backward rate against the field of

$$k_b = k_0 e^{-\frac{fx}{2kT}} \qquad 16\cdot 91$$

This gives a net rate of

$$k' = k_f - k_b = k_0 \left(e^{\frac{fx}{2kT}} - e^{-\frac{fx}{2kT}} \right) = 2k_0 \sinh \frac{fx}{2kT} \qquad 16\cdot 92$$

and hence a net forward velocity of

$$\lambda k' = 2\lambda k_0 \sinh \frac{fx}{2kT} \qquad 16.93$$

Here λ is the average distance traveled per jump, which may, or may not, equal x.[16]

Elaborations of 16·92 and 16·93 have been successfully applied to the study of a wide variety of physical problems, including viscosity, diffusion, plastic deformation, and electrochemical phenomena.[2]

[14] M. G. Evans and M. Polanyi, *Trans. Faraday Soc.*, **31**, 876 (1935).
[15] W. F. K. Wynne-Jones and H. Eyring, *J. Chem. Phys.*, **3**, 493 (1935).
[16] H. Eyring, *J. Chem. Phys.*, **4**, 283 (1936).

CHAPTER XVII

ELECTRIC AND MAGNETIC PHENOMENA*

17a. Moments Induced by an Electromagnetic Field. In order to discuss the phenomenon of optical rotatory power, as well as certain other phenomena, we need expressions for the electric and magnetic moments induced in an atomic or molecular system by an electromagnetic field. The procedure to be followed in calculating these moments will be quite similar to that in Chapter VIII in the discussion of radiation theory.

The wave functions for the unperturbed molecule will be of the form

$$\Psi^0 = \psi^0 e^{-i\frac{E}{\hbar}t}$$

Let the normal state of the molecule be Ψ_a^0. Then, in the presence of an electromagnetic field the wave function for the molecule may be written as

$$\Psi = \Psi_a^0 + \sum_b c_b(t)\Psi_b^0 \qquad 17\cdot1$$

where

$$\frac{dc_b}{dt} = -\frac{i}{\hbar}(\Psi_b^{0*}|\mathbf{H}'|\Psi_a^0)$$

and

$$\mathbf{H}' = -\sum \frac{e}{m_j c}\mathbf{A}^j \cdot \mathbf{p}^j$$

In equation 17·1 the assumption has been made that the coefficients of all wave functions except Ψ_a^0 are very small.

In developing the principles of radiation theory we made the approximation that $\mathbf{A}$ could be regarded as constant over the molecule; this assumption gave the result that the probability of a transition between two states was proportional to the matrix element for the electric dipole moment between the two states. For the discussion of optical rotatory power this approximation is insufficient. The value of $\mathbf{A}$ at any point in the molecule may be expressed by a Taylor's series expansion in terms

* See General References.

of the value of $\mathbf{A}$ and its derivatives at the origin of a coordinate system fixed in the molecule. For the x component of $\mathbf{A}$ at the position occupied by the jth particle in the molecule we will have, neglecting higher terms:

$$A_x^j = A_x^0 + x^j \left(\frac{\partial A_x}{\partial x}\right)_0 + y^j \left(\frac{\partial A_x}{\partial y}\right)_0 + z^j \left(\frac{\partial A_x}{\partial z}\right)_0 \qquad 17\cdot2$$

To this approximation the perturbation $\mathbf{H}'$ may be written as

$$\mathbf{H}' = -\frac{e}{c} \sum_j \frac{1}{m_j} \left\{ \mathbf{A}^0 \cdot \mathbf{p}^j + \tfrac{1}{2}(\nabla \times \mathbf{A})_0 \cdot (\mathbf{r}^j \times \mathbf{p}^j) + \begin{Bmatrix} \text{Terms} \\ \text{representing} \\ \text{quadripole} \\ \text{moment} \end{Bmatrix} \right\} \qquad 17\cdot3$$

The first and second terms in $\mathbf{H}'$ include the operators for the electric and magnetic dipole moments, respectively. The electric quadripole moment will be of no importance for our purposes; hence this term in $\mathbf{H}'$ will be disregarded. The matrix element $(\Psi_b^{0*}|\mathbf{H}'|\Psi_a^0)$ is therefore

$$(\Psi_b^{0*}|\mathbf{H}'|\Psi_a^0) = -\left\{ \frac{1}{c} \left(\Psi_b^{0*} \left| e \sum_j \frac{1}{m_j} \mathbf{p}^j \right| \Psi_a^0 \right) \cdot \mathbf{A}^0 \right.$$

$$\left. + \left(\Psi_b^{0*} \left| \sum_j \frac{e}{2m_j c} (\mathbf{r}^j \times \mathbf{p}^j) \right| \Psi_a^0 \right) \cdot (\nabla \times \mathbf{A})_0 \right\} \qquad 17\cdot4$$

or, since

$$(\Psi_b^{0*}|\mathbf{p}^j|\Psi_a^0) = m_j \frac{d}{dt} (\Psi_b^{0*}|\mathbf{q}^j|\Psi_a^0)$$

$$(\Psi_b^{0*}|\mathbf{H}'|\Psi_a^0) = -\left\{ \frac{iE_{ba}}{c\hbar} (b|\mathbf{R}|a) \cdot \mathbf{A}^0 + (b|\mathbf{M}|a) \cdot (\nabla \times \mathbf{A})_0 \right\} e^{i\frac{E_{ba}}{\hbar}t} \qquad 17\cdot5$$

where

$$E_{ba} = E_b - E_a$$

$$(b|\mathbf{R}|a) = \int \Psi_b^{0*} (\sum_j e \mathbf{r}^j) \Psi_a^0 \, d\tau$$

$$(b|\mathbf{M}|a) = \int \Psi_b^{0*} \left\{ \sum_j \frac{e}{2m_j c} (\mathbf{r}^j \times \mathbf{p}^j) \Psi_a^0 \, d\tau \right.$$

We now introduce explicitly the time dependence of $\mathbf{A}^0$ as

$$\mathbf{A}^0 = \tfrac{1}{2}\mathbf{A}_0^0 (e^{i\frac{\epsilon}{\hbar}t} + e^{-i\frac{\epsilon}{\hbar}t}) \qquad 17\cdot6$$

where $\epsilon = h\nu$ and ν is the frequency of the electromagnetic field which is perturbing the molecule. The coefficients $\dfrac{dc_b}{dt}$ are thus

$$\frac{dc_b}{dt} = \frac{i}{2\hbar}\left\{\frac{iE_{ba}}{c\hbar}\,(b|\mathbf{R}|a)\cdot\mathbf{A}_0^0 + (b|\mathbf{M}|a)\cdot(\nabla\times\mathbf{A}_0^0)\right\}\times$$

$$\left\{e^{i\frac{E_{ba}+\epsilon}{\hbar}t} + e^{i\frac{E_{ba}-\epsilon}{\hbar}t}\right\} \qquad 17\cdot7$$

Integrating with respect to time, we have

$$c_b = \tfrac{1}{2}\left\{\frac{iE_{ba}}{c\hbar}\,(b|\mathbf{R}|a)\cdot\mathbf{A}_0^0 + (b|\mathbf{M}|a)\cdot(\nabla\times\mathbf{A}_0^0)\right\}\times$$

$$\left\{\frac{e^{i\frac{E_{ba}+\epsilon}{\hbar}t}}{E_{ba}+\epsilon} + \frac{e^{i\frac{E_{ba}-\epsilon}{\hbar}t}}{E_{ba}-\epsilon}\right\} + \text{Constant} \qquad 17\cdot8$$

The constant in this expression for c_b is not a function of the time-dependent perturbing field and may for convenience be put equal to zero in this problem.

According to section 8g, the electric dipole moment of the system represented by the wave function Ψ is

$$\mathbf{R} = Re\,(\Psi^*|\mathbf{R}|\Psi)$$

Neglecting terms of the order of c^2, this is equal to

$$\mathbf{R}_a = Re\left\{(a|\mathbf{R}|a) + 2\sum_b c_b(a|\mathbf{R}|b)e^{-i\frac{E_{ba}}{\hbar}t}\right\} \qquad 17\cdot9$$

The first term in 17·9 represents the permanent dipole moment μ of the unperturbed molecule; the second term represents the dipole moment $\mathbf{R}_a'$ which has been induced by the perturbing field. Substituting 17·8 into 17·9, the expression for the induced dipole moment becomes

$$\mathbf{R}_a' = Re\left\{\left[\sum_b \frac{iE_{ba}}{c\hbar}\,(a|\mathbf{R}|b)(b|\mathbf{R}|a)\cdot\mathbf{A}_0^0\right.\right.$$

$$\left.\left. + (a|\mathbf{R}|b)(b|\mathbf{M}|a)\cdot(\nabla\times\mathbf{A}_0^0)\right]\left[\frac{e^{i\frac{\epsilon}{\hbar}t}}{E_{ba}+\epsilon} + \frac{e^{-i\frac{\epsilon}{\hbar}t}}{E_{ba}-\epsilon}\right]\right\} \qquad 17\cdot10$$

or, since

$$\frac{e^{i\frac{\epsilon}{\hbar}t}}{E_{ba}+\epsilon} + \frac{e^{-i\frac{\epsilon}{\hbar}t}}{E_{ba}-\epsilon} = \frac{E_{ba}\left(e^{i\frac{\epsilon}{\hbar}t} + e^{-i\frac{\epsilon}{\hbar}t}\right) - \epsilon\left(e^{i\frac{\epsilon}{\hbar}t} - e^{-i\frac{\epsilon}{\hbar}t}\right)}{E_{ba}^2 - \epsilon^2}$$

$$\mathbf{R}_a' = Re\left\{\sum_b (a|\mathbf{R}|b)(b|\mathbf{R}|a)\cdot\left[\frac{iE_{ba}^2}{c\hbar(E_{ba}^2-\epsilon^2)}\mathbf{A}_0^0\left(e^{i\frac{\epsilon}{\hbar}t}+e^{-i\frac{\epsilon}{\hbar}t}\right)\right.\right.$$

$$\left.-\frac{iE_{ba}\epsilon}{c\hbar(E_{ba}^2-\epsilon^2)}\mathbf{A}_0^0\left(e^{i\frac{\epsilon}{\hbar}t}-e^{-i\frac{\epsilon}{\hbar}t}\right)\right]$$

$$+\sum_b (a|\mathbf{R}|b)(b|\mathbf{M}|a)\cdot\left[\frac{E_{ba}}{(E_{ba}^2-\epsilon^2)}(\nabla\times\mathbf{A}_0^0)\left(e^{i\frac{\epsilon}{\hbar}t}+e^{-i\frac{\epsilon}{\hbar}t}\right)\right.$$

$$\left.\left.-\frac{\epsilon}{(E_{ba}^2-\epsilon^2)}(\nabla\times\mathbf{A}_0^0)\left(e^{i\frac{\epsilon}{\hbar}t}-e^{-i\frac{\epsilon}{\hbar}t}\right)\right]\right\} \quad 17\cdot11$$

From the relations $\mathbf{E} = -\dfrac{1}{c}\dfrac{d}{dt}\mathbf{A}$, $\mathbf{H} = \nabla\times\mathbf{A}$ between the fields $\mathbf{E}$ and $\mathbf{H}$ and the vector potential $\mathbf{A}$, we have

$$\mathbf{E}^0 = -\frac{i\epsilon}{2c\hbar}\mathbf{A}_0^0\left(e^{i\frac{\epsilon}{\hbar}t}-e^{-i\frac{\epsilon}{\hbar}t}\right)$$

$$\frac{d\mathbf{E}^0}{dt} = \frac{\epsilon^2}{2c\hbar^2}\mathbf{A}_0^0\left(e^{i\frac{\epsilon}{\hbar}t}+e^{-i\frac{\epsilon}{\hbar}t}\right) \qquad 17\cdot12$$

$$\mathbf{H}^0 = \tfrac{1}{2}(\nabla\times\mathbf{A}_0^0)\left(e^{i\frac{\epsilon}{\hbar}t}+e^{-i\frac{\epsilon}{\hbar}t}\right)$$

$$\frac{d\mathbf{H}^0}{dt} = \frac{i\epsilon}{2\hbar}(\nabla\times\mathbf{A}_0^0)\left(e^{i\frac{\epsilon}{\hbar}t}-e^{-i\frac{\epsilon}{\hbar}t}\right)$$

Using these relations, equation 17·11 reduces to

$$\mathbf{R}_a' = 2Re\left\{\sum_b \frac{E_{ba}}{(E_{ba}^2-\epsilon^2)}(a|\mathbf{R}|b)(b|\mathbf{R}|a)\cdot\mathbf{E}^0\right.$$

$$+\sum_b \frac{i\hbar E_{ba}^2}{(E_{ba}^2-\epsilon^2)\epsilon^2}(a|\mathbf{R}|b)(b|\mathbf{R}|a)\cdot\frac{d\mathbf{E}^0}{dt}$$

$$+\sum_b \frac{E_{ba}}{E_{ba}^2-\epsilon^2}(a|\mathbf{R}|b)(b|\mathbf{M}|a)\cdot\mathbf{H}^0$$

$$\left.+\sum_b \frac{i\hbar}{E_{ba}^2-\epsilon^2}(a|\mathbf{R}|b)(b|\mathbf{M}|a)\cdot\frac{d\mathbf{H}^0}{dt}\right\} \qquad 17\cdot13$$

We will be interested in the components of $\mathbf{R}_a'$ in the direction of the fields. To obtain these components, we average the expressions of the type $\mathbf{R}\mathbf{R}\cdot\mathbf{E}$ over all orientations of the molecule with respect to the field directions, assuming all orientations to be equally probable, and obtain, as in Chapter VIII, the result $\frac{1}{3}\mathbf{R} \cdot \mathbf{RE}$.   Equation 17·13 thus becomes

$$\mathbf{R}'_a = \frac{2}{3}Re\left\{\sum_b \frac{E_{ba}}{(E_{ba}^2 - \epsilon^2)} \, (a|\mathbf{R}|b) \cdot (b|\mathbf{R}|a)\mathbf{E}^0\right.$$

$$+ \sum_b \frac{i\hbar E_{ba}^2}{(E_{ba}^2 - \epsilon^2)\epsilon^2} \, (a|\mathbf{R}|b) \cdot (b|\mathbf{R}|a) \frac{d\mathbf{E}^0}{dt}$$

$$+ \sum_b \frac{E_{ba}}{(E_{ba}^2 - \epsilon^2)} \, (a|\mathbf{R}|b) \cdot (b|\mathbf{M}|a)\mathbf{H}^0$$

$$+ \sum_b \frac{i\hbar}{(E_{ba}^2 - \epsilon^2)} \, (a|\mathbf{R}|b) \cdot (b|\mathbf{M}|a) \frac{d\mathbf{H}^0}{dt} \qquad 17\cdot14$$

The induced magnetic moment $\mathbf{M}'_a$ is obtained from 17·14 by replacing $(a|\mathbf{R}|b) \cdot (b|\mathbf{R}|a)$ by $(a|\mathbf{M}|b) \cdot (b|\mathbf{R}|a)$ and $(a|\mathbf{R}|b) \cdot (b|\mathbf{M}|a)$ by $(a|\mathbf{M}|b) \cdot (b|\mathbf{M}|a)$, as is apparent from the derivation.   In taking the real part of 17·14, we see that, since

$$(a|\mathbf{R}|b) \cdot (b|\mathbf{R}|a) \equiv |(a|\mathbf{R}|b)|^2$$

is real, the coefficient of $\dfrac{d\mathbf{E}^0}{dt}$ is purely imaginary, so that its real part is zero.   Similarly, for $\mathbf{M}'_a$, the coefficient of $\dfrac{d\mathbf{H}^0}{dt}$ is zero.

$(a|\mathbf{R}|b) \cdot (b|\mathbf{M}|a)$ can be complex, so that

$$Re\{i(a|\mathbf{R}|b) \cdot (b|\mathbf{M}|a)\} = -Im\{(a|\mathbf{R}|b) \cdot (b|\mathbf{M}|a)\}$$

where Im means that we are to take the imaginary part of the term in brackets.   In calculating $\mathbf{M}'_a$, the coefficient of $\dfrac{d\mathbf{E}^0}{dt}$ can be further reduced, since

$$\sum_b \frac{i\hbar \dfrac{E_{ba}^2}{\epsilon^2}}{(E_{ba}^2 - \epsilon^2)} \, (a|\mathbf{M}|b) \cdot (b|\mathbf{R}|a)$$

$$= \frac{i\hbar}{\epsilon^2} \sum_b (a|\mathbf{M}|b) \cdot (b|\mathbf{R}|a) + \sum_b \frac{i\hbar}{(E_{ba}^2 - \epsilon^2)} \, (a|\mathbf{M}|b) \cdot (b|\mathbf{R}|a)$$

$$= \frac{i\hbar}{\epsilon^2} (a|\mathbf{M} \cdot \mathbf{R}|a) + \sum_b \frac{i\hbar}{(E_{ba}^2 - \epsilon^2)} \, (a|\mathbf{M}|b) \cdot (b|\mathbf{R}|a)$$

The first term is purely imaginary, so that its real part is zero.   We note further that, owing to the Hermitian character of $\mathbf{R}$ and $\mathbf{M}$,

$$[(a|\mathbf{M}|b) \cdot (b|\mathbf{R}|a)] = [(a|\mathbf{R}|b) \cdot (b|\mathbf{M}|a)]^*$$

so that

$$Im[(a|\mathbf{M}|b) \cdot (b|\mathbf{R}|a)] = -Im[(a|\mathbf{R}|b) \cdot (b|\mathbf{M}|a)]$$

Making use of the various relations given above, we have the final expressions for the induced moments:

$$\mathbf{R}'_a = \alpha'_a \mathbf{E}' + \gamma_a \mathbf{H}' - \frac{1}{c}\beta_a \frac{d\mathbf{H}'}{dt}$$

$$\mathbf{M}'_a = \kappa_a \mathbf{H}' + \gamma_a \mathbf{E}' + \frac{1}{c}\beta_a \frac{d\mathbf{E}'}{dt} \qquad 17\cdot15$$

The superscripts on the fields have been dropped, but the fields have been written as $\mathbf{E}'$, etc., to denote the fact that they are the total effective field at the molecule, which may not be the same as the external applied field. The quantities α'_a, κ_a, γ_a, β_a are, as may be seen from 17·14

$$\alpha'_a = \frac{2}{3h}\sum_b \frac{\nu_{ba}|(a|\mathbf{R}|b)|^2}{\nu_{ba}^2 - \nu^2}$$

$$\kappa_a = \frac{2}{3h}\sum_b \frac{\nu_{ba}|(a|\mathbf{M}|b)|^2}{\nu_{ba}^2 - \nu^2}$$

$$\gamma_a = \frac{2}{3h}\sum_b \frac{\nu_{ba}Re\{(a|\mathbf{R}|b) \cdot (b|\mathbf{M}|a)\}}{\nu_{ba}^2 - \nu^2} \qquad 17\cdot16$$

$$\beta_a = \frac{c}{3\pi h}\sum_b \frac{Im\{(a|\mathbf{R}|b) \cdot (b|\mathbf{M}|a)\}}{\nu_{ba}^2 - \nu^2}$$

where $\nu_{ba} = \dfrac{E_{ba}}{h}$ and $\nu = \dfrac{\epsilon}{h}$.

17b. Dipole Moments and Dielectric Constant. As shown in Chapter VIII, the matrix element $(a|\mathbf{M}|b)$ for the magnetic moment will in general be very much smaller than the corresponding matrix element $(a|\mathbf{R}|b)$ for the electric moment. Of the quantities α', κ, β, γ listed above, κ, β, γ will thus be much smaller than α', so that, to a first approximation, and one which is sufficient for many purposes, we may state that the effect of an electromagnetic field on a molecule which is in the state a is merely the induction of an electric dipole moment

$$\mathbf{R}'_a = \alpha'_a \mathbf{E}' \qquad 17\cdot17$$

where α'_a is the polarizability of the molecule in the state a. If the matrix element $(a|\mathbf{R}|a)$ is different from zero, that is, if the molecule possesses a permanent dipole moment μ_a, there will be an additional contribution to the polarizability arising from a partial orientation of the molecules with their dipole moments pointing along the field direction.   We may calculate this contribution to the polarizability in the following manner.

Let us consider that the molecule is subjected, not to the influence of an electromagnetic field similar to that associated with light, but to a constant electric field in the z direction, of strength E_z.   For this case, the vector potential $\mathbf{A}$ may be taken equal to zero; the scalar potential φ is $-zE_z$.   The classical Hamiltonian function for a system of charged particles will then be

$$H = H_0 - \sum_i e_i z_i E_z \qquad 17\cdot18$$

where H_0 is the Hamiltonian function for the system in the absence of an external field.   For this system, the dipole moment is

$$\mu_z = \sum_i e_i z_i = -\frac{\partial H}{\partial E_z} \qquad 17\cdot19$$

Quantum mechanically, the relation analogous to 17·19 will be

$$\mu_{a_z} = -\frac{\partial \epsilon_a}{\partial E_z} \qquad 17\cdot20$$

where ϵ_a is the energy of the molecule in the state a, this energy being expressed as a function of the perturbing field.

The quantum-mechanical method of calculating the contribution to the polarizability arising from the orientation of the permanent dipole moment of a molecule may be illustrated by the simple example of a diatomic molecule with a permanent moment μ_0 along the internuclear axis; this calculation, in fact, leads to results of quite general validity.

We treat the diatomic molecule as a rigid rotator in space; the wave functions, in the absence of a perturbing field, are

$$\psi_{J,\,M}(\theta, \varphi) = P_J^{|M|}(\cos\theta)e^{iM\varphi} \qquad 17\cdot21$$

and the associated energy levels are

$$\epsilon_0 = \frac{J(J+1)h^2}{8\pi^2 I} \qquad 17\cdot22$$

The perturbation is $-\mu_0 E_z \cos\theta$, so that the first-order perturbation energy is

$$\epsilon' = (\psi_{J,\,M}^* | -\mu_0 E_z \cos\theta | \psi_{J,\,M}) = 0 \qquad 17\cdot23$$

as may readily be seen from the known properties of the wave functions $\psi_{J,\,M}$.   In order to evaluate the second-order perturbation energy we need the values of the integrals

$$H'_{J,\,M;\,J',\,M'} = (\psi_{J,\,M}^* | -\mu_0 E_z \cos\theta | \psi_{J',\,M'}) \qquad 17\cdot24$$

These integrals are similar to those involved in the determination of the selection rules for electronic transitions in the hydrogen atom, and are zero unless $M = M'$, $J = J' \pm 1$. From the recursion formulas 4·85, we find for the squares of the pertinent integrals:

$$\left| H'_{J, M; J-1, M} \right|^2 = \mu_0^2 E_z^2 \left\{ \frac{(J + M)(J - M)}{(2J + 1)(2J - 1)} \right\}$$

$$\left| H'_{J, M; J+1, M} \right|^2 = \mu_0^2 E_z^2 \left\{ \frac{(J + M + 1)(J - M + 1)}{(2J + 1)(2J + 3)} \right\} \qquad 17\cdot25$$

The second-order perturbation energy will be

$$\epsilon''_{J, M} = \frac{\left| H'_{J, M; J-1, M} \right|^2}{\epsilon_J - \epsilon_{J-1}} + \frac{\left| H'_{J, M; J+1, M} \right|^2}{\epsilon_J - \epsilon_{J+1}} \qquad 17\cdot26$$

For $J = 0$, $M = 0$, we have

$$\epsilon''_{00} = - \frac{8\pi^2 I}{2h^2} \frac{\mu_0^2 E_z^2}{3} \qquad 17\cdot27$$

For $J \neq 0$, we obtain

$$\epsilon''_{J, M} = - \frac{8\pi^2 I \mu_0^2 E_z^2}{2h^2} \left\{ \frac{3M^2 - J(J + 1)}{J(J + 1)(2J - 1)(2J + 3)} \right\} \qquad 17\cdot28$$

According to 17·20, the z component of the dipole moment when the molecule is in the state $\psi_{J, M}$ is $\mu_{J, M, z} = - \dfrac{\partial \epsilon''_{J, M}}{\partial E_z}$. Since the energy of a state, to a first approximation, depends only on J, it will be convenient to calculate

$$\mu_{J, z} = \sum_{M=-J}^{M=+J} \mu_{J, M, z} \qquad 17\cdot29$$

Now

$$\sum_{M=-J}^{M=J} M^2 = 2(1^2 + 2^2 + 3^2 + \cdots + J^2) = \frac{J(J + 1)(2J + 1)}{3}$$

so that

$$\sum_{M=-J}^{M=J} [(3M^2 - J(J + 1)] = J(J + 1)(2J + 1)$$

$$- (2J + 1)(J)(J + 1) = 0 \qquad 17\cdot3()$$

We thus see that $\mu_{J, z} = 0$ for $J \neq 0$. For $J = 0$, we have

$$\mu_{0, z} = \frac{8\pi^2 I \mu_0^2 E_z}{3h^2}$$

The average z component of the dipole moment is thus just $\mu_{0, z}$ multiplied by the probability that the molecule will be in the state with $J = 0$. According to 15·26, this probability is equal to

$$\frac{N_0}{N} = \frac{1}{\sum_i e^{-\frac{\epsilon_i}{kT}}}$$

where ϵ_i is the energy of the ith state measured from the state with $J = 0$. If we neglect the second-order perturbation energy, we obtain, according to 15·59, the result

$$\sum_i e^{-\frac{\epsilon_i}{kT}} = \frac{8\pi^2 IkT}{h^2}$$

so that the contribution to the polarizability arising from this effect is $\frac{\mu_0^2}{3kT}$. This result is identical with that obtained from the well-known classical theory. It is to be noted that the final result $\frac{\mu_0^2}{3kT}$ is valid only for low field strengths (neglect of ϵ_i'' in ϵ_i), and high temperatures (replacement of summation by integration), but these conditions are adequately fulfilled in the usual measurements. Although this result has been here derived only for a diatomic molecule with a permanent dipole moment, a similar treatment shows that the result obtained is of general validity.

The above contribution to the polarizability arises from the partial orientation of the molecules with their permanent dipoles along the field direction. In deriving the expression for α_a', we assumed all orientations to be equally probable. The effect on α_a' of this partial orientation is of a higher order than the effects considered above and will be neglected. Our above derivation assumed the field to be stationary. If this is not true, the results must be modified. The nature of the necessary modification may be seen as follows. If the frequency of the field is much less than the frequencies associated with molecular rotation the molecule will be oriented in the manner discussed above; if the frequency of the field is much greater than the rotational frequencies the molecule will not be oriented with respect to the field, and there will be no contribution to the polarizability arising from this effect. Since molecular rotational frequencies correspond to wavelengths in the far infra-red, there will be no molecular orientation when the perturbing field has the frequency of visible light. We thus have the final formula for the dipole moment induced by an electric field

$$\mathbf{R}_a = \alpha_a \mathbf{E}'$$

with

$$\alpha_a = \frac{\mu_a^2}{3kT} + \alpha_a' \quad \text{(stationary fields)}$$

$$\alpha_a = \alpha_a' \quad \text{(visible light)}$$

where

$$\mu_a = \left| (a|\mathbf{R}|a) \right|; \quad \alpha_a' = \frac{2}{3h} \sum_b \frac{\nu_{ba} \left| (a|\mathbf{R}|b) \right|^2}{\nu_{ba}^2 - \nu^2}$$

To complete the discussion of the relation between dipole moment and dielectric constant, we consider a material medium containing N_1 molecules per cubic centimeter, all of the same kind and in the same state a (the extension to mixtures is obvious; if more than one state need be considered, it must be weighted with the appropriate Boltzmann factor). The polarization of the medium will be $\mathbf{P} = N_1\mathbf{R}$. For an isotropic medium, we may use for the effective electric field the Lorentz field

$$\mathbf{E}' = \mathbf{E} + \frac{4\pi}{3}\mathbf{P}$$

If $\mathbf{E}'$ is expressed by this relation, the polarization of the medium will be

$$\mathbf{P} = \frac{N_1\alpha\mathbf{E}}{1 - \dfrac{4\pi N_1\alpha}{3}}$$

From electromagnetic theory, we have the relations

$$\mathbf{D} = \epsilon\mathbf{E} = \mathbf{E} + 4\pi\mathbf{P}$$

where ϵ is the dielectric constant of the medium and $\mathbf{D}$ is the electric displacement vector. In terms of the polarizability, the dielectric constant will be

$$\epsilon = 1 + \frac{4\pi N_1\alpha}{1 - \dfrac{4\pi N_1\alpha}{3}}$$

or

$$\frac{\epsilon - 1}{\epsilon + 2} = \frac{4\pi N_1\alpha}{3} \qquad\qquad 17\cdot31$$

For stationary or almost stationary fields, we have

$$\frac{\epsilon - 1}{\epsilon + 2} = \frac{4\pi N_1}{3}\left(\frac{\mu^2}{3kT} + \alpha'\right) \qquad\qquad 17\cdot32$$

which is the relation used when dipole moments are determined from measurements of dielectric constants. The usefulness of a knowledge of the dipole moment in investigating the structure of a given molecule is so well known as to require no further comment at this point.

17c. The Theory of Optical Rotatory Power. In order to understand the origin of the phenomenon of optical rotatory power, we must include the higher-order terms when calculating the moments induced by an electromagnetic field. We therefore write, for the fields associated with visible light,

$$\mathbf{R} = \alpha \left(\mathbf{E} + \frac{4\pi}{3} \mathbf{P} \right) - \frac{\beta}{c} \frac{\partial}{\partial t} \mathbf{H} \qquad 17\cdot33$$

$$\mathbf{M} = \kappa \mathbf{H} + \frac{\beta}{c} \frac{\partial}{\partial t} \left(\mathbf{E} + \frac{4\pi}{3} \mathbf{P} \right) \qquad 17\cdot34$$

where $\alpha = \sum_a \rho_a \alpha'_a$, $\beta = \sum_a \rho_a \beta_a$, $\kappa = \sum_a \rho_a \kappa_a$, and ρ_a is the probability that the molecule will be in the state a. For the effective electric field we have again used the Lorentz field $\mathbf{E}' = \mathbf{E} + \frac{4\pi}{3} \mathbf{P}$; for the effective magnetic field we have set $\mathbf{H}' = \mathbf{H}$, since the magnetization is in general very small. The terms in γ_a have been neglected, since it may be shown that their inclusion would have only a second-order effect on the optical rotatory power.[1] The electric induction $\mathbf{D}$ and the magnetic induction $\mathbf{B}$ may, with the aid of 17·33 and 17·34, be calculated to be

$$\mathbf{D} = \mathbf{E} + 4\pi N_1 \mathbf{R} = \left(\frac{3 + 8\pi N_1 \alpha}{3 - 4\pi N_1 \alpha} \right) \mathbf{E} - \left(\frac{12\pi N_1 \dfrac{\beta}{c}}{3 - 4\pi N_1 \alpha} \right) \frac{\partial}{\partial t} \mathbf{H}$$

$$\mathbf{D} = \epsilon \mathbf{E} - g \frac{d}{dt} \mathbf{H} \qquad 17\cdot35$$

$$\mathbf{B} = \mathbf{H} + 4\pi N_1 \mathbf{M}$$

$$= (1 + 4\pi N_1 \kappa) \mathbf{H} + \frac{12\pi N_1 \dfrac{\beta}{c}}{3 - 4\pi N_1 \alpha} \frac{\partial}{\partial t} \mathbf{E} \quad \text{(to the first order in } \beta)$$

$$= K\mathbf{H} + g \frac{\partial}{\partial t} \mathbf{E} \qquad 17\cdot36$$

[1] E. U. Condon, *Rev. Modern Phys.* **9**, 444 1937.

where

$$\frac{\epsilon - 1}{\epsilon + 2} = \frac{4\pi N_1 \alpha}{3}$$

$$K = 1 + 4\pi N_1 \kappa$$

$$g = 4\pi N_1 \frac{\beta}{c} \frac{\epsilon + 2}{3} \qquad\qquad 17\cdot37$$

The nature of the electromagnetic field in a region free from real charges or real currents is specified by Maxwell's equations

$$\nabla \cdot \mathbf{D} = 0 \qquad\qquad \nabla \cdot \mathbf{B} = 0$$

$$\nabla {\times} \mathbf{E} = -\frac{1}{c}\frac{\partial}{\partial t}\mathbf{B} \qquad \nabla {\times} \mathbf{H} = \frac{1}{c}\frac{\partial}{\partial t}\mathbf{D} \qquad 17\cdot38$$

For any particular medium, these equations must be solved subject to relations of the type 17·35 and 17·36. Let us suppose, for the moment, that the parameter g is zero, so that $\mathbf{D} = \epsilon\mathbf{E}, \mathbf{B} = K\mathbf{H}$. From the equation for $\nabla{\times}\mathbf{E}$, we obtain, by taking the curl of both sides,

$$\nabla{\times}\nabla{\times}\mathbf{E} = -\nabla^2\mathbf{E} + \nabla\nabla\cdot\mathbf{E} = -\frac{1}{c}\frac{\partial}{\partial t}(\nabla{\times}\mathbf{B}) = -\frac{K\epsilon}{c^2}\frac{\partial^2}{\partial t^2}\mathbf{E}$$

or, since $\nabla \cdot \mathbf{E} = 0$,

$$\nabla^2\mathbf{E} = \frac{K\epsilon}{c^2}\frac{\partial^2}{\partial t^2}\mathbf{E} \qquad\qquad 17\cdot39$$

In the same manner, we find

$$\nabla^2\mathbf{H} = \frac{K\epsilon}{c^2}\frac{\partial^2}{\partial t^2}\mathbf{H} \qquad\qquad 17\cdot40$$

These equations represent waves propagated with a velocity

$$v = \frac{c}{\sqrt{K\epsilon}} = \frac{c}{n}$$

where n is the index of refraction. In non-magnetic media $K \cong 1$, so that $n^2 = \epsilon$, which is the familiar relation connecting index of refraction with dielectric constant. We will now investigate the solutions of Maxwell's equations for the case where g is not zero.

For our present purposes, we will investigate the nature of the solutions representing plane waves propagated along the z axis. The equation $\nabla \cdot \mathbf{D} = 0$ may be written as

$$\frac{\partial D_x}{\partial x} + \frac{\partial D_y}{\partial y} + \frac{\partial D_z}{\partial z} = 0 \qquad\qquad 17\cdot41$$

For our plane wave, $\dfrac{\partial D_x}{\partial x} = \dfrac{\partial D_y}{\partial y} = 0$, and so we conclude that $D_z = 0$. In the same way, the equation $\nabla \cdot \mathbf{B} = 0$ requires that $B_z = 0$; since $D_z = B_z = 0$ we must have $E_z = H_z = 0$. We now specialize our desired solution even more; we require that the solution represent right circularly polarized light.   For this type of wave we have

$$\mathbf{E} = E(\mathbf{i} \cos \psi - \mathbf{j} \sin \psi) \qquad\qquad 17\cdot42$$

where E is the amplitude of $\mathbf{E}$ and $\psi = 2\pi\nu\left(t - \dfrac{nz}{c}\right)$ is the phase of the wave of frequency ν propagated with a velocity $v = \dfrac{c}{n}$.   At $t = 0$, $z = 0$, $\mathbf{E}$ is directed along the x axis.   As t increases, $\mathbf{E}$ rotates toward the $-y$ axis, or, to an observer stationed so that the light enters his eyes, $\mathbf{E}$ rotates clockwise.   From the curl equations, we have

$$\nabla^\times \mathbf{E} = -\mathbf{i}\,\frac{\partial E_y}{\partial z} + \mathbf{j}\,\frac{\partial E_x}{\partial z}$$

$$= \frac{2\pi\nu n}{c} E\{-\mathbf{i} \cos \psi + \mathbf{j} \sin \psi\} = -\frac{1}{c}\,\frac{\partial}{\partial t} \mathbf{B}$$

or

$$\mathbf{B} = nE\{\mathbf{i} \sin \psi + \mathbf{j} \cos \psi\} \qquad\qquad 17\cdot43$$

In 17·36 we make the approximation that $K = 1$.   Then

$$\mathbf{B} = \mathbf{H} + g\,\frac{\partial \mathbf{E}}{\partial t} = \mathbf{H} - \frac{2\pi\nu g}{n} \mathbf{B}$$

or

$$\mathbf{H} = \left(\frac{n + 2\pi\nu g}{n}\right)\mathbf{B} = (n + 2\pi\nu g)E(\mathbf{i} \sin \psi + \mathbf{j} \cos \psi) \qquad 17\cdot44$$

From the curl equations, we have

$$\nabla^\times \mathbf{H} = \frac{2\pi\nu n}{c}\,(n + 2\pi\nu g)E(-\mathbf{i} \sin \psi - \mathbf{j} \cos \psi) = \frac{1}{c}\,\frac{\partial \mathbf{D}}{\partial t}$$

or

$$\mathbf{D} = n(n + 2\pi\nu g)E(\,\mathbf{i} \cos \psi - \mathbf{j} \sin \psi) = n(n + 2\pi\nu g)\mathbf{E} \qquad 17\cdot45$$

But, according to 17·35 and 17·44

$$\mathbf{D} = \epsilon\mathbf{E} - g\,\frac{\partial}{\partial t} \mathbf{H} = \epsilon\mathbf{E} - \frac{2\pi\nu g}{n} \mathbf{D}$$

or

$$\mathbf{D} = \frac{n\epsilon}{n + 2\pi\nu g} \mathbf{E} \qquad\qquad 17\cdot46$$

In order that 17·45 and 17·46 be consistent, we must have

$$n(n + 2\pi\nu g) = \frac{n\epsilon}{n + 2\pi\nu g}$$

or

$$n_R = \epsilon^{1/2} - 2\pi\nu g \qquad 17\cdot47$$

where n_R is the index of refraction for right circularly polarized light.

For left circularly polarized light, we may write **E** as

$$\mathbf{E} = E(\mathbf{i}\cos\psi + \mathbf{j}\sin\psi) \qquad 17\cdot48$$

Proceeding in exactly the same manner as above, we find that in this case the index of refraction is

$$n_L = \epsilon^{1/2} + 2\pi\nu g \qquad 17\cdot49$$

We therefore write

$$\psi_R = \psi_0 + \delta, \qquad \psi_L = \psi_0 - \delta \qquad 17\cdot50$$

where $\psi_0 = 2\pi\nu\left(t - \dfrac{nz}{c}\right)$ is the phase of a wave propagated with the

mean index of refraction $n = \epsilon^{1/2}$ and $\delta = 4\pi^2\nu^2 g\,\dfrac{z}{c}$. The superposition of right and left circularly polarized light waves of equal amplitude gives a plane polarized wave. Adding 17·42 and 17·48, we have

$$\mathbf{E} = E\{\mathbf{i}[\cos(\psi_0 + \delta) + \cos(\psi_0 - \delta)]$$
$$+ \mathbf{j}\,[-\sin(\psi_0 + \delta) + \sin(\psi_0 - \delta)]\}$$

$$= 2E\cos\psi_0\{\mathbf{i}\cos\delta - \mathbf{j}\sin\delta\} \qquad 17\cdot51$$

For $\delta = 0$, **E** is along the x axis; for $\delta > 0$, **E** has been rotated through an angle δ in the clockwise direction as viewed by an observer looking along the $-z$ axis. A medium for which δ is positive is therefore dextro-rotatory. The rotation in radians per centimeter is thus

$$\varphi' = \frac{\delta}{z} = \frac{4\pi^2\nu^2 g}{c}$$

or, according to 17·37 and 17·16,

$$\varphi' = \frac{4\pi^2\nu^2}{c}\,\frac{4\pi N_1}{c}\,\frac{\epsilon + 2}{3}\,\beta$$

$$= \frac{16\pi^2}{3ch}\,N_1\left(\frac{n^2 + 2}{3}\right)\sum_a\rho_a\sum_b\frac{\nu^2 R_{ba}}{\nu_{ba}^2 - \nu^2} \qquad 17\cdot52$$

where $R_{ba} = Im\{(a|\mathbf{R}|b)\cdot(b|\mathbf{M}|a)\}$ is the "rotatory strength" of the transition $a \rightarrow b$. From the theoretical viewpoint, the calculation of the optical rotatory power of a molecule is thus reduced to a calculation of the matrix elements $(a|\mathbf{R}|b)$ and $(b|\mathbf{M}|a)$. Since the eigenfunctions of complex molecules are not known to any high degree of accuracy, it has not as yet proved possible to determine the absolute configuration of any molecules by actual calculation. For a discussion of the attempts which have been made in this direction, as well as of related topics from this viewpoint, the reader should turn to one of the review articles in this field. It is possible, however, by a study of the symmetry properties of the rotatory strengths, to state the conditions necessary for optical activity.

The operators $\mathbf{R}$ and $\mathbf{M}$ in rectangular coordinates are

$$\mathbf{R} = e\{\mathbf{i}x + \mathbf{j}y + \mathbf{k}z\}$$

$$\mathbf{M} = \frac{eh}{4\pi mci}\left\{\mathbf{i}\left(y\frac{\partial}{\partial z} - z\frac{\partial}{\partial y}\right) + \mathbf{j}\left(z\frac{\partial}{\partial x} - x\frac{\partial}{\partial z}\right)\right.$$
$$\left. + \mathbf{k}\left(x\frac{\partial}{\partial y} - y\frac{\partial}{\partial x}\right)\right\} \quad 17\cdot53$$

If the molecule has a center of symmetry we may classify the states of the molecule as odd or even according as the wave function for a given state changes sign or retains the same sign when subjected to an inversion at the center of symmetry, that is, when each coordinate is replaced by its negative. Since the operator $\mathbf{R}$ changes sign upon inversion, we have a non-vanishing value of $(a|\mathbf{R}|b)$ only between odd and even states. The operator $\mathbf{M}$ does not change sign upon inversion; hence we have a non-vanishing value of $(a|\mathbf{M}|b)$ only between two odd or two even states. The scalar product $(a|\mathbf{R}|b)\cdot(b|\mathbf{M}|a)$ will therefore be identically zero for all states a and b, and the optical rotatory power will be zero. If the molecule has a plane of symmetry, we may again classify the wave functions as odd or even with respect to reflection in this plane. Let the plane of symmetry be the yz plane. Then, with respect to reflection in this plane, the x component of $\mathbf{R}$ is odd and the x component of $\mathbf{M}$ is even. There will be no pair of states a and b for which the x components of $(a|\mathbf{R}|b)$ and $(b|\mathbf{M}|a)$ are both different from zero. The same is true of the y and z components. A fundamental requirement for optical activity is thus that the molecule possess neither a plane nor a center of symmetry.

We now consider the values of $(a|\mathbf{R}|b) \cdot (b|\mathbf{M}|a)$ for a given molecule and its mirror image. A molecule may be transformed into its mirror image by reflection of its coordinates in any plane; this reflection is equivalent to changing from a right-handed to a left-handed coordinate system. If we reflect a molecule in the xy plane, the new value of $(a|\mathbf{R}|b) \cdot (b|\mathbf{M}|a)$ for the molecule is obtained by replacing z by $-z$ in the wave functions a and b in the corresponding expression for the original molecule. If we change z to $-z$ in both eigenfunctions and operators, the product of the matrix components will remain unchanged, since the values of the integrals involved, being pure numbers, are independent of the particular coordinate system in which they are evaluated. From the form of the operators, we see that $\mathbf{R} \cdot \mathbf{M}$ changes sign when z is replaced by $-z$; therefore $(a|\mathbf{R}|b) \cdot (b|\mathbf{M}|a)$ must change sign if we replace z by $-z$ in the eigenfunctions only. An unsymmetrical molecule and its mirror image must therefore have equal optical rotations, but with opposite signs. If a molecule is identical with its mirror image, its optical rotation must vanish. These conditions for the existence of optical activity are, of course, identical with those which have long been known.

17d. Diamagnetism and Paramagnetism. According to equation 8·15 the Hamiltonian operator for a system of charged particles in an electromagnetic field is

$$\mathbf{H} = \mathbf{H}_0 + \mathbf{H}'$$

where $\mathbf{H}_0$ is the Hamiltonian operator for the system in the absence of the field and

$$\mathbf{H}' = \sum_i \left[\frac{1}{2m_i} \left(i\hbar \frac{e}{c} \nabla_i \cdot \mathbf{A}_i + 2i\hbar \frac{e}{c} \mathbf{A}_i \cdot \nabla_i + \frac{e^2}{c^2} |\mathbf{A}_i|^2 \right) + e_i \varphi_i \right] \quad 17\cdot54$$

Let us consider a uniform magnetic field of magnitude H_z along the z axis. The potentials are

$$A_{x_i} = -\tfrac{1}{2} H_z y_i; \quad A_{y_i} = \tfrac{1}{2} H_z x_i; \quad A_z = 0; \quad \varphi = 0$$

From these values of the potentials we readily find the relations

$$\nabla_i \cdot \mathbf{A}_i = 0 \qquad |\mathbf{A}_i|^2 = \frac{H_z^2}{4}(x_i^2 + y_i^2)$$

$$\sum_i \mathbf{A}_i \cdot \nabla_i = \frac{H_z}{2} \sum_i \left(x_i \frac{\partial}{\partial y_i} - y_i \frac{\partial}{\partial x_i} \right) = \frac{H_z}{2} \frac{2\pi i}{h} \mathbf{M}_z \qquad 17\cdot55$$

where $\mathbf{M}_z$ is the operator for the z component of the angular momentum of the system. The perturbation $\mathbf{H}'$ can thus be written

$$\mathbf{H}' = -\frac{e}{2mc} H_z \mathbf{M}_z + \frac{e^2 H_z^2}{8mc^2} \sum_i (x_i^2 + y_i^2) \qquad 17\cdot56$$

If we include the interaction of the magnetic field with the electron spin, the perturbation $\mathbf{H}'$ becomes, according to 9·11,

$$\mathbf{H}' = -\frac{e}{2mc}H_z(\mathbf{M}_z + 2\mathbf{S}_z) + \frac{e^2 H_z^2}{8mc^2}\sum_i (x_i^2 + y_i^2) \qquad 17\cdot57$$

The term in H_z^2 will in general be much smaller than that in H_z and will be of importance only where the eigenvalues of $\mathbf{M}_z$ and $\mathbf{S}_z$ are zero. We will discuss the term in H_z^2, which is responsible for diamagnetism, later, and will for the present concentrate our attention on the term in H_z, which is responsible for paramagnetism.

For atoms or ions, a portion of our discussion will parallel the discussion of the Zeeman effect in Chapter IX. The paramagnetic term, for an arbitrary magnetic field $\mathbf{H}$, is

$$\mathbf{H}' = -\frac{e}{2mc}\{\mathbf{H}\cdot\mathbf{M} + 2\mathbf{H}\cdot\mathbf{S}\} \qquad 17\cdot58$$

For an atom in the state characterized by quantum numbers L and S, the first-order perturbation energy will be

$$E'(L, S) = -\frac{eh}{4\pi mc}\{\mathbf{H}\cdot\mathbf{L}^* + 2\mathbf{H}\cdot\mathbf{S}^*\} \qquad 17\cdot59$$

where $\mathbf{L}^*$ is a vector of magnitude $\sqrt{L(L+1)}$ and $\mathbf{S}^*$ is a vector of magnitude $\sqrt{S(S+1)}$. The magnetic moment for this state will be given by the relation analogous to 17·20, that is,

$$\boldsymbol{\mu}(L, S) = -\frac{\partial E'(L, S)}{\partial \mathbf{H}} = \frac{eh}{4\pi mc}\{\mathbf{L}^* + 2\mathbf{S}^*\}$$

$$= (\mathbf{L}^* + 2\mathbf{S}^*)\mu_0 \qquad 17\cdot60$$

where $\mu_0 = \dfrac{eh}{4\pi mc}$ is the " Bohr magneton." The component of $\boldsymbol{\mu}(L, S)$ along the vector $\mathbf{J}^*$ representing the total angular momentum will be

$$\mu_J(L, S) = \mu_0\{\mathbf{L}^* \cos(\mathbf{L}^*, \mathbf{J}^*) + 2\mathbf{S}^* \cos(\mathbf{S}^*, \mathbf{J}^*)\}$$

$$= g\mathbf{J}^*\mu_0 \qquad 17\cdot61$$

where

$$g = 1 + \frac{J(J+1) + S(S+1) - L(L+1)}{2J(J+1)}$$

In the presence of a magnetic field, the atom is so oriented that the projection of $\mathbf{J}^*$ along the axis of the field has the quantized values $M = J$, $J - 1 \cdots -J$. The average value of the component of the magnetic moment of a given atom along the direction of the field, provided that only the ground electronic state has an appreciable chance of being occupied, is

$$\bar{\mu} = \frac{\sum_M gM\mu_0 e^{\frac{gM\mu_0 H}{kT}}}{\sum_M e^{\frac{gM\mu_0 H}{kT}}}$$ 17·62

For small values of H, we may expand the exponential and retain only the first two terms. Then

$$\bar{\mu} = \frac{g\mu_0 \sum_M M + \frac{g^2\mu_0^2 H}{kT}\sum_M M^2}{\sum_M \left(1 + \frac{g\mu_0 MH}{kT}\right)}$$ 17·63

Since

$$\sum_M 1 = (2J+1), \quad \sum_M M = 0, \quad \sum_M M^2 = \frac{J(J+1)(2J+1)}{3}$$

equation 17·63 reduces to

$$\bar{\mu} = \frac{J(J+1)g^2\mu_0^2}{3kT}H$$ 17·64

The contribution to the magnetic susceptibility arising from the presence of permanent magnetic dipoles in an atom or ion is thus $\frac{J(J+1)g^2\mu_0^2}{3kT}$, an expression which is very similar to the contribution to the electric polarizability arising from the presence of the permanent electric dipole. This paramagnetic term vanishes for atoms with $J = 0$; for atoms in S states we have $J = S$, and the paramagnetism arises entirely from the unpaired spins. Most molecules have zero orbital angular momentum and no unpaired spins in their ground states, and thus show no paramagnetic effects. A notable exception is O_2, which has the ground state $^3\Sigma_g^-$, and thus exhibits a paramagnetic effect arising from the unpaired spins. The exact value of the paramagnetic susceptibility for molecules depends upon the nature of the coupling between the spin, orbital, and rotational angular momenta.

All atoms or molecules, regardless of whether or not they are paramagnetic, show diamagnetic effects. The perturbation energy arising from the second term in 17·56 is

$$E' = \frac{e^2 H^2}{8mc^2}\sum_i \overline{(x_i^2 + y_i^2)}$$ 17·65

where $\overline{(x_i^2 + y_i^2)}$ is the average value of $(x_i^2 + y_i^2)$. Since, to a first approximation, all directions in space will be equivalent, $\overline{x_i^2} = \overline{y_i^2} = \overline{z_i^2} = \frac{1}{3}\overline{r_i^2}$, where $\overline{r_i^2}$ is the distance of the electron from the center of gravity of the system, so that

$$E' = \frac{e^2 H^2}{8mc^2} \frac{2}{3} \sum_i \overline{r_i^2} \qquad 17\cdot 66$$

The associated magnetic moment will be $-\dfrac{e^2}{6mc^2} H \sum_i \overline{r_i^2}$, and the corresponding susceptibility is $-\dfrac{e^2}{6mc^2} \sum_i \overline{r_i^2}$, which we note to be negative. The complete magnetic susceptibility for an atom or ion will thus be

$$\kappa = -\frac{e^2}{6mc^2} \sum_i \overline{r_i^2} + \frac{J(J+1)g^2\mu_0^2}{3kT} \qquad 17\cdot 67$$

CHAPTER XVIII

SPECIAL TOPICS

18a. Van der Waals' Forces. The weak attractive forces between atoms which are not connected by ordinary valence bonds have long been known by the name of Van der Waals' forces. If the particles possess permanent dipole moments, certain forces will arise from this cause; these forces can be calculated from classical theory. Van der Waals' forces exist even if the particles are symmetrical; the origin of the forces may be most simply seen by consideration of the interaction of two hydrogen atoms when the interatomic distance is large.

For the hydrogen molecule, the wave function, in the Heitler-London approximation, may be written as

$$\psi = \psi_a(1)\psi_b(2) + \psi_a(2)\psi_b(1) \qquad 18\cdot1$$

If the internuclear distance is sufficiently large, we may assume the electrons to be definitely located on one or the other hydrogen atom, and we may write the wave function for this system as

$$\psi = \psi_a(1)\psi_b(2) \qquad 18\cdot2$$

The first-order perturbation energy will then be

$$E' = \int \psi_a^*(1)\psi_b^*(2)\mathbf{H}'\psi_a(1)\psi_b(2)\, d\tau_1\, d\tau_2 \qquad 18\cdot3$$

where

$$\mathbf{H}' = e^2\left(\frac{1}{r_{ab}} + \frac{1}{r_{12}} - \frac{1}{r_{a2}} - \frac{1}{r_{b1}}\right)$$

the symbols $\dfrac{1}{r_{ab}}$, etc., having their usual significance.

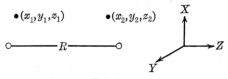

Fig. 18.1.

If, in the coordinate system as illustrated in Figure 18·1, we let (x_1, y_1, z_1) be the coordinates of electron (1) relative to nucleus a, and (x_2, y_2, z_2) the coordinates of electron (2) relative to nucleus b, the analytical expressions for the distances are

$$r_{ab} = R$$
$$r_{12} = \sqrt{(x_1 - x_2)^2 + (y_1 - y_2)^2 + (z_1 - z_2 - R)^2}$$
$$r_{a2} = \sqrt{x_2^2 + y_2^2 + (R + z_2)^2}$$
$$r_{b1} = \sqrt{x_1^2 + y_1^2 + (z_1 - R)^2}$$

18·4

Since the atoms are assumed to be far apart, $R \gg x_1$, $R \gg x_2$, etc. Since

$$\frac{1}{\sqrt{1 + \epsilon}} = 1 - \frac{\epsilon}{2} + \frac{3}{8}\epsilon^2 + \cdots$$

we obtain, upon expanding the expressions in 18·4 and retaining only the first two powers of the coordinates of the electrons, the results

$$\frac{1}{r_{ab}} = \frac{1}{R}$$

$$\frac{1}{r_{12}} = \frac{1}{R} \times$$
$$\left[1 - \frac{(x_1 - x_2)^2 + (y_1 - y_2)^2 - 2(z_1 - z_2)^2 - 2R(z_1 - z_2)}{2R^2} \right]$$

18·5

$$\frac{1}{r_{a2}} = \frac{1}{R}\left[1 - \frac{x_2^2 + y_2^2 - 2z_2^2 + 2Rz_2}{2R^2} \right]$$

$$\frac{1}{r_{b1}} = \frac{1}{R}\left[1 - \frac{x_1^2 + y_1^2 - 2z_1^2 - 2Rz_1}{2R^2} \right]$$

Combining these terms gives, for the perturbation $\mathbf{H}'$, to this approximation, the result

$$\mathbf{H}' = \frac{e^2}{R^3}\{x_1 x_2 + y_1 y_2 - 2z_1 z_2\}$$

18·6

which is the " dipole-dipole " interaction.

For $\psi_a(1)$ and $\psi_b(2)$ we take the $1s$ eigenfunctions of hydrogen. Using the perturbation above, we immediately see that the first-order perturbation energy is zero, since $\mathbf{H}'$ is an odd function of the coordinates while the ψ's are even functions of the coordinates. According to equation 7·27, the second-order perturbation energy is

$$E_0'' = \sum_{k \neq 0} \frac{H_{0k}' H_{k0}'}{E_0 - E_k}$$

18·7

where the summation is over all the states k of the hydrogen atom except the ground state. The denominator of this summation is equal to

$-\dfrac{e^2}{a_0}\left(1 - \dfrac{1}{n^2}\right)$ (since there are two hydrogen atoms), where n is the principal quantum number of the state k. The denominator of the summation thus varies from $-\dfrac{3}{4}\dfrac{e^2}{a_0}$ to $-\dfrac{e^2}{a_0}$; in order to evaluate the sum, we set the denominator equal to $-\dfrac{e^2}{a_0}$ for all terms. This gives an approximate value for the second-order perturbation energy equal to

$$E_0'' = -\frac{1}{e^2/a_0} \sum_{k \neq 0} H_{0k}' H_{k0}'$$

$$= -\frac{1}{e^2/a_0} \sum_k \{[(H_{0k}'H_{k0}') - (H_{00}'H_{00}')]\} \qquad 18\cdot8$$

$$= -\frac{1}{e^2/a_0} (H'^2)_{00}$$

since $H_{00}' = 0$ and $\sum_k (H_{0k}'H_{k0}') = (H'^2)_{00}$. In evaluating $(H'^2)_{00}$, the cross terms are zero for the same reason that H_{00}' vanished; we therefore have the result

$$(H'^2)_{00} = \frac{e^4}{R^6} \int \psi_a^*(1)\psi_b^*(2)[x_1^2 x_2^2 + y_1^2 y_2^2 + 4z_1^2 z_2^2]\psi_a(1)\psi_b(2)\, d\tau_1\, d\tau_2$$

$$= \frac{e^4}{R^6} [\overline{x_1^2 x_2^2} + \overline{y_1^2 y_2^2} + \overline{4z_1^2 z_2^2}] \qquad 18\cdot9$$

Since the $1s$ state is spherically symmetrical,

$$\overline{x_1^2} = \overline{y_1^2} = \overline{z_1^2} = \tfrac{1}{3}\overline{r_1^2}, \quad \text{etc.} \qquad 18\cdot10$$

so that

$$(H'^2)_{00} = \frac{2}{3}\frac{e^4}{R^6} \overline{r_1^2}\,\overline{r_2^2} \qquad 18\cdot11$$

According to equation 6·33, $\overline{r^2} = 3a_0^2$. The second-order perturbation energy is thus

$$E_0'' = -\frac{1}{e^2/a_0} (H'^2)_{00} = -\frac{6e^2 a_0^5}{R^6} \qquad 18\cdot12$$

By an actual summation of the series 18·7, Eisenschitz and London[1] obtained the more accurate value $E_0'' = -6.47\dfrac{e^2 a_0^5}{R^6}$; an exact pertur-

[1] R. Eisenschitz and F. London, Z. Physik, **60**, 491 (1930).

bation calculation[2] gives -6.499 as the value of the numerical coefficient.

If the expansion of $\mathbf{H}'$ is extended to include higher powers of the coordinates, the van der Waals energy contains not only the term in $\dfrac{1}{R^6}$ but also terms in $\dfrac{1}{R^8}, \dfrac{1}{R^{10}}$, etc. By a procedure similar to that carried out above, Margenau[3] obtained for the van der Waals energy the expression

$$E_0'' = -\frac{6e^2 a_0^5}{R^6} - \frac{135 e^2 a_0^7}{R^8} - \frac{1416 e^2 a_0^9}{R^{10}} \qquad 18\cdot13$$

The van der Waals energy may be expressed in terms of the polarizability by an argument due to London.[4] Instead of writing $E_0'' = -\dfrac{1}{e^2/a_0} (H'^2)_{00}$, we write $E_0'' = -\dfrac{1}{2I} (H'^2)_{00}$, where I may be taken to be the first ionization potential with the same degree of accuracy as we formerly took it equal to the ionization potential. According to 17b the polarizability of an atom in a stationary field ($\nu = 0$) is

$$\alpha = \frac{2e^2}{3h} \sum_b \frac{1}{\nu_{ab}} (a|\mathbf{r}|b) \cdot (b|\mathbf{r}|a) \qquad 18\cdot14$$

An approximate value for the polarizability is therefore

$$\alpha = \frac{2e^2}{3h} \frac{1}{\bar{\nu}_{ab}} \sum_b (a|\mathbf{r}|b) \cdot (b|\mathbf{r}|a)$$

$$= \frac{2e^2}{3h\nu_{ab}} (a|\mathbf{r}^2|a) = \frac{2e^2}{3I} \overline{r^2} \qquad 18\cdot15$$

where $\bar{\nu}_{ab}$ is an average value of ν_{ab}, and $h\bar{\nu}_{ab}$ has been replaced by I. $(H'^2)_{00}$ is thus equal to $\dfrac{3}{2} \dfrac{I^2 \alpha^2}{R^6}$; to this approximation, and the van der Waals energy is

$$E_0'' = -\frac{3}{4} \frac{I\alpha^2}{R^6} \qquad 18\cdot16$$

London has shown that, if the atoms are not equivalent, the analogous expression is

$$E_0'' = -\frac{3}{2} \frac{I_A I_B}{I_A + I_B} \frac{\alpha_A \alpha_B}{R^6} \qquad 18\cdot17$$

[2] L. Pauling and J. Beach, *Phys. Rev.*, **47**, 686 (1935).
[3] H. Margenau, *Phys. Rev.*, **38**, 747 (1931).
[4] F. London, *Z. Physik*, **63**, 245 (1930).

where I_A and α_A are the ionization constant and polarizability of atom (or molecule) A and I_B and α_B are similar quantities for atom B.

For many-electron atoms, the perturbation energy is a sum of terms of the type 18·6, with one term for each pair of electrons. Further details on the van der Waals forces in complex atoms may be found in the review article by Margenau.[5]

18b. The Quantum-Mechanical Virial Theorem.[6]   In classical mechanics, the virial theorem states that

$$\sum_i m_i \overline{\left(\frac{dx_i}{dt}\right)^2} = -\overline{\sum_i x_i F_{xi}} \qquad 18\cdot18$$

where the bars denote time averages and F_{x_i} is the x component of the force on the ith particle; the left side of this equation is $2\bar{T}$, where T is the kinetic energy of the system. This theorem also holds in quantum mechanics, as may be seen from the following argument. Schrödinger's equation for a system of particles is

$$\sum_i -\frac{h^2}{8\pi^2 m_i}\frac{\partial^2 \psi}{\partial x_i^2} + (V - E)\psi = 0 \qquad 18\cdot19$$

Operating on equation 18·19 by $x_j \psi^* \dfrac{\partial}{\partial x_j}$, we obtain

$$\sum_i -\frac{h^2}{8\pi^2 m_i} x_j \psi^* \frac{\partial^3 \psi}{\partial x_i^2\,\partial x_j} + x_j \psi^* \frac{\partial V}{\partial x_j}\psi + x_j \psi^*(V - E)\frac{\partial \psi}{\partial x_j} = 0 \qquad 18\cdot20$$

while from 18·19 we have

$$x_j \psi^*(V - E)\frac{\partial \psi}{\partial x_j} = \sum_i \frac{h^2}{8\pi^2 m_i} x_j \frac{\partial \psi}{\partial x_j}\frac{\partial^2 \psi^*}{\partial x_i^2} \qquad 18\cdot21$$

Substituting 18·21 in 18·20, and summing over j, gives

$$\sum_i -\frac{h^2}{8\pi^2 m_i}\sum_j x_j \left(\psi^* \frac{\partial^3 \psi}{\partial x_i^2\,\partial x_j} - \frac{\partial \psi}{\partial x_j}\frac{\partial^2 \psi^*}{\partial x_i^2}\right) + \psi^* \left(\sum_j x_j \frac{\partial V}{\partial x_j}\right)\psi = 0 \qquad 18\cdot22$$

It is possible to integrate the first term in equation 18·22. We have

$$\psi^{*2}\frac{\partial}{\partial x_i}\frac{\sum_j x_j \dfrac{\partial \psi}{\partial x_j}}{\psi^*} = \sum_j \left(\psi^* \frac{\partial x_j}{\partial x_i}\frac{\partial \psi}{\partial x_j} + \psi^* x_j \frac{\partial^2 \psi}{\partial x_i\,\partial x_j} - x_j \frac{\partial \psi}{\partial x_j}\frac{\partial \psi^*}{\partial x_i}\right)$$

$$= \psi^* \frac{\partial \psi}{\partial x_i} + \sum_j \left(\psi^* x_j \frac{\partial^2 \psi}{\partial x_i\,\partial x_j} - x_j \frac{\partial \psi}{\partial x_j}\frac{\partial \psi^*}{\partial x_i}\right) \qquad 18\cdot23$$

[5] H. Margenau, *Rev. Modern Phys.*, **11**, 1 (1939).
[6] J. Slater, *J. Chem. Phys.*, **1**, 687 (1933).

Therefore

$$\frac{\partial}{\partial x_i}\left[\psi^{*2}\frac{\partial}{\partial x_i}\frac{\sum_j x_j \frac{\partial \psi}{\partial x_j}}{\psi^*}\right] = 2\psi^*\frac{\partial^2 \psi}{\partial x_i^2} + \sum_j x_j\left(\psi^*\frac{\partial^3 \psi}{\partial x_i^2\,\partial x_j} - \frac{\partial \psi}{\partial x_j}\frac{\partial^2 \psi^*}{\partial x_i^2}\right) \qquad 18\cdot24$$

or

$$\sum_j x_j\left(\psi^*\frac{\partial^3 \psi}{\partial x_i^2\,\partial x_j} - \frac{\partial \psi}{\partial x_j}\frac{\partial^2 \psi^*}{\partial x_i^2}\right) = -2\psi^*\frac{\partial^2 \psi}{\partial x_i^2} + \frac{\partial}{\partial x_i}\left[\psi^{*2}\frac{\partial}{\partial x_i}\frac{\sum_j x_j \frac{\partial \psi}{\partial x_j}}{\psi^*}\right] \qquad 18\cdot25$$

When 18·25 is integrated with respect to x_i, the last term vanishes because the term ψ^{*2} is zero at $\pm \infty$. Integrating 18·22, we thus obtain

$$2\sum_i - \frac{h^2}{8\pi^2 m_i}\int \psi^*\frac{\partial^2 \psi}{\partial x_i^2}\,d\tau = -\int \psi^*\left(\sum_j x_j\cdot - \frac{\partial V}{\partial x_j}\right)\psi\,d\tau \qquad 18\cdot26$$

Since $F_{x_j} = -\dfrac{\partial V}{\partial x_j}$, this may also be written as

$$2\int \psi^*\left(\sum_i - \frac{h^2}{8\pi^2 m_i}\frac{\partial^2}{\partial x_i^2}\right)\psi\,d\tau = -\int \psi^*\,(\sum_j x_j F_{x_j})\psi\,d\tau \qquad 18\cdot27$$

or

$$2\overline{T} = -\overline{\sum_j x_j F_{x_j}} \qquad 18\cdot28$$

where the bars now represent quantum-mechanical averages.

If the potential energy arises entirely from the interactions of charged particles, the term $\overline{\sum_j x_j F_{x_j}}$ takes a particularly simple form. The potential V for such a system may be written as $V = \sum\limits_{m\neq n} V_{mn}$ with $V_{mn} = \dfrac{\epsilon_m \epsilon_n}{r_{mn}}$, where ϵ_m and ϵ_n are the charges on particles m and n a distance r_{mn} apart. We will now calculate the quantity $\sum x_j\cdot - \dfrac{\partial V_{mn}}{\partial x_j}$ for this pair of particles. Since

$$r_{mn} = \sqrt{(x_m - x_n)^2 + (y_m - y_n)^2 + (z_m - z_n)^2}$$

we have

$$\frac{\partial r_{mn}}{\partial x_m} = \frac{(x_m - x_n)}{r_{mn}}, \quad \frac{\partial r_{mn}}{\partial x_n} = -\frac{(x_m - x_n)}{r_{mn}}, \quad \text{etc.}$$

We thus obtain the result, since $\dfrac{\partial V}{\partial x_m} = \dfrac{\partial V}{\partial r_{mn}} \dfrac{\partial r_{mn}}{\partial x_m}$, etc.,

$$\sum x_j \frac{\partial V_{mn}}{\partial x_j} = -\frac{\epsilon_m \epsilon_n}{r_{mn}^3} \left\{ (x_m - x_n)^2 + (y_m - y_n)^2 + (z_m - z_n)^2 \right\}$$

$$= -\frac{\epsilon_m \epsilon_n}{r_{mn}} = -V_{mn} \qquad\qquad 18{\cdot}29$$

or, summing over all pairs

$$\sum_j x_j \cdot -\frac{\partial V}{\partial x_j} = V \qquad\qquad 18{\cdot}30$$

For this particular case, equation 18·28 becomes

$$2\bar{T} = -\bar{V} \qquad\qquad 18{\cdot}31$$

for a system of charged particles.

For a diatomic molecule, the virial theorem can be put into the following useful form. If the potential energy of the nuclei (the electronic energy) is $E(r)$, the external force required to hold the nuclei fixed at a distance r is $\dfrac{\partial E(r)}{\partial r}$. If we apply this force to the nuclei, the virial theorem $2\bar{T} = -\sum_j x_j F_{x_j}$ becomes

$$2\overline{T'} = -\overline{V'} - r\frac{\partial E(r)}{\partial r} \qquad\qquad 18{\cdot}32$$

where $\overline{T'}$ is the kinetic energy of the electrons only and $\overline{V'}$ is the potential of the electrostatic forces. Since the nuclei have no kinetic energy in this case, the energy E is equal to $\overline{T'} + \overline{V'}$. Using this relation, we may solve 18·32 for $\overline{T'}$ and $\overline{V'}$ separately, obtaining

$$\overline{T'} = -E - r\frac{\partial E}{\partial r}$$

$$\overline{V'} = 2E + r\frac{\partial E}{\partial r} \qquad\qquad 18{\cdot}33$$

The potential energy curve for a diatomic molecule can be represented with reasonable accuracy by the Morse curve

$$E(r) = D\{1 - e^{-a(r-r_e)}\}^2$$

or

$$E(r) = D\{-2e^{-a(r-r_e)} + e^{-2a(r-r_e)}\} \qquad\qquad 18{\cdot}34$$

where the energy zero has been chosen so that $E(r) = 0$ when $r = \infty$. For purposes of illustration, let us take $D = 100$ kcal., $a = r_e = 1$. The resulting curves for E, $\overline{T'}$, $\overline{V'}$ are plotted in Figure 18·2. At $r = \infty$, $E = \overline{T'} = \overline{V'} = 0$. As the internuclear distance is decreased, the kinetic energy first decreases, then increases rapidly as the nuclei are brought closer together. This increase in kinetic energy is more than

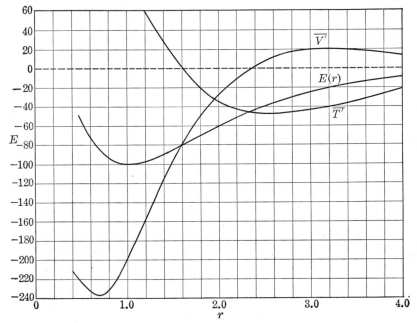

FIG. 18·2.   Energy relations for a diatomic molecule.

compensated for by the decrease in potential energy, leading to the formation of a stable system. It is of particular interest that at the equilibrium position $2\overline{T'} = -\overline{V'}$; that is, the kinetic energy of the electrons is $-\frac{1}{2}$ the electrostatic potential energy, so that the binding energy E is equal to $\frac{1}{2}\overline{V'} = -\overline{T'}$.

18c. The Restricted Rotator. Of considerable importance for the study of the internal motions of complex molecules as well as for the study of the motion of molecules in crystals is the problem of the energy levels of a rotator moving under the influence of a potential field. As the simplest example, we consider a rigid rotator whose moment of inertia is I, moving in a sinusoidal potential field of the form

$$V(\varphi) = \frac{V_0}{2}(1 - \cos n\varphi) \qquad \textbf{18·35}$$

where φ is the angle of rotation. The wave equation for this system is

$$\frac{d^2\psi(\varphi)}{d\varphi^2} + \frac{8\pi^2 I}{h^2}\left[E_r - \frac{V_0}{2}(1 - \cos n\varphi)\right]\psi(\varphi) = 0 \qquad 18\cdot36$$

Making the substitutions,

$$x = \frac{n\varphi}{2}$$

$$\theta = \frac{8\pi^2 I V_0}{n^2 h^2} \qquad 18\cdot37$$

$$a_r = \frac{32\pi^2 I}{n^2 h^2}\left(E_r - \frac{V_0}{2}\right)$$

this equation reduces to Mathieu's differential equation

$$\frac{d^2\psi(x)}{dx^2} + (a_r + 2\theta\cos 2x)\psi(x) = 0 \qquad 18\cdot38$$

the solutions of which are far from simple. We may, however, consider the limiting cases, where the motion resembles that of a free rotator or that of a harmonic oscillator. For $a_r \gg 2\theta$ the equation becomes

$$\frac{d^2\psi}{dx^2} + a_r\psi = 0 \qquad 18\cdot39$$

which has the solutions

$$\psi = e^{\pm irx} = e^{\pm ir\frac{n\varphi}{2}} \qquad 18\cdot40$$

where r is a positive integer, including zero. From the symmetry of the potential field, we must have $\psi(\varphi) = \psi\left(\varphi + \frac{2\pi}{n}\right)$. This requires that r be restricted to even integers. Since $a_r = r^2$ the energy levels are

$$E_r - \frac{V_0}{2} = \frac{n^2 h^2 r^2}{32\pi^2 I} \qquad r = 0, 2, 4, 6 \cdots \qquad 18\cdot41$$

For the various values of n, we have

$$n = 1 \qquad E_m - \frac{V_0}{2} = \frac{h^2}{8\pi^2 I}m^2, \quad m = 0, 1, 2, 3, 4 \cdots$$

$$n = 2 \qquad E_m - \frac{V_0}{2} = \frac{h^2}{8\pi^2 I}m^2, \quad m = 0, 2, 4, 6 \cdots$$

$$n = 3 \qquad E_m - \frac{V_0}{2} = \frac{h^2}{8\pi^2 I}m^2, \quad m = 0, 3, 6, 9 \cdots$$

For $n > 1$, only $\dfrac{1}{n}$ th of the energy levels for the free rotator are allowed. The connection between this fact and the origin of the symmetry number (section 15e) in rotational partition functions is obvious. These energy levels are doubly degenerate.

For the opposite case, $a_r \ll 2\theta$, the wave function will have appreciable values only for $x \cong 0$, so that we may write

$$\frac{d^2\psi}{dx^2} + [a_r + 2\theta(1 - 2x^2)]\ \psi = 0 \qquad 18\cdot42$$

which is the wave equation for the harmonic oscillator. The energy levels are given by the relation $a_r = 2(2r + 1)\sqrt{\theta} - 2\theta$, so that

$$E_r = (r + \tfrac{1}{2})h\nu_0, \quad r = 0, 1, 2, 3 \cdots \qquad 18\cdot43$$

where $\nu_0 = \dfrac{n}{2\pi}\sqrt{\dfrac{V_0}{2I}}$. For the intermediate case $a_r \sim \theta$ the energy levels will not be well approximated by either of the above equations. However, the Mathieu equation has been solved exactly for certain values of θ; the eigenvalues a_r are tabulated by Wilson[7] for values of θ from 0 to 40. We reproduce in Table 18·1 the exact eigenvalues a_r for the first seven levels for $\theta = 4, 9, 16$, and 36, together with the values calculated by the above expressions for the limiting cases (in parentheses). Values above the line were calculated by the harmonic oscillator approximation; those below the line were calculated by the free rotator approximation.

TABLE 18·1

EIGENVALUES a_r OF THE MATHIEU FUNCTION

$\theta = 4$		$\theta = 9$		$\theta = 16$	
−4.2805	(−4.000)	−12.262	(−12.000)	−24.259	(−24.000)
2.7469	(4.000)	− 1.3588	(0.000)	− 9.3341	(− 8.000)
6.8291	(4.000)	7.9828	(4.000)	4.3712	(4.000)
16.452	(16.000)	17.303	(16.000)	16.819	(16.000)
16.150	(16.000)	20.161	(16.000)	26.009	(16.000)
36.229	(36.000)	37.157	(36.000)	39.315	(36.000)
36.230	(36.000)	37.21	(36.000)	40.22	(36.000)

$\theta = 36$	
−60.256	(−60.000)
−37.303	(−36.000)
−15.467	(−12.000)
5.1467	(12.000)
24.379	(16.000)
42.118	(36.000)

[7] E. B. Wilson, *Chem. Revs.*, 27, 31 (1940).

APPENDIX

I. PHYSICAL CONSTANTS

These values of the important physical constants are taken from the tabulation of R. Birge, *Rev. Modern Phys.*, **13**, 233 (1941). Many of the numerical values used in the text are based on slightly different values for certain of the physical constants; these differences are not significant.

Velocity of light	$c = 2.99776 \times 10^{10}$ cm. $\cdot$ sec.$^{-1}$
Charge on electron	$e = 4.8025 \times 10^{-10}$ abs. e.s.u.
Ratio, charge to mass of electron	$\dfrac{e}{m} = 1.7592 \times 10^{7}$ abs. e.m.u. $\cdot$ gm.$^{-1}$
Planck's constant	$h = 6.6242 \times 10^{-27}$ erg $\cdot$ sec.
Ratio	$\dfrac{h}{e} = 1.3793 \times 10^{-17}$ erg $\cdot$ sec. $\cdot$ e.s.u.$^{-1}$
Mass of electron	$m = 9.107 \times 10^{-28}$ gm.
Mass of proton	$M_p = 1.6725 \times 10^{-24}$ gm.
Mass of hydrogen atom	$M_H = 1.6734 \times 10^{-24}$ gm.
Ratio	$\dfrac{M_p}{m} = 1836.5.$
Boltzmann constant	$k = 1.3805 \times 10^{-16}$ erg $\cdot$ degree^{-1}.
Gas constant	$R = 8.3144 \times 10^{7}$ erg $\cdot$ deg.$^{-1} \cdot$ mol.$^{-1}$
	$= 1.9865$ cal. $\cdot$ deg.$^{-1} \cdot$ mol.$^{-1}$
Avogadro's number	$N = 6.0228 \times 10^{23}$ mol.$^{-1}$
Rydberg constant for H	$R_H = 109{,}677.581$ cm.$^{-1}$
Rydberg constant for ∞ mass	$R_\infty = 109{,}737.303$ cm.$^{-1}$
Bohr radius $\left(\dfrac{h^2}{4\pi^2 m e^2}\right)$	$a_0 = 0.5292 \times 10^{-8}$ cm.
Bohr magneton $\left(\dfrac{eh}{4\pi mc}\right)$	$\beta = 0.9273 \times 10^{-20}$ erg $\cdot$ gauss^{-1}

1 electron volt $= 1.6020 \times 10^{-12}$ erg $\cdot$ molecule$^{-1} = 23{,}052$ cal. $\cdot$ mol.$^{-1}$
$\qquad\qquad = 12395 \times 10^{-8}$ cm. $= 8067.5$ cm.$^{-1}$

$\dfrac{e^2}{a_0} = 2R_\infty = 27.205$ e.v.

II. VECTOR NOTATION

The concept of a vector as a quantity having both magnitude and direction is quite familiar, as is the parallelogram rule for vector addition. If **A** is any vector, and A_1, A_2, and A_3 are the projections of this vector along the x, y, and z axes, respectively, $\mathbf{A}$ may be written as the vector sum

$$\mathbf{A} = \mathbf{A}_1 + \mathbf{A}_2 + \mathbf{A}_3 \qquad \text{II·1}$$

It is convenient to define a set of unit vectors $\mathbf{i}$, $\mathbf{j}$, $\mathbf{k}$, which are vectors of unit length directed along the x, y, and z axes, respectively, of a rectangular coordinate system. If we now let A_x be the magnitude of $\mathbf{A}_1$, we have $\mathbf{A}_1 = \mathbf{i}A_x$, etc., so that, in terms of the unit vectors and the components A_x, A_y, A_z we have

$$\mathbf{A} = \mathbf{i}A_x + \mathbf{j}A_y + \mathbf{k}A_z \qquad \text{II·2}$$

There are two types of products of vectors, the scalar product and the vector product. If $|A|$ and $|B|$ are the absolute magnitudes of the two vectors $\mathbf{A}$ and $\mathbf{B}$, and θ is the angle between them, then the scalar product $\mathbf{A} \cdot \mathbf{B}$ (" $\mathbf{A}$ dot $\mathbf{B}$ ") is defined as

$$\mathbf{A} \cdot \mathbf{B} = |A||B| \cos \theta \qquad \text{II·3}$$

In terms of the components of $\mathbf{A}$ and $\mathbf{B}$, the scalar product is

$$\mathbf{A} \cdot \mathbf{B} = A_x B_x + A_y B_y + A_z B_z \qquad \text{II·4}$$

As an example of the use of the scalar product, consider the motion of a particle through a small distance $d\mathbf{s}$, subjected to a force $\mathbf{F}$ which makes an angle θ with the direction of motion. The work done by the force is the product of the component of the force along the direction of motion times the distance through which the particle moves, or, in vector notation, $dW = \mathbf{F} \cdot d\mathbf{s}$.

The vector product $\mathbf{A} \times \mathbf{B}$ (" $\mathbf{A}$ cross $\mathbf{B}$ ") is a vector $\mathbf{C}$ perpendicular to the plane of $\mathbf{A}$ and $\mathbf{B}$. If $\mathbf{A}$ is rotated into $\mathbf{B}$ through an angle less than 180°, the direction of $\mathbf{C}$ is that in which a right-handed screw would move if given a similar rotation. The magnitude of $\mathbf{C}$ is defined to be $|C| = |A||B| \sin \theta$, where θ is the angle between $\mathbf{A}$ and $\mathbf{B}$. In terms of the components of $\mathbf{A}$ and $\mathbf{B}$ the vector product is

$$\mathbf{A} \times \mathbf{B} = \mathbf{i}(A_y B_z - A_z B_y) + \mathbf{j}(A_z B_x - A_x B_z) + \mathbf{k}(A_x B_y - A_y B_x)$$

$$= \begin{vmatrix} \mathbf{i} & \mathbf{j} & \mathbf{k} \\ A_x & A_y & A_z \\ B_x & B_y & B_z \end{vmatrix} \qquad \text{II·5}$$

From the definition of the direction of $\mathbf{C} = \mathbf{A} \times \mathbf{B}$, it is obvious that $(\mathbf{A} \times \mathbf{B}) = -(\mathbf{B} \times \mathbf{A})$. Angular momenta can be quite simply expressed in terms of the vector product. If $\mathbf{r}$ is the vector distance from a fixed point to a particle of mass m moving with the velocity $\mathbf{v}$, it can readily be seen from the definition of the vector product that the angular momentum of the particle relative to the fixed point is $\mathbf{r} \times m\mathbf{v} = m(\mathbf{r} \times \mathbf{v})$.

Many physical laws assume a particularly simple form when written in terms of the vector differential operators. We define a vector operator ∇ (" del "), which, in rectangular coordinates, is

$$\nabla = \mathbf{i}\,\frac{\partial}{\partial x} + \mathbf{j}\,\frac{\partial}{\partial y} + \mathbf{k}\,\frac{\partial}{\partial z} \qquad \text{II·6}$$

Operating on a scalar function φ, this operator generates a vector called the " gradient " of φ:

$$\nabla\varphi = \mathbf{i}\,\frac{\partial\varphi}{\partial x} + \mathbf{j}\,\frac{\partial\varphi}{\partial y} + \mathbf{k}\,\frac{\partial\varphi}{\partial z} \qquad \text{II·7}$$

The scalar product of ∇ and a vector $\mathbf{A}$ gives a scalar function known as the " divergence " of $\mathbf{A}$:

$$\nabla \cdot \mathbf{A} = \frac{\partial A_x}{\partial x} + \frac{\partial A_y}{\partial y} + \frac{\partial A_z}{\partial z} \qquad \text{II·8}$$

The vector product of ∇ and a vector $\mathbf{A}$ gives a new vector called the " curl " of $\mathbf{A}$:

$$\nabla{\times}\mathbf{A} = \begin{vmatrix} \mathbf{i} & \mathbf{j} & \mathbf{k} \\[2mm] \dfrac{\partial}{\partial x} & \dfrac{\partial}{\partial y} & \dfrac{\partial}{\partial z} \\[3mm] A_x & A_y & A_z \end{vmatrix} \qquad \text{II·9}$$

Of particular interest in quantum mechanics is the operator formed by taking the scalar product of ∇ with itself:

$$\nabla \cdot \nabla \equiv \nabla^2 = \frac{\partial^2}{\partial x^2} + \frac{\partial^2}{\partial y^2} + \frac{\partial^2}{\partial z^2} \qquad \text{II·10}$$

The operator ∇^2 (" del squared ") is usually called the Laplacian operator.

III. THE OPERATOR ∇^2 IN GENERALIZED COORDINATES

In rectangular coordinates, the operator ∇^2 is given by the relation $\nabla^2 = \dfrac{\partial^2}{\partial x^2} + \dfrac{\partial^2}{\partial y^2} + \dfrac{\partial^2}{\partial z^2}$. Because of the frequent occurrence of this operator in quantum mechanics, we will show by means of a physical interpretation how this operator can be transformed to coordinate systems which are not rectangular. The only coordinate systems that we shall consider are those in which the three coordinate surfaces cut each other at right angles. Such coordinates are known as orthogonal coordinates. Let these othogonal coordinates be q_1, q_2, q_3. The distance ds_1 perpendicular to the surface q_1 = constant, between the two points (q_1, q_2, q_3) and $(q_1 + dq_1, q_2, q_3)$, will not in general be equal to dq_1 but may be written as $ds_1 = h_1 dq_1$, where h_1 may be a function of the coordinates. The distance between the points (q_1, q_2, q_3) and $(q_1 + dq_1, q_2 + dq_2, q_3 + dq_3)$ will therefore, since the coordinate surfaces are perpendicular, be

$$(ds)^2 = (ds_1)^2 + (ds_2)^2 + (ds_3)^2$$
$$= h_1^2 (dq_1)^2 + h_2^2 (dq_2)^2 + h_3^2 (dq_3^2) \qquad \text{III·1}$$

Comparing this with the corresponding expression in rectangular coordinates

$$(ds)^2 = (dx)^2 + (dy)^2 + (dz)^2$$
$$= \left(\frac{\partial x}{\partial q_1} dq_1 + \frac{\partial x}{\partial q_2} dq_2 + \frac{\partial x}{\partial q_3} dq_3 \right)^2$$
$$+ \left(\frac{\partial y}{\partial q_1} dq_1 + \frac{\partial y}{\partial q_2} dq_2 + \frac{\partial y}{\partial q_3} dq_3 \right)^2$$
$$+ \left(\frac{\partial z}{\partial q_1} dq_1 + \frac{\partial z}{\partial q_2} dq_2 + \frac{\partial z}{\partial q_3} dq_3 \right)^2 \qquad \text{III·2}$$

we find

$$h_1^2 = \left(\frac{\partial x}{\partial q_1} \right)^2 + \left(\frac{\partial y}{\partial q_1} \right)^2 + \left(\frac{\partial z}{\partial q_1} \right)^2$$

$$h_2^2 = \left(\frac{\partial x}{\partial q_2} \right)^2 + \left(\frac{\partial y}{\partial q_2} \right)^2 + \left(\frac{\partial z}{\partial q_2} \right)^2 \qquad \text{III·3}$$

$$h_3^2 = \left(\frac{\partial x}{\partial q_3} \right)^2 + \left(\frac{\partial y}{\partial q_3} \right)^2 + \left(\frac{\partial z}{\partial q_3} \right)^2$$

the other coefficients being necessarily equal to zero.

Now suppose that the coordinate space is completely filled with a fluid whose density at the point (q_1, q_2, q_3) is $\rho(q_1, q_2, q_3)$. Suppose further that the motion of the fluid at any point is determined by a velocity potential $V(q_1, q_2, q_3)$ such that the velocity in any direction is given by the value $-\dfrac{dV}{ds}$, where ds is a displacement in the given direction. Let us calculate the rate of accumulation of fluid in a small element of volume bounded by the surfaces $q_1 = q_1^0, q_1 = q_1^0 + dq_1; q_2 = q_2^0, q_2 = q_2^0 + dq_2;$ $q_3 = q_3^0, q_3 = q_3^0 + dq_3$ (Figure III·1). Since the sides of the volume element are infinitesimal, we may assume that V is constant over any one surface. Now consider the surface $q_1 = q_1^0$. The rate of flow perpendicular to this surface is

$$-\frac{dV}{ds_1} = -\frac{1}{h_1}\frac{\partial V}{\partial q_1} \qquad\qquad \text{III·4}$$

and the area of the surface is $h_2 h_3\, dq_2\, dq_3$. Hence the amount of fluid flowing through this side in unit time is

$$\rho\left(-\frac{dV}{ds_1}\right) h_2 h_3\, dq_2\, dq_3 = -\rho\,\frac{h_2 h_3}{h_1}\frac{\partial V}{\partial q_1}\, dq_2\, dq_3 \qquad \text{III·5}$$

The rate at which fluid is flowing in through the other side is

$$\rho\,\frac{h_2 h_3}{h_1}\frac{\partial V}{\partial q_1}\, dq_2\, dq_3 + \frac{\partial}{\partial q_1}\left\{\rho\,\frac{h_2 h_3}{h_1}\frac{\partial V}{\partial q_1}\right\} dq_2\, dq_3\, dq_1 \qquad \text{III·6}$$

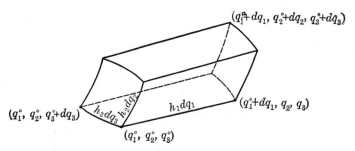

Fig. III·1.

so that the rate of accumulation of fluid due to this pair of surfaces is

$$\frac{\partial}{\partial q_1}\left\{\rho\,\frac{h_2 h_3}{h_1}\frac{\partial V}{\partial q_1}\right\} dq_1\, dq_2\, dq_3 \qquad\qquad \text{III·7}$$

The other two pairs of surfaces contribute

$$\frac{\partial}{\partial q_2}\left\{\rho\,\frac{h_1 h_3}{h_2}\frac{\partial V}{\partial q_2}\right\} dq_1\, dq_2\, dq_3 \qquad\qquad \text{III·8}$$

and

$$\frac{\partial}{\partial q_3}\left\{\rho\,\frac{h_1 h_2}{h_3}\frac{\partial V}{\partial q_3}\right\} dq_1\, dq_2\, dq_3 \qquad\qquad \text{III·9}$$

so that the total rate of accumulation is

$$\left[\frac{\partial}{\partial q_1}\left\{\rho\,\frac{h_2 h_3}{h_1}\frac{\partial V}{\partial q_1}\right\} + \frac{\partial}{\partial q_2}\left\{\rho\,\frac{h_1 h_3}{h_2}\frac{\partial V}{\partial q_2}\right\}\right.$$
$$\left. +\frac{\partial}{\partial q_3}\left\{\rho\,\frac{h_1 h_2}{h_3}\frac{\partial V}{\partial q_3}\right\}\right] dq_1\, dq_2\, dq_3 \qquad \text{III·10}$$

The rate of accumulation of fluid per unit volume at any point is just the rate of change of density at that point. Hence, since the element of volume is

$$d\tau = ds_1\,ds_2\,ds_3 = h_1h_2h_3\,dq_1\,dq_2\,dq_3 \qquad\text{III·11}$$

the rate of change of density is

$$\frac{\partial\rho}{\partial t} = \frac{1}{h_1h_2h_3}\left[\frac{\partial}{\partial q_1}\left(\rho\,\frac{h_2h_3}{h_1}\frac{\partial V}{\partial q_1}\right) + \frac{\partial}{\partial q_2}\left(\rho\,\frac{h_1h_3}{h_2}\frac{\partial V}{\partial q_2}\right)\right.$$
$$\left. + \frac{\partial}{\partial q_3}\left(\rho\,\frac{h_1h_2}{h_3}\frac{\partial V}{\partial q_3}\right)\right] \qquad\text{III·12}$$

If we carry out the same analysis in rectangular coordinates, we find

$$\frac{\partial\rho}{\partial t} = \frac{\partial}{\partial x}\left(\rho\,\frac{\partial V}{\partial x}\right) + \frac{\partial}{\partial y}\left(\rho\,\frac{\partial V}{\partial y}\right) + \frac{\partial}{\partial z}\left(\rho\,\frac{\partial V}{\partial z}\right)$$
$$= \nabla\cdot(\rho\nabla V) \qquad\text{III·13}$$

Since the value of $\dfrac{\partial\rho}{\partial t}$ is independent of the particular coordinate system we use, we conclude that, in general,

$$\nabla\cdot(\rho\nabla V) = \frac{1}{h_1h_2h_3}\left[\frac{\partial}{\partial q_1}\left(\rho\,\frac{h_2h_3}{h_1}\frac{\partial V}{\partial q_1}\right) + \frac{\partial}{\partial q_2}\left(\rho\,\frac{h_1h_3}{h_2}\frac{\partial V}{\partial q_2}\right)\right.$$
$$\left. + \frac{\partial}{\partial q_3}\left(\rho\,\frac{h_1h_2}{h_3}\frac{\partial V}{\partial q_3}\right)\right] \qquad\text{III·14}$$

Taking now the special case $\rho = $ constant, we find the expression for the operator $\nabla\cdot\nabla \equiv \nabla^2$ to be

$$\nabla^2 = \frac{1}{h_1h_2h_3}\left[\frac{\partial}{\partial q_1}\left(\frac{h_2h_3}{h_1}\frac{\partial}{\partial q_1}\right) + \frac{\partial}{\partial q_2}\left(\frac{h_1h_3}{h_2}\frac{\partial}{\partial q_2}\right)\right.$$
$$\left. + \frac{\partial}{\partial q_3}\left(\frac{h_1h_2}{h_3}\frac{\partial}{\partial q_3}\right)\right] \qquad\text{III·15}$$

In particular, if we use rectangular coordinates, equation III·15 becomes

$$\nabla^2 = \frac{\partial^2}{\partial x^2} + \frac{\partial^2}{\partial y^2} + \frac{\partial^2}{\partial z^2} \qquad\text{III·16}$$

In rectangular coordinates, the operator for the kinetic energy of a particle is

$$\mathbf{T} = -\frac{h^2}{8\pi^2 m}\left(\frac{\partial^2}{\partial x^2} + \frac{\partial^2}{\partial y^2} + \frac{\partial^2}{\partial z^2}\right) \qquad\text{III·17}$$

We thus conclude that, in generalized coordinates, the operator for the kinetic energy of a particle is

$$\mathbf{T} = -\frac{h^2}{8\pi^2 m}\,\nabla^2 \qquad\qquad \text{III·18}$$

where ∇^2 is given by equation III·15. Equation III·18 may also be verified by a direct transformation of III·17.

We give below a few of the most important coordinate systems, including the equations for the transformation from rectangular coordinates, the explicit expression for ∇^2, and the value of the volume element

$$d\tau = ds_1\,ds_2\,ds_3 = h_1 h_2 h_3\,dq_1\,dq_2\,dq_3$$

1. Polar Coordinates.

$$x = r\sin\theta\cos\varphi \qquad y = r\sin\theta\sin\varphi \qquad z = r\cos\theta$$

$$\nabla^2 = \frac{1}{r^2}\frac{\partial}{\partial r}\left(r^2\frac{\partial}{\partial r}\right) + \frac{1}{r^2\sin\theta}\frac{\partial}{\partial\theta}\left(\sin\theta\frac{\partial}{\partial\theta}\right) + \frac{1}{r^2\sin^2\theta}\frac{\partial^2}{\partial\varphi^2}$$

$$d\tau = r^2\sin\theta\,dr\,d\theta\,d\varphi$$

2. Cylindrical Coordinates.

$$x = r\cos\theta \qquad y = r\sin\theta \qquad z = z$$

$$\nabla^2 = \frac{1}{r}\frac{\partial}{\partial r}\left(r\frac{\partial}{\partial r}\right) + \frac{1}{r^2}\frac{\partial^2}{\partial\theta^2} + \frac{\partial^2}{\partial z^2}$$

$$d\tau = r\,dr\,d\theta\,dz$$

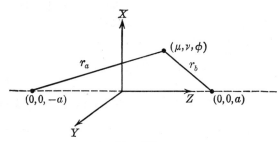

Fig. III·2.

3. Elliptical Coordinates (Figure III·2). (φ measured from xz plane.)

$$x = a\sqrt{(\mu^2 - 1)(1 - \nu^2)}\,\cos\varphi \qquad \mu = \frac{r_a + r_b}{R}$$

$$y = a\sqrt{(\mu^2 - 1)(1 - \nu^2)}\,\sin\varphi \qquad \nu = \frac{r_a - r_b}{R}$$

$$z = a\mu\nu \qquad\qquad\qquad\qquad (R = 2a)$$

$$\nabla^2 = \frac{4}{R(\mu^2 - \nu^2)}\left[\frac{\partial}{\partial\mu}\left\{(\mu^2 - 1)\frac{\partial}{\partial\mu}\right\} + \frac{\partial}{\partial\nu}\left\{(1 - \nu^2)\frac{\partial}{\partial\nu}\right\}\right.$$

$$\left. + \frac{\mu^2 - \nu^2}{(\mu^2 - 1)(1 - \nu^2)}\frac{\partial^2}{\partial\varphi^2}\right]$$

$$d\tau = \frac{R^3}{8}(\mu^2 - \nu^2)\,d\mu\,d\nu\,d\varphi$$

IV. DETERMINANTS AND THE SOLUTION OF SIMULTANEOUS LINEAR EQUATIONS

A determinant, it will be recalled, is defined by the equation

$$\begin{vmatrix} a_{11} & a_{12} & a_{13} & \cdots & a_{1n} \\ a_{21} & a_{22} & a_{23} & \cdots & a_{2n} \\ a_{31} & a_{32} & a_{33} & \cdots & a_{3n} \\ & & & & \\ & & & & \\ & & & & \\ a_{n1} & a_{n2} & a_{n3} & \cdots & a_{nn} \end{vmatrix} = \sum(-1)^\nu P_\nu\,(a_{11}a_{22}a_{33}\cdots a_{nn}) \qquad \text{IV·1}$$

where P_ν is the operator which permutes the second subscripts and ν is the number of interchanges of pairs of subscripts involved in P_ν. From the definition, it is readily seen that the determinant vanishes if two rows or two columns are identical, since interchange of two identical rows or columns changes the sign of the determinant but leaves its value unchanged.   If we denote the above determinant by A, we can define a set of numbers A_{im} by the relation

$$A = \sum_{i=1}^{n} a_{im}A_{im} \qquad \text{IV·2}$$

From this definition, it is obvious that $\sum_{i=1}^{n} a_{ik}A_{im} = 0$ for $k \neq m$, since, if $a_{ik} = a_{im}$ for all i, the determinant is identically zero, and, by IV·2, $\sum_{i=1}^{n} a_{ik}A_{im}$ is the determinant which has $a_{ik} = a_{im}$ for all i.

If we have a set of simultaneous equations

$$a_{11}x_1 + a_{12}x_2 + a_{13}x_3 + \cdots + a_{1n}x_n = c_1$$
$$a_{21}x_1 + a_{22}x_2 + a_{23}x_3 + \cdots + a_{2n}x_n = c_2$$
$$\vdots \qquad\qquad\qquad\qquad \text{IV·3}$$
$$a_{n1}x_1 + a_{n2}x_2 + a_{n3}x_3 + \cdots + a_{nn}x_n = c_n$$

we can obtain a solution in the following manner.   We multiply the first equation by A_{11}, the second by A_{21}, etc., and add, obtaining

$$\sum_{i=1}^{n} a_{i1}A_{i1}x_1 + \sum_{i=1}^{n} a_{i2}A_{i1}x_2 + \cdots + \sum_{i=1}^{n} a_{in}A_{i1}x_n = \sum_i c_iA_{i1} \qquad \text{IV·4}$$

But $\sum_{i=1}^{n} a_{i1}A_{i1} = A$ and $\sum_{i=1}^{n} a_{im}A_{i1} = 0$ for $m \neq 1$, so that

$$Ax_1 = \sum_i c_iA_{i1} \qquad \text{or} \qquad x_1 = \frac{\sum_i c_iA_{i1}}{A} \qquad \text{IV·5}$$

The quantity $\sum_i c_iA_{i1}$ is just the determinant in which a_{i1} has been replaced by c_i.   The values of the other x's are found in exactly the same manner.   The general result is

$$x_n = \frac{\sum_i c_iA_{in}}{A} \qquad \text{IV·6}$$

A solution exists only if $A \neq 0$, or, if $A = 0$, a solution exists only if all the c's are zero.   Conversely, we may say that, if all the c's are zero, then a solution (aside from the trivial solution $x_1 = x_2 = \cdots = x_n = 0$) exists only if $A = 0$.   This last statement is the one of particular importance in quantum mechanics.

V. THE EXPANSION OF $\dfrac{1}{r_{ij}}$

In terms of the distances r_i and r_j and the angle γ between the vectors from the origin to the two particles, the distance r_{ij} between the two particles is

$$r_{ij} = \sqrt{r_i^2 + r_j^2 - 2r_ir_j \cos \gamma} \qquad \text{V·1}$$

If we let $r_>$ be the greater of r_i and r_j, and $r_<$ be the lesser, then

$$r_{ij} = r_>\sqrt{1 + x^2 - 2x \cos \gamma} \qquad \text{V·2}$$

where $x = \dfrac{r_<}{r_>}$.   Let us now look for an expansion of $\dfrac{1}{r_{ij}}$ of the type

$$\frac{1}{r_{ij}} = \frac{1}{r_>} \frac{1}{\sqrt{1 + x^2 - 2x \cos \gamma}} = \frac{1}{r_>} \sum_n a_nP_n (\cos \gamma) \qquad \text{V·3}$$

If we square both sides of this expansion, multiply by $\sin \gamma \, d\gamma$, and integrate over γ from $\gamma = 0$ to $\gamma = \pi$, we obtain, by 4·53, the result

$$\frac{1}{x}\log\frac{(1+x)}{(1-x)} = \sum_n \frac{2}{2n+1}a_n^2 \qquad \text{V·4}$$

But, by an expansion, we have

$$\frac{1}{x}\log\frac{(1+x)}{(1-x)} = \sum_n \frac{2}{2n+1}x^{2n} \qquad \text{V·5}$$

so that we conclude that $a_n = x^n$, and the expansion of $\dfrac{1}{r_{ij}}$ in terms of $P_n(\cos\gamma)$ is

$$\frac{1}{r_{ij}} = \frac{1}{r_>}\sum_n x^n P_n(\cos\gamma) \qquad \text{V·6}$$

We must now express $P_n(\cos\gamma)$ as a function of the θ's and φ's of the two particles. Considering this as a function of θ_i and φ_i, we may expand it in terms of the orthogonal functions $P_l^{|m|}(\cos\theta_i)\,e^{im\varphi_i}$. $P_n(\cos\gamma)$ is a solution of the equation

$$\frac{1}{\sin\theta_i}\frac{\partial}{\partial\theta_i}\left(\sin\theta_i\frac{\partial P_n}{\partial\theta_i}\right) + \frac{1}{\sin^2\theta_i}\frac{\partial^2 P_n}{\partial\varphi_i^2} + n(n+1)P_n = 0 \qquad \text{V·7}$$

since this equation remains unchanged under any rotation. The general solution of this equation is a linear combination of the functions $P_n^{|m|}(\cos\theta_i)\,e^{im\varphi_i}$, so that we may express $P_n(\cos\gamma)$ as

$$P_n(\cos\gamma) = \sum_{m=-n}^{m=+n} A_{nm}P_n^{|m|}(\cos\theta_i)\,e^{im\varphi_i} \qquad \text{V·8}$$

where, by 4·53,

$$A_{nm} = \frac{2n+1}{4\pi}\frac{(n-|m|)!}{(n+|m|)!}\int P_n(\cos\gamma)\,P_n^{|m|}(\cos\theta_i)\,e^{-im\varphi_i}\,d\tau \qquad \text{V·9}$$

We also can expand $P_n^{|m|}(\cos\theta_i)\,e^{-im\varphi_i}$ in terms of the functions $P_n^{|k|}(\cos\gamma)\,e^{ik\varphi}$ as

$$P_n^{|m|}(\cos\theta_i)\,e^{-im\varphi_i} = \sum_{k=-n}^{k=+n} B_{nk}P_n^{|k|}(\cos\gamma)\,e^{ik\varphi} \qquad \text{V·10}$$

where

$$B_{nk} = \frac{2n+1}{4\pi}\frac{(n-|k|)!}{(n+|k|)!}\int P_n^{|m|}(\cos\theta_i)\,e^{-im\varphi_i}P_n^{|k|}(\cos\gamma)\,e^{-ik\varphi}\,d\tau \qquad \text{V·11}$$

Equation V·10 must hold for $\gamma = 0$, that is, for $\theta_i = \theta_j$, $\varphi_i = \varphi_j$. Then

$$P_n^{|m|}(\cos\theta_j)\,e^{-im\varphi_j} = \sum_{k=-n}^{k=+n} B_{nk}P_n^{|k|}(1)\,e^{ik\varphi} = B_{n0}P_n^0(1) \qquad \text{V·12}$$

since $P_n^k(1) = 0$ for $k \neq 0$. $P_n^0(1) = 1$; from V·12 and V·11 we have

$$\frac{2n+1}{4\pi} \int P_n^{|m|}(\cos\theta_i) e^{-im\varphi_i} P_n(\cos\gamma)\, d\tau = P_n^{|m|}(\cos\theta_j) e^{-im\varphi_i} \quad \text{V·13}$$

so that

$$A_{nm} = \frac{(n-|m|)!}{(n+|m|)!} P_n^{|m|}(\cos\theta_j) e^{-im\varphi_i} \quad \text{V·14}$$

Combining V·6, V·8, and V·14, we have the final result

$$\frac{1}{r_{ij}} = \sum_{n=0}^{\infty} \sum_{m=-n}^{m=+n} \frac{(n-|m|)!}{(n+|m|)!} \frac{r_<^n}{r_>^{n+1}} P_n^{|m|}(\cos\theta_i) P_n^{|m|}(\cos\theta_j) e^{im(\varphi_i-\varphi_i)} \quad \text{V·15}$$

Equation V·15 may alternatively be expressed as

$$\frac{1}{r_{ij}} = \sum_{n=0}^{\infty} \sum_{m=-n}^{m=+n} \frac{2}{2n+1} \frac{r_<^n}{r_>^{n-1}} \Theta_n^{|m|}(\theta_i)\Theta_n^{|m|}(\theta_j) e^{im(\varphi_i-\varphi_i)} \quad \text{V·16}$$

$$\frac{1}{r_{ij}} = \sum_{n=0}^{\infty} \sum_{m=-n}^{m=+n} \frac{4\pi}{2n+1} \frac{r_<^n}{r_>^{n+1}} Y_n^m(\theta_i, \varphi_i) Y_n^{m*}(\theta_j, \varphi_j) \quad \text{V·17}$$

VI. PROOF OF THE ORTHOGONALITY RELATIONS

The most important single theorem in group theory is that giving the orthogonality relation between the irreducible matrix representations of any group. As stated in Chapter 10, this theorem is

$$\sum_R \Gamma_i(R)_{mn} \sqrt{\frac{l_i}{h}}\, \Gamma_j(R)_{m'n'} \sqrt{\frac{l_j}{h}} = \delta_{ij}\delta_{mm'}\delta_{nn'} \quad \text{VI·1}$$

where l_i and l_j are the dimensions of the representations and h is the order of the group. We wish to give a simple proof of this theorem, following essentially the method of Speiser.[1] Before we can begin the actual proof of the orthogonality relations, we need several preliminary theorems.

THEOREM 1. If we have two sets of variables $x_1' \cdots x_n'$ and $y_1' \cdots y_m'$, then every bilinear form

$$f = \sum_{i=1}^{n} \sum_{j=1}^{m} c_{ij} x_i' y_j' \quad \text{VI·2}$$

of these variables can be reduced to the normal form

$$f = \sum_{k=1}^{r} x_k y_k \quad \text{VI·3}$$

---

[1] A. Speiser, *Theorie der Guppen von endlicher Ordnung*, Springer, Berlin, 1927.

where $r \leq n$, $r \leq m$, by a suitable linear transformation of the variables x_i' and y_j'.

Proof. The product

$$\frac{1}{c_{11}} \left(\sum_{i=1}^{n} c_{i1} x_i' \right) \left(\sum_{j=1}^{m} c_{1j} y_j' \right) \qquad \text{VI·4}$$

contain all the terms in f which involve either x_1' or y_1'. If we make the substitutions

$$x_1 = \frac{1}{\sqrt{c_{11}}} \sum_{i=1}^{n} c_{i1} x_i'$$

$$y_1 = \frac{1}{\sqrt{c_{11}}} \sum_{j=1}^{m} c_{1j} y_j' \qquad \text{VI·5}$$

we may write f as

$$f = x_1 y_1 + \sum_{i=2}^{n} \sum_{j=2}^{m} d_{ij} x_i' y_j' \qquad \text{VI·6}$$

We can, without loss of generality, assume that $n < m$. After $(n-1)$ substitutions of the type VI·5, we will have obtained the result

$$f = x_1 y_1 + x_2 y_2 + \cdots + x_{n-1} y_{n-1} + \sum_{j=n}^{m} g_{nj} x_n' y_j' \qquad \text{VI·7}$$

We now make the final substitutions

$$x_n = x_n' \qquad y_n = \sum_{j=n}^{m} g_{nj} y_j' \qquad y_j = y_j' \qquad (j > n)$$

Equation VI·7 then reduces to

$$f = \sum_{i=1}^{n} x_i y_i \qquad \text{VI·8}$$

which is the desired result. As the determinants of the transformations on the x''s and y''s are different from zero, the transformations have reciprocals. In certain special cases the normal form VI·8 may contain less than n terms.

Let us now take a set of variables $x_1' \cdots x_n'$ which form a basis for an irreducible representation $\Gamma_{x'}$ of a group. We also take a set of variables $y_1' \cdots y_m'$ which form a basis for an irreducible representation $\Gamma_{y'}$ of the same group. We have then

THEOREM 2. If $\Gamma_{x'}$ and $\Gamma_{y'}$ are two irreducible representations of a group there is no bilinear form of the variables x_i' and y_j' which is always invariant when both the x_i' and the y_j' are subjected to some operation R of the group unless $\Gamma_{x'}$ is identical with $\Gamma_{y'}$.

Proof. We shall prove this theorem only for the type of groups in which we have been interested, namely, those representing transformations of coordinates. The corresponding matrix representations involve only unitary matrices; for simplicity, we will assume that the matrices are real. According to Theorem 1, any bilinear form

$$f = \sum_{i=1}^{n} \sum_{j=1}^{m} c_{ij} x_i' y_j' \qquad \text{VI·9}$$

can be reduced to the form

$$f = \sum_{k=1}^{r} x_k y_k \qquad \text{VI·10}$$

by a suitable transformation. We consider that the matrices of the representations $\Gamma_{x'}$ and $\Gamma_{y'}$ have been subjected to the same transformation, so that we have obtained the corresponding new representations Γ_x and Γ_y which have the x's and y's as their bases. We now require that f be invariant when both the x's and the y's have been operated on by some operation R of the group.

$$Rx_k = \sum_{s=1}^{n} \Gamma_x(R)_{sk} x_s$$
$$\qquad\qquad\qquad\qquad \text{VI·11}$$
$$Ry_k = \sum_{t=1}^{m} \Gamma_y(R)_{tk} y_t$$

If we operate on the x's only in equation VI·10, we have

$$f = y_1 \sum_{s=1}^{n} \Gamma_x(R)_{s1} x_s + y_2 \sum_{s=1}^{n} \Gamma_x(R)_{s2} x_s + \cdots + y_r \sum_{s=1}^{n} \Gamma_x(R)_{sr} x_s \quad \text{VI·12}$$

Arranging this according to the x's we have

$$f = x_1 \sum_{k=1}^{r} \Gamma_x(R)_{1k} y_k + \cdots + x_n \sum_{k=1}^{r} \Gamma_x(R)_{nk} y_k \qquad \text{VI·13}$$

When we operate on the y's, equation VI·13 must reduce to equation VI·10. This requires that

$$\sum_{k=1}^{r} \Gamma_x(R)_{ik} R y_k = y_i \qquad i = 1 \cdots r$$

which is equivalent to the requirement that

$$R \sum_{k=1}^{r} \Gamma_x(R)_{ik} y_k = y_i$$

or

$$R^{-1} y_i = \sum_{k=1}^{r} \Gamma_x(R)_{ik} y_k \qquad i = 1 \cdots r \qquad \text{VI·14}$$

For the real unitary matrix representations we have been considering, the matrix of the inverse transformation is obtained from the original matrix by simply interchanging rows and columns. By definition, therefore

$$R^{-1}y_i = \sum_{k=1}^{m} \Gamma_y(R)_{ik}y_k \qquad i = 1 \cdots m \qquad \text{VI·15}$$

Comparing VI·14 and VI·15, we see that VI·10 will be invariant only if $m = r$. By interchanging the order of operations, we could prove in the same way that VI·10 will be invariant only if $n = r$. Again comparing VI·15 and VI·14, we see that VI·10 is invariant only if $\Gamma_x(R)_{ik} = \Gamma_y(R)_{ik}$ for $i, k = 1 \cdots r$. Equation VI·10 is, therefore, invariant only if Γ_x and Γ_y are identical.

We now have the necessary background for the proof of the orthogonality relations. Taking the sets of functions $x_1 \cdots x_n, y_1 \cdots y_n$, which are the bases for the irreducible representations Γ_x and Γ_y, we have

THEOREM 3. If Γ_x is not identical with Γ_y, then

$$\sum_{r} \Gamma_x(R)_{ij}\Gamma_y(R)_{kl} = 0$$

for all values of i, j, k, l.

Proof. Referring to the definition of the direct product given in Chapter 10, we see that the mn functions x_sy_t form a basis for a representation $\Gamma_x\Gamma_y$ of the group of dimension mn. If we denote these mn functions by $z_1 \cdots z_r$ $(r = mn)$ and the corresponding representation by $\Gamma_z = \Gamma_x\Gamma_y$, then the r^2 matrix elements of $\Gamma_z(R)$ are $\Gamma_x(R)_{ij}\Gamma_y(R)_{kl}$ $(i, j = 1 \cdots n; k, l = 1 \cdots m)$. If we now operate on z_s by one of the operations R of the group, we have

$$Rz_s = \sum_{t=1}^{r} \Gamma_z(R)_{ts}z_t \qquad \text{VI·16}$$

Summing over all the operations R of the group, we have

$$f = \sum_{R} Rz_s = \sum_{R}\sum_{t=1}^{r} \Gamma_z(R)_{ts}z_t \qquad \text{VI·17}$$

Let A be any operation of the group. Then

$$Af = \sum_{R} ARz_s = \sum_{R} Rz_s = f$$

since AR is always an operation of the group and the operation by A merely changes the order of the summation. Now f is a linear form of the z's, and hence a bilinear form of the x's and y's. But we have just seen that there is no such form f which is invariant under an operation of the group. Since $Af = f$, we must, therefore, conclude that f is identically zero. This can be true only if $\sum_R \Gamma_z(R)_{ts}$ is identically zero for all values of t and s. Referring to the correlation between the elements of $\Gamma_2(R)$ and those of $\Gamma_x(R)$ and $\Gamma_y(R)$, we thus see that the theorem is true.

Now taking the sets of functions $x_1 \cdots x_r$, $y_1 \cdots y_r$, which are bases for the representation Γ, and noting that according to Theorem 2 the function

$$f = \sum_{k=1}^{l} x_k y_k$$

is invariant under operations of the group, we can prove

THEOREM 4.

$$\sum_R \Gamma(R)_{ij}\Gamma(R)_{ij} = \frac{h}{l} \; ; \quad \sum_R \Gamma(R)_{ij}\Gamma(R)_{mn} = 0 \qquad (ij) \neq (mn)$$

where h is the order of the group and l is the dimension of the representation.

Proof. The function $f = \sum_{k=1}^{l} x_k y_k$ is invariant. We operate on f with some operation R, sum over all operations of the group, obtaining

$$\sum_R Rf = \sum_R \sum_{k=1}^{l} \sum_{s=1}^{l} \sum_{t=1}^{l} \Gamma(R)_{sk}\Gamma(R)_{tk}x_s y_t = hf \qquad \text{VI·18}$$

The coefficient of $x_s y_t$ must vanish if $s \neq t$, so we immediately have the relation

$$\sum_R \Gamma(R)_{sk}\Gamma(R)_{tk} = 0 \qquad s \neq t \qquad \text{VI·19}$$

Now $\sum_R R^{-1}f = \sum_R Rf$, since each operation is contained once and only once in both summations. Recalling that the inverse matrices are obtained by interchanging rows and columns in the original matrix, we have

$$\sum_R Rf = \sum_R R^{-1}f = \sum_R \sum_{k=1}^{l} \sum_{s=1}^{l} \sum_{t=1}^{l} \Gamma(R)_{ks}\Gamma(R)_{kt}x_s y_t$$

which gives us immediately the relation

$$\sum_R \Gamma(R)_{ks}\Gamma(R)_{kt} = 0 \qquad s \neq t \qquad \text{VI·20}$$

Equation VI·18 is thus reduced to

$$\sum_R Rf = \sum_R \sum_{k=1}^{l} \sum_{j=1}^{l} \Gamma(R)_{jk}\Gamma(R)_{jk}x_j y_j = hf \qquad \text{VI·21}$$

This requires that

$$\sum_R \sum_{k=1} \Gamma(R)_{jk} \Gamma(R)_{jk} = h \qquad (j = 1 \cdots l) \qquad \text{VI·22}$$

Considering the inverse transformation, we also obtain

$$\sum_R \sum_{k=1} \Gamma(R)_{kj} \Gamma(R)_{kj} = h \qquad (j = 1 \cdots l) \qquad \text{VI·23}$$

From VI·22 and VI·23, we see that $\sum_R \Gamma(R)_{jk} \Gamma(R)_{jk}$ is independent of both k and j. Therefore

$$\sum_R \Gamma(R)_{jk} \Gamma(R)_{jk} = \frac{h}{l}$$

Combining the results of Theorems 3 and 4, we have the desired relation

$$\sum_R \Gamma_i(R)_{mn} \sqrt{\frac{l_i}{h}} \, \Gamma_j(R)_{m'n'} \sqrt{\frac{l_j}{h}} = \delta_{ij} \delta_{mn'} \delta_{nn'} \qquad \text{VI·24}$$

VII. THE SYMMETRY GROUPS AND THEIR CHARACTER TABLES

Most simple molecules will have a certain degree of symmetry; that is, there will be certain transformations of coordinates which leave the atoms of the molecule in a configuration in space which is indistinguishable from the former configuration. The possible transformations of this type will be either rotation about an axis of symmetry, reflection in a plane of symmetry, inversion in a center of symmetry, or various combinations of these transformations. If two such transformations are carried out successively, the configuration will be that which could be obtained from some other transformation. The set of transformations which do not alter the configuration of the atoms in a molecule thus form a group, the group of the symmetry operations for the molecule. We include in this appendix the character tables for most of the symmetry groups which are likely to occur in problems of molecular structure.[1, 2, 3]

The notation used for the operators which transform a symmetrical molecule into itself is the following:

E = the identity operation, which leaves each particle in its original position.

[1] J. Rosenthal and G. Murphy, *Rev. Modern Phys.*, **8**, 317 (1936).

[2] H. Sponer and E. Teller, *Rev. Modern Phys.*, **13**, 75 (1941).

[3] R. Mulliken, *Phys. Rev.*, **43**, 279 (1933).

C_n = rotation about an axis of symmetry by an angle $\dfrac{2\pi}{n}$. In problems of molecular structure, the values of n which will be of particular interest are $n = 1$ (no symmetry axis), 2, 3, 4, 5, 6, and ∞. ($n = 7, 8$, etc., are possible values but probably occur only occasionally; these groups are not included in the tables.)

σ = reflection in a plane of symmetry. The symmetry planes are further classified as follows. If the plane is perpendicular to the principal axis of symmetry (the axis with the largest value of n), reflection in this plane is denoted by σ_h. If the plane contains the principal axis, reflection in this plane is denoted by σ_v. If there are axes with $n = 2$ perpendicular to the principal axis, and if the plane contains the principal axis and bisects the angle between two of these 2-fold axes, reflection in this plane is designated by σ_d.

S_n = rotation about an axis by $\dfrac{2\pi}{n}$ followed by a reflection in a plane perpendicular to the axis of rotation.

i = inversion in a center of symmetry.

The symmetry groups are designated by the following notation. We may divide them into three main types:

I. The Rotation Groups. These are symmetry groups which have one symmetry axis which is of a higher degree than any other symmetry axis. This axis is considered to be the z coordinate axis. The following groups belong to this general class:

A. The molecule possesses an axis of symmetry only. The groups of interest are $C_1, C_2, C_3, C_4, C_5, C_6$. The possible operations are found as follows. For the group C_6, with a 6-fold axis, all powers of C_6 are likewise symmetry operations. We thus have the operations

$$C_6, \quad C_6^2 = C_3, \quad C_6^3 = C_2, \quad C_6^4 = C_3^2, \quad C_6^5$$

B. The molecule has the symmetry operations C_n and σ_v. The manner in which the operations are found will be discussed later. The possible groups are $C_{2v}, C_{3v}, C_{4v}, C_{5v}, C_{6v}$.

C. The molecule has the symmetry operations C_n and σ_h. The possible groups are $C_{1h}(C_s), C_{2h}, C_{3h}, C_{4h}, C_{5h}, C_{6h}$.

D. The molecule has the symmetry operation S_n. The possible groups are $S_2(C_i), S_4, S_6(C_{3i})$.

E. The molecule has $2n$ 2-fold axes perpendicular to the principal n-fold axis. These axes are denoted by C', C_2'', etc. The notation for this type of group is D_n. The possible groups are $D_2(V), D_3, D_4, D_5, D_6$.

F. The molecule has the symmetry operations D_n and σ_d. The possible groups of interest are $D_{2d}(V_d), D_{3d}$.

G. The molecule has the symmetry operations D_n, σ_d, and σ_h. The possible groups are $\mathbf{D}_{2h}(\mathbf{V}_h)$, $\mathbf{D}_{3h}$, $\mathbf{D}_{4h}$, $\mathbf{D}_{5h}$, $\mathbf{D}_{6h}$.

A number of the above groups can be expressed quite simply as the combination of some other group of symmetry operations plus the inversion i. These are

$$\mathbf{C}_{4h} = \mathbf{C}_4 {\times} i \qquad \mathbf{D}_{2h} = \mathbf{D}_2 {\times} i$$
$$\mathbf{C}_{6h} = \mathbf{C}_6 {\times} i \qquad \mathbf{D}_{4h} = \mathbf{D}_4 {\times} i$$
$$\mathbf{S}_6 = \mathbf{C}_3 {\times} i \qquad \mathbf{D}_{6h} = \mathbf{D}_6 {\times} i$$
$$\mathbf{D}_{3d} = \mathbf{D}_3 {\times} i$$

II. Groups of Higher Symmetry. These are groups which have no unique axis of high symmetry but which have more than one n-fold axis where $n > 2$. The groups of interest are

$\mathbf{T}$ = the group of operations which sends a regular tetrahedron into itself. $\mathbf{T}_h = \mathbf{T} {\times} i$.

$\mathbf{O}$ = the set of operations which sends a cube or a regular octahedron into itself. $\mathbf{O}_h = \mathbf{O} {\times} i$.

$\mathbf{T}_d$ = the symmetry group of CH_4.

III. Groups with the Symmetry Operation C_∞.

$\mathbf{C}_{\infty v}$ = the group of the symmetry operations of a heteronuclear diatomic molecule.

$\mathbf{D}_{\infty h}$ = the group of the symmetry operations of a homonuclear diatomic molecule.

The symmetry operations for the rotation groups can most easily be found by means of the stereographic projection diagrams. For the group $\mathbf{C}_{4v}$, this takes the form of Figure VII·1. The square in the center represents the 4-fold axis. Starting with point 1, where the $+$ indicates that it is above the plane of the paper, we can obtain the points 3, 5, and 7 by applying the operations C_4, C_4^2, and C_4^3 to this point. Applying the operation σ_v to point 1 we obtain point 2; from this point we obtain the points 4, 6, and 8 by the rotations. These eight points are all that can be obtained from a single point by any combination of C_4 and σ_v. From the diagram, we see that this set of points also possesses the symmetry elements σ_d, where σ_d represents a reflection in a plane which bisects the angle between the original σ_v planes of symmetry.

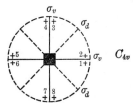

FIG. VII·1. Stereographic projection diagram for the group C_{4v}.

Diagrams of this type are given in Figure VII·2 for all the rotation groups. The principal n-fold axis is represented by the n-sided shaded

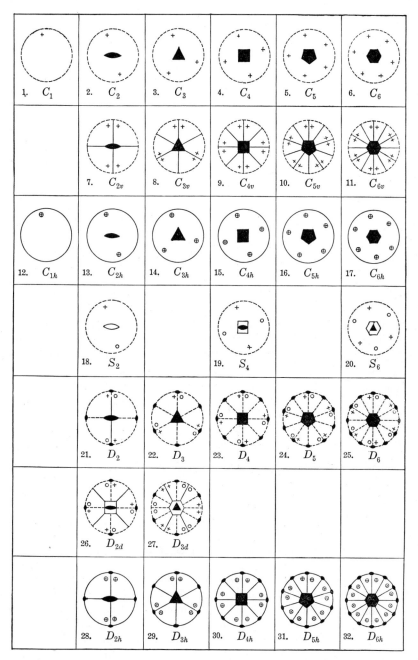

Fig. VII·2. Stereographic projection diagrams for the simple point groups.

figure in the center of the diagrams. S_n axes are represented by open n-sided figures. If the symmetry operation σ_h is present, the large circle is full; otherwise the large circle is dotted. The planes σ_v and σ_d are denoted by full lines. Two-fold axes perpendicular to the principal axis are denoted by the symbol for a 2-fold axis placed at the ends of the line through the center of the circle. The symbol $+$ represents a point above the plane of the paper; the symbol $\bigcirc$ represents a point below the plane of the paper. All these points can be obtained from any one of them by application of the various symmetry operations. As the exact significance of the various symmetry groups can be better seen by means of examples, in Table VII·1 we show molecules belonging to the various symmetry groups.

In the character tables, the operations of the various groups are collected into classes. For example, the group $\mathbf{C}_{3v}$ has three classes: the class of E, the class of the two 3-fold axes, and the class of the three planes of symmetry. This may readily be verified from the definition of a class and the stereographic projection diagrams.

The characters of the irreducible representations of the groups of most frequent occurrence are integers. For certain of the groups of low symmetry, particularly the $\mathbf{C}_n$ groups, complex characters occur. When they do, the irreducible representations can be taken in pairs, the characters of one member being the complex conjugates of the corresponding characters of the other member of the pair. Such a pair of representations is essentially equivalent to a single doubly degenerate representation.[3] When applying the orthogonality rules to such representations, the rule

$$\sum_R \chi^j(R)\chi^i(R) = h\delta_{ij}$$

must be replaced by

$$\sum_R [\chi^j(R)]^*\chi^i(R) = h\delta_{ij}$$

etc. Also, it is to be recalled that, if $\omega = e^{\frac{2\pi i}{6}}$, for example, then

$$1 + \omega + \omega^2 + \omega^3 + \omega^4 + \omega^5 = 0$$

Non-degenerate representations are designated by the letters A and B. The A's are symmetrical and the B's are antisymmetrical with respect to rotation about the principal axis of symmetry, that is, about the z axis. Doubly degenerate representations are denoted by E and triply degenerate representations by T. The characters of the groups of the type $\mathbf{D}_{6h} = \mathbf{D}_6 \times i$ are not given explicitly. They may readily be found in the manner illustrated by Table 14·7 for the group $\mathbf{D}_{6h}$. These representations are denoted by the symbols A_{1g} and A_{1u}, etc., the g representations being symmetrical and the u representations being antisymmetrical with respect to inversion.   The transformation properties of the coordinates x, y, z, the products of coordinates x^2, y^2, z^2, xy, xz, yz, and the rotations R_x, R_y, R_z, about the x, y, z axes, respectively, are also given.   If the operation i is present, the coordinates belong to the u representations while the rotations and products of coordinates belong to the g representations, as may be seen from Table 14·7.

TABLE VII·1

EXAMPLES OF MOLECULES BELONGING TO VARIOUS SYMMETRY GROUPS*

$\mathbf{D}_{\infty h}$	H_2, O_2, C_2H_2, CO_2
$\mathbf{C}_{\infty v}$	CO, HCl
$\mathbf{C}_{2v}$	H_2O, SO_2, H_2S, cis-$C_2H_2Cl_2$
$\mathbf{C}_{3v}$	NH_3, PCl_3, CH_3Cl
$\mathbf{C}_{2h}$	$trans$-$C_2H_2Cl_2$
$\mathbf{D}_{3d}$	" Staggered " C_2H_6
$\mathbf{D}_{3h}$	" Eclipsed " C_2H_6
$\mathbf{D}_{6h}$	C_6H_6
$\mathbf{T}_d$	CH_4
$\mathbf{O}_h$	SF_6

* See also E. B. Wilson, *J. Chem. Phys.*, **2**, 432 (1934).

The characters themselves are easily found for any group by application of the four rules given in Chapter X.   It may perhaps be of value to determine the transformation properties of the coordinates and rotations in several instances.   For C_{2v}, for example, the various operations on the vector r, with components x, y, z, give us the matrix equations

$$E \begin{pmatrix} x \\ y \\ z \end{pmatrix} \equiv \begin{pmatrix} 1 & 0 & 0 \\ 0 & 1 & 0 \\ 0 & 0 & 1 \end{pmatrix} \begin{pmatrix} x \\ y \\ z \end{pmatrix} \qquad \sigma_v \begin{pmatrix} x \\ y \\ z \end{pmatrix} \equiv \begin{pmatrix} 1 & 0 & 0 \\ 0 & -1 & 0 \\ 0 & 0 & 1 \end{pmatrix} \begin{pmatrix} x \\ y \\ z \end{pmatrix}$$

$$C_2 \begin{pmatrix} x \\ y \\ z \end{pmatrix} \equiv \begin{pmatrix} -1 & 0 & 0 \\ 0 & -1 & 0 \\ 0 & 0 & 1 \end{pmatrix} \begin{pmatrix} x \\ y \\ z \end{pmatrix} \qquad \sigma_v' \begin{pmatrix} x \\ y \\ z \end{pmatrix} \equiv \begin{pmatrix} -1 & 0 & 0 \\ 0 & 1 & 0 \\ 0 & 0 & 1 \end{pmatrix} \begin{pmatrix} x \\ y \\ z \end{pmatrix}$$

σ_v = reflection in xz plane.

σ_v' = reflection in yz plane.

Each coordinate therefore belongs to an irreducible representation, x to B_1, y to B_2, and z to A_1.   The products of the coordinates belong to the representation of the direct product of the irreducible representations involved; for example, xy belongs to $B_1B_2 = A_2$.   The various rotations may be indicated by curved arrows as indicated in Figure VII·3. Operating on these arrows with the symmetry operations, we have

$$E \begin{pmatrix} R_x \\ R_y \\ R_z \end{pmatrix} \equiv \begin{pmatrix} 1 & 0 & 0 \\ 0 & 1 & 0 \\ 0 & 0 & 1 \end{pmatrix} \begin{pmatrix} R_x \\ R_y \\ R_z \end{pmatrix} \qquad \sigma_v \begin{pmatrix} R_x \\ R_y \\ R_z \end{pmatrix} \equiv \begin{pmatrix} -1 & 0 & 0 \\ 0 & 1 & 0 \\ 0 & 0 & -1 \end{pmatrix} \begin{pmatrix} R_x \\ R_y \\ R_z \end{pmatrix}$$

$$C_2 \begin{pmatrix} R_x \\ R_y \\ R_z \end{pmatrix} \equiv \begin{pmatrix} -1 & 0 & 0 \\ 0 & -1 & 0 \\ 0 & 0 & 1 \end{pmatrix} \begin{pmatrix} R_x \\ R_y \\ R_z \end{pmatrix} \qquad \sigma_v' \begin{pmatrix} R_x \\ R_y \\ R_z \end{pmatrix} = \begin{pmatrix} 1 & 0 & 0 \\ 0 & -1 & 0 \\ 0 & 0 & -1 \end{pmatrix} \begin{pmatrix} R_x \\ R_y \\ R_z \end{pmatrix}$$

so that R_x belongs to B_2, R_y to B_1, and R_z to A_2.

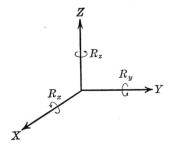

FIG. VII·3.

When we have degenerate representations the procedure is sometimes less simple. For example, for $\mathbf{D}_{3h}$, we have the matrices

$$E \sim \begin{pmatrix} 1 & 0 & 0 \\ 0 & 1 & 0 \\ 0 & 0 & 1 \end{pmatrix} \qquad S_3 \sim \begin{pmatrix} -\dfrac{1}{2} & \dfrac{\sqrt{3}}{2} & 0 \\ -\dfrac{\sqrt{3}}{2} & -\dfrac{1}{2} & 0 \\ 0 & 0 & -1 \end{pmatrix}$$

$$\sigma_h \sim \begin{pmatrix} 1 & 0 & 0 \\ 0 & 1 & 0 \\ 0 & 0 & -1 \end{pmatrix} \qquad C_2' \sim \begin{pmatrix} 1 & 0 & 0 \\ 0 & -1 & 0 \\ 0 & 0 & -1 \end{pmatrix}$$

$$C_3 \sim \begin{pmatrix} -\dfrac{1}{2} & \dfrac{\sqrt{3}}{2} & 0 \\ -\dfrac{\sqrt{3}}{2} & -\dfrac{1}{2} & 0 \\ 0 & 0 & 1 \end{pmatrix} \qquad \sigma_v \sim \begin{pmatrix} 1 & 0 & 0 \\ 0 & -1 & 0 \\ 0 & 0 & 1 \end{pmatrix}$$

We thus see that z belongs to the non-degenerate representation A_2'', and that the pair of coordinates (x, y) belongs to the degenerate representation E'. The product z^2 belongs to $A_2''A_2'' = A_1'$, the pair (xz, yz) belongs to $A_2''E' = E''$. The products x^2, y^2, and xy must belong to $E'E' = E' + A_1' + A_2'$. If we consider any vector of unit length, then $x^2 + y^2 + z^2 = 1$. Since z^2 belongs to A_1', the combination $x^2 + y^2$ must belong to A_1'. This leaves us xy and the combination $x^2 - y^2$ to be assigned to $E' + A_2'$; we conclude that the pair $(x^2 - y^2, xy)$ belongs to E'. These conclusions may be verified by working out the transformation matrices for the vector with components $x^2 + y^2$, $x^2 - y^2$, xy. In a similar manner, we find that R_z belongs to A_2', the pair of rotations (R_x, R_y) belongs to E''.

1.

C_1	E
A	1

2.

C_2			E	C_2
x^2, y^2, z^2, xy	R_z, z	A	1	1
xz, yz	x, y R_x, R_y	B	1	-1

3.

C_3			E	C_3	C_3^2	
$x^2 + y^2, z^2$	R_z, z	A	1	1	1	
(xz, yz) $(x^2 - y^2, xy)$	(x, y) (R_x, R_y)	E	$\begin{matrix}1 \\ 1\end{matrix}$	$\begin{matrix}\omega \\ \omega^2\end{matrix}$	$\begin{matrix}\omega^2 \\ \omega\end{matrix}$	$(\omega = e^{\frac{2\pi i}{3}})$

4.

C_4			E	C_2	C_4	C_4^3
$x^2 + y^2, z^2$ $x^2 - y^2, xy$	R_z, z	A	1	1	1	1
		B	1	1	-1	-1
(xz, yz)	(x, y) (R_x, R_y)	E	$\begin{matrix}1 \\ 1\end{matrix}$	$\begin{matrix}-1 \\ -1\end{matrix}$	$\begin{matrix}i \\ -i\end{matrix}$	$\begin{matrix}-i \\ i\end{matrix}$

5.

C_5			E	C_5	C_5^2	C_5^3	C_5^4	
$x^2 + y^2, z^2$	R_z, z	A	1	1	1	1	1	
(xz, yz)	(x, y) (R_x, R_y)	E'	$\begin{matrix}1 \\ 1\end{matrix}$	$\begin{matrix}\omega \\ \omega^4\end{matrix}$	$\begin{matrix}\omega^2 \\ \omega^3\end{matrix}$	$\begin{matrix}\omega^3 \\ \omega^2\end{matrix}$	$\begin{matrix}\omega^4 \\ \omega\end{matrix}$	$(\omega = e^{\frac{2\pi i}{5}})$
$(x^2 - y^2, xy)$		E''	$\begin{matrix}1 \\ 1\end{matrix}$	$\begin{matrix}\omega^2 \\ \omega^3\end{matrix}$	$\begin{matrix}\omega^4 \\ \omega\end{matrix}$	$\begin{matrix}\omega \\ \omega^4\end{matrix}$	$\begin{matrix}\omega^3 \\ \omega^2\end{matrix}$	

6.

C_6			E	C_6	C_3	C_2	C^2	C_6^5
$x^2 + y^2, z^2$	R_z, z	A	1	1	1	1	1	1
		B	1	-1	1	-1	1	-1
(xz, yz)	(x, y) (R_x, R_y)	E' $\{$	1	ω	ω^2	ω^3	ω^4	ω^5 $(\omega = e^{\frac{2\pi i}{6}})$
			1	ω^5	ω^4	ω^3	ω^2	ω
$(x^2 - y^2, xy)$		E'' $\{$	1	ω^2	ω^4	1	ω^2	ω^4
			1	ω^4	ω^2	1	ω^4	ω^2

7.

C_{2v}			E	C_2	σ_v	σ_v'
x^2, y^2, z^2	z	A_1	1	1	1	1
xy	R_z	A_2	1	1	-1	-1
xz	R_y, x	B_1	1	-1	1	-1
yz	R_x, y	B_2	1	-1	-1	1

8.

C_{3v}			E	$2C_3$	$3\sigma_v$
$x^2 + y^2, z^2$	z	A_1	1	1	1
	R_z	A_2	1	1	-1
$(x^2 - y^2, xy)$ (xz, yz)	(x, y) (R_x, R_y)	E	2	-1	0

9.

C_{4v}			E	C_2	$2C_4$	$2\sigma_v$	$2\sigma_d$
$x^2 + y^2, z^2$	z	A_1	1	1	1	1	1
	R_z	A_2	1	1	1	-1	-1
$x^2 - y^2$		B_1	1	1	-1	1	-1
xy		B_2	1	1	-1	-1	1
(xz, yz)	(x, y) (R_x, R_y)	E	2	-2	0	0	0

10.

C_{5v}			E	$2C_5$	$2C_5^2$	$5\sigma_v$	
$x^2 + y^2, z^2$	z	A_1	1	1	1	1	
	R_z	A_2	1	1	1	-1	$x = \dfrac{2\pi}{5}$
(xz, yz)	(x, y) (R_x, R_y)	E_1	2	$2\cos x$	$2\cos 2x$	0	
$(x^2 - y^2, xy)$		E_2	2	$2\cos 2x$	$2\cos 4x$	0	

11.

C_{6v}			E	C_2	$2C_3$	$2C_6$	$3\sigma_d$	$3\sigma_v$
$x^2 + y^2, z^2$	z	A_1	1	1	1	1	1	1
	R_z	A_2	1	1	1	1	-1	-1
		B_1	1	-1	1	-1	-1	1
		B_2	1	-1	1	-1	1	-1
(xz, yz)	(x, y) $\big\}$ (R_x, R_y)	E_1	2	-2	-1	1	0	0
$(x^2 - y^2, xy)$		E_2	2	2	-1	-1	0	0

12.

C_{1h}			E	σ_h
x^2, y^2, z^2, xy	R_z, x, y	A'	1	1
xz, yz	R_x, R_y, z	A''	1	-1

13.

C_{2h}			E	C_2	σ_h	i
x^2, y^2, z^2, xy	R_z	A_g	1	1	1	1
	z	A_u	1	1	-1	-1
xz, yz	R_x, R_y	B_g	1	-1	-1	1
	x, y	B_u	1	-1	1	-1

14.

$C_{3h} = C_3 {\times} \sigma_h$			E	C_3	C_3^2	σ_h	S_3	$(\sigma_h C_3^2)$
$x^2 + y^2, z^2$	R_z	A'	1	1	1	1	1	1
	z	A''	1	1	1	-1	-1	-1
$(x^2 - y^2, xy)$	(x, y)	$E' \Big\{$	1	ω	ω^2	1	ω	ω^2
			1	ω^2	ω	1	ω^2	ω
(xz, yz)	(R_x, R_y)	$E'' \Big\{$	1	ω	ω^2	-1	$-\omega$	$-\omega^2$
			1	ω^2	ω	-1	$-\omega^2$	$-\omega$

$\left(\omega = e^{\frac{2\pi i}{3}}\right)$

15. $$C_{4h} = C_4 {\times} i$$

16. $$C_{5h} = C_5 {\times} \sigma_h$$

17. $$C_{6h} = C_6 {\times} i$$

18.

S_2			E	i
$x^2, y^2, z^2, xy,$ xz, yz	R_x, R_y, R_z	A_g	1	1
	x, y, z	A_u	1	-1

19.

S_4			E	C_2	S_4	S_4^3
$x^2 + y^2,\ z^2$	R_z	A	1	1	1	1
	z	B	1	1	-1	-1
(xz, yz) $(x^2 - y^2,\ xy)$	(x, y) (R_x, R_y)	$E\ \Big\{$	1 1	-1 -1	i $-i$	$-i$ i

20. $$S_6 = C_3 \times i$$

21.

D_2			E	C_2^z	C_2^y	C_2^x
$x^2,\ y^2,\ z^2$		A_1	1	1	1	1
xy	$R_z,\ z$	B_1	1	1	-1	-1
xz	$R_y,\ y$	B_2	1	-1	1	-1
yz	$R_x,\ x$	B_3	1	-1	-1	1

22.

D_3			E	$2C_3$	$3C_2'$
$x^2 + y^2,\ z^2$		A_1	1	1	1
	$R_z,\ z$	A_2	1	1	-1
(xz, yz) $(x^2 - y^2,\ xy)$	(x, y) (R_x, R_y)	E	2	-1	0

23.

D_4			E	C_2	$2C_4$	$2C_2'$	$2C_2''$
$x^2 + y^2,\ z^2$		A_1	1	1	1	1	1
	$R_z,\ z$	A_2	1	1	1	-1	-1
		B_1	1	1	-1	1	-1
		B_2	1	1	-1	-1	1
(xz, yz) $(x^2 - y^2,\ xy)$	(x, y) (R_x, R_y)	E	2	-2	0	0	0

24.

D_5			E	$2C_5$	$2C_5^2$	$5C_2'$	
$x^2 + y^2,\ z^2$		A_1	1	1	1	1	
	$R_z,\ z$	A_2	1	1	1	-1	
(xz, yz)	(x, y) (R_x, R_y)	E_1	2	$2\cos x$	$2\cos 2x$	0	$\left(x = \dfrac{2\pi}{5}\right)$
$(x^2 - y^2,\ xy)$		E_2	2	$2\cos 2x$	$2\cos 4x$	0	

D_6			E	C_2	$2C_3$	$2C_6$	$3C_2'$	$3C_2''$
$x^2 + y^2,\ z^2$		A_1	1	1	1	1	1	1
	$R_z,\ z$	A_2	1	1	1	1	-1	-1
		B_1	1	-1	1	-1	1	-1
		B_2	1	-1	1	-1	-1	1
$(xz,\ yz)$	$(x,\ y)$ $(R_x,\ R_y)$	E_1	2	-2	-1	1	0	0
$(x^2 - y^2,\ xy)$		E_2	2	2	-1	-1	0	0

25.

D_{2d}			E	C_2	$2S_4$	$2C_2'$	$2\sigma_d$
$x^2 + y^2,\ z^2$		A_1	1	1	1	1	1
	R_z	A_2	1	1	1	-1	-1
$x^2 - y^2$		B_1	1	1	-1	1	-1
xy	z	B_2	1	1	-1	-1	1
$(xz,\ yz)$	$(x,\ y)$ $(R_x,\ R_y)$	E	2	-2	0	0	0

26.

27. $\quad\quad\quad\quad\quad\quad\quad\quad \mathbf{D}_{3d} = \mathbf{D}_3{\times}i$

28. $\quad\quad\quad\quad\quad\quad\quad\quad \mathbf{D}_{2h} = \mathbf{D}_2{\times}i$

$\mathbf{D}_{3h} = \mathbf{D}_3{\times}\sigma_h$			E	σ_h	$2C_3$	$2S_3$	$3C_2'$	$3\sigma_v$
$x^2 + y^2,\ z^2$		A_1'	1	1	1	1	1	1
	R_z	A_2'	1	1	1	1	-1	-1
		A_1''	1	-1	1	-1	1	-1
	z	A_2''	1	-1	1	-1	-1	1
$(x^2 - y^2,\ xy)$	$(x,\ y)$	E'	2	2	-1	-1	0	0
$(xz,\ yz)$	$(R_x,\ R_y)$	E''	2	-2	-1	1	0	0

29.

30. $\quad\quad\quad\quad\quad\quad\quad\quad \mathbf{D}_{4h} = \mathbf{D}_4{\times}i$

31. $\quad\quad\quad\quad\quad\quad\quad\quad \mathbf{D}_{5h} = \mathbf{D}_5{\times}\sigma_h$

32. $\quad\quad\quad\quad\quad\quad\quad\quad \mathbf{D}_{6h} = \mathbf{D}_6{\times}i$

T			E	$3C_2$	$4C_3$	$4C_3'$	
Active		A	1	1	1	1	
Active		E $\Big\{$	1	1	ω	ω^2	$\left(\omega = e^{\frac{2\pi i}{3}}\right)$
			1	1	ω^2	ω	
Active	$(R_x,\ R_y,\ R_z)$ $(x,\ y,\ z)$	T	3	-1	0	0	

33.

34. $\quad\quad\quad\quad\quad\quad\quad\quad \mathbf{T}_h = T{\times}i$

35.

O			E	$8C_3$	$3C_2$	$6C_2$	$6C_4$
Active		A_1	1	1	1	1	1
Inactive		A_2	1	1	1	-1	-1
Active		E	2	-1	2	0	0
Active	(R_x, R_y, R_z) (x, y, z)	T_1	3	0	-1	-1	$+1$
Active		T_2	3	0	-1	$+1$	-1

36.

$$O_h = O \times i$$

37.

T_d			E	$8C_3$	$3C_2$	$6\sigma_d$	$6S_4$
Active		A_1	1	1	1	1	1
Inactive		A_2	1	1	1	-1	-1
Active		E	2	-1	2	0	0
Active	(R_x, R_y, R_z)	T_1	3	0	-1	1	-1
Active	(x, y, z)	T_2	3	0	-1	-1	1

38.

$C_{\infty v}$			E	$2C_\varphi$	σ_v
$x^2 + y^2, z^2$		A_1	1	1	1
	z	A_2	1	1	-1
(xz, yz)	(x, y) (R_x, R_y)	E_1	2	$2\cos\varphi$	0
$(x^2 - y^2, xy)$		E_2	2	$2\cos 2\varphi$	0
		..	. . . .		

39.

$D_{\infty h}$			E	$2C_\varphi$	C_2'	i	$2iC_\varphi$	iC_2'
$x^2 + y^2, z^2$		A_{1g}	1	1	1	1	1	1
		A_{1u}	1	1	1	-1	-1	-1
		A_{2g}	1	1	-1	1	1	-1
	z	A_{2u}	1	1	-1	-1	-1	1
(xz, yz)	(R_x, R_y)	E_{1g}	2	$2\cos\varphi$	0	2	$2\cos\varphi$	0
	(x, y)	E_{1u}	2	$2\cos\varphi$	0	-2	$-2\cos\varphi$	0
$(x^2 - y^2, xy)$		E_{2g}	2	$2\cos 2\varphi$	0	2	$2\cos 2\varphi$	0
		E_{2u}	2	$2\cos 2\varphi$	0	-2	$-2\cos 2\varphi$	0
		..	. . . .					

VIII. SOME SPECIAL INTEGRALS

1. $\displaystyle \int x^n e^{ax}\, dx = \frac{x^n e^{ax}}{a} - \frac{n}{a} \int x^{n-1} e^{ax}\, dx$

2. $\displaystyle \int_0^\infty x^n e^{-ax}\, dx = \frac{n!}{a^{n+1}}, \quad n > -1, a > 0$

3. $\displaystyle\int_0^\infty e^{-ax^2}\,dx = \frac{1}{2}\sqrt{\frac{\pi}{a}}$

4. $\displaystyle\int_0^\infty x^2 e^{-ax^2}\,dx = \frac{1}{4}\sqrt{\frac{\pi}{a^3}}$

5. $\displaystyle\int_0^\infty x^{2n} e^{-ax^2}\,dx = \frac{1\cdot 3\cdots(2n-1)}{2^{n+1}}\sqrt{\frac{\pi}{a^{2n+1}}}$

6. $\displaystyle\int_0^\infty x e^{-ax^2}\,dx = \frac{1}{2a}$

7. $\displaystyle\int_0^\infty x^3 e^{-ax^2}\,dx = \frac{1}{2a^2}$

8. $\displaystyle\int_0^\infty x^{2n+1} e^{-ax^2} = \frac{n!}{2a^{n+1}}$

9. $\displaystyle\int_1^\infty e^{-ax}\,dx = \frac{e^{-a}}{a}$

10. $\displaystyle\int_1^\infty x e^{-ax}\,dx = \frac{e^{-a}}{a^2}\,(1+a)$

11. $\displaystyle\int_1^\infty x^2 e^{-ax}\,dx = \frac{2e^{-a}}{a^3}\left(1+a+\frac{a^2}{2}\right)$

12. $\displaystyle\int_1^\infty x^n e^{-ax}\,dx = \frac{n!\,e^{-a}}{a^{n+1}}\sum_{k=0}^{n}\frac{a^k}{k!}\equiv A_n(a)$

13. $\displaystyle\int_{-1}^{+1} e^{-ax}\,dx = \frac{1}{a}\,(e^a - e^{-a})$

14. $\displaystyle\int_{-1}^{+1} x e^{-ax}\,dx = \frac{1}{a^2}\left\{e^a - e^{-a} - a(e^a + e^{-a})\right\}$

15. $\displaystyle\int_{-1}^{+1} x^n e^{-ax}\,dx = (-1)^{n+1}A_n(-a) - A_n(a)$

IX. GENERAL REFERENCES

A. *Classical Mechanics*

    W. BYERLY, *Generalized Coördinates*, Ginn, 1916.

    G. JOOS, *Theoretical Physics*, Blackie, 1934.

    H. B. PHILLIPS, *Vector Analysis*, Wiley.

    J. SLATER and N. FRANK, *Introduction to Theoretical Physics*, McGraw-Hill, 1933.

B. *Quantum Mechanics*

    P. DIRAC, *Quantum Mechanics*, Oxford, 1935.

    S. DUSHMAN, *Elements of Quantum Mechanics*, Wiley, 1938.

    H. HELLMANN, *Einführung in die Quantenchemie*, Deuticke, Leipzig, 1937.

E. KEMBLE, *Fundamental Principles of Quantum Mechanics*, McGraw-Hill, 1937.

L. PAULING and E. B. WILSON, *Introduction to Quantum Mechanics*, McGraw-Hill, 1935.

V. ROJANSKY, *Introductory Quantum Mechanics*, Prentice-Hall, 1942.

A. SOMMERFELD, *Atombau und Spektrallinien*, Vieweg, Braunschweig, 1939.

C. *Atomic Structure and Spectroscopy*

E. U. CONDON and G. SHORTLEY, *Theory of Atomic Spectra*, Cambridge, 1935.

S. DUSHMAN, Chapter II in TAYLOR'S *Treatise on Physical Chemistry*, Van Nostrand, 1942.

G. HERZBERG, *Atomic Spectra and Atomic Structure*, Prentice-Hall, 1937.

L. PAULING and S. GOUDSMIT, *The Structure of Line Spectra*, McGraw-Hill, 1930.

H. WHITE, *Introduction to Atomic Spectra*, McGraw-Hill, 1934.

D. *Group Theory*

J. E. ROSENTHAL and G. M. MURPHY, " Group Theory and Molecular Vibrations," *Rev. Modern Phys.*, **8**, 317 (1936).

A. SPEISER, *Theorie der Gruppen von endlicher Ordnung*, Springer, Berlin, 1927.

E. WIGNER, *Gruppentheorie*, Vieweg, Braunschweig, 1931.

E. *Molecular Structure and Molecular Spectroscopy*

D. DENNISON, " Infra-Red Spectra," *Rev. Modern Phys.*, **12**, 175 (1940).

G. GLOCKLER, " The Raman Effect," *Rev. Modern Phys.*, **15**, 112 (1943).

G. HERZBERG, *Molecular Spectra and Molecular Structure*, Prentice-Hall, 1939.

L. PAULING, *Nature of the Chemical Bond*, Cornell, 1940.

O. K. RICE, *Electronic Structure and Chemical Binding*, McGraw-Hill, 1940.

H. SPONER, *Molekülspektren*, Springer, Berlin, 1936.

H. SPONER and E. TELLER, " Electronic Spectra," *Rev. Modern Phys.*, **13**, 75 (1941).

J. H. VAN VLECK and A. SHERMAN, " Quantum Theory of Valence," *Rev. Modern Phys.*, **7**, 174 (1935).

F. *Statistical Mechanics and Reaction Rates*

R. H. FOWLER, *Statistical Mechanics*, Cambridge, 1936.

R. H. FOWLER and E. A. GUGGENHEIM, *Statistical Thermodynamics*, Cambridge, 1939.

S. GLASSTONE, K. J. LAIDLER, and H. EYRING, *Theory of Rate Processes*, McGraw-Hill, 1941.

R. B. LINDSAY, *Physical Statistics*, Wiley, 1941.

J. MAYER and M. MAYER, *Statistical Mechanics*, Wiley, 1940.

R. C. TOLMAN, *Principles of Statistical Mechanics*, Oxford, 1938.

G. *Electric and Magnetic Phenomena, Optical Activity*

E. U. CONDON, " Optical Rotatory Power," *Rev. Modern Phys.*, **9**, 432 (1937).

R. H. FOWLER and E. A. GUGGENHEIM, *Statistical Thermodynamics*, Cambridge, 1939, Chapter XIV.

W. KAUZMANN, J. WALTER, and H. EYRING, ' Optical Activity," *Chem. Revs.*, **26**, 339 (1940).

J. G. KIRKWOOD, " Polarizability Theory of Optical Activity," *J. Chem. Phys.*, **5**, 479 (1937).

C. P. SMYTH, *Dielectric Constant and Molecular Structure*, Chemical Catalog Co., 1931.

E. STONER, *Magnetism and Atomic Structure*, Dutton, 1926.

J. H. VAN VLECK, *Electric and Magnetic Susceptibilities*, Oxford, 1932.

INDEX